Doctrinal Instruction in Early Islam

Islamic History and Civilization

STUDIES AND TEXTS

VOLUME 174

The titles published in this series are listed at *brill.com/ihc*

Doctrinal Instruction in Early Islam

The Book of the Explanation of the Sunna by Ghulām Khalīl (d. 275/888)

By

Maher Jarrar

in collaboration with

Sebastian Günther

BRILL

LEIDEN | BOSTON

Cover illustration: “Abū Zayd preaches in the mosque of Samarqand,” Paris, Bibliothèque Nationale, Arabic ms. 5847, fol.84., *The Maqamāt of al-Ḥarīrī* (d. 516 AH/1122 CE), illustrated by Yaḥyā ibn Mahmūd al-Wāsiṭī (7th c. AH/13th c. CE), Charles Schefer Collection. Reproduced with kind permission of the Bibliothèque Nationale de France.

The Library of Congress Cataloging-in-Publication Data is available online at http://catalog.loc.gov
LC record available at http://lccn.loc.gov/2020009928

Typeface for the Latin, Greek, and Cyrillic scripts: “Brill”. See and download: brill.com/brill-typeface.

ISSN 0929-2403
ISBN 978-90-04-42904-8 (hardback)
ISBN 978-90-04-42905-5 (e-book)

This book is printed on acid-free paper and produced in a sustainable manner.

For Rima and Bassam

Contents

Acknowledgments IX
Notes on Transliteration and Style XI
Abbreviations XIII

Introduction 1

1 Ghulām Khalīl: Life, Career, and Image as a Scholar 10

2 The *Kitāb Sharḥ al-sunna*: Textual Evidence, Transmission, and Authorship 28

3 The Third/Ninth Century: The Veneration of Aḥmad b. Ḥanbal and the Proliferation of Creeds 65

4 Toward Common Ground: The People of the Sunna and the Community 96

Epilogue: Doctrinal Instruction in Times of Political Change 142

Translation of *The Book of the Explanation of the Sunna* 153

Appendix I: List of Editions and Translations 191
Appendix II: List of Traditions Transmitted on the Authority of Ghulām Khalīl 201
General Bibliography 214
General Index 239
Index of Book Titles 249

Arabic Edition 251

Bibliography for the Arabic Edition 339
Index for the Arabic Edition 371

Acknowledgments

In 2001, my colleague and friend Sebastian Günther and I started work on a unique manuscript that has been preserved in the Dār al-Kutub al-Ẓāhiriyya Library in Damascus, listed there under the title *Kitāb Sharḥ al-sunna* by Ghulām Khalīl. We were strongly encouraged by my *Doktorvater* and mentor, Professor Josef van Ess, University of Tübingen, to edit critically and translate this important Arabic text, as it appears to contain one of the earliest Muslim creeds, dating back to the second half of the second/eighth century.

It was a particularly fortunate coincidence that we also had the privilege of reading parts of the Arabic manuscript with my late mentor, Professor Ihsan Abbas, during a short visit he paid to Beirut in 2001, and it was a real pleasure to enjoy his company and benefit from his precious comments and insights.

The preliminary outcome of this research was an article in German published in 2003.[1] Since then, we have intermittently continued pursuing this research project, unfortunately subject to frequent interruptions by other academic and administrative obligations, and to the unstable political situation in Lebanon and the wider Middle East region.

In 2008, with the help of a grant awarded to us by the Gerda Henkel Foundation, we were able to concentrate once again our academic efforts on this research project. We gratefully acknowledge this financial support from the Gerda Henkel Foundation here, as it enabled us to meet in person in Göttingen twice, in the summers of 2008 and 2010, in order to revamp our project ideas and continue our collaboration and academic conversation.

The importance of this research project also found new affirmation in 2014, when I was asked by *Encyclopaedia of Islam, THREE*, to write the entry on Ghulām Khalīl. Furthermore, my sabbatical leave from the American University of Beirut in 2017 considerably helped me to do the necessary groundwork and reading for this research project, which turned out to be more complex the more primary sources were discovered and compared.

It is my pleasure to acknowledge Sebastian Günther's comprehensive commitment to this project, his valuable advice and intellectual stimulation, and most of all his inestimable support in bringing this project to fruition. This study is the rewarding outcome of our joint collaboration and ongoing conversation.

1 Jarrar and Günther, Ġulām Ḫalīl.

I owe my sincere thanks also to a number of colleagues and friends for their help at various stages of the project. First of all, I wish to sincerely thank Professor Tarif Khalidi, mentor and dear colleague at the American University of Beirut, for agreeing to take a critical look at the English translation of the text of *Kitāb Sharḥ al-sunna*. I am deeply grateful to him for his most valuable advice in revising this translation.

Likewise, I wish to express my heartfelt gratitude to my colleague and friend at the American University of Beirut, Mahmoud Youness, for his unremitting faith in this project. Mahmoud painstakingly read and revised a first draft of the English translation and made a number of very helpful suggestions to improve its language and style. I also wish to thank Hussein Abdulsater, University of Notre Dame, Indiana, in whose judiciousness I have complete confidence.

I am indebted to my former student Ali Rida Rizek, Institute of Arabic and Islamic Studies, University of Göttingen, for his insightful comments and his thoughtful proofreading of the Arabic text.

Special thanks are due to Amina al-Hasan, Hiba al-Malih, and Hisham Ahmad, from the Manuscript Division at the Asad National Library, Damascus, for their kind and generous help. At the American University of Beirut's Jafet Library, I greatly benefited from the assistance of Samar Mikati-Kaissi, Archives and Special Collections Librarian, and Carla Chalhoub, Head of Access Services.

Mention needs to be made of the invaluable technical assistance offered by Dorothee Lauer and Jana Newiger, Institute of Arabic and Islamic Studies, University of Göttingen, especially in the final stages of preparing this book manuscript for publication. Elizabeth Crawford, Göttingen deserves my sincere gratitude for her thorough editorial help and her patience in fine-tuning the English text of this book.

A warm and very cordial word of thanks goes to Teddi Dols, Brill's Islamic History and Civilization (IHC) Series Editor, and to Daniel Sentance, freelance copy editor with Brill, for their invaluable support in bringing this book to fruition.

Finally, I would like to express genuine thanks to the anonymous assessor for her most detailed, helpful, and inspiring comments. It is also my great pleasure to record a sincere expression of gratitude to Hans Hinrich Biesterfeldt, Professor Emeritus at the University of Bochum, for accepting this publication in Brill's IHC series.

Maher Jarrar
Beirut, August 2019

Notes on Transliteration and Style

We adhere to the following transliteration system for Arabic script, which is based on the scheme used in Brill's *Encyclopaedia of the Qurʾān*:

Consonants

ʾ	d	ḍ	k
b	dh	ṭ	l
t	r	ẓ	m
th	z	ʿ	n
j	s	gh	h
ḥ	sh	f	w
kh	ṣ	q	y

Vowels

Long vowels	Short	Diphthongs
ā	a	aw
ū	u	ay
ī	i	

-a (-at in *iḍāfa*)
bi-l-kitāb *but* lil-masjid
b. and bt.
iyy (final form ī)
no initial hamza, e.g., *al-amr*
al and (-)l- (e.g. *al-kitāb*; *wa-l-kitāb*; no sun letters)
Abū l-Walīd; fī l-Qurʾān
ʿAbdallāh *but* ʿAbd al-Raḥmān
uww (final form ū)
baytuhu, only in poetry, if desirable, *baytuhū*

Proper names, technical terms, and geographic designations that are common in English are either not transliterated or used in simplified transliteration. Examples of such words include Cairo, Baghdad, Kufa, Sunni and Sunnites, as well as Quran (not Qur'an) and Sura. Examples of words in simplified transliteration are: ʿAbbasids, Ismaʿili and Ismaʿilis, Shiʿi, Shiʿite, Shiʿites.

Quranic references are noted thus: Q 50:1 or Q 73:2–6, i.e., the number of the Sura in Arabic numerals, followed directly by a colon, which is followed by the verse numbers in Arabic numerals. Quranic verse numbering follows the text now generally known as the "Cairo" or "Egyptian" official version of 1342/1923–1924.

The standard system of dating all post-Hijri events is Hijri/Christian, e.g., 786/1384–1385 and 786–796/1484–1493. Pre-Islamic dates, if not made obvious by the context in which they are used, are indicated by "CE" or "BCE."

References in the footnote apparatus are given, from their very first appearance on, in brief form. The full bibliographical data of all publications cited may be found in the bibliography included at the end of each contribution. Note that the Arabic article "al-" is disregarded in the alphabetical ordering of the bibliographical entries, while "ibn" is taken into account. For typographical reasons, the names of books and articles in English are written in lower case. For abbreviations of frequently cited periodicals and reference works, see the following list of abbreviations.

Abbreviations

ActaAntHung	*Acta Antiqua Academiae Scientiarum Hungaricae*
AHR	*The American Historical Review*
AI	*Annales Islamologiques*
AIUON	*Annali dell'Istituto Universitario Orientale di Napoli*
AJISS	*American Journal of Islamic Social Sciences*
AKM	Abhandlungen für die Kunde des Morgenlandes
AO	*Acta Orientalia*
AO-H	*Acta Orientalia (Academiae Scientiarum Hungaricae)*
Arabica	*Arabica: Revue d'Études Arabes*
ARW	*Archiv für Religionswissenschaft*
AS	*Arabian Studies*
ASP	*Arabic Sciences and Philosophy*
ATS	Arabistische Texte und Studien
AUU	*Acta Universitatis Upsaliensis*
BASOR	*Bulletin of the American School of Oriental Research*
BEO	*Bulletin d'Études Orientales de l'Institut Français de Damas*
BGA	Bibliotheca Geographorum Arabicorum
BI	Bibliotheca Islamica
BIFAO	*Bulletin de l'Institut Français d'Archéologie Orientale du Caire*
BJMES	*British Journal of Middle Eastern Studies*
BO	*Bibliotheca Orientalis*
BSA	*Budapest Studies in Arabic*
BSOAS	*Bulletin of the School of Oriental and African Studies*
BTS	Beiruter Texte und Studien
BzI	Beiträge zur Iranistik
CER	*Comparative Education Review*
CRAI	*Comptes-rendus des Séances de l'Académie des Inscriptions et Belles-Lettres*
CSSH	*Comparative Studies in Society and History*
DA	Diskurse der Arabistik
Der Islam	*Der Islam. Zeitschrift für Geschichte und Kultur des islamischen Orients*
DIR	*De Institutione Regia*
EI^1	*Encyclopaedia of Islam*, 1st ed., Leiden 1913–1938
EI^2	*Encyclopaedia of Islam*, 2nd ed., Leiden 1954–2004
EI^3	*Encyclopaedia of Islam*, 3rd ed., Leiden 2007–
EIr	*Encyclopaedia Iranica*, London 1982–
EQ	*Encyclopaedia of the Qurʾān*, Leiden 2001–2006

ER	*Encyclopaedia of Religion*, ed. M. Eliade, New York 1986
ERE	*Encyclopaedia of Religions and Ethics*
FCIW	The Formation of the Classical Islamic World
FIS	Freiburger Islamstudien
GAL S	*Brockelmann, C., Geschichte der arabischen Litteratur*, 2 vols. + 3 suppl. vols., Leiden 1937–1943
GAS	*Sezgin, F., Geschichte des arabischen Schrifttums*, vols. i–ix, Leiden 1967–1984, Frankfurt/M. 2000–2015
GMS	Gibb Memorial Series
HCMR	History of Christian-Muslim Relations
HMEIR	*Harvard Middle Eastern and Islamic Review*
HO	Handbuch der Orientalistik
IA	*İslâm Ansiklopedisi*
IBLA	*Revue de l'Institut des Belles Lettres Arabes, Tunis*
IC	*Islamic Culture*
IHC	Islamic History and Civilization
IJMES	*International Journal of Middle Eastern Studies*
ILS	*Islamic Law and Society*
IOS	*Israel Oriental Studies*
IPTS	Islamic Philosophy, Theology and Science
IQ	*The Islamic Quarterly*
Iran	*Iran. Journal of the British Persian Studies*
IU	Islamkundliche Untersuchungen
JA	*Journal Asiatique*
JAH	*Journal of Asian History*
JAIS	*Journal of Arabic and Islamic Studies*
JAL	*Journal of Arabic Literature*
JAOS	*Journal of the American Oriental Society*
JCLS	*The Journal of Catholic Legal Studies*
JE	*Jewish Encyclopaedia*
JESHO	*Journal of the Economic and Social History of the Orient*
JHI	*Journal of the History of Ideas*
JIS	*Journal of Islamic Studies*
JNES	*Journal of Near Eastern Studies*
JQR	*The Jewish Quarterly Review*
JQS	*Journal of Quranic Studies*
JRAS	*Journal of the Royal Asiatic Society*
JSAI	*Jerusalem Studies in Arabic and Islam*
JSS	*Journal of Semitic Studies*
MFOB	*Mélanges de la Faculté Orientale de l'Université St. Joseph de Beyrouth*

MIC	Makers of Islamic Civilization
MIDEO	*Mélanges de l'Institut Dominicain d'Études Orientales du Caire*
MO	*Le Monde Oriental*
MSOS	*Mitteilung des Seminars für Orientalische Sprachen, Westasiatische Studien*
MSR	*Mamlūk Studies Review*
Muséon	*Le Muséon. Revue des Études Orientales*
MUSJ	*Mélanges de l'Université Saint-Joseph*
MW	*The Muslim World*
NKJV	*New King James Version of the Bible*
OC	*Oriens Christianus*
OLA	Orientalia Lovaniensia Analecta
OLZ	*Orientalistische Literaturzeitung*
OOM	Oxford Oriental Monographs
Oriens	*Oriens. Zeitschrift der Internationalen Gesellschaft für Orientforschung*
Orientalia	*Orientalia. Commentarii Periodici Pontifici Instituti Biblici*
PEW	*Philosophy East and West*
Qanṭara	*al-Qanṭara. Revista de Estudios Arabes*
QSA	*Quaderni di Studi Arabi*
RAC	*Reallexikon für Antike und Christentum*
RCEA	*Répertoire Chronologique d'Épigraphie Arabe*
REJ	*Revues des Études Juives*
REI	*Revue des Études Islamiques*
REMMM	*Revue du Monde Musulman et de la Méditerranée*
RHR	*Revue de l'Histoire des Religions*
RIMA	*Revue de l'Institut des Manuscrits Arabes*
RMM	*Revue des Mondes Musulmans et de la Méditerranée*
RO	Res Orientales
ROC	*Revue de l'Orient Chrétien*
ROr	*Rocznik Orientalistyczny*
RSCL	Routledge Studies in Classical Islam
RSO	*Rivista degli Studi Orientali*
RSQ	Routledge Studies in the Qurʾan
SALL	Studies in Arabic Language and Literature
SGKIO	Studien zur Sprache, Geschichte und Kultur des islamischen Orients
SI	*Studia Islamica*
SIr	*Studia Iranica*
SRSME	SOAS/Routledge Studies on the Middle East
ThG	van Ess, J., *Theologie und Gesellschaft im 2. und 3. Jahrhundert Hidschra: Eine Geschichte des religiösen Denkens im frühen Islam*, 6 vols., Berlin 1991–1996.

TRE, ThRE	*Theologische Realenzyklopädie*
WI	*Die Welt des Islams*
WKAS	Wörterbuch der Klassischen Arabischen Sprache, Wiesbaden 1970–
WO	*Welt des Orients*
WZKM	*Wiener Zeitschrift für die Kunde des Morgenlandes*
ZAL	*Zeitschrift für Arabische Linguistik*
ZDMG	*Zeitschrift der Deutschen Morgenländischen Gesellschaft*
ZfDA	*Zeitschrift für deutsches Altertum und deutsche Literatur*
ZGAIW	*Zeitschrift für Geschichte der arabisch-islamischen Wissenschaften*
ZMR	*Zeitschrift für Missions- und Religionswissenschaft*
ZS	*Zeitschrift für Semitistik*

Introduction

> If one confines oneself to the traditions of the Messenger of God—may peace and blessings be upon him—and to the consensus of the Community, one shall prevail over all innovators. Moreover, one's body is relieved of its tensions and one's religion remains intact, should God so wish … Such is the remedy, the unambiguous account, the clear truth, and the illuminating source of light.
>
> GHULĀM KHALĪL, *Kitāb Sharḥ al-sunna*, § 84

∴

During the third/ninth century, the various factions of Sunni Muslims had a marked predilection for creeds. This preponderant tendency reflected the intensity of the struggle over communal identity, integrity, and the accuracy of faith, which was defined, according to their understanding, by the exemplum of the Prophet Muhammad and his Companions (*aṣḥāb*, *ṣaḥāba*). The mark of the "genuine believer," then, according to Ghulām Khalīl's creed, as well as creeds by other third-century Sunni traditionalists, was that one entrusted one's religion to the Companions, since religion was but strict "obedience" and due compliance, or *taqlīd*.[1] Consequently, the main threat to this truth came from heretical innovations of any kind.

The "victory" claimed by the traditionalists as a result of the *miḥna*—the inquisition against the traditionalists that began under the ʿAbbasid caliph al-Maʾmūn (r. 198–218 AH/813–833 CE) and which was suspended in 234/848–849[2]—prompted them to strive for power in the social sphere. Accordingly, the practice of composing religious creeds (*ʿaqīda*, *iʿtiqād*) in line with the basic tenets that were promulgated by Aḥmad b. Ḥanbal (d. 241/855) assumed its ascendancy.

In fact, one of the watershed moments that facilitated the writing and propagation of creeds in the third/ninth century is closely related to the "triumph

1 By the term "traditionalists" (*asḥāb al-ḥadīth*), as Makdisi explains, "is meant that which comprises the traditionalists [lit. people of the Sunna] among the jurisconsults, even though they may not be tradition-experts." Makdisi, Significance 4–6; see also Frank, Elements 142, fn. 3.

2 See chapters 3 and 4.

 | DOI:10.1163/9789004429055_002

of Sunnism,"[3] which also expressed itself through the fervent activities of the *ḥadīth* scholars in collecting and classifying *ḥadīth* "canonical" compendia, and the production of biographical dictionaries of the *ḥadīth* scholars.[4] Moreover, it was at this juncture that "al-Shafiʿi's paradigm"[5] was exercising its effective and formative influence.[6]

The existence of an "Other" as a constituting factor in the self-image of a person or group is of fundamental importance in writing a creed, since it emphasizes the exclusivity of belonging to one's very specific group. Creeds were also used as a means to evince a link between the "present" Community, as the recipients, and the glorious and wholesome "past" of the forebears and their "living traditions." This strategy lies at the heart of a process of idealization of the early Muslim Community.

Given this general political-dogmatic context of third/ninth-century Iraq, the present book examines in depth the creed written by the Basran and Baghdadi Sunni preacher Abū ʿAbdallāh Aḥmad b. Muḥammad b. Ghālib al-Bāhilī, known as Ghulām Khalīl (d. 275/888). This creed has been edited and translated several times, including a translation into English by a Salafi publishing house in England in 1995.[7] All these editions and translations, however, attribute the creed to al-Ḥasan b. ʿAlī al-Barbahārī (d. 329/941), a Hanbali leader and demagogue.[8] It is precisely this attribution of authorship, evident already in the medieval Arabic sources and uncritically accepted and elaborated on by several modern scholars, Eastern and Western, that sparked the interest that precipitated the present book project. The second motivation for the study may be summarized as an aspiration to understand just how this "living tradition" of the forefathers has prompted some contemporary Salafis to adopt and propagate a creed that was first published in the third/ninth century.[9]

---

3 Watt, *Formative period* 251; see also Khalidi, *Arabic historical thought* 111.

4 For the canonical compendia, see Brown, *Canonization* 47–60; Stewart, Developments 146–148; and for the biographical dictionaries Lucas, *Constructive critics* 287–326.

5 El Shamsy, *Canonization* 176–182.

6 Ibid., 195–201.

7 For a list of editions and translations, see appendix 1. For an appraisal of the much-debated terms "Salafi" and "Salafiyya," cf. Shinar, Salafiyya viii, 900–906; Meijer, *Global Salafism* 3–9; Wiktorowicz, Anatomy; Lauzière, *Making* 5–10; and Bin Ali, *Roots* 1–13.

8 See Cook, *Commanding right* 164.

9 The suggestion that "the thinking of the fundamentalist Islamic intellectuals and of the great masses of ordinary Muslims is still dominated by the standard traditional Islamic world-view and the corresponding self-image of Islam" (Watt, *Islamic fundamentalism* 1) seems somewhat simplistic and does not adequately consider the numerous complex elements inherent in the ongoing social process of the reception of a "living tradition," where aspects of this tradition carry new energy and presence in all spheres of life.

Thus, the present publication broaches multilayered themes with the aim of specifying the parameters of this creed in terms of the complex relationship between its content and its origin. It also tackles the question of what might have led Salafis, financed by certain Saudi foundations, to adopt the doctrinal standpoints of a particular creed and, perhaps more importantly, to pursue its "institutionalization" as a religious ideology.

1 The Creed and Its Contents

In order to provide insight into the material, I delineate here some of the main ideas communicated by Ghulām Khalīl in his creed. Like most creeds of the third/ninth century, Ghulām Khalīl's creed is an obstreperous amalgamation of different dogmatic points. Foremost, the creed calls upon its readers to think of themselves as the true and righteous adherents of the Community of the Prophet and his Companions, as distinguished from all other Muslim groups and schisms. It moreover describes with authority certain tenets and behaviors required of the believer, at a time when, according to the author, signs of heresy were abundant, diverse, and historically contingent. In this regard, the creed not only presents a statement of faith and a guide for determining belief and unbelief but also aims to regulate social behavior. Ghulām Khalīl's creed perceives itself, so to speak, as a way of life or a "manual of orthopraxy," distinguished by a tone that is, in general, polemical. This can be observed in all its articles of faith, whether pertaining to ritual ablution, marriage, or other symbolic practices, as well as in articles that stress the correctness of the faith or remonstrate against theological disputations.

Perhaps on account of the overall purpose of his book—to inculcate in fellow Muslims a strict creed—Ghulām Khalīl appears to have paid little attention to creating a more systematic arrangement of the material presented. The book is thus a rather axiomatic work, in which formal sets of doctrine have been listed, and in some cases briefly explained, without any tangible thematic strategy. Although the tenets appear to be randomly assembled, the following topics emerge as the creed's main thematic layers:

1.1 *Right of Entry*

The Community is designated by a title that is charged with significance and associated with some Prophetic traditions; it is described as the *ahl al-sunna wa-l-jamāʿa* (the People of the Sunna and the Community, or "the majority community"),[10] a label that distinguishes this group of transmission-based tra-

10 Stewart, Developments 144–146.

ditionalists (with its various factions) from all other groups. Just as the early Community was led by the Prophet and his Companions, so this creed claims right over tenets concerning the articulation of orthodoxy and strict adherence to the Sunna and the Community, whose backbone is formed by the Companions of the Prophet.

Both the Sunna and the Community have already determined the principles of religion (*amr al-dīn*), according to which all are called upon to comply with and to follow the path of the previous generations, affirm their actions, and submit to the Will of God. Above all, human reason is incapable of fathoming the intentions of God's revelation. Moreover, the Sunna should not be subject to analogy, neither can it be grasped by parables, nor yet is it dictated by the prejudices of men. Rather, it is the unconditional assent to the traditions of the Messenger of God; one should ask neither "why," nor "how." One of the basic principles is to confirm the position taken by Aḥmad b. Ḥanbal during the *miḥna* toward the Quran: It "is the Speech of God, His revelation (*tanzīl*), and His light. It is not created. For the Quran is of God. Whatever is of God is not created" (§ 12).

1.2 *Tenets of Faith*

The creed elaborates on the doctrine of predestination by confirming that "God is prescient of everything from eternity, of what has not been and what is to be, having them all counted and numbered. Denying His knowledge of what has not been and what is to be renders one an unbeliever in the Almighty" (§ 33). One has to patiently accept God's decree and His divine justice, and believe in God's fate, the good and the bad, the sweet and the bitter.

1.3 *Events and Realities of the Day of Judgment*

The reality of the Day of Judgment and its description become, as it were, a guarantee of the objectivity of salvation and a culmination of one's life. It was a standard practice in early Sunni creeds to enumerate the stations after death. This itinerary was meant to target all those theologians who deny that Paradise and Hell have already been created, or who deny certain tenets that the Sunnis affirm regarding the Hereafter. The creed asserts the tortures of the grave, the portents upon death, and the punishment in Hell. On the Day of Resurrection, God will restore to life all creation. He restores them to the very state in which they died. He then holds them to account as He pleases.

1.4 *Communal Aspects*

Faithful to the traditional way of life of the early Community, the creed emphasizes the importance of solidarity and of communal prayers. In this regard, it espouses a slogan that was adopted from the early Murjiʾa, who proposed to postpone judgment about the battles among the early Companions. This slogan is generalized and appears now in the form of a plea for abstention from giving a verdict about the belief of other Muslims in the Community: "A Muslim who has never bore false witness against anyone …, we merely ask for God's mercy on his behalf" (§ 22). "We withhold testimony as to someone's true belief until he complies with the laws and codices (*sharāʾiʿ*) of Islam" (§ 26).[11]

Another important aspect has to do with the tendency to refuse to earn a living or to engage in business transactions, which prevailed in the first/seventh and second/eighth centuries among many pious Muslims and found expression in the third/ninth century among scrupulous Sufis. The mainstream Sunni understanding in the third/ninth century, however, was to confirm the lawfulness of earning one's living and the legitimacy of commerce and economic commissions in general.[12]

1.5 *Praxis*

More often than not, rules that fall under this category are polemical in nature and intended as an attack on the "unorthodox" practices of other groups. Hence it is of great importance that a true member of *al-sunna wa-l-jamāʿa* abide by some prescribed rules that visibly, so to speak, validate his true status. It is part of the Sunna, for instance, to pass the wetted hands over the shoes in ritual ablution. Likewise, it is part of the Sunna to shorten prayers while traveling. Such rules of practice also cover aspects pertaining to stoning in case of adultery, funeral prayers, marriage, prohibition of *mutʿa* (temporary marriage), and conditions of bloodshed.

1.6 *Innovators and Their Novelties*

Basing his format on the famous tradition about the "seventy-two sects,"[13] Ghulām Khalīl quotes a statement by the early Muslim scholar ʿAbdallāh b. al-Mubārak (d. 181/797) explaining that "the origin of seventy-two deviating sects are four: the Qadariyya, the Murjiʾa, the Shiʿa, and the Khawarij; the seventy-two deviations branched from these four" (§ 144). On the contrary, however, the *ahl al-sunna wa-l-jamāʿa* belong to a consecrated Community that follows the righteous path of the Prophet and his Companions, and they abjure the wicked

11 See van Ess, Political ideas 154.

12 See chapter 4.

13 van Ess, *Der Eine* i, 74–77, van Ess, Constructing Islam.

beliefs and practices of the abovementioned heretical groups. Moreover, the creed explicitly tags Jahmis and the Muʿtazila as unbelievers who should be treated as such.

1.7 *Contra Theology*

The creed forwards a repudiation of all possible expressions and ideas that are based on human reasoning and speculation. It accentuates that "truth is that which comes from God, and that the Sunna is that of the Messenger of God, and the Community is defined by the consensus of the Companions of the Messenger of God" (§ 84). Outside of these three sources, there is no proper guidance to the truth.

Accordingly, one should not delve into trivia and should abide, rather, by the "ancient conviction (*dīn ʿatīq*)," since "the source of all heresy, unbelief, doubt, innovation, misguidance, or perplexity in matters of religion is theological disputation" (§ 61). Heretics and innovators deployed reasoning by analogy (*qiyās*), and they fancied their limited understanding and subjective opinion (*raʾy*) fit to fathom the omnipotence of the Lord (§ 71).

1.8 *Political Theology*[14]

Among the fundamental points that have found consensus among Sunni Muslims is that a kind of amnesty applies to the civil strife (*fitna/fitan*) that tainted the history of the early Community. For Sunnis, disputes over these events posed an immediate threat to their unity. By the late second/eighth and early third/ninth centuries, an accord had been reached concerning the Companions, their ranks, and their virtues. Ghulām Khalīl's creed reiterates this conformity and considers it imperative to "refrain from discussing the wars among ʿAlī, Muʿāwiya, ʿĀʾisha, Ṭalḥa, al-Zubayr, and those who were with them" (§ 101). One should not argue about them, but rather leave their affairs to God alone.

To avoid any possible civil strife that might lead to dissension (*furqa*), it is incumbent upon the members of the Community to obey the ruler, pay taxes to him, carry out *jihād* under his authority, and perform the daily prayers, as well as the Friday prayers led by him, whether the rulers are righteous or

---

14 By political theology is meant "the problems arising out of the early political controversies which split up the Muslims into several groups and ultimately resulted into the emergence of many dogmas," quoting Ahmed, Some aspects 53. Van Ess argues that the "three elements, historiography, theology and political thought, appeared at the same time and so early that they became incorporated into the search for identity which preoccupied the early community and continues up to our day." Political ideas 154. See also Moosa, Muslim political theology; Ben Achour, *Aux fondements* 12–13.

dissolute. To fight authority (*al-sulṭān*), or to revolt against it, is forbidden, even if such authority were despotic.

1.9 *Maxims*

The creed also replicates sayings regarding the importance of the Sunna and its adherents as a path to salvation. These sayings are attributed to certain Companions, Successors, and early authorities from among the ranks of the Muslim *Urgemeinde*, including direct predecessors from the second/eighth century who served as models (*aṣḥāb sunna*).

2 Outline and Summary

In light of the aspects outlined above, the present publication begins with four chapters, an epilogue, and two appendices. These parts of the book are followed by a critical edition of the Arabic text and, finally, an English translation.

Chapter 1 deals with the life of Ghulām Khalīl and his career as a preacher. Two main subjects are highlighted here: first, his persecution of the Sufis of Baghdad in 264/877–878; and second, his affiliation with the ʿAbbasids and his maintaining of a close relationship with the mother of the regent al-Muwaffaq, which fulfilled an ideological function in the service of the state.

Chapter 2 describes the unique Damascene manuscript that is the primary basis of this study. It deals with the textual evidence as well as the process of its transmission up to the fifth/eleventh century. This chapter also examines the question of the authorship of the creed, as it has been attributed since Ibn Abī Yaʿlā (d. 536/1131) not to Ghulām Khalīl but instead to the Hanbali leader al-Ḥasan b. ʿAlī al-Barbahārī (d. 329/941); Ibn Abī Yaʿlā cited it in its entirety in his *Ṭabaqāt al-Ḥanābila*. The chapter also reviews the opinions of earlier twentieth-century Western scholars who dealt with this issue, beginning with Louis Massignon, the French scholar who confirmed Ghulām Khalīl's authorship. The confusion in modern scholarship begins with Henri Laoust in 1958, who accepted the medieval attribution of the creed to al-Barbahārī. Since then, most modern Western scholars have relied on Laoust's opinion without adopting a critical stance. The chapter concludes by setting the terms of the argument, in that it presents three points of internal and three of external textual evidence that assert Ghulām Khalīl's authorship.

Chapter 3 investigates and explains the proliferation of Sunni creeds in the third/ninth century, and provides a classification of these creeds and a detailed comparative study of their tenets. The analysis centers on the conceptual field of the tenets and tries to clarify the ways in which Ghulām Khalīl's creed is similar to or different from other creeds of that time.

Chapter 4 begins by studying the terminology adopted by Ghulām Khalīl, concentrating on two principle terms, the Sunna and the Community. It also explains the meaning of the title, *Kitāb Sharḥ al-sunna*. The second part of the chapter then broaches a thematic study of that book and examines the terminology and the conceptual framework of the twelve main themes that the book addresses.

The epilogue examines the question of what assumptions Ghulām Khalīl operated on in propagating his creed. The issues explored here include the questions: For whom was this creed written, and what were its horizons? The epilogue also explores how Sunni creeds generally function and how their mode of reception is to be understood. It is important to keep in mind that Ghulām Khalīl was writing at a time when two major changes left indelible marks on the third century. The first was the triumph of traditionalism in the aftermath of the *miḥna*; the second was the product of a chequered ʿAbbasid rule weakened by the civil wars between brothers al-Amīn and al-Maʾmūn in 195–198/811–813 and in the period of anarchy in 247–256/861–870, followed by the Zanj revolt in Basra. In this turbulent politico-dogmatic context, Ghulām Khalīl's creed appears to have aimed at redounding to the ideological authority of the "victorious" traditionists in two ways: first, by reaching out to the waves of refugees from the rural areas who moved to Baghdad in the wake of these events; and second, by claiming a role that was mutually beneficial to the ʿAbbasids as well as to the traditionalists, a tactic with which Ghulām Khalīl attempted to consolidate and to legitimate ʿAbbasid rule. Moreover, with his appeal to the imminence of a messianic figure, Ghulām Khalīl was mobilizing existing ideological symbols in order to promulgate the advent of a new era under the rule of his charismatic patron, the victorious al-Muwaffaq bi-Llāh, "the Blessed of God," then the de facto regent of the ʿAbbasid caliphate for most of the reign of his brother, the caliph al-Muʿtamid (r. 256–279/870–892).

Appendix 1 is a survey of the different editions of the creed. It takes up again the question posed at the beginning of this introduction: What prompted some contemporary Salafis to adopt and propagate a creed first published in the third/ninth century? In point of fact, this creed, albeit in its attribution to the Hanbali al-Ḥasan b. ʿAlī al-Barbahārī, was adopted by the Council of Senior Ulema in the Kingdom of Saudi Arabia as a quasi-official catechism to be taught at seminaries for *daʿwa*, or Islamic mission, sponsored by the Saudi establishment in different parts of the world to promote its ideology.

The attribution of this creed to al-Ḥasan b. ʿAlī al-Barbahārī, a direct student of one of Aḥmad b. Ḥanbal's disciples, is one of the main factors that legitimate it in contemporary Salafi circles. Moreover, the creed displays a conservative tone. It vehemently adjures strict submission to the ruler (*walī al-amr*) and proscribes any action against him.

To address certain of these observations, and to contextualize them in view of Ghulām Khalīl's general transmission activities, the second appendix identifies and offers translations of some 22 traditions transmitted in the medieval sources on the authority of Ghulām Khalīl.

Yet, in spite of the confused authorship that was attached—deliberately, it seems—to Ghulām Khalīl's creed, or, perhaps more probably because of this very confusion, the creed has been reclaimed and has found wide circulation among some contemporary Salafis, a fact that underscores the ongoing vitality of the "living tradition" and its doctrinal instructions.

CHAPTER 1

Ghulām Khalīl: Life, Career, and Image as a Scholar

1 Biographical Information

Abū ʿAbdallāh Aḥmad b. Muḥammad b. Ghālib al-Bāhilī, known as Ghulām Khalīl (d. 275/888), was originally from Basra. He was a client (*mawlā*) of the Bāhila clan, which had moved to Iraq through Syria during the course of the Islamic expansion and had settled in the vicinity of Basra,[1] specifically in al-Baṭāʾiḥ, the marshlands on the east side of the Tigris,[2] and in al-ʿĀliya, the highlands in Basra.[3] Louis Massignon affiliates Ghulām Khalīl with the latter. Part of the Bāhila clan seems to have taken part in the Zanj revolt (255–270/869–883) under the leadership of a certain Sulaymān b. Jāmiʿ.[4] The Bāhila clan generally held anti-Shiʿi attitudes.[5]

Nothing is known about Ghulām Khalīl's early years in Basra. We are somewhat better informed about the later years of his active life in Baghdad, where he appears to have been of the same generation as the disciples of Aḥmad b. Ḥanbal (d. 241/855), noted theologian and the eponym of the most traditionalist of the four Sunni schools of law. Among those disciples are Aḥmad's two sons, Ṣāliḥ (d. 265/878) and ʿAbdallāh (d. 290/902), and his cousin Ḥanbal b. Isḥāq (d. 273/886), as well as Abū Bakr al-Marrūdhī (d. 275/888).

Although Ghulām Khalīl recurrently cites Aḥmad b. Ḥanbal in the *K. Sharḥ al-sunna*, it cannot be ascertained whether he actually studied with him. Nor do the sources offer any statement describing Ghulām Khalīl's relationship with Aḥmad b. Ḥanbal or his followers. Nonetheless, both Qawwām al-Sunna,[6] Abū l-Qāsim Ismāʿīl (d. 535/1140), a Shafiʿi traditionist (*muḥaddith*) from Isfahan, and Ibn Taymiyya (d. 728/1328), the noted Hanbali theologian and jurisconsult from Syria, state that Ghulām Khalīl was a disciple (*ṣāḥib*) of Aḥmad b. Ḥanbal.[7] It is of special note, however, that not a single author of a Han-

1 Cf. Ibn Ḥazm, *Jamhara* 245–247; Caskel, Bāhila.

2 Al-ʿAlī, *Khiṭaṭ al-Baṣra* 191. See also Streck and El-Ali, al-Baṭīḥa.

3 Al-ʿAlī, *Khiṭaṭ al-Baṣra* 82; Massignon, Explication du plan de Basra 66.

4 Al-Ṭabarī, *Tārīkh* ix, 521–523.

5 Massignon, Explication du plan de Kufa 60.

6 It is also possible to read his epithet as Qiwām al-Sunna, meaning the "pillar of the Sunna"; see also "Qiwām al-Dīn" in Ibn al-Fuwaṭī, *Majmaʿ* iii, 470–568.

7 Qawwām al-Sunna, *al-Ḥujja* ii, 475; Ibn Taymiyya, *Sharḥ ḥadīth al-nuzūl* 163–164, while counting disciples of Aḥmad whose names were "Muḥammad."

 | DOI:10.1163/9789004429055_003

bali *ṭabaqāt* work, the biographical dictionaries of Hanbali scholars, makes any mention at all of Ghulām Khalīl.

Yet there are two reports that might shed light on Ghulām Khalīl's religio-political stances, in that they give some indication of his attitudes toward the *miḥna*, the "inquisition" instituted by the ʿAbbasid caliph al-Maʾmūn (r. 813–833) to enforce the doctrine that the Quran was the created (rather than the uncreated or eternal) word of God. The first account is quoted by the Hanbali jurisconsult, theologian, and historian Ibn al-Jawzī (d. 597/1201), reporting that Ghulām Khalīl transmitted a poem in ʿAbbādān by Abū Jaʿfar al-Khawwāṣ that celebrates the end of the *miḥna* and the heroic position taken in it by "the hero of Islam" (*fatā l-Islām*), Aḥmad b. Ḥanbal.[8]

The second account is quoted by the Shafiʿi traditionist and historian al-Dhahabī (d. 748/1348), on the authority of Aḥmad b. Kāmil (d. 350/961),[9] a student of Ghulām Khalīl. This report states first that Ghulām Khalīl had related having heard from al-ʿAbbās b. ʿAbd al-ʿAẓīm (d. 246/860)[10] that the Basran traditionist ʿAlī b. ʿAbdallāh al-Madīnī (d. 234/849, known as Ibn al-Madīnī) had had a dream in which he delivered a sermon at the pulpit of the prophet David. Ibn al-Madīnī is also said to have told al-ʿAbbās b. ʿAbd al-ʿAẓīm that he would have wished the pulpit had been that of the prophet Job, since David had been severely tested with regard to his religion (*dīn*, in reference to Q 38:24–25; cf. Hebrew Scripture 2 Samuel 11). Eventually, al-ʿAbbās comments on this dream by saying that ʿAlī b. al-Madīnī had failed during the *miḥna*, which was in his view comparable to one of the divine tests that David had faced. The content and the message of this account indicate that this anecdote is one of those reports that were later put in circulation to belittle ʿAlī b. al-Madīnī for his conduct during the *miḥna*.[11]

These few pieces of biographical information can be summarized as follows:

On the one hand, there is evidence that Ghulām Khalīl venerated Aḥmad b. Ḥanbal. Yet it is difficult to say anything more definite about whether he was a disciple of Ibn Ḥanbal, and whether or not he was among the companions (*aṣḥāb*) who comprised the first generation of the Hanbali *madhhab*.[12] On

8 Ibn al-Jawzī, *Manāqib Aḥmad* ii, 170.

9 Al-Dhahabī, *Siyar* xi, 51; al-Dhahabī comments on the report by stating that Ghulām Khalīl is untrustworthy.

10 Al-Dhahabī, *Siyar* xii, 302.

11 Al-Khaṭīb al-Baghdādī, *Tārīkh* xiii, 430–438; Jadʿān, *al-Miḥna* 154, 225–227. Part of the complex background of the story is that ʿAlī b. al-Madīnī, when threatened with physical punishment should he refuse to give up his traditional beliefs in the createdness of the Quran, had renounced these beliefs. Cf. also *ThG* iii, 470 and 475.

12 Cf. Hallaq, *Origins* 150–167.

the other hand, Ghulām Khalīl was older than the great Hanbali theologian and dogmatist Abū Bakr al-Khallāl (d. 311/923), whose book on the doctrine of "orthodox" faith gained significant influence. Thus, Ghulām Khalīl's scholarly activities fall into the core period of the development and gradual textual fixation of the conservative Hanbali creeds. Indeed, his creed seems to link the development of creeds written in the first half of the third/ninth century with those of the great dogmatists of the fourth/tenth century.

The question as to whether Ghulām Khalīl was a Hanbali, as has often been claimed since Massignon,[13] cannot be conclusively answered on the basis of this evidence.[14] What is clear, however, is that his *K. Sharḥ al-sunna* was penned by an author who was a strict adherent of the Sunna.

2 The Epithet

No conclusive explanation is given in the sources for the epithet "Ghulām Khalīl" by which Aḥmad b. Muḥammad b. Ghālib al-Bāhilī of Basra came to be known. "Ghulām" could refer to a "boy," an "apprentice," or an "adherent" of an elder (hitherto unidentified) *shaykh* or scholar named Khalīl. Yet, two forms of the name are attested in the sources: Ghulām Khalīl and Ghulām al-Khalīl.

Modern scholars have made several attempts to explain the names Ghulām Khalīl and Ghulām al-Khalīl, respectively. Louis Massignon, for example, refers to a statement made by one of Ghulām Khalīl's students, Aḥmad b. Kāmil (d. 350/961), who reportedly said that Ghulām Khalīl used to "vocalize" his speech.[15] Massignon concludes from this that Ghulām was a student of the prominent Basran grammarian al-Khalīl b. Aḥmad al-Farāhīdī (d. 170/786).[16]

13 The following individuals all consider him a Hanbali: Massignon, *Recueil* 212; Massignon, Explication du plan de Basra 74; Massignon, *Passion* i, 80–81; Schacht, *Der Islam* 40; Grunebaum, *Der Islam* 141; *GAS* i, 511; Nwyia, *Exégèse coranique* 317; Madelung, al-Kharrāz 1083b; Ernst, *Words of ecstasy* 97; Schimmel, Qibla of the lights 60; Knysh, *Islamic mysticism* 57; de Crussol, *Role de la raison*, 256.

14 Jarrar and Günther, Ġulām Ḫalīl 12, 19. See also Gramlich, *Alte Vorbilder* 383, fn. 20, who calls him a "Jurist und Prediger streng traditionalistischer Schule," although it is clear that he was not, in fact, a jurist. Furthermore, *ThG* iv, 284; van Ess, Sufism 26; van Ess, *Der Eine* i, 285–286. Melchert, Ḥanābila 361, however, sees strong evidence for a connection with Hanbalism; on this issue see Jarrar, Ghulām Khalīl.

15 Al-Khaṭīb al-Baghdādī, *Tārīkh* vi, 248.

16 Massignon, Explication du plan de Basra 74.

Although al-Farāhīdī apparently died even before Ghulām Khalīl was born, Massignon's assumption is appealing since one of the preaching sessions that Ghulām Khalīl gave in Basra shows him as an eloquent orator. Referring to him as Ghulām al-Khalīl may have been meant to indicate that he was a preacher who delivered his admonitions in fluent and articulate language.[17]

Josef van Ess suggests that "Ghulām al-Khalīl" could be an honorific title meaning "Servant of Abraham," though he does not provide any evidence to corroborate this idea.[18] Nonetheless, it is rather unlikely that Ghulām would be given such an honorific title, derived from *khulla* (divine love),[19] as was bestowed upon the ancient prophet Abraham. This can be concluded from the fact that Ghulām Khalīl was an outright opponent of Sufis, who were known to hold such ideas (see "The *Miḥna* against the Sufis," below). There is, however, another interesting report, quoted by the Moroccan scholar al-Ḥasan al-Yūsī (d. 1102/1691), who attributed it to the famous Arab grammarian and lexicographer al-Aṣmaʿī (d. ca. 213/828).[20] The account belongs to the genre of those anecdotes, ample in the sources, about prototypical so-called *ʿubbād* lovers—people who devoted themselves entirely to the love of God. In this story, the young believer (*ʿābid*) introduces himself as a Ghulām following the religion (*dīn*) of the prophet Abraham (Ibrāhīm), while alluding to Abraham's hospitality.[21] It remains unclear, however, whether this story helps explain the appellation "al-Khalīl," as nothing is mentioned in the sources regarding Ghulām Khalīl's hospitality as a particular character trait.

Although the question of Ghulām's epithet has remained unsettled thus far, the table below offers a chronology of references to those sources that mention the second part of Ghulām's epithet, either without or with the definite article:

---

17 For the use of *fuṣḥā* (pure, articulate language) in classical Arabic oratory, see Jones, *Power* 90.

18 *ThG* iv, 285.

19 Massignon, *Essai* 177, 195. See, however, al-Jāḥiẓ's argument about the difference between *khulla* (derived from "fraternity, friendhip, and sincerity") and *khalla* (meaning "need, hardship and poverty"). Abraham's appellation relates to the second term; cf. Risāla fī l-radd ʿalā l-Naṣārā, *Rasāʾil* iii, 337–341.

20 Al-Yūsī, *Zahr al-akam* i, 234–235.

21 On Ibrāhīm's hospitality, see al-Thaʿlabī, *ʿArāʾis* 108; al-Ghazālī, *Iḥyāʾ* 461, 465, 466 (*ādāb al-ḍiyāfa*); Ibn Qayyim al-Jawziyya, *Majmūʿ al-rasāʾil* 73–79. In the Jewish literature, Abraham is the paragon of hospitality; cf. Ward, Works of Abraham 286–289; van Bekkum, Many nations 285.

Khalīl	al-Khalīl
– Al-Dīnawarī, (d. 333/944, direct student), *al-Mujālasa* vii, 236	– Ibn Abī Ḥātim (d. 327/938), *al-Jarḥ* ii, 73
– Al-Dārquṭnī (d. 385/995), *al-Ḍuʿafāʾ* 122	
– Ibn al-Nadīm (d. ca. 380/990), *al-Fihrist* 186	– Ibn Ḥibbān (d. 354/965), *K. al-Majrūḥīn* i, 150
– Ibn al-Faraḍī (d. 403/1012), *Tārīkh* i, 217	– Ibn ʿAdī (d. 365/975), *al-Kāmil* i, 322
– Al-Khaṭīb (d. 462/1069), *Tārīkh* vi, 335; xiii, 617	– Al-Sarrāj (d. 378/988), *al-Lumaʿ* 498–499
– Al-Ṭarṭūshī (d. 520/1126), *Sirāj al-mulūk* 369	– Al-Dārquṭnī (d. 385/995), *Suʾālāt al-Ḥākim* 90
– Al-Qāḍī ʿIyāḍ (d. 544/1149), *Tartīb* iv, 283	– Abū Ṭālib al-Makkī (d. 386/996), *Qūt al-qulūb* ii, 1106
– Ibn ʿAsākir (d. 571/1175), *Tārīkh* xli, 467	– Al-Ḥākim al-Naysābūrī (d. 405/1014), *Maʿrifat ʿulūm* ii, 207
– Ibn al-Jawzī (d. 597/1201), *al-Ḍuʿafāʾ* i, 88, iii, 161; *al-Quṣṣāṣ* 296; *Manāqib Aḥmad* 484	– al-Sulamī (d. 412/1021), *Masāʾil* 55
– Ibn Taymiyya (d. 728/1327), *Sharḥ ḥadīth al-nuzūl* 163–164; *al-Istighātha* 636–637	– Ḥamza al-Sahmī (d. 427/1035), *Tārīkh Jurjān* i, 109
– al-Dhahabī (d. 748/1348), *Siyar* xi, 51; xiii, 284–285; xiv, 71	– Abū Nuʿaym (d. 430/1038), *Ḥilya* x, 250; *al-Mustakhraj* i, 60
	– al-Qushayrī (d. 465/1072), *al-Risāla* ii, 404
	– al-Hujwīrī (d. ca. 465/1072), *Kashf* 349, 421
	– al-Ghazālī (d. 505/1111), *Iḥyāʾ* 1797
	– Qawwām al-Sunna (d. 535/1140), *al-Ḥujja* ii, 475
	– Najm al-Dīn al-Nasafī (d. 537/1142), *al-Qand* 197
	– Ibn al-Jawzī (d. 597/1201), *Talbīs* 1011, 1034–1038 (al-Khalīl); *al-Muntaẓim* xii, 265
	– Ibn Ḥajar al-ʿAsqalānī (d. 852/1448), *Lisān* i, 617

Aḥmad b. Kāmil, one of Ghulām's direct students and the first transmitter of *K. Sharḥ al-sunna*, as well as Aḥmad b. Marwān al-Dīnawarī, another of Ghulām's direct students, refer to their teacher as "Ghulām Khalīl." Still, the majority of the Arabic sources specified in the table above give Ghulām the appellation al-Khalīl, among them two early authors, as well as all the authors of works that deal with mysticism.

In addition, al-Dārquṭnī refers to Ghulām Khalīl (without the definite article) on one occasion, and on another, this time on the authority of al-Ḥākim al-Naysābūrī, Ghulām al-Khalīl. Ibn al-Jawzī, in turn, uses both forms, each of them twice. It is therefore impossible at this point to say with any certainty which form of the name is the more original or plausible. In the present study, the name "Ghulām Khalīl" is used throughout, as this is the name that appears on the title page of the Damascus manuscript of the *K. Sharḥ al-sunna*.

3 Scholarship

3.1 *Teachers*

Al-Khaṭīb al-Baghdādī lists the following as Ghulām Khalīl's teachers:[22]

(1) Dīnār b. ʿAbdallāh (d. 229/843),[23] of Abyssinian origin, who claimed that he was a servant of the much older Prophet's Companion Anas b. Mālik (d. 91–93/709–711). The sources agree in calling him "useless" (*tālif*) and a fabricator of weak traditions (*mawḍūʿāt*). Ghulām Khalīl reports that he had met with Dīnār b. ʿAbdallāh sometime after 210/825–826 (*sanat biḍʿ wa-ʿashr*) in al-Ahwāz. Ghulām Khalīl indicates as well that, in the same year, he had also met a certain Khirāsh in Basra, and that he had transmitted from both Dīnār b. ʿAbdallāh and Khirāsh.[24] Ghulām Khalīl transmits nine traditions from Dīnār b. ʿAbdallāh (see appendix II, 2, 3, 10a, 10b, 12, 18, 19, 20, 21).

(2) Muḥammad b. Maslama al-Madīnī (d. 216/831),[25] a Maliki jurisprudent and one of Mālik's direct students.

22 Al-Khaṭīb al-Baghdādī, *Tārīkh* vi, 245; see also al-Dhahabī, *Siyar* xiii, 282.

23 Ibn ʿAdī, *al-Kāmil* iv, 5; Ibn Ḥibbān, *K. al-Majrūḥīn* i, 295; al-Dhahabī, *Siyar* x, 376; Ibn Ḥajar, *Lisān* iii, 426.

24 Al-Khaṭīb al-Baghdādī, *Tārīkh* ix, 359, vi, 246, mentions that Ghulām Khalīl had studied with Dīnār b. ʿAbdallāh in Baghdad.

25 Al-Qāḍī ʿIyāḍ, *Tartīb* iii, 131.

(3) Qurra b. Ḥabīb al-Baṣrī (d. 224/838),[26] known as a trustworthy teacher of al-Bukhārī (for a tradition on his behalf see appendix II, 14).

(4) Sahl b. ʿUthmān, most probably studied under Abū Masʿūd al-ʿAskarī (d. 235/849), a "trustworthy" teacher of Muslim b. al-Ḥajjāj.

(5) Shaybān b. Farrūkh al-Baṣrī (d. 236/850),[27] known as a trustworthy teacher of Muslim b. al-Ḥajjāj and Abū Dāwūd al-Sijistānī (for a tradition on his behalf see appendix II, 16).

(6) Sulaymān b. Dāwūd al-Shādhakūnī al-Baṣrī (d. 334/848),[28] known as an authority on the reliability of traditionists. Although he himself was regarded as a weak traditionist, Aḥmad b. Ḥanbal is said to have admired him.

The following teachers are mentioned in other sources:

(7) Ibn Ḥibbān states[29] that Ghulām Khalīl studied with ("heard from") the Medinese Ismāʿīl b. Abī Uways (d. 226/840 or 227/841),[30] one of the main disciples of Mālik. Ismāʿīl b. Abī Uways was considered weak in *ḥadīth* transmission. Ibn Ḥibbān reports that Ghulām Khalīl transmitted from him a small collection of prophetic traditions (*ṣaḥīfa*) compiled by al-Bukhārī on the authority of Ibn Abī Uways, which contained 80 *ḥadīth*s from the noted scholar of prophetic traditions Ibn Shihāb al-Zuhrī (d. 124/741–742), although he had not studied this collection with Ibn Abī Uways in person.

(8) Yazīd b. Ṣāliḥ, known as a weak traditionist. It is said that Ghulām Khalīl transmitted from him a certain fabricated incantation (*ḥirz*)[31] on the authority of Abū Dujāna, a Companion of the Prophet Muhammad.[32] Al-Dhahabī contends that Ghulām Khalīl invented this account.[33]

(9) Ibn al-Jawzī relates[34] a poem (using a chain of transmission identical to the *samāʿ* chain on the first page of *K. Sharḥ al-sunna*)[35] which an otherwise unkown Abū Jaʿfar al-Khawwāṣ recited to Ghulām Khalīl in

---

26 Al-Dhahabī, *Siyar* x, 426.

27 Ibid., xi, 101.

28 Al-Khaṭīb al-Baghdādī, *Tārīkh* x, 55; al-Dhahabī, *Siyar* x, 679.

29 Ibn Ḥibbān, *K. al-Majrūḥīn* i, 150–151.

30 Al-Qāḍī ʿIyāḍ, *Tartīb* iii, 151; al-Dhahabī, *Siyar* x, 391.

31 See appendix II, 11.

32 Ibn ʿAbd al-Barr, *al-Istīʿāb* iv, 1644.

33 Al-Dhahabī, *Mīzān* iv, 429; Ibn Ḥajar, *Lisān* viii, 498.

34 Ibn al-Jawzī, *Manāqib Aḥmad* ii, 170; al-Suyūṭī, *al-Muḥāḍarāt* 365.

35 Abū Bakr Aḥmad b. Kāmil b. Khalaf b. Shajara (d. 350/961) ← Abū l-Ḥasan Muḥammad b. al-ʿAbbās b. al-Furāt (d. 384/994) ← Abū Isḥāq Ibrāhīm b. ʿUmar b. Aḥmad al-Barmakī (d. 445/1053).

ʿAbbādān. The event is said to have taken place after the *miḥna* against Aḥmad b. Ḥanbal during the reign of al-Mutawakkil. Although this does not necessarily mean that al-Khawwāṣ taught Ghulām Khalīl, it suggests that they might have been acquaintances.

3.2 *Further Teachers*

Twenty-two traditions in the sources transmitted by Ghulām Khalīl were identified (appendix II). Consequently, in addition to the names of his possible teachers listed above, the following ten are to be noted, assuming that the *isnād* chains provided by Ghulām Khalīl are sound and not fabricated:

(10) ʿAbdallāh b. Yazīd al-Ramlī (appendix II, 4).
(11) ʿAlī b. Ḥammād (appendix II, 8).
(12) Muḥammad b. ʿAbdallāh, Abū Zayd al-Madanī (appendix II, 13).
(13) Muḥammad b. ʿAbdallāh al-ʿUmarī[36] (appendix II, 7).
(14) Muḥammad b. Ibrāhīm al-Bayyāḍī (appendix II, 5).
(15) Muḥammad b. Ibrāhīm b. al-ʿAlāʾ[37] (appendix II, 1), from Damascus. He settled in ʿAbbādān for some time.[38] His name appears twice as informant of Ghulām Khalīl in traditions cited by Abū l-Shaykh al-Iṣbahānī (d. 369/979).[39]
(16) Muḥammad b. Sulaymān (appendix II, 15).
(17) Maḥmūd b. Ghaylān (d. 249/863;[40] appendix II, 22).
(18) ʿUthmān b. Abī Shayba[41] (appendix II, 17).
(19) Thawbān b. Saʿīd (died after 245/859;[42] appendix II, 6).

3.3 *Students*

Al-Khaṭīb al-Baghdādī mentions three students of Ghulām Khalīl:[43]

(1) Abū Bakr Aḥmad b. Kāmil b. Khalaf b. Shajara (d. 350/961). Ibn Kāmil was also a prominent student of al-Ṭabarī (d. 310/923) before becoming a renowned scholar himself.[44] He held the office of judge in Kufa for

36 Al-Dhahabī, *Mīzān* i, 142; Ibn Ḥajar, *Lisān* i, 618. For al-ʿUmarī, see Ibn Ḥibbān, *K. al-Majrūḥīn* ii, 282.
37 Ibn Ḥibbān, *K. al-Majrūḥīn* ii, 301; Ibn Ḥajar, *Tahdhīb* ix, 14.
38 Ibn Ḥibbān, *K. al-Majrūḥīn* ii, 301; Ibn Ḥajar, *Tahdhīb* ix, 14.
39 See appendix II, no. 1.
40 Al-Dhahabī, *Siyar* xii, 223.
41 Al-Ṭuraythīthī, *Musalsalāt* 127b.
42 Ibn Abī Ḥātim, *al-Jarḥ* ii, 470 no. 1909.
43 Al-Khaṭīb al-Baghdādī, *Tārīkh* vi, 245; see also al-Dhahabī, *Siyar* xiii, 282.
44 Al-Khaṭīb al-Baghdādī, *Tārīkh* v, 587; Rosenthal, *History* 1, 7, 15, 18, 65–67, 107.

some time.[45] Ibn Kāmil was an expert in more than one field of study and authored books in Quranic studies, including a book on exegesis, a book on *variae lectiones* (*qirāʾāt*), a book on intonation and pauses in the Quran (*al-waqf*), and another on uncommon terms in the Quran (*gharīb*). In legal theory, he wrote a book on the conditions for verifying legal documents (*shurūṭ*) and an abridgment of it (*al-shurūṭ al-ṣaghīr*),[46] as well as a book on the rules of war and of dealings with non-Muslims (*siyar*).[47] Moreover, he compiled a book on the lives of judges with accounts about them (*Akhbār al-quḍāt*) and another about the poets (*Akhbār al-shuʿarāʾ*). He also compiled a book in jurisprudence based on the legal opinion (*madhhab*) of Ibn Jarīr al-Ṭabarī.[48] When his student, the famous traditionist al-Dārquṭnī (d. 385/996), was asked if Ibn Kāmil was a Jariri (a follower of the legal school of Ibn Jarīr al-Ṭabarī), he explained that Ibn Kāmil had taken issue with Ibn Jarīr's *madhhab* and had chosen a stance of his own. Al-Dārquṭnī also accused him of lax transmission of *ḥadīth* reports.[49] Ibn Abī al-Wafāʾ (d. 775/1373) dedicates an entry to him. He lists him, however, among the Hanafi scholars.[50] Importantly, Aḥmad b. Kāmil makes an addition to the text of *K. Sharḥ al-sunna*, inserting his own "signature" in the text by introducing from a direct teacher of his an account on Fuḍayl b. ʿIyāḍ. This addition might also be read as an indication to the possible fact that the text of *K. Sharḥ al-sunna* is a "recension" of Ibn Kāmil's transmission, which was prepared by Muḥammad b. al-ʿAbbās b. al-Furāt (d. 384/994), the transmitter from Ibn Kāmil (see article 115 in the text). It was possible to identify four traditions that Aḥmad b. Kāmil transmitted on the authority of Ghulām Khalīl.[51]

(2) Muḥammad b. Makhlad (d. 331/942).[52]

(3) ʿUthmān b. Aḥmad b. al-Sammāk (d. 344/955).[53]

---

45 Al-Khaṭīb al-Baghdādī, *Tārīkh* v, 587, communicates that he became judge of Kufa directly before Abū ʿUmar Muḥammad b. Yūsuf; the latter was appointed in 301/913 judge of the east side of Baghdad, as well as of other places, including areas of al-Sawād (the alluvial land of the Euphrates and Tigris), Syria, Mecca and Medina (al-Ḥaramān), and Yemen. Al-Khaṭīb al-Baghdādī, *Tārīkh* iv, 636–637.

46 Ibn al-Nadīm, *al-Fihrist* (ed. Flügel) 23, (ed. Tajaddud) 35; Yāqūt, *Muʿjam* i, 420; al-Dāwūdī, *Ṭabaqāt* i, 66.

47 Al-Khaṭīb al-Baghdādī, *Tārīkh* v, 589.

48 Ibn al-Nadīm, *al-Fihrist* (ed. Flügel) 235, (ed. Tajaddud) 292.

49 Al-Sahmī, *Suʾālāt* xxi, 165; al-Khaṭīb al-Baghdādī, *Tārīkh* iv, 589.

50 Ibn Abī al-Wafāʾ, *al-Jawāhir* i, 238.

51 See appendix II, 10a, 10b, 14, 20, 21.

52 Al-Khaṭīb al-Baghdādī, *Tārīkh* iv, 499; al-Dhahabī, *Siyar* xv, 679.

53 Al-Khaṭīb al-Baghdādī, *Tārīkh* xiii, 190; al-Dhahabī, *Siyar* xv, 444.

Fourteen more students of Ghulām Khalīl are mentioned in other sources:

(4) ʿAbdallāh b. Masarra (d. 286/899),[54] father of the Andalusian philosopher and mystic.

(5) ʿAbd al-Raḥmān b. Muḥammad al-Tamīmī (al-Yaḥmudī;[55] appendix II, 9).

(6) Aḥmad b. Marwān al-Dīnawarī (d. 333/944),[56] the author of *al-Mujālasa wa-jawāhir al-ʿilm*, in which he transmits a *ḥadīth* directly from Ghulām Khalīl[57] (appendix II, 6).

(7) Aḥmad b. Muḥammad b. Hammām (appendix II, 8).

(8) ʿAlī b. Yūsuf b. Ayyūb al-Daqqāq.[58] Al-Khaṭīb dedicates an entry to him that includes only a *ḥadīth* that he transmitted on the authority of his teacher (appendix II, 22).

(9) ʿAlī b. Dāwūd Abū l-Ḥasan al-Warthānī, originally from Azerbaijan, but resided in al-Mizza.[59]

(10) Ilyās b. Idrīs al-Kassī (appendix II, 19).

(11) Isḥāq b. Muḥammad al-Kaysānī (d. 319/931;[60] appendix II, 15).

(12) Ismāʿīl b. al-Faraj (appendix II, 12).

(13) Maysara b. ʿAbd Rabbih.[61] Maysara was also a student of the ascetic Abū Sulaymān Dāwūd b. al-Muḥabbar (d. 206/821).[62]

(14) Muʿādh b. Yūsuf al-Jurjānī (appendix II, 17).

(15) Usayd b. Muḥammad, from Balkh (appendix II, 3).

(16) Yaʿqūb b. Muḥammad al-Balkhī (appendix II, 18).

(17) A certain Abū ʿĪsā (appendix II, 4).

It is impossible at this point to determine which subjects Ghulām Khalīl taught these students. Nonetheless, looking at the provenance of his students, one notes that Ghulām Khalīl's renown as a scholar was widespread at the time.

54 Ibn al-Faraḍī, *Tārīkh* i, 179, no. 650.
55 Ibn Ḥajar, *Lisān* v, 133 no. 4695.
56 Al-Dhahabī, *Siyar* xv, 427.
57 Al-Dīnawarī, *al-Mujālasa* vii, 236.
58 Al-Khaṭīb al-Baghdādī, *Tārīkh* xiii, 617.
59 Ibn ʿAsākir, *Tārīkh* xli, 467.
60 Al-Qazwīnī, *al-Tadwīn* ii, 281.
61 Al-Dhahabī, *Mīzan* iv, 231; *ThG* iv, 285.
62 Al-Khaṭīb al-Baghdādī, *Tārīkh* ix, 326.

4 Image as Scholar and Preacher

Ghulām Khalīl appears in the sources as a rather controversial figure, primarily in connection with the persecution (*miḥna*) that he inflicted on the Sufis of Baghdad, which will be discussed later in this volume. Otherwise, he is known as an ascetic and a popular preacher (*qāṣṣ, wāʿiẓ*) who had a poor reputation as a traditionist. Preachers were generally highly respected in his hometown of Basra for their eloquence.[63] Al-Dhahabī thought highly of Ghulām Khalīl and praised him as a knowledgeable scholar (*ʿālim*), ascetic, and preacher.[64] Moreover, he commended him for his "soundness of belief" (*ṣiḥḥat al-muʿtaqad*).

Most accounts of Ghulām Khalīl's life stem from his student Ibn Kāmil. Ibn Kāmil speaks highly of his asceticism (*zuhd*) and scrupulosity (*waraʿ*),[65] and says that he was eloquent and used to speak classical Arabic with all grammatical endings (*kāna faṣīḥan yuʿribu l-kalām*), and that he used to dye his hair with henna. Ibn Kāmil also report that Ghulām Khalīl's diet consisted of plain vegetables and broad beans (*bāqillāʾ*),[66] which most probably earned him the appellation "al-Bāqillānī" among the Hanafis of northeastern Iran, a name that appears in a transmission chain in some copies of *K. al-Sawād al-aʿẓam* by al-Ḥakīm al-Samarqandī (d. 342/953).[67]

Ibn Ḥibbān (d. 354/965) reports that "he was a renunciant" (*kāna yataqashshaf*),[68] an image of him that predominates in the sources.[69] Ibn al-Nadīm (d. 380/990) counts him among the ascetics and mystics, and mentions four books that he is reported to have authored, *K. al-Duʿāʾ* ("Supplication"), *K. al-Inqiṭāʿ ilā Allāh* ("Devotion to and preoccupation with God"), *K. al-Ṣalāt* ("Prayers"), and *K. al-Mawāʿiẓ* ("The book of sermons or exhortations").[70] This evidence caused Massignon to maintain that Ghulām Khalīl's ascetic tendencies represent the ascetic teachings of the old movement in Basra.[71]

---

63 Al-Jāḥiẓ, *al-Bayān* i, 291.

64 Al-Dhahabī, *Siyar* xiii, 283.

65 Al-Ḥākim, *al-Madkhal* i, 150.

66 Al-Khaṭīb al-Baghdādī, *Tārīkh* vi, 248; Ibn al-Jawzī, *al-Muntaẓam* xii, 267; Ibn al-Athīr, *al-Kāmil* xi, 310; for the putridity of *al-bāqillāʾ*, see al-Jāḥiẓ, *al-Ḥayawān* iii, 356–358; cf. *ThG* ii, 176.

67 MS American University of Beirut, fol. 29.

68 Ibn Ḥibbān, *K. al-Majrūḥīn* i, 150.

69 Al-Ḥākim, *al-Musnad* i, 60; al-Dhahabī, *Siyar* xiii, 282; Ibn Taymiyya, *al-Istighātha* 637.

70 Ibn al-Nadīm, *al-Fihrist* (ed. Flügel) 186, (ed. Tajaddud) 237.

71 Massignon, *Passion* i, 22, before "the doctrinal development by the young group that Muḥāsibī, who came from Basra, organized in Baghdad and that Junayd began to direct"; *ThG* iv, 283; Knysh, *Islamic mysticism* 61.

Ghulām Khalīl's role as a popular preacher stands out in his career. The prophetic traditions (*ḥadīth*s) were definitely not "his forte," as Ibn Ḥibbān (d. 354/965) puts it.[72] Ghulām Khalīl is also said to have "plagiarized" the traditions of Sulaymān b. Bilāl (d. 172/788)[73] from ʿAbdallāh b. Shabīb,[74] who, in turn, is said to have embezzled them from Shādhān,[75] while the latter is called their original "falsifier."[76] The famous traditionist and author of one of the six canonical *ḥadīth* compilations, Abū Dāwūd al-Sijistānī (d. 275/889),[77] corroborates this information, as he had looked into Ghulām Khalīl's traditions and found 400 *ḥadīth*s that were entirely "forged," both the chains of transmission (*asānīd*) as well as the texts (*mutūn*).[78] Another celebrated early *ḥadīth* expert, however, Ibn Abī Ḥātim (d. 327/938), relates from his father that although Ghulām Khalīl transmitted deliberately forged *ḥadīth*s (*munkara*) from unidentified authorities (*shuyūkh*), he was nonetheless not to be considered a fabricator, but rather an "upright man."[79] Yet, despite Ibn Abī Ḥātim's positive opinion, Ghulām Khalīl's reputation as a traditionist remained infamous. Later scholars thoroughly impugned his methods of transmission, described him as an outright liar, and charged him with plagiarism.[80] In fact, the *ḥadīth* scholars accused Ghulām Khalīl of fabricating traditions in order to exhort the common people and soften their hearts.[81] Al-Ḥākim al-Naysābūrī comments on this opinion by saying, "We invoke the protection of God against asceticism that leads to such a [degraded] position."[82] Yet Ibn Taymiyya contends that although Ghulām Khalīl had a temperament of devotion and asceticism, he nonetheless "also showed a lack of knowledge; this is why it is related that he used to put together *ḥadīth*s encouraging moral excellence (*faḍāʾil*)."[83]

---

72 Ibn Ḥibbān, *K. al-Majrūḥīn* i, 150: "*lam yakun al-ḥadīth shaʾnah*."

73 Al-Dhahabī, *Siyar* vii, 425–427.

74 Al-Khaṭīb al-Baghdādī, *Tārīkh* xi, 149–151.

75 Ibn ʿAdī, *al-Kāmil* viii, 271–273.

76 Ibn ʿAdī, *al-Kāmil* viii, 272; al-Khaṭīb al-Baghdādī, *Tārīkh* vi, 247.

77 Brown, *Canonization* 148–149.

78 Al-Khaṭīb al-Baghdādī, *Tārīkh* vi, 247–248. It is unclear from the text whether Ghulām Khalīl himself had brought his books to Abū Dāwūd for consultation, or whether someone else had brought them to Abū Dāwūd's attention.

79 Ibn Abī Ḥātim, *al-Jarḥ* ii, 73.

80 Ibn ʿAdī, *al-Kāmil* i, 322; al-Dārquṭnī, *al-Ḍuʿafāʾ* 122; al-Dārquṭnī, *Suʾālāt al-Ḥākim* 90; Ibn al-Jawzī, *al-Ḍuʿafāʾ* i, 88, 161; al-Dhahabī, *Mīzān* i, 141, ii, 438; Ibn Ḥajar, *Lisān* i, 617–619.

81 Al-Khaṭīb al-Baghdādī, *Tārīkh* iv, 247; Ibn al-Jawzī, *al-Muntaẓam* xii, 266; al-Dhahabī, *Siyar* xiii, 284; Massignon, *Essai* 101.

82 Al-Ḥākim al-Naysābūrī, *al-Madkhal* 1150.

83 Ibn Taymiyya, *al-Istighātha* 637.

In fact, Ghulām Khalīl's career as a preacher who evokes religious precepts through recourse to political power while suffusing his speeches with the specialized vocabulary of the sacred language of traditions, was not unique.[84] In fact, *ḥadīths* formed the basis for the ideological jargon of the day, all (rivalling) religious groups produced traditions that would support their dogmatic stances.

Ibn al-Jawzī (d. 597/1200), himself a preacher, relates—in a chapter on the odd ways of "some ignorant preachers" who wanted to attract the common people—two anecdotes about how Ghulām Khalīl employed mimicry during his sermons in Baghdad.[85]

It seems that Ghulām Khalīl used to frequent Basra and give sermons there. Al-Hamdānī (d. 334/945) also provides a report about an oration Ghulām Khalīl had given there five years before the revolt of the Zanj. Al-Hamdānī reports:[86]

> Muḥammad b. Aḥmad al-Qahmī al-Simsār transmitted to me, he said, Ibrāhīm b. Ismāʿīl al-Qahmī transmitted to me, he said:
>
> It was in Basra sometime before the year 250/864–865 when I saw in its congregational mosque a densely packed assembly. So I asked what is the event? I was told, "[this is] the preaching session (*ḥalqa*) of Ghulām Khalīl." So, I moved in and heard some of his speech exhorting the people. Then Ghulām Khalīl turned to the congregation and said:
>
> "O people of Basra, make your wives accustomed to bare-footedness: as if I hear the clatter of their anklets on camel saddles." Then he turned to a group of people from Basra, of whom he knew that they traded in Ṣanʿāʾ and resided there; they used to be called the Ṣanʿānis. Then [he turned to] Banū Miskīn, Banū Budhayl, Banū Ḥarb, and others,[87] saying, "O People of Ṣanʿāʾ! Solid stones, only solid stones would be of use to you. O people! The first city to fall into ruins from among the Muslim cities will be

84 We were able to collect twelve traditions attributed to Ghulām Khalīl in the sources, see appendix II.

85 Ibn al-Jawzī, *K. al-Quṣṣāṣ* 296–297; see also 320, where Ibn al-Jawzī cites an anecdote about the stupidity of a porter who attends Ghulām Khalīl's preaching sessions; asked "who is Muḥammad?," he replys that "he is the son of the Blessed and Exalted." ʿAbd al-Fattāḥ Kilito noted the similarity of the preaching session to the visual performances of the *maqāma*, and the close relationship to the spectacle and to imitation. Cf. his *Séances* 58. The examples he cites are those of Ghulām Khalīl, although he is not mentioned by name.

86 Al-Hamdānī, *al-Iklīl* viii, 5–6; Massignon, *Passion* i, 22, 63; Massignon, Explication du plan de Basra 74.

87 The text does not make clear whether the tribes were from Yemen or from Basra.

Basra, followed by Ṣanʿāʾ; it will be destroyed about 40 years after Basra's destruction." [And things] came to pass similar to what he said.

Ghulām Khalīl's visions, with their pictorial images and vivid descriptions, rich in fantasy and apocalyptic tone, recall the mourings and exhortations of the "the Prophets of disaster" of the Hebrew Scripture.

Such prophecies, which form a trope about the destruction of Basra, seem to have been circulating for quite some time in Ghulām Khalīl's day.[88] Interestingly, the comment of the narrator at the end of the report hints at the fact that Ghulām Khalīl's vision had been fulfilled. Conceivably, if the narrator is calculating the 40 years mentioned in Ghulām Khalīl's "prophecy'" from the destruction wreaked upon Basra during the later revolt of the Zanj (which began in 255/869),[89] he might have been also hinting at the disastrous situation that overwhelmed Sanaa and its districts in the last decade of the third/ninth century. The latter happened as a result of three factors: the long-lasting wars between the local tribes, the involvement of Zaydi claimants, the fierce attacks of the Qarmaṭians around 293/905, and the drought that pervaded the region.[90]

In short, Ghulām Khalīl appears in these narratives as a charismatic preacher, quite as al-Dhahabī described him when he called him a "master of Baghdad" (*shaykh Baghdād*) and a man of "admirable sublimity" (*jalāla ʿajība*) and "authoritative somberness" (*ṣawla mahība*). In fact, sermons and public admonitions (*tadhkīr*), as forms of religious communication, were important tools of power manipulation in early Islam.[91]

It is therefore of little surprise that parts of Ghulām Khalīl's influence seem to have resulted from his close contact at court. For example, al-Dhahabī mentions that the mother of the ʿAbbasid regent al-Muwaffaq[92] used to treat Ghulām Khalīl favorably.[93] This is notable since al-Muwaffaq was the de facto ruler during the caliphate of his brother al-Muʿtamid (r. 256–279/870–892).

---

88 Massignon, Explication du plan de Basra 74.

89 Basra was captured in Shawwāl 257 / September 871; its inhabitants were massacred, and massive destruction was visited upon the city. Popovic, *Revolt* 60–65.

90 Al-Ṣanʿānī, *Tārīkh Ṣanʿāʾ* 73–88; ʿImād al-Dīn Idrīs, *Tārīkh al-Yaman* 52–61; Yaḥyā b. al-Ḥusayn, *Anbāʾ al-zaman* 38–54.

91 ʿAthamina, al-Qasas 69–72; Armstrong, *Quṣṣāṣ*, chap. 5.

92 Al-Masʿūdī, *Murūj* v, 134, and Massignon, *Passion* i, 80, give the name of al-Muwaffaq's mother as "Asḥar"; Kennedy, al-Muwaffaḳ, indicates that she was a slave girl named Umm Isḥāq.

93 Al-Dhahabī, Siyar xiii, 284: *"wa-kānat tamīl ilayhi wālidat al-Muwaffaq wa-kadhālika al-dawla wa-l-ʿawāmm"*; Massignon, *Passion* i, 81.

Furthermore, al-Qāḍī ʿIyāḍ (d. 544/1149) quotes an interesting report from al-Farghānī's (d. 362/973)[94] lost history. According to this account, Ghulām Khalīl—while at a banquet of some notable together with the Maliki *qāḍī* Ismāʿīl b. Isḥāq al-Azdī (d. 282/896)[95]—was cursing the judges, calling them "denizens of Hell-fire." When the people left the banquet, the Maliki *qāḍī* said to Ghulām Khalīl, "But you yourself were sitting together with those whom you were rebuking and promising Hell-fire, because they keep company with the rulers (*aṣḥāb al-sulṭān*)."[96] This account by Ismāʿīl b. Isḥāq reveals a certain enmity, evident also in another of his accounts on Ghulām Khalīl, wherein he calls the latter a liar.[97]

Incidentally, Ismāʿīl b. Isḥāq also originated from Basra and played a significant role during the supremacy of al-Muwaffaq,[98] who is known also as al-Nāṣir (the Victorious) because of his successful military achievements.[99] Ismāʿīl b. Isḥāq had been the chief judge of Baghdad for a long time,[100] and it was he who was entrusted with the case against the Sufis, then instigated by Ghulām Khalīl.

Both Ismāʿīl b. Isḥāq and Ghulām Khalīl were influential in the ʿAbbasid administration, Ismāʿīl as chief judge with close relations to three caliphs, and Ghulām Khalīl as "propagandist." Moreover, both were strict devotees of the Sunna.[101] Nonetheless, it seems that the ill feeling between them was caused by the "odd ways" in which Ghulām Khalīl cited *ḥadīth*s, the "authoritative somberness" that he enjoyed, and the rivalry in the circles of power that the two scholars frequented at the court.

---

94 Abbott, *Studies* i, 112–116.

95 Wakīʿ, *Akhbār* iii, 280; al-Khaṭīb al-Baghdādī, *Tārīkh* vii, 272; al-Qāḍī ʿIyāḍ, *Tartīb* iv, 276.

96 Al-Qāḍī ʿIyāḍ, *Tartīb* iv, 283; al-Hujwīrī, *Kashf* 349.

97 Al-Khaṭīb al-Baghdādī, *Tārīkh* vi, 246.

98 Tillier, Qāḍīs 48, argues, "For several decades, the appointment of the empire's *qāḍīs* clearly depended upon the caliphate. But the dangerous Zanj revolt, which ravaged the south of Iraq from 255/869, prompted the regent to intervene directly in the judicial system."

99 Al-Khaṭīb al-Baghdādī uses the verbs "*ghalaba ʿalā al-Muwaffaq*" and "*tamakkana min al-Nāṣir*." *Tārīkh* vii, 278, 279. ʿAbdallāh b. al-Muʿtazz calls al-Muwaffaq "al-Nāṣir" in a panegyric dedicated to him. Al-Ṣūlī, *Ashʿār* 127. See also al-Masʿūdī, *Murūj* v, 135; al-Masʿūdī, *al-Tanbīh* 367. Al-Qaysī, al-Dīnār 263–275, references an inscription on gold dinars minted between 271/884–885 and 275/888–889.

100 Melchert, Religious policies 329–330, 339–341.

101 Al-Khalīlī, *al-Irshād* 608, reports that "*aṣḥāb al-ḥadīth*" in Khorasan and Rayy used to invoke God for him. Al-Qāḍī ʿIyāḍ counts him, together with the other famous members of his family, as "*rijāl Sunna*." *Tartīb* iv, 277. He also mentions a "*K. al-Sunan*" among his books. *Tartīb* iv, 292. Both printed books of his that we were able to consult, *Aḥkām al-Quran* and *Aḥādīth Ayyūb al-Sakhtiyānī*, reveal his adherence to the methods of the traditionists.

5 The *Miḥna* against the Sufis

According to Abū Saʿīd Ibn al-Aʿrābī (d. 341/952), a Sufi master from Basra and author of perhaps the first, though lost, collection of Sufi biographies and dicta, *Ṭabaqāt al-nussāk* ("The generations of the devout"), the persecution of the Sufis took place upon Ghulām Khalīl's arrival from Wāsiṭ,[102] which was at that time "essentially a pietistic Ḥanbalite center."[103] The traditional religious scholars (*ahl al-āthār*) told him of the Sufi slogan "We love our Lord and He loves us, hence He delivers us from our fear through the dominance of our love to Him," as well as about other "hideous sayings" (*shanāʿāt*).[104] Ibn al-Aʿrābī added to this that Ghulām Khalīl's position was that "fear is more proper on our side" (*al-khawf awlā binā*); a notion expressed also in his *K. Sharḥ al-sunna*.[105]

Ghulām Khalīl then used his influence at court to denounce the teaching of certain Sufis who were said to have gone beyond the traditionally accepted—that is, the Quranic—terminology of the love of God (*ḥubb*, Q 5:54)[106] by describing their relationship with the divine as "passionate love" (*ʿishq*).[107] The Sufis thus accused were first brought before the caliph al-Muʿtamid.[108] The interrogation ended in a formal ostracism of those Sufis whom Ghulām Khalīl now charged with heresy (*zandaqa*). This trial came to be known in the sources as "the persecution instituted by Ghulām Khalīl" (*miḥnat Ghulām Khalīl*).[109]

Ibn Taymiyya, relying on Abū Saʿīd b. al-Aʿrābī's lost *Ṭabaqāt al-nussāk*, dates Ghulām Khalīl's *miḥna*[110] sometime after 263/876–877 (*sanat biḍʿ wa-sittīn wa-miʾatayn*),[111] while *biḍʿ* (a "few") can refer to a number between three and

102 Al-Dhahabī, *Siyar* xiii, 284.
103 Massignon, *Passion* i, 60.
104 On the concepts of *ḥubb* and *ʿishq* in early Sufism, see Bell and Al Shafie, *Treatise* li–lviii (for al-Ḥallāj); Lumbard, From *ḥubb* to *ʿishq*.
105 Item 58 of the English translation.
106 Cf. al-Hujwīrī, *Kashf* 547.
107 Ibn al-Jawzi, *Talbīs* 1011; Karamustafa, *Sufism* 12.
108 Al-Dhahabī, *Siyar* xiv, 71. Abdel-Kader, *Life* 38, says that "Ghulām Khalīl raised the case against the ṣūfīs before the Khalīf al-Muwaffaq [*sic*]." Böwering, Early Sufism 55, mentions that the accusation was made before al-Muwaffaq. This information, however, is not attested in the sources. Ernst, *Words of ecstasy* 97–98, has both al-Muwaffaq and the caliph taking part in the trial.
109 Abū Nuʿaym, *Ḥilya* x, 250; al-Khaṭīb al-Baghdādī, *Tārīkh* vi, 335; Ibn al-Jawzī, *Talbīs* 1011, 1034–1038; al-Dhahabī, *Siyar* xiv, 71. Ernst, *Words of ecstasy* 101, argues that the tense political situation had an effect on the accusation of heresy and the subsequent trial.
110 Al-Dhahabī, *Siyar* xiv, 235, calls it *nawba* (misfortune, calamity).
111 Ibn Taymiyya, *al-Istighātha* 636–637.

nine.[112] Al-Dhahabī, however, on the authority of the traditionist Abū Nuʿaym (d. 430/1038), dates this persecution to the year 264/877–878,[113] although Abū Nuʿaym in his earlier report in his *Ḥilya* actually does not mention a year.[114] The date, however, that al-Dhahabī offers seems plausible, since Ghulām Khalīl appears to have left Wāsiṭ in 264/877–878, upon the attack of the Zanj early in the month of Jumādā I, and their entrance into the city in Rabīʿ II.[115] This view also sets a possible date for the recording of *K. Sharḥ al-sunna* since Ghulām Khalīl's mention in article 99 of those who advocate longing (*shawq*) and love (*maḥabba*), refers to a group that he was already aware of.

Between 70 and 75 Sufis, among them Abū l-Ḥusayn al-Nūrī, al-Kharrāz, Abū Ḥamza, Ruwaym,[116] and Sumnūn al-Muḥibb, were summoned by the "censor" (*muḥtasib*).[117] The Grand Judge of Baghdad, the Maliki Ismāʿīl b. Isḥāq, conducted the interrogation.[118]

It is interesting to note in this context Melchert's argument that one of the consequences of this trial was that the Sufi master Abū l-Qāsim al-Junayd (d. 271/892)—a contemporary of Ghulām Khalīl—then developed "a language to deal with mystical experience that would not offend more old-fashioned ascetics."[119]

---

112 Al-Farāhīdī, *K. al-ʿAyn* i, 144; Abū ʿUbayda, *Majāz* ii, 119; see Jarrar, Exegetical designs; Massignon dates it around 266/878, *Passion* i, 75, 80.

113 Al-Dhahabī, *Siyar* xiv, 71.

114 Abū Nuʿaym, *Ḥilya* x, 250; see also al-Khaṭīb al-Baghdādī, *Tārīkh* vi, 335–336; Ibn al-Jawzi, *Talbīs* 1034.

115 Al-Ṭabarī, *Tārīkh* ix, 534–540.

116 According to al-Dhahabī, *Siyar* xiv, 235, Ghulām Khalīl said, "I personally heard him say, 'Between God and myself there is no veil'"; cf. also Gramlich, *Alte Vorbilder* i, 494.

117 Officially appointed by the caliph or his vizier to ensure correct ethical behavior, detect offences, and punish offenders. Cf. Cook, *Commanding right* 471.

118 See on this *miḥna* and the fate of these Sufis: al-Sarrāj, *al-Lumaʿ* 498–499; Gramlich, *Die Nahrung* ii, 530; al-Sulamī, *Masāʾil* 55; Abū Nuʿaym, *Ḥilya* x, 250; al-Khaṭīb al-Baghdādī, *Tārīkh* vi, 335–336; al-Qushayrī, *al-Risāla* ii, 404; al-Ghazālī, *Iḥyāʾ* 1797; Gramlich, *Muḥammad al-Ghazzālīs Lehre* 719; al-Ṭarṭūshī, *Sirāj al-mulūk* i, 369; al-Hujwīrī, *Kashf* 349, 421; Ibn al-Jawzī, *Talbīs* 1011, 1034–1038; ʿAṭṭār, *Tazkerat ul-awliyāʾ* ii, 48; al-Dhahabī, *Siyar* xiii, 284–285, xiv, 71; Massignon, *Passion* i, 80–81; Abdel-Kader, *Life* 37–40; Nwyia, *Exégèse coranique* 317–319; Ernst, *Words of ecstasy* 97–101; Gramlich, *Alte Vorbilder* i, 383; Melchert, Transition 65–70; Melchert, Ḥanābila 360–362; *ThG* iv, 281–283; Gramlich, *Lebensweise* 71; Schimmel, Qibla of the lights 60–61; van Ess, Sufism 26–28; Böwering, Early Sufism 54–56; Knysh, *Islamic mysticism* 61–63; Karamustafa, *Sufism* 11–12, 21–23; de Crussol, *Role de la raison* 256 (quoting P. Nwyia); van Ess, *Der Eine* i, 285–288.

119 Melchert, Transition 66; Melchert, Sufis 239.

6 Death and Burial

Ghulām Khalīl died in Baghdad on Sunday, 21 Rajab 275 / Monday, 29 November 888.[120] Eyewitness reports of his funeral clearly give the impression that Ghulām Khalīl, at the end of his life, was a person of renown. Ibn Kāmil states that the markets of Baghdad closed during the funeral. Men, women, and children came out to pray for the deceased.[121] The corpse was then taken in a coffin to Basra, where Ghulām Khalīl was buried and a mausoleum (*qubba*) built over his grave.[122] The exact location of his grave is unknown. He might have been buried in the cemetery of the Bāhila tribe.[123]

Ibn al-Munādī (d. 346/957),[124] a Hanbali scholar who was 18 years old at the time of Ghulām Khalīl's death, was an eyewitness to the funeral.[125] He first describes how the prayer was performed in the house of the deceased in Dār al-Kalbī in Baghdad. Thereafter, the coffin was carried to the banks of the River Tigris, from where it was shipped on a boat down to Basra. Many people walked along the riverbank near the boat, accompanying it to Kalawādhā, a village about two kilometers south of Baghdad.[126] Whenever the boat passed by a group of mourners, they would pray for the dead, giving a sign and bowing their heads in reverence.

120 Al-Khaṭīb al-Baghdādī, *Tārīkh* vi, 248.
121 See also Ibn al-Athīr, *al-Kāmil* xi, 310.
122 Al-Khaṭīb al-Baghdādī, *Tārīkh* vi, 248–249.
123 Cf., Massignon, Explication du plan de Basra 71.
124 Al-Dhahabī, *Siyar* xv, 361; al-ʿUlaymī, *al-Manhaj* ii, 245–247.
125 Al-Khaṭīb al-Baghdādī, *Tārīkh* vi, 248–249.
126 Yāqūt, *Muʿjam* iv, 477.

CHAPTER 2

The *Kitāb Sharḥ al-sunna*: Textual Evidence, Transmission, and Authorship

The *Kitāb Sharḥ al-sunna* belongs to the *ʿaqīda* (creed) genre, a type of literature meant to determine Islamic doctrine. In it, Ghulām Khalīl expressly addresses the *ahl al-sunna wa-l-jamāʿa* (adherents of the Sunna and the Muslim, or "majority," community) and adjures them to obey strictly all principles established in his book.[1] It is the only book by him to have been preserved.[2] Although its authorship has been a matter of much debate in both medieval and modern scholarship, this study hopes to authenticate conclusively Ghulām Khalīl's authorship, an issue this chapter will explore in depth.

1 The Damascus Manuscript

The Damascus manuscript of the *K. Sharḥ al-sunna* is a unicum. It is included in the first part (fols. 1a–19b) of a collection of manuscripts (*majmūʿ*) with the call number 3750.[3] Originally preserved in al-Madrasa al-ʿUmariyya,[4] today a division of the Dār al-Kutub al-Ẓāhiriyya Library in Damascus,[5] it was moved in 1984, when that institution transferred its manuscripts to the collections at the Asad National Library, also in Damascus.

The composite manuscript "Ẓāhiriyya 3750" comprises 13 Arabic manuscripts, 166 folios in total, 17.5×13 cm,[6] with 15 to 24 lines in each folio, and a margin of about 2 cm.[7] The compiler of the Damascus manuscript catalogue,

1 See *K. Sharḥ al-sunna*, nos. 88, 90, 91, 92, 136, 146, 148.

2 Ibn al-Nadīm does not mention it, *al-Fihrist* (ed. Flügel) 186; *al-Fihrist* (ed. Tajaddud) 237.

3 Al-Sawwās, *Fihris* 60–66; *GAS* i, 511. Sezgin's claim that Ibn Taymiyya made mention of it in his *Majmūʿ al-rasāʾil al-kubrā* i, 410, is inaccurate. The work mentioned there is, in fact, the *K. al-Sunna* by al-Khallāl.

4 Al-Ḥimṣī, al-Madrasa al-Ẓāhiriyya 129; al-Sawwās, *Fihris* 10–11.

5 Its construction started on 5 Jumāda I, 676/4 October 1277; it was concluded in Ṣafar 677/June 1278; cf. al-Ḥimṣī, al-Madrasa al-Ẓāhiriyya 129.

6 According to the measurement taken by M. Jarrar together with the staff at the al-Ẓāhiriyya in summer 2017; the original measurements given by al-Sawwās, *Fihris* 61, as 26×18 cm, are incorrect.

7 Al-Sawwās, *Fihris* 60–61.

 | DOI:10.1163/9789004429055_004

Yāsīn Muḥammad al-Sawwās, mentions that the *K. Sharḥ al-sunna* is the first in that collection, and that it consists of 7 folios (fols. 13–19). However, this information is incorrect. In fact, the text of the *K. Sharḥ al-sunna* manuscript starts on folio 1 and ends on folio 19b; folio 20a is left blank. There is an additional *samāʿ* (audition or attendance) certificate on folio 20b.[8]

Al-Sawwās describes the text as a "very good transcript" (*nuskha jayyida*), written in a clear *naskhī* script.[9] He adds that the treatises (*rasāʾil*) in this composite manuscript were copied between the sixth/twelfth and seventh/thirteenth centuries, and that the third treatise was written by al-Ḥāfiẓ ʿAbd al-Ghanī al-Maqdisī (d. 600/1204).[10] He notes that the names of the scribes of the other treatises are unknown, but again, this information is not completely accurate, since the name of the scribe of the *K. Sharḥ al-sunna* appears in the *samāʿ* certificate at the end of the book, as will be explained further below.

1.1 *Transmission*

Importantly, the Damascus manuscript of the *K. Sharḥ al-sunna* contains a *riwāyat al-kitāb*—that is, an authentication of the names of those scholars who audited teaching sessions in which the *K. Sharḥ al-sunna* was taught, and who themselves later taught, and thus transmitted, the text. This *riwāyat al-kitāb*, replicated below, is given twice, once on the title page and again on the first page. On the title page, the *riwāyat al-kitāb* lists five generations of Baghdadi scholars who, over a period of 300 years, transmitted the text on the authority of the author himself.[11]

The author:
Abū ʿAbdallāh Aḥmad b. Muḥammad b. Ghālib al-Bāhilī, Ghulām Khalīl
[d. 275/888]
↓
(2) Abū Bakr Aḥmad b. Kāmil b. Khalaf b. Shajara [260–350/873–961]
↓
(3) Abū l-Ḥasan Muḥammad b. al-ʿAbbās b. al-Furāt [319–384/931–994]
↓

8 Al-Albānī, *Fihris* 497, no. 1400, states that it covers 19 folios.

9 Al-Sawwās, *Fihris* 61.

10 Al-Dhahabī, *Siyar* xxi, 443; Leder, Dokumente 59, 63–66.

11 The names in the *samāʿ* certificate are mostly unpunctuated and unvocalized. Several close readings of these name lists in the original manuscript have revealed a few errors in our previous study, Jarrar and Günther, Ġulām Ḫalīl 13, which have been corrected here.

(4) Abū Isḥāq Ibrāhīm b. ʿUmar b. Aḥmad al-Barmakī [361–445/971–1053]
↓
(5) Abū Ṭālib ʿAbd al-Qādir b. Muḥammad b. Yūsuf [430–516/1038–1122]
↓
(6) Abū l-Ḥusayn ʿAbd al-Ḥaqq b. ʿAbd al-Khāliq [494–575/1100–1179]

The same information is given again on the first page of the manuscript, although now in more detail. Here, the text runs as follows:

> The trustworthy master and *imām* Abū l-Ḥusayn ʿAbd al-Ḥaqq b. ʿAbd al-Khāliq transmitted to us by way of reading aloud (*qirāʾatan*). He said:
> Abū Ṭālib ʿAbd al-Qādir b. Muḥammad b. Yūsuf transmitted to us in the Friday mosque, while we were listening (*wa-naḥnu nasmaʿu*). It was read out before him (*qīla lahū*) that:
> Shaykh Abū Isḥāq Ibrāhīm b. ʿUmar b. Aḥmad al-Barmakī transmitted to you, from among what he had authorized you to transmit—an authorization publically known. He [confirmed it by] saying, "Yes." He stated:
> Abū l-Ḥasan Muḥammad b. al-ʿAbbās b. Aḥmad b. al-Furāt—may God have mercy on him—informed us in his book, and it was transmitted [to us] by way of reading aloud from a book of his (*wa-min kitābihi quriʾa*). He said:
> Abū Bakr Aḥmad b. Kāmil b. Khalaf b. Shajara al-Qāḍī transmitted to us by way of hearing it read out before him (*qirāʾatan ʿalayhi*), while he said to me:
> "Transmit this book on my authority from beginning to end."

It is clear that this chain of transmission is an integral part of the text. Moreover, it is written in the same hand as the main text. Other details have been reported about these transmitters in the sources. These details are presented below, with the chain in reverse order—that is, from the earliest to the most recent transmitters:

(1) The first and earliest transmitter was Aḥmad b. Kāmil. He was given a copy of the book by the author himself and told, "Transmit this book on my authority from beginning to end." If the biographical data is correct, Ibn Kāmil was no more than 15 years old, or even younger, when he received permission from the author to transmit this book. This may seem quite a young age to be entrusted with transmission of such a text, but it was not at all unusual in early Muslim scholarship.[12]

12 Cf. Hirschler, *Written word* 39, 48–49; Ibn Kāmil's teacher, al-Ṭabarī, had encouraged Ibn

(2) Ibn al-Furāt was the second transmitter. He is said to have been a "trustworthy" transmitter who spent his days reading and attending teaching sessions, and his nights copying books. Moreover, he is reported to have copied a vast number of works. First, he would double-check them together with a woman serving in his house; then, he would check them again with the respective teacher (*shaykh*). Ibn al-Furāt is known to have owned a library of "rare books."[13]

(3) From him, Abū Isḥāq al-Barmakī received permission to transmit the text. Al-Barmakī was a jurisconsult and a student of the Hanbali scholars Ibn Baṭṭa al-ʿUkbarī (d. 387/997)[14] and Ibn Ḥāmid (d. 403/1012), the foremost leader of the Hanbali school.[15] From Ibn Baṭṭa, al-Barmakī transmitted *al-Sharḥ wa-l-ibāna ʿalā uṣūl al-sunna wa-l-diyāna*.[16] He held the chair of the teaching circle Ḥalqat al-Barāmika,[17] which was founded by his father, Abū Ḥafs (d. 387/997), in the al-Manṣūr mosque in Baghdad,[18] a position later occupied by Abū Yaʿlā al-Farrāʾ (d. 458/1066), one of the great historical authorities of the Hanbali *madhhab* of Sunni law.[19] Al-Khaṭīb al-Baghdādī, who was al-Barmakī's student, says that al-Barmakī was a legal scholar (*faqīh*) and jurisconsult (*muftī*)[20] following the *madhhab* of Aḥmad b. Ḥanbal. Ibn Abī Yaʿlā describes him as an ascetic (*nāsik, zāhid*).[21]

(4) From him, Shaykh Abū Ṭālib ʿAbd al-Qādir b. Muḥammad received the right to transmit this work.[22] Abū Ṭālib belonged to a renowned Baghdadi family of scholars that produced a number of traditionists.[23] He studied with the best teachers of his day, and he is said to have been trustworthy and reliable in his scholarly work.[24] Abū Ṭālib's father, Muḥammad

---

Kāmil to have his nine-year-old son study with him and recalled that he himself "served as prayer leader when he was eight, and studied (lit. "wrote down") traditions of the Prophet when he was nine." Rosenthal, *History* i, 15.

13 Al-Khaṭīb al-Baghdādī, *Tārīkh* iv, 207; Ibn al-Jawzī, *al-Muntaẓam* xiv, 371.

14 Al-Khaṭīb al-Baghdādī, *Tārīkh* vii, 63; Ibn Abī Yaʿlā, *Ṭabaqāt* (al-ʿUthaymīn) iii, 352.

15 Ibn Abī Yaʿlā, *Ṭabaqāt* (al-ʿUthaymīn) iii, 309.

16 Laoust, *Profession* cxlviii, cli.

17 Makdisi, *Rise* 17–18; Makdisi, *Ibn ʿAqīl and culture* 27.

18 On the west side of the Tigris. Le Strange, *Baghdad* 33–37.

19 Laoust, Ibn al-Farrāʾ iii, 765–766.

20 Al-Khaṭīb al-Baghdādī, *Tārīkh* vii, 63.

21 Ibn Abī Yaʿlā, *Ṭabaqāt* (al-ʿUthaymīn) iii, 352; al-Dhahabī, *Siyar* xvii, 606.

22 Abū Ṭālib also transmitted Ibn Baṭṭa's *al-Sharḥ wa-l-ibāna* from al-Barmakī. Laoust, *Profession* cxlviii.

23 Ibn Nuqṭa, *Takmila* vi, 308–312.

24 Ibn al-Jawzī, *al-Muntaẓam* xvii, 211; al-Dhahabī, *Siyar* xix, 386.

b. ʿAbd al-Qādir (d. 479/1086), was considered an honorable shaykh and strict man in matters of the Sunna.[25]

(5) ʿAbd al-Ḥaqq,[26] called *imām* in the chain of transmitters (*isnād*), was a son of the well-known traditionist ʿAbd al-Khāliq b. Aḥmad.[27] He transmitted traditions from the celebrated Abū l-Wafāʾ b. ʿAqīl (d. 513/1119), a Hanbali jurist with rationalist leanings,[28] and he had explicit permission (*ijāza*) to do so.[29] He was also a teacher of Ibn al-Jawzī.[30] It was Abū Ṭālib (see no. 4 above), his father's first cousin,[31] who granted him permission to transmit the text in a teaching session he audited (*samāʿan*).

(6) Abū l-Qāsim ʿAbdallāh b. Ḥamza b. Abī Ṭāhir b. Sānū [*sic*], known as *al-shaykh al-imām al-ṣāliḥ* (the pious master and imam), is last in this scheme of transmission. He studied the book with ʿAbd al-Ḥaqq. His name is otherwise unattested in the sources thus far.

On the very last page of the manuscript (fol. 19v), the name ʿAbdallāh b. Ḥamza appears again. This additional note is part of a kind of attendance sheet used in higher Muslim education to attest the names of those present in the given teaching session, or *samāʿ* assembly. Importantly, in this note of attendance ʿAbdallāh b. Ḥamza gives the date of the teaching session that the Damascus manuscript contains as "the year 506/1112 or sometime later." Furthermore, the respective *samāʿ* certificate names another 14 participants in this teaching session. Although the certificate does not record the location of this lecture, the names of the attendees indicate that it took place in Baghdad. ʿAbdallāh b. Ḥamza reproduced the following note about this assembly:

> The reproduction of the audition (*ṣūrat al-samāʿ*) which I copied from the original [is as follows]: ʿAbdallāh b. Ḥamza b. Sānū wrote: "The book in its entirety was taught [lit. heard] in a session of al-Shaykh Abū Ṭālib—may God grant him support—with his maternal nephews present, while Muḥammad b. Nāṣir b. Muḥammad b. ʿAlī was reading, [the session was attended by]:
> Abū l-Qāsim ʿAbdallāh,
> Abū l-Maʿālī,
> Abū l-Fatḥ Yūsuf, the sons of Aḥmad b. al-Faraj al-Daqqāq,

25 Ibn al-Jawzī, *al-Muntaẓam* xvi, 265.
26 Ibn al-Dubaythī, *Dhayl* iv, 219; al-Dhahabī, *Siyar* xx, 552.
27 Al-Dhahabī, *Siyar* xx, 279.
28 Makdisi, *Ibn ʿAqīl* 17–43.
29 Makdisi, *Ibn ʿAqīl* 44.
30 Ibn al-Jawzī, *al-Mashyakha* 186–187.
31 Ibn al-Dubaythī, *Dhayl* iv, 219.

and by
Abū Manṣūr al-Jawālīqī,
Abū l-Dulaf,
Abū l-Fa[…] al-Ḥannāṭ al-Muqri',
Abū l-Faraj 'Abd al-Khāliq b. Aḥmad b. 'Abd al-Qādir, and his son
'Abd al-Ḥaqq b. 'Abd al-Khāliq,
Yaḥyā b. 'Alī al-Ḥannāṭ,
Abū l-Faḍl al-Mukharrimī,
Ṣāfī al-Muṭayyin,
Hazārasb al-Harawī,
Aḥmad b. Muḥammad al-Fayrūmī,
Ḥusayn b. Ibrāhīm (or Adham),
Muḥammad b. Aḥmad b. Muḥammad b. Dāwūd al-Iṣbahānī.
This [took place] in the year six or more[32] and five hundred."

In other words, in 506/1112 "or later" (*aw akthar*), 'Abd al-Ḥaqq (b. 494/1100) was a boy of only about twelve years. The *samāʿ* certificate indicates that he accompanied his father, 'Abd al-Khāliq (d. 548/1153), to this teaching session. Thus, Abū l-Qāsim 'Abdallāh b. Ḥamza b. Abī Ṭāhir b. Sānū, the scribe, must have studied the book directly with 'Abd al-Ḥaqq at a later date. 'Abdallāh b. Ḥamza received permission to transmit it from 'Abd al-Ḥaqq and copied the text of the book, along with the original certificate of the teaching session that 'Abd al-Ḥaqq had attended together with his father. With regard to the date, it should be noted that in a *naskhī* script without diacritical points, the respective number could be read as either "six," "seven," or "nine," which might explain 'Abdallāh b. Ḥamza's uncertainty on this point.

Among the auditors of this teaching session whose names are given in the attendance sheet, eight names can be determined with certainty, and one only with some caution. As we elucidate in the following, this session, which, as noted above, had gathered around al-Shaykh Abū Ṭālib, assembled members of both the Abū Ṭālib and the Abū l-Faḍl b. Nāṣir families:

– Muḥammad b. Nāṣir b. Muḥammad b. 'Alī (d. 550/1155) is known as Abū l-Faḍl b. Nāṣir al-Salāmī.[33] Among other celebrated teachers, he studied with Abū l-Wafā' b. 'Aqīl,[34] as well as with Abū Ṭālib al-Yūsufī, in whose presence he was reading the book. He also studied language and *adab* with al-Tabrīzī

32 With no diacritical points.
33 Al-Samʿānī, *al-Ansāb* vii, 208.
34 Makdisi, *Ibn 'Aqīl* 17, 44.

(d. 502/1108), together with Abū Manṣūr al-Jawālīqī, who was also in attendance at this teaching session (see below). Abū l-Faḍl b. Nāṣir was the maternal uncle of the al-Daqqāq brothers,[35] who were also present. He is highly praised by his student Ibn al-Jawzī, who "heard" from him the *Musnad* of Aḥmad b. Ḥanbal. Abū l-Faḍl b. Nāṣir's name also appears in Ibn al-Jawzī's chain of transmission for the Qadiri creed.[36] Ibn al-Jawzī describes him as trustworthy, precise, and committed to the Sunna.[37] Originally a follower of the Ashʿari school of theology and of the Shafiʿi school of law, Abū l-Faḍl later became an adherent of the Hanbali school of law. Only one of the five books that are attributed to him in the sources[38] has been published: *K. al-Tanbīh*, which is a follow-up to and emendation of Abū ʿUbayd Aḥmad al-Harawī al-Fāshānī's (d. 401/1010) book on uncommon words in the prophetic traditions (*gharīb al-ḥadīth*).[39]

- Abū l-Qāsim ʿAbdallāh, Abū l-Maʿālī, and Abū l-Fatḥ Yūsuf are the sons of Aḥmad b. al-Faraj al-Daqqāq. These three brothers are the nephews of Abū l-Faḍl b. Nāṣir, as is stated by Ibn al-Dubaythī in his biographical entry on Abū l-Maʿālī Muḥammad (d. 564/1168).[40] The sources contain biographical entries only for Abū l-Maʿālī and for a fourth brother, Abū Manṣūr Muḥammad (d. 575/1179),[41] whose name does not appear in this *samāʿ* certificate.
- Abū Manṣūr al-Jawālīqī (d. 539/1144 or 540/1145), was a renowned Hanbali philologist and lexicographer.[42] Ibn al-Jawzī describes him as a follower of the Sunna.[43] He had accompanied Abū l-Faḍl b. Nāṣir al-Salāmī for several years, during which they both studied language and *adab* under al-Tabrīzī. Ibn al-Najjār mentions that the "people used to say that Ibn Nāṣir would become the linguist of Baghdad and al-Jawālīqī its traditionist, but things turned out otherwise."[44]

---

35 Ibn al-Dubaythī, *Dhayl* i, 177.

36 Makdisi, *Ibn ʿAqīl* 9.

37 Ibn al-Jawzī, *al-Mashyakha* 129; al-Dhahabī, *Siyar* xx, 267; see also Ibn al-Jawzī, *al-Muntaẓam* xviii, 103; Ibn Rajab, *Dhayl* ii, 51.

38 Among them a book on the virtues (*manāqib*) of Aḥmad b. Ḥanbal and a refutation of those who claim that the articulation (*lafẓ*) of the Quran is created; Ibn Rajab, *Dhayl* ii, 58–59; al-ʿUlaymī, *al-Manhaj* iii, 152.

39 Ed. Ḥusayn Bānāja, Riyadh, 1429/2008.

40 Ibn al-Dubaythī, *Dhayl* i, 177.

41 Ibid., i, 186.

42 Ibn al-Anbārī, *Nuzha* 293; al-Dhahabī, *Siyar* xx, 89; Ibn Rajab *Dhayl* ii, 1.

43 Ibn al-Jawzī, *al-Muntaẓam* xviii, 47.

44 Al-Dimyāṭī, *al-Mustafād* 40.

- Abū l-Dulaf has remained unidentified so far. Although it seems odd to have the definite article *al-* attached to the surname Dulaf,[45] this name form is attested in the sources. Ibn al-Dubaythī, for example, mentions a certain Abū l-Dulaf Muḥammad b. Hibatallāh b. ʿAlī[46] from the Hanbali quarter of Bāb al-Azaj,[47] who was a brother of a traditionist. This latter person known as Abū l-Dulaf was a secretary to the ʿAbbasid administration and a poet. He was appointed as "overseer" (*nāẓir*) in the *sawād* of Dujayl, the fertile area of al-Ahwāz in southern Iraq, and had connections to Ṣadaqa b. Manṣūr al-Mazyadī,[48] the ruler of al-Ḥilla (a city on the northern bank of the Euphrates River) and a bitter enemy of both al-Mustaẓhir[49] and his son al-Mustarshid.[50] When, upon the death of al-Mustaẓhir, Abū l-Ḥasan ʿAbdallāh, the son of the caliph al-Mustaẓhir bi-Llāh, turned against his brother al-Mustarshid in 512/1118, Abū l-Dulaf worked for him as secretary. However, Abū l-Dulaf was arrested during this affair, defamed, and incarcerated. He died in 513/1119 and was buried initially in the cemetery of Darb al-Khabbāzīn, a quarter in Baghdad. Later, his body was moved to the cemetery at Bāb Ḥarb, the cemetery where Aḥmad b. Ḥanbal was buried.

  Notwithstanding this information, it can by no means be concluded that the Abū l-Dulaf mentioned in the *samāʿ* certificate is identical to Abū l-Dulaf, the ʿAbbasid secretary and poet; the scrupulous traditionist circle studying the *K. Sharḥ al-sunna* would hardly have welcomed his company.
- Abū l-Faraj ʿAbd al-Khāliq b. Aḥmad b. ʿAbd al-Qādir (d. 548/1153)[51] was the father of Abū l-Ḥusayn ʿAbd al-Ḥaqq (d. 575/1179), whose name appears in the first *samāʿ* certificate list as someone who also attended this teaching session.
- Abū l-Faḍl al-Mukharrimī is most probably Abū l-Faḍl ʿAlī b. al-Mubārak al-Mukharrimī (d. 552/1172),[52] the son of the Hanbali Abū Saʿd (d. 513/1119),[53] who founded a *madrasa* in Bāb al-Azaj, in which his student the Sufi master

45 One would directly think of the poet Abū Dulaf al-ʿIjlī (d. 226/840), al-Dhahabī, *Siyar* x, 563, and of Abū Dulaf al-Khazrajī (died after 331/943), cf. Minorsky, Abū Dulaf.

46 Ibn al-Dubaythī, *Dhayl* ii, 146; al-Ṣafadī, *al-Wāfī* v, 153.

47 Le Strange, *Baghdad* 296–299; al-Samʿānī, *al-Ansāb* i, 197.

48 Zettersteen, Ṣadaḳa b. Manṣūr.

49 Ibn al-Dubaythī, *Dhayl* iii, 432–433.

50 Hillenbrand, al-Mustars͟hid vii, 733–735.

51 Ibn al-Jawzī, *al-Mashyakha* 139–140; al-Dhahabī, *Siyar* xx, 279.

52 Ibn al-Dubaythī, *Dhayl* iv, 520.

53 Ibn al-Jawzī, *al-Muntaẓam* 17, 183; Ibn Rajab, *Dhayl* i, 366.

'Abd al-Qādir al-Jīlī (or al-Jīlānī) resided. Abū Sa'd's name figures in a Hanbali *silsila* of Sufis.[54]

– Hazārasb al-Harawī (d. 515/1121). Both al-Silafī and Ibn al-Jawzī describe him as trustworthy. Ibn al-Jawzī adds that he was a follower of the Sunna who died young.[55] George Makdisi writes of him, "We do not know how old Hazārasb was at the time of his death. Not yet a master of *hadith*, he was still an advanced student, but he had a 'book' with biographical information on transmitters of *hadith*."[56]

The *K. Sharḥ al-sunna* ends on folio 19 verso. Folio 20 recto is empty.[57] Folio 20 verso seems to have included only a certificate of another teaching session centered in the middle of the page, but annotations were added (latitudinally and vertically) that are unrelated to the original book. Moreover, a piece of white paper was glued at the upper left margin that covered the ending of this *samā'* certificate.[58] What remains to be deciphered from this certificate reads as follows:

> The entire book *Sharḥ al-sunna* was heard [i.e., taught] in the audition session of al-Shaykh al-Imā[m ...] b. 'Abd al-Qādir b. Muḥammad b. Yūsuf, in a similar manner (*naḥwa*) to his audition from Abū Ṭāl [...] 'Abd al-Razzāq b. 'Abd al-Qādir b. Abī Ṣāliḥ al-Jīlī, his son 'Abd al-Raḥīm, and Abū [...] b. Mas'ūd b. Ḥamza al-Nahramallī [*sic*], and Abū l-Ḥasan 'Alī b. Hilāl. This took place on the ninth of Muḥarram in the year 568 [i.e., 31 August 1172] in the school [...].

One might assume that the person here named "al-Shaykh al-Imā[m ...] b. 'Abd al-Qādir b. Muḥammad b. Yūsuf" is a son of Abū Ṭālib 'Abd al-Qādir b. Muḥammad,[59] even though there is no proof of such a relationship. The *samā'* certificate in question refers to one of the sessions that he had given.

Furthermore, 'Abd al-Razzāq b. 'Abd al-Qādir b. Abī Ṣāliḥ al-Jīlī (d. 603/1206),[60] whose name is mentioned in the certificate, is the son of the celebrated

54 Makdisi, *Ibn 'Aqīl* 216.

55 Al-Silafī, *al-Wajīz* 74, 76–77; Ibn al-Jawzī, *al-Muntaẓam* xvii, 202; see also al-Dhahabī, *al-'Ibar* ii, 405.

56 Makdisi, Diary 178–179.

57 An error seems to have occurred while binding the folios, resulting in tipping in folio 22 before 21.

58 This was verified during M. Jarrar's visit to the Asad National Library, Damascus.

59 Abū Ṭālib 'Abd al-Qādir had many sons and grandsons; cf. Ibn Nuqta, *Takmila* vi, 308–313; al-Na''āl, *Mashyakha* 18–19.

60 Ibn al-Dubaythī, *Dhayl* iv, 184; Ibn Rajab, *Dhayl* iii, 75.

Sufi master ʿAbd al-Qādir al-Jīlī.[61] He was a Hanbali, like his father, a legist (*faqīh*), and a traditionist; furthermore, he was a direct student of Abū l-Faḍl b. Nāṣir al-Salāmī (d. 550/1155), who, as has been shown above, had received formal permission to transmit the *K. Sharḥ al-sunna*. Whether or not ʿAbd al-Razzāq al-Jīlī actually had an opportunity to transmit the book directly from Abū l-Faḍl al-Salāmī remains uncertain. It is possible, however, that ʿAbd al-Razzāq al-Jīlī was requesting formal permission (*ijāza*) from this particular Ibn ʿAbd al-Qādir b. Muḥammad b. Yūsuf to transmit the book, while one of his sons, ʿAbd al-Raḥīm b. ʿAbd al-Razzāq al-Jīlī (d. 606/1209),[62] was apparently present and studied the *K. Sharḥ al-sunna* along with his father.

In conclusion, the *K. Sharḥ al-sunna* was first transmitted by a Quran scholar and legist—that is, by Ibn Kāmil. The next transmission was confirmed with written permission (*ijāza*) by a meticulous and trustworthy *ḥadīth* transmitter, copyist, and bibliophile, Ibn al-Furāt. With the third transmitter, Abū Isḥāq al-Barmakī, the book enters one of the major Hanbali teaching circles established in the al-Manṣūr mosque on the western side of Baghdad, known as "the bastion of the Traditionalist movement."[63] Moreover, it was the fight over the chair of this mosque that started an infamous controversy between Abū l-Wafāʾ b. ʿAqīl and his rival, al-Sharīf Abū Jaʿfar.[64]

Although it is not clearly stated in the sources, the fourth transmitter, Abū Ṭālib ʿAbd al-Qādir, belonged to the Hanbali school; at least, he seems to have been a Hanbali: from his teacher, al-Barmakī, he transmitted a number of reports telling of dreams in which the Prophet urges the person having the dream to follow the example of Aḥmad b. Ḥanbal.[65] From Abū Ṭālib on, the *K. Sharḥ al-sunna* was in circulation for the next hundred years primarily in the limited circle of his family, other relatives, and close associates, all of whom belonged to the proto-Sunni *ḥadīth* folk.[66] Three of the respective transmitters—Ibn Nāṣir al-Salāmī, Abū Manṣūr al-Jawālīqī, and Hazārasb—are explicitly labeled as "followers of the Sunna." One of the main transmitters, Abū l-Ḥusayn ʿAbd al-Ḥaqq b. ʿAbd al-Khāliq, on whose authority the book was read in three audition sessions, was a student of Abū l-Wafāʾ b. ʿAqīl. The other

61 Chabbi, ʿAbd al-Qādir al-Jīlānī; Laoust, *Profession* cxix–cxxi.

62 Ibn al-Dubaythī, *Dhayl* iv, 89.

63 Makdisi, *Rise* 15–16; Makdisi, *Ibn ʿAqīl* 27.

64 Makdisi, *Ibn ʿAqīl* 24–43.

65 Ibn al-Jawzī, *Manāqib Aḥmad* ii, 388, 390, 394, 398 (in which the dreamer is Abū Dāwūd al-Sijistānī, d. 275/889, the famous compiler of one of the six canonical books).

66 For the term "proto-Sunni," see Zaman, *Religion* 1–2; and for the "*ḥadīth*-folk," Hodgson, *Venture* i, 263, 335, etc.

three, the aforementioned al-Jawālīqī, Abū l-Faḍl al-Mukharrimī, and ʿAbd al-Razzāq al-Jīlī, were adherents of the Hanbali school; with the latter, it seems that the *K. Sharḥ al-sunna* became available in the Hanbali teaching circle (*ḥalqa*) at the Bāb al-Azaj *madrasa*.

1.2 *Excerpts*

The first excerpt is found at the end of another Damascus manuscript, *al-Tanbīh wa-l-radd ʿalā ahl al-ahwāʾ wa-l-bidaʿ*, a treatise on heresiography by Muḥammad b. Aḥmad al-Malaṭī al-Shāfiʿī (d. 377/987), preserved in the Ẓāhiriyya Library (no. 2968) in 87 folios, 14×19 cm. The manuscript is numbered from 1 to 175, and some excerpts were added in a different script. They extend over three pages (172, ll. 10–175), without mentioning a source for these additions. There is no transmission chain, no author's name, no book title, nor any information about the date when this text was copied. The *samāʿ* certificates, however, attest to the fact that the copy was in circulation in Damascus between 414/1023 and 431/1039,[67] and that it was acquired by Abū l-Bayān b. al-Ḥawrānī (d. 551/1156).[68] It is Ibn al-Ḥawrānī who describes on the cover page the contents of the manuscript, indicating that al-Malaṭī's text is followed by folios (*awrāq*) containing points of excellence (*maḥāsin*) in praise of the Sunna (*min madḥ al-sunna*), along with fascicles that contain a creed from Aḥmad b. Ḥanbal.

The passages in the folios on the Sunna, as contained in this manuscript, are clearly quotations from *K. Sharḥ al-sunna* taken mainly from its last section, although some phrases also relate to the middle part of it. Importantly, however, as a close comparison shows, in those cases in which the text reproduced in these folios and the text of *K. Sharḥ al-sunna* differ, the closest match is, more often than not, the text of the work attributed to al-Barbahārī. In other words, the passages in the folios appear to be quotations from the well-known version of *Sharḥ Kitāb al-sunna* quoted by Ibn Abī Yaʿlā (d. 536/1131) in his *Ṭabaqāt al-Ḥanābila*. Therefore, the passages on the Sunna contained in these leaflets appear to have been added sometime after 526/1131, the year when Ibn Abī Yaʿlā died.

67 See al-Malaṭī, *al-Tanbīh* (ed. Dedering) w-z; (ed. al-Kawtharī) 8–9.

68 Al-Subkī, *Ṭabaqāt* vii, 318–319.

2 The Question of Authorship

2.1 *Medieval Attribution to al-Barbahārī*

Abū Yaʿlā l-Farrāʾ (d. 458/1066) was apparently the first to attribute this book to the "demagogue" Hanbali leader al-Ḥasan b. ʿAlī al-Barbahārī (d. 329/941).[69] No such claim is found in the Arabic sources prior to his. Abū Yaʿlā twice quotes from *K. Sharḥ al-sunna*, providing the definition of *ʿaql* (reason; cf. the translation item 55), and he attributes the work both times to al-Barbahārī. In the first instance, he writes, "It was mentioned by Abū Muḥammad al-Barbahārī, 'Reason is not an object of acquisition but rather a matter of Divine favor.' He mentioned this in his *Sharḥ al-sunna*, in a fascicle (*juzʾ*) that I came across (*waqaʿa ilayya*)."[70] The passage cited is the last part of a longer paragraph that Abū Yaʿlā also quotes in his *K. al-ʿUdda*, saying, "Abū Muḥammad al-Barbahārī said in *Sharḥ al-sunna* …"[71]

Abū Yaʿlā studied with a daughter of the first transmitter of the *K. Sharḥ al-sunna*, Abū Bakr Aḥmad b. Kāmil (d. 350/961).[72] Had he heard the book from him, he would surely have mentioned his transmission of it, as he usually does, and as he does in the case of his *K. Ibṭāl al-taʾwīlāt*. In that case, he confirms, "Abū Isḥāq al-Barmakī showed me (*akhraja ilayya*) a 'fascicle' (*juzʾ*) containing accounts by Abū l-Ḥasan b. Bashshār."[73]

Abū Yaʿlā's use of the phrase "that I came across," without further identification, raises doubt about the provenance of the book he used. These suspicions would appear to be confirmed by a close look at the way in which Abū Yaʿlā's son, Ibn Abī Yaʿlā (d. 536/1131), introduces the book. Three points are significant here. First, Ibn Abī Yaʿlā cites the *K. Sharḥ al-sunna* in his *Ṭabaqāt al-Ḥanābila* under a title that is slightly, yet significantly, different. Here, Ibn Abī Yaʿlā states that he quotes from *Sharḥ Kitāb al-sunna* (instead of *Kitāb Sharḥ al-sunna*).[74] This alteration of wording is conspicuous. Second, throughout the *Ṭabaqāt*, Ibn Abī Yaʿlā gives the transmission chains by which he connects himself with the authors of the books he quotes. Third, yet no less importantly, when Ibn Abī Yaʿlā copies from a book, he generally mentions the respective author by name

---

69 Ibn al-Jawzī, *al-Muntaẓam* xiv, 14–15; al-Dhahabī, *Siyar* xv, 90–93; Melchert, al-Barbahārī; Hurvitz, Authority.

70 Abū Yaʿlā al-Farrāʾ, *al-ʿIdda* i, 84–85; from him Ibn Taymiyya, *Bughya* 258.

71 Abū Yaʿlā al-Farrāʾ, *al-ʿIdda* i, 94.

72 Ibn Abī Yaʿlā, *Ṭabaqāt* (al-Fiqī) ii, 196, (al-ʿUthaymīn) iii, 366.

73 Abū Yaʿlā al-Farrāʾ, *Ibṭāl* i, 142.

74 Ibn Abī Yaʿlā, *Ṭabaqāt* (al-Fiqī) ii, 18; (al-ʿUthaymīn) iii, 36.

and, at times, the titles of the books and chapters from which he quotes, as the following instances demonstrate:[75]

(1) Ibn Abī Yaʿlā's citations authenticated by a chain of transmission:
- A creed (*ʿaqīda*) attributed to Aḥmad b. Ḥanbal on the authority of a certain Abū l-ʿAbbās al-Iṣṭakhrī.[76]
- The *masāʾil* ("questions" on legal opinions) that Abū Bakr Aḥmad b. Muḥammad al-Marrūdhī (d. 275/888), a leading disciple of Ibn Ḥanbal, transmitted from the latter.[77]
- The *masāʾil* that al-Athram al-Iskāfī (died between 261/874 and 273/886) transmitted from Ibn Ḥanbal, as well as excerpts of a creed he had addressed to *ahl al-thaghr*.[78]
- The events of Ibn Ḥanbal's inquisition (*al-miḥna*) as narrated by Sulaymān al-Sijzī.[79]
- Excerpts from the *masāʾil* that ʿAbd al-Malik al-Maymūnī (d. 274/887) transmitted from Aḥmad b. Ḥanbal.[80]
- A creed (*ʿaqīda*) attributed to Aḥmad b. Ḥanbal on the authority of ʿAbdūs b. Mālik (d. ca. 250/864).[81]
- Excerpts from the *masāʾil* that Muḥammad b. ʿAwf al-Ḥimṣī (d. 272/885) transmitted from Aḥmad b. Ḥanbal; the texts were dictated to him (*amlā ʿalayya*) based on a manuscript transcribed by Aḥmad al-Sinjī, where the latter provided his chain of transmitters.[82]
- Excerpts from a creed attributed to Aḥmad b. Ḥanbal, transmitted on the authority of Muḥammad b. Yūnus al-Sarakhsī.[83]
- A creed of Aḥmad b. Ḥanbal, contained in a letter addressed to Musaddad b. Musarhad al-Baṣrī (d. 228/842).[84]
- A book on prayers (*Kitāb fī l-ṣalāt*) transmitted on the authority of Muhannā b. Yaḥyā al-Shāmī.[85]

---

75 The lists are by no means exhaustive; their purpose is to support our argument.

76 Ibn Abī Yaʿlā, *Ṭabaqāt* (al-Fiqī) i, 24–36, (al-ʿUthaymīn) i, 55–74; compare with al-Dhahabī, *Siyar* xi, 286, 302; translated by Watt, *Islamic creeds* 33–40; on the attribution of this creed to al-Iṣṭakhrī, see chapter 3 (C.5).

77 Ibn Abī Yaʿlā, *Ṭabaqāt* (al-Fiqī) i, 56–58, (al-ʿUthaymīn) i, 137–141.

78 Ibn Abī Yaʿlā, *Ṭabaqāt* (al-Fiqī) i, 66–74, (al-ʿUthaymīn) i, 162–167.

79 Ibn Abī Yaʿlā, *Ṭabaqāt* (al-Fiqī) i, 163–167, (al-ʿUthaymīn) i, 438–443.

80 Ibn Abī Yaʿlā, *Ṭabaqāt* (al-Fiqī) i, 213–215, (al-ʿUthaymīn) ii, 93–95.

81 Ibn Abī Yaʿlā, *Ṭabaqāt* (al-Fiqī) i, 241–246, (al-ʿUthaymīn) ii, 166–174; al-Dhahabī, *Tārīkh* v, 1179.

82 Ibn Abī Yaʿlā, *Ṭabaqāt* (al-Fiqī) i, 311–313, (al-ʿUthaymīn) ii, 339–343.

83 Ibn Abī Yaʿlā, *Ṭabaqāt* (al-Fiqī) i, 329–330, (al-ʿUthaymīn) ii, 392–394.

84 Ibn Abī Yaʿlā, *Ṭabaqāt* (al-Fiqī) i, 341–345, (al-ʿUthaymīn) ii, 426–432.

85 Ibn Abī Yaʿlā, *Ṭabaqāt* (al-Fiqī) i, 348–380, (al-ʿUthaymīn) ii, 437–476; for Muhannā, Ibn ʿAsākir, *Tārīkh* 61, 310.

- A poem containing a creed by Abū Dāwūd al-Sijistānī's son, ʿAbdallāh (d. 316/928).[86]
- A creed on the authority of Abū ʿAlī Muḥammad b. Aḥmad al-Hāshimī (d. 428/1036).[87]

(2) Ibn Abī Yaʿlā's citations with explicit reference to book and/or chapter titles:
- A quote from *K. al-Sunna* by al-Khallāl.[88]
- A quote from *al-Majmūʿ* by Abū Ḥafṣ al-Barmakī (d. 387/997).[89]
- A quote from the book of al-Makkī (i.e., Abū Ṭālib al-Makkī in his *Qūt al-qulūb*).[90]
- A quote from Abū Nuʿaym (i.e., al-Iṣfahānī in his book *Ḥilyat al-awliyāʾ*).[91]
- A quote from a certain *K. al-Zakāt* transmitted on the authority of ʿUmar b. Ḥayyawayh (d. 382/992).[92]
- A long excerpt on the authority of Aḥmad b. Ṣāliḥ from one of the books of his grandfather, Aḥmad b. Ḥanbal.[93]
- A long excerpt from a book by Ibn Shāqillā (d. 369/979) that Ibn Abī Yaʿlā had studied in a manuscript copy written by his father, who in turn had copied it from the manuscript in the handwriting of Ibn Shāqillā, who had questioned Abū Sulaymān al-Dimashqī on the *aḥādīth al-ṣifāt*—that is, the traditions that depict God and His attributes in an anthropomorphic language.[94]

Considering his essentially consistent and precise method of citation, it is quite uncharacteristic that Ibn Abī Yaʿlā does not refer to the source from which he quotes the *Sharḥ Kitāb al-sunna*, which he attributes to al-Barbahārī. Likewise, it is striking that he does not mention his own chain of transmission and thus the way he obtained knowledge of this book.

Having said this, however, one notices that Ibn Abī Yaʿlā cites a report just before mentioning the *Sharḥ Kitāb al-sunna*, quoting from it at length. This

86 Ibn Abī Yaʿlā, *Ṭabaqāt* (al-Fiqī) ii, 53–54, (al-ʿUthaymīn) iii, 100–101.
87 Ibn Abī Yaʿlā, *Ṭabaqāt* (al-Fiqī) ii, 182–185, (al-ʿUthaymīn) iii, 336–339.
88 Ibn Abī Yaʿlā, *Ṭabaqāt* (al-Fiqī) i, 50, (al-ʿUthaymīn) i, 120.
89 Ibn Abī Yaʿlā, *Ṭabaqāt* (al-Fiqī) i, 221, (al-ʿUthaymīn) ii, 115; he is the father of Abū Isḥāq al-Barmakī, who appears in the transmission chain on the first page of the manuscript of Ghulām Khalīl's *K. Sharḥ al-sunna*; see also other citations from Abū Ḥafṣ al-Barmakī from his *K. al-Majmūʿ* (al-ʿUthaymīn) iii, 626.
90 Ibn Abī Yaʿlā, *Ṭabaqāt* (al-Fiqī) i, 231, (al-ʿUthaymīn) ii, 145.
91 Ibn Abī Yaʿlā, *Ṭabaqāt* (al-Fiqī) i, 231, (al-ʿUthaymīn) ii, 145.
92 Ibn Abī Yaʿlā, *Ṭabaqāt* (al-Fiqī) ii, 17, (al-ʿUthaymīn) iii, 32.
93 Ibn Abī Yaʿlā, *Ṭabaqāt* (al-Fiqī) ii, 65, (al-ʿUthaymīn) iii, 122.
94 Ibn Abī Yaʿlā, *Ṭabaqāt* (al-Fiqī) ii, 128–138, (al-ʿUthaymīn) iii, 227–243.

report is cited on the authority of ʿAlī al-Qurashī,[95] who transmitted it from a certain al-Ḥasan al-Ahwāzī, and the latter from Abū ʿAbdallāh al-Ḥumrānī.[96] It concerns an alleged confrontation between al-Barbahārī and the famous theologian Abū l-Ḥasan al-Ashʿarī (d. 324/935 or 936), which prompted the latter to write his *K. al-Ibāna ʿan uṣūl al-diyāna* ("The elucidation concerning the principles of religion").[97] Interestingly, the report in question is also mentioned by al-Ḥasan b. ʿAlī al-Ahwāzī (d. 446/1055) in his short treatise *Mathālib b. Abī Bishr*, in which he defames al-Ashʿarī.[98] Moreover, the renowned historian and follower of al-Ashʿarī, Ibn ʿAsākir (d. 571/1176), dedicates lengthy sections in his *Tabyīn* to refuting accusations by al-Ahwāzī against al-Ashʿarī;[99] he also calls al-Ḥasan b. ʿAlī al-Ahwāzī a liar.[100] Likewise, al-Dhahabī mentions that al-Ahwāzī was a *sālimī* (i.e., an anthropomorphist) and a fanatic Sunni (*min ghulāt al-sunna*),[101] who had transmitted "odious falsities" (*abāṭīl samija*).[102] Al-Dhahabī cautions against accepting his transmissions and ends the entry by stating, "May God forgive him."[103] It should be mentioned in this regard that al-Barbahārī had close ties to the anthropomorphist group.[104]

---

95 Al-ʿUthaymīn, who is the editor of the second edition of *Ṭabaqāt al-Ḥanābila*, *Ṭabaqāt* iii, 37, makes a guess at the identity of ʿAlī al-Qurashī, associating him with Abū l-Ḥasan al-Hakkārī (d. 480/108); al-Dhahabī, *Siyar* xix, 67; Allard, however, could not identify him. Pamphlet 135, fn. 2.

96 Ibn Ḥajar, *Lisān* ix, 111, calls him "*majhūl*" and refers to Ibn ʿAsākir in his *Tabyīn*; al-Ahwāzī describes him, in his *Mathālib* 155 (154, French translation—Allard writes his name "al-Ḥamrānī") as "a scholar in language with superior knowledge in grammar, metrics, vocabulary, *akhbār* and poetry."

97 Allard, *Problème* 48, 52; Makdisi says, "The anecdote may be of a recent date and attributed to al-Barbahārī." *Ibn ʿAqīl et la résurgence* 296, fn. 4.

98 Allard, Pamphlet 157–158; al-Dhahabī, *Siyar* xv, 90; and from him al-Ṣafadī, *al-Wāfī* xii, 147; van Ess, *Der Eine* ii, 747.

99 Ibn ʿAsākir, *Tabyīn* 364–430; McCarthy, *Theology* 188–204; Ibn ʿAsākir, *Tārīkh* xiii, 143–148.

100 Ibn ʿAsākir, *Tabyīn* 415, 416; al-Dhahabī, *Tārīkh* ix, 679.

101 Al-Dhahabī, *Tārīkh* ix, 678; Ibn ʿAsākir and al-Dhahabī say that he was a *sālimī*—that is, a follower of the doctrine of the Baṣran Abū l-Ḥasan b. Sālim (and his father Abū ʿAbdallāh), who propounded extreme anthropomorphism (*tashbīh* and *tajsīm*); see also Ibn Taymiyya, *Majmūʿ fatāwā*, v, 124, 556; Ibn Taymiyya, *Minhāj*, ii, 499; Ibn ʿAsākir, *Tabyīn* 366–367, 369, *Ḥashwiyya*; al-Isfarāyīnī, *al-Tabṣīr* 133, also calls them *Ḥashwiyya*; for a catalogue of their beliefs, Abū Yaʿlā, *al-Muʿtamad* 217–222; al-Jīlānī, *al-Ghunya* i, 191–192; see Allard, Pamphlet 132; Makdisi, Ashʿarī and the Ashʿarites i, 54–55; Böwering, *Mystical vision* 89–96; Sobieroj, *Ibn Ḫafīf* 307–308; Baldick, *Mystical Islam* 52.

102 Al-Dhahabī, *Siyar* xviii, 14.

103 Al-Dhahabī, *Siyar* xviii, 13–18; al-Khaṭīb al-Baghdādī, *Tārīkh* ix, 677–681; Allard, Pamphlet 129–132.

104 Böwering, *Mystical vision* 97.

In view of Ibn Abī Yaʿlā's method of writing and general practice of indicating his chains of transmitters, it can be assumed that the reason he does not provide a chain of transmission for the book he uses (and which he attributes to al-Barbahārī) is that he is still relying on the chain of transmission he has mentioned just before. This would lead the reader to al-Ḥasan al-Ahwāzī as the source for the information in question. Yet, as we have just noted above, several well-known medieval scholars suspected al-Ḥasan al-Ahwāzī of fabrication and mention that the story he told about the alleged meeting between al-Barbahārī and al-Ashʿarī was just another one of his inventions.[105]

Taken together, these various pieces of information make it reasonable to suggest that al-Ḥasan al-Ahwāzī was most probably the first person who intentionally attributed the *Sharḥ Kitāb al-sunna* to al-Barbahārī. Moreover, if this is the case, it would explain why Ibn Abī Yaʿlā, as well as his father before him, neglects to make any explicit mention of a chain of transmission with regard to *Sharḥ Kitāb al-sunna*. Apparently, they were well aware of the uncertainty of its attribution to al-Barbahārī. Moreover, except for Ibn Abī Yaʿlā, no other early source contains any mention of a *Sharḥ Kitāb al-sunna* or a *Kitāb Sharḥ al-sunna* authored by al-Barbahārī, who is known mainly as a popular preacher (*wāʿiẓ*) and, as John Kelsay puts it, a "marauding zealot,"[106] rather than a dogmatist or a man of letters.[107]

2.2 *Modern Scholars' Attribution*

2.2.1 Louis Massignon

Louis Massignon (d. 1962) was apparently the first in modern scholarship to attribute the *K. Sharḥ al-sunna* to Ghulām Khalīl. In his 1929 collection of unpublished texts, Massignon reproduces a few excerpts from the Ẓāhiriyya manuscript (19 lines altogether).[108] In introducing these "extracts from his *kitāb*

105 Badawī, *Madhāhib* i, 515.

106 Kelsay, Comparison 358; Cook, *Commanding right* 164, points to his charismatic style of preaching and calls it "demagoguery and trouble-making."

107 Hurvitz, Authority 37–38, argues that "he was clearly not a typical leader of a *madhhab*, because he was not mentioned by contemporary or later Hanbalis as a notable jurist." Hurvitz also says that he was depicted by authors of biographies of Hanbali jurists and *ḥadīth* experts "as a minor intellectual figure." Al-Dhahabī, *al-ʿIbar* ii, 33, states that al-Barbahārī had authored books, but he does not mention any titles; also al-Ṣafadī, *al-Wāfī* xii, 147, mentions only "*Sharḥ al-sunna*." Laoust, al-Barbahārī i, 1039, since he accepted the attribution of "*K. al-Sunna*," as he calls it, to al-Barbahārī, writes that he was a "theologian," and "both a traditionist (*ʿālim*), and a jurist (*faḳīh*)"; nonetheless, Laoust does not give any titles of books possibly written by him.

108 Massignon, *Recueil* 213–214; see also Schacht, *Der Islam* 40; Grunebaum, *Der Islam im Mittelalter* 141.

sharḥ al sonnah", Massignon writes that Ghulām Khalīl belonged to the "ḥanbalite rite," and that "the ḥanbalites have long paid attention to his little Sunni manual (*manuel de sunnisme*)." This statement is probably based on the number of Hanbali names that appear in the later part of the transmission chain on the first page of the manuscript, as well as in the transmission certificate. In a footnote, Massignon refers to "a verbatim copy" with the title "*sharḥ kitāb al sonnah*" by al-Barbahārī, included in al-Farrā''s *Ṭabaqāt al-Ḥanābila*.[109] Moreover, Massignon made extensive use of the manuscript attributed to Ghulām Khalīl for *The passion of al-Hallaj*. Van Ess also made extensive use of *K. Sharḥ al-sunna*, relying on the Damascus manuscript and attributing the text to Ghulām Khalīl.[110]

The audition certificates examined above, in addition to Massignon's attribution of the text to Ghulām Khalīl, lead one to conclude that the author of the *K. Sharḥ al-sunna* as contained in the Ẓāhiriyya manuscript is Ghulām Khalīl. Yet certain modern scholars dispute this attribution, basing their views on the information given by Ibn Abī Yaʿlā, which they interpret as Ibn Abī Yaʿlā's attribution of *K. Sharḥ al-sunna* to al-Barbahārī. In the following, we take a closer look at these opinions.

2.2.2 Henri Laoust

In 1957, while preparing his work on Ibn Baṭṭa's profession of faith for publication, Henri Laoust (d. 1983) published a study on the early Hanbali professions of faith in *Mélanges Louis Massignon*, in which he attributes the *K. al-Sunna* (sic!) to al-Barbahārī.[111] Laoust refers in this context to a report "echoed" in the *Ṭabaqāt al-Ḥanābila*, stating that al-Ashʿarī must have composed his *Ibāna* after having a lively discussion with al-Barbahārī.

Although earlier on in his study Laoust addresses "the problem of the authenticity of these different professions of faith" attributed to Aḥmad b. Ḥanbal,[112] he is silent on the question of whether the attribution of this particular creed to al-Barbahārī is authentic. Likewise, he disregards the extracts from the *Kitāb Sharḥ al-sunna* by Ghulām Khalīl that had already been published at that time by Massignon.

In his 1958 book on Ibn Baṭṭa, Laoust considers "the *Kitāb as-Sunna* by al-Barbahārī," as he terms it, "the most celebrated hanbalite profession of faith

109 Fn. 2, "Copié textuellement ap. *sharḥ kitāb al sonnah* de Barbahārī."

110 *ThG* iv, 282–283, 285, 685; van Ess, Sufism 26–27; van Ess, *Der Eine* i, 285.

111 Laoust, Premières professions 22.

112 Ibid., 14.

in the beginning of the fourth century."[113] In contrast, in a footnote he somewhat shyly mentions "the influence exerted on al-Barbahārī by the *Šarḥ Kitāb as-sunna* by Aḥmad Ġulām Ḫalīl," referring the reader to Massignon's *Textes inédits*.[114]

Laoust also notes the "somewhat aberrant" condemnation of the "incarnationism of Ḥulūlīya,"[115] which appears in the book of the "hanbalite" Ghulām Khalīl as well as in works by Ibn Baṭṭa and al-Barbahārī.[116] With this cursory mention, it seems, the matter is settled for Laoust. He then makes extensive use of the book in producing very useful comparisons of Ghulām Khalīl/al-Barbahārī with Ibn Baṭṭa's profession of faith.[117]

It is, nonetheless, rather peculiar that Laoust does not take notice of the fact that Ibn Baṭṭa never mentions al-Barbahārī by name, nor refers to the book ascribed to him either in his shorter creed *al-Sharḥ wa-l-ibāna* or in the longer *al-Ibāna*. In his book on Ibn Baṭṭa (1959), Laoust repeats the same information and once more refers to the report about the "lively discussion" between al-Barbahārī and al-Ashʿarī, as a result of which the latter "would have composed his *Ibāna*."[118] In 1982 Laoust returns once more to the book which he calls *K. al-Sunna*, reiterating his position.[119] He states here that

> the restoration of law as he conceived it [i.e., al-Barbahārī in the text Laoust attributes to him] was to be done, not by armed rebellion against the established authorities, but by a missionary action, by putting into practice, through "the duty of good council (*naṣīḥa*)" and "commanding the right," on the spot and without hesitation, to resort to popular demonstrations.

113 Laoust, *Profession* xxiii.

114 Ibid., xxix, fn. 61.

115 There is actually no mention of either incarnationism or of the Ḥulūlīya in Ghulām Khalīl's text; possibly, Laoust is referring to his condemnation of "those who advocate longing (*shawq*) and love (*maḥabba*)," 99 in our translation.

116 Laoust, *Profession* lviii; see also Laoust, al-Barbahārī i, 1039.

117 See also Laoust, al-Barbahārī i, 1040. In fact, the sources do not count al-Barbahārī among Ibn Baṭṭa's teachers; only Ibn Abī Yaʿlā mentions two general reports about al-Barbahārī introduced with "*samiʿtu al-Barbahārī yaqūl*," *Ṭabaqāt* (al-Fiqī) ii, 43, (al-ʿUthaymīn) iii, 76; and Laoust, *Profession* xliv–xlivii. But this does not necessarlily mean that he studied with him; Ibn Baṭṭa might have heard these two sayings in one of the public admonition sessions of the latter.

118 Laoust, Hanbalisme 82.

119 Laoust, *Schismes* 126–127.

Nonetheless, Laoust fails to notice that al-Barbahārī was actually launching operational aggressions not with good council, but rather "with the sword," paying no heed to the authorities or the interests of the community. Thus, Laoust's study of the book and its alleged authorship remain unsatisfactory.[120]

2.2.3 Michel Allard

In his study on al-Ashʿarī (1965), Michel Allard (d. 1976) takes the discussion a step further in the direction laid down by Laoust, his teacher. Building his argument on the report by al-Ḥasan al-Ahwāzī as it appears in Ibn Abī Yaʿlā's *Ṭabaqāt al-Ḥanābila*,[121] and accepting it at face value, Allard writes that the *Risāla fī istiḥsān al-khawḍ fī ʿilm al-kalām* (*Risāla II*, as he refers to it) was "very consciously directed by al-Ashʿarī against the Ḥanābila. But this conclusion leads to another point that concerns the approximate place and time of its composition."[122]

Risāla II refutes plain *taqlīd* (conformism and due compliance) and encourages the use of speculative argumentation (*kalām*). It was first published in Hyderabad in 1344/1925, then edited by McCarthy and republished in 1953.[123] This is noteworthy because McCarthy, and later Makdisi,[124] question the veracity of its attribution to al-Ashʿarī,[125] and Allard partially agrees with them.[126] Nonetheless, Allard connects *Risāla II* with al-Barbahārī's assumed authorship of the *K. al-Sunna* (sic!), and ventures further to argue:

> And how not to think of al-Barbahārī and his violent attacks against *kalām* with which he filled his *Kitāb al-Sunna*, when we read at the beginning of the *Risāla II* the description of a group of ignorants against whom al-Ashʿarī wants to write? Isn't it al-Barbahārī who proclaims that "religion is but servile imitation (*taqlīd*)"?[127]

---

120 Gilliot, Textes arabes anciens, commenting on the second edition of the text attributed to al-Barbahārī by al-Qaḥṭānī (1996), writes, "Selon Laoust, la profession de foi de B [al-Barbahārī] rappelle celle que Ghulām Khalīl avait lui-même [Sic.] composée," 223, no. 97.

121 Allard, Problème 45–46.

122 Allard, *Problème* 208; van Ess, *Der Eine* i, 100, relies on Allard but is more cautious, fn. 7.

123 McCarthy, *Theology*, Arabic section 87–97.

124 Makdisi, Ashʿarī and the Ashʿarites i, 19–26.

125 McCarthy, *Theology* xxvi.

126 Allard, *Problème* 51, "Mais il est difficile de tirer de là une conclusion nette, étant donné que nous ignorons le contenu réel de trop nombreux traités et que leurs titres ont pu varier." Allard, however, makes no mention of Makdisi's article.

127 Allard, *Problème* 208, "Et comment ne pas penser à Barbahārī, et aux violentes attaques contre le kalam dont il a rempli son *Kitāb al-Sunna*, quand on lit, au début de la *Risāla II*, la description du groupe d' ignorants contre qui al-Ašʿarī veut écrire? N' est-ce pas Barbahārī

Moreover, Allard uses al-Ḥasan al-Ahwāzī's anecdote to establish the attribution of *al-Ibāna* to al-Ashʿarī,[128] an attribution that has been called into question since Goldziher.[129] No mention of Ghulām Khalīl is made in the entire discussion; yet, one notices again the weakness of the arguments put forward by Allard, built on rather poor textual foundations.

It is not part of my argument here to propound speculations concerning the attributions of either *al-Ibāna* or *Risāla II*.[130] But the question arises as to the motives that allegedly would have driven al-Ashʿarī to a confrontation with al-Barbahārī.

Laoust, and Allard after him, indiscriminately speculated the ascription of *Sharḥ Kitāb al-sunna* to al-Barbahārī. Allard relied on al-Ahwāzī's anecdote for his argumentation. As we understand it, *Risāla II* constitutes a rebuttal deploring the positions of the prevailing Hanbali approach, which had found expression in a number of creeds and books in the aftermath of Aḥmad b. Ḥanbal's tribulation. Had *Risāla II* been addressed to one person in particular, the addressee would have been one of the main advocates of this movement at that time, say, Abū Bakr al-Khallāl (d. 311/923), instead of a populist activist such as al-Barbahārī, who was not even counted among the learned scholars, nor known to have written a book.[131] Thus, it is more probable that *Risāla II* constitutes a refutation of the positions promoted by the "tradionalist faction," rather than a text nominally targeting a particular representative or author.

Al-Ashʿarī seems rather likely as a target of the misleading information that this report tried to disseminate. After all, in the process of forming authoritative, unified, and acceptable[132] theology among the *ahl al-sunna*, al-Ashʿarī represented a turning point at a critical "interpretive" juncture[133] of "collision of the two approaches to the scripture": the "anthropomorphic" and the "lit-

---

qui proclame que «la religion n'est qu'imitation servile (*taqlīd*)»." See also pp. 104–105, 230, 259; and Laoust, *Profession* xxix.

128 Allard, *Problème* 51–53; Melchert, *Formation* 152, quotes the anecdote with a caution: "The story is rejected by Ibn ʿAsākir, but on grounds that Michel Allard considers inadequate"; Turner, *Inquisition* 144, and fn. 125 on p. 203, cites, after Melchert, al-Barbahārī's supposed response and notes, "This statement is an uncomfortable parallel to Aḥmad's response during his trial."

129 Cf. Makdisi, Ashʿarī and the Ashʿarites i, 42–44; McCarthy, *Theology* 231–232; Gimaret, Document majeur 218.

130 It is noteworthy that the author in his defense of *kalām* refers to the substantive branches (*furūʿ*) of *al-tawḥīd wa-l-ʿadl*; Frank, al-Ashʿarī's "Kitāb *al-ḥathth ʿalā l-baḥth*" 138.

131 Cf. Melchert, *Formation* 150.

132 Dallal, Ghazali 786.

133 We are relying on Sherman Jackson's introduction to *On the boundaries*.

eralist" approaches toward the Quranic statements about God.[134] Indeed, the contrived doctrine that al-Ashʿarī famously proposed in this regard was disapproved strongly by all sides: the Hanbalis as well as the hard-line anthropomorphists and literalists.[135]

By introducing the name of al-Barbahārī in his well-tailored, allusive report, al-Ahwāzī's purpose appears to have been threefold: (1) to belittle al-Ashʿarī by claiming that his only rival was al-Barbahārī; (2) to recognize al-Barbahārī, a *sālimī* companion, as an established scholar; and (3) to lessen the significance of *Risāla II* by implying that it was addressed to a single person by name, as opposed to being a refutation of widespread doctrines. It is noteworthy, moreover, that *Sharḥ Kitāb al-sunna* is a creed whose audience are the learned at large. Its content, whether concerning the position approving of plain *taqlīd*, or its other "ideological" commitments, summarizes tenets that had been circulating among the tradionalists throughout the third/ninth century.

2.2.4 Richard M. Frank

In 1988, Richard M. Frank published a new edition of the *Risāla fī istiḥsān al-khawḍ fī ʿilm al-kalām* (*Risāla II*, attributed to al-Ashʿarī) under the title *al-Ḥaththʿalā l-baḥth*.[136] This edition is based on a manuscript of *al-Ghunya* by the Ashʿarī theologian Abū l-Qāsim Salmān al-Anṣārī (d. 512/1118).[137] In an article that appeared in 1991, Frank refutes Makdisi's doubts about the attribution of *Risāla fī istiḥsān* to al-Ashʿarī, and examines select thematic aspects and elements in that text. Relevant to our discussion here is the fact that Frank, following Laoust and Allard, accepts the veracity of the report by al-Ḥasan al-Ahwāzī about the purported meeting between al-Barbahārī and al-Ashʿarī, as well as the attribution of the book to al-Barbahārī.[138] Moreover, Frank uncritically relies on the *Sharḥ Kitāb al-sunna* as attributed to al-Barbahārī in drawing his conclusions.[139] To corroborate his ideas, Frank adduces once again the practice of *taqlīd*, which, contrary to the position of al-Barbahārī, is vehemently condemned in *al-Ḥaththʿalā l-baḥth*, as Frank notes. The issue of *taqlīd* will

134 Knysh, "Orthodoxy" 56, 60–61.

135 For the later development of the Ashʿari school and its view of "Hanbalism," see Makdisi, Ashʿarī and the Ashʿarites i, 37–39.

136 In al-Ashʿarī's "Kitāb *al-ḥaththʿalā l-baḥth*" 84, Frank explains that "The title given in the Hyderabad edition is plainly spurious, a descriptive pseudo-title."

137 Ibid., 83. Meanwhile, the book has been edited in two volumes in Cairo, 2010.

138 In footnote 53 on page 161 of Frank's article, read "al-Iṣṭakhrī" instead of "al-Barbahārī."

139 Frank, al-Ashʿarī's "Kitāb *al-ḥaththʿalā l-baḥth*" 99, 114, 117–119, 121–122; Frank, Elements 153, 171–173, 175, 177.

be addressed in more detail later on in our discussion; it suffices here to say that, in this particular case, Frank's argumentation remains unconvincing.[140]

2.2.5 Alexander Knysh

Giving an example of a "collision of the two approaches to the scripture," noted above, Knysh also relies on the startling anecdote about al-Barbahārī and al-Ashʿarī, which he takes at face value. Knysh, unfortunately unaware of the literature on the subject,[141] quotes al-Dhahabī's entry on al-Barbahārī in *Siyar aʿlām al-nubalāʾ*. He highlights the "pious agnosticism and literal-mindedness" of al-Barbahārī, which "eventually resulted in his embracing an 'anthropomorphist' concept of God that was eventually condemned in a special decree issued by the Caliph al-Rāḍī." Knysh concludes, "Al-Barbahārī's position is succinctly formulated by sympathetic al-Dhahabī who quotes one of the Hanbali's statements."[142] Importantly, however, shortly after al-Dhahabī's reference to the anecdote of al-Barbahārī and al-Ashʿarī in the *Siyar*, he provides certain quotations from the book as attributed to al-Barbahārī (these quotations are identical to items 10 to 12 in our translation). This passage, however, stresses the refusal to posit "how" or "why" concerning God's attributes. It does not declare any "anthropomorphist" views, nor does al-Dhahabī, in this particular instance, divulge such stances. Moreover, al-Dhahabī is known to have sternly attacked the anthropomorphist posture of Abū l-Ḥasan al-Ahwāzī—that is, the one who had put the abovementioned anecdote into circulation. Besides, this anecdote is introduced by al-Dhahabī with *qīla* ("it was said"), a formula used in the medieval Arabic sources in cases when no reliable source for a given piece of information was available or might be given. Put differently, al-Dhahabī appears here to distance himself from the content of the report he then offers.

2.2.6 Christopher Melchert

In the attempt to arrive at a more satisfactory account of the authorship of the *K. Sharḥ al-sunna*, the work of Christopher Melchert, one of the leading scholars in the field of Islamic studies, must be included in the discussion.[143]

---

140 Cf., however, Dallal, Ghazali 773–787; a critical review of Richard Frank's *al-Ghazali and the Ashʿarite school.*

141 Knysh mentions that he owes the reference to Professor Michael Cook, "Orthodoxy" 57, fn. 21.

142 Knysh, "Orthodoxy" 61.

143 Relying on the attribution of the book to al-Barbahārī by Ibn Abī Yaʿlā in his *Ṭabaqāt* and on Laoust/Allard's acknowledgment, the following scholars have accepted the attribution to al-Barbahārī without providing explanation: Makdisi, *Ibn ʿAqīl et la résurgence* 327, fn. 1;

Melchert has dealt with the issue of the attribution of the *K. Sharḥ al-sunna* to al-Barbahārī on more than one occasion. Indeed, he has published important results in this regard based on examinations of this text as quoted in Ibn Abī Yaʿlā's *Ṭabaqāt* and, since 2001, by referring to an edition of the book that also attributes it to al-Barbahārī.[144]

In his 1992 dissertation, Melchert mentions that "Ibn Abī Yaʿlā preserves a long creedal statement from al-Barbahārī, evidently an excerpt from his commentary on ʿAbd Allāh's *Kitāb al-Sunnah*."[145] The reader is not provided with further information about this particular "ʿAbd Allāh." Is ʿAbdallāh b. Aḥmad b. Ḥanbal meant here, who authored a *K. al-Sunna*? This, at least, is suggested by the entry of the name "ʿAbd Allāh b. Aḥmad b. Ḥanbal" in the index of the dissertation, which points to page 152, where the name "ʿAbd Allāh" appears.

It is noteworthy, as well, that Melchert does not offer a critical comparison of the two books in question, the *K. al-Sunna* (by ʿAbdallāh b. Aḥmad b. Ḥanbal) and the *Sharḥ Kitāb al-sunna* (as attributed to al-Barbahārī). Nor is the reader informed of any reasons that might have moved al-Barbahārī to write a commentary on the *K. al-Sunna*.

To address the arguments Melchert has raised in his various studies adequately, we present the following six points for consideration.

(1) As mentioned already, the title page of the Ghulām Khalīl manuscript gives the title of the work as "*K. Sharḥ al-sunna*." Moreover, the author of the work very clearly explains that this book is about the meaning of "the Sunna" as a concept and doctrine (not just about a particular book with *Sunna* in its title), and that it will be of central significance for *dīn* (religion and way of life) and for Islam in general (see chapter 3). What is more, Abū Yaʿlā gives the title of the work he attributed to al-Barbahārī as "*Sharḥ al-sunna*." It was Abū Yaʿlā's son, Ibn Abī Yaʿlā, who first supplied the puzzling information that al-Barbahārī had written a "*Sharḥ Kitāb al-sunna*," giving the impression that he was commenting on the aforementioned book. This apparently subtle but

Makdisi, *Ibn ʿAqīl* 92, 108, "al-Barbahārī drew attention to the dangers of going deeply into the study of the divinity," and he quotes item 31 in our translation; Gardet, Dīn 295; Nagel, *Rechtleitung* 265; Bell, *Love theory* 48–50; Abrahamov, "Bi-lā kayfa" doctrine 366; Daiber, Creed 107, 123, 124; Juynboll, Some new ideas 106, 112; Mughni, *Ḥanbalī movements* 107; Juynboll, Sunna 880; Schmidtke, Creeds 481; Brown, *Canonization* 141–142; Brown, Faithful dissenters 130; Turner, *Inquisition* 149, and fn. 158 on p. 206; Hoover, Creed; Temel, Uṣūl al-sunna 44 (he is using the edition which appeared in Riyadh 1993 [1414], but does not mention the name of the editor [Abū Yāsir Khālid b. Qāsim al-Raddādī]).

144 Edited by Muḥammad b. Saʿīd al-Qaḥṭānī, 3rd printing (Cairo, 1416/1996).

145 Dissertation 272, under the supervision of George Makdisi, Pennsylvania 1992; revised and published as Melchert, *Formation* 152 (we will be referring to this book again later).

essential misrepresentation by both father and son, Abū Yaʿlā and Ibn Abī Yaʿlā, seems to lie at the heart of the confusion among modern scholars regarding the nature and the authorship of the text quoted by these two Hanbali scholars, and its dependence on an earlier author.

(2) Melchert makes another cursory mention of al-Barbahārī's creed in an article from 1996 in which he refers to a statement from the creed regarding giving counsel (*naṣīḥa*) to any Muslim, righteous or otherwise.[146] Not until an article in 2001 does Melchert embark on a critical discussion of "*Šarḥ 'Kitāb al-Sunna*'," as he refers to it,[147] attempting a textual analysis of a few issues raised in this text. It is here that Melchert first considers the possibility that "either the later Ḥanbalī leader thoroughly agreed with Ġulām Ḫalīl on a range of questions and reproduced his statement practically verbatim, or the attribution to Ġulām Ḫalīl is erroneous. Nothing in the *Šarḥ* could have been written only in the tenth century."[148] Both alternatives are plausible.[149] We believe that internal evidence from the *K. Sharḥ al-sunna* enables us to argue with reasonable certainty that it is indeed the work of Ghulām Khalīl.

As for the last observation in Melchert's statement (referring to the fact that many of the "orthodox" creeds had been developed in the second/eighth and third/ninth centuries, and were available in the third/ninth century), there is much evidence in the sources to support this view. In fact, in the third/ninth century these tenets of faith had become a common good for the *ahl al-ḥadīth* and the adherents of the Sunna in general. They had been included in a number of written creeds both in the third century and later—with textual nuances and thematic variations according with the particular position of the compiler of the work.

(3) Melchert adds to the aforementioned statements, "Apparently in favour of its attribution to Ġulām Ḫalīl is its specific warning against those who speak of *šawq* (longing) and *maḥabba* (love), which Abū Ḥamza had introduced in Baghdad as technical terms."[150] This textual evidence, taken from the *K. Sharḥ*

146 Melchert, Transition 68.

147 Melchert, Ḥanābila 361–365; however, in Adversaries 251, fn. 132, he refers to the *K. al-Sunna* attributed to Ghulām Khalīl and quotes Massignon's remark that it is extremely similar to that of the later Hanbali al-Barbahārī.

148 Melchert, Ḥanābila 361.

149 The first possibility was put forward by Massignon and adopted by van Ess, *Der Eine* ii, 1363; although van Ess attributes the text to al-Barbahārī whenever he cites it, see *Der Eine*, Index ii, 1451. Although van Ess discusses Ghulām Khalīl's book in a separate entry, his comment on p. 285, fn. 44, is noteworthy as he asks here, "Hat Barbahārī einfach die „Schule" des Ġulām Ḫalīl mitsamt ihrer Programmschrift übernommen?"

150 Melchert, Ḥanābila 361.

al-sunna is, in fact, another argument in support of our proposal that Ghulām Khalīl was the author of this work, and not al-Barbahārī. Nonetheless, Melchert continues with the statement that "the document seems more likely to be al-Barbahārī's, not Ġulām Ḫalīl's, for several reasons."[151] He then notes that the text's "stress on *ḥadīṯ* from the Prophet, not Companions, is inconsistent with Hanbali works of the ninth century, which lay equal stress on *ḥadīṯ* from Companions." This conclusion, however, is not entirely accurate, since the *K. Sharḥ al-sunna* abundantly invokes *ḥadīth*s and sayings from the Companions, the Successors, and their followers. Some of these sayings are integrated within the text without referring to the specific name of the authority. Examples include ʿUmar b. al-Khaṭṭāb (3, 103, 141), Ubayy b. Kaʿb and ʿAbdallāh b. al-Ṣāmiṭ (40), ʿAbdallāh b. ʿUmar (14), al-Ḥasan al-Baṣrī (137), al-Zuhrī (158), and al-Awzāʿī/Makḥūl (48), as well as a plentitude of authorities and ascetics from the second/eighth century.[152]

(4) Melchert considers the mention of the Muʿtazila by Ghulām Khalīl, writing:[153]

> It names two Muʿtazila, Abū Huḏayl (d. 235/849–850?) and Hišam al-Fuwaṭī (fl. first half 3rd/9th cent.), as arch-heretics. The Muʿtazila are nowhere near so prominent in the various creeds of Aḥmad ibn Ḥanbal himself, corroborating the recent finding that the classical Muʿtazili school formed only near the end of the ninth century; that is, after the death of Ġulām Ḫalīl.[154]

Melchert then narrows down his statement in the footnote on the same page, where he writes, "Only half the creeds even mention the Muʿtazila, twice to reject their doctrine concerning responsibility for actions, once for equating sin with unbelief."[155] As a matter of fact, one also encounters mention of the Muʿtazila and refutations of certain of their views in the works of al-Bukhārī

151 Melchert, Ḥanābila 362.

152 The numbers in parentheses after each named individual relate to the items in our translation of the *K. Sharḥ al-sunna*. Recent scholarship has demonstrated not only Aḥmad b. Ḥanbal but also other authors of third/ninth-century creeds "express the adherence to the precedent of the Prophet's companions" and, at times, that of the Successors. Moreover, this trend continued in Hanbali legal tradition from the fourth/tenth century onward. Cf. Bin Ramli, From tradition 167–171, 79–83.

153 Melchert, Ḥanābila 362.

154 In Adversaries 240, Melchert contends, "The *Muʿtazila* evidently did become a more pressing concern to *Ḥanābila* in the last quarter of the ninth century."

155 Melchert, Ḥanābila 362, fn. 52.

(d. 256/869),[156] Ḥarb/al-Iṣṭakhrī[157] (Ḥarb was a student of Aḥmad b. Ḥanbal),[158] Ibn Hāniʾ al-Naysābūrī (d. 275/888),[159] and ʿAbdallāh b. Aḥmad (d. 290/902).[160] More significantly, however, there is also Ibn Qutayba's (d. 276/889) book, *Taʾwīl mukhtalif al-ḥadīth*, which, as Michael Cook puts it, was "a product of a debate culture [in] a period of acute polarisation between the elitist religion of the theologians and the populist religion of the traditionists."[161] In it, Ibn Qutayba mentions some of the important scholars of the Muʿtazila by name and refutes their views by recourse to the Quran and the Hadith.

(5) Melchert raises another argument against the attribution of *K. Sharḥ al-sunna* to Ghulām Khalīl in his considerations of the formula *al-amr bi-l-maʿrūf wa-l-nahy ʿan al-munkar* (commanding right and forbidding wrong—the Quranic command to the Muslim community to encourage righteous and discourage immoral behavior).[162] Melchert writes:

> The text names as a duty ordering the good and prohibiting evil. This was al-Barbahārī's way, as we shall see, but in contravention of the previous Ḥanbalī tradition as represented by Abū Bakr al-Ḫallāl and Aḥmad himself. It was also not the way of Ġulām Ḫalīl, who did not take it upon himself to correct abuses but rather persuaded the ruler to lend him the power of the state.[163]

Contrary to what Melchert claims, the opposite must be concluded from the text of *K. Sharḥ al-sunna*. Whereas al-Barbahārī, as the sources portray him, was a major advocate and devotee of fanatic and indeed brutal activism, the text itself suggests something entirely different. In fact, it proclaims quietism and obedience to the ruler, as the following quotations from the book illustrate:

---

156 Al-Bukhārī, Khalq afʿāl al-ʿibād 11.

157 Ibn Abī Yaʿlā, *Ṭabaqāt* i, 32. Nothing is known about al-Iṣṭakhrī; his *ʿaqīda* is quoted by Ibn Abī Yaʿlā with an *isnād* that passes through al-Barmakī (one of the transmitters of Ghulām Khalīl's *K. Sharḥ al-sunna*). The creed attributed to al-Iṣṭakhrī is a verbatim copy of the creed written by Ḥarb b. Ismāʿīl al-Kirmānī (d. 280/893). It is also mentioned by Ibn Taymiyya, who likewise attributes it to al-Iṣṭakhrī, *al-Ṣārim* 573; al-Dhahabī, *Siyar* xi, 302–303, cites excerpts from it with an *isnād* that differs from that given by Ibn Abī Yaʿlā; al-Dhahabī, *Siyar* xi, 286, criticizes its *isnād*.

158 Ḥarb al-Kirmānī, *K. al-Sunna* 64.

159 Ibn Hāniʾ al-Naysābūrī, *Masāʾil* ii, 163.

160 ʿAbdallāh b. Aḥmad, *K. al-Sunna* 103, 58; and see Melchert, Adversaries 240, fn. 41.

161 Cook, Ibn Qutayba 44–45.

162 Cf., in this regard, Laoust's argument above.

163 Melchert, Ḥanābila 362.

> Whoever rebels against a Muslim ruler is a dissident (*khārijī*) who has renounced allegiance with the Muslim community and opposed the prophetic tradition.
>
> no. 18
>
> To fight authority (*al-sulṭān*), or to revolt against it is forbidden, even if it is despotic.
>
> no. 19
>
> It is your religious duty to command right and forbid wrong, unless someone's sword or rod is to be feared.
>
> no. 106
>
> Commanding right and forbidding wrong ought to be effected first by action [lit., by the hand], [then] verbally [lit., by the tongue], and [if this is not possible, then] by inner abhorrence [lit., by the heart]; it is not to be effected by violent means [lit., by the sword].
>
> no. 109
>
> If nothing suspicious is apparent, then your fellow Muslim's privacy is not to be breached.
>
> no. 110[164]

Statements of this kind by no means represent the spirit of an outright militant, "muscular Ḥanbalī."[165] Rather, they correspond to Ghulām Khalīl's characteristics as an eloquent and successful preacher; controversial, but with good connections to those in power at the time, as the sources portray.

(6) Another of Melchert's confutations concerning Ghulām Khalīl's authorship of the *K. Sharḥ al-sunna* is his statement that "al-Barbahārī warns against those who assert that one sees God in this world, then warns against thinking about God (*al-fikra fī Allāh*)."[166] On the one hand, there is indeed an evident connection between "he who 'claims to see his Lord in this worldly abode'" (30) and some Basran renunciants, as Melchert emphasizes. On the other hand, however, and in order to clarify this issue, one must recall that a number of these "renunciants," mentioned by al-Ashʿarī (d. 324/935) and the theologian

164 See in the translation also nos. 15, 19, 115.

165 Cook, *Commanding right* 116.

166 Melchert, Ḥanābila 265.

and mystic Abū Naṣr al-Sarrāj al-Ṭūsī (d. 378/988),[167] lived during the second/eighth century, and not only in the third/tenth century. This may call to mind names such as Kahmas b. al-Ḥasan (d. 149/767),[168] as well as a group of former students of ʿAbd al-Wāḥid b. Zayd (d. 177/793?).[169] Such discomfited visions seem to have been frequent among some Basran Sufis of the third/ninth century as well. Al-Sarrāj refers, for example, to al-Ṣubayḥī from Basra,[170] a contemporary of Sahl al-Tustarī (d. 283/896), and to one of the disciples of Sahl al-Tustarī, who had visions of Satan seated on God's throne.[171] One must recall, in this regard, Ghulām Khalīl's persecution of the Sufis, whom he had accused of deviating from "the right path." This is to note also that reproving such beliefs squarely belonged to his worldview.

The question readily suggests itself as to whether item (31), "Contemplating God—blessed and exalted be He—is an innovation according to the saying of the Prophet—may peace and blessings be upon him—"reflect upon creation, but do not reflect upon God." For, contemplating God kindles doubt in one's heart," refers exclusively to the Sufis.

Much evidence suggests that the reproach against him who 'claims to see his Lord in this worldly abode' also targeted extreme Sunni anthropomorphists[172] and some speculative theologians, as the traditions circulating during the second/eighth and third/ninth centuries indicate.[173]

In conclusion it must be noted that, while discussing our 2003 article on Ghulām Khalīl[174] in his entry on al-Barbahārī in the *Encyclopaedia of Islam* THREE, Melchert revises some of his earlier findings. He contends, "No anachronism patently rules out attribution to Ghulām Khalīl," and he offers examples from the text to that effect. Again, Melchert advances the argument of the "fierce opposition to speculative theology, [which] is also consistent with stories of al-Barbahārī's hostility to Abū l-Ḥasan al-Ashʿarī (d. 324/935–936) and Muʿtazilī hostility to him, whereas Ghulām Khalīl is not known independently for hostility to *kalām*."[175]

167 See also al-Qushayrī's comment, *al-Risāla* ii, 524.
168 Al-Ashʿarī, *Maqālāt* 214; Abū Nuʿaym, *Ḥilya* vi, 211; *ThG* ii, 100.
169 Van Ess argues for an earlier date. *ThG* ii, 96–100. See also Massignon, *Essai* 191–197; Pellat, *Milieu Basrien* 99–105.
170 Al-Sulamī, *Ṭabaqāt* 329–331; al-Sīrjānī, *al-Bayāḍ wa-l-sawād* 219.
171 Al-Sarrāj, *al-Lumaʿ* 544–545; Böwering, *Mystical vision* 80–81.
172 Al-Shahristānī, *al-Milal* 45.
173 Cf. the comments on nos. 29–31 in the Arabic text.
174 Jarrar and Günther, Ġulām Ḫalīl 11–36.
175 Melchert, al-Barbahārī.

We have already established several arguments against the authenticity of the report about al-Barbahārī's quarrels with al-Ashʿarī, but the contention that "Ghulām Khalīl is not known independently for hostility to *kalām*" has no firm ground, since his *K. Sharḥ al-sunna* is replete with warnings against involvement in theological disputations, polemics, and cavil.

2.3 *External Textual Evidence*

In the pursuit of a more reliable account of the attribution of the *K. Sharḥ al-sunna* to Ghulām Khalīl, it is important to survey all relevant internal and external textual evidence. While the internal evidence will be discussed in detail in chapter 3, which examines the book's various themes, we shall take a closer look in the following section at two particularly conspicuous instances of external textual evidence.

2.3.1 Al-Imām Qawwām al-Sunna

One piece of data relates to the Shafiʿi scholar Qawwām al-Sunna (d. 535/1140) from Isfahan, a strict adherent to the Sunna.[176] Toward the end of his book *al-Ḥujja*, Qawwām al-Sunna lists the authors of the Sunni creeds quoted in his work. He names 27 persons who had "made public their tenets and beliefs and had expressed what their minds embrace concerning the significance of the Sunan." Among the names recorded, he specifies "Aḥmad b. Muḥammad b. Ghālib, known as Ghulām Khalīl, the disciple (*ṣāḥib*) of Aḥmad b. Ḥanbal," but no mention is made of al-Barbahārī, either in this list or elsewhere in the book.[177]

The last chapters of *al-Ḥujja* include sections in which Qawwām al-Sunna summarizes tenets and articles of faith from Sunni creeds. He does so without identifying his sources—except in the final part,[178] where, importantly, we do find verbatim quotations from the text of the *K. Sharḥ al-sunna*.

It may seem almost impossible to trace the actual source of a specific tenet, as the Muslim authors tend to copy from each other in the spirit of strict observance in matters pertaining to the respective creeds. Nonetheless, a few citations indicate that these are faithful excerpts from the *K. Sharḥ al-sunna*, particularly when the diction and the sequence of the respective tenets are compared, as the following examples demonstrate:

---

176 Al-Samʿānī, *al-Ansāb* iii, 368–369 (al-Samʿānī was his student); al-Dhahabī, *Siyar* xx, 80–86; the editor's introduction, *al-Ḥujja* i, 31–58.

177 Qawwām al-Sunna, *al-Ḥujja* ii, 475.

178 "Excerpts from *kutub al-sunna*," Qawwām al-Sunna, *al-Ḥujja* ii, 492–532.

Sharḥ al-sunna	*al-Ḥujja*
11, 10	2:432, 1–3
واعلم، رحمك الله، أنّ الكلام في الربِّ مُحدث وهو بدعة وضلالة، ولا يُتكلّمُ في الربّ إلّا بما وصف به نفسه في القرآن، وما بيّن رسولُ الله، صلّى الله عليه وسلّم، لأصحابه. وهو، جلّ ثناؤه، واحدٌ ﴿ليس كَمِثْلِهِ شيءٌ وهُوَ السَّميعُ البَصير﴾ (الشورى 11/42)، ربُّنا أوّلٌ بلا متى، وآخِرٌ بلا مُنتهى، ﴿يَعلَمُ السِرّ وأَخْفَى﴾ (طه 7/20)، وعلى عرشه استوى، وعلمُه بكلِّ مكان لا يخلو من علمه مكان، ولا يقول في صفات الربّ كيف ولِـمَ إلّا شاكٌّ في الله.	وقالوا: الكلام في الربّ، عزّ وجلّ، بدعة لأنّه لا يجوز أن يُتكلّم في الربّ، عزّ وجلّ، إلّا بما وصف به نفسه في القرآن، وما بيّنه رسول الله، صلّى الله عليه وسلّم. وهو، جلّ ثناؤه، الأول بلا ابتداء والآخر بلا انتهاء، يعلم السرّ وأخفى، وعلى عرشه استوى، وعلمُه بكلِّ مكان ...
29	2:435, 10–14
وكلّ ما سمعت من الآثار ممّا لم يبلغه عقلُك، نحو قول رسول الله، صلّى الله عليه وسلّم ...	وكلّ ما سمعه المرء من الآثار ممّا لم يبلغه عقلُه، نحو ...
36	2:436, 7–10
وكلُّ شيءٍ ممّا أوجب الله عليه الفناء يَفنى، إلّا الجنّة والنّار والعرش والكرسي واللوح والقلم والصُّور، ليس يفنى شيء من هذا أبدًا.	وكلّ شيء كتب عليه الفناء، وليس تفنى الجنة والنار والعرش والكرسي واللوح والقلم والصّور، ليس يفنى شيء من هذه الأشياء.
13f	2:437, 7–8
والإيمان بالصِّراط على جهنّم، يأخذ الصّراطُ من شاء الله، ويجوز من شاء الله، ويسقط في جهنّم من شاء الله، ولهم أنوارٌ على قدر إيمانهم.	والصراط حقّ يجوز عليه من شاء الله، ويسقط في جهنّم من شاء الله، ولهم أنوار على قدر أعمالهم.

(*cont.*)

al-Ḥujja	*Sharḥ al-sunna*
2:437, 9–12	9
والسنّة إنّما هي التصديق لآثار رسول الله، صلّى الله عليه وسلّم، وترك معارضتها بكيف ولِمَ.	واعلم، رحمك الله، أنّه ليس في السنّة قياسٌ، ولا تُضرب لها الأمثال، ولا تُتّبع فيها الأهواء. وهو التّصديق بآثار رسول الله، صلّى الله عليه وسلّم، بلا كيف ولا شرح؛ لا يُقال لما وكيف.
2:440, 5–11	4
لأنّ الدين إنّما جاء من قِبَل الله تعالى، لمْ يوضع على عقول الرجال وآرائهم، قد بيّن رسول الله، صلّى الله عليه وسلّم، السنّة لأمّته وأوضحها لأصحابه، فمن خالف أصحابَ رسول الله، صلّى الله عليه وسلّم، في شيء من الدين فقد ضلّ.	واعلم، رحمك الله، أنّ الذي جاء من قِبلِ الله، تبارك وتعالى، لم يوضع على عقول الرّجال وآرائهم، وعلمُهُ عند الله وعند رسوله، فلا تتّبع شيئًا بهواك فتمرقَ من الدين فتخرجَ من الإسلام، فإنّه لا حجّةَ لك، فقد بيّن رسولُ الله، صلّى الله عليه وسلّم، لأُمّته السنّة وأوضحها لأصحابه، وهم الجماعة وهم السّواد الأعظم، والسّواد الأعظم الحقّ وأهله، فمن خالف أصحابَ رسول الله، صلّى الله عليه وسلّم، في شيء من أمر الله فقد كفر.

2.3.2 Later Hanbalis

One would expect that the Hanbalis relied heavily on this book (attributed to al-Barbahārī). Yet this was not the case, except for the late Hanbali authors of *Ṭabaqāt* works, who reworked the materials offered by Ibn Abī Yaʿlā.[179] The following observations must be pointed out in this regard. First, the apparently earliest quotation from the *Sharḥ Kitāb al-sunna* (attributed here to al-Barbahārī) after Ibn Abī Yaʿlā was made by Ibn Ḥamdān al-Ḥarrānī al-Ḥanbalī

179 Ibn Mufliḥ (d. 884/1479), *al-Maqsad* i, 228–230; al-ʿUlaymī (d. 928/1521), *al-Manhaj* ii, 226–236; Ibn al-ʿImād (d. 1089/1678), *Shadharāt* iv, 159–162.

(d. 695/1296)[180] in his theological creed *Nihāyat al-mubtadiʾīn*.[181] Ibn Ḥamdān loosely quotes a part of the text (see no. 38) concerning retaliation on the Day of Resurrection among all Creation. He expressly says in this regard, "This was mentioned by al-Barbahārī."

Ibn Ḥamdān also offers a textual addition here that is found neither in the manuscript of *K. Sharḥ al-sunna* nor in Ibn Abī Yaʿlā's *Ṭabaqāt*. This addition concerns the notion that retaliation "even from a stone which had afflicted distress to a man, is but right." Ibn Ḥamdān does not name his source for this addition, and it can only be speculated at this point that this quotation, if it were actually extracted from a respective book attributed to al-Barbahārī, might have been quoted from a version of the *Ṭabaqāt* that has not survived.

Second, Ibn Taymiyya quotes the respective text directly from Abū Yaʿlā. Ibn Taymiyya does not give a title for the book that he used as his source. He simply writes, "And it was related from al-Barbahārī."[182]

Third, Ibn Taymiyya's student, the Syrian Shafiʿi scholar al-Dhahabī, cites a passage (see no. 4 in our edition) and expressly notes that it is from the *K. Sharḥ al-sunna*, although without indicating the name of the author.[183] The same quotation appears again in his entries on al-Barbahārī in two of his other books.[184]

Fourth, Ibn Rajab al-Ḥanbalī (d. 795/1392) and Ibn Ḥajar al-ʿAsqalānī (d. 852/1448) refer to al-Barbahārī in their respective commentaries on al-Bukhārī's compendium of prophetic traditions, both entitled *Fatḥ al-bārī*. They do so without mentioning the book. Whereas Ibn Rajab offers a direct quotation (see no. 63 in our edition),[185] Ibn Ḥajar provides merely a non-verbatim indication (no. 103).[186]

This extratextual evidence concerning the reception of the *K. Sharḥ al-sunna*, or of parts of it, by later scholars makes it clear: There are some 150 years between the initial attribution of the book to al-Barbahārī (by Ibn Abī Yaʿlā, in his *Ṭabaqāt al-Ḥanābila*) and the first quotation attributed to him (by the seventh/thirteenth-century Ibn Ḥamdān in his creed, *Nihāyat al-mubtadiʾīn*). In other words, these observations add weight, from a different perspective, to the argument that Ghulām Khalīl is indeed the author of this book.

180 Van Ess, Bibliographische Notizen 127–130.
181 Ibn Ḥamdān al-Ḥarrānī al-Ḥanbalī, *Nihāyat al-mubtadiʾīn* 57.
182 Ibn Taymiyya, *Bughya* 258.
183 Al-Dhahabī, *Tārīkh* vii, 572 (with variations in the reading that differ from both the manuscript and the *Ṭabaqāt*).
184 Al-Dhahabī, *al-ʿUluww* 222–223; al-Dhahabī, *Siyar* xv, 91.
185 Ibn Rajab, *Fatḥ al-bārī* v, 135 (Mawāqīt al-ṣalāt).
186 Ibn Ḥajar, *Fatḥ al-bārī* xi, 276–277 (al-Raqāʾiq 81).

2.4 *Internal Textual Evidence*

2.4.1 Apocalyptic Notions

One of the principles advocated in the *K. Sharḥ al-sunna* supports the general Muslim belief about the second coming of Jesus. It does so, however, in a peculiar way, as the following quotation shows:

> [Belief in] the Antichrist, and the descent of Jesus, son of Mary, who will come down and kill the Antichrist. He will marry and perform the ritual prayer behind the forthcoming Messianic Leader (*al-Qāʾim*) from amongst Muḥammad's Household. He will die and be buried by Muslims.
> § 13j

The first part of this testimonial (save the unusual statement that Jesus will marry) is rather common and well attested in several works of Sunni traditions and creeds.[187] The second part, however, in particular the use of the phrase *al-Qāʾim min Āl Muḥammad*, is unusual for a Sunni—or, for that matter, Hanbali—creed.[188] Curiously enough, the recent editions of the text attributed to al-Barbahārī that we have been able to consult thus far, as well as the English and the Swedish translations, pass in silence over this special phrase and its significance.

The title *al-Qāʾim* (the Riser, Resurrector or Redresser)[189] carries considerable apocalyptic significance. It was in common use among the various early Hashimi and Shiʿi factions during the early second/eighth century, and it formed part of the ʿAbbasid propaganda during the years of the underground mission of the *daʿwa*.[190] In fact, it has been in continual use by the Ismaʿilis and the Twelver Shiʿis up to the present. It is noteworthy, moreover, that in article no. 73 of the creed, the *K. Sharḥ al-sunna* offers the ultimate recognition of "excellence and virtue (*faḍl*)" to the bloodline of Hāshim. It is from the ranks of this clan that *al-Qāʾim al-Mahdī* will rise, an idea crucial to ʿAbbasid ideology and identity.[191] It seems indeed quite feasible, therefore, that a preacher

187 See the comments on § 13b in the Arabic text of the creed.

188 For the use of the terms "al-Qāʾim" and "al-Mahdī" by Sunnis and Shiʿis in relation to the second coming of Jesus as a sign of the eschatological events, Reynolds, Jesus.

189 Hussain, *Occultation* 12–19; Modarressi, *Crisis* 56, 60, 62, 86–89; Arjomand, Crisis 493–495; Arjomand, Consolation 560; Madelung, al-Ḳāʾim.

190 *Akhbār al-dawla* 51, 52, 199, 200, 238, 288, 317 (for the author of this book, see Daniel, Anonymous 419–439); al-Dūrī, al-Fikra al-mahdiyya 124, 127, 128; Madelung, New documents 343, in a letter attributed to al-Maʾmūn.

191 *Akhbār al-dawla* 51–52, 238.

supporting the ʿAbbasid authorities and ideology, like Ghulām Khalīl, would emphasize such a claim in a creed, especially in the troubled times he lived in.[192]

2.4.2 The Prophet's Intercession

Ibn Abī Yaʿlā reports, "Al-Barbahārī never convened a session without mentioning that God Almighty will seat Muhammad—may peace and blessings be upon him—[next to Himself] on the Throne."[193] The reference is to Q 17:79, "Perhaps your Lord will resurrect you in a commendable station (*al-maqām al-maḥmūd*)." This specific interpretation, favored by al-Barbahārī, is based on a prophetic tradition cited by the Quran commentator Mujāhid b. Jabr (d. 104/722).[194] In contrast, the majority of traditionists interpreted it as referring to Muhammad's intercession (*shafāʿa*) on the Day of Judgment in favor of believers culpable of grave faults.[195] Although Aḥmad b. Ḥanbal does not relate Mujāhid's tradition in his *Musnad*, his son ʿAbdallāh contends that his father accepted its veracity.[196] Abū Bakr al-Marrūdhī (d. 275/888), Aḥmad's student, as well as other Hanbali scholars, were very rigid in their views and treatment of those who refused this *ḥadīth*, accusing them of belonging to the Jahmis and calling them unbelievers.[197] The interpretation of this Quranic verse was a matter of dispute in the second/eighth and third/ninth centuries, and in 317/929 the issue developed into an open fight in Baghdad between the Hanbalis and their adversaries.[198]

If one were to accept the attribution of the book to al-Barbahārī, who adopted excessively anthropomorphist positions,[199] one would expect to find textual evidence in this creed, proclaiming the tenet that Muhammad would sit on the Throne on the Day of Judgment. But no mention of this at all is to be

192 See the epilogue of this study.

193 Ibn Abī Yaʿlā, *Ṭabaqāt* ii, 44 (al-Fiqī) iii, 76 (al-ʿUthaymīn); Melchert, al-Barbahārī.

194 Al-Ṭabarī, *Tafsīr* xv, 47, 51–54; al-Dhahabī, *al-ʿArsh* ii, 153; *ThG* iv, 403–404; and with an attribution to traditionists other than Mujāhid, Abū Yaʿlā, *Ibṭāl al-taʾwīlāt* i, 476–478; al-Jīlānī, *al-Ghunya* i, 150–151; al-Suyūṭī, *al-Durr* ix, 423, 427.

195 Al-Ṭabarī, *Tafsīr* xv, 44–50; Laoust, al-Barbahārī i, 1039.

196 Al-Khallāl, *al-Sunna* i, 210–212, 243–244; Abū Yaʿlā, *Ibṭāl al-taʾwīlāt* i, 478; al-Dhahabī, *al-ʿArsh* ii, 214–220, 316–317; and see *ThG* ii, 642.

197 Al-Khallāl, *al-Sunna* i, 231–248 (from a letter by al-Khallāl which he had read publically in Tarsus); it is an item in Ibn Baṭṭa's creed, *al-Sharḥ wa-l-ibāna* 61; see also Ibn Abī Yaʿlā, *al-Iʿtiqād* 37–40.

198 Ibn al-Athīr, *al-Kāmil* vii, 57; Ibn Kathīr, *al-Bidāya* xii, 85–86; Rosenthal, *History* i, 72; *ThG* ii, 642.

199 Most probably because of his links to the Basran Salimis.

found in the book. This is particularly striking in the article that expressly deals with Muhammad's intercession (see no. 13e in the translation).

2.4.3 Ibn Kāmil's Addition

Chapter 1 has already referred to an addition that Aḥmad b. Kāmil, the first transmitter of *K. Sharḥ al-sunna* from Ghulām Khalīl, makes in the text, by stating explicitly his name (*qāla Aḥmad b. Kāmil*), and then giving his chain of transmission.[200] The question arises why Ibn Kāmil, who was a student of al-Ṭabarī and who was present at his deathbed,[201] would then want to transmit a book authored by al-Barbahārī (if he were the author of this text, as certain later Hanbali scholars claim), although al-Barbahārī's enmity toward al-Ṭabarī is well attested in the sources,[202] specifically in the matter of the commendable station (*al-maqām al-maḥmūd*) that we discussed earlier. The answer to this question is part of the conclusion to this chapter.

3 Conclusion

Abū Yaʿlā was the first to attribute this book to the Hanbali agitator and demagogue al-Ḥasan b. ʿAlī al-Barbahārī. He did so, however, without revealing his source for this attribution. Likewise, his son Ibn Abī Yaʿlā attributed the work to al-Barbahārī when he incorporated the text in his *Ṭabaqāt al-Ḥanābila*. Contrary to his usual method of citing his sources, Ibn Abī Yaʿlā refrains in this particular case from specifying a source. Nor does he provide a chain of transmission indicating that al-Barbahārī is, as Ibn Abī Yaʿlā claims, the author of the quoted text. Rather, he quotes the text verbatim after having mentioned a report by al-Ḥasan b. ʿAlī al-Ahwāzī (d. 446/1055) about a direct confrontation between al-Barbahārī and Abū l-Ḥasan al-Ashʿarī. This confrontation between the two scholars, it is claimed, caused the latter to write his book *al-Ibāna*. Given this evidence, it seems at least feasible to conclude that a work by al-Ḥasan al-Ahwāzī was probably Ibn Abī Yaʿlā's actual source for the quoted text of *K. Sharḥ al-sunna*, since al-Ḥasan al-Ahwāzī was, as shown in the analysis above, apparently the first scholar who deliberately attributed this work to al-Barbahārī.

Only 159 years after the initial attribution of the book to al-Barbahārī, we encounter the first quotation of the text attributed to al-Barbahārī by Ibn Ḥam-

200 See §115.
201 Ibn ʿAsākir, *Taʾrīkh* lii, 203.
202 See Rosenthal, *History* 72; Melchert, al-Barbahārī.

dān al-Ḥarrānī al-Ḥanbalī (d. 695/1296), followed by Ibn Taymiyya (d. 728/1328), and other late Muslim authors.

In modern scholarship, Massignon in 1929 was the first to make use of the Ẓāhiriyya manuscript, which twice expressly names Ghulām Khalīl as the author of the text it contains. Massignon refers in a footnote to "a verbatim copy" with the title "*Sharḥ kitāb al sonnah*" by al-Barbahārī, which is to be found in Ibn Abī Yaʿlā's *Ṭabaqāt al-Ḥanābila*.

Henri Laoust uncritically adopted in 1957 the attribution of the text to al-Barbahārī. He also accepted, without any serious deliberation, the anecdote reported by al-Ḥasan al-Ahwāzī about a meeting between al-Barbahārī and Abū l-Ḥasan al-Ashʿarī. Laoust's student, Michel Allard, as well as Richard Frank and other modern scholars, uncritically accepted Laoust's view of al-Ḥasan al-Ahwāzī's account as a historically trustworthy piece of information.

Our refutation of the ascription of the *K. Sharḥ al-sunna* to al-Barbahārī and the reasoning in favor of Ghulām Khalīl as its author are based on three major arguments. First, the book's chain of transmission (*riwāyat al-kitāb*), which is an integral part of the text and which was written in the same hand as the main text of the *K. Sharḥ al-sunna*, presents a list of five generations of scholars—several of them renowned Hanbalis—who, over a period of three centuries, identify Ghulām Khalīl as the author of the text.

Second, external textual evidence, based above all on the quotations by Qawwām al-Sunna (d. 535/1140) from Isfahan, explicitly mentions Ghulām Khalīl as the author of a Sunni creed. Moreover, al-Dhahabī's phrase commending Ghulām Khalīl for the soundness of his belief (*ṣiḥḥat al-muʿtaqad*) points, most probably, to the *Iʿtiqād* ("Creed") that he had authored.

Third, internal textual evidence pertaining to explicit pieces of information in the text of *K. Sharḥ al-sunna* itself shows clear divergence from al-Barbahārī's views in three significant points:

(1) Reference to the eschatological figure "*al-Qāʾim min Āl Muḥammad*," a notion entirely strange to the Hanbali Sunni milieu. It is, conversely, part of the ideological idiom of the ʿAbbasids, whom Ghulām Khalīl had served as preacher and propagandist.

(2) The repeated insistence on the duty of good council (*naṣīḥa*) and that "commanding right and forbidding wrong" is the duty of the authorities alone. This view expresses the opposite of what the day-to-day militant activities of al-Barbahārī exhibit, with his operations "with the sword" instead of good council.

(3) The absence of any textual evidence for the tenet so significant to al-Barbahārī, claiming that Muhammad will sit on the Throne on the Day of Judgment. Moreover, antithetical to the rudimentary anthropomorphism

of al-Barbahārī (and the *sālimī*s in general, for that matter), the textual information in the *K. Sharḥ al-sunna* about God's attributes speaks of a rather moderate anthropomorphic position, and is in line with the doctrine prevalent among the traditionists of the third/ninth century.

CHAPTER 3

The Third/Ninth Century: The Veneration of Aḥmad b. Ḥanbal and the Proliferation of Creeds

1 Proto-Sunnis at the Turn of the Century

After the death of the caliph Hārūn al-Rashīd in 193/809, the rivalry between his two sons, the heir apparent al-Amīn (r. 193–198/809–813), and the second in succession al-Maʾmūn (r. 198–218/813–833), speedily ignited, and phantoms and plots were seen lurking around every corner between Iraq and Khorasan. It was not long before civil war broke out in the ʿAbbasid house between the two brothers, a civil war that lasted for three years (195–198/811–813) and which ended with the murder of the caliph al-Amīn. As Tayeb El-Hibri posits, "The murder of al-Amīn was a drastic offense to various collective social and cultural attitudes. It stands on its own as the first of its kind in the restored ideal political order of the caliphate."[1]

Al-Maʾmūn's policies during his reign presented a major rupture in the prevailing ideology and strategies of the ʿAbbasids. He espoused sympathy for the ʿAlid cause, and some time between 2 and 5 Ramaḍān 201 / 23 and 27 March 817, he appointed the eighth ʿAlid imam, ʿAlī al-Riḍā (d. Ṣafar 203 / September 818), as heir to the caliphate.[2] Shortly thereafter, he also ordered that the official color of the ʿAbbasids be changed from black to green.[3] The *Abnāʾ* of Baghdad,[4] the descendants of the Perso-Arab generation, were dismayed by al-Maʾmūn's policies,[5] and "came to define themselves in opposition to the others, who happened to be the rabble of Baghdad and the followers of al-Maʾmūn and his new *daʿwa*."[6] El-Hibri propounds in this regard that "Baghdad had been a city of the *Abnāʾ* and maintained residues of political hostility to the successors of al-Amīn."[7]

---

1 El-Hibri, *Reinterpreting Islamic historiography* 35.
2 Yücesoy, *Messianic beliefs* 70, 90–96.
3 Cooperson, *Classical Arabic biography* 73–75; Yücesoy, *Messianic beliefs* 79.
4 Kennedy, *Armies* 80, 92 (fn. 164), 96.
5 Cooperson, *Classical Arabic biography* 25–31.
6 Cf. Turner, Abnāʾ al-dawla 2, 16. Yücesoy, *Messianic beliefs* 133, stresses the idea of *tajdīd* (religious renewal).
7 El-Hibri, *Reinterpreting Islamic historiography* 9. Turner, Abnāʾ al-dawla 22, contends, however, that "their interests and ties of loyalties were too diffuse to maintain it once the compelling reasons to identify as such were removed."

 | DOI:10.1163/9789004429055_005

The sense of turbulence caused by al-Ma'mūn's controversial religious policies was palpable, and his policies antagonized many groups and factions in society, including the proto-Sunni *ʿulamāʾ*. Al-Ma'mūn's *irjāʾ* and Jahmi inclinations,[8] his proclivity for the Muʿtazila, his hostile attitude toward proto-Sunnis and, above all, his initiating the *miḥna* ("inquisition") against the proto-Sunni *ʿulamāʾ* (in Rabīʿ I 218 / April 833)[9] by proclaiming the doctrine of the "created Quran" in the *miḥna* letters caused sweeping division, especially in Baghdad, where he resided as of Ṣafar 204 / August 819.

The *miḥna* represented a clear and unswerving confrontation between the caliph and the proto-Sunni *ʿulamāʾ*. Inextricably linked with the *miḥna*, however, was al-Ma'mūn's claim to interpretive authority as the rightly guiding leader (*imām al-hudā*). The exact meaning and implications of this pronouncement are still a point of discussion in modern scholarship.[10]

It seems, however, that there was more at stake in the variety of military and political hues forwarded by al-Ma'mūn. Observed from a distance, the civil war and the subsequent, mostly unprecedented, policies implemented by al-Ma'mūn presented a drastic crisis in the ʿAbbasid caliphate and a kairotic juncture,[11] entailing a dynamic moment of political action and of rupture with the potential for radical change and the anticipation of a "messianic event."[12]

The *miḥna* lasted for 15 years, during which time Aḥmad b. Ḥanbal, descendant of the Baghdad faction of the *Abnāʾ* and the chief representative of *ahl al-ḥadīth*, was frequently interrogated. Eventually, he was imprisoned for 28 months during the reign of al-Muʿtaṣim (r. 218–227/833–842) and flogged in the presence of the caliph.[13] Ironic consequences of the *miḥna* were the ineluctable triumphal spirit that took hold among the proto-Sunnis and the veneration of Ibn Ḥanbal by the *ʿulamāʾ* and the masses alike. As Cooperson has observed,

8 *ThG* iii, 157; Cooperson, *Classical Arabic biography* 33. *Irjāʾ* refers here to identifying faith with the confession of belief to the exclusion of acts, as well as to the legitimacy of the caliph regardless of his acts or disrepute.

9 Hinds, Miḥna; Melchert, *Ahmad ibn Hanbal* 8–16.

10 How this might actually be interpreted is still a matter of debate. See Zahniser, Insights 14–16; Nagel, *Staat* i, 193–194, 248–253, 307–310; and Crone and Hinds, *God's caliph* 94. Zaman refutes Crone and Hinds's arguments that Ma'mūn was assuming for himself the prerogatives of the Shiʿi imam; cf. his *Religion and politics* 109–112. See also Cooperson, *Classical Arabic biography* 27–67; Cooperson, *al-Ma'mun* 45–47; and Hurvitz, Miḥna 102–109. Yücesoy, *Messianic beliefs* 86–87, 133, stresses the messianic nuance, while Turner, *Inquisition* 15, sees no proof that "he was Shiʿite."

11 Relying on the usage of the term as proposed by Walter Benjamin, cf. Lindroos, *Now-time* 12, 31, and 43–45.

12 Madelung, New documents 343–345. See also Yücesoy, *Messianic beliefs* 59–80.

13 Cooperson, *Classical Arabic biography* 110–128; Turner, *Inquisition* 93–105.

"For many of his contemporaries, it was Ibn Ḥanbal who came closest to fulfilling the mission God had entrusted to the *ahl al-ḥadīth*."[14] In 234/848–849, al-Mutawakkil (r. 232–247/847–861) suspended the *miḥna* and offered his support to the proto-Sunnis.[15] Al-Masʿūdī reports that al-Mutawakkil ordered that all theological speculations and polemics be ended. The caliph also ordered that people assent and follow in religious matters in blind adherence and strict conformance (*bi-l-taslīm wa-l-taqlīd*), and that the traditionists spread their knowledge (*bi-l-taḥdīth*) and proclaim the *sunna wa-l-jamāʿa*.[16]

The formula *al-sunna wa-l-jamāʿa* in this context refers to a "political preference." Closely connected with this usage is *ahl al-sunna wa-l-jamāʿa*, a term that was already in use as a self-designation by a faction of the proto-Sunnis sometime during the last quarter of the second/eighth century.[17] Morover, as Juynboll contends, the appellative *ṣāḥib sunna wa-jamāʿa* may also be interpreted as "highlighting the bearer of a political preference."[18] Van Ess notes furthermore that the formula *ahl al-sunna wa-l-jamāʿa* had been circulating in eastern Iran,[19] and suggests that Sufyān al-Thawrī (d. 161/778) had used it.[20] Illustrative in this regard is the fact that al-Maʾmūn, in his first letter announcing the *miḥna*, speaks of those who had claimed "adherence to the *sunna* … and proclaimed that they make an outward show of being the people of divine truth, the [real] religion and the community of Muslims (*dīn* and *jamāʿa*)."[21] Although the usage of the expression in this letter is somewhat vague, it nevertheless refers to a group that constructed its identity by reference to a combination of these concepts—a development that eventually attracted a solid body of adherents during the *miḥna* and its aftermath.[22] And it is around this time that Aḥmad b.

14 Cooperson, *Classical Arabic biography* 109.

15 Cf. Ibn al-Jawzī, *al-Muntaẓam* xi, 206–208; al-Dhahabī, *Tārīkh* v, 746. Hinds, Miḥna vii, 4b, writes, "Certainly, it appears to have been Jumāda I–II 234/Jan.–Feb. 849 that al-Mutawakkil prohibited argument about the Qurʾān and sent instructions to this effect throughout his domains." See also Melchert, Religious policies 321–322.

16 Al-Masʿūdī, *Murūj* v, 5.

17 Stewart, Developments 144.

18 Juynboll, Excursus 320; and see Lucas, *Constructive critics* 323–324.

19 Van Ess, *Der Eine* ii, 1275.

20 Ibid., 1273, 1278.

21 Al-Ṭabarī, *Tārīkh* viii, 632 (Eng. trans. xxxii, 202); Nagel, *Rechtleitung* 259; Cooperson, *Classical Arabic biography* 33.

22 Nawas, Appellation 22, argues that "the first and most important tenet of Sunnism was established in opposition to the caliph's will and a momentous step was taken in the crystallization of Sunnism as we now know it—*ahl al-sunna wa-l-jamāʿa*." This view, however, seems questionable as Zaman posits that the *miḥna* actually affirmed the role of the caliphs in religious matters as commensurate with that of religious scholars.

Ḥanbal used the expression in the form *ahl al-sunna wa-l-jamāʿa wa-l-āthār*.[23] The term *al-sunna wa-l-jamāʿa* also appears in two creeds attributed to Ibn Ḥanbal—namely, the *Iʿtiqād* of Musaddad b. Musarhad and the *Iʿtiqād* of al-Andarābī, as well as the *Iʿtiqād* by Ḥarb al-Kirmānī/al-Iṣṭakhrī.[24]

Recent scholarship has emphasized that the process of formation of the proto-Sunni trends goes back to the second/eighth century[25] and, moreover, that the *aṣḥāb al-ḥadīth* were devoted to the dogmatic principles of the *ahl al-sunna*. It is also stressed that they defined their identity by maintaining the authority of *ḥadīth*. Furthermore, ʿAbbasid caliphs prior to al-Maʾmūn had aligned themselves with these trends and offered them caliphal patronage.[26] Put more concretely, the *miḥna* avowed the role of the caliphs in religious matters parallel to that of religious scholars, as Muhammad Zaman has pointed out.[27]

As is evident from numerous statements of belief, some common doctrinal principles prevailed among the proto-Sunnis during the last part of the second/eighth century and began to be consolidated during the third/ninth century, among which three propositions can be recognized: (1) a sympathetic attitude toward the Umayyads, (2) political quietism, and (3) a positive attitude toward the Companions of the Prophet.[28] Also remarkable in this regard is the piety-mindedness that characterized many of them.[29] Moreover, as Christopher Melchert has demonstrated, "A mystical element of traditionalist piety is its refusal to expel people from the community for wrong actions, sins."[30]

---

23 Watt, *Formative period* 268. For a survey on the formation of the concept and the worldview of the *ahl al-sunna wa-l-jamāʿa*, cf. Nagel, *Rechtleitung* 224–293.

24 For Musaddad b. Musarhad, see Ibn Abī Yaʿlā, *Ṭabaqāt* (al-Fiqī) i, 345, and (al-ʿUthaymīn) ii, 432. For Ḥarb al-Kirmānī/al-Iṣṭakhrī, see Ḥarb al-Kirmānī, *K. al-Sunna* 62; Ibn Abī Yaʿlā, *Ṭabaqāt* (al-Fiqī) i, 31, (al-ʿUthaymīn) i, 65. For al-Andarābī, see Ibn Abī Yaʿlā, Ṭabaqāt (al-Fiqī) i, 294, (al-ʿUthaymīn) ii, 293; Ibn al-Jawzī, *Manāqib* i, 286, 304; (al-Sarakhsī), Ibn Abī Yaʿlā, *Ṭabaqāt* (al-Fiqī) i, 329, and (al-ʿUthaymīn) ii, 392.

25 Zaman, *Religion and politics* 59, 208–213. Melchert, *Formation* 1, argues that "the traditionalists had separated out from *aṣḥāb al-raʾy* in the later eighth century." See Melchert, Piety 434.

26 Zaman, *Religion and politics* 11, 70, 103–105.

27 Ibid., 49–59, 82, 114.

28 Ibid., 49–51; Khalidi, *Arabic historical thought* 111; Cooperson, *Classical Arabic biography* 112–117; Lucas, *Constructive critics* 255–266.

29 Melchert, Piety 426–430; cf. also Salem, *Emergence* 14–22.

30 Melchert, Piety 431.

2 Tenets of Faith (*iʿtiqādāt*)

From early in Islamic history, schisms informed the gradual shaping and the ongoing process of forming identities within the Muslim community. Wensinck has noted that questions of faith—whether it is alone sufficient for salvation—and of the relation of works to faith were already debated at an early date. Later, in the second/eighth and third/ninth centuries, disputation over predestination and free will, the justice of God and His essence became common themes of religious discourse.[31] Also, doctrinal conformity was not yet regulated. Controversies spread far and wide, covering a broad spectrum of issues and doctrines. What is more, many a theological factor was influenced by politics during disputes taking place both in public sessions and at the court.

In various ways, these ideas grew out of the debates that early proto-Sunni *ʿulamāʾ* had initiated against those who were deemed heretics. By the late second/eighth and third/ninth centuries, certain names came to be singled out as representatives of the proto-Sunni movement, including Ayyūb al-Sakhtiyānī (d. 131/748), Yūnus b. ʿUbayd (d. 140/757), ʿAbdallāh b. ʿAwn (d. 151/768), al-Awzāʿī (d. 157/774), Sufyān al-Thawrī (d. 161/778), Ḥammād b. Salama (d. 167/783), Ḥammād b. Zayd (d. 179/795), Mālik b. Anas (d. 179/796), ʿAbdallāh b. al-Mubārak (d. 181/797), and Sufyān b. ʿUyayna (d. 198/814). Their views were seen as having been nourished by their own pious experience in the community and, as perceived by their later adherents, by the abiding interaction between scripture and the living tradition. Their sayings and practices came to form a model, alongside the arsenal of proof-texts of the *ḥadīth* and opinions of the early forebears, the *al-salaf al-ṣāliḥ*.[32]

All of the aforementioned individuals were hostile to the *aṣḥāb al-raʾy* (advocates of personal reasoning in matters pertaining to religious law; the proto-Sunnis usually refer with this label to those who follow Abū Ḥanīfa)[33] and struggled against what they perceived as their heresies.[34] Not all of them, however, were traditionists (*muḥaddithūn*), and the Syrian al-Awzāʿī and the Basran Ayyūb al-Sakhtiyānī, who belonged to the circle of Ibn Sīrīn, for example, were jurists. Yet they both represented a frame of reference: al-Awzāʿī saw the origin

31 Wensinck, *Muslim creed* chapter one and p. 59.

32 ʿAbdallāh b. al-Mubārak and Abū Isḥāq al-Fazārī were also distinguished by their piety and active participation in *jihād*; cf. Jarrar, Martyrdom 319–322; and see now Salem, *Emergence* 1–14.

33 Cf. Melchert, *Formation*, 13–15; El Shamsy, *Canonization* 22–31; Stewart, Developments 146–149.

34 On the "polemics of naming" and the "social roles and creation of normativity," see Turner, *Inquisition* 26–41.

of all evil in the early Qadaris;[35] and al-Sakhtiyānī stood firmly against them and even emphasized the idea of hope (*rajāʾ*) for every sinner who belongs to the community.[36]

A catch-all narrative, which took on the character of an early catechism, was attributed to ʿAbdallāh b. al-Mubārak by Ghulām Khalīl.[37] Under the rubric of an alleged prophetic tradition, one that became widespread in later generations, Ibn al-Mubārak specifies "the origin of seventy-two deviating sects" in four sects: the Qadaris, the Murjiʾa, the Shiʿa, and the Kharijites. Attempts were also made to indicate the innovations that threatened the doctrinal authority and to clarify those tenets to which the proto-Sunnis had acquiesced and which informed the main traits of the Sunna.[38]

Indeed, these *ʿulamāʾ* lacked a uniform concept encompassing all of the decisive dogmatic issues; however, they came to represent a body that formed a standard reference and whose attitudes were adopted by the later *ahl al-sunna*. It seems that, as is usual, the early codification of statements of faith appeared in simple formulae based on enumeration. Abū Isḥāq al-Fazārī relates, from al-Awzāʿī (d. 157/774), the simple dictum "It used to be said, the Companions of Muhammad—may peace and blessings be upon him—and the Successors in good acts, agreed on (*kāna ʿalayhā*) five things: adhering to the *sunna*, complying with the *sunna*, populating the mosques, reciting the Quran, and Jihād in God's path."[39] Sufyān b. ʿUyayna (d. 198/814) relates another plain saying accentuating ten points.[40]

Reports about the dogmatic positions of early *ʿulamāʾ* had often been quoted since the mid-third/ninth century by authors from the circle of the *aṣḥāb al-ḥadīth*, especially in the aftermath of the *miḥna*, when creeds (*ʿaqāʾid, iʿtiqādāt*) attributed to some of these early authorities had been put in circulation.

As Wensinck puts it, these creeds "are enumerations of the articles of belief"[41] and were basically meant to be easily accessible literalistic thoughts on core beliefs and practices, setting forth with authority certain articles of belief that were the products of the flurry of discourse with opponents. In general,

35 Cf. *ThG* i, 67–69, 72–74.

36 Cf. *ThG* ii, 347–352.

37 Eng. trans. §§88 and 144. In some sources, it is attributed to Yūsuf b. Asbāṭ (d. 196/812); see our comments on §88 in the Arabic text.

38 Cf. Laoust, *Schismes* 449; Juynboll, Excursus 321; van Ess, *Der Eine* i, 74–77; van Ess, Constructing Islam.

39 Al-Marwazī, *Taʿẓīm* 679; al-Lālakāʾī, *Sharḥ* i, 36.

40 al-Lālakāʾī, *Sharḥ* i, 89.

41 Wensinck, *Muslim creed* 1. See furthermore Watt, *Islamic creeds* 3–12; Schmidtke, Creeds; Hoover, Creed; van Ess, *Der Eine* ii, 1208–1212.

although they made efforts to collect, arrange, and scaffold material, they often did not reveal any internal organization or governing principle. Rather, they put singular emphasis on precepts and formularies concerning refutations of erroneous beliefs and derailed developments, and expounded upon the questions of what one should believe, how one should practice, and how to be silent and obey. These were essential in the process of forging a community identity based on "who we are" (like what distinguishes "us" from "other groups"), and were often meant as tenets. In other words, they were not intended merely for rote memorization but had to be practiced. Indeed, these creeds offered a syncretic sense of obligations and correct ritual practice, since orthopraxy occupies meaningful space and time in everyday life and acquires a particular significance when the prescribed acts of worship are performed.

3 Classification of Third/Ninth-Century Creeds and Tenets

Twenty creeds and tenets have been collected which are attributed to authorities who died before the fourth/tenth century and include articulations of their position on controversial issues that they deemed heresy. Before we examine these, three comments seem appropriate as an introduction. First, with the propagation of creeds during the third/ninth century, authors of later centuries were induced to put together aphorisms attributed in the sources to *ʿulamāʾ* of the second/eighth century, and to present them in the form of creeds. Second, creeds during the third/ninth century not only proliferated rapidly on an unprecedented scale but also came to be manipulated as part of a legitimating discourse that became heated in the rivalry for influence among various Sunni trends. Moreover, some of these creeds represented an attempt to show fealty to a certain group, or teacher, as well as to gain prestige. This insight is made clear in a feigned attempt put under the name of Ibn ʿUkāsha al-Kirmānī (died after 225/839; D.11 below). Third, one must be particularly cautious when dealing with the *iʿtiqādāt* attributed to Ibn Ḥanbal, as they represent the various trends that were competing within the Hanbali movement of the third/ninth century (or even later), such that some of the presumed authors cannot be identified. Some of these creeds reveal crude anthropomorphist tendencies, as well as other tenets that can hardly be attributed to Ibn Ḥanbal (e.g., Abū l-ʿAbbās al-Iṣṭakhrī/Ḥarb b. Ismāʿīl al-Kirmānī, C.5 below).

Some of the creeds mentioned in the sources were transmitted, either partially or completely, by later scholars, in which case chains of transmission are attached. Moreover, the Shafiʿi traditionist Qawwām al-Sunna from Isfahan (d. 535/1140) enumerated a list of the creeds of the *ahl al-salaf* that he had consulted or heard of.[42] Henri Laoust in 1957 produced a list of Hanbali creeds that were quoted by Ibn Abī Yaʿlā.[43] Some tenets concerning dogmatic matters (*iʿtiqādāt*) can also be culled from quaestiones and responsa (*masāʾil wa-ajwiba*)—that is, works of religious instruction organized for use in curricula.[44] In the third/ninth century, many *masāʾil* collections of a legal nature were put into circulation on the authority of Ahmad b. Ḥanbal.[45] The *masāʾil* of Ḥarb b. Ismāʿīl al-Kirmānī (d. 280/893), known as al-Sīrjānī,[46] as given in his *K. al-Sunna*, are useful in this regard,[47] although it should be emphasized that Ḥarb b. Ismāʿīl gives a creed (*iʿtiqād*) at the beginning of his book[48] that is a verbatim copy of the one attributed to Abū l-ʿAbbās Aḥmad b. Jaʿfar b. Yaʿqūb al-Iṣṭakhrī (C.5 below).

The following list augments Henri Laoust's list of creeds attributed to earlier authorities:

(A) Ostensibly second-century *iʿtiqādāt*

(1) Al-Awzāʿī, ʿAbd al-Raḥmān b. ʿAmr (d. 157/774); Syrian. He was a highly acclaimed jurisprudent and traditionist and the founder of a school of law.[49] His student Baqiyya b. al-Walīd (d. 197/812) used to say that whoever praises al-Awzāʿī is an adherent of the *sunna* (*ṣāḥib sunna*), and whoever slanders him is an adherent of heretic novelties (*ṣāḥib bidʿa*).[50] Qawwām al-Sunna mentions that his *iʿtiqād* was transmitted by Abū Isḥāq al-Fazārī (d. 186/802).[51] It seems, however,

42 Qawwām al-Sunna, *al-Ḥujja* ii, 473–477.

43 See also Melchert, *Ahmad ibn Hanbal* 83–85.

44 *Masāʾil* and *ajwiba* represent an early method of transmitting legal opinions. For the early *masāʾil* from ʿAṭāʾ (d. 115/733) by Ibn Jurayj (d. 150/767), see Motzki, *Origins* 79–82; see also Spectorsky, Sunna 52; Cook, *Commanding right* 88; Melchert, *Ahmad ibn Hanbal* 65–69; among the early Shīʿa they were an indispensable link to the authoritative knowledge of the imam (cf. e.g. Modarressi, *Introduction* 101–108; Modarressi, *Tradition* 347, 381–382). For questions-and-answers as a genre, see Daiber, Masāʾil wa-Adjwiba, and for their use as pedagogical devices, Günther, Eine Erkenntnis 75.

45 Cf. Melchert, Traditionist-jurisprudents 389–395; Bin Ramli, From tradition 166–175.

46 Yāqūt, *Muʿjam al-buldān* iii, 296 (al-Sīrjān).

47 The material concerning *iʿtiqādāt* was recently extracted and edited under the title *Kitāb al-Sunna* (Beirut 2014).

48 Al-Kirmānī, *K. al-Sunna* 33–62.

49 Ibn ʿAsākir, *Tārīkh* xxxv, 147–228; Schacht, al-Awzāʿī; Hallaq, *Origins* 170–176; Judd, Competitive hagiography 26–31; Juynboll, *Encyclopedia of canonical ḥadīth* 140–144.

50 Ibn ʿAsākir, *Tārīkh* xxxv, 176.

51 Qawwām al-Sunna, *al-Ḥujja* ii, 474. See also Ibn Baṭṭa, *al-Ibāna* (al-Īmān) ii, 882; and cf. Ibn ʿAsākir, *Tārīkh* xxxv, 200–202, where he relates items on the authority of Baqiyya b. al-Walīd, although without mentioning that they form part of a creed.

that this *iʿtiqād* was culled from the responses of al-Awzāʿī to questions posed by al-Fazārī, as is clear from extracts by al-Lālakāʾī.[52]

(2) Sufyān al-Thawrī (d. 161/778); Kufan. A venerated traditionist, renunciant, Quran interpreter, and jurisprudent who was hostile to the *aṣḥāb al-raʾy*.[53] Al-ʿIjlī (d. 261/874) describes him as *ṣāḥib sunna wa-ttibāʿ*.[54] Qawwām al-Sunna[55] mentions that he dictated his *iʿtiqād* to Shuʿayb b. Ḥarb (d. 196/811 or 197/812).[56] Both al-Lālakāʾī (d. 418/1027) and al-Ṭuyūrī (d. 500/1106) quote the *iʿtiqād* on the authority of Shuʿayb b. Ḥarb, but with a different chain of transmission and decisive text variations. Also, al-Lālakāʾī's text starts with the phrase "Tell me a *ḥadīth* from the *sunna*" (*ḥaddithnī bi-ḥadīthin min al-sunna*), whereas al-Ṭuyūrī's reads, "Tell me what is the *sunna*" (*akhbirnī mā l-sunna*).[57]

(3) Sufyān b. ʿUyayna (d. 198/814 in Mecca); Kufan. Qawwām al-Sunna mentions that his *iʿtiqād* was related by a certain Muḥammad b. Isḥāq al-Thaqafī.[58] Al-Lālakāʾī, however, quotes excerpts on the authority of a certain Bakr b. al-Faraj.[59] Ibn ʿUyayna was a famous and widely respected *ḥadīth* scholar. Al-Dhahabī describes him as *ṣāḥib sunna wa-ttibāʿ*.[60]

(B) Pre-*miḥna* creeds

(4) A creed by al-Ḥumaydī, Abū Bakr ʿAbdallāh (d. 219/834); Meccan.[61] A five-page creed entitled *Uṣūl al-sunna* is given at the end of his *Musnad*.[62] Al-Ḥumaydī is known as a compiler of a *musnad*.[63] He

52 Al-Lālakāʾī, *Sharḥ* i, 89, ii, 5, 60–61.

53 Al-Dhahabī, *Siyar* vii, 229–279; *ThG* i, 221–228; Motzki, *Origins* 58–62 and index; Spectorsky, Sufyān al-Thawrī; Judd, Competitive hagiography 31–37.

54 Al-ʿIjlī, *al-Thiqāt* 192.

55 Qawwām al-Sunna, *al-Ḥujja* ii, 473.

56 Al-Dhahabī, *Siyar* ix, 188–190.

57 Al-Lālakāʾī, *Sharḥ* i, 87–88; al-Ṭuyūrī, *al-Ṭuyūriyyāt* ii, 539–542; cf. Abū Nuʿaym, *Ḥilya* vii, 34–35.

58 Qawwām al-Sunna, *al-Ḥujja* ii, 474. If al-Sarrāj al-Naysābūrī (d. 313/925; cf. al-Dhahabī, *Siyar* xiv, 388) is meant here, he did not hear directly from Sufyān b. ʿUyayna.

59 Al-Lālakāʾī, *Sharḥ* i, 89. Cf. also sayings by various transmitters in Abū Nuʿaym, *Ḥilya* vii, 295.

60 Al-Dhahabī, *Siyar* viii, 466. See also on Sufyān b. ʿUyayna, Motzki, *Origins* 59–62 and index; Spectorsky, Sufyān b. ʿUyayna; Juynboll, *Encyclopedia of canonical ḥadīth* 568–621.

61 Al-Dhahabī, *Siyar* x, 616–621; al-Mizzī, *Tahdhīb* xiv, 511–515.

62 Al-Ḥumaydī, *al-Musnad* ii, 357–362.

63 Brown, *Hadith* 28–31.

is one of the main transmitters from Sufyān b. ʿUyayna,[64] and he was also a student of al-Shāfiʿī. Al-Bukhārī studied with him, and Ibn Ḥanbal regarded him as an *imām*. Temel notes that this is the first known work with the title of "*uṣūl*."[65] Most probably, the terminology was influenced by al-Shāfiʿī. The creed by ʿAbdūs b. Mālik (no. 7 below) also starts with the term *uṣūl* (*uṣūl al-sunna ʿindanā*), and Ibn Abī Ḥātim al-Rāzī (no. 17 below), in the creed that he relates on the authority of Abū Zurʿa al-Rāzī and Abū Ḥātim al-Rāzī, also mentions the teachings of the *ahl al-sunna* pertaining to *uṣūl al-dīn*.

(C) Creeds attributed to Aḥmad b. Ḥanbal (d. 241/855)[66]

(5) A creed attributed to Aḥmad b. Ḥanbal (Laoust, *ʿAqīda 1*) on the authority of a certain Abū l-ʿAbbās Aḥmad b. Jaʿfar b. Yaʿqūb al-Iṣṭakhrī.[67] Ibn Abī Yaʿlā[68] transmits this creed through a *sanad* that goes back to a certain Ibn Zūrān.[69] Al-Dhahabī quotes eight lines from al-Iṣṭakhrī's creed that reveal anthropomorphist language.[70] Al-Dhahabī comments on it by saying,

> And he mentioned things similar to these unacceptable examples [that are cited above]; things that—by God—were not uttered by the Imam—may God damn its fabricator. One of the most abhorred things is his maxim, "Whoever claims that he does not approve of due compliance (*taqlīd*; i.e., strict conformance) and does not emulate anyone in his religion is a wrongdoer (*fāsiq*)."

64 Juynboll, *Encyclopedia of canonical ḥadīth* 569b.

65 Temel, Uṣūl al-sunna 45; van Ess, *Der Eine* ii, 1209.

66 It is remarkable that most of the *asānīd* of the creeds attributed to Aḥmad b. Ḥanbal contain names of unspecified transmitters whose exact pronunciation was uncertain in the sources.

67 Laoust, *Profession* 12; translated by Watt, *Islamic creeds* 33–40.

68 Ibn Abī Yaʿlā, *Ṭabaqāt* (al-Fiqī) i, 24–36 (al-ʿUthaymīn) i, 54–72; Ibn Taymiyya, *al-Ṣārim* 573, quotes a phrase about the ranking of the Companions. See also Ibn Qayyim al-Jawziyya, *Ḥādī al-arwāḥ* 63–64 (citing Ibn Abī Yaʿlā's *Ṭabaqāt*).

69 This name should be read as Ibn Zūzān (d. after 330/941–942), Ibn ʿAsākir, *Tārīkh* li, 211–213; al-Dhahabī, *Siyar* xv, 334. The transmitter from Ibn Zūzān according to al-Dhahabī, *Siyar* xi, 302–303, who cites excerpts from the creed, is ʿAbdallāh b. Muḥammad b. Jaʿfar al-Nahāwandī (as in Ibn ʿAsākir, *Tārīkh* xxxii, 175), not Aḥmad b. ʿAbdallāh al-Mālikī, as the name appears in the *isnād* given by Ibn Abī Yaʿlā. If Ibn Zūzān had actually met a certain Abū l-ʿAbbās al-Iṣṭakhrī, about whom no biographical information is available, and if his attribution of the creed to him is not a mistake (or a forgery) by Ibn Zūzān, that would mean that this al-Iṣṭakhrī must have died in the last quarter of the third/ninth century.

70 Al-Dhahabī, *Siyar* xi, 302–303; and see also al-Dhahabī's comment, xi, 286, who criticizes its *isnād*.

> The enemy of God. Look at the ignorance of the traditionists how they transmit this fable (*al-khurāfa*) without commenting on it.

Interestingly, however, the same creed is transmitted on the authority of Ḥarb b. Ismāʿīl al-Kirmānī (d. 280/893) in his *K. al-Sunna*,[71] by a certain, yet otherwise unidentifiable, Abū l-Qāsim. Ibn Taymiyya observes reticence in the wording of the creed, arguing that this belongs to Ḥarb's diction and not Ibn Ḥanbal's.[72] In fact, whereas Ḥarb al-Kirmānī al-Sīrjānī is acknowledged in the sources as a student of Aḥmad b. Ḥanbal, nothing is known about Abū l-ʿAbbās al-Iṣṭakhrī. This observation, however, does not solve the problem concerning the authorship of this particular *iʿtiqād*. At the end of the creed, Ḥarb al-Kirmānī/Abū l-ʿAbbās al-Iṣṭakhrī designates a section to catalog the various "heretic" groups and their innovations,[73] along with their names and basic principles.[74] Yet it is not clear whether this section was originally part of the *iʿtiqād*, since the previous section ends with, "Hold to that [i.e., what the author elaborated earlier], study it and teach it, and success will be granted by God."[75] Importantly, this example of straightforward instruction very much resembles the typical closing sentence of a creed.

Ḥarb's book was known, however, to Abū l-Qāsim al-Balkhī al-Kaʿbī (d. 319/931), who had written a rebuttal to invalidate it.[76] Al-Rāmahurmuzī (d. 360/970) also appears to have known Ḥarb's book, as he says of Ḥarb that he "had listened [to many *ḥadīth*] and neglected to apply comprehension (*istibṣār*) [...] where he displayed arrogance,"[77] and he refers to al-Kaʿbī's refutation.

---

71 See the introduction of *K. al-Sunna* by its editor, Āl Ḥamdān 27–28.

72 Ibn Taymiyya, *al-Istiqāma* i, 73–74; Ibn Qayyim al-Jawziyya, likewise, quotes the *iʿtiqād* and attributes it to Ḥarb b. Ismāʿīl al-Kirmānī; see his *Ḥādī al-arwāḥ* 447–454.

73 Shorter lists of "heretic" groups appear in the creeds by ʿAbdūs b. Mālik (only four) and the Rāzīs.

74 Cf. van Ess, *Der Eine* i, 281–282.

75 Ḥarb al-Kirmānī, *K. al-Sunna* 62; Ibn Abī Yaʿlā, *Ṭabaqāt* (al-Fiqī) i, 31 (al-ʿUthaymīn) i, 66. In his translation of al-Iṣṭakhrī's creed, Watt does not include the section enumerating the innovators; see his *Islamic creeds* 39.

76 Yāqūt, *Muʿjam al-buldān* iii, 296 (al-Sīrjān); van Ess, *Der Eine* i, 331–332; El Omari, Accommodation 237–239, 251; El Omari, *Theology* 20.

77 Al-Rāmahurmuzī, *al-Muḥaddith* 309; translated by El Omari, Accommodation 237. The person meant, however, is Ḥarb al-Sīrjānī and not "the secretary," meaning al-Balkhī al-Kaʿbī, as El Omari maintains.

The edited text of Ḥarb's *K. al-Sunna* corrects a number of odd readings that appear in Ibn Abī Yaʿlā's *Ṭabaqāt*,[78] while certain other issues (which are beyond the scope of this study) still seem to await a solution. Nonetheless, one question deserves to be addressed here, concerning the dating of the text: Toward the end of the catalog enumerating the various "innovations" in the second section, the claim is made that the *aṣḥāb al-raʾy*[79] call the *aṣḥāb al-sunna* "*nābita*" and "*ḥashwiyya*".[80] This indicates that the *aṣḥāb al-raʾy* and the Hanafi scholars of Iran used to give the name *al-nābita* to the *ahl al-sunna* in Iran during the second half of the third/ninth century,[81] to which group both Ḥarb al-Kirmānī and Abū l-ʿAbbās al-Iṣṭakhrī belong.

(6) A creed by al-Ḥasan b. Ismāʿīl al-Rabaʿī (Laoust, *ʿAqīda II*);[82] the *sanad* as given by Ibn Abī Yaʿlā goes through al-Mubārak [b. ʿAbd al-Jabbār Ibn al-Ṭuyūrī (d. 500/1107)[83]] ← ʿAbd al-ʿAzīz al-Azajī (d. 444/1052)[84] ← Abū Bakr al-Mufīd (d. 378/988)[85] ← al-Ḥasan b. Ismāʿīl al-Rabaʿī. As is clear from the chain of transmission, al-Rabaʿī must have lived during the fourth/tenth century, and it is unlikely that he had heard the report directly from Ibn Ḥanbal.

(7) A creed attributed to Ibn Ḥanbal (Laoust, *ʿAqīda III*) on the authority of ʿAbdūs b. Mālik (d. around 250/864), Baghdadi,[86] with a *sanad* attested by all the sources that goes through al-Mubārak [b. ʿAbd al-

78 The Nuṣayriyya, for example, a reading accepted by van Ess, *Der Eine* i, 281, is read as al-Bakriyya, which makes more sense since the ascription of "*al-qawl bi-l-ḥabba wa-l-qīrāṭ*," which is attributed to them, is also attributed to al-Bakriyya a few pages later. The cryptic sentence concerning the Rafidis, saying that they "*yukaffirūn al-aʾimma al-arbaʿa, ʿAlī, ʿAmmār, al-Miqdād and Salmān*," is to be read as "*yukaffirūn al-aʾimma illā*."

79 The author mentions the Muʿtazila by name in a previous section; he differentiates between them and the *aṣḥāb al-raʾy*, those who "*yattakhidhūna Abā Ḥanīfa wa-man qāla bi-qawlihi imāman wa-yadīnūna bi-dīnihim* ..." Ibn Abī Yaʿlā, *Ṭabaqāt* (al-Fiqī) i, 35 (al-ʿUthaymīn) i, 71; Ḥarb al-Kirmānī, *K. al-Sunna* 69.

80 Ibn Abī Yaʿlā, *Ṭabaqāt* (al-Fiqī) i, 36 (al-ʿUthaymīn) i, 73; Ḥarb al-Kirmānī, *K. al-Sunna* 72.

81 The term was used by Abū l-Qāsim al-Balkhī to describe the *ahl al-ḥadīth*, El Omari, Accommodation 232, 243.

82 Laoust, *Profession* 12; Ibn Abī Yaʿlā, *Ṭabaqāt* (al-Fiqī) i, 130–131 (al-ʿUthaymīn) i, 349–350; Ibn al-Jawzī, *Manāqib* i, 324–326 (with the same *sanad* as that of Ibn Abī Yaʿlā; al-ʿUthaymīn i, 349, fn. 3), mentions that the creed had been transmitted with the same *sanad* by al-Silafī in his *al-Mashyakha al-baghdādiyya*.

83 Ibn Ḥajar, *Lisān* vi, 452.

84 Al-Dhahabī, *Siyar* xviii, 18.

85 Ibid., xvi, 270.

86 Laoust, *Profession* 13; Ibn Abī Yaʿlā, *Ṭabaqāt* (al-Fiqī) i, 241–246, (al-ʿUthaymīn) ii, 166–174; al-Dhahabī, *Tārīkh* v, 1179; Ibn al-Jawzī, *Manāqib* i, 296–298, 316–324.

Jabbār Ibn al-Ṭuyūrī (d. 500/1107)[87]] ← ʿAbd al-ʿAzīz al-Azajī (d. 444/1052)[88] ← ʿAlī b. Bushrān (d. 415/1024)[89] ← ʿUthmān Ibn al-Sammāk (d. 344/955)[90] ← an unidentified Sulaymān b. Muḥammad (or Muḥammad b. Sulaymān) al-Minqarī ← ʿAbdūs b. Mālik. Very little is known about ʿAbdūs.[91] He is supposed to have related responsa (*masāʾil*) from Aḥmad b. Ḥanbal.[92]

(8) A creed by Muḥammad b. Ḥabīb al-Andarābī, Balkh (Laoust, *ʿAqīda IV*).[93] Whereas Ibn Abī Yaʿlā quotes the same creed—almost verbatim—under the name of Muḥammad b. Yūnus al-Sarakhsī,[94] Ibn al-Jawzī gives the name of al-Sarakhsī as the main transmitter from al-Andarābī.[95]

(9) A creed (Laoust, *ʿAqīda* V) by Muḥammad b. ʿAwf Abū Jaʿfar al-Ḥimṣī (d. 272/885), who is an authority on the *ḥadīth*s of the Syrians and was praised by ʿAbdallāh b. Aḥmad b. Ḥanbal.[96] He transmitted from Ibn Ḥanbal by way of dictation (*amlā ʿalayya*); the excerpts were copied from the handwriting of Aḥmad al-Sinjī,[97] where the latter gave his *isnād*.[98]

(10) A creed by Ibn Ḥanbal (Laoust, *ʿAqīda VI*) in the form of a letter addressed to Musaddad b. Musarhad al-Baṣrī (d. 228/842),[99] which is transmitted by a certain Aḥmad b. Muḥammad al-Tamīmī al-Zarandī by Ibn Abī Yaʿlā (and al-Bardhaʿī by Ibn al-Jawzī).[100] Musad-

87 Ibn Ḥajar, *Lisān* vi, 452.

88 Al-Dhahabī, *Siyar* xviii, 18.

89 Ibid., xvii, 311.

90 Ibid., xv, 444.

91 Al-Khaṭīb al-Baghdādī, *Tārīkh* xii, 417.

92 Ibn Abī Yaʿlā, *Ṭabaqāt* (al-Fiqī) i, 241, (al-ʿUthaymīn) ii, 166.

93 Laoust, *Profession* 13; Laoust, al-Andarānī (*ʿAqīda IV*); Ibn Abī Yaʿlā, *Ṭabaqāt* (al-Fiqī) i, 294–295 (al-Andarānī), (al-ʿUthaymīn) ii, 293–295 (al-Andarābī); Ibn al-Jawzī, *Manāqib* i, 286, 304–307 (al-Andarābī).

94 Ibn Abī Yaʿlā, *Ṭabaqāt* (al-Fiqī) i, 329–330, (al-ʿUthaymīn) ii, 392–394.

95 Ibn al-Jawzī, *Manāqib* i, 324.

96 Ibn ʿAsākir, *Tārīkh* lv, 47–51; al-Dhahabī, *Siyar* xii, 613–616; al-Mizzī, *Tahdhīb* xxvi, 236–240.

97 *Ṭabaqāt* (al-Fiqī) i, 311 al-Shinjī.

98 Laoust, *Profession* 13; Ibn Abī Yaʿlā, *Ṭabaqāt* (al-Fiqī) i, 311–313, (al-ʿUthaymīn) ii, 339–343; cf. Ibn al-Jawzī, *Manāqib* i, 298. He also transmitted *masāʾil* from Ibn Ḥanbal.

99 Laoust, *Profession* 13–14; Ibn Abī Yaʿlā, *Ṭabaqāt*, with a *sanad* that goes from Ibn Baṭṭa back to an unidentified ʿAlī (al-Fiqī) i, 341–345 (al-ʿUthaymīn) ii, 426–432; Ibn al-Jawzī, *Manāqib* i, 309–316.

100 Ibn Taymiyya mentions that the veracity of this letter from Aḥmad to Musaddad has been questioned due to the fact that the first transmitter is unknown. *Majmūʿ fatāwā* v, 375, 379–380, 396.

dad was a renowned traditionist who had compiled a *musnad*. Al-Bukhārī and Abū Dāwūd, among others, related from him in their books, and he was praised by Ibn Ḥanbal.[101]

(D) Other creeds of the third/ninth century

(11) A creed by Muḥammad b. ʿUkāsha al-Kirmānī (d. after 225/839).[102] The sources agree that he was a "fabricator of traditions" and a "liar." When asked about the vision/dream that al-Kirmānī claims to have had, Abū Zurʿa remarked, "He was a liar who did not even know how to lie."[103] Al-Malaṭī (d. 377/987) introduces the creed attributed to him at the beginning of his *al-Tanbīh*,[104] with a formula that is quite strong and confident, as he states, "It had been asserted on the authority of Muḥammad b. ʿUkāsha that the 'roots of the *sunna*' (*uṣūl al-sunna*) that had been agreed upon by the learned (*al-fuqahāʾ*) were ..."[105] He then enumerates 23 names of tradionists, all of whom are reported to have said, "We met the Companions of the Prophet, and they used to say ..." Al-Malaṭī then quotes a short creed, which is followed by a spurious report in which Muḥammad b. ʿUkāsha recounts that on three consecutive nights he had a vision of the Prophet in a dream in which he read to him his creed while the Prophet approved of it.

Al-Malaṭī also claims that when al-Mutawakkil asked Aḥmad b. Ḥanbal to explain (or "make known") the *sunna wa-l-jamāʿa* for him (*aẓhirnī ʿalā*), and what he had written down from his teachers (*aṣḥāb*), on the authority (*mimmā katabūhu ʿan*) of the Successors on the authority of the Companions of the Prophet, Ibn Ḥanbal then related to him Ibn ʿUkāsha's report.

Ibn ʿAsākir also quotes both the creed and the dream in his biographical dictionary in the entry on Umayya b. ʿUthmān al-Dimashqī,[106] who is known to Ibn ʿAsākir solely through this report on Ibn ʿUkāsha al-Kirmānī. At the end of the entry, Ibn ʿAsākir posits that Aḥmad b. Isḥāq al-Sukkarī had attributed the report to Munabbih[107] b. ʿUthmān al-Dimashqī (d. after 212/827), and not to Umayya

101 Al-Dhahabī, *Siyar* x, 591–595; van Ess, *Der Eine* i, 281.

102 Ibn ʿAsākir, *Tārīkh* lxxxv, 229–230; Qawwām al-Sunna, *al-Ḥujja* ii, 475.

103 Ibn Ḥajar, *Lisān* vii, 350–355.

104 Al-Malaṭī, *al-Tanbīh* 11–13.

105 Ibn ʿAsākir, *Tārīkh* ix, 300.

106 Ibid., ix, 299–302.

107 The confusion might have been due to the ambiguity (*taṣḥīf*) of the letters of the names in Arabic.

b. ʿUthmān, and furthermore comments, "And this is actually the right [attribution]." Nonetheless, Ibn ʿAsākir makes no mention of this report in the respective entry on Munabbih, nor does the name of Muḥammad b. ʿUkāsha appear there.[108]

In his entry on Umayya, Ibn ʿAsākir writes, "Muḥammad b. ʿUkāsha reported the creed from Umayya ([*ḥakā ʿanhu*] *uṣūl al-sunna*), as it has been said (*ʿalā mā qīla*) [i.e., about Muḥammad b. ʿUkāsha]." Ibn ʿAsākir's use of this choice of words is a deliberate attempt to draw attention to the unspecified nature of the report attributed to Ibn ʿUkāsha.

Ibn ʿAsākir provides three transmission chains for the creed. Two of these pass through ʿAlī b. Mūsā b. al-Simsār (d. 433/1041)[109] to reach the first narrator after Ibn ʿUkāsha—namely, Abū Jaʿfar Muḥammad b. Sulaymān al-Baṣrī. It is the latter who reports that "Ibn ʿUkāsha came to Basra in the year 225/839 and I heard him say," which means that he studied with him. The third chain of transmission, however, goes back to Abū Isḥāq Ibrāhīm b. Muḥammad al-Burūdī, who reports in Basra in 301/913 that he had directly heard the creed from Ibn ʿUkāsha (*ḥaddathanā*).

It is important to note that the creed does not go back to Umayya b. ʿUthmān al-Dimashqī, but rather, as mentioned above, starts with an introduction stating that it represents "the consensus that has been reached by [those members] of *ahl al-sunna wa-l-jamāʿa* that I have seen (*raʾaytu*) and heard from amongst the learned (*wa-samiʿtu min ahl al-ʿilm*)."[110] Ibn ʿUkāsha then mentions the name of Umayya b. ʿUthmān while enumerating a list of more than 30 authorities from various geographic regions, among whom are the totality of the students (*ʿāmmat aṣḥāb*) of a certain Ibn al-Mufriṭ.[111]

(12) Abū Thawr, Ibrāhīm b. Khālid (d. 240/854); Baghdadi.[112] Al-Lālakāʾī quotes, on the authority of Idrīs b. ʿAbd al-Karīm (d. 292/904),[113] a letter from Abū Thawr responding to a man in Khorasan who had asked him about faith. Abū Thawr is a well-known jurisconsult

108 Ibn ʿAsākir, *Tārīkh* lx, 273–276; Ibn al-Bannā, *al-Mukhtār* 233–234.

109 Ibn ʿAsākir, *Tārīkh* xliii, 255–257. (Ibn ʿAsākir reports that he harbored Shīʿī tendencies that amount to *rafḍ*.)

110 Ibid., ix, 300.

111 It was not possible to identify Ibn al-Mufriṭ. Perhaps "al-Mufriḍ" is a more correct reading of this name; cf. al-Samʿānī, *al-Ansāb* xi, 425.

112 Al-Lālakāʾī, *Sharḥ* i, 101–102.

113 Al-Dhahabī, *Siyar* xiv, 45.

(*faqīh*), famous for his reliance on *ra'y*. He studied with al-Shāfiʿī in Baghdad and is said to have followed his teachings.[114] Nevertheless, the traditionists celebrate him as a "defender of the *sunna*." His contemporary, Abū Bakr al-Aʿyan (d. 240/854),[115] quotes Aḥmad b. Ḥanbal as stating, when he was asked about Abū Thawr, "I have known him for 50 years for his adherence to the *sunna*," and putting him in a rank with Sufyān al-Thawrī.[116] Ibn Ḥibbān also considered him a "defender of the *sunna*."[117]

(13) Abū Rajā' Qutayba b. Saʿīd (d. 240/854), from Balkh. Qawwām al-Sunna mentions[118] that his *iʿtiqād* was related by Abū l-ʿAbbās al-Sarrāj (d. 313/925).[119] Abū Rajā' was highly praised by *ḥadīth* experts as well as the compilers of the six books transmitted from him. When he visited Baghdad in 216/831, both Aḥmad b. Ḥanbal and Ibn Maʿīn went to meet with him.[120] Ibn Sayyār al-Marwazī (d. 268/881)[121] describes him as *ṣāḥib sunna wa-jamāʿa*.[122]

(14) A creed by ʿAlī b. ʿAbdallāh b. al-Madīnī (d. 243/849), from Basra.[123] A highly respected traditionist;[124] Abū ʿUbayd stated, "Religious knowledge (*ʿilm*—not just *ḥadīth*) has ended up with four": Abū Bakr Ibn Abī Shayba (d. 235/849 in Kufa), Aḥmad b. Ḥanbal (d. 241/855 in Baghdad), ʿAlī b. al-Madīnī (d. 234/849 in Samarra), and Yaḥyā b. Maʿīn (d. 233/848 in Medina).[125] His affirmative answer during the *miḥna*, however, stirred the anger of Aḥmad b. Ḥanbal and caused a wave of antagonism against him among the traditionists.[126]

(15) A creed by Muḥammad b. Ismāʿīl al-Bukhārī (d. 256/870) from Bukhara. Al-Lālakā'ī cites an *iʿtiqād* attributed to him on the authority of a certain Abū Muḥammad ʿAbd al-Raḥmān b. Muḥammad al-

---

114 Schacht, Abū Thawr.
115 Al-Dhahabī, *Siyar* xii, 119.
116 Ibid., xii, 73; al-Subkī, *Ṭabaqāt* ii, 74; see also Melchert, *Formation* 73.
117 Cf. al-Subkī, *Ṭabaqāt* ii, 74.
118 Qawwām al-Sunna, *al-Ḥujja* ii, 475; cf. also al-Karābīsī, *Shiʿār* 40–41.
119 Al-Dhahabī, *Siyar* xiv, 388.
120 Ibid., xi, 14–24; Juynboll, *Encyclopedia of canonical ḥadīth* 449–453.
121 Al-Dhahabī, *Siyar* xii, 609–611.
122 Ibid., xi, 19.
123 Al-Lālakā'ī, *Sharḥ* i, 97–101. Only one name in the chain of transmission could be identified—namely, Abū Muḥammad ʿAbdallāh b. Ghannām (d. 297/909), a grandson of Ḥafṣ b. Ghiyāth; see al-Dhahabī, *Siyar* xiii, 558.
124 Al-Dhahabī, *Siyar* xi, 41–59.
125 From Melchert, *Formation* 13.
126 Al-Dhahabī, *Siyar* xi, 55–57.

Bukhārī who had related it to a student in al-Shāsh (i.e., Tashkent in today's Uzbekistan).[127] The alleged author, al-Bukhārī, is the compiler of the leading canonical collection of Sunni traditions.[128] Despite his eminence and authority, al-Bukhārī was forced to leave Nishapur toward the end of his life on account of his statement that the physical recitation of the Quran is created (*masʾalat al-lafẓ*).[129]

(16) A creed by Abū Zurʿa ʿUbayd Allāh b. ʿAbd al-Karīm al-Rāzī (d. 264/878)[130] and Abū Ḥātim Muḥammad b. Idrīs al-Rāzī (d. 277/890),[131] which was transmitted on the authority of both scholars by Abū Ḥātim's son,[132] the celebrated *rijāl* author Abū Muḥammad ʿAbd al-Raḥmān (d. 327/938).[133] Both Abū Zurʿa and Abū Ḥātim were illustrious traditionists from the ancient city of Rayy near Tehran.

(17) Sahl al-Tustarī (d. 283/896), the Sufi master of Tustar who is counted among the *ahl al-sunna*.[134] Al-Lālakāʾī[135] relates items of a creed on the authority of Abū l-Qāsim ʿAbd al-Jabbār b. Shīrān al-ʿAbdī.[136]

(18) Abū Aḥmad b. Abī Usāma al-Qurashī al-Harawī, unidentified thus far.[137]

4 Comparison

The various tenets of the creeds will be delineated in chapter 4, when we come to study *K. Sharh al-sunna* by Ghulām Khalīl. To facilitate the current part of our investigation, however, let us first tease out the main items that appear in the early *iʿtiqādāt* (group A).

As argued above, the spontaneous beginnings were enumerations of a general nature, which came, more often than not, as responses to questions posed

127 Al-Lālakāʾī, *Sharḥ* i, 102–104.
128 Brown, *Canonization* 64–71.
129 Ibid., 66, 74–81.
130 Al-Dhahabī, *Siyar* xiii, 65–85.
131 Ibid., xiii, 247–263.
132 Al-Lālakāʾī, *Sharḥ* i, 104–109; al-Dhahabī, *Siyar* xiii, 260.
133 Dickinson, *Development* 11–40.
134 Böwering, *Mystical vision* 65–66.
135 Al-Lālakāʾī, *Sharḥ* i, 109.
136 His name in al-Lālakāʾī's *Sharḥ* appears as "Ibn Shīrāz"; cf. Ibn Nuqṭa, *Takmila* iii, 465; Ibn Ḥajar, *Tabṣīr* ii, 798; Ibn ʿAsākir, *Tārīkh* lii, 45, relates on his authority a saying by al-Tustarī; Böwering does not mention him among the disciples and associates of al-Tustarī.
137 Qawwām al-Sunna, *al-Ḥujja* ii, 476–477.

by students. The straightforward structure and style of these questions and responses—expressed either orally (in teaching sessions) or in written form (for example, in letters)—is still preserved in the *iʿtiqādāt* attributed to al-Awzāʿī, Sufyān al-Thawrī, and Sufyān b. ʿUyayna.

4.1 *Tenets Common among Three Creeds*

The following section studies in particular the *iʿtiqādāt* of al-Awzāʿī, Sufyān al-Thawrī, and Sufyān b. ʿUyayna, with emphasis on certain individual issues expressed in their tenets.

4.1.1 An Indignant Excoriation of the *Qadar* "Heresy"[138]

The question of *qadar* (advocating "free will" since God cannot be the source of evil), with its political implications, had been deliberated since the times of the Umayyads in Syria, as well as in Basra, mainly among proto-Sunni *ʿulamāʾ*, and continued to preponderate in the later centuries. Among the earliest advocates of this view were Maʿbad al-Juhanī al-Baṣrī (d. 83/704), Ghaylān al-Dimashqī (d. ca. 112/730), Ṣāliḥ b. Suwayd (d. ca. 112/730), and Makḥūl al-Dimashqī (d. 113/731). Al-Awzāʿī stood in opposition to the Qadaris and campaigned against delving into these subtleties.[139] By the time of Ibn Ḥanbal, this disagreement with Qadari views had become the standard position of the proto-Sunnis.

The formula from Sufyān al-Thawrī, "Patiently accept God's decree, and believe in God's fate, the good and the bad, the sweet and the bitter," is also attested in *al-Fiqh al-absaṭ*[140] attributed to Abū Ḥanīfa (Abū Muṭīʿ al-Balkhī, d. 199/814).[141]

4.1.2 The Nature of Faith and Its Relation to Works[142]

There is in the creeds of the proto-Sunnis an oft-cited formula that runs as follows: "Faith consists in [a.] verbal profession and action, given equal prece-

138 Al-Awzāʿī: al-Lālakāʾī, *Sharḥ* i, 89; Ibn ʿAsākir, *Tārīkh* xxxv, 202; al-Thawrī: al-Lālakāʾī, *Sharḥ* i, 87; al-Ṭuyūrī, *al-Ṭuyūriyyāt* ii, 541 (the citations from the Quran that are attributed to al-Thawrī in the *iʿtiqād* version of al-Lālakāʾī do not appear in this version); Ibn ʿUyayna: al-Lālakāʾī, *Sharḥ* i, 89 (*ithbāt al-qadar*).

139 Ibn Baṭṭa, *al-Ibāna* ii, 881, 882.

140 See on this our comments on the Arabic text, § 40.

141 Rudolph, *al-Māturīdī* 53–64.

142 Al-Awzāʿī: Ibn Baṭṭa, *al-Ibāna* ii, 882 (for the question "Are you a believer?"); Abū Nuʿaym, *Ḥilya* vi, 143–144; al-Lālakāʾī, *Sharḥ* i, 89, ii, 60–61; al-Thawrī: al-Lālakāʾī, *Sharḥ* i, 87; al-Ṭuyūrī, *al-Ṭuyūriyyāt* ii, 540; Ibn ʿUyayna: al-Lālakāʾī, *Sharḥ* i, 89; Abū Nuʿaym, *Ḥilya* vii, 295.

dence, and [b.] intention and [its] fulfilment. Belief admits of increase and diminution."[143] The question of the nature of faith and its relation to Islam (as complete submission to God through internalizing the confession of faith, *shahāda*),[144] and the significance of faith to good works, were matters of debate as early as the third part of the first/seventh century and were entangled with an egalitarian call for the rights of new converts. The early Murji'a, adherents of an overarching variety of politico-theological views who upheld this doctrine, promoted an understanding that identified knowledge in the heart, and the confession of faith, with belief to the exclusion of works.[145] This, at least, was the position adopted by Abū Ḥanīfa (d. 150/767),[146] against which a majority of early proto-Sunni *ʿulamāʾ* had committed themselves, including al-Awzāʿī, Sufyān al-Thawrī, and Sufyān b. ʿUyayna. Other questions were also related to this assortment of views, such as whether belief decreases and increases (as al-Thawrī proposed) by acts of good work, and whether doubt about one's belief could be admitted (as al-Awzāʿī saw it).[147]

4.2 *Tenets Common in Two Creeds*

This section studies tenets apparent in the *iʿtiqādāt* of Sufyān al-Thawrī and Sufyān b. ʿUyayna.

4.2.1 Giving Preference to Abū Bakr and ʿUmar

Giving preference to Abū Bakr and ʿUmar (*taqdīm al-shaykhayn*), as it is articulated in the *iʿtiqād* attributed to both al-Thawrī and Ibn ʿUyayna,[148] seems to have been a matter of consensus from an early date. This consensus appears first as part of views held by the Murji'a since both caliphs lived before the first great schism (*furqa*, *fitna*),[149] but was adopted later by the *ahl al-ḥadīth*.[150] The second part of the clause, however, seems contrived.[151] It concerns the question

143 Cf. the comments on the Arabic text, §§13k and 144; cf. also Pessagno, Murji'a 384–386.

144 Izutsu, *Concept* 57–66.

145 Ibid., 83–92.

146 *ThG* i, 194–198 (letter to ʿUthmān al-Battī); iv, 563–569.

147 The issue of "*istithnā*'"; cf. Izutsu, *Concept* 193–194; Madelung, Early Sunnī doctrine 240–243.

148 Al-Thawrī: al-Lālakā'ī, *Sharḥ* i, 101; al-Ṭuyūrī, *al-Ṭuyūriyyāt* ii, 540; Ibn ʿUyayna: al-Lālakā'ī, *Sharḥ* i, 89.

149 Cf. Sālim b. Dhakwān (d. ca. 100/719), *Sīra* 118; *Kitāb al-Irjā'*, which is attributed to Ḥasan b. Muḥammad b. al-Ḥanafiyya (flourished during the reign of ʿAbd al-Malik b. Marwan, 65–86/685–705), and could be dated toward the mid-second/eighth century, cf. *ThG* i, 177; Cook, Activism 20.

150 Nagel, *Rechtleitung* 236–240. Cf. Sālim b. Dhakwān, *Sīra* 118.

151 Ibn Ḥajar, *Lisān* i, 312, mentions that al-Thawrī used to give precedence to ʿAlī; see also Madelung, Origins 519, fn. 4.

of excellence among the Companions and the arrangement of ʿAlī and ʿUthmān in rank and preference. This view remained contested among the *ahl al-sunna* in the third/ninth century, although Ibn Ḥanbal had opted to count ʿAlī as the fourth caliph.[152]

4.2.2 The Question of the Createdness of the Quran

The question of the createdness of the Quran found its first expression during the Umayyad period with Jaʿd b. Dirham and al-Jahm b. Ṣafwān. However, it developed over time to become more complex, as Madelung has shown.[153]

In the *iʿtiqād* of Ibn ʿUyayna, it appears as a simple assertion that the Quran is God's speech (*kalām Allāh*),[154] without offering more arguments to support this view.[155] However, at the time of al-Thawrī, the matter became more complex, since there are additions in two respects. In the version transmitted by al-Lālakāʾī, one reads that the Quran is "uncreated," and that "whoever says otherwise is an unbeliever."[156] In the version by al-Ṭuyūrī, it is stated that it is God's speech that "He has uttered and has revealed to His messenger—may peace and blessings be upon him; you [i.e., Shuʿayb b. Ḥarb] should disavow (*tabraʾu min*) whoever says it is created, and whoever expresses disbelief regarding His names (*alḥada*)."[157] Noteworthy is the distinction between *fa-huwa kāfir* and *tabraʾu min*. A more important question posed by Madelung is whether it is likely that al-Thawrī "should have given such prominence to the doctrine concerning the Koran and have formulated it, long before the *miḥna*, in these terms."[158]

---

152 Ibn Abī Yaʿlā, *Ṭabaqāt* (*iʿtiqād* Ibn ʿAwf al-Ḥimṣī), (al-Fiqī) i, 313, (al-ʿUthaymīn), ii, 343; and a report from Warīza al-Ḥimṣī, claiming that he asked Aḥmad after the latter had made clear the four schema ranking "*aẓhara al-tarbīʿ*," (al-Fiqī) i, 393, (al-ʿUthaymīn) ii, 502; al-Khallāl, *al-Sunna* ii, 411–412, in a report quoting a number of Ibn Ḥanbal's students; al-Khallāl, *al-Sunna* ii, 426; and Ibn Ḥarb al-Kirmānī in the form of a question addressed to Ibn Ḥanbal, al-Kirmānī, *al-Sunna* (excerpts from his *masāʾil*) 255–256; see also Ahmed, Some aspects 56–61.

153 Madelung, Origins 504–525; *ThG* iv, 625–630; Martin, Createdness i, 467–471.

154 Al-Lālakāʾī, *Sharḥ* i, 89.

155 See also the more detailed opinion attributed to Ibn ʿUyayna in Ibn Taymiyya, *Sharḥ* 120.

156 Al-Lālakāʾī, Sharḥ i, 87; in Abū Nuʿaym, *Ḥilya* vii, 30, "*man zaʿama anna ʿqul: huwa Allāhu aḥadʾ makhlūq fa-qad kafara bi-llāh ʿazza wa-jalla.*"

157 Al-Ṭuyūrī, *al-Ṭuyūriyyāt* ii, 542.

158 Madelung, Origins 519.

4.3 *Tenets Apparent in Only One Creed*

4.3.1 Al-Awzāʿī

In directions such as "Forebear with the *sunna*," "Comply with the *sunna* and avoid innovations," and "We follow the *sunna* wherever it turns," al-Awzāʿī emphasizes the concept of the Sunna,[159] which, as Juynboll has argued, began to be identified exclusively with *sunnat al-nabī* toward the end of the first/seventh century.[160] The term also denotes a commendable path to follow and a praiseworthy precedence. Furthermore, it could refer to the living tradition of the community, including a variety of creditable behavior that could be molded on the model of the Prophet Muhammad, as well as those of Abū Bakr and ʿUmar, the caliphs, and pious and righteous men of the earliest generation of Muslims, or the accepted path of a certain community of believers.[161] The term did not necessarily evoke the authority of *ḥadīth*, which, nonetheless, was still in the process of being consolidated. Thus, it seems that one of the fundamental rationales for the pro-Umayyad al-Awzāʿī in invoking the term was to express the concerns of a body of believers who shared common views and practices which labeled them as different from other groups within the community—say, the Qadaris, the Murji'a, and other "innovators"—be it on the political or the theological level. Here, we encounter the increasing importance of al-Awzāʿī's call "to adhere to the Community (*luzūm al-jamāʿa*)," and to populate the mosques.

Furthermore, al-Awzāʿī's *iʿtiqād* underscores a prohibition of polemics (*al-jidāl*) and delving [into trivia] (*al-taʿammuq*).[162] The prohibition of these two practices is repeatedly mentioned in *ḥadīth*s and dicta attributed to the Successors. Interestingly, it is also attested in the *K. Sharḥ al-sunna* of Ghulām Khalīl.[163]

4.3.2 Al-Thawrī

4.3.2.1 *Paradise Promised to Ten Companions*

In Sufyān al-Thawrī's *iʿtiqād*, there is a mention of the ten Companions who were promised entry to Paradise (*al-ʿashara al-mubashshara bi-l-janna*).[164] Al-Lālakāʾī's version relates simply that they are ten, from the Quraysh tribe. Al-

159 Cf. Bravmann, *Spiritual background* 123–129, 160–166; Jarrar, *Die Prophetenbiographie* 4–12.

160 Juynboll, *Muslim tradition* 30.

161 Cf. Boekhoff-van der Voort, Concept 27–33.

162 Ghulām Khalīl, *Sharḥ* § 85; Dutton, *Origins* 20.

163 Ghulām Khalīl, *Sharḥ* §§ 9, 49, 61, 133, 136.

164 Al-Lālakāʾī, *Sharḥ* i, 87; al-Ṭuyūrī, *al-Ṭuyūriyyāt* ii, 540; for the concept, Wensinck, al-ʿAshara al-mubashshara; *ThG* i, 21–22; Yazigi, Ḥadīth al-ʿashara.

Ṭuyūrī's version, however, specifies ten Companions by name, whereas the names of Abū ʿUbayda b. al-Jarrāḥ and ʿAbd al-Raḥmān b. ʿAwf had been a matter of dispute. Also, some such lists mention one of these two Companions and dismiss the other.[165]

4.3.2.2 *Praying behind the Ruler*

Al-Thawrī's *iʿtiqād* mentions the tenet that became common in early creeds—namely, "to pray behind every [ruler], good or wicked."[166] It appears in *al-Fiqh al-absaṭ*, attributed to Abū Ḥanīfa,[167] and in works by Aḥmad b. Ḥanbal, as well as in certain other sources, including the *K. Sharḥ al-sunna* by Ghulām Khalīl.[168] The creed asserts that prayers other than Friday prayers and the prayers of the two feasts are to be performed only behind him whom he trusts from the *ahl al-sunna wa-l-jamāʿa*.

4.3.2.3 *Ritual Ablution*

Al-Thawrī's *iʿtiqād* also include two points relating to ritual practice, one of which is "passing the wetted hands over the shoes in ritual ablution" (*al-masḥ ʿalā l-khuffayn*).[169] This obligation appears to have permeated early proto-Sunni creeds[170] and to have become an article of orthopraxy at an early time. Abū Ḥanīfa is believed to have advised, when asked about the *sunna wa-l-jamāʿa*,[171] "to give preference to the two *shaykhs* [i.e., Abū Bakr and ʿUmar], to love the two sons-in-law [of the Prophet, i.e., ʿUthmān and ʿAlī], and to uphold [the concept of] *al-masḥ ʿalā l-khuffayn*."

The tenet of *al-masḥ* was the subject of much controversy among the various Muslim factions. This dispute appears to have been instigated by the exegetical uncertainty among the Companions of the Prophet concerning Q 5:6 (*al-Māʾida*).[172] Juynboll maintains that "probably just after the Prophet's demise, the *masḥ* issue became a lively point of discussion, if not already during his

165 Cf. the commentary on the Arabic text of Ghulām Khalīl §14.

166 Only in the version of al-Lālakāʾī, *Sharḥ* i, 88, is there an addition about *jihād* with the ruler; see on this our comments on the Arabic text, §§115 and 144.

167 See also al-Ḥakīm al-Samarqandī (d. 342/953), *al-Sawād al-aʿẓam* (MS. American University of Beirut), fol. 12, 14, 21.

168 Concerning the mention of *jihād*, cf. our comments on the Arabic text, §144.

169 In Abū Nuʿaym, *Ḥilya* vii, 208, a tradition about *al-masḥ* on the authority of Ibn ʿUyayna.

170 See our comments on §24 in the Arabic text; and also al-Ḥakīm al-Samarqandī (d. 342/953), *al-Sawād al-aʿẓam* (MS. American University of Beirut), fols. 21.

171 Al-Kāsānī, *Badāʾiʿ* i, 7; see Juynboll, (Re)Appraisal 337.

172 Cf. Pellat, al-Masḥ ʿalā ʾl-khuffayn; Jarrar, Ibn Abī Yaḥyā 208.

lifetime."[173] Mālik b. Anas also seems not to have been clear about the practice of *al-masḥ* as an established *ʿamal* as "a broader concept which includes not only *sunna* established by the Prophet but also the *ijtihād* of later authorities," as Dutton maintains.[174] Dutton also argues that "Mālik appears to have changed his mind during his life, which suggests that no particular practice had gained predominance in Madina by that time."[175]

The *masḥ* issue also became yet another parting of the ways in the performance of ritual practices between the *ahl al-sunna* and Shiʿis.[176] Early proto-Sunni traditionists and *fuqahāʾ* endorsed the *masḥ*, whereas the Zaydis and the Imamis disapproved of it.[177] Nonetheless, Sulaymān b. Jarīr al-Raqqī, the head of the Jariri branch of the Zaydis, as well as the Batris, admitted *masḥ*.[178]

Studying an illustrative example of a major *ḥadīth* cluster on *masḥ* with al-Aʿmash as the common link in these text transmissions, Juynboll notes that "it is not a case of *tawātur*, but rather an accumulated bunch of mostly well-known traditions, for which Muslim *ḥadīth* experts used the technical term *mashhūr*, all brought together under one seemingly comprehensive label."[179]

The other point in al-Thawrī's *iʿtiqād* relevant to components of prayer strongly advises "not to read the *basmala* out loud at the beginning of prayers."[180] This issue also became a matter of debate among the early *fuqahāʾ*, as Haider has shown in a meticulous study.[181]

4.3.3 Sufyān b. ʿUyayna

In the *iʿtiqād* attributed to Sufyān b. ʿUyayna, seven points relate to events on the Day of Judgment. These are to be found also in almost all of the later creeds.[182]

173 Juynboll, (Re)Appraisal 337.
174 Dutton, *Origins* 2.
175 Ibid., 40–41.
176 See an anecdote concerning the ʿAbbasid caliph al-Manṣūr in al-Azdī, *Tārīkh* 212; and cf. Wensinck, *Muslim creed* 158–160.
177 Al-Hādī, *al-Aḥkām* i, 67; Ibn al-Murtaḍā, *al-Baḥr* ii, 68–72; al-Ṣadūq, *Man lā yaḥḍuruh* i, 40; al-Ṭūsī, *al-Istibṣār* i, 76–77.
178 Strothmann, *Kultus* 21–46; Jarrar, Ibn Abī Yaḥyā 209–211.
179 Juynboll, (Re)Appraisal 336.
180 Al-Lālakāʾī, *Sharḥ* i, 87.
181 Haider, *Origins* 57–94; id., Muʿāwiya 48–54.
182 See the comments on §§ 13, 36, and 37 in the Arabic text.

5 Development of Tenets and Their Distribution

The *iʿtiqādāt* of the second/eighth century attempted to recapitulate and confute some of the fundamental controversial questions that were raised during the formative period. Yet, during the third/ninth century—and as a result of the *miḥna*—importance was given to certain other aspects of the matter, which became even more poignant. Thus, the development of confessional creeds came to be one of the main features of the third/ninth century, as certain scholars made significant efforts to redefine and delineate the premises of a normative "orthodoxy" anchored in the Sunna. Following Sherman Jackson, we are inclined to perceive that which is needed to establish "orthodoxy" as, above all, authority. This authority "may be formal or *informal*," depending on reputation.[183]

This having been said, two caveats need to be made. First, those very early creeds were composed in a milieu characterized by a "zero-orthodoxy," as Knysh has put it.[184] The efforts of Aḥmad b. Ḥanbal in collecting and assorting *ḥadīth*s and his endeavor to base items of faith, conduct, and practice on the authority of the Prophet and his Companions, exemplified predilection for the authoritative Sunna as the only "authentic" source of knowledge. Moreover, with al-Mutawakkil's avowal of *al-sunna wa-l-jamāʿa*, devotion to the Sunna and a heightened "*sunna*-consciousness" prevailed.[185] Second, the creeds vary in length, and there is no clear guiding principle in the configuration of the respective manuals. They are mostly arranged at random, shifting from one point concerning the unity of God or His attributes to another, or concerning the theoretical conception of belief, to addressing an item of religious practice, and then eventually turning again to a previous item concerning faith. It is noteworthy, however, that the authors of these creeds avoided any rhetorical dimensions and expressed themselves most clearly through "the teachings of the Prophet and his Companions" (as the respective texts were collected and explained by the proto-Sunnis), as well as through the teachings of other specific individuals. The authors of these creeds laid emphasis on the fixation of new thematic items and teachings of the pious forebears (*salaf*). These teach-

---

183 Jackson, *Boundaries* 29–30. See also Ben Achour, *Aux fondements* 7, where he argues that "orthodoxy" needs the solidarity of the *ʿulamāʾ*, the sultan, and the masses; on the process of the formation of this early "orthodoxy," 2–9, 18–20.

184 Knysh, "Orthodoxy" 64: "Any pondering on the data of the Revelation, any deviation from its narrow pragmatic and literal interpretation, from the established religious practice, were to be rejected as deplorable 'innovations'."

185 See also Ben Achour, *Aux fondements* 22.

ings were supported by verses from the Quran and prophetic *ḥadīth*s. Hence an *iʿtiqād* came to resemble, to a certain degree, an exercise in exegesis.

The following outline of major tenets featuring in these *iʿtiqādāt* shall help us further clarify their major characteristics, including their thematic similarities and shared doctrines. For example, three of the *iʿtiqādāt* start with a reference to the Companions, the Successors, the *salaf*, or other earlier scholars, apparently to lend their creeds more legitimacy and authority:

- Al-Rabaʿī: "Aḥmad b. Ḥanbal, the imam of the *ahl al-sunna*, who endured the *miḥna*, told me, 'Ninety[186] men from among the Successors, the imams of the Muslims, the imams of the forbearers (*al-salaf*), and the legists of the provinces all have agreed that …' "[187]
- Ḥarb al-Kirmānī/al-Iṣṭakhrī: "These are the teachings (*madhāhib*) of the people of learning, the *aṣḥāb al-athar*, and the *ahl al-sunna*,[188] who held fast to its veins and those who are known by it [i.e., known for their adherence to the Sunna], and who are sought after in matters pertaining to it. [And this has been so] from [the time] of the Companions of the Prophet—may peace and blessings be upon him—till our present day, and I have caught up with a number of the *ʿulamāʾ* of al-Ḥijāz and al-Shām and others, who follow these teachings."
- Al-Bukhārī: "I met more than a thousand men of the people of learning from the people of al-Ḥijāz, Mecca, Madina, Kufa, Basra, Wāsiṭ, Baghdad, Syria and Egypt. I met them often, one generation after the other …"[189]

One issue, which will be dealt with in greater detail in the epilogue, must nonetheless be mentioned here—namely, that none of the abovementioned creeds addresses the practice of "commanding right and forbidding wrong" (*al-amr bi-l-maʿrūf wa-l-nahy ʿan al-munkar*).

The following overview identifies central themes apparent in third/ninth-century tenets of faith, with authors indicated.[190]

186 Ibn al-Jawzī, *Manāqib* i, 324, "seventy."

187 Ibn Abī Yaʿlā, *Ṭabaqāt* (al-Fiqī) i, 130, (al-ʿUthaymīn) i, 349; Cooperson, Ibn al-Jawzī, *Manāqib* i, 327, understood the Successors and Imamas to be part of the "seventy jurisprudents from different towns."

188 In a similar formula at the end of the creed he refers to "*ahl al-sunna wa-l-jamāʿa*."

189 Al-Bukhārī enumerates a list of names belonging to various provinces, al-Lālakāʾī, *Sharḥ* i, 102.

190 Names in round brackets refer to the creeds attributed to Ibn Ḥanbal; names between square brackets to other creeds of the third/ninth century.

A) **Central importance of the *sunna wa-l-jamāʿa*:**

A.1. Religion (*al-dīn*) consists of the Quran, tradition and Sunna.
(Ḥarb al-Kirmānī/al-Iṣṭakhrī)

A.2. The Companions are the source of knowledge in matters religious.
(ʿAbdūs b. Mālik)

A.3. Everyone is called upon to comply (*ittibāʿ* or *iqtidāʾ*).
(ʿAbdūs b. Mālik)

A.3.1. Conformism and due compliance in religious matters (*al-taqlīd fī l-dīn*).
(Ḥarb al-Kirmānī/al-Iṣṭakhrī)

A.4. The essence of the Sunna is to adhere to the Community.
[al-Tustarī]

A.5. All innovation (*bidʿa*) commits one to misguidance.
(ʿAbdūs b. Mālik) [al-Bukhārī]

A.6. The Sunna is not a matter of analogy, nor may it be grasped by parables, nor yet is it dictated by the inclinations of men.
(ʿAbdūs b. Mālik; al-Andarābī/al-Sarakhsī; Ibn ʿAwf al-Ḥimṣī)

A.7. In matters of religion, "why" is not to be asked, nor is "how."
[Ibn al-Madīnī; Rāzīs]

A.8. The Sunna explicates the Quran.
(ʿAbdūs b. Mālik)

B) **Faith:**

B.1. Belief that there is no God but God and that Muhammad is His messenger (*al-shahāda*); and confirm all what has been brought by the prophets and messengers.
(al-Andarābī/al-Sarakhsī)

B.2. Faith consists in [a.] verbal profession and in works, and giving equal precedence, and [b.] intention and its fulfillment.
(Ḥarb al-Kirmānī/al-Iṣṭakhrī; al-Rabaʿī; ʿAbdūs b. Mālik; Ibn ʿAwf al-Ḥimṣī; al-Sarakhsī) [al-Ḥumaydī; al-Bukhārī = verbal profession and action; Rāzīs]

B.3. Faith admits of increase and diminution; increasing as God wishes and diminishing until it is no more.
(Ḥarb al-Kirmānī/al-Iṣṭakhrī+ *istithnāʾ*; Musaddad) [al-Ḥumaydī; Ibn al-Madīnī]

B.4. Do not have doubt concerning your belief.
(al-Andarābī/al-Sarakhsī) [al-Tustarī]

B.5. Predestination: persevere in upholding God's decree and believe in God's fate, the good and the bad, the sweet and the bitter.
(Ḥarb al-Kirmānī/al-Iṣṭakhrī; al-Rabaʿī, first part only; ʿAbdūs b. Mālik;

Ibn ʿAwf al-Ḥimṣī; Musaddad; al-Sarakhsī) [al-Ḥumaydī; Ibn al-Madīnī; al-Bukhārī; Rāzīs; al-Tustarī]

B.6. Penitence is a religious duty.
(ʿAbdūs b. Mālik; Ibn ʿAwf al-Ḥimṣī) [Ibn al-Madīnī]

C) God and His attributes:

C.1. Creation of the heavens and earths.
(Ḥarb al-Kirmānī/al-Iṣṭakhrī)

C.2. God's Throne.
(Ḥarb al-Kirmānī/al-Iṣṭakhrī + abundant details; Rāzīs) [al-Ḥumaydī]

C.2.1. The Chair is the place of His feet.
(Ḥarb al-Kirmānī/al-Iṣṭakhrī)

C.3. God's attributes: anthropomorphic traditions.
(Ḥarb al-Kirmānī/al-Iṣṭakhrī; Ibn ʿAwf al-Ḥimṣī; Musaddad) [al-Ḥumaydī]

C.4. Created Adam in His image.
(Ḥarb al-Kirmānī/al-Iṣṭakhrī; Ibn ʿAwf al-Ḥimṣī)

C.5. Spoke to Moses.
(Ḥarb al-Kirmānī/al-Iṣṭakhrī; Musaddad)

C.6. God took Abraham as friend (*khalīl*).
(Musaddad)

C.7. The Quran is God's uncreated speech.
(Ḥarb al-Kirmānī/al-Iṣṭakhrī; al-Rabaʿī; ʿAbdūs b. Mālik + *lafẓ* and *waqf*; al-Andarābī/al-Sarakhsī; Musaddad (details); Ibn ʿAwf al-Ḥimṣī) [al-Ḥumaydī; Ibn al-Madīnī; Rāzīs + *lafẓ* and *waqf*]

D) Caliphate

D.1. Excellence and precedence of the Arabs.
(Ḥarb al-Kirmānī/al-Iṣṭakhrī)

D.2. The Caliphate is the prerogative of the Quraysh.
(Ḥarb al-Kirmānī/al-Iṣṭakhrī)

E) The Community:

E.1. The Companions: Excellence of the Companions; mention their virtues, and take no notice of their shortcomings. More so, none of them you should mention except favorably.
(Ḥarb al-Kirmānī/al-Iṣṭakhrī; al-Rabaʿī; ʿAbdūs b. Mālik; al-Andarābī/al-Sarakhsī; Ibn ʿAwf al-Ḥimṣī; Musaddad; al-Sarakhsī) [al-Ḥumaydī; al-Bukhārī; al-Tustarī]

E.1.1. Ranking the best after the Prophet.

Ḥarb al-Kirmānī/al-Iṣṭakhrī = Abū Bakr, ʿUmar, ʿUthmān, ʿAlī (some stopped at ʿUthmān)
Al-Rabaʿī = Abū Bakr, ʿUmar, ʿUthmān, ʿAlī
Musaddad = Abū Bakr, ʿUmar, ʿUthmān, ʿAlī + Ṭalḥa, al-Zubayr, Saʿd (Ibn Abī Waqqāṣ), Saʿīd (Ibn Nufayl), Ibn ʿAwf, Abū ʿUbayda b. al-Jarrāḥ
ʿAbdūs b. Mālik = Abū Bakr, ʿUmar, ʿUthmān + *aṣḥāb al-shūrā* + *ahl Badr* from among the *muhājirūn* + *ahl Badr* from amongst the *Anṣār*; who ever met him for a year, a month, a day, an hour, or have seen him
Al-Andarābī/al-Sarakhsī = Abū Bakr, ʿUmar, ʿUthmān + ʿAlī, Ṭalḥa, al-Zubayr, Ibn ʿAwf, Ibn Abī Waqqāṣ, Ibn Nufayl and all other Companions
Ibn ʿAwf al-Ḥimṣī = Abū Bakr, ʿUmar, ʿUthmān, ʿAlī (+ question whether Ibn Ḥanbal stopped at ʿAlī);
Ibn al-Madīnī = Abū Bakr, ʿUmar, ʿUthmān + ʿAlī, Ṭalḥa, al-Zubayr, Ibn ʿAwf, Saʿd b. Mālik + who ever met him for a year, a month, a day, an hour, or have seen him;
Rāzīs = Abū Bakr, ʿUmar, ʿUthmān, ʿAlī

E.2. It is forbidden to fight or to revolt against them, even if they were despotic.
(Ḥarb al-Kirmānī/al-Iṣṭakhrī; al-Rabaʿī; ʿAbdūs b. Mālik; al-Andarābī/al-Sarakhsī) [Ibn al-Madīnī; al-Bukhārī = *lā yarā l-sayf aʿlā ummat*[i] *Muḥammad*; Rāzīs; al-Tustarī]

E.2.1. The civil war: Forbearance in case of civil war (*fitna*) and shun partisanship.
(Ḥarb al-Kirmānī/al-Iṣṭakhrī; al-Andarābī/al-Sarakhsī)

E.2.2. Fighting dissidence and its conducts (*al-khawārij*).
(ʿAbdūs b. Mālik) [Ibn al-Madīnī]

E.3. Conduct within the Community

E.3.1. Preserving the prayers and Friday prayers (abandoning prayers equals unbelief)
[ʿAbdūs b. Mālik; al-Ḥumaydī (prayer, fasting, and pilgrimage; Musaddad); Ibn al-Madīnī]

E.3.2. Judging fellow Muslims: Do not bear false witness against Muslim brethren.
(al-Rabaʿī; ʿAbdūs b. Mālik)

E.3.3. Withhold testimony as to someone's true belief until he complies with the laws and codices (*sharāʾiʿ*) of Islam; hope and fear for him.
(Ḥarb al-Kirmānī/al-Iṣṭakhrī; ʿAbdūs b. Mālik; al-Andarābī/al-Sarakhsī; Ibn ʿAwf al-Ḥimṣī) [Ibn al-Madīnī; al-Bukhārī; al-Rāzī]

E.3.4. Offering funeral prayers to the deceased from among the Community.

('Abdūs b. Mālik; Ibn 'Awf al-Ḥimṣī; Musaddad) [Ibn al-Madīnī; al-Tustarī]

E.4. Hypocrisy and unbelief (citing *ḥadīths*).
('Abdūs b. Mālik; Ibn 'Awf al-Ḥimṣī) [Ibn al-Madīnī]

E.5. Gain and commerce (*al-makāsib*) are permissible.
(Ḥarb al-Kirmānī/al-Iṣṭakhrī; al-Andarābī/al-Sarakhsī)

E.6. Prohibition of *ra'y* and *qiyās*.
(Ḥarb al-Kirmānī/al-Iṣṭakhrī)

E.7. Apprehension of theological disputation, of polemics, and argumentation.
(Al-Raba'ī; 'Abdūs b. Mālik) [Ibn al-Madīnī; al-Tustarī]

F) Orthopraxy:

F.1. To pass the wetted hands over the shoes in ritual ablution (*al-masḥ 'alā l-khuffayn*).
(al-Andarābī/al-Sarakhsī; Musaddad) [al-Tustarī]

F.2. Prayer

F.2.1. Abandoning prayers equals unbelief.
('Abdūs b. Mālik) [Ibn al-Madīnī]

F.2.2. Second call for prayer (*al-iqāma*), only once.[191]
(Musaddad)

F.2.3. Raising hands in *takbīr* (i.e., declaring *Allāhu akbar*, God is great), (*raf' al-yadayn*).[192]
(Musaddad)

---

191 Ibn Hāni' al-Naysābūrī, *Masā'il* i, 40; al-Marwazī, *Ikhtilāf* 175–176; al-Jaṣṣāṣ, *Sharḥ* i, 548–558; Juynboll, Iḳāma.

192 Raising the hands at the beginning of prayer, commencing with the first *takbīra* (*takbīrat al-iḥrām*), has found general consensus by all Muslim factions. However, raising the hands during prayer at other junctures thereafter, such as prostration and when rising to the sitting position, is disputed. The matter has been a case of contention since an early time. For Mālik b. Anas, see Dutton, *Origins* 46. For Ibn Ḥanbal, see al-Kawsaj, *Masā'il* i, 515, no. 187; Abū Dāwūd, *Masā'il Aḥmad* i, 50–51; Ibn Hāni' al-Naysābūrī, *Masā'il* i, 49–50; Ṣāliḥ b. Aḥmad, *Masā'il* 152, no. 549; 324–325, nos. 1244–1246; Ibn al-Mundhir al-Naysābūrī, *al-Ishrāf* ii, 26–28. See furthermore al-Baghawī, *Juz' al-masā'il* 15 (approving *raf'* after prostration). Al-Bukhārī compiled a book of traditions confirming *raf'* (see bibliography). For the Zaydis, see Aḥmad b. 'Īsā, *Ra'b al-ṣad'* i, 233–237; al-Jaṣṣāṣ, *Sharḥ* i, 597–607; Ibn Qudāma, *al-Mughnī* ii, 170–174; and Fierro, Polémique 69–90. The caliph al-Ma'mūn in 216/831 introduced an additional three *takbīrāt* at the end of prayers. This measure was first initiated in his army. Al-Ṭabarī, *Tārīkh* viii, 626; Ibn Kathīr, *al-Bidāya* xi, 55–56.

F.2.4. Pronouncing Amen after the Fāṭiḥa.[193]
(Musaddad)
F.2.5. Shortening prayers while traveling.
(al-Andarābī/al-Sarakhsī)
F.2.6. Two prostrations upon entering the mosque (*taḥiyyat al-masjid*).
(Musaddad)
F.2.7. Night prayer—odd number (*al-witr*), only one *rakʿa*.[194]
(Musaddad)
F.2.8. Number of *takbīrāt* in funerals.
(al-Andarābī/al-Sarakhsī; Musaddad)
F.3. Stoning (*al-rajm*).
(ʿAbdūs b. Mālik) [Ibn al-Madīnī]
F.4. Marriage and divorce.
F.4.1. Marriage becomes legal with a guardian and two just witnesses.
(Musaddad)
F.4.2. Prohibition of temporary marriage (*al-mutʿa*).
(Musaddad)
F.4.3. Divorce (thrice).
(Musaddad)

G) Eschatology:
G.1. The descending of Jesus (al-Mahdī and/or *al-dajjāl*).
(ʿAbdūs b. Mālik; Musaddad) [Ibn al-Madīnī]
G.2. The Horn (*al-Ṣūr*).
(Ḥarb al-Kirmānī/al-Iṣṭakhrī; Musaddad)
G.3. Resurrection and Afterlife.
G.3.1. Belief in the veritable truth of Paradise and Hell, and in their being created.
(al-Iṣṭakhrī/Ḥarb; ʿAbdūs b. Mālik (cites *ḥadīths*); Ibn ʿAwf al-Ḥimṣī (cites *ḥadīths*); Musaddad) [Ibn al-Madīnī (cites *ḥadīths*); Rāzīs]
G.3.2. Paradise Virgins do not die at Resurrection.
(al-Iṣṭakhrī)

193 Whereas Sufyān al-Thawrī was of the opinion that "Amen" should not be pronounced, al-Shāfiʿī, Ibn Ḥanbal, and others said that it should be pronounced loudly; cf. al-Marwazī, *Ikhtilāf* 105. See also al-Kawsaj, *Masāʾil* i, 547, nos. 210–211; Abū Dāwūd, *Masāʾil Aḥmad* i, 49; Ibn Hāniʾ al-Naysābūrī, *Masāʾil* i, 45; Ṣāliḥ b. Aḥmad, *Masāʾil* 149; Ibn al-Mundhir al-Naysābūrī, *al-Ishrāf* ii, 23–24; al-Jaṣṣāṣ, *Sharḥ* i, 594–596.

194 According to Aḥmad in Abū Dāwūd, *Masāʾil Aḥmad* i, 94, and Ibn Hāniʾ al-Naysābūrī, *Masāʾil* i, 99, he did not recommend a single *rakʿa*.

G.3.2. Souls will be retained in the grave.
(Musaddad)

G.3.3. Belief in the torment of the grave (some mention **Munkar** and **Nakīr**).
(Ḥarb al-Kirmānī/al-Iṣṭakhrī; ʿAbdūs b. Mālik; al-Andarābī/al-Sarakhsī; Ibn ʿAwf al-Ḥimṣī; Musaddad) [Ibn al-Madīnī]

G.3.4. Belief in the Balance (*al-mīzān*) on the Day of Resurrection.
(Ḥarb al-Kirmānī/al-Iṣṭakhrī; ʿAbdūs b. Mālik; Ibn ʿAwf al-Ḥimṣī; Musaddad) [Ibn al-Madīnī; Rāzīs]

G.3.5. Tablet and Pen.
(Ḥarb al-Kirmānī/al-Iṣṭakhrī)

G.3.6. Thin Bridge (*al-ṣirāṭ*) stretched over the Fire.
(Ḥarb al-Kirmānī/al-Iṣṭakhrī; Musaddad) [Rāzīs]

G.3.7. Belief in the Prophets' sanctum (*ḥawḍ*).
(Ḥarb al-Kirmānī/al-Iṣṭakhrī; ʿAbdūs b. Mālik; al-Andarābī/al-Sarakhsī; Ibn ʿAwf al-Ḥimṣī; Musaddad) [Ibn al-Madīnī; Rāzīs]

G.3.9. God speaks to each individual on the Day of Judgment; no veils then, and no mediators.
(ʿAbdūs b. Mālik; Ibn ʿAwf al-Ḥimṣī) [Ibn al-Madīnī]

G.3.10. Belief in the Prophet's intercession on behalf of the sinners on the Day of Judgment.
(Ḥarb al-Kirmānī/al-Iṣṭakhrī; ʿAbdūs b. Mālik; al-Andarābī/al-Sarakhsī; Ibn ʿAwf al-Ḥimṣī; Musaddad) [Ibn al-Madīnī; Rāzīs]

G.3.11. Some people will be brought out of the Fire after they have been burnt and charred.
(ʿAbdūs b. Mālik; Ibn ʿAwf al-Ḥimṣī; al-Iṣṭakhrī/Ḥarb; al-Sarakhsī) [Ibn al-Madīnī]

G.3.12. Belief in the Beatific Vision of God on the Day of Resurrection.
(Ḥarb al-Kirmānī/al-Iṣṭakhrī; ʿAbdūs b. Mālik; Ibn ʿAwf al-Ḥimṣī) [al-Ḥumaydī; Rāzīs]

G.3.13. The Prophet has seen God [during the Nocturnal Journey].
(ʿAbdūs b. Mālik; Ibn ʿAwf al-Ḥimṣī)

CHAPTER 4

Toward Common Ground: The People of the Sunna and the Community

1 The *Ahl al-Sunna wa-l-Jamāʿa*

It is important at the beginning of this chapter to recapitulate the particular meaning of the term *sunna*, which became current during the third/ninth century. What stands out are the significant aspects that came to define this term, which was also used in relation to some particular adherents of the *ahl al-ḥadīth* in the form of *ṣāḥib sunna*,[1] denoting a devotee of the Sunna.[2] Gautier H.A. Juynboll argued that over the years "the definition of the appellative was subject to modification," thus "*ṣāḥib sunna wa-jamāʿa* may be interpreted as highlighting the bearer's political preference."[3] We have seen in chapter 3, for example, that Baqiyya b. al-Walīd (d. 197/812) used to say that whoever praises al-Awzāʿī is an adherent of the Sunna (*ṣāḥib sunna*), and whoever slanders him is an adherent of novelties (*ṣāḥib bidʿa*).[4] It is clear, in this particular case, that *ṣāḥib sunna* refers to a position congruent with the acceptance of a correct creed, whose holder stands distinguished as an enthusiast of the Sunna and in contradistinction to innovators. In this sense, a *ṣāḥib sunna* is a devotee of the dogmatic principles of the *ahl al-sunna*, such that he sees his distinctiveness in his upholding of a set of beliefs to which he devotes his life.[5]

1 Juynboll, Excursus 321, underscores the fact that "*ṣāḥib ḥadīth* and *ṣāḥib sunna* are never to be equated automatically, at least not at first, nor during the entire second/eighth or third/ninth centuries."

2 Nawas, Appellation 18, argues that only "about 3% of the ulama of the early and classical period were called a *ṣāḥib sunna*"; the majority (about half of them) lived and died during the pivotal third/ninth century.

3 Juynboll, Excursus 320.

4 Ibn ʿAsākir, *Tārīkh* xxxv, 176.

5 Ḥanbal b. Isḥāq claims that his cousin Aḥmad b. Ḥanbal had used the epithet *ṣāḥib sunna* during the *miḥna* in a private session with the caliph al-Muʿtaṣim to describe a certain Ṣāliḥ al-Rashīdī (cf. Ḥanbal ibn Isḥāq, *Dhikr miḥnat Aḥmad* 48). This information, however, seems odd, as Ṣāliḥ, Aḥmad's son, does not mention it when he narrates the same event. Furthermore, both Abū Nuʿaym, *Ḥilya* ix, 199, and al-Dhahabī, *Siyar* xi, 248, quote Ṣāliḥ b. Aḥmad. In al-Dhahabī, *Siyar* xi, 248, Aḥmad seems not to have known him: "*qad samiʿtu bi-hi.*" Furthermore, van Ess identifies Ṣāliḥ al-Rashīdī as the son of the caliph Hārūn al-Rashīd, cf. *Der Eine* ii, 1274.

 | DOI:10.1163/9789004429055_006

Richard Frank has pointed out that "the Ḥanbalites sometimes speak of 'sunnah' meaning not simply the texts but the texts taken integrally with their own interpretation of them. They refer, that is, to their interpretation of the texts as 'sunnah.'"[6] This rightly suggests that the tag *ṣāḥib sunna* refers to someone who holds fast to a certain set of doctrines that distinguishes him from other members, who belong to the general label of *ahl al-ḥadīth* and *ahl al-sunna*.[7]

Josef van Ess maintains that the first use of the term apparently goes back to Sufyān al-Thawrī (d. 161/778), and that it was taken up by ʿAbdallāh b. al-Mubārak (d. 181/797) and introduced in Baghdad by Ibn Ḥanbal and in Basra by Ghulām Khalīl.[8]

Indeed a catch-dictum, which is a kind of early conviction, was attributed to ʿAbdallāh b. al-Mubārak by Ghulām Khalīl.[9] Under the rubric of an alleged prophetic tradition, which became widespread in later generations, Ibn al-Mubārak specifies "the origin of seventy-two deviating sects" in four sects—namely, the Qadaris, the Murji'a, the Shiʿa, and the Kharijites. Ibn al-Mubārak then attempts to indicate the innovations that threatened the doctrinal authority of the *ahl al-sunna* and to clarify those tenets that the proto-Sunnis had acquiesced to and that informed the main traits of the Sunna, so that whoever abjures the mentioned innovations and closely follows the precepts specified in his dictum is truly a "*ṣāḥib sunna*."[10]

The profound significance of this matter is, in effect, articulated by Ghulām Khalīl in a number of pointers that he elucidates in his *K. Sharḥ al-sunna*,[11] and which he calls the character traits or principles of the Sunna (*khiṣāl al-sunna*).[12] Ghulām Khalīl expressly addresses the *ahl al-sunna wa-l-jamāʿa* and appeals to

---

6 Frank, Elements 149.

7 Based on a quantitative approach, Nawas, Appellation 20, concludes that "*sunna* is obviously not equated with hadith. To the contrary, the evidence seems to corroborate Goldziher's finding that initially *sunna* referred to a general 'standard of correctitude' that was subsequently restricted to the conduct of the Prophet as exemplar and norm." See, however, Lucas, *Constructive critics* 195–197.

8 Van Ess, *Der Eine* ii, 1273–1274.

9 Cf. the English translation, § 144. In certain sources, this dictum is attributed to Yūsuf b. Asbāṭ (d. 196/812); see the comments on § 88 (Arabic text).

10 See § 144; Juynboll, Excursus 321; and van Ess, *Der Eine* i, 74–77.

11 See §§ 86, 88, 104, 115, 117, 122, 132, 143, and 148. Among the traits that establish the Sunna according to the Basran judge ʿAbdallāh b. Siwār al-ʿAnbarī (d. 228/842) are: "The precedence of Abū Bakr, ʿUmar and ʿUthmān, showing love to all the Companions, refraining from mentioning their shortcomings, and having great hope for them due to their company to the Messenger of God—may peace and blessings be upon him; and that faith consists in both, verbal profession and action." Cf. Ḥarb al-Kirmānī, *K. al-Sunna* 264, no. 508.

12 See § 143.

them to adhere strictly to all the principles given in his book if they want to be seen as a "*ṣāḥib sunna*."[13] The designation *ahl al-sunna wa-l-jamāʿa* was an appellation already in use at that time, as we have seen earlier.

2 The Book Title *Sharḥ al-sunna*

The term *sharḥ*—meaning "elucidation" or "explication," as evident in certain works dated to toward the end of the second/eighth century in relation to the Sunna—was apparently used to indicate an entire set of doctrines. The *ḥadīth* scholar and mystic ʿAbdallāh b. al-Mubārak, for example, is reported to have praised Abū Bakr b. ʿAyyāsh (d. 193/808), the renowned Kufan Quran reciter,[14] saying, "He had never seen someone more capable of *elucidating* the Sunna (*ashraḥ lil-sunna min*) than Abū Bakr b. ʿAyyāsh."[15] However, the term *ashraḥ* is rather odd here, and al-Dhahabī (d. 748/1347) reads it as *asraʿ ilā l-sunna*, meaning that he was "promptly ready to adopt [a tenet considered part of] the Sunna."[16] But al-Sakhāwī (d. 643/1245), again, also has *ashraḥ*.[17]

Although the sources confirm that Ibn ʿAyyāsh was unreliable as a transmitter of *ḥadīth*s, they nonetheless agree that he was an imam in matters of the Sunna.[18] Ibn ʿAyyāsh was an ʿUthmānī, as Abū Dāwūd al-Sijistānī claims.[19] Yet the sources mention an opinion attributed to him, according to which one should not doubt the caliphate of ʿAlī[20]—a view that can probably be explained by Ibn ʿAyyāsh's Kufan origin.[21] Given his declared position on some basic tenets, it seems that he was concerned to clarify some of these creeds by basing his explanation on the Quran (as he did when he claimed that the

13 It is also noteworthy that according to Ghulām Khalīl the Companions of Prophet Muhammad are the People of the Sunna and the Community (*ahl al-sunna wa-l-jamāʿa*), and they are, moreover, the Community and the vast majority (*al-sawād al-aʿẓam*). Cf. §§2, 4.

14 Ibn ʿAdī, *al-Kāmil* v, 40–47; Abū Nuʿaym, *Ḥilya* viii, 303–313; and al-Mizzī, *Tahdhīb* xxxiii, 129–135.

15 Al-Lālakāʾī, *Sharḥ* i, 73.

16 Al-Dhahabī, *Siyar* viii, 496; id., *Maʿrifat al-qurrāʾ* i, 135.

17 Al-Sakhāwī, *Jamāl al-qurrāʾ* ii, 497.

18 Ibn al-Jazarī states that Ibn ʿAyyāsh was counted "among the leaders of the *ahl al-sunna*" (*min aʾimmat ahl al-sunna*); cf. his *Ghāyat al-nihāya* i, 295.

19 Al-Ājurrī, *Suʾālāt* i, 228, no. 274.

20 Ibn ʿAdī, *al-Kāmil* v, 40; Abū Nuʿaym, *Ḥilya* vii, 307.

21 See also Ibn ʿAyyāsh's positive attitude toward the Rāfiḍa when Hārūn al-Rashīd, with specific reference to a *ḥadīth*, asked him if the Rāfiḍa should be killed. Cf. Ibn ʿAdī, *al-Kāmil* v, 42.

caliphate of Abū Bakr is mentioned in the Quran).[22] Remarkably, Ibn ʿAyyāsh is also supposed to have advised the caliph Hārūn al-Rashīd to seek out the faction "*al-ʿiṣāba*," who gave preference to Abū Bakr and ʿUmar in order to honor them.[23] Furthermore, he also used to say that the Quran is the uncreated speech of God, and whoever says otherwise should be considered *zindīq* and be killed.[24] Most interesting, however, is his definition of the Sunna, as he says, "The Sunna in relation to Islam is more precious than the relation of Islam to other religions" (*al-sunna fī l-Islām aʿazz min al-Islām fī sāʾir al-adyān*).[25] To corroborate this study about the usage of the term *sharḥ al-sunna* with more evidence, we draw attention to certain other creeds with the same title. *Sharḥ al-sunna* as a book title also appears in a work by the celebrated student of al-Shāfiʿī, Ismāʿīl b. Yaḥyā l-Muzanī (d. 264/878), an Egyptian contemporary of Ghulām Khalīl.[26] Furthermore, the well-known *ḥadīth* compiler Abū Dāwūd al-Sijistānī (d. 275/888) titles the first chapter of his *K. al-Sunna*, "*Sharḥ al-sunna*." (Here, the author gives two versions of the famous prophetic tradition of "the 72 sects" in Islam.[27]) Likewise, Muḥammad b. Aḥmad al-Malaṭī (d. 377/987) titles a chapter of his book *al-Tanbīh*, "*Bāb mā shuriḥa min bayān al-sunna*."[28]

It should also be noted, however, that some creeds of the third/ninth century use the idiom *uṣūl al-sunna* as an accessible explanation of their content, as demonstrated in the present study.[29] An example is seen in a creed by al-Ḥumaydī (d. 219/834) that bears the title *Uṣūl al-sunna*. Likewise, both the rather dubious creed attributed to ʿUkāsha al-Kirmānī (d. after 225/839) as well as the creed by ʿAbdūs b. Mālik (d. around 250/864) start with the same heading. Ibn Abī Ḥātim al-Rāzī (d. 277/890), in turn, mentions "the teachings of *ahl al-sunna* pertaining to *uṣūl al-dīn*," while Ibn Baṭṭa (d. 387/997) in his creed combines both terms, *sharḥ* and *uṣūl*.[30]

---

22 Ibn ʿAdī, *al-Kāmil* v, 41; al-Dhahabī, *Tārīkh* iv, 1262.

23 Ibn ʿAdī, *al-Kāmil* v, 41.

24 For the use of the term *zindīq*, see *ThG* i, 136, 416–426. Ibn ʿAdī, *al-Kāmil* v, 45; al-Dhahabī, *Siyar* vii, 499; al-Dhahabī, *Tārīkh* iv, 1263.

25 Ibn ʿAdī, *al-Kāmil* v, 45; al-Lālakāʾī, *Sharḥ* i, 73.

26 Heffining, Al-Muzanī *EI*², vii, 822. The book *Sharḥ al-sunna* is not, however, mentioned in the entry. Sezgin mentions a creed by al-Muzanī on the authority of Aḥmad b. Ḥanbal (MS. Shuhayd ʿAlī, 3/2763; cf. *GAS* i, 493). A copy of this manuscript is preserved at the Islamic University in Medina and was used by Jamāl ʿAzzūn for his edition. Cf. his *Ismāʿīl b. Yaḥyā* 50. Interestingly, the title *Sharḥ al-sunna* was derived from the *samāʿ*-chain at the beginning of the manuscript.

27 Abū Dāwūd al-Sijistānī, *al-Sunan* vii, 5–7.

28 Al-Malaṭī, *al-Tanbīh* 11.

29 See also Temel, Uṣūl al-sunna 44–51; and van Ess, *Der Eine* ii, 1209.

30 *Al-Sharḥ wa-l-ibāna ʿalā ūṣūl al-sunna wa-l-diyāna*. On p. 5, he says that the last part of his

3 Thematic Study

In his *K. Sharḥ al-sunna*, Ghulām Khalīl sets out to explicate the meaning of the Sunna and its central role for both *dīn* (religion and way of life) and Islam, as the author puts it. His exposition is introduced by some pointers, so to speak, meant to help establish the "correct" creed, concordant with the truth and the Sunna.[31] This is declared to be executed without any inquiry as to "how" or "why," since theological disputations, controversy, and polemics would render the heart dubious.[32] Instead, Ghulām Khalīl cites verses of the Quran and prophetic traditions, often referring to axioms and dicta accredited to Companions and Successors, as well as traditionists, whose sayings had been accepted as part of the Sunna. In the following we shall identify and analyze certain main tenets of his creed, and delineate the main themes given therein.

As noted in chapter 3 concerning the arrangement and scaffolding of creeds in general,[33] one major point must be underlined in this context, relating to the fact that Ghulām Khalīl paid little attention in his book to any systematic ordering of the materials. It thus represents, rather, a work in which formal sets of principles have simply been listed and briefly commented on for the Muslim community, with no discernable strategic thematic arrangement nor attention paid to literary style. Moreover, the *K. Sharḥ al-sunna* displays a rather superficial thematic structure and little sense of internal literary coherence. The arrangement of themes is sometimes repetitive and, more often than not, there is no clear relationship to the material preceding or following a certain topic.

The distinct themes of the book relate mainly to religious belief and practice, while a considerable part of it addresses matters of communal significance. Finally, there resonates a clear polemical, ideological tone throughout the text, which reflects the bitterness and obstinacy of the doctrinal tensions and controversies at the time.[34]

Ghulām Khalīl's creed starts with an authoritative, imperative voice in the second-person plural, "know" (*iʿlamū*), thus apparently addressing the Muslim

---

book comprises *"Sharḥ al-sunna min ijmāʿ al-aʾimma wa-ittifāq al-umma"*; and see p. 47. Likewise, al-Lālakāʾī titles his book *Sharḥ uṣūl iʿtiqād ahl al-sunna*, thus combining both terms. George Makdisi rightly noted that all these expressions are "terms with Traditionalist resonance"; cf. Makdisi, Ibn ʿAqīl 75.

31 In two instances, he uses the phrase in the positive sense, *min al-sunna* ("it belongs to the Sunna"), and in one other instance in the negative, *laysa min al-sunna*, ("it does not belong to the Sunna"). See §§1, 19, and 149.

32 See §§9 and 11.

33 See chapter 3, "Development of Tenets and Their Distribution."

34 For a thematic arrangement of the tenets, see the index of the Arabic text.

community as a whole. The author, however, switches throughout the text from this plural form to the more personal second-person singular, "know" (*iʿlam*). The singular is used to introduce no fewer than 38 articles of the creed[35]—not until § 88 is the plural used again. Other articles of the creed start with an authoritative demand, in the forms "believe in" (*al-īmān bi*) and "believe that" (*al-īmān anna*).[36]

4 Islam and *Īmān*

Ghulām Khalīl begins his *K. Sharḥ al-sunna* with an unusual doctrinal statement, as he declares, "Islam is the Sunna, and the Sunna, Islam." (Interestingly, in § 152,[37] he attributes this statement to a certain Bishr al-Ḥārith—probably referring to the ascetic and *ḥadīth* scholar Bishr b. al-Ḥārith al-Ḥāfī, d. 227/841–842.) The statement is contrived, however, as it is nowhere attested in the classical sources. In any case, it is a puzzling aphorism and, what is more, both of its key constituents—Islam and the Sunna—would need to be defined more closely.

The Sunna, according to Ghulām Khalīl, is to be sought from,

> the Companions of the Prophet—may God bless him and have mercy upon all of them—[who] are the foundation upon which Islam has been established; they are the People of the Sunna and the Community of the Righteous (*ahl al-sunna wa-l-jamāʿa*). Whoever does not seek guidance from them is misled and is an innovator.[38] …
>
> For, the Sunna and the Community of the Righteous have, both, already determined the principles of religion (*amr al-dīn*), rendering it manifest. Accordingly, everyone is called upon to comply.[39]

Ghulām Khalīl then elucidates the idea that the Sunna is nothing but *āthār*—that is, traditions relating the deeds and the utterances of the Prophet Muhammad. This understanding associates the Sunna with all the traditions that were

---

35 See §§ 4, 5, 7, 8, 9, 10, 21, 26, 32, 46, 51, 53, 56, 59, 60, 61, 63, 65, 68, 69, 71, 72, 74, 75, 77, 80, 81, 82, 83, 85 (in the text), 89, 90, 98, 100, 102, 115, 125, 126.

36 Sometimes, "*bi-anna*" is used and then translated as "believe that." For these instances, see §§ 13, 33, 38, 40, 42, 43, 44, 45, 50, 52, 54, 62, 67, 70, 105, and 150.

37 Cf. Gilliot, Représentation 156.

38 See § 2.

39 See § 3.

related by the Prophet and his Companions, as Ghulām Khalīl quotes the prophetic saying "Take refuge in my Sunna and in the Sunna of the rightly guided caliphs, and hold fast to both."[40]

The author clarifies further that one is asked to give

> unconditional assent to the traditions of the Messenger of God—may peace and blessings be upon him—without asking "how" nor making any inquiry whatsoever; "why" is not to be asked, nor is "how."[41]

He also underlines the fact that whoever

> (a) denies a verse in the Book of God; (b) denies anything from the traditions (*āthār*) of the Messenger of God—may peace and blessings be upon him; (c) sacrifices for other than God; or (d) prays to other than God ... is a deserter from Islam.[42]

Furthermore,

> Should you hear someone casting doubt on prophetic traditions, know that his commitment to Islam is doubtful; his opinion and his belief are repugnant. As a matter of fact, the target of his doubt is but the Prophet—peace be upon him—and his Companions. For, it is through these traditions that we have come to know God, the Messenger of God—peace be upon Him—and the Quran, and we have come to know good and evil, and this world and the Hereafter.[43] You are to submit and be content with what the traditions, and their advocates (*ahl al-āthār*), convey. Refrain therefore [from argument], and be silent.[44]

Specifically at stake in his *Sharḥ* is the author's objective of emphasizing those basic doctrinal tenets from the Sunna to which every Muslim "should adhere" (*fa-min al-sunna an* ...) and upon which they should expound. These tenets constitute the central points that Ghulām Khalīl claims to have exposed in his book.[45] Accordingly, he even claims that

40 See § 76.
41 See § 9.
42 See § 28.
43 See § 48.
44 See § 61; see also §§ 97, 135.
45 Although Ghulām Khalīl does not use the term *uṣūl al-sunna*, the tenets he enumerates are to be understood as such.

> he who believes in *what is in this book*, and adopts it as a solid conviction, freeing his heart of all doubts and suspicions. Such is the adherent of the Sunna (*ṣāḥib sunna*), and the one who merits salvation, should God so wish.[46]

All of this leads us to the question: What exactly does Ghulām Khalīl understand the term "Islam" to mean? In Sunni traditionist contexts, the relationship between Islam and *īmān* (belief, faith) was a matter of much dispute.[47] Izutsu has observed that it "was one of the most important theoretical problems that … the newly-born Muslim community [faced]."[48] Commenting on the *ḥadīth* "An adulterer when he commits adultery is not a believer (or in a state of belief; *lā yaznī l-zānī wa-huwa muʾmin*),"[49] Abū ʿAbdallāh al-Marwazī (d. 294/906), the Shafiʿi traditionist from Nishapur,[50] maintains that the *aṣḥāb al-ḥadīth* and the *ahl al-sunna wa-l-jamāʿa* are divided into three groups as to their understanding of the relationship between Islam and *īmān*.[51] The first group, which makes a distinction between Islam and *īmān*, contends that the

---

46 See § 88.

47 It is not easy to render the term *īmān* properly into English since it denotes both a person's verbal confession and his or her inner conviction. See, among others, Smith, *Understanding* 115–134, 275–281. In his *Concept*, Izutsu uses the term "belief" in the title of his study as well as in his exposé in chapter five. Yet he leaves the term *īmān* untranslated throughout his publication. The term "faith" as used in the present publication refers to the inner conviction that encompasses verbal profession (*qawl*) and work (*ʿamal*), as well as intention (*niyya*) and its fulfillment (*iṣāba*).

48 Izutsu, *Concept* 57.

49 Al-Marwazī, *Taʿẓīm* 487–508. The same applies to one who steals, drinks wine (*khamr*), or kills; cf. Ibn Ḥanbal, *al-Musnad* xvi, 161, no. 10216; al-Bukhārī, *Ṣaḥīḥ* 1418 (*K. al-Ashriba*, no. 5578); and 1684 (*K. al-Ḥudūd*, no. 6808).

50 Abū ʿAbdallāh al-Marwazī was born in Baghdād in 202/817 and raised in Nishapur. He lived and died in Samarqand. Cf. al-Dhahabī, *Siyar* xiv, 33–40; and Halm, *Die Ausbreitung* 44, 103.

51 For a detailed discussion on the doctrine of the *ahl al-sunna* as it is portrayed in *K. al-Īmān* by Abū ʿUbayd (d. 224/839), see Madelung, Sunnī doctrine. See also Pessagno, The Murjiʾa. For a survey of the position of Aḥmad b. Ḥanbal, see Ahmed, Aḥmad b. Ḥanbal. Al-Khallāl, *al-Sunna* iii, 564–608, gives a review of Ibn Ḥanbal's opinion. See on this also Abū Yaʿlā in his *K. Masāʾil al-īmān* 152–159. There, he cites from a *K. al-Īmān* by Ibn Ḥanbal; cf. ibid., 165, 377. Al-Marwazī, however, already knew that a certain *K. al-Īmān* was attributed to Ibn Ḥanbal; cf. his *Taʿẓīm* 577. Al-Marwazī also maintains that two opinions on the question of *īmān* had been reported about Ibn Ḥanbal; cf. ibid., 527. Ibn Abī Yaʿlā, *al-Iʿtiqād* 24, maintains that *īmān* and *islām* are two expressions conveying different meanings: *islām* refers to the profession of faith in both its parts as well as its assent by the heart, while *īmān* refers to all the acts of devotion (*ṭāʿāt*).

Prophet had excluded the adulterer from the category of belief (*azāla ʿanhu ism al-īmān*) without removing him from the category of Islam, nor denying him its name (i.e., being a Muslim).[52] The second group, Abū ʿAbdallāh al-Marwazī holds, are those who likewise distinguish between Islam and *īmān* but nonetheless called the adulterer a Muslim since he still maintains the verbal confession (*li-iqrārihi bi-Llāh*). Yet they removed him from the category of belief, although his unbelief (*kufr*) does not amount to disbelief in God (*kufr bi-Llāh*).[53] The third group, however, al-Marwazī concludes, represents the vast majority (*al-sawād al-aʿẓam*) from among the *ahl al-sunna wa-l-jamāʿa* and the *aṣḥāb al-ḥadīth*. They equate Islam and *īmān* and perceive both expressions as names (or categories) that have one and the same meaning.[54] Indeed, they understand them as being equivalent to the *dīn* (religion as a Godly order). Consequently, whosoever fails to perform any one of the religious obligations (*farāʾiḍ*) or commits an act that is prohibited (i.e., adultery, drinking wine, or killing someone), falls into a lesser state concerning his Islam and *īmān*. He does so, however, without this development leading to any diminution (*nuqṣān*) with regard to his verbal confession (*li-iqrārihi bi-Llāh*).[55]

It is also worth noting in this context that a deed or work (*ʿamal*) is regarded by al-Marwazī as an integral part of both Islam and *īmān*.[56] Succinctly put, it seems that al-Marwazī formed his theory in reliance on the debates he perhaps had with representatives of the Murjiʾa of Samarqand, where he lived.[57] The Murjiʾa confirm that *īmān* encompasses Islam, yet they limit the category of *īmān* to a mere "inward" assent (*taṣdīq*) of its precepts.[58]

These explanations from al-Marwazī are very interesting since the principle that apparently prevailed in his time was that the majority of the *ahl al-sunna wa-l-jamāʿa* (a) differentiated between Islam and *īmān* and (b) maintained that belief admits of increase and diminution.[59] In fact, although al-Marwazī does

52 Al-Marwazī, *Taʿẓīm* 506.

53 Ibid., 517.

54 Ibn ʿAbd al-Barr, *al-Tamhīd* ix, 247, maintains that the majority of Mālik's followers also equate Islam with *īmān*. See also Ibn Ḥazm, *al-Fiṣal* iii, 109. The same understanding is also attributed to Sufyān al-Thawrī; cf. Ibn Rajab, *Jāmiʿ* i, 107.

55 Al-Marwazī, 533–534, see also ibid. 341, 344, 416, 424, 506, and 529–534.

56 Al-Marwazī, 416, 533, and others.

57 Al-Khaṭīb, *Tārīkh* v, 508, also uses the term in a way that points to such a provenance.

58 Al-Marwazī, *Taʿẓīm* 806. See also Ibn ʿAbd al-Barr, *al-Tamhīd* ix, 247. Furthermore, cf. Izutsu, *The concept* 64–82; van Ess, *TuG* i, 194–195, 202; and Rudolph, *Al-Māturīdī* 49, 89, 111.

59 Ibn Ḥanbal is reported to have said that belief decreases till nothing remains of it; cf. al-

not explicitly separate Islam from *īmān*, he does (c) admit the possibility of increase and diminution of belief. Furthermore, he explains that (d) diminution of belief occurs in relation to a preceding increase, but does not entail a reduction of the verbal confession (*iqrār*), which represents the origin or root (*al-aṣl*).[60] Therefore, as al-Marwazī argues, increase and diminution of belief happen solely in relation to its branches (*shuʿab*).[61]

Although Ibn Taymiyya in his *K. al-Īmān* adopts some of al-Marwazī's arguments, he dedicates a long section to refuting al-Marwazī's views concerning the equation of Islam with *īmān*.[62] Izutsu, however, who had thoroughly delineated the position of Ibn Taymiyya on the question of Islam and *īmān*,[63] seems not to have noticed this aspect, or at least makes no mention of al-Marwazī's position in his respective study.

It is difficult to know precisely the position of Ghulām Khalīl on this matter. But his puzzling formula "Islam is the Sunna, and the Sunna, Islam" does seem to point clearly to a position similar to that of al-Marwazī, which apparently also prevailed among adherents of Mālik b. Anas.[64]

Importantly, in his *Sharḥ al-sunna* Ghulām Khalīl also pairs the two terms—Islam and Sunna—in two instances[65] when defining faith as consisting of verbal profession (*qawl*) and work (*ʿamal*)—these two being equally important—as well as intention (*niyya*) and its fulfillment (*iṣāba*).[66] Like al-Marwazī, Ghulām Khalīl also admits the possibility of an increase or a diminution of belief.[67] Lastly, in yet another tenet he equates Islam with Sunna with regard to a person's estrangement from them whenever innovations arise and spread.[68]

However, whereas al-Marwazī categorizes his arguments and details them in specific chapters, Ghulām Khalīl—apparently because of the abridged nature of his creed that would be used as a guide of plain and simple doctrinal instruction—does not develop his points of view concerning central terms

Kawsaj, *Masāʾil* ix, 4847, and also ix, 4748. Sufyān b. ʿUyayna, however, apparently used to say that it can increase. But he would not fault those who claim that it only decreases; cf. Abū Dāwūd, *Masāʾil* 364; and Ṣāliḥ b. Aḥmad, *Masāʾil* 346–347.

60 Al-Marwazī, *Taʿẓīm* 703, gives the simile of a palm tree which—even if some branches or leaves were cut off—would still be named a palm tree.

61 See also al-Marwazī, *Taʿẓīm* 712–713, 753. For the branches (*shuʿab*) of belief, see al-Marwazī, *Taʿẓīm* 423 and the following pages.

62 Ibn Taymiyya, *K. al-Īmān* 310–326.

63 Izutsu, *Concept* 59–66, and 71–75.

64 Cf. fn. 55 above.

65 See §§ 26 and 152.

66 See § 13k (on intention, *niyya*). Cf. also Daiber, Creed 113–114.

67 See §§ 13k and 144.

68 See § 71.

used therein. Nor does he explain in any detail the terminological constituents defining belief or the relation of these terms to each other.

With these premises in mind, one can perhaps better understand why Ghulām Khalīl writes in the form of condensed dicta. Thus, the common reader of this creed might remain unaware of, or might fail to recognize, the distinct nuances and gradations inherent in the respective religious terms and expressions. Yet instruction in theological subtleties and doctrinal sophistication of Islamic belief appear not to have been Ghulām Khalīl's prime objective in writing this creed after all.

Seen from this perspective, the dictum "Islam is the Sunna and the Sunna, Islam" acquires conspicuous significance vis-à-vis a more stringent interpretation of religion and faith on the one hand, and an unwavering rejection of innovations (*bidaʿ*) on the other. The latter point, as we have seen earlier, was one of the main, explicit impulses prompting our author to write his *Sharḥ*, fusing doctrine, orthopraxy, and (religious) obedience into one and the same scheme.

5 Heresy and the Accusation of Unbelief

Takfīr, the practice of declaring another Muslim a heretic or an unbeliever, is an act of religious castigation, a category of exclusion involving excommunication that exceeds the boundaries of theological tolerance.[69] According to Izutsu, it means "literally declaring somebody—who, in this case, is an actual member of the community and passes for a believer—to be a *kâfir*, and condemning him as such."[70] He explains further, "More generally, however, *takfîr* was still largely a matter of practical significance, a handy tool of party-politics."[71] The concept played an important role in the thought of the Kharijites;[72] yet, as van Ess explicates, "The Muʿtazila were actually those who generously practiced *takfīr*, especially in their polemic against the anthropomorphists and the determinists."[73]

Ghulām Khalīl broaches the subject of *takfīr*, arguing that it was first instigated by the sectarians after the murder of the third caliph, ʿUthmān b. ʿAffān, in 35/656, to be later adopted as a weapon by the Jahmis:

69 Jackson, *Boundaries* 3–4.
70 Izutsu, *Concept* 11. See also Björkmann, Kāfir; and Adang et al., *Accusations* 1–6.
71 Izutsu, *Concept* 17.
72 Izutsu, *Concept*; and *ThG* iv, 674.
73 Van Ess, *Der Eine* ii, 1287.

(71) Such was the [understanding of] religion up to the caliphate of ʿUmar, and such it was during the reign of ʿUthmān. When ʿUthmān was murdered, however, disagreement and innovations prevailed, and people [split into] factions (*aḥzāb*) and sects (*firaq*). Some, when it all started, held fast to the Truth and called to it. Thus, things remained in order until the fourth generation of the caliphate of the line of so-and-so. Afterwards, the times turned, people drastically changed, and innovations were rampant. Advocates of paths other than righteousness and the Community multiplied. Tribulations took place over matters that neither the Messenger of God—may peace and blessings be upon him—nor his Companions addressed. They instigated factionalism, which the Prophet of God forbade. They called one another unbelievers, each advocating their own cause while accusing others of unbelief. Thereupon, the hotheaded, the uncouth, and the ignorant were led astray. They tempted people with worldly matters and intimidated them with worldly punishment. By such intimidation and temptation, people were led to follow them through desire for worldly goods.

(74) Know—may God's mercy be upon you—that disproving the views of the Jahmiyya [was a matter for] the learned (*ahl al-ʿilm*) until, during the caliphate of so-and-so, the lowly rabble (*ruwaybiḍa*) rendered the discourse public, discrediting thereat the traditions of the Prophet—may peace and blessings be upon him—and adopting [reasoning by] analogy (*qiyās*) and [subjective legal] opinion (*raʾy*), ultimately accusing dissenters of unbelief.

This rejoinder is most probably targeted against the Jahmis and Muʿtazila during the "inquisition" (*miḥna*). With "the caliphate of so-and-so," Ghulām Khalīl is, in all likelihood, referring to the caliph al-Maʾmūn, who imposed the doctrine of the createdness of the Quran, which, as the proto-Sunnis emphasized, was prompted and enforced by the Jahmis.[74]

In addition to the statements quoted above, Ghulām Khalīl attacks the common populace on another occasion in his book, claiming that the "source of every innovation is but riffraff crowds who follow every croaking [agitator] and sway with every blowing wind."[75] The striking feature in Ghulām

74 Martin, Createdness i, 468. For the Jahmi convictions of al-Maʾmūn, see *ThG* iii, 157, 449; and for Ibn Abī Duwād, *ThG* iii, 481. For how the Jahmis were conceived by the Hanbalis, see Watt, *Formative period* 144–145.

75 See §80. The wording resembles a sentence in a sermon of ʿAlī b. Abī Ṭālib; cf. his *Nahj*

Khalīl's position toward the riffraff among the common people (*al-ʿāmma*) is the parallel he draws with the derision that both al-Maʾmūn, in his "inquisition" letters, and al-Jāḥiẓ[76] show toward the "seditious and heretical ignorance of the common people and their leaders."[77] Thus Ghulām Khalīl gives the impression that, by adopting the jargon used in the official caliphal letters to attack the proto-Sunnis, he was directly reacting to the respective accusation voiced by the caliph, by turning it around and leveling it against his adversaries.

By accusing sectarians, including the Jahmis, of having initiated *takfīr* in the community, Ghulām Khalīl puts himself on the defensive while attempting to explain his position on the matter. In fact, his basic approach toward his fellow Muslims in the community appears almost forbearing, as the following tenets demonstrate:

> (22) A Muslim who has never borne false witness against anyone, nor has been seen to have done anything, good or bad, yet about whom it cannot be known how his life will end, we are to hope and fear for him. Nor do we know whether he will repent to God upon death, or what God will ordain for him at the time, should he die as a Muslim. We merely ask for God's mercy on his behalf; it is his sins that make us fear for him. For no sin is beyond repentance for any worshipper.
>
> (26) Know that this world (*dunyā*) is an abode of belief (*īmān*) and Islam. Thus, the Community of Muhammad—may peace and blessings be upon him—includes believers who entrust themselves to Islam insofar as the legal rulings they follow, inheritance, and funeral prayers are concerned. We withhold testimony as to someone's true belief until he complies with the laws and rules (*sharāʾiʿ*) of Islam. Falling short in this regard renders a person less of a believer till he dies. As to his faith, God alone—exalted is He—knows it, be it complete or less so; unless he disregards the laws of Islam openly.

In this, Ghulām Khalīl follows the Murjiʾi understanding that became a mainstream creed among the *ahl al-sunna* in general[78]—namely, "to deem not a

---

496, no. 147. See also al-Yaʿqūbī, *Tārīkh* ii, 243; al-Khaṭīb al-Baghdādī, *Tārīkh* vi, 379; and Ibn ʿAsākir, *Tārīkh* xiv, 18, l, 252.

76 Al-Jāḥiẓ, Istiḥqāq iv, 212.

77 Cooperson, *Classical Arabic biography* 38.

78 Al-Bukhārī in al-Lālakāʾī, *Sharḥ* i, 103; Ḥarb, *al-Sunna* 64, n. 96 (with the addition "or

member of the People of the Qibla a non-Muslim," and "to hope and fear for him and ask for God's mercy on his behalf; it is his sins that make us fear for him."[79] This overall tolerant declaration had been surcharged with additional restrictions before it found acceptance among the proto-Sunnis, who admitted the increase and decrease in matters of belief as well as direct relationships between belief and deeds,[80] as demonstrated by a saying attributed to Sufyān b. ʿUyayna (d. 198/814).[81] According to the Meccan al-Ḥumaydī (d. 219/834), *kufr* consists in forsaking the five pillars upon which Islam is built: the confession of faith, prayer, almsgiving, fasting in Ramadan, and pilgrimage.[82] Likewise, Aḥmad b. Ḥanbal (d. 241/855) reportedly explained that "whoever relinquishes the daily prayers is an unbeliever."[83]

Ghulām Khalīl's lenience embraces even those Muslims who are neglectful with regard to "the laws and rules (*sharāʾiʿ*) of Islam," since he regards them as falling short of being an integral believer (*nāqiṣ al-īmān*), a label that already had been used by Sufyān b. ʿUyayna, as well as by al-Shāfiʿī (d. 204/820),[84] and which had found general acceptance by the later *ahl al-sunna wa-l-jamāʿa*.[85] Ghulām Khalīl thus affirms that one should,

> (28) Deem not a member of the People of the Qibla a non-Muslim, except if he (a) denies a verse in the Book of God; (b) denies anything from the

---

exclude him from Islam for a work he has done unless there is a *ḥadīth* about that"). See also al-Ḥasan b. Ismāʿīl al-Rabaʿī (Laoust, *ʿAqīda II*), Ibn Abī Yaʿlā, *Ṭabaqāt* (al-Fiqī) i, 130–131, (al-ʿUthaymīn) i, 349–350; Ibn al-Madīnī in al-Lālakāʾī, *Sharḥ* i, 99; al-Ṭaḥāwī, *al-ʿAqīda*, 31; Ibn Abī al-ʿIzz, *Sharḥ* 318–319; al-Ashʿarī, *Maqālāt* 293; al-Ismāʿīlī, *al-Iʿtiqād* 175; Ibn Baṭṭa, *al-Sharḥ wa-l-ibāna* 63; al-Malaṭī, *al-Tanbīh* 13; Ibn ʿAsākir, *Tārīkh* ix, 301 (in a creed attributed to a certain Ibn ʿUkāsha al-Kirmānī); and al-Ījī, *Sharḥ al-mawāqif* viii, 371. Cf. also Melchert, *Ahmad ibn Hanbal* 86.

79 This formulation is associated with the name of Abū Ḥanīfa (d. 150/767), "Do not bear witness of any of them for a sin he has committed"; cf. *ThG* i, 201, 210; and "to hope and fear for them," Abū Muqātil al-Samarqandī (d. 208/823), *al-ʿĀlim* 587; as well as al-Tamīmī, *al-Ṭabaqāt al-saniyya* i, 176.

80 Izutsu, *Concept* 179–194.

81 Abū Nuʿaym, *Ḥilya* vii, 295–296.

82 Al-Ḥumaydī, *al-Musnad* ii, 547.

83 Ibn Hāniʾ, *Masāʾil* ii, 156. See also the creed by ʿAbdūs b. Mālik in Ibn Abī Yaʿlā, *Ṭabaqāt* (al-Fiqī) i, 243; (al-ʿUthaymīn) ii, 172; Ibn al-Madīnī, al-Lālakāʾī, *Sharḥ* i, 98; Ḥanbal b. Isḥāq, "Juzʾ Ḥanbal," *K. al-Fitan* 247; al-Marwazī, *Taʿẓīm* 885–900.

84 Al-Bayhaqī, *Manāqib al-Shāfiʿī* i, 392. The Murjiʾi, Saʿīd b. Sālim al-Qaddāḥ (d. ca. 190/805; al-Dhahabī, *Siyar* ix, 319), used to ridicule those who used the term (*nāqiṣ al-īmān*), al-ʿUqaylī, *al-Ḍuʿafāʾ* ii, 108, no. 579.

85 Ibn ʿAbd al-Barr, *al-Tamhīd* ix, 243; and Ibn Taymiyya, *al-ʿAqīda al-Wāsiṭiyya* 268–269.

traditions (*āthār*) of the Messenger of God—may peace and blessings be upon him; (c) sacrifices for other than God; or (d) prays to other than God.

Should he commit any of the above, you must deem him, then, a deserter from Islam. Otherwise, he remains a Muslim believer, nominally—but not in reality.

Significant in his wording, however, is the phrase "nominally—but not in reality" (*bi-l-ism lā bi-l-ḥaqīqa*). It is also noteworthy that no such terminology is found in the early creeds; it seems to be specific to Ghulām Khalīl. This manner of expression, however, gives the impression of being aimed at Abū Ḥanīfa since this view (which equates the name and the reality that it refers to in relation to belief) is apparent in the *K. al-ʿĀlim wa-l-mutaʿallim* (put together by Abū Ḥanīfa's student Abū Muqātil al-Samarqandī, d. 208/823–824),[86] as well as Abū Ḥanīfa's epistle to his student ʿUthmān al-Battī.[87] The expression is likewise to be found in *al-Fiqh al-akbar II*,[88] a work first attributed to Abū Ḥanīfa in the second half of the fourth/tenth century.[89] The respective dispute about the status of belief and the legal verdict accompanying its classification was dealt with in later generations under the rubric of "*al-asmāʾ wa-l-aḥkām*."[90]

So much for Ghulām Khalīl's general approach to accusations of unbelief. Yet it is salient that there are cases where he tagged individuals or groups as unbelievers (sing. *kāfir*).[91] These statements in his book are, again, cases that fall within the general proto-Sunni principles, as the following table illustrates.

86 Abū Ḥanīfa, *al-ʿĀlim* 577–578.

87 *ThG* i, 195–196.

88 Wensinck, *Muslim creed* 192, art. 11, "Neither do we banish him from the field of faith, nay, we call him really faithful; he may be faithful of bad behavior, not an infidel."

89 *ThG* i, 207.

90 Al-Shahrastānī, *al-Milal* 43; Fakhr al-Dīn al-Rāzī, *Muḥaṣṣal* 181–183; al-Ījī, *Sharḥ al-Mawāqif* viii, 351.

91 Al-Zuʿkurī, a quietist Salafi authority from Yemen (see appendix II), noted in his introduction to his edition on al-Barbahārī's *Sharḥ al-sunna* (as he attributes the book to al-Barbahārī), quoting his teacher Muqbil b. Hādī al-Wādiʿī (see appendix II), that there is "some liberty" (*iṭlāq*) in the book with regard to accusations of unbelief. *Fatḥ al-bārī* 22.

§	Ghulām Khalīl's *Sharḥ al-sunna*	Other creeds
4		– Ḥarb/al-Iṣṭakhrī, *al-Sunna* 54, no. 75 (Watt, *Creeds* 38, no. 13)
	[Whoever] Challenge the authority of the Companions and dissent from them (*man khālafa aṣḥāb rasūl Allāh—ṣ—fī shay'in min amr al-dīn*).	Whoever criticizes the Companions ... is an innovator, a Rāfiḍī, malignant, and a wicked opponent ... He must be corrected and punished by the authorities. They may not pardon him, but must punish him and ask him to repent. If he repents, that is accepted from him. If he does not repent, his punishment is renewed and he should stay at prison indefinitely, until he dies or goes back (to correct belief).
		– ʿAbdūs, Ibn Abī Yaʿlā, *Ṭabaqāt* (al-Fiqī) i, 245; (al-ʿUthaymīn) ii, 172, labels as innovator (*mubtadiʿ*) those who deprecate (*intaqaṣa*) the Companions.
		– ʿAlī b. ʿAbdallāh b. al-Madīnī, al-Lālakā'ī, *Sharḥ* i, 100, the same wording as ʿAbdūs's.
12		– Abū Thawr, al-Lālakā'ī, *Sharḥ* i, 102
	Dispute that the Quran is uncreated.	Al-Qadariyya and those who say the Qur'ān is created are unbelievers, they must repent or else be killed (*ḍuribat aʿnāquhum*).
		– Ḥarb/al-Iṣṭakhrī, *al-Sunna* 52–53, nos. 66–69 (Watt, *Creeds* 37, no. 10)
		Whoever supposes that the Quran is created, he is a Jahmi, an unbeliever. Whoever supposes that the Quran is the Speech of God, but suspends judgment and does not say it is uncreated, he is worse than the first. Whoever supposes that our utterance of the Quran, and our reciting of it is created, while the Quran is the Speech of God, is a Jahmi, noxious, and an innovator. He who does not charge these people, as well as all Jahmis, of unbelief, is, then, one of them.
		– Musaddad, Ibn Abī Yaʿlā, *Ṭabaqāt* (al-Fiqī) i, 342; (al-ʿUthaymīn) ii, 427–428

(*cont.*)

§	Ghulām Khalīl's *Sharḥ al-sunna*	Other creeds
		The Quran is God's speech uncreated, whoever says it is created is an unbeliever in God the Almighty. He, who does not charge him with unbelief, he is, then, unbeliever. (See also under "Jahmis" in this table.) – Abū Zurʿa al-Rāzī, al-Lālakāʾī, *Sharḥ* i, 106 and 108 (both Abū Zurʿa al-Rāzī and Abū Ḥātim al-Rāzī) The Murjiʾa and Qadaris are devious innovators, and the Jahmis are unbelievers. Whoever says that the Quran is created commits unbelief that leads one to renounce the religion (*yanqul ʿan al-milla*). Whoever doubts the unbelief of such a person, from among those who have understanding, is also an unbeliever. Whoever doubts about whether the Quran is uncreated, he is a Jahmi, whoever stops unknowingly, should be instructed and treated as an innovator, but will not be accused of unbelief. Whoever says "My utterance of the Quran is created," is a Jahmi. – Al-Ḥumaydi, *al-Musnad* ii, 547, labels him as an innovator (*mubtadiʿ*) (quoting Sufyān).
33	Deny God's knowledge of what has not been and what is to be.	
60	Deny the Visio Beatifica.	– Ibn Ḥanbal, *Masāʾil Abū Dāwūd* 353.
125	The Rafidis, the Muʿtazila, and the Jahmis. For they all revolve around the denial of God's attributes (*taʿṭīl*) and around (*zandaqa*) heresy.	– Musaddad, Ibn Abī Yaʿlā, *Ṭabaqāt* (al-Fiqī) i, 343, (al-ʿUthaymīn) ii, 429.
54	Moses heard God's very speech in a voice that struck his ears. The voice came from God and from God alone. To maintain otherwise is an act of unbelief.	– Ibn Ḥanbal, *Masāʾil Abū Dāwūd* 353. – Al-Malaṭī, *al-Tanbīh* 100 "Jahm denied that God talked to Moses." – Al-Ājurrī, *al-Sharīʿa* iii, 1109.

(*cont.*)

§	Ghulām Khalīl's *Sharḥ al-sunna*	Other creeds
77		– Ḥarb, *al-Sunna* 64, n. 96.
	The Jahmis, because they contemplated the essence of the Lord, introducing "why" and "how," forsook tradition, adopted reasoning by analogy, and measured religion by the yardstick of their subjective opinions. See also 78.	The Jahmis are the enemies of God. They allege that the Quran is created, that God did not speak to Moses, that God does not speak, cannot be seen, that He is in no place, and that he does not possess throne and a stool. They are unbelievers, *zanādiqa*, and enemies of God, so beware of them. – Musaddad, Ibn Abī Yaʿlā, *Ṭabaqāt* (al-Fiqī) i, 343, (al-ʿUthaymīn) ii, 428 The Jahmis are unbelievers. They should be called to repent, and if they do not repent, they should be killed. There is a consensus among the learned (*ahl al-ʿilm*) whom we have met that whoever makes such a statement, if he does not repent, should not be married to a Muslim woman, his rulings are not permissible, and the animals he slaughters are unlawful. – Abū Zurʿa al-Rāzī, al-Lālakāʾī, *Sharḥ* i, 106.
145	There has spread an innovation which amounts to disbelief in God Almighty, a) Whoever proclaims it is an indisputable unbeliever: Those who believe in the Return [of the dead Imam] (*rajʿa*) before the Day of Resurrection, that ʿAlī b. Abī Ṭālib is alive and will return, and likewise Muḥammad b. ʿAlī, Jaʿfar b. Muḥammad, and Mūsā b. Jaʿfar; b) And posit the Imamate; c) And claim that they know the Unseen.	

Several other issues merit our attention:

(1) Another creed, by Muḥammad b. ʿAwf, Abū Jaʿfar al-Ḥimṣī (d. 272/885), considers whoever claims that both Paradise and Hell are not yet created, and whoever denies the anthropomorphic traditions about God's fingers and hands, is an unbeliever who shall repent or else be killed.[92] Interest-

92 Laoust, *ʿAqīda* v; Ibn Abī Yaʿlā, *Ṭabaqāt* (al-Fiqī) i, 312, (al-ʿUthaymīn) ii, 341–342.

ingly, on this issue Ghulām Khalīl confirms "the veritable truth of Paradise and Hell and of their being created" (§ 13h).[93] Yet he does not accuse those who deny this tenet of unbelief.[94]

(2) As for anthropomorphic traditions, Ghulām Khalīl does not directly accuse those who oppose them as unbelievers. Nonetheless, he classifies them as Jahmis (§§ 27, 29, 74). The differentiation between the two labels, however, is too facile, and the end result is the same.

(3) The same applies to the Jahmis, who do not say that God punishes people in the Fire (§ 62). What must be emphasized in this regard, however, is that Ghulām Khalīl does not share the position so conspicuously expressed by Musaddad and Ḥarb al-Kirmānī/al-Iṣṭakhrī, to the effect that whoever does not charge these people with unbelief, should himself be considered an unbeliever.

It should be noted that Ghulām Khalīl's attitude changes in the course of his exposé, and the inflexibility increases regarding the consequences pertaining to the repudiation of, or reluctance to accept, items of creed delineated in his book. Thus, he stresses,

> (92) Fear God, then, and abide by that ancient and pristine state-of-affairs *that I have expounded herein, in this book*, for you. May God grace with his mercy the servant—and the servant's parents—who reads *this book*, circulates it, acts upon it, advocates it, and argues from it. For it is the way (*dīn*; or "the maintained order") of God and the way of the Messenger of God—may peace and blessings be upon him.

In the same item, he even goes so far as to equate the legal status of someone who contests an item of his book with the legal status of one who holds in doubt even a single letter in the book of God and who thus departs outright from the way of God.

Ghulām Khalīl reiterates the same ideas time and again in different forms.[95] This recurrent insistence on the authoritative status of "his book" seems unique. Yet there is at least one other instance which we cite for comparison

---

93 Ghulām Khalīl adds that "Paradise and Fire shall never cease to exist and shall, forever and for all eternity, remain together with God—blessed and exalted is He." See on this issue Demichelis, *Fanāʾ al-nār* 392–394.

94 Same as Ibn al-Madīnī, al-Lālakāʾī, *Sharḥ* i, 100; Ḥarb/Iṣṭakhrī confirm that whoever denies that they are created or that they will perish is an innovator and *zindīq*, *K. al-Sunna* 48; and al-Iṣṭakhrī by Ibn Abī Yaʿlā, *Ṭabaqāt* (al-Fiqī) i, 28, (al-ʿUthaymīn) i, 60.

95 See §§ 88, 90, 91, 136, 146, 148.

in this respect—namely, the opening lines of the creed that appears at the beginning of the responsa (*Masāʾil*) of Ḥarb al-Kirmānī (d. 280/893). This said, however, it must be noted that in the latter case the creed is attributed to a collective entity of predecessors. Al-Kirmānī's creed is introduced with the following statement:

> This is the doctrine of the leaders of the people of knowledge (*ahl al-ʿilm*), the traditionists (*aṣḥāb al-athar*), and the *ahl al-sunna*, i.e., those who have been known by it, who have been emulated in regards to it, since the time of the Prophet—may peace and blessings be upon him—till our very day. All those, whose acquaintance I have made from amongst the scholars of Iraq, the Hijaz, and Syria, as well as others, follow this doctrine. Whoever contradicts one of these doctrines calls it into question, or discredits the one who believes in it, is but an innovator who has deviated from the community and strayed from the course of the Sunna and the track of the truth.[96]

With a slight twist, Ghulām Khalīl was thus able to introduce a modification of perspective in order to make a self-predication and to label his creed not only as a representation of the views of previous generations of the learned and the *ahl al-sunna*, but, what is more, to compare the authority of his book with that of the Quran and the Sunna.

Crucial for our understanding of Ghulām Khalīl's attitude toward *takfīr* is his use of the terms *ṣāḥib bidʿa* (innovator) and *ṣāḥib hawā* (sectarian), since both are employed in a manner that equates them with unbelief. This becomes clear as Ghulām Khalīl states,

> (91) Fear God, then, O servant of God. Assent to [what is in] this book; submit and entrust yourself to it. Conceal not, from anyone of the People of the Qibla, what is in it. God might well, through it, rescue those bewildered from their confusion, the innovator (*ṣāḥib bidʿa*) from innovation, or the misguided from error, that they may be saved …
>
> (148) Whoever assents to what is in *this book*, upholding it, and seeks guidance in it, and does not doubt or reject even a letter therein, is thereby an

96 Ḥarb al-Kirmānī, *K. al-Sunna* 33, no. 1; al-Iṣṭakhrī by Ibn Abī Yaʿlā, *Ṭabaqāt* (al-Fiqī) i, 24, (al-ʿUthaymīn) i, 55.

> adherent of the Sunna and the *jamāʿa*. He is accomplished in the Sunna, and the Sunna is complete through him.
>
> Whoever abjures a letter in *this book*, or casts doubt upon it, or wavers [in accepting it in full], is but a sectarian (*ṣāḥib al-hawā*).
>
> Whoever abjures, or holds in doubt, a letter in the Quran, or anything that is related on the authority of the Messenger of God—may peace and blessings be upon him—shall meet God—exalted is He—as a denier of truth. Therefore, fear God, beware of Him, and attend to your faith.

In the second/eighth and the third/ninth centuries, the lines differentiating the terms *bidʿa*, *hawā*, and *kufr*[97] were quite thin.[98] While Jackson proposes a very useful categorization of "theological deviance, from outright Unbelief (*kufr*) to unsanctioned (though non-damning) innovation (*bidʿa*) to honest mistakes and misunderstandings,"[99] it seems necessary to specify in more detail the variations and distinctions in the ways these terms were used and to draw comparisons and continuities, respectively. Although *hawā* was, more often than not, used to describe sectarians of different sorts, the exact meaning of *bidʿa* (innovation)—as well as the legal position of an innovator—are much more difficult to pin down.[100] Be that as it may, what does merit emphasis here is that Ghulām Khalīl uses the term *bidʿa* no fewer than 22 times in his creed.[101] In fact, he starts his book with the warning,

97 Al-Ḥasan b. ʿAbd al-ʿAzīz al-Jarawī (d. 257/870; al-Dhahabī, *Siyar* xii, 334) reports that al-Shāfiʿī used to strongly forbid discussing sectarian schemes (*al-kalām fī l-ahwāʾ*); and that he used to say, "If one of them was contradicted by his colleague, he would accuse him of unbelief (*kafarta*), whereas the right thing is to tell him that he is in error (*akhṭaʾta*)," al-Lālakāʾī, *Sharḥ* i, 165, no. 302. It is in the same spirit that the Shafiʿi, Qawwām al-Sunna uses *ḍalla* (deviated) instead of *kafara*, in an item that he is most probably quoting from Ghulām Khalīl's *K. Sharḥ al-sunna*. It is also worth noting the category of "unbelief that does not rule a person as digresser from religion" (*lā yukhrij min al-milla*). See, for example, the ruling based on exegetic opinion given by Ibn ʿAbbās concerning Q 2:44 (rejecting divine sovereignty), al-Marwazī, *Taʿẓīm* 518–523; Ibn Baṭṭā, *al-Ibāna* i, 734–737. The concept was used by the Ṣufriyya from amongst the Kharijites, cf. Laoust, *Schismes* 46, 446.

98 In later centuries, books on innovations dealt mainly with the denunciation of social habits and innovations introduced in rituals, cf. Fierro, Treatise 206–207.

99 Jackson, *On the boundaries* 3–4. See a classification by Rispler, Toward a new understanding 324–328.

100 Lewis, Some observations 52–54; Laoust, *Schismes* 118, 447; *ThG* iv, 674–680; Adang et al., *Accusations* 6. For later periods see Brentjes, Vocabulary 147; and Levanoni, *Takfīr* in Egypt 156.

101 See *bidʿa* in the index of termini at the end of the Arabic translation.

> (2) All innovation (*bidʿa*) is misguidance, and all misguidance and its adherents lead to Hellfire.

He instructs further,

> (5) Know that when people bring about an innovation, they of necessity forfeit what corresponds to it in the Sunna. Therefore,
>
> Beware of novelties, since every novelty is an innovation, and innovations, one and all, lead one astray. Every innovation is a deviation. Deviation and its adherents belong to Hellfire.
>
> Beware of insignificant novelties, as even the insignificant ultimately becomes momentous. For whatever innovation has been practiced by this Community began as a minor innovation having the semblance of truth, but in no time it grew malignant, deluding meanwhile whoever adhered to it and was trapped in it. And yet it spread, becoming a religion (*dīn*) with adherents of its own, who deviated from the Straight Path and thus forsook Islam.

Ghulām Khalīl presents his classification of the levels of innovation more or less as a rule of thumb, rather than as a clear taxonomy with corresponding legal implications. Yet it also becomes clear that, in his view, the most "malignant innovations" are those that he classifies as plain unbelief (as mentioned in the table above).

Interestingly, the model employed by Ghulām Khalīl corresponds to that expressed by Ibn Ḥanbal in his various books. Josef van Ess points to this dynamic use of terms when observing that "innovator was the term that was chosen in the long run instead of 'unbeliever,' *takfīr* was replaced by *tabdīʿ*."[102] Yet, we must ask here: What were the actual legal implications of *takfīr* at that time? Van Ess contends in this respect,

> To call someone *kāfir* was probably just a verbal affront under Baghdadi terms; only in closed small communities such as the Ibāḍiyya—and perhaps the Muʿtazila of Basra—did one undertake legal and social consequences.[103]

102 *ThG* iv, 678.

103 *ThG* iii, 137; and see iv, 422.

As the evidence adduced in the table above indicates (although it represents only a limited number of samples), killing and excommunication were proposed as possible punishments. In one case, in fact, both forms of penalty are mentioned, thus allowing an alternative to killing.[104] For Ghulām Khalīl, excommunication was unquestionably the first and main consequence of relevant accusations, rather than killing, as he makes clear in his book.[105] Most assuredly, because of his close personal connections with the authorities, Ghulām Khalīl was in a position to commence formal persecution and to initiate taking "innovators" for official examination, as is clearly attested by the trial he is said to have instigated against the Sufis.

6 The Authority of the Companions

To better understand Ghulām Khalīl's strategy in explicating the tenets of the Sunna, it is useful at this point to take a closer look at his views concerning the Companions. Following the exonerating consensus among the *ahl al-sunna* in the third/ninth century[106]—adopted from the early Murji'a and the dogmatic formulation ascribed to Abū Ḥanīfa[107]—Ghulām Khalīl also affirms that the Companions are exalted models to be emulated and honored. He avows the excellence, merits, accomplishments, and moral precedence of the Companions. His attitude toward the Companions can be summarized as follows:

The Companions as a source of guidance:

> (2) They are the People of the Sunna and the Community (*ahl al-sunna wa-l-jamāʿa*). He who does not seek guidance from them is misled and is an innovator. All innovation (*bidʿa*) is misguidance, and all misguidance and its adherents lead to Hellfire.[108]

The Companions as a source of truth:

---

104 Musaddad, Ibn Abī Yaʿlā, *Ṭabaqāt* (al-Fiqī) i, 343, (al-ʿUthaymīn) ii, 428.

105 See §§123, 124, 128, 129, 130. See also al-Bayhaqī, *al-Qaḍāʾ* ii, 705–724.

106 See Ibn Saʿd, *Ṭabaqāt* ii, 126–127; Ibn Ḥanbal, *Faḍāʾil al-ṣaḥāba* i, 47–61; al-Ashʿarī, *Maqālāt* 294; al-Ashʿarī, *Risāla* 299–305; Muranyi, Ṣaḥāba viii, 828b; and Afsaruddin, *Excellence* 36–43.

107 Cf. *ThG* i, 194.

108 See also §§8, 86, and 114.

> (4) … The Prophet has shown his Community the Sunna and explicated it to his Companions, who are the Community and the vast majority (*al-sawād al-aʿẓam*). The vast majority, in turn, represent the truth and its adherents. Therefore, he who dissents from the Companions of the Prophet—may peace and blessings be upon him—in anything pertaining to God's command, becomes an unbeliever.

The Companions as symbols of inviolability:

> (101) Refrain from discussing the wars among ʿAlī, Muʿāwiya, ʿĀʾisha, Ṭalḥa, al-Zubayr, and those who were with them. Do not argue about them, and leave their affair to God alone—blessed and exalted is He. The Messenger of God—may peace and blessings be upon him—said: "Do not disparage my Companions and my in-laws, whether on the male side or on the female."

Accordingly,

> (113) One should "not make their lapses or their wars part of your conversation."

The Companions as a source of authority and blessing:

> (6) One should adhere to traditions on their authority, not omit it or prefer anything to it, lest you fall into Hellfire. (8) … Whoever claims that the Companions of Muhammad—may peace and blessings be upon him—have left certain parts of Islam unexplicated, has called them liars.

> (74) Only those, within the Community, are saved who (a) firmly adhere to what the Prophet—may peace and blessings be upon him—has said, to his authority, and to the authority of his Companions; (b) do not find fault in any of them; (c) do not bypass their authority; are content with what they deemed worthy of contentment; and (d) are not disinclined from their path or their teaching; and (e) know that theirs was the true Islam and the true faith.

> (84) Truth is that which comes from God; the Sunna is that of the Messenger of God—may peace and blessings be upon Him; and "the community [is defined by] the consensus" (*wa-l-jamāʿa mā jtamaʿa ʿalayhi*) of the Companions of the Messenger of God—may peace and blessings be upon

> him—during the caliphate of Abū Bakr and ʿUmar. If one confines [oneself] to the traditions of the Messenger of God—may peace and blessings be upon him—and to the consensus of the community, one shall prevail over all innovators.[109]

Ghulām Khalīl's understanding of *ijmāʿ* comes close to Ibn Ḥanbal's position,[110] as well as that of Ibn Ḥazm (d. 456/1063).[111] Although all the Companions are—according to Ghulām Khalīl—equal in merit, he advances a certain gradation within their ranks following the distinction common among *ahl al-sunna* at his time.[112]

(1) Basing his judgment on a widespread tradition from ʿAbdallāh b. ʿUmar,[113] Ghulām Khalīl states that the best of all, after the death of the Prophet, are Abū Bakr, then ʿUmar, and then ʿUthmān.[114] Al-Dhahabī, however, cites another, defective *ḥadīth* that Ghulām Khalīl transmits from Muḥammad b. ʿAbdallāh al-ʿUmarī, a weak traditionist,[115] going back to Mālik, with the following *matn*: "Follow the example of those two who will come after me, Abū Bakr and ʿUmar."[116]

(2) Next in rank, after the first three caliphs, are ʿAlī, Ṭalḥa, al-Zubayr, Saʿd b. Abī Waqqās, Saʿīd b. Zayd b. Nufayl, and ʿAbd al-Raḥmān b. ʿAwf; all of them are seen as fit to be caliphs.

(3) Following these in rank are the people of the first generation of Muslims, the first Immigrants [to Medina] (*al-Muhājirūn al-awwalūn*) and the Supporters (*al-Anṣār*). These are the ones who performed the ritual prayers in the direction of the two *qiblas*, i.e., Jerusalem first and Mecca afterward.

(4) The next in rank are those who were in the company of the Prophet for a day, a month, or a year.[117]

---

109 See also §71 (the 72 sects tradition).

110 See, e.g., Abū Yaʿlā, *al-ʿUdda* 1060–1063.

111 Ibn Ḥazm, *al-Iḥkām* iv, 146–147; Turkī, *Munāẓarāt* 173–178.

112 Muranyi, Ṣaḥāba viii, 827–829; and Kern, Companions i, 388–390.

113 Madelung, Häresiographie 224; Madelung, *Succession* 224.

114 See §14.

115 Ibn Ḥibbān, *K. al-Majrūḥīn* ii, 282.

116 Al-Dhahabī, *Mīzān* i, 142; Ibn Ḥajar, *Lisān* i, 618. See also appendix II, no. 7, in the present study.

117 §14.

The Basran prejudice against ʿAlī b. Abī Ṭālib is made manifest in Ghulām Khalīl's classification, since he does not mention him among the three caliphs. Rather, he defers him to the second group in rank, which includes the names of ten Companions who, according to some traditions, were promised Paradise (*al-ʿashara al-mubashshara*).[118] Furthermore, Ghulām Khalīl quotes the following saying by two Kufan traditionists in order to underscore the merit and preference of ʿUthmān over ʿAlī:

> (146) Ṭuʿma b. ʿAmr[119] and Sufyān b.ʿUyayna[120] said: "Whoever lingers on the question [of the preference] of ʿUthmān and ʿAlī (*waqafa ʿinda ʿUthmān wa-ʿAlī*) is but a Shīʿī, not to be considered fit for testimony, nor addressed in speech, nor foregathered."

Ghulām Khalīl adds to the above that,[121]

> Whoever prefers ʿAlī to ʿUthmān is a Rafidi, for he has disputed the command of the Companions of the Messenger of God—may peace and blessings be upon him. Whoever, in contrast, gives preference to the [first] three [Successors to Muhammad] over the rest of them (*jamāʿa*) (i.e., the Companions of Muhammad), and asks mercy for these, and takes no notice of their shortcomings, is on the path to guidance [by the standard] of *this book*.

In fact, the matter of the preference (*al-tafḍīl*) for ʿUthmān over ʿAlī was a subject of dispute among the *ahl al-sunna*. It was not until the third/ninth century that a certain consensus in the matter was reached.[122] Yet there are other accounts that do not mention ʿAlī among the rightly-guided caliphs.[123] Aḥmad b. Ḥanbal seems to have differentiated between personal merit and the office of the caliphate and to have favored ʿUthmān over ʿAlī (according to Ibn ʿUmar's tradition),[124] although some traditions report that he had declared *tarbīʿ*[125] (i.e.,

118 See § 147. Cf. also al-Khallāl, *al-Sunna* ii, 355–369; Massignon, *Passion* iii, 192, fn. 64; *ThG* i, 21–22.

119 Died 169/785 or 178/794; cf. al-Mizzī, *Tahdhīb* xiii, 383.

120 Died 198/814; Juynboll, *Encyclopedia of canonical ḥadīth* 568–621.

121 This second part of the saying appears to be an addition by Ghulām Khalīl, as it ends with a reference to "*this book*."

122 Zaman, *Religion* 50–51, 169; *ThG* iv, 698–699; and van Ess, Political ideas 155.

123 Cf. al-Khallāl, *al-Sunna* ii, 371–429.

124 Ḥarb al-Kirmānī, *K. al-Sunna* 355–359; al-Khallāl, *al-Sunna* ii, 396–404.

125 Ṣāliḥ, *Masāʾil* 99; al-Khallāl, *al-Sunna* ii, 423; Ibn Abī Yaʿlā, *Ṭabaqāt* (al-Fiqī) i, 45, (al-

accepting all four first caliphs in historical sequence of their caliphates[126]), as a criterion for preference.[127] Madelung argues that Aḥmad b. Ḥanbal had adopted the second option later in his life.[128] An account by Abū Jaʿfar Ḥamdān b. ʿAlī[129] explains this change in Aḥmad's position as a result of his keenness to reach conciliation with the Kufans.[130]

The discussion above reveals two issues. Firstly, Ghulām Khalīl ascribed a very special and honorable role to the Companions as the foundation upon which "Islam" was built and, consequently, as the main source for guidance after the Prophet, beside the Quran. For him, they are the representatives of the Community, and consensus (*ijmāʿ*) is limited to them alone. Secondly, Ghulām Khalīl belonged to a minority of scholars who still did not abide by the consensus regarding the position of ʿAlī in the question of *tafḍīl*.

7 Conformance and Submission without Questioning

Ghulām Khalīl's position is essentially as follows:
(a) True religion is to be sought from the Prophet and his Companions through strict conformance and due compliance (*al-taqlīd*), and
(b) Theological disputation and its propagators are prohibited, including polemics, controversy, reasoning by analogy, and debates over matters of religion.[131]

In chapter 3, we referred to al-Mutawakkil's edict issued in 234/848–849, when he suspended the *miḥna* and made three declarations, with severe consequences for disobedience: that all theological speculation and polemics be ended; that the people be instructed to adhere blindly to and conform strictly with (*bi-l-taslīm wa-l-taqlīd*) the example of the Prophet and his Companions; and that the traditionists should spread their knowledge and proclaim *al-sunna wa-l-jamāʿa*.[132]

ʿUthaymīn) i, 99–100, (al-Fiqī) i, 393, (al-ʿUthaymīn) ii, 501–502. For the *tarbīʿ* in Syria, see al-Ghassānī, *Akhbār* 43; and Ibn Ḥanbal, *al-Masāʾil* i, 385.

126 For the caliphate of ʿAlī, cf. al-Khallāl, *al-Sunna* ii, 341–354.

127 Abū Dāwūd, *Masāʾil* 370; al-Ghassānī, *Akhbār* 41; al-Khallāl, *al-Sunna* ii, 408 ("who ever adds ʿAlī in *tafḍīl* is a *ṣāḥib sunna*").

128 Madelung, Häresiographie 223–224; Zaman, *Religion* 51–52.

129 Died 271/884; cf. Ibn Abī Yaʿlā, *Ṭabaqāt* (al-Fiqī) i, 308, (al-ʿUthaymīn) ii, 334.

130 Al-Khallāl, *al-Sunna* ii, 373.

131 See §133.

132 Al-Masʿūdī, *Murūj* v, 5.

It seems that due compliance (*al-taqlīd*) and strict conformance in the two abovementioned points by Ghulām Khalīl, as well as in the edict by al-Mutawakkil, can be understood as being restricted to matters pertaining to dogmatic-theological issues. Directly related to the concept of *taqlīd*, however, is that of *al-ittibāʿ* (blind adherence). At the beginning of his treatise, Ghulām Khalīl argues in this regard,

> (3) For the Sunna and the Community have, both, already determined the principles of religion (*amr al-dīn*), rendering it manifest. Accordingly, everyone is called upon to comply (adhere blindly "*al-ittibāʿ*").

Therefore, both *taqlīd* and *ittibāʿ* are, for Ghulām Khalīl, the basis upon which religion (*al-dīn*) is established. In fact, during the second/eighth and third/ninth centuries both *taqlīd* and *ittibāʿ* belonged to the distinctive features of the traditionists' normativity in binding themselves uncritically to the authority of the Prophet and his Companions, and a good number of reports attested in the sources affirm these stances.[133]

In this connection, two remarks from third/ninth-century authorities Aḥmad b. Ḥanbal and Isḥāq b. Rāhawayh (d. 238/853) are to be noted.[134] When asked about al-Awzāʿī and Mālik b. Anas, Aḥmad b. Ḥanbal is reported to have answered:

> Do not entrust your religion (*lā tuqallid dīnaka*; in the sense of not following blindly in matters of religion) to anyone of them.[135] [Rather,] follow what has been transmitted on the authority of the Prophet—may peace

133 Al-Shāfiʿī refers to *taqlīd* of the Companions in many instances. In *al-Umm* viii, 763–764 (*ikhtilāf Mālik wa-l-Shāfiʿī fī al-ʿaqīqa*), he argues, "Whatever is found in the Book of God and the Sunna, and whoever hears it, is obliged to accept it unquestioningly. If, however, we did not find [evidence from the Book of God and the Sunna], we look into the sayings of the Companions, or [the saying] of one of them. Thereafter, we look into the sayings of the *aʾimma*, Abū Bakr, ʿUmar, or ʿUthmān, since it is more preferable to us to follow strict conformance (*idhā ṣirnā ilā l-taqlīd aḥabbu ilaynā*)." For al-Shāfiʿī's debt to Aḥmad and the Iraqi school in general—the works of both al-Shaybānī and Bishr al-Marīsiī—in his use of the term *taqlīd* and the associated methodological rigor, see El Shamsy, Rethinking 4–8.

134 On Isḥāq b. Rāhawayh, see Spectorsky, Sunna 51.

135 It is noteworthy, however, that Ishāq b. Rāhawayh is reported to have said, "Should al-Thawrī, al-Awzāʿī, and Mālik agree on a matter, then it is considered a sunna." Cf. al-Dhahabī, *Siyar* vii, 116.

> and blessings be upon him—and his Companions. [As for] the Successors after them, one has the choice [to follow them, or to follow what one finds appropriate].[136]

In a similar saying attributed to Aḥmad b. Ḥanbal, the term *ittibāʿ* is used instead of *taqlīd*.[137] On his part, Isḥāq b. Rāhawayh is said to have stated, while commenting on the dictum "My pronouncement of the Quran is created,"

> We are but adherents of unquestioning submission and strict conformance (*aṣḥāb ittibāʿ wa-taqlīd*) to our *aʾimma* and forebears; we do not bring about after them any novelty (*ḥadath*) which is not found in the Book of God, in the Sunna of his Prophet, or is not attested by an imam.[138]

It is clear from the quotations above that *taqlīd* and *ittibāʿ* are used by Aḥmad b. Ḥanbal and Isḥāq b. Rāhawayh with identical meaning. Later scholars, however, attempted to differentiate between these terms in describing the practice of jurisconsults within developed schools of law. Ibn ʿAbd al-Barr (d. 463/1070), for example, contends,

> *Taqlīd* among the scholars is different from *ittibāʿ*; for *taqlīd* means that you follow someone according to what has become manifest to you concerning the superiority of his statement and the veracity of his (*madhhab*). *Ittibāʿ* [in contrast] is that you follow his statement without having realized it, or having understood its significance or its meaning,[139] which amounts to a "servile imitation of other jurisconsults."

As Richard Frank rightly notes, "This insistence on *taqlīd* in all religious matters as the total and unquestioning submission to the authority of God and the Prophet ... has primarily to do with another level of theological knowing and with the formal elaboration of doctrinal theses."[140] This particular appeal to *taqlīd* has been further elucidated by Christopher Melchert, who argues,

---

136 Ibn Dāwūd, *Masāʾil* 369, no. 1793. See also Ṣāliḥ, *Masāʾil* 162–163, "Should there have been a variance among the Companions on a particular issue, one has the preference to choose from among their accounts, but not to rely on an account of a Successor in that particular matter."

137 Ibn Dāwūd, *Masāʾil* 368, no. 1789.

138 Al-Khallāl, *al-Sunna* vii, 110.

139 Ibn ʿAbd al-Barr, *Jāmiʿ* ii, 37.

140 Frank, Knowledge 37, fn. 1.

> The *taqlīd* that traditionalists did advocate had to do with the Prophet and his Companions, not the teachings of later jurisprudents. So, for example, when Aḥmad repudiates those who deny *taqlīd*, he has in mind not a party that has come up with new solutions to juridical problems, but one that, to his mind, does not wish to follow the Prophet and his Companions. His position was certainly that one should not ask theological questions that the pious ancestors were not known to have asked, nor adopt juridical positions contrary to what they were known to have adopted.[141]

Yet it should be emphasized here that Aḥmad b. Ḥanbal's understanding of *taqlīd* is nowhere expounded clearly. The two instances cited by Frank and Melchert are not direct sayings of Aḥmad b. Ḥanbal's; rather, they are pronouncements that appear in the creeds of Ghulām Khalīl and al-Iṣṭakhrī/Ḥarb al-Kirmānī.[142] Moreover, Ibn Ḥanbal seems to have been more cautious since he speaks of "sound *taqlīd*," as a quotation from al-Bukhārī indicates:

> Some people have adopted theological discourse (*hādhā l-kalām*); so they were divided into sorts that I am unable to count, without [having] understanding (*baṣar*), and without [relying on] sound conformance (*taqlīd yaṣiḥḥu*).[143]

Exactly what this "sound conformance" means is difficult to pinpoint.[144] In any case, it seems that the understanding of *taqlīd* as an uncritical acquiescence propagated by Ghulām Khalīl was a stringent yardstick that average folk should adhere to. As he argues in this regard,

> (74) One's religion is best entrusted to them. For one should acknowledge that religion (*al-dīn*) is but strict conformity (or due compliance "*al-taqlīd*"); indeed, it is to follow the example of the Companions of Muhammad—may peace and blessings be upon him.

---

141 Melchert, *Formation* 17–18.

142 Frank, Elements 149; Melchert, *Formation* 18; see al-Dhahabī's pitiless comment concerning al-Iṣṭakhrī/Ḥarb al-Kirmānī's notion of *taqlīd* in chapter three, C.5. in the present volume.

143 Al-Bukhārī, *Khalq afʿāl al-ʿibād* 59.

144 Cf. Ibn Ḥāmid's (d. 403/1012) detailed delineation of Aḥmad's methodology in matters pertaining to *fiqh*, *Tahdhīb al-ajwiba* 17–35; see also Abū Yaʿlā, *al-Masāʾil al-uṣūliyya* 52–55.

Dīn is undoubtedly one of the most difficult terms to deal with; whereas Tilman Nagel understands it as the Godly order, or *Gott gewollte Ordnung*,[145] Izutsu notes that in the Quran *dīn* "has two opposite faces, one positive and the other negative. On its positive side, it means 'to subdue, oppress, govern by power,' and on its negative side it means 'to submit, yield, to be obedient and submissive,' in the sense of individual *ṭāʿa*."[146] Izutsu concludes his illuminating exposé by affirming that *dīn* "originates from a purely personal obedience."[147] According to Ghulām Khalīl, however, *dīn* is a matter of due compliance and blind adherence to "the ancient religion" (*al-dīn al-ʿaṭīq*) that prevailed until the end of ʿUthmān's caliphate (cf. §§85 and 92; see also §71). For Ghulām Khalīl, this was the "golden time," when the Sunna and the consensus of the *jamāʿa* was established—both having set the precedence for the "Godly order" and the established custom; since *dīn* "was not intended in compliance with men's reason or their opinions,"[148] lest novelties and innovations become a *dīn*, a maintained order "with adherents of its own, who deviated from the Straight Path and, thus, forsook Islam."[149] In this sense, *dīn* is commensurate with an arrangement of precepts that one should adhere to and follow.[150]

In another bold and uncompromising conclusion, Ghulām Khalīl claims that his own book represents the religion of God and His Prophet (*dīn Allāh wa-dīn rasūl Allāh*).[151] He emphasizes this point on several occasions.[152] Unsurprisingly, the case that Ghulām Khalīl brings up here is stringent. Further proof in this regard is provided by statements studied above, including Ghulām Khalīl's declaration that "Islam is the Sunna and the Sunna, Islam."

8 Obeying the Rulers

One of the central traits distinguishing early creeds is their insistence on the concept of submission to the ruler. This avowal seems to have been ubiqui-

---

145 Nagel, *Staat* 13–15, or, "The totality of all in the revealed divine law-rooted modes of behavior of the creatures" (163), and see the following pages.

146 Izutsu, *God and man* 222; see also Brodeur, Religion.

147 Izutsu, *God and man* 229, as opposed to *millah*, which is *dīn* completely reified.

148 See §4.

149 See §5.

150 According to Ḥarb al-Kirmānī, *al-dīn* is "the Book of God, traditions (*āthār*), *sunan* and sound accounts transmitted from trustworthy men through authentic, strong, well-known and widespread narratives"; cf. his *K. al-Sunna* 59, no. 87.

151 See §92.

152 See §§88, 90, 91, 146, 148.

tously expressed in a variety of early Islamic sources in view of the fact that the caliphate of Muʿāwiya was seen by the early community of proto-Sunnis as the end of the civil war (*fitna*). The year 40–41/660–661, in which formal allegiance was paid to Muʿāwiya as caliph, came to be called in the sources "the year of [unification of] the community" (*ʿām al-jamāʿa*).[153] Several *ḥadīth*s from early Companions of the Prophet contain the behest to submit to authority in all cases and circumstances.[154] Indeed, such submission was understood as a founding precept of the political theology of proto-Sunnis, who held that legitimacy resides in the office of the caliph and that it is incumbent upon Muslims to obey authority, whether the authority acts uprightly or sinfully. Ghulām Khalīl quotes the widespread dictum, attested in several *ḥadīth* compendia, "Obeying is the prerogative of the rulers (*aʾimma*) in whatever pleases God and merits His approval."[155]

It is clear that Ghulām Khalīl in this respect is following the main convictions current in the third/ninth century among the *ahl al-sunna* about obedience to the caliphal authority, notably expressed by Aḥmad b. Ḥanbal and other early scholars. In their basic form, these precepts, as apparent in Ghulām Khalīl's *K. Sharḥ al-sunna*, maintain that[156]

> whoever succeeds to the caliphate with unanimous approval and consent is the Commander of the Faithful. None is excused in spending even a single night without accepting the ruler's authority, be the ruler righteous or dissolute (*barran aw-fājiran*). Moreover, pilgrimage and military expeditions with the ruler are valid; and Friday prayers led by him are lawful. Whoever rebels against a Muslim ruler is a dissident who has renounced allegiance to the Muslim community and opposed the

153 Khalīfa b. Khayyāṭ, *Tārīkh* 203; Abū Yaʿlā, *al-Muʿtamad* 237–238; Hinds, Muʿāwiya I 265; Madelung, *Succession* 326.

154 Cf., e.g., the saying of Makḥūl (died between 112/730 and 118/736), al-Lālakāʾī, *Sharḥ*, iv, 1299, no. 2299; and al-Awzāʿī (d. 157/774), al-Lālakāʾī, *Sharḥ* iv, 1301, no. 2302; in *al-Fiqh al-absaṭ* 609–610, attributed to Abū Ḥanīfa; the *iʿtiqād* of Sufyān al-Thawrī (d. 161/778), al-Lālakāʾī, *Sharḥ* i, 88, al-Ṭuyūrī, al-*Ṭuyūriyyāt*, ii, 539, only in the version of al-Lālakāʾī there is an addition about *jihād* with the ruler. Abū Yūsuf, *K. al-Kharāj* 80–83; Yūsuf b. Asbāṭ (d. 196/812), in Ḥarb al-Kirmānī, *K. al-Sunna* 151; al-Muḥāsibī, *al-Makāsib* 79, 83, 108; al-Bukhārī, *al-Ṣaḥīḥ* 1765 (*K. al-Aḥkām, bāb al-samʿ wa-l-ṭāʿa*); Muslim, *al-Ṣaḥīḥ* 1469 (*K. al-Imāra*); al-Ṭabarī, *Tafsīr* vii, 183–184 (commenting on Q 4:59). See also translation below §§15, 19, and 115. Furthermore, see Cook, *Commanding right* 52–67; and Abou El Fadl, *Rebellion* 112–131.

155 See §15.

156 See §§15–21 and 115.

> Prophetic tradition. To fight authority (*al-sulṭān*), or to revolt against it, is forbidden, even if he were despotic. The Sunna prohibits fighting against authority (*al-sulṭān*), for therein lies corruption, both religious and worldly.
>
> The injustices of the rulers do not lessen God's duties ordained and communicated through His Prophet. Attend the Friday prayer with them, and join arms in *jihād* with them. In all acts of devotion be their partner. Evidently, your intention is other than theirs.

Thus far, there is agreement in the earliest creeds on these principles.[157] It is important to note, however, that the creed of ʿAbdūs b. Mālik diverges in that it additionally recognizes the rule of the usurper. He writes:[158]

> Whoever revolts against an Imam from amongst the Muslim Imams—who had been agreed upon and whose caliphate has been approved by Muslims—whether by way of assent (*bi-l-riḍā*), or by way of force (*ghalaba*), then his revolt amounts to driving a wedge among the Muslims, and to violating the traditions from the Messenger of God. When he dies, he shall die a death which amounts to a *jāhilī* death (i.e., he dies as if he had never been a Muslim). It is not legitimate for anyone to fight against the ruler or to revolt against him. Whoever does so is an innovator, who does not follow the path of the Sunna.
>
> … Being obeyed is the prerogative of the rulers (*aʾimma*) and the Commander of the Faithful, be the ruler righteous or otherwise (*barran aw-fājiran*). Whether one succeeds to the caliphate with unanimous approval and consent, or uses force to become caliph, he becomes the Commander of the Faithful.

This is one of the rather interesting instances of accepting the rule of a usurper in clear and articulated diction in early Sunni creeds. It is not, moreover, as far as can be said at this point, attested in any of the dicta or responsa transmitted from Aḥmad b. Ḥanbal.[159]

Finally, it is also made clear by Ghulām Khalīl that one should invoke God for the ruler:

---

157 Crone, *God's rule* 135–136; Stewart, Developments 151.

158 Ibn Abī Yaʿlā, *Ṭabaqāt* (al-Fiqī) i, 244, (al-ʿUthaymīn) ii, 170–171; Abū Yaʿlā, *al-Muʿtamad* 238–239.

159 On this point, cf. Abou El Fadl, *Rebellion* 119, 158, and 323.

(115) Whenever you find a man invoking God against (*yadʿū ʿalā*) the ruler (*al-sulṭān*), you should know that he is a man of sectarian tendencies. [Conversely,] whenever you find a man invoking God for (*yadʿū li-*) the ruler, you should know that he is as an adherent of the Sunna—if God so wishes. For Fuḍayl said, "If I were to invoke God only once, I would invoke Him for the ruler."

9 Anthropomorphism[160]

It has long been maintained that anthropomorphic tendencies found expression and circulation in early Quranic exegesis and the *ḥadīth* literature.[161] Wesley Williams argues that "at an early period Islam possessed a tradition of 'transcendent anthropomorphism' similar in many ways to that articulated in ANE (Ancient Near Eastern/Semitic) and biblical sources."[162] Williams also contends that "during and immediately following the *Miḥna* ..., anthropomorphism achieved 'orthodox' recognition."[163]

The indices of early anthropomorphism are variegated and have been studied in some detail by modern scholars. Particularly interesting for the third/ninth century is the accusation of *tashbīh* leveled by al-Jāḥiẓ against the traditionists (*muḥaddithūn*) in his *Risāla fī nafy al-tashbīh* (written around 220/835),[164] in which he states, "The anthropomorphists have become influential because of the support of the masses."[165] Williams has also demonstrated that Aḥmad b. Ḥanbal had affirmed anthropomorphic views,[166] some of which were

160 For a distinction between the terms *tashbīh* and anthropomorphism, see Williams, Body 30.
161 *ThG* iv, 373–381; and van Ess, Tashbīh x, 341–344.
162 Williams, Body 22.
163 Williams, Aspects 442.
164 Hurvitz, Miḥna 97; Williams, Aspects 450–452.
165 Hurvitz, Miḥna 98. See also al-Jāḥiẓ, Khalq al-Qurʾān iii, 300; and Williams, Aspects 453.
166 The general evidence concerning Aḥmad b. Ḥanbal's anthropomorphic views notwithstanding, one must be cautious in verifying some specific dicta he has been credited with, either in the various creeds whose authors ascribed the sayings to Aḥmad b. Ḥanbal, or the material attributed to him in *K. al-Radd ʿalā l-zanādiqa wa-l-jahmiyya*, which has been called into doubt by al-Dhahabī; cf. al-Dhahabī, *Siyar* xi, 287; Melchert, *Aḥmad ibn Ḥanbal* 101; Holtzman, Aḥmad b. Ḥanbal. Al-ʿAjamī, the editor of the book, attempts in two sections of his introduction to demonstrate that *al-Radd* was written by Aḥmad b. Ḥanbal, cf. his *al-Radd* 84–116. Some of the reports in *K. al-Sunna*, transmitted by his son ʿAbdallāh, were also believed to represent ʿAbdallāh's own views, rather than those of his father.

blatant.[167] Williams furthermore contends, "The God of 9th–10th-century Sunnism was theophanous and corporeal."[168]

Looking again at Ghulām Khalīl's *Sharḥ*, it is noticed that the material he cites concerning God's attributes falls in line with the customary usage prevalent among the traditionalists of the third/ninth century. He states, for example,

> (11) He—may He be praised—is One, ﴿Nothing resembles His Likeness. He is the All-Hearing, All-Seeing﴾ (Q 42:11).[169] Our Lord is the First, albeit [asking] "when" is never appropriate to him; He is the Last, albeit speaking of an ending is never appropriate to him. ﴿He knows what is kept secret or even more deeply concealed﴾ (Q 20:7). On His Throne He rests; His knowledge is all-encompassing; nothing escapes it. No one but a sceptic posits a "how" or a "why" as regards God's attributes.
>
> (29) You may hear some prophetic traditions that surpass your comprehension, such as:
> (a) "The hearts of God's servants are held between two fingers of the Merciful (*al-Raḥmān*)."
> (b) "God—blessed and exalted is He—descends to the world's Heavenly sphere. He also descends on the Day of ʿArafa (i.e., the ninth day of the month of Pilgrimage) and on the Day of Resurrection."
> (c) "Hellfire will not cease receiving [the damned], until God—may His praise be glorified—places His foot upon it."
> (d) God's saying to his servant, "Walk toward me, and I shall hurry toward you."
> (e) "God—blessed and exalted is He—descends on the Day of ʿArafa."
> (f) "God created Adam in His image."
> (g) The saying of the Prophet—may peace and blessings be upon him, "I saw my Lord in the best form (*ṣūra*)"; and other such traditions.

According to these traditions, assent, belief, delegation, and satisfaction are incumbent upon Muslims. One must not interpret anything merely in accordance with one's whims. For belief is obligatory. Whimsical interpretation or rejection thereof renders one a Jahmi. This is clear also in the following of Ghulām Khalīl's statements:

167 Williams, Aspects 443–450.
168 Ibid., 454.
169 Q 42:11 (Khalidi's translation, modified).

(30) Whoever claims to see his Lord in this worldly abode is an unbeliever.

(50) Believe that the Messenger of God—peace be upon him—was carried on a journey by night to Heaven [the Nocturnal Journey]. He arrived at the Throne and spoke to God—blessed and exalted is He.

(135) If you hear a man saying, upon hearing the traditions of the messenger of God, "Merely glorify God," then know that he is a Jahmi whose intention is to dismiss, and to reject, by way of this utterance, the traditions of the messenger of God. When he comes across traditions of the *visio* of God, and the descent of God, and suchlike, he claims to be glorifying God and arguing for His transcendence. Doesn't he thus dismiss the traditions of the messenger of God—may peace and blessings be upon him? Should he retort, "God is far too transcendent, we believe, to move from one place to another?" Then he has claimed that he knows God better than anyone else does.[170] Be wary, then, of these, for the majority of people, the vulgar and otherwise, entertain such beliefs.

This instructional directory does not necessarily translate into an adherence to the circles of crude Hanbali anthropomorphists. It is definitely milder than the raucous suppositions preached by certain Hanbali authors, such as Ḥarb al-Kirmānī/al-Iṣṭakhrī during the third/ninth century and al-Barbahārī at the beginning of the fourth/tenth century. We already encountered a sample of al-Barbahārī's crude anthropomorphism in his insistence on interpreting Q 17:79 (Perhaps your Lord will resurrect you in a commendable station), as meaning that in the Hereafter God will seat Muhammad next to Himself on the throne. It is thus interesting to note that an edict of the caliph al-Rāḍī from 323/935 condemned the "crude" anthropomorphist views of al-Barbahārī and his Hanbali associates.[171]

Having said this, Ghulām Khalīl's acceptance of the statement "God created Adam in His image,"[172] along with § 60 in the *Sharḥ* on the Beatific Vision, is compatible with the prevalent interpretation among the Hanbalis, which was contested by Mālik b. Anas.[173]

---

170 English translation in Frank, Elements 161.

171 Ibn al-Athīr, *al-Kāmil* vii, 114; *ThG* iv, 381; and Williams, Aspects 454.

172 See the comments on the Arabic text. Cf. also *ThG* iv, 377–383; Williams, Aspects 443; and Williams, Body 34–37.

173 Dutton, *Origins* 19–20.

However, what brings Ghulām Khalīl closer to a more radical dogmatic position is his insistence that God spoke to Moses "with a voice." Three verses in the Quran explicitly confirm God's speech to Moses.[174] These passages caused much exasperation for Muslim exegetes;[175] nonetheless, the opinion that God spoke to Moses "with a voice" has also been preserved on the authority of Aḥmad b. Ḥanbal.[176] Ghulām Khalīl's position, however, remains milder in this respect than that of Ḥarb al-Kirmānī/al-Iṣṭakhrī, which maintains that "God spoke to Moses from His mouth."[177]

> (13a) Belief in the *visio* of God on the Day of Resurrection. [Believers] will see God with their very eyes, He will judge [them], without a veil and without a mediator.

> (54) Believe that God—blessed and exalted is He—is the One who spoke to Moses, son of Amram, on the Day of the Mount (*al-Ṭūr*). Moses heard God's very speech in a voice that struck his ears. The voice came from God and from God alone. To maintain otherwise is an act of unbelief.

Ghulām Khalīl's use of the *bi-lā kayfa* formula is in line with Aḥmad b. Ḥanbal's principle, as evident in a response to his cousin Ḥanbal b. Isḥāq.[178] While Williams in his study of Ibn Ḥanbal's creed confirms that "scholars are almost unanimous in attributing to Ibn Hanbal the use of the ancient *balkafa* formula,"[179] relying on al-Jāḥiẓ in his *Risālat al-nābita*, written about 225/839–840,[180] Williams avows also that "the text clearly implies, however, that the Nābita did not use this formula. According to al-Jahiz, one of the differences between the Nābita and the earlier anthropomorphists (*aṣḥāb al-ḥadīth*) was the Nābitas' refusal to qualify their statements with *balkafa*."[181]

---

174 ﴿And God spoke to Moses in plain speech﴾ (Q 4:164); ﴿When Moses came to Our appointment and his Lord spoke to him﴾ (Q 7:143); ﴿I have preferred you above mankind with My mission and My speech﴾ (Q 7:144).

175 *ThG* iv, 619–620; and see Muqātil, *Tafsīr* i, 423; Abū Ḥanīfa, *al-Fiqh al-akbar* 620; al-Akhfash, *Maʿānī* i, 270; Ibn Qutayba, *Taʾwīl* 111; Ibn Abī Ḥātim, *Tafsīr* i, 1119–1120; al-Māturīdī, *Taʾwīlāt* i, 528; al-Māturīdī, *K. al-Tawḥīd* 120–122; and al-Ṭabarī, *Tafsīr* vii, 689–692.

176 ʿAbdallāh b. Aḥmad, *al-Sunna* i, 280, no. 533. It is not found in his *ʿaqīda* to Musaddad b. Musarhad, where it is plainly stated, "*wa-anna Allāha kallama Mūsā taklīmā*"; cf. Ibn Abī Yaʿlā, *Ṭabaqāt* (al-Fiqī) i, 344, (al-ʿUthaymīn) ii, 430.

177 Ḥarb al-Kirmānī, *al-Sunna* 53, 220–222; Ibn Abī Yaʿlā, *Ṭabaqāt* (al-Fiqī) i, 29.

178 Al-Lālakāʾī, *Sharḥ* ii, 502, no. 777.

179 Williams, Aspects 448.

180 Al-Qāḍī, Earliest "Nābita" 41.

181 Williams, Aspects 452–453, and 462, fn. 145.

In fact, we should note here also that some of the pre-Nābita—earlier anthropomorphists among those traditionists mentioned by al-Dārimī (d. 280/893) and Ibn Abī Ḥātim (d. 327/938)—used to apply the *balkafa*. The first attribution to Mālik b. Anas (d. 179/796) is the dictum explaining Q 20:5 "How [in relation to God's sitting on the Throne] is incomprehensible (al-*kayf ghayr maʿqūl*), [His mounting] firmly (*istiwāʾ*) is not unknown, believing in it is obligatory, and posing questions about it is an innovation."[182]

Furthermore, Ibn Abī Ḥātim adduces that al-Awzāʿī, Sufyān al-Thawrī, Mālik b. Anas, and Layth b. Saʿd, when asked about traditions that refer to God's attributes, used to say, "Transmit it (*amirrūhā*, lit. let it pass) as it is without asking how (*bi-lā kayfa*)."[183]

That views of this kind were not entertained by Aḥmad b. Ḥanbal, as Williams argues (following Schacht), but were espoused later by al-Ashʿarī,[184] is not entirely accurate. Rather, in adopting the *bi-lā kayfa* axiom[185] and the use of temperate anthropomorphic terminology in general, Ghulām Khalīl remains in line with the milder anthropomorphist understanding of the early *ahl al-ḥadīth*, thus keeping a distance from crude Hanbali positions in this regard.

10 The Shiʿa

A *ḥadīth* attributed to the sixth Imam, al-Ṣādiq, stresses the belief that both *mutʿa* and *rajʿa* are basic tenets for the true followers of the Imams.[186] Ghulām Khalīl makes the refutation of both tenets part of his creed, and declares their beliefs tantamount to unbelief (*kufr*). Thus, he instructs:

> (72) Know that (*mutʿa*), that is temporary marriage, and making licit (*istiḥlāl*)[187] are strictly forbidden (*ḥarām*) until the Day of Resurrection.

182 Al-Dārimī, *al-Radd ʿalā l-jahmiyya* 55, no. 104. For a translation of a different version attributed to Mālik, see Abrahamov, "Bi-lā kayfa" 366. Abrahamov's claim that, "according to al-Barbahārī, the origin of this doctrine is the teaching of Mālik b. Anas (d. 795) and other *fuqahāʾ*," is not accurate, since Ghulām Khalīl in this phrase is referring to the issue of *khalq al-Qurʾān* rather than the issue of the attributes. The latter he mentioned directly in the preceding sentence. Abrahamov relies on Laoust in accepting the attribution of *K. Sharḥ al-sunna* to al-Barbahārī.

183 Ibn Abī Ḥātim, *al-ʿIlal* v, 468.

184 Williams, Aspects 448; Frank, Elements 155; and Abrahamov, *Anthropomorphism* 7.

185 See §§ 9, 11, 47 and 77.

186 Al-Mufīd, *al-Masāʾil al-sarawiyya* 30; al-Ṣadūq, *Man lā yaḥḍurhu l-faqīh* iii, 299, no. 4583; Crow, Death 65–66; and Turner, *Islam without Allah?* 217.

187 Having a woman married through some legal strategem in order to make licit her return to her former husband after having been thrice divorced.

(145) There has spread an innovation which amounts to disbelief in God Almighty,

(a) Whoever proclaims it is an indisputable unbeliever: Those who believe in the Return [of the dead Imam] (*raj'a*) before the Day of Resurrection, that 'Alī b. Abī Ṭālib is alive and will return, and likewise Muḥammad b.'Alī, Ja'far ibn Muḥammad, and Mūsā b. Ja'far;
(b) And posit the Imamate;
(c) And claim that they know the Unseen.

11 *Mut'a*: Temporary Marriage

In reproving *mut'a*, Ghulām Khalīl agrees with the universal Sunni attitude during the third/ninth century.[188] Sunni Muslims maintained that Q 4:23 was abrogated and, moreover, that it did not relate to the matter of marriage anyway.[189] Yet, in this context one ought not to exclude the possibility that this matter conveys a reported attempt to legalize *mut'a* reminiscent of al-Ma'mūn—who was, however, discouraged by Yaḥyā b. Aktham (d. 242/857).[190]

12 *Raj'a*: Eschatological Return

The *raj'a*[191] (the return of a dead person to life, or of a concealed Imam, in order to reign before the Day of Judgment[192]), was a widespread belief among early Shi'i sects.[193] This belief was, more often than not, mentioned together with the concept of the *ghayba* (the temporary disappearance of the Imam, who would ultimately reappear at the end of eschatological times).[194] In the

188 See the comments on § 47 (Arabic text); and Gribetz, *Strange bedfellows* 111–113.

189 Gribetz, *Strange bedfellows* 6–21. Most of the canonical *ḥadīth* books have a chapter on the prohibition of temporary marriage.

190 Al-Khaṭīb al-Baghdādī, *Tārīkh* xvi 291–292. Al-Ma'mūn was in Syria more than once; the trip most often referred to is his passage on his way to launch a campaign against the Byzantines in 215/830, al-Ṭabarī, *Tārīkh* viii, 623.

191 Crow, Death 44–45, 63–64; Sachedina, *Messianism* 166–173; Kohlberg, Radj'a viii, 371–373; Amir-Moezzi, Raj'a.

192 It was coupled with the idea of vengeance on the adversaries, al-Qummī, *al-Maqālāt* 70–71; Makḥūl al-Nasafī, *al-Radd* 85; Sachedina, *Islamic messianism* 168–169; Turner, *Islam without Allah?* 219–228; Amir-Moezzi, Raj'a.

193 Hodgson, Early Shî'a 6–8; Modarressi, *Crisis* 47, fn. Sunni writers such as Ibn Sa'd in his *Ṭabaqāt* were aware of the concept; cf. Takim, *Heirs* 116.

194 Hodgson and MacDonald, Ghayba; Turner, "Tradition" 175, contends that "doctrine of the

respective article of faith, Ghulām Khalīl seems to have restricted his focus particularly to the Imamis (known, as of the early fourth/tenth century, as the *Ithnā ʿAshariyya*, or Twelver Shiʿa),[195] since he lists in the *Sharḥ* only ʿAlī b. Abī Ṭālib, Muḥammad b. ʿAlī al-Bāqir (d. 112/732), Jaʿfar b. Muḥammad al-Ṣādiq (d. 148/765), and Mūsā b. Jaʿfar al-Kāẓim (d. 183/799), excluding other Shiʿi Imams who were adopted by other factions. Indeed, this particular belief had been associated with the three Imams enumerated by Ghulām Khalīl. Other sources also attest to the fact that some divisions among the Imamis accepted the conviction that these Imams would actually return.[196]

It is not quite clear when exactly this concept was extended to include all Twelve Imams,[197] nor when it ceased to be restricted to the belief of a minority in the return (*rajʿa*) of one of the abovementioned Imams. Be that as it may, Ghulām Khalīl appears to have been well informed about these views prevalent among the Imamis, even though he does not mention a particular belief in the *rajʿa* after Mūsā al-Kāẓim (and the belief in his return by the *Wāqifa* sect).

If we take the date of Ghulām Khalīl's persecution of the Sufis in 264/877–878 as an *ante quem* ostensible date for writing his *K. Sharḥ al-sunna*—that is, some three to four years after the minor occultation of the twelfth Imam, Muḥammad b. al-Ḥasan al-ʿAskarī—Ghulām Khalīl still seems to have been unaware of the latter's occultation.

13 *Sabb al-Ṣaḥāba*: Impeaching the Companions

One more point worth mentioning is another issue that Ghulām Khalīl raises against the Shiʿa. It pertains to the Shiʿi preference for ʿAlī, their rejection of the first three caliphs, and their rebuking of the Companions of the Prophet,

rajʿa—including the twin notions of the *ghayba* and *ẓuhūr* of the Hidden Imam—is for the most part a secondary importation into Shiʿism, introduced in the second and third centuries A.H. by adherents of one or more of the various anarcho-mystical sects known as the *ghulāt*."

195 Kohlberg, From Imāmiyya; Kohlberg, *Shīʿism* xvi.

196 For the claim that al-Bāqir was believed by some Shiʿi factions to be the Mahdi, cf. al-Baghdādī, *al-Farq* 59–60 (for his sources concerning the Shiʿa, see van Ess, *Der Eine* i, 678, 696–700). For the *rajʿa* of al-Ṣādiq and al-Kāẓim, see Modarressi, *Crisis* 56 (Jaʿfar al-Ṣādiq), 60–62 (Mūsā al-Kāẓim), and 88–91.

197 Sachedina, *Islamic messianism* 167; Turner, *Islam without Allah?* 215–218.

including his in-laws (*akhtān wa-aṣhār*;[198] i.e., all of the Prophet's sons-in-law, fathers-in-law, and brothers-in-law).[199]

Since the middle of the second/eighth century the principle of the uprightness of all the Companions of the Prophet had become a general precept among proto-Sunnis. This seems to have been first propagated by the Murjiʾa, aiming at reconciliation after the schisms that had wracked the community as a result of the events of the civil wars.[200] By the early third/ninth century, the uprightness of all the Companions became a unanimously accepted doctrine among the *ahl al-sunna*, as the early Muslim creeds attest.[201] Apart from the fact that Ghulām Khalīl does not use the term *sabb al-Ṣaḥāba*, or *shatm* (to revile),[202] his phraseology on this point is similar to that of other creeds.

14 *Makāsib*: Earnings for Living

The acquisition of profit (*kasb*) and commerce were topics of much discussion among jurists during the second/eighth century. Generally, the early jurists maintained a positive, favorable attitude toward gain and amassing capital, as Goitein puts it.[203] One of the earliest books devoted to this subject was authored by the Kufan jurist Muḥammad b. al-Ḥasan al-Shaybānī (d. 189/804). Although the preserved version of this text is an abridgment by Muḥammad b. Samāʿa (d. 233/847) of al-Shaybanī's original work,[204] it nonetheless reflects the kernel of early ideas and the views of its original author. Moreover, al-Shaybānī "maintains that *kasb* is a religious obligation, analogous to the obligation of seeking knowledge." He adds further that, "if only people would be content with what suffices for them, and direct their attention to [their] surplus wealth, and direct [this surplus wealth] toward the matter of their eternal life, it would be

198 See § 61. For the in-laws of the Prophet, Ibn Isḥāq, *Sīra* (Ḥamīdullāh) 228–250; Ibn Kathīr, *Sīra* iv, 575–615; Ibn Ḥajar, *Fatḥ* vii, 85–86; most probably, along with the first three caliphs, Muʿāwiya is alluded to here, since the Prophet married his sister Umm Ḥabība Ramla bt. Abī Sufyān; cf., Ibn Isḥāq, *Sīra* (Ḥamīdullāh) 241; Ibn ʿAbd al-Barr, *al-Istīʿāb* iv, 1843, no. 3344.

199 Kohlberg, Some Imāmī Shīʿī views 143–175.

200 *ThG* iv, 696–700.

201 Cf., e.g., Ibn Ḥanbal, *al-Masāʾil* ii, 357–361; ʿAbdallāh b. Aḥmad, *al-Sunna* ii, 543; Ḥarb al-Kirmānī, *K. al-Sunna* 66; al-Khallāl, *al-Sunna* ii, 490–495; and Watt, *Islamic creeds* 38.

202 See Wiederhold, Blasphemy 41–45.

203 Quoted according to Bonner, *Kitāb* 410.

204 Ibid., 412. A third layer was added by al-Sarakhsī as a commentary, cf. ibid., 413–414.

better for them."[205] Michael Bonner noticed that al-Shaybānī seems to say more about poverty and charity than about acquisition and gain: "The 'economy of poverty' which emerges from Shaybānī's doctrines contrasts sharply with early Islamic thinking in the tradition of *ʿilm tadbīr al-manzil* economics."[206]

The question of the lawfulness of earning one's living and the legitimacy of commerce and economic commissions in general had been of significance among the pious and renunciants of the second/eighth and third/ninth centuries. This moral scrupulousness (*waraʿ*) was a way of life that questioned the very notion of working for a living, since one should rely only on God (*tawakkul*) as the guarantor of all provision.[207] What is more, one should abstain from all dubious activities (*shubuhāt*).[208] Some of these pious abstainers from worldly life and possessions went so far as to condemn all such related activities vigorously. In its earlier forms, the trend was not new among early pious ascetics. Ḥasan al-Baṣrī (d. 110/728), for example, showed distrust toward those who accumulated wealth and possessions,[209] preaching a strict ideal of poverty.[210] Other Basran proto-Sunni mystics (Sufis) were also known for repudiating gain,[211] as was the Kufan 'Abdak al-Ṣūfī.[212] This trend seems to have taken an austere form in eastern Iran, represented by the exemplum of Shaqīq al-Balkhī (d. 194/810),[213] who propagated the disavowal of earning a livelihood altogether (*tark al-makāsib*).[214] But this conviction and way of life found acceptance also in Iraq by the mystics among the Muʿtazila, the so-called *ṣūfiyyat al-Muʿtazila*, who flourished during the first half of the third/ninth century.[215]

A rejoinder against this severe understanding was advocated by the mystic and prolific writer al-Muḥāsibī (d. 243/857), who argued for a more perceptive view based on piety, humility, self-examination, and continuous observance of one's undertakings and doings. Al-Muḥāsibī argued that to declare acquisition as forbidden and illicit (*taḥrīm al-makāsib*) is to admit weakness. Accordingly, although he emphasized abstinence and asceticism, he nonetheless rejected the extreme worldviews and conduct of Shaqīq al-Balkhī and the *ṣūfiyyat al-*

205 Ibid., 419.
206 Ibid., 410.
207 Reinert, *Lehre* 37.
208 Cf. al-Makkī, *Qūt al-qulūb* iv, 216–231; Gramlich, *Die Nahrung* iii, 684–721.
209 Cahen, Kasb.
210 Ritter, Studien 20–25.
211 Melchert, Basran origins 230–231.
212 *ThG* i, 228–229.
213 Massignon, *Essai* 228–229; Reinert, *Lehre* 80–85; and *ThG* ii, 545–547.
214 Massignon, *Passion* iii, 227; al-Muḥāsibī, *al-Makāsib* 61; Reinert, *Lehre* 172.
215 *ThG* iv, 716–717.

Muʿtazila, for possession in itself is nothing immoral; the important thing is how one feels about it and deals with it.[216] The prohibition against earning a living (*taḥrīm al-makāsib*) then found firm ground in eastern Iran with the mystic Aḥmad b. Ḥarb (d. 234/849) and his student Muḥammad b. Karrām (d. 255/869), the founder of the Karrāmiyya school,[217] whose teachings were fervently refuted by al-Ḥakīm al-Tirmidhī (d. 320/932).[218]

These developments are important to keep in mind when considering Ghulām Khalīl's views on *kasb* (§§102 and 103) and his reproach of those who renounce commerce altogether. Here, Ghulām Khalīl falls in line with the generally accepted Sunni position. In other words, Ghulām Khalīl's views on the matter are similar to those expressed by both al-Muḥāsibī and Aḥmad b. Ḥanbal, which were taken over by later Sunni traditionists and jurists such as Ibn Abī l-Dunyā (d. 281/894) in *Iṣlāḥ al-māl* and al-Khallāl (d. 311/923) in *al-Hathth ʿalā l-tijāra*. Along these lines, we must note as well that *kasb* is mentioned in only one creed of those contemporaneous to Ghulām Khalīl's—namely, that of Ḥarb al-Kirmānī/al-Iṣṭakhrī.[219]

More interestingly, Ghulām Khalīl appears not to have worried about earning his living. He was a preacher whose income was guaranteed by the state. Also, he was enmeshed in circles close to the ruling class and used to frequent banquets of the notables.

15 Reason

Not least of all, Ghulām Khalīl's definition of *al-ʿaql* is of special interest in our context. He gives a cursory definition of it, describing reason as "inborn":

> (55) Reason is inborn. To each is given [of reason] a share willed by God. Humans are as diverse in their reason as are the particles in the skies (*mithla l-dharra fī l-samāwāt*). Proportionate to their allotted share [of reason], [an amount of] work is demanded. Reason, thus, is not an object of acquisition but rather a matter of Divine favor (*faḍl*).

---

216 Ibid., iv, 197–198.

217 Van Ess, *Ungenützte Texte* 30–32; Bonner, *Kitāb* 423–426.

218 Radtke, Theologien 564–565. See also al-Ḥākim al-Samarqandī (d. 342/953), *al-Sawād al-aʿẓam* §48. Rudolph, *al-Māturīdī* 119.

219 Ḥarb al-Kirmānī, *K. al-Sunna* 57–58; Ibn Abī Yaʿlā, *Ṭabaqāt al-Ḥanābila* (al-Fiqī) i, 30, (al-ʿUthaymīn) i, 64–65.

This use of the term *mawlūd* (inborn) is quite intriguing. Since the early sources—whether literary, theological, or philosophical—state that the term *gharīzī* (or prime-instinctual) was used as a definition for *ʿaql*,[220] *mawlūd* in this context most probably means that it is a primarily created intellect given by God as a particular gift to humans, distinguishing human beings from one another.

In fact, al-Muḥāsibī defines *ʿaql* as *"gharīza yūladu al-ʿabdu bi-hā,"* which means an inborn instinct.[221] The term *mawlūd* is also used by Ghulām Khalīl's older contemporary al-Jāḥiẓ (d. 255/869) in *K. al-Buldān*, where he says, "The inborn intellect[222] is finite, whereas experiential reason has no limits."[223] This demarcation between an "inborn reason" and "experiential reason" comes near to al-Muḥāsibī's second part of the definition, in which he contends that this prime instinct is augmented gradually through cognition of those means that establish or conjure up the intelligible (*thumma yazīdu fīhi maʿnā baʿda maʿnā bi-l-asbāb al-dālla ʿalā l-maʿqūl*). This gradual increase in knowledge through induction is actually comparable to experiential reasoning. In fact, al-Jāḥiẓ seems to have used al-Muḥāsibī's definition, since he uses a definition that appears in *K. Māʾiyyat al-ʿaql*;[224] or else both of them are using the same source.

Nonetheless, al-Muḥāsibī accentuates the specific meaning of his argument by explaining that this cognition (*maʿrifa*) derives, in fact, from the intellect and is not an acquired knowledge (*ʿilm muktasab*).[225] This rejoinder is most

220 Al-Muḥāsibī, *Māʾiyyat al-ʿaql* 205, 201, 203–205; *ThG* iv, 206–207. It is also a light that resides in the heart, cf. al-Muḥāsibī, *Māʾiyyat al-ʿaql* 204; Massignon, *Essai* iii, 17. Al-Shāfiʿī in his *Risāla*, mentions that intellects (*ʿuqūl*) are "installed" by God (*rakkabahā fīhim*), Lowry, *Early Islamic legal theory* 313. Abū Yaʿlā, *al-ʿUdda* i, 83–84, claims that Aḥmad b. Ḥanbal likewise considered *al-ʿaql* to be a *gharīza*. See also Ibn Taymiyya, *Bughya* 257; Ibn Taymiyya, *al-Radd* 94, 276. Makdisi, *Ibn ʿAqīl and culture* 92, writes, "A predecessor of Ibn ʿAqil, Barbahari (d. 329/941) seems to have this identification in mind when he states that reason is created (*mawlūd*). Barbahari is no doubt alluding to the first principles of reason." In accepting the authorship of al-Barbahārī, Makdisi is following his teacher Laoust.

221 Al-Muḥāsibī, *Māʾiyyat al-ʿaql* 205.

222 Khalidi, *Arabic historical thought* 107, has "The created mind."

223 Al-Jāḥiẓ, *K. al-Buldān* 465 (al-Awṭān wa-l-buldān iv, 112): *"al-ʿaql al-mawlūd mutanāhī al-ḥudūd, wa-ʿaql al-tajārib lā yūqafu minhu ʿalā ḥadd."* In his Fī ḥujjaj al-nubuwwa iii, 237, al-Jāḥiẓ uses the term *gharīza*.

224 "An argument is of two sorts: clear witnessing or a subjugating tradition (*ʿiyān ẓāhir aw khabar qāhir*)," cf. al-Muḥāsibī, *Māʾiyyat al-ʿaql* 232; al-Jāḥiẓ, Fī ḥujaj al-nubuwwa iii, 225–226.

225 De Crussol argues that "al-Muḥāsibī relies on revelation, and discovers through the grace of *ʿaql* what is intelligible and useful, that is to say reasonable," *Role* 252; "Good and evil are 'objective' and inherent to the created order; *ʿaql* has the legitimate right to seek to define them," ibid., 253.

probably directed against those such as Abū l-Hudhayl al-ʿAllāf (d. ca. 227/841) who argued that reason is tantamount to understanding and reasoning, which is the faculty of acquiring knowledge.[226]

Again, it seems necessary to keep these intellectual developments of early Islam in mind in order to appreciate Ghulām Khalīl's understanding of the matter. In fact, Ghulām Khalīl is refuting the idea of an "acquired reason," and in doing this he is most probably following al-Muḥāsibī. Al-Muḥāsibī, however, relying on a prophetic tradition, speaks of attaining reason by means of obeying God.[227]

Al-Muḥāsibī also expressly refers to inference (*istidlāl*),[228] understanding (*fahm*),[229] insight (*naẓar*),[230] and perspicacity (*baṣīra*).[231] Nowhere does he speak of an "experiential *ʿaql*." It is, therefore, interesting to note as well a saying attributed to the Basran Muʿāwiya b. Qurra (d. 113/731):[232] "Reason is of two sorts, experiential reason and reason by nature (*ʿaql tajārib wa-ʿaql naḥīza*[233])."[234]

It is in the context of "acquired reason" that one appreciates the delineation proposed by Abū l-Ḥusayn b. Wahb al-Kātib in his *K. al-Burhān*, written after 335/946 and circulated as *K. Naqd al-nathr* with an attribution to Qudāma b. Jaʿfar (d. 337/948).[235] Ibn Wahb argues that there are two kinds of reason. The first is endowed (*mawhūb*), which God has created as a natural disposition in the human beings, and the second, acquired (*maksūb*), which man derives from experimentation (*tajriba*), lessons (*ʿibar*), morals (*adab*), and insight (*naẓar*).[236] Such a differentiation between the levels of reason was later elaborated by al-Ghazālī, who distinguished between four meanings for reason (*ʿaql*), the first of which is the *gharīza*, and the third, experiential reason.[237] Another classification is given by Qawwām al-Sunna (d. 535/1140), who, like al-Ghazālī, was a Shafiʿi scholar from eastern Iran. According to him, the first

226 Al-Ashʿarī, *Maqālāt* 480–481. Cf. *ThG* iii, 250.
227 Al-Muḥāsibī, *al-Waṣāyā* 86–87.
228 Al-Muḥāsibī, *Māʾiyyat al-ʿaql* 206, 225, 232.
229 Ibid., 208.
230 Ibid., 237.
231 Ibid., 210.
232 Al-Dhahabī, *Siyar* v, 153–155.
233 Nature (*naḥīzat al-rajul ṭabīʿatuhu*), cf. Ibn Manẓūr, *Lisān* v, 415 under "n.ḥ.z."; Ibn Taymiyya, *al-Radd* 94.
234 Ibn Abī al-Dunyā, *al-ʿAql* 17.
235 See the introduction by the editor, Ḥafnī Muḥammad Sharaf.
236 Ibn Wahb, *al-Burhān* 53–54; (ps.-Qudāma), *Naqd al-nathr* 6–7.
237 Al-Ghazālī, *Iḥyāʾ* 109–110; id., *Miʿyār* 286–287; Leaman, *Introduction* 153–154.

reason is inborn and naturally disposed (*mawlūd, maṭbūʿ*); this is the reason of the human being, which distinguishes man in excellence from all other creatures, and it is the place of religious obligation (*al-taklīf*). The second is that of affirmation (*taʾyīd*), which comes together with and is related to belief (*al-īmān*); and the third is that of experiential reasoning.[238]

Ghulām Khalīl argues further that men are diverse with regard to their reason and intellectual capacities. Accordingly, their deeds or works (sing. *ʿamal*) differ in this world, as do their rewards in the Hereafter. The idea that God will reward human beings according to the reason bestowed on them appears in traditions attributed to the Prophet Muhammad, as well as in a tradition by Imam al-Bāqir, who attributes it to Moses.[239]

---

238 Qawwām al-Sunna, *al-Ḥujja* i, 320; see also ii, 429, were he quotes the second part of Ghulām Khalīl's item.

239 Al-Barqī, al-*Maḥāsin* 194. The Shiʿi concepts of *ʿaql* reveal generally a more Gnostic tone and seem to have been influenced by Neoplatonic nuances, as van Ess argues; cf. his *ThG* ii, 119.

EPILOGUE

Doctrinal Instruction in Times of Political Change

In the preceding chapters, we have investigated the themes and structure of the *K. Sharḥ al-sunna* by Ghulām Khalīl (d. 275/888), as well as its relationship to other Sunni creeds from the third/ninth century. This study has yielded detailed insights into the themes and nature of early Muslim creeds and has delineated the various constituents that inform these texts. In the process, we have seen that the early creeds constitute a genre that consolidates key doctrinal ideas taken from previous generations, and that most of these tenets appear to have found consensus among the early *ahl al-sunna*. Notably, most of these dogmatic materials are known to have been adopted by Aḥmad b. Ḥanbal (d. 241/855), the vastly influential "trendsetter" in the flourishing of the scholarly genre of Sunni Muslim creeds.

Furthermore, we revisited the question of the authorship of *K. Sharḥ al-sunna* and found that it was, in fact, possible to establish substantial evidence against the uncertainties and doubts held by several modern scholars concerning Ghulām Khalīl's authorship of this book. Four steps have been instrumental in this regard: (a) close scrutiny of the relevant external evidence available in the classical Arabic sources, (b) a reassessment of the different arguments offered by modern scholars, (c) an examination of internal data drawn from the *K. Sharḥ al-sunna* itself, and (d) the inclusion of circumstantial data from a variety of sources. As a result of this inclusive approach, our research conclusions now attest that the third/ninth-century scholar and preacher Ghulām Khalīl was indeed the author of the *K. Sharḥ al-sunna*, rather than the Hanbali activist al-Ḥasan b. ʿAlī al-Barbahārī (d. 329/941).

In his book *Der Eine und das Andere*, Josef van Ess propounds an engaging reflection that deserves closer attention in this context. He asks, "Hat Barbahārī einfach die ‚Schule' des Ġulām Ḫalīl mitsamt ihrer Programmschrift übernommen?" (Did al-Barbahārī simply adopt Ghulām Khalīl's "school," along with its programmatic text?).[1] It is true that both scholars enjoyed ubiquitous success among the masses, in spite of the fact that they had distinct backgrounds and followed different agendas. Yet we must also ask why al-Barbahārī would have decided to adopt this specific creed from among the various creeds readily

1 Van Ess, *Der Eine* i, 285, fn. 44.

DOI:10.1163/9789004429055_007

available during the third/ninth century. Would it not have better served his "ideological" preferences to settle on a creed that clearly embraced a hard-line position on anthropomorphism, one that avoided the rather quietist approach advanced by Ghulām Khalīl? One might expect at least that al-Barbahārī would have made changes to Ghulām Khalīl's creed to make it serve his conservative outlook more effectively.

While the creeds generally tend to have common doctrinal points—since they draw on a shared repository prevalent among the *ahl al-sunna* in the third/ninth century—there was no urgent need for the authors of creeds to take over a given creed in its entirety, particularly if it diverged in major points from one's own mindset. In fact, all the creeds we studied in chapter 3, without exception, reveal certain peculiar thematic and dogmatic aspects effecting a specific textual arrangement and presentation of ideas, and thus impart a measure of information about their intended audience. We will come back to this point later in this epilogue.

Ghulām Khalīl's life and career were marked by the political instability in the ruling ʿAbbasid house. After the assassination of al-Mutawakkil (r. 247–248/861–862), the crisis found its expression in the forceful interference of Turkish soldiers in the affairs of the state,[2] culminating in a civil war between al-Mustaʿīn (r. 248–252/862–866), the caliph in Baghdad, and his cousin al-Muʿtazz (r. 252–255/866–869) in Samarra.[3] During this war, which lasted for about a year, Baghdad was besieged by the Turkish soldiers, and its environs suffered greatly. The result was extensive devastation and a drastic decline in the rural economy.[4]

Spurred on by this almost anarchic situation, the Saffarids[5] were able to vanquish the Tahirids, governors for the ʿAbbasids in northeast Iran, posing a serious threat to the caliphate. Yaʿqūb al-Ṣaffār (d. 275/879), founder of the later Saffarid empire, tried to gain control over Iraq but was defeated in a battle near Baghdad in Rajab 262 / April 876. More importantly, the revolt of the Zanj (255–270/869–883) in southern Iraq is regarded as the most threatening menace that the ʿAbbasid caliphate faced during the reigns of al-Muhtadī (r. 255–256/869–870) and al-Muʿtamid (r. 256–279/870–892). It eventually resulted in the total destruction of Basra.[6]

2 Gordon, *Thousand swords* 75–104.
3 Kennedy, *Armies* 126–149; Kennedy, *Prophet* 169–173.
4 Gordon, *Thousand swords* 90; Waines, Third century internal crisis 299.
5 Bosworth, Ṣaffārids viii, 795–798.
6 Popovic, *Revolt* 60–65; Kennedy, *Armies* 148–158; Kennedy, *Prophet* 177–179.

These fateful crises at the heart of the empire left their marks on the community, which had to contend with the breakdown of order and equilibrium. Indeed, it witnessed the critical moment of the ushering in of a new balance of power. It is against this background that we must situate Ghulām Khalīl's creed as an attempt to serve the "ideational system" of the state, while at the same time reflecting the mood that prevailed in the community.[7]

Periods of transition are usually intense moments in history that stimulate reaction in the field of religious and doctrinal instruction. As was argued in chapter 3, the controversy kindled by al-Ma'mūn over ʿAbbasid state ideology, as well as other momentous political issues and matters pertaining to political theology, had galvanized an uncompromising rejoinder on the part of the *ahl al-sunna*, represented by Aḥmad b. Ḥanbal. The aftermath of the *miḥna* witnessed a proliferation in Sunni creeds. Tarif Khalidi, for example, contends that it was approximately in the second half of the third/ninth century "that the ʿAbbasids, and after a hundred years or more of dramatic shifts in religious policy, seemed at last to be adopting what was eventually to become Sunni 'orthodoxy.'"[8]

Concentrating on the social function of creeds and their reception by various audiences, questions arise regarding to whom these creeds were addressed, and how their mode of reception is to be understood. In the absence of unequivocal data in the sources, it is rather difficult to draw definite conclusions in this regard. We shall therefore begin our concluding reflections on the matter by looking at the authors of early Islamic creeds, paying particular attention to their geographic provenance.

Transoxania

– Muḥammad b. Ḥabīb al-Andarābī (creed 8), from Balkh, the center of Murji'a activities;[9]
– Abū Rajā' Qutayba b. Saʿīd (d. 240/854), from Balkh (creed 13);
– Muḥammad b. Ismāʿīl al-Bukhārī (d. 256/870). Renowned traditionist and author of what came to be, among Sunnis, the most respected canonical *ḥadīth* compendium. He spent long periods of his life in Bukhara, and his creed (creed 15) was related on the authority of a traditionist from Bukhara, who related it to a student in Shāsh, Transoxania.

7 Watt, *Islam* 2–3.
8 Khalidi, *Arabic historical thought* 111.
9 Madelung, Early Murji'a 36–39.

Iran

- Ḥarb al-Kirmānī (d. 280/893). He lived in Sirjan, and it is important to note that a refutation of his book (creed 1) came from Khorasan, penned by the Muʿtazili theologian Abū l-Qāsim al-Balkhī al-Kaʿbī (d. 319/931);
- The two Rāzīs, Abū Zurʿa ʿUbayd Allāh (d. 264/878) and Abū Ḥātim Muḥammad (d. 277/890), who both flourished in Rayy;
- Abū Thawr, Ibrāhīm b. Khālid (d. 240/854). He was from Baghdad, but his creed (12) is preserved in a response letter he wrote to a man in Khorasan who had asked him about faith.

Iraq

- Musaddad b. Musarhad (d. 228/842), from Basra. His creed is preserved in a letter from Aḥmad b. Ḥanbal addressed to him (creed 10, in chapter 3);
- ʿAlī b. ʿAbdallāh b. al-Madīnī, from Basra. He died in Samarra in 243/849 (creed 14);
- ʿAbdūs b. Mālik (d. ca. 250/864), from Baghdad. He attributes his creed to Aḥmad b. Ḥanbal (creed 7).

Syria

- Muḥammad b. ʿAwf Abū Jaʿfar (d. 272/885). He was from Hims, Syria.

Let us also keep in mind the dynamic factor of mobility, and the scholarly networks associated with travel and acquisition of knowledge, within the cosmopolitan Arabo-Islamic cultural sphere. Most authors, including those named above, undertook journeys in search of knowledge. However, the sources yield no clear indications as to where they resided when composing their respective creeds. As a correlate, these creeds must have diffused broadly in various parts of the Islamic empire. Even more certainly, each of these creeds must have been composed with a specific audience in mind—in most cases, the *ahl al-sunna* in the respective localities where the authors in question lived.

Five of the authors mentioned above flourished in either North Iran or Transoxania, both areas where Hanafis, followers of the Murjiʾa, and a variety of rationalists and semi-rationalists were abundant. It is particularly interesting to note that a number of the transmitters of Ghulām Khalīl in the field of *ḥadīth* came from northern Iran (see appendix 11). These creeds were significantly characterized by an urgent need to facilitate a solid and substantial religious education, achieved through discussing and identifiying uncompromising tenets of doctrine against what was considered religious “innovation.”

Apparently, these creeds as means of doctrinal construction were often meant primarily for a rather learned audience among the authors’ coreligionists, aiming to expound the traditional rules of faith and evince what distinguishes "us" from the "other." Creeds generally infuse a sense of obligation and an urge to follow "the correct" ritual practice, to observe the boundaries of social interaction, and not to trespass against the right requirements of orthopraxy. Also significant is the insistence expressed in these creeds on forbidding any questioning as to "why" and "how," or for that matter, any indulgence in theological disputations.

Crucial to the dissemination of knowledge in the Islamic cultural sphere was the intertwined relationship between oral lecturing and the process of writing, authorized by the teacher/transmitter. Accordingly, these creeds circulated first among scholars of the same guild. But, as is in the very nature of the genre, they appear to have been read both publicly and privately, and often publicized in congregations at mosques, or in other religious and/or educational gatherings.

An attempt to explain the proliferation of creeds during the third/ninth century must take the conversion rate into consideration. Indeed, it seems that it had reached a "slight peak" during this century. Richard Bulliet once estimated that in Iran, the 34 percent making up the "late majority" converted between 820 and 875.[10] More recently, however, Bulliet revised his estimate, contending, "Iran in the third/ninth century saw a rapid growth of Islam but was very far from being a predominantly Muslim country until the end of the century."[11] As for Iraq, Bulliet states that around 260/873–874 "the curve of conversion showed a slight peak or bulge."[12]

Creeds and other confessional statements are particularly effective in the instruction of new converts. In addition, they are similarly important in polemics against all sorts of "heresies" often carried over, consciously or not, by these converts from their previous religious milieus into the Muslim intellectual and religious discourse. Wilferd Madelung noticed that Sunni traditionalism was strongly established in particular in Bukhara and influenced the local Hanafi creed,[13] which attracted eastern converts to Islam.[14]

Ghulām Khalīl's career flourished between Basra and Baghdad during the middle of the third/ninth century. However, as we have seen, there is not much definite information about his life. Al-Khaṭīb al-Baghdādī does indicate that he lived in Baghdad from an early age and that he studied there.[15] Nonetheless,

10 Bulliet, *Conversion* 51–52.

11 Bulliet, *Cotton* 32.

12 Bulliet, *Conversion* 73.

13 Madelung, Early Murji'a 39.

14 Madelung, *Religious trends* 19.

15 Al-Khaṭīb al-Baghdādī, *Tārīkh* vi, 246.

the little gleaned from the sources about Ghulām Khalīl's life does not permit of definite conclusions about when exactly he authored his *K. Sharḥ al-sunna*.

Looking at internal evidence in his book, we would argue that he apparently wrote this creed sometime between the death of the caliph al-Mutawakkil in Shawwāl 247 / December 861—since the text indicates rather clearly that the caliph was dead when the book was written (see §79)—and 264/877–878—that is, the date of Ghulām Khalīl's persecution of the Sufis. These dates seem to fall within the supremacy of al-Muwaffaq, Abū Aḥmad Ṭalḥa b. Jaʿfar, son of the caliph al-Mutawwakil and a slave girl, Umm Isḥāq (or Asḥar), and regent and virtual ruler of the caliphate as of Ṣafar 257 / January 871[16] and throughout the reign of his half brother al-Muʿtamid (r. 256–279/870–892).[17]

As attested by the *samāʿ* certificates at the beginning and end of the book, the *K. Sharḥ al-sunna* was circulated in the learned circles of Baghdad during the third-sixth/ninth-twelfth centuries. It was also known to Qawwām al-Sunna in Isfahan, and must have been circulated later in Damascus, where the only surviving manuscript of this creed has been preserved. But taking into consideration that Ghulām Khalīl was a preacher—a public voice, so to speak, who represented "low" Sufism,[18] which touched on the pious sensibilities in the religious culture of the masses—one would expect certain items of the creed to have been used frequently during his sermons (even though it was undesirable for the preacher to prolong a sermon and risk boring his audience[19]). Preaching was not restricted to an audience of common people (*qāṣ al-ʿāmma*),[20] as preachers also used to sermonize to men of the state and other notables.[21] In the case of Ghulām Khalīl—the "master of Baghdad" (*shaykh Baghdād*), a man of "admirable sublimity" (*jalāla ʿajība*) and "authoritative somberness" (*ṣawla mahība*), who was treated favorably by the mother of the ʿAbbasid regent al-Muwaffaq and admired by both state officials (*al-dawla*) and the common folk (*al-ʿawāmm*), as al-Dhahabī informs us[22]—it is highly probable that the reception of his creed was not limited to the closed circles of the learned, and that he also used to teach his creed (or tenets thereof) in formal assemblies (conceivably, in the palace as well).

16 Gordon, *Thousand swords* 141, and 250, fn. 5.

17 Al-Muʿtamid's mother is called Fityān—al-Khaṭīb al-Baghdādī, *Tārīkh* v, 99; and see Kennedy, al-Muʿtamid ʿAlāʾllāh.

18 Khalidi, *Arabic historical thought* 211, "low" Sufists who managed "to transmit their message of rededication and moral reform to the urban masses."

19 A statement attributed to Aḥmad b. Ḥanbal; cf. Ibn al-Jawzī, *Quṣṣāṣ* 369.

20 Ibid., 167.

21 Ibid., 193.

22 Al-Dhahabī, *Siyar* xiii, 284; Massignon, *Passion* i, 81.

New converts to Islam are another audience that would have been quite receptive to this kind of doctrinal instruction. As we have seen, Ghulām Khalīl wrote his creed during a time when the conversion rate was reaching a "slight peak," to use Bulliet's words again, around 260/873–874. However, there is a further factor that suggests yet another possible audience. Let us recall here that political disorder had irreversibly damaged the rural economy through "the destruction of rural life and damage to the irrigation based agricultural system."[23] In the aftermath of the civil war between al-Mustaʿīn and al-Muʿtazz, waves of refugees from rural areas moved to Baghdad. Others must have come in from Basra during the revolt of the Zanj. As David Waines has argued, "The destruction to rural life wrought by this conflict was then compounded by the conflict of large segments of the rural population against the ruling order."[24] Waines observes furthermore, "The destruction of rural districts consequent upon the 'civil war' and siege of Baghdad in 251/865 wiped out any notion that the government's reciprocal function of protection could be honoured."[25] It is at such times of turmoil and uncertainty that it becomes vitally necessary to regulate the "ideational system" and the public teaching of "correct" doctrinal, moral, and political views, guarding against all manner of religious and political errors.

William M. Watt has contended that the function of Islamic creeds "is to preserve some balance in the ideational synthesis on which Islamic society is based … In so far as a set of dogmas is accepted, it preserves the balance and comprehensiveness of an ideational system (such as the Qurʾanic one) and thereby contributes to the integration of the society based on this ideational system."[26] This is especially the case, Watt argues, "when the religious institution, which produces the dogmatic formulations, is in alliance with a political or ruling institution."[27] In fact, considerations of this kind provide additional historical evidence of the importance of Ghulām Khalīl's creed.

The essential question remains, however, as to whether Ghulām Khalīl's creed enjoyed state patronage, and whether it was perhaps commissioned by an appeal from the palace. If this was the case, it would not have been a unique instance in that time and cultural milieu.[28] There is, for example, clear histor-

23 Waines, Third century internal crisis 299.
24 Ibid., 295.
25 Ibid., 299.
26 Watt, *Islam* 223.
27 Ibid., 174.
28 El-Hibri, *Reinterpreting* 124, writes, "The fact that the caliphs from al-Mutawakkil onward

ical attestation of one such event in Transoxania, when the Samanid prince Ismāʿīl b. Aḥmad (r. 279–295/892–907) reportedly commissioned the writing of a Sunni dogma that was eventually authored in 290/902 by al-Ḥākim al-Samarqandī (d. 342/953).[29]

This gives rise to the next question: Who might have encouraged Ghulām Khalīl to write and publish such a creed? Support may have been instigated by either the regent al-Muwaffaq himself, or by al-Muwaffaq's mother, who is known to have been Ghulām Khalīl's patron. In fact, Hugh Kennedy has shown that al-Muwaffaq and his son Abū l-ʿAbbās, later the caliph al-Muʿtaḍid (r. 279–289/892–902), played a vital role in propagating the official writing of accounts favorable to their rule.[30] Interestingly enough, there are in fact two points in the *K. Sharḥ al-sunna* that make this creed particularly pro-ʿAbbasid in tenor. The first point concerns the political disorder within the ʿAbbasid ruling house, as well as the socioeconomic crises and the wars against the Zanj and Yaʿqūb al-Ṣaffār—that is, events that were critical in raising apocalyptic expectations. Wilferd Madelung has observed that many Islamic apocalyptic *ḥadīth*s served a war of propaganda.[31] As we saw in chapter 2,[32] the idea of *al-Qāʾim al-Mahdī* (the Riser, Resurrector, or Redresser) was central to ʿAbbasid ideology and identity formation, and it fashioned part of the ʿAbbasid propaganda during the years of the underground mission, the ʿAbbasid *daʿwa*. The idea of *al-Qāʾim al-Mahdī* was revived and continued to prevail among the ʿAbbasids from the reign of al-Maʾmūn onward.[33]

By inducing the belief in the coming of *al-Qāʾim min Āl Muḥammad* (the Resurrector from among Muḥammad's House), Ghulām Khalīl was propagating a possible restitution of the caliphate in the figure of his charismatic patron, the victorious ʿAbbasid prince and military leader al-Muwaffaq, who had acted as regent throughout most of his brother's reign and who in 261/875 was given a place in the succession of the caliphate after al-Muʿtamid's son.[34] Between 266/879 and 270/883, al-Muwaffaq took command of the war against the Zanj

embraced orthodox creeds and worked to institutionalize them made the *ʿulamāʾ* more deferential to the position of the caliphs as symbolic religious leaders and protectors of orthodox religious law"; this contention, however, cannot be substantiated in the sources.

29 Madelung, *Religious trends* 30.

30 Kennedy, Caliphs 26, 33–35; Kennedy, *Prophet* 180.

31 Madelung, ʿAbd Allāh b. al-Zubayr 293.

32 See also Jarrar, Ghulām Khalīl.

33 Madelung, New documents 345.

34 Kennedy, *Prophet* 174.

and appointed his son Abū l-ʿAbbās to lead the campaign.[35] Al-Muwaffaq emerged victorious and claimed the title of *al-Nāṣir* (the Victorious).

This understanding of these political developments as connected with Ghulām Khalīl's activities and writing is strongly supported by a statement in the *K. Sharḥ al-sunna*, according to which the coming of *al-Qāʾim* is anticipated. It is bolstered furthermore by the general ideological interests of the ʿAbbasids to spread expectancy of an imminent renewal of ʿAbbasid society.

It is interesting to note furthermore that all the editors of the *Kitāb Sharḥ al-sunna* who have attributed the text to al-Barbahārī[36] have passed in silence over the fact that the concept of *al-Qāʾim min Āl Muḥammad* is a particularly Shiʿi/ʿAbbasid precept. It is also of note that all the respective editors have been affiliated in one way or another with the Salafi Saudi establishment.[37] Only Ṣāliḥ al-Fawzān, a member of the Council of Senior Ulema in the Kingdom of Saudi Arabia,[38] has attempted to explain this particular point. His explanation, however, aims to make it consistent with a general Salafi understanding, as he states,[39]

> The Qāʾim is the Mahdī, Muḥammad b. ʿAbdallāh. His name is identical with the name of the Messenger [of God]—may peace and blessings be upon him—; and the name of his father is identical with the name of the father of the Messenger [of God]. He belongs to the house/progeny (*bayt*) of al-Ḥasan b. ʿAlī—may God be pleased with him. It was said that the wisdom in this [in the fact that *al-Qāʾim* belongs to the progeny of al-Ḥasan b. ʿAlī], and God knows best, is that when al-Ḥasan renounced the caliphate in favor of Muʿāwiya—may God be pleased with him—in order to prevent bloodshed [among the Muslims], God, as an act of graciousness (*akramahu Allāh*), granted him that the Mahdi should be from his own progeny.[40]

Ṣāliḥ al-Fawzān's explanation is peculiar in that it restricts the expectation of *al-Qāʾim al-Mahdī* to the progeny of al-Ḥasan b. ʿAlī, who, according to Sunni

---

35 Hellige, *Die Regenschaft* 39–44; Kennedy, *Armies* xv, 151–155; Kennedy, Caliphs 179; Gordon, *Thousand swords* 142.

36 This pertains to the nine editions we were able to consult on this point.

37 For an appraisal of the much-debated terms "Salafi" and "Salafiyya," cf. Shinar, Salafiyya; Wiktorowicz, Anatomy; Lauzière, *Making* 5–10; and Bin Ali, *Roots* 1–13.

38 See appendix 1, no. 9.

39 Al-Fawzān, *Sharḥ al-sunna* 92.

40 It is noteworthy that Ṣāliḥ al-Fawzān does not mention this explanation in his chapter on al-Mahdī; cf. his book *al-Irshād ilā ṣaḥīḥ al-iʿtiqād* 169–170.

understanding, had "wisely opted" to peacefully end the devastating war within the early Muslim community by abdicating his rights to the caliphate.[41] Moreover, Ṣāliḥ al-Fawzān's way of explaining early Islamic history disparages the Twelver Imami belief that *al-Qāʾim* is the Twelfth Imam from the progeny of al-Ḥusayn b. ʿAlī—that is, Muḥammad b. al-Ḥasan al-Mahdī, who is said to have entered major occultation in 329/940.

The second point is that Ghulām Khalīl's *K. Sharḥ al-sunna* is the only creed from among those written in the third/ninth century that explicitly expresses interest in the practice of "commanding right and forbidding wrong" (*al-amr bi-l-maʿrūf wa-l-nahy ʿan al-munkar*). Ghulām Khalīl underscores the fact that this duty should only be commenced by the authorities, whether the ruler is "righteous or dissolute" (*barran aw-fājiran*), and regardless of the ruler's legitimacy. The importance of this instruction must be highlighted. This is another point in which Ghulām Khalīl's creed well serves the concerns of the ʿAbbasid ruling house, during an extended period of conflict concerning the legality of those claimants who attempted to seize the office of the caliph.[42]

Moreover, his creedal point about political quietism had become a widely accepted item in catechist literature at an early stage. Ghulām Khalīl's insistence on the legitimacy of the ruler, however, and his individual responsibility in implementing and securing *al-amr bi-l-maʿrūf wa-l-nahy ʿan al-munkar* delineates "clever politicking" as much as it does an indubitable urge to assert the legality of the ʿAbbasid ruler, in a time of an extended quandary over the imperative concern of the legitimacy of the ruler. In effect, it bolsters the justification of ʿAbbasid supremacy. Let us not forget that this kind of "ideational" propaganda was launched at a time of crisis, when a new, radical, and formidable period of equilibrium in power was being ushered in along with a "messianic event," eventually represented by "the rising star" of al-Muwaffaq.[43]

Ghulām Khalīl's strategy seems to have been well designed. In order to successfully reach the broadest possible audience among the traditionists, and to attain space for promulgating a pro-ʿAbbasid stance, he apparently aimed to connect his creed to the living legacy bequeathed by Aḥmad b. Ḥanbal, the

41 Called in Sunni sources *ʿām al-jamāʿa*; see above chapter 4, "Obeying the Rulers." For al-Ḥasan's abdication, cf. Madelung, *Succession* 321–327; Jafri, *Origins* 130–157; and Dakake, *Charismatic community* 74–75.

42 The idea of holy war (*jihād*) was also invested in the "official propaganda" widely disseminated in the "official" versions, written under the patronage of al-Muwaffaq and his son, the future caliph al-Muʿtaḍid; see Kennedy, Caliphs 30, 34–35.

43 For the messianic aura with which several early ʿAbbasid caliphs attempted to surround their reign, see Khalidi, *Arabic historical thought* 96–97.

venerated authority of conservative Islam, to whom he refers six times in his book.[44] Additionally, Ghulām Khalīl probably also hoped to attract the same popular support that the traditionists, as well as the Hanbali masses, generally enjoyed.

These two points demonstrate once again the uniqueness of Ghulām Khalīl's creed. In all the other items of his creed, he espoused tenets that had been approved by Ibn Ḥanbal and had already become standard doctrines among the *ahl al-sunna* during Ghulām Khalīl's time. It is, therefore, no surprise that the *K. Sharḥ al-sunna* eventually found wide circulation among Hanbali scholars in later generations, as the respective chains of transmission attest. It also becomes clearer now how the eminent significance that this creed had gained appears to have attracted an attempt at forgery, when it was attributed to the Hanbali activist Abū Muḥammad al-Barbahārī in the fifth/eleventh century. While this attribution created for modern scholars a great deal of ambiguity and doubt about the authorship of the text, the contemporary Salafi-Wahhabi movement endorsed its ascription to al-Barbahārī and adopted this creed as a standard textbook in the curriculum of mission or *daʿwa* institutions around the world as well as in Saudi Arabia, financed by the Saudi religious establishment.[45]

All this illustrates why the interest in "orthodox" creeds persists to this day. As William M. Watt once argued,

> Dogma has a negative side, of course, as well as a positive one. It excludes from the society, or at least from full participation in the life of the society, those who do not accept it. This is especially the case when the religious institution which produces the dogmatic formulations, is in alliance with a political or ruling institution.[46]

44 §§12, 16, 41, 75, 78, 122.

45 See appendix 1.

46 Watt, *Islam* 174.

Translation of *The Book of the Explanation of the Sunna*

The trustworthy master and prominent scholar (al-Shaykh al-Imam) Abū l-Ḥusayn ʿAbd al-Ḥaqq b. ʿAbd al-Khāliq transmitted to us by having the text read in his presence (*qirāʾatan*): Abū Ṭālib ʿAbd al-Qādir ibn Muḥammad ibn Yūsuf transmitted to us in an audited session (*wa-naḥnu nasmaʿu*) in the congregational mosque. It was said to him (*qīla lahu*): Shaykh Abū Isḥāq Ibrāhīm b. ʿUmar b. Aḥmad al-Barmakī transmitted to you, among what he had authorized you to transmit, an authorization that was publically known, he replied, "Yes." He said: Abū l-Ḥasan Muḥammad b. al-ʿAbbās b. Aḥmad b. al-Furāt—may God have mercy on him—informed us in his book, and it was transmitted [to us] by way of an audited transmission (*wa-min kitābihi quriʾa*). He said: Abū Bakr Aḥmad b. Kāmil ibn Khalaf b. Shajara the judge transmitted to us by way of direct reading before him (*qirāʾatan ʿalayhi*); and he said to me: Transmit this book on my authority from beginning to end.

Abū ʿAbdallāh Aḥmad b. Muḥammad b. Ghālib al-Bāhilī—may peace and blessings be upon him—said:

> Praise be to God, Who guided us to Islam, bestowed it upon us, and brought us forth in the best community; we thus ask Him for success in that which He loves and pleases Him, and for protection from that which He loathes and angers Him.

1 Sunna and Community[1]

(1) Know that Islam is the Sunna, and the Sunna, Islam. Either is well founded within the other. It is of the essence of the Sunna to adhere to the Community (*jamāʿa*).

Verily, whoever turns away, and distances himself from the Community has unfastened the tie of Islam from around his neck, leading astray both himself and others.

1 The editors introduced thematic subheadings and numbers for thematic units, and chose a text format that distinguishes between dogmatic instruction (regular font) and creedal confirmation (*italics*).

 | DOI:10.1163/9789004429055_008

(2) The Companions of the Prophet—may God bless him and have mercy upon all of them—are the foundation upon which Islam was established. They are the People of the Sunna and the Community (*ahl al-sunna wa-l-jamāʿa*).

He who does not seek guidance from them is misled and is an innovator. All innovation (bidʿa) *is misguidance, and all misguidance and its adherents lead to Hellfire.*

(3) ʿUmar b. al-Khaṭṭāb—may God have mercy upon him—said, "None is excused for straying away all the while imagining that he is being righteous. Nor is one excused for straying from right guidance, deeming it all the while misguidance. For all matters have already been made clear, proof (*ḥujja*) stands conclusive, and no room for excuse is at all possible."

For the Sunna and the Community have, both, already determined the principles of religion (amr al-dīn)*, rendering it manifest. Accordingly, everyone is called upon to comply.*

2 The Companions

(4) Know—may God have mercy upon you—that what God—blessed and exalted is He—has revealed was not intended to comply with men's reason or their opinions. Rather, the knowledge thereof pertains solely to God and to His messenger.

Verily, let not your inclinations be your guide, lest you slip away from religion and abandon Islam. For you would have no proof.

The Prophet has shown his Community the Sunna and explicated it to his Companions, who are the Community and the vast majority (*al-sawād al-aʿẓam*). The vast majority, in turn, represent the truth and its adherents.

Therefore, he who dissents from the Companions of the Prophet—may peace and blessings be upon him—in anything pertaining to God's command, becomes an unbeliever.[2]

3 Heretical Innovation

(5) Know that when people bring about an innovation, they of necessity forfeit what corresponds to it in the Sunna. Therefore,

2 Cf. German translation in von Grunebaum, *Der Islam im Mittelalter* 141.

Beware of novelties, since every novelty is an innovation, and innovations, one and all, lead one astray. "Every innovation is a deviation. Deviation and its adherents belong to Hellfire."

Beware of insignificant novelties, as even the insignificant ultimately becomes momentous. For whatever innovation has been practiced by this Community began as a minor innovation having the semblance of truth, but in no time it grew malignant, deluding meanwhile whoever adhered to it and was trapped in it. And yet, it spread, becoming a religion (dīn) *with adherents of its own, who deviated from the Straight Path and, thus, forsook Islam.*

(6) Consider—may God have mercy on you—every one of your contemporaries, whose discourse you have listened to. Do not rush or get involved in an issue until you inquire whether the Companions of the Prophet—may God bless him and have mercy upon all of them—had something to say about it.[3]

Should you find a tradition on their authority, adhere to it. Do not omit it nor prefer anything to it, lest you fall into Hellfire.

4 Deviation from the Right Path

(7) Know that deviating from the right path can take one of two courses: the one whereby a man loses track, albeit well-intentioned—his straying from the path should not guide us, for he is doomed; the other whereby a man actively opposes the truth, diverging from the pious who preceded him. Such is the misguided one who engenders nothing but misguidance. Such is the obdurate Satan (*marīd*)[4] of this Community.

Whosoever recognizes him is obligated to caution people and make his case known, lest anyone would follow his innovation and be doomed.

(8) Know—may God have mercy upon you—that a worshipper's adherence to Islam remains incomplete until he follows [the path of the previous generations], affirms [their actions], and submits [to the will of God].

Whoever claims that the Companions of Muhammad—may peace and blessings be upon him—left certain parts of Islam unexplicated has called them liars. No other dissension from the Companions is more grievous, nor can an accusation be more perjurious.

---

3 Cf. Frank, al-Ashʿarī's *"Kitāb al-ḥathth"* 117, item 6.

4 Cf. Q 23:3.

Such is [the work of] the innovator, the misguided one who engenders but misguidance, and originates in Islam things alien to it.

5 Confirming God's Attributes

(9) Know—may God have mercy upon you—that the Sunna is not subject to analogy, nor can it be grasped by parables, nor yet is it dictated by the prejudices of men. Rather, it is the unconditional assent to the traditions of the Messenger of God—may peace and blessings be upon him—without asking "how" or making any inquiry whatsoever; "why" is not to be asked, nor is "how."[5]

Theological disputations, controversy, polemics, and cavil (mirāʾ) *were introduced of late* (muḥdath) *and spark doubt in the heart—even though this may be concordant with the truth—and the Sunna as argued by him who engages in it.*

(10) Know—may God have mercy upon you—that discourses regarding the Lord are novelties, indeed innovations and misguidance.

No argument about God is permitted except as He describes Himself in the Quran, and what the Prophet has explained to his Companions.[6]

(11) He—may He be praised—is One, ﴾Nothing resembles His Likeness. He is the All-Hearing, All-Seeing﴿.[7] Our Lord is the First, albeit [asking] "when" is never appropriate to Him; He is the Last, albeit speaking of an ending is never appropriate to Him. ﴾He knows what is kept secret or even more deeply concealed﴿ (Q 20:7). On His Throne He rests, His knowledge is all-encompassing; nothing escapes it.

No one but a sceptic posits a "how" or a "why" as regards God's attributes.

(12) "The Quran is the Speech of God, His revelation (*tanzīl*), and His light. It is not created. For the Quran is of God. Whatever is of God is not created." Thus spoke Mālik b. Anas and Aḥmad b. Ḥanbal, as well as the jurists before and after.

Disputing this is unbelief.

---

5 Cf. French translation in Allard, *Problème*, 106; German translation in von Grunebaum, *Der Islam im Mittelalter* 141.

6 Cf. Frank, al-Ashʿarī's *"Kitāb al-ḥathth"* 118, item 10; Knysh, "Orthodoxy" 61.

7 Q 42:11. Khalidi, *Qur'an* (modified).

6 Further Articles of Faith

(13) Belief in:

a. The *visio* of God on the Day of Resurrection. [Believers] will see God with their very eyes, He will judge [them], without a veil and without a mediator.[8]

b. The Balance on the Day of Resurrection, wherewith good and evil are weighed. It has a pair of scales and a tongue.

c. The torment of the grave, and in Munkar and Nakīr.

d. The Prophets' pool (*ḥawḍ*); for every prophet a pool, except for Ṣāliḥ, whose pool is the udder of his she-camel.

e. The Prophet's intercession on behalf of the sinners on the Day of Resurrection, and as they cross the Narrow Bridge (*al-ṣirāṭ*) stretched over the Fire. He (i.e., Muhammad) brings them out of the depths of Hell (*jahannam*). All prophets are entitled to intercede [on this Day]—likewise, men of righteousness, martyrs, and the virtuous. Thereafter, God has additional favors to offer those whom He elects. Thus, they may be brought out of the Fire after they have been burnt and charred.

f. The Narrow Bridge [stretching] over Hell. Whomever God wills shall follow that bridge. Whomever God wishes shall fall into Hell. They are endowed with light in accordance with their faith.

g. The prophets and the angels.

h. The veritable truth of Paradise and Hell, and in the fact that they were created. Paradise is in the Seventh Heaven, the uppermost limit of which is God's Throne. The Fire is under the seventh, lowermost level of the earthly dominion (*al-arḍ*). Both are already created. God has known beforehand the number of the inhabitants of Heaven and those who will enter it, and the number of the inhabitants of the Fire and those who will enter it. Paradise and the Fire shall never cease to exist and shall, forever and for all eternity, remain together with God—blessed and exalted is He.

i. Adam was once in the created, everlasting Paradise, that he was expelled [from it] after he disobeyed God.

j. The Antichrist, and the descent of Jesus, son of Mary, who will come down and kill the Antichrist. He will marry and perform the ritual prayer behind the forthcoming messianic Leader (*al-Qāʾim*) from among Muhammad's Household. He will die and be buried by Muslims.

---

8 Cf. French translation in Allard, *Problème* 104.

k. Faith consists in verbal profession and in works [given equal precedence], and intention and [its] fulfilment. Belief admits of increase and diminution, increasing as God wishes and diminishing until it is no more.

7 Ranks of the Companions and Their Virtues

(14) The best of all, after the death of its Prophet, in this Community are:

Abū Bakr, ʿUmar, and ʿUthmān. This was related to us on the authority of Ibn ʿUmar, who said, "We used to say, while the Messenger of God—God bless him and grant him peace—was still among us, that the best people after the Prophet were Abū Bakr, ʿUmar, and ʿUthmān. The Prophet would listen without objecting."

Then, following them in rank, ʿAlī, Ṭalḥa, al-Zubayr, Saʿd [ibn Abī Waqqās], Saʿīd [b. Zayd b. Nufayl], and ʿAbd al-Raḥmān b. ʿAwf; all of them fit to be caliphs.

Then following these in rank, the Companions of the Messenger of God—God bless him and grant him peace—i.e., the people of the first generation, to whom belong the first Immigrants (*al-muhājirūn al-awwalūn*) and the Supporters (*anṣār*). They are the ones who performed the ritual prayers in the direction of the two Qiblas [Jerusalem then Mecca].

Then, following these in rank, those who were in the company of the Messenger of God—may peace and blessings be upon him—for a day, a month, or a year or more or less.

You ought to ask God to have mercy upon every single one [of them], mention their virtue, and make no mention of their shortcomings. Moreover, you should mention none of them except favorably, for the Prophet has said, "If my Companions are ill-mentioned [in your presence], refrain from doing so." Furthermore, Ibn ʿUyayna said, "Whoever utters a bad word about the Companions of the Messenger of God—may peace and blessings be upon him—is a sectarian (ṣāḥib hawā)*."*

8 Obeying the Ruler

(15) Obeying is the prerogative of the rulers (*aʾimma*) in whatever pleases God and merits His approval. Whoever succeeds to the caliphate with unanimous approval and consent is the Commander of the Faithful.

None is excused for spending even a single night without accepting the ruler's authority, be the ruler righteous or dissolute (barran aw fājiran).

(16) Pilgrimage and military expeditions with the ruler are already an established practice.

Furthermore, Friday prayers led by him are lawful. The prayer should be followed by six prostrations (*rakʿas*), performed in pairs—as Aḥmad b. Ḥanbal stated.

(17) The caliphate, i.e. the succession [to the Prophet], is the prerogative of Quraysh until the day on which Jesus, son of Mary, descends.

(18) Whoever rebels against a Muslim ruler is a dissident (*khārijī*) who has renounced allegiance to the Muslim Community and opposed the prophetic tradition. He shall die in a state of ignorance [*mīta jāhiliyya*; like the Arabs prior to Islam].

(19) To fight authority (*al-sulṭān*), or to revolt against it is forbidden, even if it is despotic—this is the import of the Prophet's saying to Abū Dharr, "Hold fast, even if the ruler is an Abyssinian slave";[9] and his saying to the Supporters (*anṣār*), "Hold fast until you join me [on the Day of Resurrection] at my pool." The Sunna prohibits fighting against authority (*sulṭān*), for therein lies corruption, both religious and worldly.

(20) Fighting dissidents (*khawārij*) is licit, in case they compromise Muslim lives and properties. However, should they cease to fight, [the sultan] is not to pursue them, put to death their wounded, confiscate their chattels (*fay'ahum*), kill their captives, or track down their runaways.

(21) Know—may God have mercy upon you—that none may be obeyed if this entails disobeying God, Almighty and Majestic.

9 Judging Fellow Muslims

(22) A Muslim who has never bore false witness against anyone, nor was seen to have done anything, good or bad, yet it can still not be known about him how his life will end—we are to hope and fear for him. Nor do we know whether he will repent to God upon death, or what God will ordain for him at the time, should he die as a Muslim. We merely ask for God's mercy on his

9 Cf. Abou El Fadl, *Rebellion and violence* 119.

behalf. It is his sins that make us fear for him. For no sin is beyond repentance for any worshipper.

10 Stoning

(23) Stoning is legitimate.[10]

11 Licenses for Performed Prayer

(24) It is in keeping with the Sunna to pass the wetted hands over the shoes [in ritual ablution]. Likewise, it is of the Sunna to shorten prayers while traveling. As for fasting while traveling, it is up to the traveler to fast or break fasting. [Finally,] it is acceptable to pray in trousers.

12 Hypocrisy

(25) Hypocrisy means that you openly display Islam while concealing your unbelief.

(26) Know that this world (*dunyā*) is an abode of belief (*īmān*) and Islam. Thus, the Community of Muhammad—may peace and blessings be upon him—includes believers who entrust themselves to Islam insofar as the legal rulings they practice, inheritance, and funeral prayers are concerned.

We withhold testimony as to someone's true belief until he complies with the laws and codices (*sharāʾiʿ*) of Islam. Falling short in this regard renders a person less of a believer until he dies. As to his faith, God alone—exalted is He—knows it, be it complete or less so; unless he disregards the laws of Islam openly.

13 Funeral Prayer

(27) It is of the Sunna to offer the deceased among the People of the Qibla the funeral prayer [including] (a) a person stoned to death; (b) fornicators, male

10 In the sense that it is rightly ordained by God (*al-rajmu ḥaqq*).

and female; (c) anyone who committed suicide; (d) the rest of the People of the Qibla; and (e) drunkards and so on. Offering them the funeral prayer is of the Sunna.

14 Leaving Islam

(28) Deem not a member of the People of the Qibla a non-Muslim, except if he (a) denies a verse in the Book of God; (b) denies anything from the traditions (*āthār*) of the Messenger of God—may peace and blessings be upon him; (c) sacrifices for other than God; or (d) prays to other than God.

Should he commit any of the above, you must deem him, then, a deserter from Islam. Otherwise, he remains a Muslim believer, nominally—but not in reality.

15 God's Attributes

(29) You may hear some prophetic traditions that surpass your comprehension, such as:

a. "The hearts of God's servants are held between two fingers of the Merciful one (*al-Raḥmān*)."
b. "God—blessed and exalted is He—descends to the world's heavenly sphere. He also descends on the Day of ʿArafa (i.e., the ninth day of the month of Pilgrimage) and on the Day of Resurrection."
c. "Hellfire will not cease receiving [the damned], until God—may His praise be glorified—places His foot upon it."
d. God's saying to his servant, "Walk toward me, and I shall hurry toward you."
e. "God—blessed and exalted is He—descends on the Day of ʿArafa."
f. "God created Adam in His image."
g. The saying of the Prophet—may peace and blessings be upon him, "I saw my Lord in the best countenance (*ṣūra*)"; and other such traditions.

According to these traditions, assent, belief, delegation, and satisfaction are incumbent upon you. Do not interpret anything in accordance with your whims. For belief in them is obligatory. Whimsical interpretation or rejection thereof renders one a Jahmi.[11]

11 Partial translation in French: Allard, *Problème* 106; in English: Frank, Elements 161.

(30) Whoever claims to see his Lord in this worldly abode is an unbeliever.

(31) Contemplating God—blessed and exalted is He—is an innovation according to the saying of the Prophet—may peace and blessings be upon him, "Reflect upon creation, but do not reflect upon God." For contemplating God kindles doubt in one's heart.[12]

16 God's Command and Prescience

(32) Know that vermin, predators, and animals all alike—including the smallest ants—are under God's command.

They do nothing except by God's permission—blessed and exalted is He.

(33) It is incumbent upon you to believe that God—blessed and exalted is He—is prescient of everything from eternity, of what has not been and what is to be, having them all counted and numbered. Denying His knowledge of what has not been and what is to be renders one an unbeliever in the Almighty.

17 Marriage

(34) No marriage is valid without the presence of [the bride's] guardian, two just witnesses, and a dowry, small or large. Should [the bride] lack a guardian, the ruler (*al-sulṭān*) shall be her guardian. If a man divorces his wife thrice, "She shall not be licit to him again until she marries another husband."[13]

18 Conditions for Bloodshed

(35) Shedding the blood of a Muslim who bears witness that "there is no God but God, and Muḥammad is the Messenger of God, His servant and His messenger" is lawful in only three [cases]: (a) adultery while within the bounds of marriage (*iḥṣān*); (b) apostatizing after having believed; and (c) killing a believer. One will be killed for these crimes.

---

12 Cf. Makdisi, *Ibn ʿAqil and culture* 108; Melchert, Ḥanābila 365.

13 Q 2:230.

Otherwise and until the Hour of Judgment, it is never lawful for a Muslim to shed the blood of a fellow Muslim.

19 The Day of Resurrection

(36) All will perish that God decreed to perish, except for Heaven and Hell, the Throne and the Chair,[14] the Tablet, the Pen, and the Trumpet. None of these will ever perish.

(37) Then, on the Day of Resurrection God will restore to life all creation. He restores them to the very state in which they died. He then holds them to account as He pleases: a party to Paradise, another to the blazing fire of Hell. To the rest of the creation He says, "Dust you shall be."

(38) Belief in retaliation (*qiṣāṣ*, Q 2:178–179) on the Day of Resurrection [whereby it is equally ordained] among all creation, humans, predators, and vermin all alike—even among the smallest ants—until God restores to each their due, "To the People of Paradise from the People of the Fire; and to the People of the Fire from the People of Paradise; further, to the People of Paradise among each other, and to the People of the Fire among each other."

(39) Work in sincerity to God, accept what God ordains (*qaḍāʾ*) in contentment, to believe in the words of God Almighty and All-powerful.

(40) Patiently accept God's decree, and believe in God's fate, the good and the bad, the sweet and the bitter. God knows all that His servants will do, and all that they are destined to be. None escapes His knowledge. Nothing on earth or in the heavens can exist, if it is not known to him.

You ought to know that whatever has befallen you, was not meant to have missed you; and whatever has missed you, was not meant to have befallen you; and that there is no creator beside God.

14 For the Quranic terms, God's "throne" and "chair," see Sadan, Kursī; *ThG* iv, 407–411.

20 Funeral Prayer

(41) "The formula 'God is greater than everything' (*takbīr*) should be pronounced four times over the body of a deceased." Thus spoke Mālik b. Anas, Sufyān alThawrī, al-Ḥasan b. Ṣāliḥ [b. Ḥayy], Aḥmad b. Ḥanbal, and other jurists; and thus stated the Messenger of God—peace be upon him.

21 Rain and Angels

(42) Believe that, with every drop [of rain], an angel descends from heaven, placing it wherever God commands.

22 The Dead Hear

(43) Believe that the polytheists [killed in the Battle of Badr and] placed in the *Qalīb* [dry well] actually did hear the Prophet's words—peace be upon him.

23 Divine Compensation

(44) Believe that if a man falls sick, God rewards him for his suffering. A martyr likewise is rewarded for having been killed.

24 Children's Suffering

(45) Believe that "children feel pain whenever something afflicts them in the abode of this world." [Contrary to] Bakr, the nephew of ʿAbd al-Wāḥid, who claims that "they do not." He has lied.

25 Divine Justice

(46) Know that none enters Paradise except by God's mercy. When God inflicts punishment, it is but for one's sins, [the severity of the punishment] varying accordingly. Should God torment the inhabitants of the heavens and the earthly terrains, the righteous and the wicked alike, He cannot be said to torment them unjustly.

(47) It is not permitted to say of "God—blessed and exalted is He—that he acts unjustly." To be unjust is to take what is not one's own. To God—praised be He—however, belong the creation and the command; the creation is His, and the abode likewise. ﴾He cannot be questioned about what He does. It is they who are questioned﴿ (Q 21:23).

Moreover, "why" is not to be asked, nor is "how."
None intervenes between God and His creation.

26 Authority of Quran and Sunna

(48) Should you hear someone casting doubt on prophetic traditions, know that his commitment to Islam is doubtful; his opinion and his belief are repugnant. In fact, the target of his doubt is but the Prophet—peace be upon him—and his Companions. For it is through these traditions that we have come to know God, the Messenger of God—peace be upon Him—and the Quran, and we have come to know good and evil, and this world and the Hereafter.[15]

Verily, the Quran stands more in need of the Sunna than the other way round.

27 Fate

(49) Disputation (*kalām*), debate (*jidāl*), and controversy (*khuṣūma*) on the question of fate, above all, are prohibited in the view of all groups. For fate is God's mystery. The Lord—blessed and exalted is He—prohibited the prophets from discussing fate. Likewise, the Prophet—may peace and blessings be upon him—forbade controversial discussions of fate.[16] Moreover, scholars and people of piety deplored and prohibited it.

Therefore, you are to assent, acknowledge, and have faith. Believe in everything the Messenger of God—peace be upon him—said, and remain silent concerning everything else.

15 French translation in Allard, *Problème* 107.
16 French translation in ibid., 112.

28 The Night Journey

(50) Believe that the Messenger of God—peace be upon him—was carried on a journey by night to Heaven [the Nocturnal Journey]. He arrived at the Throne and spoke to God—blessed and exalted is He. He further entered Paradise and peered into Hell. He saw the angels and the prophets paraded before him. Awake, he saw the canopies (*surādiqāt*) of the Throne, the Chair, and everything in the heavens and the earthly terrains. Gabriel had him mount the *Burāq* (the heavenly riding beast) and roam the heavens. It is on that night that the ritual prayers were made obligatory to him (*furiḍat lahū*). On that same night, he returned to Mecca. This took place before the hijra.

29 Destiny of the Souls in the Hereafter

(51) Know that the souls of the martyrs dwell in lanterns beneath the Throne, and roam Paradise at leisure; the souls of the faithful are beneath the Throne, while the souls of the unbelievers and the wicked are in [the well of] Barahūt.[17]

30 The Grave and Its Torments

(52) Believe that the deceased is made to sit in his grave, whereupon God sends the soul (*rūḥ*) [back] to him so that [the two angels] Munkar and Nakīr might question him about faith and the relevant laws. His soul is then painlessly and deftly extricated. He retains knowledge of his visitors. If he is a believer, he is comforted in his grave, while a wicked person is punished as God wills.

31 Pairing

(53) Know that pairing (*al-tazwīj*) [i.e., granting parents children of both sexes] is a matter of Divine decree and predestination.

---

17 Yāqūt, *Muʿjam al-buldān* i, 405, ii, 92; see Rentz, Barhūt.

32 God's Speech

(54) Believe that God—blessed and exalted is He—is the One who spoke to Moses, son of Amram, on the Day of the Mount (*al-Ṭūr*). Moses heard God's very speech in a voice that struck his ears. The voice came from God and from God alone.

To maintain otherwise is an act of unbelief.

33 Reason

(55) Reason (*al-ʿaql*) is inborn. To each is given [of reason] a share willed by God. Humans are as diverse in their reason as are the particles in the skies (*mithl al-dharra fī l-samāwāt*). Proportionate to their allotted share [of reason], [an amount of] work is demanded. Reason, thus, is not an object of acquisition but rather a matter of Divine favor (*faḍl*).[18]

34 God's Justice

(56) Know that God has preferred some of his servants over others in matters religious and worldly. This is but Justice. It cannot be described as injustice or partiality.

Whoever says that God favors the believer and the unbeliever alike is an innovator. Rather, God favors the believer over the unbeliever, the obedient over the disobedient, and the infallible over the forsaken. This is but Justice, and His justice is His very favor; He gives whomever He wishes and denies whomever He wishes.

35 Counsel to Muslims

(57) It is illicit in religious matters to withhold your counsel from Muslims, whether pious or dissolute, in religious matters. To withhold it is to cheat the Muslims, and to cheat the Muslims is to corrupt religion, and, further, to corrupt religion is to betray God, His Messenger, and the believers.[19]

---

18 Cf. Makdisi, *Ibn ʿAqil and culture* 92.

19 Cf. Melchert, Transition 68.

(58) God—blessed and exalted is He—is ﴾All-Hearing and All-Seeing﴿, and ﴾All-Hearing and All-Knowing﴿.[20] ﴾Both His hands are spread forth (*mabsūṭatān*)﴿.[21] Before having created humankind, He had knowledge of their disobedience, His knowledge having comprehended them. However, His prescience did not bar Him from guiding them to Islam and, thereby, favoring them in His generosity, graciousness, and favor—praise is due to Him.[22]

36 The Portents upon Death

(59) Know that the portents upon death are three: It will be said, "Rejoice, O beloved of God, in God's contentment [with you] and in Paradise," and it will be said, "O enemy of God, prepare to receive the dreadful tidings of God's anger and of the Fire"; and it will further be said, "Rejoice, O servant of God, in Paradise after having accepted Islam." This is the view of Ibn ʿAbbās.

37 Visio Beatifica

(60) Know that the first to gain sight of God in Paradise are the blind, then men, and then women—with their very eyes, they gain sight of Him. As the Messenger of God—peace be upon him—said, "You shall see your Lord the way you see the moon on a full moon night. Seeing Him shall not bring you harm."

To believe this is incumbent upon you, and to deny it is unbelief.

38 Argumentation Causes Unbelief

(61) Know—may God's mercy be upon you—that the source of all heresy (*zandaqa*), unbelief, doubt, innovation, misguidance, or perplexity [in matters of] religion, is theological disputation (*kalām*)[23] and its proponents, the propagators of pointless argumentation (*jadal*), cavil (*mirāʾ*), and controversy (*khuṣūma*). How astonishing it is of men to dare to venture into argumentation, controversy, and cavil when God—blessed and exalted is He—says, "None disputes the revelations of God save the unbelievers" (Q 40:4).

---

20 Q 22:61, 2:181, and other verses.

21 Q 5:64.

22 Partial French translation in Allard, *Problème* 104.

23 Cf. French translation in ibid., 112.

Hence, you are to submit and be content with what the traditions, and their advocates (ahl al-āthār), *convey. Refrain therefore [from argument], and be silent.*

39 The Punishment in Hell

(62) Believe that God the Almighty punishes people in the Fire, while they are shackled, incarcerated, and chained, with fire in their bowels, and encompassing them above and below. Whereas the Jahmis, among whom is Hishām al-Fuwaṭī, contend that "God punishes by the Fire," which is a blatant rebuttal of God and His Messenger.

40 Three of the Five Pillars of Islam

40.1 *Ritual Prayers*

(63) Know that the ordained prayers are five. Their number does not admit increase, nor does it admit shortening at their ordained times. While traveling, two prostrations are enough in all the prayers except for the sunset prayer (*maghrib*).

Whoever claims that [the number of] prayers is more than five is an innovator. Whoever claims they are less is, likewise, an innovator. God accepts none of it outside its designated time, unless one has forgotten. He who forgets them is excused, but must perform them as soon he remembers. During travel, the two prayers may be performed together, if one wishes to do so.

40.2 *Almsgiving*

(64) Almsgiving is [deducted], according to the Messenger of God—may peace and blessings be upon him—from [the surplus of] gold, silver, fruits, grains, beans, and domesticated animals. To take the responsibility of distributing it personally is permitted; and it is also permitted to delegate said responsibility to the ruler.

40.3 *The Profession of Faith*

(65) Know that the first principle of Islam is to bear witness that "there is no God but God and Muḥammad is His servant and His messenger."

(66) Whatever God says is just as He says. Whatever He says is beyond dispute. And whatever He says He abides by.

(67) Believe in all the divinely revealed laws.[24]

41 Lawful Commerce

(68) Know that commerce is lawful (*ḥalāl*). Whatever is sold in the markets of Muslims—whatever is sold in accordance with the laws established by the Book, Islam, and the Sunna, untainted by duplicity, injustice, wrongdoing, or disagreement with the Quran or with generally established norms—is permitted.

42 Anxiety and Fear

(69) Know—may God's mercy be upon you—that it befits the servant of God to live this worldly life with anxiety, for no one knows how one will die,[25] how one's life will be sealed, or how one meet God—even if one has done everything that is good.

However, should one take the path of indulgence, one should not abandon hope in God—exalted is He—at the moment of death. Rather, one should keep good faith in God—blessed and exalted is He.

One ought to fear one's misdeeds. For should God be merciful to him, it is God's favor; should He punish him, it is for his own faults.

43 The *Jamāʿa* vs. Corruption

(70) Believe that God made known to his Prophet all that shall transpire in his Community until the Day of Resurrection.

(71) Know that the Messenger of God—may peace and blessings be upon him—stated: "My Community (*ummatī*) shall divide into 73 sects, all of which [belong] in the Fire, save one, and that is the Community (*jamāʿa*)." He was asked, "And who are they, O Messenger of God?" He answered, "Those who follow what I myself and my Companions now [uphold]."

24 This is a reference to the profession of faith as evident in Q 2:285.

25 I.e., no one knows their state upon death, nor what beliefs they hold at the time.

Such was the [understanding of] religion up to the caliphate of ʿUmar, and such it was during the reign of ʿUthmān. When ʿUthmān was murdered, however, disagreement and innovations prevailed, and people [split into] factions (*aḥzāb*) and sects (*firaq*). Some, when it all started, held fast to the Truth and called to it. Thus, things remained in order until the fourth generation of the caliphate of the line of so-and-so. Afterward, the times turned, people drastically changed, and innovations were rampant. Advocates of paths other than righteousness and the Community multiplied. Tribulations took place over matters that neither the Messenger of God—may peace and blessings be upon him—nor his Companions addressed. They instigated factionalism, which the Prophet of God forbade. They called one another unbelievers, each faction advocating their own cause while accusing others of unbelief. Thereupon, the hotheaded, the uncouth, and the ignorant were led astray. They tempted people with worldly matters and intimidated them with worldly punishment. By such intimidation and temptation, people were made to follow them through desire for worldly goods.

Therefore, the Sunna and its followers came to be suppressed, with innovations arising and spreading abroad. So, those have unwittingly committed unbelief and in more way than one. They deployed [reasoning by] analogy (*qiyās*),[26] and they fancied their [limited] understanding fit to fathom the omnipotence of the Lord—as manifest in His signs, His ordainments, and in what He commanded and forbade. Whatever suited their [limited] understanding they accepted, and whatever did not they rejected.

Islam became estranged (*gharīb*), the Sunna became estranged, and the people of the Sunna were more like strangers in fear for their daily existence.[27]

44 Temporary Marriage

(72) Know that (*mutʿa*), that is temporary marriage, and making licit (*istiḥlāl*)[28] are strictly forbidden (*ḥarām*) until the Day of Resurrection.

26 For the complex meaning of the term *qiyās*, see *ThG* iv, 661–662.

27 Cf. German translation, van Ess, *Der Eine* i, 100.

28 Having a woman married through some legal stratagem in order to make licit her return to her former husband after having been thrice divorced.

45 Excellence and Virtues

(73) You should recognize the excellence and virtue (*faḍl*) of the line of Hāshim because of their kinship to the Messenger of God—may peace and blessings be upon him.

Furthermore, you should acknowledge the excellence of Quraysh, the Arabs, and all their subdivisions, and therefore [acknowledge] their elevated status in Islam. [And bear in mind,] "A client (*mawlā*) [of an Arab clan] is considered one of them."

You should also acknowledge the rights of all other people in Islam. Give the Supporters (*anṣār*) their due, and [heed] the injunction of the Messenger of God—may peace and blessings be upon him—regarding them.

Forget not the Household of the Prophet. Acknowledge their excellence. Acknowledge, likewise, the excellence of his Medinan neighbors.

46 The Jahmis, Analogy (*qiyās*), and Subjective Opinion (*raʾy*)

(74) Know—may God's mercy be upon you—that refuting the views of the Jahmis [was a matter for] the learned (*ahl al-ʿilm*) until, during the caliphate of so-and-so, the lowly rabble (*ruwaybiḍa*) rendered the discourse public, discrediting the traditions of the Prophet—may peace and blessings be upon him—adopting [reasoning by] analogy (*qiyās*) and [subjective legal] opinion (*raʾy*), and ultimately accusing dissenters of unbelief. Thus, the ignorant, the senseless, and the unqualified subscribed to their ideas until, unknowingly, they became unbelievers. The Community, thereupon, was, in certain respects, doomed, in other respects, swayed by heresy, in further respects, committed to injustice, and in yet further respects, rendered innovative. Only those, within the Community, are saved who

a. firmly adhere to what the Prophet—may peace and blessings be upon him—said, to his authority, and to the authority of his Companions;
b. do not find fault in any of them;
c. do not bypass their authority, but are content with what they deemed worthy of contentment;
d. are not disinclined from their path or their teaching; and
e. know that theirs was the true Islam and the true faith.

Therefore, one's religion is best entrusted to them. For one should acknowledge that religion is but strict conformity (*taqlīd*; or due compliance); indeed, it is to follow the example of the Companions of Muhammad—may peace and blessings be upon him.

(75) Know that to say "My utterance of the Quran is created" renders one an innovator. To remain silent, to abstain from averring that it is "created," or "uncreated"—renders one a Jahmi. Thus said Aḥmad b. Ḥanbal.[29]

(76) The Prophet of God—may peace and blessings be upon him—said: "Whoever among you survives me shall witness serious contention. Beware, therefore, of novelties, for these are misguidance, and adopt my Sunna and the Sunna of the rightly guided caliphs, and hold fast to both."

47 The Jahmis

(77) Know that the Jahmis were doomed when they:
a. contemplated [the essence of] the Lord, introducing "why" and "how";
b. forsook tradition;
c. adopted [reasoning by] analogy; and
d. measured religion by the yardstick of their subjective opinions.
Hence, they publically adhered to blatant unbelief, branding everyone else an unbeliever, ultimately, and were thus obliged to deny all of God's attributes.[30]

(78) Some scholars, among whom was Aḥmad b. Ḥanbal—may God be pleased with him—said, "A Jahmi is an unbeliever, not to be counted among the People of the Qibla. To shed a Jahmi's blood is permissible; to allow him to inherit or to be inherited is not licit.[31] For he has renounced the Friday prayer, the communal prayer, and charity (*ṣadaqa*)."

(79) They (i.e., the Jahmis):
a. proclaimed that "whoever does not say 'The Quran is created' is an unbeliever";
b. justified killing people belonging to the Community of the Prophet—may peace and blessings be upon him—contradicting those who came before them;
c. tested people regarding matters that neither the Prophet—may peace and blessings be upon him—nor any of his Companions had discussed;
d. intended that both local and Friday mosques be abandoned;

---

29 Cf. French translation in Allard, *Problème* 104; English translation in Brown, *Canonization* 142.
30 Cf. French translation in Allard, *Problème* 104.
31 Cf. French translation in ibid., 111.

e. enfeebled Islam;
f. suspended *jihād*;
g. provoked dissent;
h. challenged established traditions;
i. cast doubt on abrogation (*al-mansūkh*) and appealed to equivocate [Quranic verses] in arguments;
j. turned people skeptical in their established opinions and beliefs; and
k. indulged in controversy concerning their Lord.
l. They denied the punishment in the grave, the pool, and intercession [of the Prophet on the Day of Judgment], ultimately proclaiming that heaven and hell were not created.
m. They denied much of what the Messenger of God—may peace and blessings be upon him—said, justifying, thereby, their labeling as "unbelievers" and the shedding of blood. For to deny a verse from the Book of God is to deny it in its entirety, and to deny a tradition from the Messenger of God—may peace and blessings be upon him—is to deny the whole body of traditions. The denier thereof is an unbeliever in God Almighty.

They held sway for a lengthy period, and on top of it had the ruler's support. The sword and the whip were theirs to use in furthering their ends, and the study of the Sunna and the *jamāʿa* was effaced and thereby [almost] perished—at any rate was suppressed—because of their spread of much innovation and theological disputation, and because of their swelling ranks. They organized assemblies, made their opinions public, and wrote books. They enticed people, seeking political power for themselves. It was so grave a trial that none endured whom God did not secure. Indeed, those frequenting their sessions ended up, at the very least, doubtful of their own faith, followers of them, or claiming they were right. Not knowing whether they [themselves] were right or in the wrong, they became skeptics.

People suffered grievously (*halaka*) until the days of [the caliph] Jaʿfar, known as al-Mutawakkil. Through him, God extinguished innovations and made manifest the truth, upon which the People of the Sunna gained the upper hand. They spoke their mind freely, unintimidated, despite their meagre numbers and despite the continued prevalence of the people of innovation up to our present day. Indeed, the chief representations of misguidance (*aʿlām al-ḍalāla*) and what they have set down (*wa-l-rasm*) were followed still and advocated by some,[32] unrestrained and unrebuked.

32 The original text bears some ambiguity.

48 The Sources of Innovation

(80) Know that the source of every innovation is but "riffraff crowds who follow every croaking [agitator] and sway with every blowing wind." Whoever is like this has no shred of piety (*lā dīn lahu*). God—blessed and exalted is He—said ﴿... But they fell into dispute only after knowledge had come to them, out of mutual envy ...﴾ (Q 45:17). They are indeed the learned-turned-wicked, the people of greed and innovation.

49 The Advocates of Truth

(81) Know that there continues to be a group of the People of Truth and the Sunna (*ahl al-ḥaqq wa-l-sunna*), whom God guides and through whom He guides others and revives prophetic traditions (*sunan*). They are those who, despite their meagre numbers, are described by God at times of disagreement as ﴿those to whom the Book was revealed and after clear signs were sent to them﴾, and these were an exception: ﴿Then God guided the believers to the truth regarding which they differed, by His leave. God guides whomsoever He wills to a path that is straight﴾ (Q 2:213). The Messenger of God—may peace and blessings be upon him—said: "There will always be in my Community a group openly upholding the Truth, untouched by deserters, [and persevering] until God's will prevails (*ya'tiya amru Allāh*)."

50 Knowledge and the Learned

(82) Know—may God have mercy upon you—that to transmit copious traditions (*kathrat al-riwāya*) does not render one learned. Rather, to be learned is to commit to action knowledge and prophetic traditions,[33] limited as one's knowledge might be.

No matter how vast is his knowledge, if he contradicts the Book and the prophetic traditions, then he is all the same an innovator.

33 Cf. French translation in Allard, *Problème* 109, Allard translates "*al-ʿilm*" as "la science."

51 The Authority of the Sunna and the Community

(83) Know—may God have mercy upon you—that the deployment, in matters religious, of [subjective legal] opinion, [of reasoning by] analogy, and of interpretation unrooted in the Sunna and the Community, is [a sign of] speaking without knowledge about God.

Whoever speaks ignorantly about God is an impostor.[34]

(84) Truth is that which comes from God; the Sunna is that of the Messenger of God—may peace and blessings be upon him; and the Community [is defined by] the consensus of the Companions of the Messenger of God—may peace and blessings be upon him—during the caliphate of Abū Bakr and ʿUmar.

If one confines oneself to the traditions of the Messenger of God—may peace and blessings be upon him—and to the consensus of the Community, one shall prevail over all innovators. Moreover, one's body is relieved of its tensions and one's religion remains intact, should God so wish. This is because the Messenger of God—may peace and blessings be upon him—said: "My Community (ummatī) *shall be dispersed …"*[35] *He—may peace and blessings be upon him—further indicated for us those who will be saved when he said: "[Those who follow] what I myself and my companions today [uphold]."*

Such is the remedy, the unambiguous account, the clear truth, and the illuminating source of light.

52 The "Ancient Religion"

(85) The Messenger of God—may peace and blessings be upon him—said, "Beware of delving into trivia (*taʿammuq*), beware of pretentiousness (*tanaṭṭuʿ*); abide, rather, by your ancient conviction (*dīn ʿatīq*)."[36]

Know that "ancient" [designates the period extending] from the death of the Messenger of God—may peace and blessings be upon him—to the murder of ʿUthmān b. ʿAffān. His murder marks the first division and the first disagreement [among Muslims]. Thereupon, the Community was at war, and was riven by divisions; it was overtaken by greed, and by worldly desires and inclinations.

---

34 Cf. Q 38:86 for the term *mutakallif*; Khalidi translates it as "one who dissembles."

35 This is a reference to a tradition mentioned above (71).

36 For *taʿammuq*, see Mālik b. Anas's opinion in Dutton, *Origins* 20. See also Dallal, Origins 341–359, esp. 343.

53 Novelties and Innovators

(86) None is entitled to innovate, if it departs from the practice of Companions of Muhammad, the Messenger of God—may peace and blessings be upon him. Nor is anyone entitled to promote the cause of erstwhile innovators. Indeed, [in such an instance] one would be no better than said innovators themselves.

To claim the above, or adopt it, is to squarely reject the Sunna, oppose the Community, and give license to innovations. Iblīs himself is not as detrimental to this Community as he is.

(87) When one comes to know the things that the people of innovation have relinquished from the Sunna and the way they have deviated [from the Community], and he holds fast to that which they have renounced, it is sure that he is an adherent of the Sunna and of the Community.

Indeed, he is worthy of being followed, supported, and safeguarded. He is one of those whom the Messenger of God—may peace and blessings be upon him—bid us [respect and protect].

54 How Innovations Spread

(88) Know—may God have mercy upon you—that innovations originate through four points of entry, out of which 72 [heretical] passions ensue. Then, each of these innovations [branches out again] until they add up to 2,800 propositions, all of which are misguided, and all of which are in the Fire. But there is one exception:

He who believes in what is in this book, *and adopts it as a solid conviction, freeing his heart of all doubts and suspicions. Such is the adherent of the Sunna* (ṣāḥib sunna)*, and the one who merits salvation, should God so wish.*

55 Disavowing the Authority of the Quran and Prophetic Tradition

(89) Know—may God have mercy upon you—that innovations would not come to pass if people paused when encountering them, or declined to add to them in any respect. Likewise, innovations would not come to pass if people did not engender discourses out of [material] not mentioned in the tradition of the Messenger of God—may peace and blessings be upon him—or his Companions.

(90) Know—may God have mercy upon you—that as soon as the servant [of God] abjures anything that God—exalted is He—has revealed, he replaces belief with unbelief. It is the same if he takes the liberty to add to—or, for that matter, subtract from—what God has said, or the Messenger of God—may peace and blessings be upon him—has urged.[37]

So, fear God, may God have mercy upon you. Take heed to yourself. Beware of excess in matters of religion, for excess is utterly foreign to the path of Truth.

All that I have prescribed for you *in this book* is on the authority of God, the Messenger of God—may peace and blessings be upon him—and his Companions, their Successors, and the third and fourth generations.

(91) Fear God, then, O servant of God. Assent to [what is in] *this book*; submit and entrust yourself to it. Conceal not, from anyone of the People of the Qibla, what is in it. Through it, God might well rescue those bewildered from their confusion, the innovator from innovation, or the misguided from error, that they may be saved.

(92) Fear God, then, and abide by that ancient and pristine state of affairs *that I have expounded herein, in this book*, for you. May God grace with his mercy the servant—and the servant's parents—who reads this book, circulates it, acts upon it, advocates it, and argues from it. For it is the way (*dīn*; or "the maintained order") of God and the way of the Messenger of God—may peace and blessings be upon him. To endorse whatever is inconsistent with the content of this book is to depart outright from the way of God; it is rather to reject it altogether.

It is as if, when a servant, believing what God—blessed and exalted is He—says, one and all, nevertheless holds one letter in doubt; he, all the same, rejects all that God—blessed and exalted is He—says, and is therefore an unbeliever. Similarly, the profession [of faith—namely, that] "there is no God but God"—is never accepted, unless pronounced in sincerity and with total certainty. God, likewise, does not accept [upholding] the Sunna, when parts of it are cast aside. To cast aside parts of the Sunna is to relinquish it altogether.

(93) Submit, therefore. Wrangle not, nor haggle, for it is nowhere to be found in God's religion. [Bear in mind that] these present times of yours are, especially, evil times.

37 Cf. Frank, al-Ashʿarī's *"Kitāb al-ḥathth"* 118, item 9.

(94) So, fear God alone. If civil war (*fitna*) arises, take refuge in the innermost part of your house, run away from the places of discord, and beware of partisanship. All fights among Muslims for [the sake] of this world are *fitna*—that is, civil war.

(95) Fear God, then, and God alone, Who Has no partner. In times of civil strife, do not get involved, nor engage in fighting, nor be led by your passions. Be not a partisan, nor have [private] hopes, nor have a heart for anything pertaining to them. For it is said: "To have a liking for the doings of some people, be they good or bad, is [well-nigh] to sharing in their act."

May God help us all to do as He pleases, and may He shield us all from disobeying Him.

56 Things to Be Avoided

(96) Observe the stars only sparingly, [and solely] as an aid to determining the times of prayer.

Leave all else to one side, for it invites heresy.

(97) Beware of engaging in theology or keeping the company of its practitioners. Hold fast, rather, to prophetic traditions and to traditionalists (*ahl al-āthār*). Address your inquiries to them, keep their company, and acquire knowledge from them.

(98) Know that the best worship of God is to fear God, to tread the path of awe, grief, anxiety, and timidity before Him—blessed and exalted is He.

(99) Beware the company of those [Sufis] who advocate longing (*shawq*) and love (*maḥabba*) and those who admit privacy with women.

Those who follow the [Sufi] path; for they are all misguided.

(100) Know—may God have mercy upon you—that God—blessed and exalted is He—enjoined His worship on all creation. He then graciously endowed whomever He wished with Islam, a favor from Him.

(101) Refrain from discussing the wars among ʿAlī, Muʿāwiya, ʿĀʾisha, Ṭalḥa, al-Zubayr, and those who were with them. Do not argue about them and leave their affair to God alone—blessed and exalted is He. The Messenger of God—may peace and blessings be upon him—said: "Do not disparage my Compan-

ions and my in-laws, whether on the male side or on the female." He said also, "God—blessed and exalted is He—looked upon the [Muslim] fighters at Badr and said, 'Do as you please, for I have [already] forgiven you.'"

57 Property and Commerce

(102) Know—may God have mercy upon you—that you have no license to a Muslim's property, unless he gladly consents. If a man has come to possess illicit monies, a license is not thereby given to take of it, absent his leave. For he might repent and wish to give the monies back to their legitimate owner, in which case your depriving him of his money would be illicit.

(103) In matters of gain, or commerce (*al-makāsib*), whatever proves to be valid to you is unqualifiedly permissible; whatever proves invalid, or illicit [is not]. Should they have been invalid, or illicit, you are entitled to what merely sustains you. You should not say, "I renounce commerce altogether and take what is given." Hitherto, such was not the practice of the Companions nor of the learned. ʿUmar [b. al-Khaṭṭāb]—may God be pleased with him—said, "A gain involving some blemish is better than being in a position of need."

58 Prayer behind Jahmis

(104) You are permitted to perform the five daily prayers behind whomever you might pray behind, unless he be a Jahmi. For he denies God's attributes (*muʿaṭṭil*). If it so happens that you pray behind such a man, you ought to perform your prayer again. If it was the Friday prayer, with a Jahmi as the imam, who is also the ruler (*sulṭān*), then pray behind him and perform your prayer again afterward. But if your imam, whether or not a ruler, is an adherent of the Sunna, then pray behind him; and do not perform it again.

59 Virtues of Abū Bakr and ʿUmar

(105) Believe that Abū Bakr and ʿUmar are buried in ʿĀʾisha's chamber together with the Messenger of God—may peace and blessings be upon him. Should you visit the tomb, then it is mandatory to greet them [by saying, "May God's peace and blessings be upon both of you"], after having greeted the Messenger of God—may peace and blessings be upon him.

60 Communal Duties

(106) It is your religious duty to command right and forbid wrong (*al-amr bi-l-maʿrūf wa-l-nahī ʿan al-munkar*), unless someone's sword or rod is to be feared.

(107) Likewise, [it is your religious duty] to greet with the greeting of peace all the servants of God.

(108) Whoever fails, without excuse, to attend the Friday prayers and the communal prayer in the mosque is an innovator. [Valid] excuses include a debilitating sickness, whereby it is not possible to attend the mosque, and fear of an oppressive ruler. Every other excuse is invalid.

Whoever stands behind the imam, without following him (fa-lam yaqtadī bihi), *his prayer is invalid.*

(109) Commanding right and forbidding wrong ought to be effected first by action (lit. by the hand), [then] verbally (lit. by the tongue), and [if this is not possible], then by inner abhorrence (lit. by the heart); it is not to be effected by violent means (lit. by the sword).

(110) If nothing suspicious is apparent, then your fellow Muslim's privacy is not to be breached.

(111) Every claim to esoteric knowledge (*ʿilm al-bāṭin*), unsubstantiated by the Quran and the Sunna, is an innovation and a misguidance. It should be neither observed nor propagated by anyone.

61 Marriage Contracts

(112) A woman offering herself to a man is not de jure licit for him (*lā taḥillu lahu*), unless [a contract has been arranged] in the presence of a guardian, two just witnesses, and a dowry. They are both to be punished if he satisfies his desire for her in any manner (*nāl*[a] *minhā shay*[ʾan]).

62 Disparaging the Companions and Their Traditions

(113) If you meet a man disparaging the Companions of the Messenger of God—may peace and blessings be upon him—you should know that he is a

man of wicked speech and innovative tendencies. For the Messenger of God—may peace and blessings be upon him—has said: "If my Companions are disparaged, refrain." The Prophet knew what lapses they were going to make after his death. Nevertheless, he only praised them, saying: "Let my Companions be. Speak only well of them." Do not make their lapses or their wars any part of your conversation. Leave to one side whatever had escaped your knowledge. Do not [even] listen to anyone discussing these affairs, for your heart is sure to be infected if you listen.

(114) Should you hear someone disparaging prophetic traditions, choosing other than these traditions, then hold his [belief in] Islam to be suspect. Form a suspicion that he is a sectarian innovator (*ṣāḥib hawā*).

63 Authority of the Rulers

(115) Know that the injustices of the ruler do not lessen God's duties ordained and communicated through His Prophet—may peace and blessings be upon him. The ruler stands to answer [before God] for his injustice, [whereas] your voluntary [acts] and devotion under his rulership stand undiminished (*tāmm*), if God so wishes. This is to say: [attend] the Friday prayer with them, and join in *jihād* with them. In all acts of devotion be their partner, since your intention is other than theirs.

Whenever you find a man invoking God against (*yadʿū ʿalā*) the ruler (*sulṭān*), you should know that he is a man of sectarian tendencies. [Conversely,] whenever you find a man invoking God for the ruler's welfare (*yadʿū li-*), you should know that he is as an adherent of the Sunna—if God so wishes. For Fuḍayl has said, "If I were to invoke God only once, I would invoke Him for the ruler."

As for **Aḥmad b. Kāmil,**[38] he said: "Al-Ḥusayn b. Muḥammad b. al-Ṭabarī informed me that Mardawayh al-Ṣāʾigh said, 'I heard Fuḍayl saying: "If I were to invoke God only once, I would invoke Him for the ruler." Thereupon he was asked, "Explain further, Abū ʿAlī." He answered, "If I were to address [the invocation] to myself, its [benefit] would not go beyond me. If, however, I were to address it to the ruler, it would render him upright, and with him the people and the country would become upright too. Thus, we were ordered to invoke God for, not against, the rulers, even if they are unjust and oppressive; they alone

38 He is the first transmitter of this book from Ghulām Khalīl.

bear the responsibility for their injustice and their oppression, whereas their uprightness benefits them and the Muslims alike."'"

(116) Never speak of any of the Mothers of the Believers [i.e., the Prophet's wives], except what is good.

64 Performing Religious Duties with the Community

(117) If you see a man taking good care to observe his religious duties (*farāʾiḍ*) with the Community, whether or not with the ruler, then know that he is an adherent of the Sunna, if God so wishes.

Conversely, if you see a man careless to observe his religious duties with the Community, even if he supports the ruler, then know that he is a sectarian.

65 Lawful and Unlawful Things

(118) What is lawful is that which you have witnessed and sworn that it is so; likewise with the unlawful. Whatever is unsettled in your chest is a semblance of truth. That which is manifestly hidden is hidden; that which is manifestly unveiled is unveiled.

66 Charges against Different Sects

(119) If you hear a man broaching the topic of anthropomorphism, or claiming that another is an anthropomorphist, then hold him suspect, and know that he is a Jahmi. And if you hear a man claiming that another is a Nasibi,[39] then know that he is a Rafidi. Moreover, if you hear a man enjoining others to discuss God's unicity, or asking for an explanation thereof, then know that he is a Muʿtazili. If you hear a man claiming that someone is a predestinarian, or discussing predestination, or justice (*ʿadl*) of God, then know that he is a Qadari. All of these are novel designations (*asmāʾ muḥdatha*) invented by sectarians.

(120) ʿAbdallāh b. al-Mubārak said, "Never accept from the people of Kufa any tradition concerning the [Imami Shiʿa] (*rafḍ*); nor accept from the people of

39 *Nāṣib* is a disparaging epithet given by Shiʿis to Sunnis. See al-Qāḍī, Earliest "Nābita" 27–61.

Syria (*al-Shām*) any tradition concerning rebellion (*sayf*); nor accept from the people of Basra any tradition concerning free will (*qadar*); nor accept from the people of Khorasan any tradition concerning postponement of Divine decree (*irjāʾ*); nor accept from the people of Mecca any tradition concerning exchange *in specie* (*ṣarf*); nor accept from the people of Medina any tradition concerning singing (*ghināʾ*). Do not accept any of the above traditions from these groups."

67 The Adherents of the Sunna vs. Sectarian Innovators

(121) If you see a man revering Abū Hurayra, Anas b. Mālik, Usayd b. Ḥuḍayr, then know that he is an adherent of the Sunna (*ṣāḥib sunna*), if God so wishes.

(122) If you see a man revering Ayyūb [al-Sakhtiyānī], Ibn ʿAwn, Yūnus b. ʿUbayd, ʿAbdallāh b. Idrīs al-Awdī, al-Shaʿbī, Mālik b. Mighwal, Yazīd b. Zurayʿ, Muʿādh b. Muʿādh, Wahb b. Jarīr, Ḥammād b. Salama, Ḥammād b. Zayd, al-Ḥajjāj b. al-Minhāl, Aḥmad b. Ḥanbal, and Aḥmad b. Naṣr—and he speaks well of them and follows their doctrine (*qawl*)—then know that he is an adherent of the Sunna, if God so wishes.

(123) If you see a man sitting with one of the sectarians, then warn him and acquaint him with the facts. Should you see him again in the company of the sectarian, then avoid him, for he also is a sectarian.

(124) If you meet a man who, upon hearing a tradition, rejects it and [prefers to rely exclusively on] the Quran, then do not doubt that he is a man who has embraced heresy; so leave his company.

(125) Know that all sectarianisms (*ahwāʾ*) are vile, and all result in rebellion. The vilest of these (*ardāhā wa-akfaruhā*) include the Rafidis, the Muʿtazila, and the Jahmis. For they all revolve around the denial of God's attributes (*taʿṭīl*) and around heresy (*zandaqa*).

(126) Know that whoever finds fault with any of the Companions of Muhammad—may peace and blessings be upon him—then he is [in effect] intending that for Muhammad himself. He has done him harm in his very grave.

(127) Should you observe in someone any innovation, then avoid him, for whatever he conceals is bound to be more than whatever he has revealed.

(128) If you see a follower of the Sunna who is vile in his manner (*ṭarīq*) and in his conduct (*madhhab*), who is dissolute, wicked, sinful, and misguided, and cleaves, nevertheless, to the Sunna, then do not shun his company, and sit with him, for you are not impaired by his sins. Conversely, if you see a man who is devout, pious, austere in his ways, passionate in his worship, [but who, nevertheless,] is a sectarian, then shun his company, refrain from meeting with him, or, for that matter, listening to him. Do not even walk alongside him in the street. I fear that you might come to appreciate his conduct and thus be ruined with him.

(129) Yūnus b. ʿUbayd once saw his son leave a sectarian's [house]. So, he enquired of him: "My son, where have you come from?" He answered: "From the house of so-and-so …" [Whereupon,] he responded: "My son, I would rather see you come out of the house of an indecent person than see you come out of the house of so-and-so. I would even rather that you face God as a fornicator, a thief, a sinner, or unfaithful, than having you face Him with the beliefs of so-and-so." Do you not see that Yūnus b. ʿUbayd well knew that the indecent person would not divert his son from his religious beliefs, whereas the innovator would do so, to the point where he would render him an unbeliever? Be wary, especially, of these present times of yours. Scrutinize and be selective with your associates and your companions, and whoever you listen to [or sit with]. For, except for those with divine protection, people seem to have apostasized from their religion.

(130) Pay attention, if you come across a man speaking well of Ibn Abī Duʾād, Bishr al-Marīsī, Thumāma, Abū l-Hudhayl, Hishām al-Fuwaṭī, or any of their partisans. Beware of him, for he must be an innovator. For all these persons, here mentioned above, were apostates. And this man of yours, who spoke well of them, must belong to the same group as they, and so abandon his company.

(131) Inquisitions of faith in Islam are an innovation. Today, however, people are put to trial for upholding the Sunna; [the Prophet] said: "This knowledge [i.e., the Sunna] is as binding as religion; scrutinize, then, and be selective with whomever you take your religion from."

(132) Accept not traditions except from people whose testimony you accept. Scrutinize the person, then; if he be an adherent of the Sunna, learned and trustworthy, then feel free to note down [what he transmits]. Otherwise, abandon him.

68 Enjoining Theological Disputation

(133) If you want to remain an adherent of the truth and to belong to the people of the Sunna before you, then be wary of theological disputation and its propagators. Be wary, as well, of polemics, disputation, [reasoning by] analogy, and debates over matters religious. Listening to these, even if you accepted none of it, is bound to sow doubt in your heart. You might as well have accepted it. For heresies, innovations, sectarianism, and misguidance, one and all, have their source in theological disputation, controversy, polemics, and analogy. These are the gateways of innovation, doubts, and heresy. So fear God for yourself; hold fast to traditions and to people of traditions and due compliance (*taqlīd*; or strict conformance). For religion is but strict conformance. Our predecessors left us with no confusion; follow them, then, and spare yourself the effort. Do not go beyond traditions, or beyond the people of traditions.

(134) Abstain from [pondering] ambiguous verses, and make no analogies. Nor exert yourself in seeking counterarguments against innovators, for you were commanded to remain silent. Offer them not the opportunity to hold sway over you.[40] Don't you know that Muḥammad b. Sīrīn, with all his learning, not once replied to an innovator, nor ever listened to a verse from the book of God [recited] by him? Upon enquiry, he said, "I fear that he would distort it, which would bring unease to my heart."[41]

(135) If you hear a man saying, upon hearing the traditions of the messenger of God, "Merely glorify God," then know that he is a Jahmi whose intention is to dismiss, and to reject, by way of this utterance, the traditions of the messenger of God. When he comes across traditions of the *visio* of God, and the descent of God, and suchlike, he claims to be glorifying God and arguing for His transcendence. Doesn't he thus dismiss the traditions of the messenger of God—may peace and blessings be upon him? Should he retort, "God is far too transcendent, we believe, to move from one place to another?" Then he has claimed that he knows God better than anyone else does.[42] Be wary, then, of these, for the majority of people, the vulgar and otherwise, entertain such beliefs.[43]

---

40 Cf. English translation in Melchert, Traditionist-jurisprudents 396.

41 For the last three lines, cf. Melchert, *Formation*, 152; Melchert, Ḥanābila 367.

42 English translation in Frank, Elements 161.

43 Cf. ibid., 161.

(136) If you were approached by someone enquiring, of his own accord,[44] about an issue *in this book*, then talk to him and offer guidance. If, however, he approaches you argumentatively, then be cautious. For debate gives rise to dispute, polemics, quarrel, controversy, and antagonism, all of which lead away from the right path, and all of which you were strictly prohibited from engaging in. It has not come to our knowledge that any of our jurists and learned authorities have ever engaged in debate, polemics, or controversy.

(137) Al-Ḥasan al-Baṣrī [once] said, "A wise man does not quarrel, nor does he flatter, but rather disseminates his wisdom. If it is accepted, he praises God; if not, he also praises Him."

(138) A man once came to al-Ḥasan and asked, "Shall we debate religion?" upon which al-Ḥasan responded, "I know my religion. If you have lost yours, then go seek it."

(139) Just outside his chamber, the Messenger of God—may peace and blessings be upon him—once heard some people arguing. One of them was saying, "Did God not say so-and-so?" and another, "Did God not say so-and-so?" Thereupon, the Prophet indignantly came out in anger and said, "Were you thus ordered to behave? Or, was I sent to you for this? To set one part of the book of God against another?" Thus, he prohibited disputation.

(140) Ibn ʿUmar disliked disputation, and so did Mālik b. Anas, and those above him in status and those below, up till this day. [Leave these to one side,] God's words are far greater than any of His creation, for He—blessed and exalted is He—said, ﴾None disputes the revelations of God save the unbelievers﴿ (Q 40:4).

(141) A man asked ʿUmar, "What are ﴾those that speed forth, at full speed﴿? (Q 79:2)." He responded, "If you were headshaved, I would have beheaded you."

(142) The Prophet—may peace and blessings be upon him—said, "A believer does not argue, nor does argument, on the Day of Judgment, bring any benefit to him who argues. Abandon disputation."

(143) Nor is it permissible for a Muslim to designate someone an adherent of the Sunna unless [the Muslim] verifies that he embodies the character traits

44 Could be also read as "*mustarshid*," i.e., seeking guidance; cf. Arabic text.

of the Sunna. Nor is he to be designated an adherent of the Sunna before he embodies the Sunna in its totality.

69 Origins of Innovations

(144) ʿAbdallāh b. al-Mubārak said,[45] "The origin of seventy-two deviating sects are four: the Qadaris, the Murjiʾa, the Shiʿa, and the Kharijites. From these four branched the seventy-two deviations.

Whoever gives precedence to Abū Bakr, ʿUmar, and ʿUthmān over all [other] the Companions of the messenger of God, and speaks only well of the rest of them, and invokes God for them, has departed from Shiʿism altogether.

Whoever says, 'Faith consists in both verbal profession and works, admitting of increase and diminution,' has departed from *Irjāʾ* altogether.

Whoever says, '[It is permissible] to pray behind every [ruler], good or wicked, and participate in the duty of *jihād* with any caliph,' and shuns rebellion by the sword against the ruler—but rather invokes God on his behalf—has departed from the doctrine of the Kharijites altogether.

Whoever says, 'All that befalls man, good or ill, is from God, ﴿He leads astray whom He wills and guides whom He wills﴾' (Q 74:31), has departed from the Qadaris altogether. Such a person, then, is an adherent of the Sunna."

(145) There has spread an innovation that amounts to disbelief in God Almighty,

(a) Whoever proclaims it is an indisputable unbeliever: Those who believe in the Return [of the dead Imam] (*rajʿa*) before the Day of Resurrection, that ʿAlī b. Abī Ṭālib is alive and will return, and likewise Muḥammad b. ʿAlī, Jaʿfar b. Muḥammad, and Mūsā b. Jaʿfar;
(b) And posit the Imamate;
(c) And claim that they know the Unseen.

Be wary of them, then, for they and whoever admits this are unbelievers in God, Almighty.

(146) Ṭuʿma b. ʿAmr and Sufyān b. ʿUyayna said: "Whoever holds back on the question [of the preference] of ʿUthmān and ʿAlī (*waqafa ʿinda ʿUthmān wa-ʿAlī*) is but a Shiʿi; he is not to be considered fit for testimony, nor to be addressed in speech, nor to be associated with."

45 Cf. Juynboll, Excursus 321; German translation in van Ess, *Der Eine* i, 74–75.

Whoever prefers ʿAlī to ʿUthmān is Rafidi, for he has disputed the command of the Companions of the Messenger of God—may peace and blessings be upon him. Whoever, in contrast, gives preference to the [first] three [Successors to Muḥammad] over the rest of them (*jamāʿa*) (i.e., the Companions of Muhammad), and asks mercy for these, and does not remark on their shortcomings, is on the path to guidance [by the standard] of *this* book.

70 Elements of the Sunna

(147) To accept the Sunna [entails]:

(a) that you bear witness that the ten Companions (*ʿashara*) whom the Messenger of God—may peace and blessings be upon him—testified that they are worthy of Paradise, are indeed in Paradise. Have no doubt of this.

(b) that you reserve the invocation ["May peace and blessings be upon him"] only for the Messenger of God—may peace and blessings be upon him—and his Household.

(c) that you know that ʿUthmān b. ʿAffān was unjustly killed and that his killer was in the wrong.

(148) Whoever assents to what is in this book, upholding it, and seeks guidance in it, and does not doubt or reject even a letter therein, is thereby an adherent of the Sunna and the *jamāʿa*. He is accomplished in the Sunna, and the Sunna is complete through him.

Whoever abjures a letter in this book, or casts doubt upon it, or wavers [in accepting it in full] is but a sectarian (*ṣāḥib al-hawā*).

Whoever abjures, or holds in doubt, a letter in the Quran, or anything that is related on the authority of the Messenger of God—may peace and blessings be upon him—shall meet God—exalted is He—as a denier of truth. Therefore, fear God, beware of Him, and attend to your faith.

(149) It is of the Sunna to withhold support from anyone acting in disobedience of God, be they people of charity, in particular, or anyone else. No one is to be obeyed if this entails disobedience of God; pay him no heed. Rather, detest it for the sake of God—blessed and exalted is He.

(150) Believe that repentance is a religious duty. Servants of God ought to repent, whether the misdeed is major or minor.

(151) The Prophet—may peace and blessings be upon him—testified that some [of his Companions] are destined for Paradise. Whoever does not likewise

testify is an innovator, misguided, and skeptical of the sayings of the Prophet—may peace and blessings be upon him.

71 The Sunna in the Words of Some Authorities

(152) Mālik b. Anas said, "Whoever adheres to the Sunna and abstains from denigrating the Companions of the Messenger of God—may peace and blessings be upon him—shall, upon death, join the Company of "prophets, men of righteousness, martyrs, and the virtuous" (Q 4:69), even if he falls short in good deeds."

(153) Bishr [b.] al-Ḥārith said, "Islam is the Sunna, and the Sunna, Islam."

(154) Fuḍayl b. ʿIyāḍ said, "Whenever I see one of the people of the Sunna, it is as if I have seen one of the Companions of the Messenger of God—may peace and blessings be upon him. Whenever, conversely, I see one of the people of innovation, it is as if I have seen one of the hypocrites."

(155) Yūnus b. ʿUbayd said: "How amazing it is to come by someone advocating the Sunna today; more amazing, however, is to come by someone who responds and accepts it."

(156) Ibn ʿAwn kept saying, while on his deathbed, "The Sunna! The Sunna! Beware of innovation!" until he died.

(157) Abū ʿAbdallāh Ghulām Khalīl said, "A friend of mine died. He was then seen in a dream saying, 'Tell Abū ʿAbdallāh to adhere to the Sunna, for it was the first thing God enquired of me.' "

(158) Abū l-ʿĀliya said, "Whoever dies [having lived] according to the Sunna, with no suspicion surrounding him, is a man of righteousness."

(159) [Finally,] it is said, "Deliverance is to be found in adherence to the Sunna."

APPENDIX I

List of Editions and Translations

This appendix concisely reviews the twelve Arabic editions of the *K. Sharḥ al-sunna* (in its attribution to al-Barbahārī) that have been identified so far, along with one Arabic-language study of this text and two translations into European languages.

Apart from the academic study by Hiba Shibārū-Sinnū, a PhD thesis written under the supervision of Ahyaf Sinnū at the Université Saint-Joseph in Beirut in 1980, the *K. Sharḥ al-sunna* has found wide circulation, especially in Salafi circles, and has been published in different editions (including several reprints). Interestingly, certain of these editions were originally given as oral lectures at Salafi-Wahhabi seminars, and some of them have also been distributed on cassettes and in audio-visual commentaries on YouTube.

In what follows, we take a closer look at the book publications in particular, most of which were edited by Saudi Arabian Salafi *ʿulamāʾ* who are near to, or are members of, the Council of Senior Ulema founded in 1971,[1] as in the case of Shaykh Ṣāliḥ b. Fawzān al-Fawzān (see below). In two cases, the editors are Egyptian Salafis living in Saudi Arabia; in one case, the editor is a Salafi shaykh from Yemen who is affiliated with a Saudi-sponsored institution. There is little wonder that this should be the case, since the book advocates a strict obedience to the ruler (*waliyy al-amr*), a tenet dear to the hearts of the Saudi establishment.[2]

It is noteworthy that the first Arabic edition was undertaken by Muḥammad Saʿīd al-Qaḥṭānī (b. 1956),[3] a student of Muḥammad Quṭb (d. 2014)[4] and the author of a book that had a significant influence on the nascent Ṣaḥwa group in Saudi Arabia[5]—namely, *al-Walāʾ wa-l-barāʾ fī l-Islām* ("Allegiance and repudiation in Islam," 1984).[6] Also, al-

1 Bligh, Saudi religious elite 39; see also Lacroix, *Awakening Islam* 74.

2 Atawneh, Is Saudi Arabia a theocracy? 26–28; Alshamsi, *Islam* 7 (Saudi constitution, art. 6); for the discourse of the Saudi reformists on obedience to the ruler, see 45, 60–61, 97, 207, and 19–20; Lacroix, *Awakening Islam* 74, 141, 203.

3 Alshamsi, *Islam* 86, 108, 114; Lacroix, *Awakening Islam* 55, 162, 205, 249.

4 The brother of Sayyid Quṭb. In 1971 he left for Saudi Arabia, where he was appointed professor at the Faculty of Sharia in Mecca. Lacroix, *Awakening Islam* 53–56; Alshamsi, *Islam* 58–61.

5 The Wahhabi Sahwa in Saudi Arabia refers to "the hybrid that took shape when the political and cultural aspects of the ideology [of the Egyptian Muslim Brothers who have been teaching in Saudi Arabia since the 1960s] encountered the religious concepts of Wahhabism," which burgeoned in the 1980s and challenged the Saudi establishment. Lacroix, Between revolution and apoliticism 63, 76, 78; Lacroix, *Awakening Islam* 37–201.

6 For his concept of *al-walāʾ wa-l-barāʾ*, see Atawneh, Is Saudi Arabia a theocracy? 726; Bin Ali, *Roots* 77–80, 206, 236–243.

 | DOI:10.1163/9789004429055_009

Qaḥṭānī is one of the Sahwi *'ulamā'* who signed the memorandum of 1991, asking for political change and reform in Saudi Arabia.[7] He was imprisoned in March 1995 and eventually lost his teaching position at Umm al-Qura University in Mecca in June 1996, along with 50 other Sahwis.

The new edition of the *K. Sharḥ al-sunna* (attributed to al-Barbahārī) by Abū Yāsir Khālid b. Qāsim al-Raddādī (1993) was first published after al-Qaḥṭānī had fallen from grace with the religious Saudi establishment between 1991 and 1993.

As indicated in the epilogue to this study, the *K. Sharḥ al-sunna* has become a recognized textbook in the curriculum of *da'wa*[8] institutions in Saudi Arabia, as well as in other similar institutes around the world financed by the Saudi religious establishment. Looking at the issue of the book's authorship from this perspective, the rationale behind the decision of those previous editors to insist on the attribution of the book to the Hanbali activist al-Barbahārī becomes clearer. Still, none of these editors has offered any straightforward proof for this attribution, nor have they undertaken an in-depth internal textual study of the book. Moreover, the respective editors have passed in silence over the messianic title *al-Qā'im min Āl Muḥammad.*

Interestingly enough, however, a certain Azhari, as he identifies himself on the internet, has published on a Sufi website a refutation of the attribution of the book to al-Barbahārī.[9] As part of this refutation, this otherwise anonymous author examines the editions of both al-Qaḥṭānī and al-Raddādī. Moreover, he expresses his irritation that these two editors include in their introductions to the book unsubstantiated accusations against the Ash'aris.[10]

Our chronological list of identified Arabic editions and commentaries of the *K. Sharḥ al-sunna* (attributed to al-Barbahārī) is descriptive and does not include detailed remarks on the nature and quality of the respective publications. This is in appreciation of the fact that—with the exception of Shibārū-Sinnū's work—these editors apply the traditional method of annotation (*sharḥ*) rather than a text-critical approach. Our main interest thus lies in highlighting the manner in which these editors dealt with the specific issue of the authorship of the *K. Sharḥ al-sunna.*

---

7 Alshamsi, *Islam* 99–110.

8 Canard, Da'wa; Da'wa is mentioned in article 23 of the Basic Law of Saudi Arabia. Guillemin-Puteaux, Religious legitimacy 1.

9 http://cb.rayaheen.net/showthread.php?tid=15275.

10 Ash'ari theology is the official doctrine taught at Al-Azhar; cf., 'Abd al-Razzāq, *Falsafat* i, 53–60. See also a relevant statement by Shaykh al-Azhar Aḥmad al-Ṭayyib on April 22, 2015 (https://www.alarabiya.net/ar/arab-and-world/egypt/2015/04/22/-الطيب-يجيب-سؤال-لماذا-يتبنى-الأزهر-المذهب-الأشعري-؟).

An asterisk indicates that the respective publication was inaccessible to us, so that we were unable to comment on this book in more detail.

1 Arabic Editions and Commentaries

(1) **Shibārū-Sinnū**, Hiba. Abū Muḥammad al-Barbahārī: *ʿAqīdatuhu wa-musāhamatuhu fī l-ḥayāt al-ʿāmma*, 269 pages. Unpublished MA thesis. Beirut: Université Saint-Joseph, 1980.

The author undertakes a detailed study of the creed as included in Ibn Abī Yalā's *Ṭabaqāt al-Ḥanābila*. Accordingly, the authorship of al-Barbahārī is taken at face value. Mention of Ghulām Khalīl is restricted to the cursory remark on page 36 taken from Henri Laoust's entry on al-Barbahārī in the *Encyclopedia of Islam*, where Laoust contends, "His creed recalls that composed by Aḥmad Ghulām Khalīl (died 275/888), an opponent of the extremist Sufism.".[11]

The thesis is divided into three parts. Part I includes a descriptive survey of the Sunni schools of law, the *madhāhib ahl al-sunna* (pp. 15–20), and the doctrines of the *ahl al-sunna* (pp. 20–26). Part II deals with al-Barbahārī's life and career (pp. 27–63), and part III comprises a study of the names of authorities mentioned in the text, as well as the terminology used in the text. Finally, the author provides an edition of the text (pp. 132–167), followed by a glossary of the vocabulary (pp. 169–237), and various indices. In general, the author relies heavily on the scholarship produced by Laoust.

(2)* **Al-Qaḥṭānī**, Muḥammad Saʿīd Sālim.[12] *Sharḥ al-sunna*. Al-Dammām: Dār Ibn al-Qayyim, 1408/1987 (Third reprint, Cairo, 1416/1996).[13]

(3) **Al-Raddādī**, Abū Yāsir Khālid b. Qāsim. *Sharḥ al-sunna*. First edition, 156 pages: al-Madīna al-Munawwara: Maktabat al-Ghurabāʾ al-Athariyya, 1414/1997. Second edition, Riyadh: Dār al-Salaf and Dār al-Ṣumayʿī, 1421/2000.[14]

Al-Raddādī argues that there was a distortion of the text and replacement of names (*taḥrīf wa-tabdīl*) at the beginning of the manuscript, in which the name of al-Barbahārī was replaced by that of Ghulām Khalīl. He then introduces the transmission chain

11 Laoust, al-Barbahārī 1039a.

12 Alshamsi, *Islam* 86–88, 114; Lacroix, *Awakening Islam* 56, 162, 204–205, 249. For his biography, see, https://ar.islamway.net/lessons/scholar/238.

13 Unfortunately, I was unable to consult either of the two editions.

14 I was able to consult only the first edition.

of the book as it appears on the first page of the manuscript and proceeds to refute the attribution to Ghulām Khalīl by advancing the following arguments (pp. 42–45):

(a) Ghulām Khalīl was considered a liar. Moreover, Ghulām Khalīl died in 275/888, whereas the author of the book states, "All that I have prescribed for you *in this book* is on the authority of God, the Messenger of God—may peace and blessings be upon him—and his Companions, their Successors, and the third and fourth generations." Consequently, this means that the author must have been al-Barbahārī, since he died in the fourth/tenth century, in 329/940.

(b) The first transmitter of the book, Ibn Kāmil, might have transmitted from Ghulām Khalīl. Nonetheless, at that time he would have been only 15 years old. It is more probable and more suitable (*awlā wa-aḥrā*) that Ibn Kāmil transmitted from al-Barbahārī. Therefore, it must have been due to the *miḥna* that al-Barbahārī's name was removed from the text by some copyist and replaced with that of Ghulām Khalīl for fear of persecution should a copy of a book related to al-Barbahārī be found in the possession of the copyist.

(c) Even though the transmission chain states explicitly that Ghulām Khalīl had instructed Ibn Kāmil, "Transmit this book on my authority from beginning to end," that does not prove in any way that Ghulām Khalīl is the author, since Ghulām Khalīl was a well-known "liar," and the possibility should therefore not to be ruled out that he had "stolen" the book.

(d) Most of those who wrote biographies of al-Barbahārī attributed a book entitled *Sharḥ al-sunna* to him.

(e) A number of later renowned authors (*a'imma*) made use of citations from the book while attributing it to al-Barbahārī. Examples of this are the citations in Ibn Abī Yaʿlā's, Ibn Taymiyya's, and al-Dhahabī's works.

It is noteworthy that al-Raddādī, while presenting the biography of al-Barbahārī, refuses to accept the veracity of the report given by al-Ḥasan b. ʿAlī al-Ahwāzī. He bases his decision in this regard on respective views offered by Ibn Taymiyya and al-Dhahabī (pp. 22–23).

Al-Raddādī then evaluates the first edition of the book undertaken by al-Qaḥṭānī and lists a number of mistakes and typographical errors in that edition (pp. 46–50). The last section of al-Raddādī's introduction is dedicated to the shortcomings of al-Barbahārī's book. In summary, they relate to the following points:

(a) repetition and lack of order in the presentation of themes;

(b) citation of unsound (*wāhiya*) and weak traditions;

(c) reservation toward the author's insistence on the fact that everything he prescribes in his book is mandatory (*ilzām*);

(d) a comment on the statement "If you see a follower of the Sunna who is vile in his manner (*ṭarīq*) and in his conduct (*madhhab*), who is dissolute, wicked, sinful, and misguided, but cleaves, nevertheless, to the Sunna, then do not shun his company." (§ 128 in our translation). Al-Raddādī also argues that the author is not trying to mitigate the seriousness of committing sins (*maʿāṣī*), but rather is accentuating the danger of innovations and their effects.

(4) **Al-Najmī**, Aḥmad b. Yaḥyā,[15] *Irshād al-sārī fī Sharḥ al-sunna lil-Barbahārī*,[16] 305 pages [2002].

Originally, oral lectures given to his students in 1419/1998 during a summer course (*Dawrat al-Shaykh ʿAbdallāh b. Muḥammad al-Qarʿāwī*) in the province of Ṣāmiṭah in Jāzān, southwestern Saudi Arabia, near the Yemeni border.

Al-Najmī was, however, unable to finish his lectures during the respective summer course and thus promised one of his students he would send him his entire explication in written form. Based on this writing, concluded on 22 Rajab 1422 / 9 October 2001, the student, Ḥasan b. Muḥammad b. Manṣūr Daghrīrī, edited his teacher's book and published it.[17] Daghrīrī takes the attribution of the book to al-Barbahārī for granted and relies on both al-Qaḥṭānī and al-Raddādī in writing al-Barbahārī's biography.

(5) **Al-ʿUbaylān**, ʿAbdallāh b. Ṣāliḥ.[18] *Al-Nubadh ʿalā Sharḥ al-sunna*, 111 pages. Reviewed and revised by His Eminence the General Muftī of the Arab Kingdom of Saudi Arabia al-Shaykh ʿAbd al-ʿAzīz b. ʿAbdallāh Āl al-Shaykh.[19] Kuwait: Ghirās lil-Nashr, 1423/2003.

As the title of this publication indicates, the book consists of brief "digests" (*nubadh*) intended as commentary on specific themes in *K. Sharḥ al-sunna* by al-Barbahārī, whose authorship is taken for granted.

In the short preface of this publication, written by several of al-ʿUbaylān's students (*majmūʿa min ṭalabat al-ʿilm*), it is mentioned that these digests were originally oral lectures given by Shaykh al-ʿUbaylān during a course in Ḥāʾil (northwest of Medina), although the dates of these lectures are not given. These unspecified students state that

15 Died 1429/2008; for his biography, see the introduction by the editor, 18–24; see also https://www.sounna.com/spip.php?article223 (in French).
16 Online: http://subulsalam.com/site/kutub/AhmedNajmi/02IrchadSari.pdf.
17 The date that the editor gives at the end of the text, p. 305, is: 6.11.1422/January 20, 2002.
18 He belongs to the Jami movement (Lacroix, *Awakening Islam* 211–221), and as such al-ʿUbaylān is loyal to the Saudi ruling family, Lacroix, *Awakening Islam* 214, 217; Alshamsi, *Islam* 111. For his biography cf. http://www.kulalsalafiyeen.com/vb/showthread.php?t=2880.
19 For his biography, see Lacroix, *Awakening Islam* 169 and 319, fn. 90.

their editorial work was restricted to omitting repetitive phrases, providing references for prophetic traditions and verifying statements attributed to certain scholars.

Al-ʿUbaylān's exposé reiterates basic "purist Salafi" doctrines concerning the importance of the Sunna, the meaning of the *jamāʿa*, i.e., "what the Prophet and his Companions have agreed on" (pp. 23–28), the method (*manhaj*) of the *ahl al-sunna* concerning reasoning and deductive argumentation (*al-naẓar wa-l-istidlāl*; pp. 40–42), the method of the *ahl al-sunna* concerning God's attributes (pp. 43–44), the refutation of the methods of the innovators (pp. 50–94), and finally, an elucidation on the refusal of strict adherence and blind imitation (*ittibāʿ* and *taqlīd*; pp. 94–99), a common denominator among Salafi positions in general and those of Wahhabis in particular.

In this section, al-ʿUbaylān refers to Ibn Taymiyya (d. 728/1337),[20] Ibn Qayyim al-Jawziyya (d. 751/1450),[21] Muḥammad al-Amīn al-Shanqīṭī (d. 1972), and Shaykh ʿAbd al-Raḥmān b. Ḥasan Āl al-Shaykh (d. 1869), grandson of Muḥammad b. ʿAbd al-Wahhāb and head of the religious establishment during the Second Saudi State (1235–1309/1819–1891).

(6) **Al-Jummayzī**, ʿAbd al-Raḥmān b. Aḥmad.[22] *Sharḥ al-sunna*, in 176 pages. Riyadh: Maktabat Dār al-Minhāj, 1426/2005.

Al-Barbahārī's authorship is, again, taken for granted. Al-Jummayzī explains that he embarked on this new edition because of the mistakes appearing in the two editions by al-Qaḥṭānī (1408/1987 and 1416/1996) and the three editions by al-Raddādī (the third being that of 1421/2000). He then gives a list of those mistakes (pp. 14–18). In arguing for al-Barbahārī's authorship of the book (pp. 25–30), he more or less repeats the main arguments made by al-Raddādī.

(7) **Salīm**, ʿAmr ʿAbd al-Munʿim.[23] *Sharḥ al-sunna wa-Riyāḍ al-janna, sharḥ wa-tartīb Sharḥ al-sunna*, 504 pages. Riyadh and Cairo: Dār Ibn al-Qayyim lil-Nashr wa-l-Tawzīʿ and Dār Ibn ʿAffān, 1426/2005.

Salīm's introduction (pp. 5–17) consists nearly entirely of a biography of al-Barbahārī. The editor does not address the problem of the authorship in his publication, which follows the method of a traditional annotation (*sharḥ*).

---

20 See Atawneh, Wahhābī legal theory 4–13.

21 Mustafa, *On taqlīd* 1–27.

22 Egyptian who lives and works in the Kingdom of Saudi Arabia, cf. http://www.ahlalhdeeth.com/vb/showthread.php?t=73767.

23 Egyptian; cf. http://www.ahlalhdeeth.com/vb/showthread.php?threadid=752.

(8) **Ibn Ṣāliḥ**, Jumʿa. *Ghāyat al-munya ʿalā Sharḥ al-sunna*, 280 pages; *wa-ʿalayhā taʿlīqāt* [with comments and annotations] by al-Shaykh Nāṣir al-Dīn al-Albānī,[24] al-ʿAllāma al-Shaykh al-Fawzān, and al-ʿAllāma al-Shaykh Muḥammad b. Ṣāliḥ al-ʿUthaymīn.[25] Introduction by Aḥmad b. Sabālik. Cairo: Maktabat Alfā, 1428/2007.

In his short introduction, Ibn Ṣāliḥ repeats the arguments set forth by al-Raddādī in order to prove the authorship of al-Barbahārī.

(9) **Al-Fawzān**, Ṣāliḥ b. Fawzān b. ʿAbdallāh.[26] *Sharḥ al-sunna*, in 448 pages. Cairo: Maktabat al-Hadī al-Muḥammadī, 1429/2008.[27]

Al-Fawzān also takes the authorship of al-Barbahārī for granted. He dedicates his introduction (pp. 5–10) to an explanation of his view that al-Barbahārī's *ʿaqīda* belongs to the books of the earliest Salaf (*al-salaf al-aqdamūn*) in the fields of *ʿaqīda* and *tawḥīd*. The last three pages of the introduction (pp. 7–10) offer a defense of these two concepts.[28]

(10) **Al-Madkhalī**, Rabīʿ b. Hādī ʿUmayr.[29] *ʿAwn al-bārī bi-bayān mā taḍammanahu Sharḥ al-sunna lil-Imām al-Barbahārī*, 494 pages. Algeria and Cairo: Dār al-Muḥsin and Dār al-Imām Aḥmad, second edition 1436/2015.[30] (First edition: 1432/2010).[31]

This book was edited by one of al-Madkhalī's Algerian students, Abū ʿAbd al-Muḥsin Layāmīn Amkrāz al-ʿAnnābī (from the Algerian coastal city of Annaba). This student mentions that he had written the text down from lectures given by Shaykh al-Madkhalī,

24 Brown, *Canonization* 321–331; Lacroix, Between revolution and apoliticism 58–80.

25 Al-ʿUthaymīn belongs to the "heart of the Wahhabi religious institution." Lacroix, *Awakening Islam* 111, and index 372; and Alshamsi, *Islam* 55, 100.

26 Ṣaliḥ al-Fawzān is a member of the Council of Senior Ulema in the Kingdom of Saudi Arabia, who serves on many committees. Lacroix, *Awakening Islam* 169, 203; see also Meijer (ed.), *Global Salafism*, index 451; Bin Ali, *Roots* 220–226.

27 Originally audio lessons: https://www.youtube.com/watch?v=VZ-7uuAgCrw.

28 For the importance of the notions of "*Sunna* and *Tawḥīd*" in fundamentalist doctrines, Peters, Islamischer Fundamentalismus 224–227; Bin Ali, *Roots* 22–23, posits that "the main concern of modern Salafi discourse is *aqidah* rather than law (*fiqh*)."

29 See Meijer, Politicising 377–382; Alshamsi, *Islam* 111; Lacroix, *Awakening Islam* 102, 213–219; Bonnefoy, *Salafism in Yemen* 54, 91–96, 171–172.

30 Originally audio lessons: https://www.youtube.com/watch?v=RrC-yUMlnFQ.

31 We were unable to consult the book, but we did obtain a PDF of the introduction of the second edition, pp. 3–27.

without, however, indicating the time and place of these lectures. It is noted that they were recorded on cassettes (not specified whether audio or audio-visual) that extended over 20 hours.[32]

Al-ʿAnnābī explains furthermore that he is relying in his introduction (pp. 3–27) on the findings of both al-Raddādī and al-Jummayzī, and offers a few comments on these two editions (pp. 24–27).

(11) **Al-Ḥajūrī al-Zuʿkurī**, Abū Muḥammad ʿAbd al-Ḥamīd b. Yaḥyā b. Zayd.[33] *Fatḥ al-bārī ʿalā Sharḥ al-sunna lil-Barbahārī*, 639 pages. Ṣaʿda, North Yemen: Dār al-Ḥadīth bi-Dammāj,[34] 1433/2011.

Al-Zuʿkurī taught and explicated the book to his students in 1431/2009[35] in the Dār al-Ḥadīth, a Salafī institute in Dammāj in the province of Ṣaʿda, North Yemen.[36] The institute was founded by Muqbil b. Hādī al-Wādiʿī (d. 2001), originally a Zaydi who converted to the quietist Salafi movement (in 1979) and a close companion of Rabīʿ b. Hādī al-Madkhalī (cf. no. 10 above).[37]

Al-Zuʿkurī mentions that he was asked by some of his non-Arab students (*al-ikhwa al-aʿājim*) to write a commentary so that they could better understand what they had studied with him. He clarifies that he had used in his commentary the explications and annotations (*shurūḥ*) of both Aḥmad b. Yaḥyā al-Najmī and Ṣāliḥ al-Fawzān, which originally were audio expositions.

He also mentions that, while he was preparing the final draft, he came upon an unpublished commentary of the text by his teacher Yaḥyā (i.e., Yaḥyā b. ʿAlī al-Ḥajūrī),[38] and that he made use of it.

Al-Barbahārī's authorship of the book is taken for granted. Interesting, though, is al-Zuʿkurī's observation regarding what he calls "the liberty" evident in this book in levying accusations of unbelief, *iṭlāq al-takfīr* (pp. 21–22).

---

32 *ʿAwn al-bārī* 3–4.

33 Born in 1392/1972 in Kushar in the province of Ḥajja in northern Yemen (al-Maqḥafī, *Muʿjam buldān* ii, 1346). He is a student of Muqbil b. Hādī al-Wādiʿī (see fn. 16). For his biography, see https://alzoukory.com/pageother.php?catsmktba=50.

34 Bonnefoy, *Salafism in Yemen* 144–152; see the website of Dar-ul-Hadith: https://dammaaj.wordpress.com/.

35 Al-Zuʿkurī, *Fatḥ al-bārī* 15.

36 For Dammāj, see al-Maqḥafī, *Muʿjam buldān* i, 619–620.

37 Bonnefoy, Violence 338–339; Bonnefoy, *Salafism in Yemen* 54, 56 and index 312; Brown, Classical and global jihad 94–95.

38 Bonnefoy, *Salafism in Yemen* 72–73, and index 308.

(12) **Ibn ʿAbduh**, Abū Yaḥyā Muḥammad.[39] *Sharḥ al-sunna*, 2 vols., 793 pages.[40] Cairo: No publishing house, 1435/2014.

Ibn ʿAbduh does not refer to any of the editions that had appeared prior to his work. He takes al-Barbahārī's authorship for granted and dedicates several pages (pp. 13–20) in his introduction to enumerating some shortcomings in the book concerning the citations of prophetic traditions.

2 Translations into European Languages

2.1 *English Translations*

(a) *Explanation of the Creed, by Abu Muhammad al-Hasan ibn Alee ibn Khalaf al-Barbahari (d. 329H) rahimahu Allah*, 135 pages, including appendices and index. Translated by Abu Talhah Daawood ibn Ronald Burbank.[41] Birmingham: Al-Haneef Publications, 1995.

The publisher's foreword states,

> The translation was based upon the Arabic edition of *Sharh as-sunnah* produced by Khaalid ar-Radaadee. While translating ar-Radaadee's footnotes to the Arabic text, Abu Talhah added additional notes relying on the taped lectures of Shaikh Saaleh as-Suhaimee's[42] explanation of *Sharh as-sunnah*. In addition, Abu Talhah also made use of excerpts from Muhammad ibn Saʿeed al-Qahtaanee's Arabic edition of the *Sharh as-sunnah*.
>
> p. 4

(b) *Explanation of the Sunna*, in two volumes with a commentary by Shaykh Dr. Saalih al-Fawzan, published by Dar Makkah International in 2014.

2.2 *French Translations*

(a) *L'Explication de la Sunnah*, 1–2, expliqué et commenté par Shaykh Salih b. Fawzan al-Fawzan. Livres Al-Bayyinah 2013.

---

39 See his website: http://abu-yahyaa.blogspot.com/.

40 While we were able to obtain a PDF of the introduction to this book (pp. 3–25), the full text of this publication was inaccessible to us.

41 British convert to Islam (d. 2011).

42 Ṣāliḥ al-Suḥaymī, Meijer, Politicising 382. For his website, see http://sohaymi.com/.

(b) *Sharḫ as-Sounna Par l'Imâm Aboû Mouhammad al-Hassan Ibn 'Alî Ibn Khalâf al-Barbahârî*, published as PDF book http://bibliotheque-islamique-coran-sunna.over-blog.com/article-telecharger-sharh-kitab-sounna-par-l-imam-al-barbahari-pdf-word-68896608.html

2.3 *Swedish Translation*

Sharh-us-Sunna [*Förklaringen av Sunnah*], 48 pages. Författare: Imâm Abû Muhammad al-Hasan bin Khalaf al-Barbahârî. Översättare (och ev. Fotnoter): Abû Mûsâ al-Albânî. Layout: 'Abdulateef Allundî. www.darulhadith.com

The translator gives 18.5.1423/29.7.2002 as the date and Trelleborg, Sweden, as the place of the translation.

2.4 *Bahasa Indonesian Translations*

http://ibnusarijan.blogspot.com/2008/07/syarh-kitab-syarhus-sunnah-al-barbahari.html (Sumatra)

3 Audio-Visual Resources on the Internet

(1) Al-Qaḥṭānī, Māhir b. Ẓāfir (audio): https://www.youtube.com/watch?v=a8zdA-dGJMs.
(2) Al-ʿAql Nāṣir b. ʿAbd al-Karīm al-ʿAlī[43] (audio): https://audio.islamweb.net/audio/index.php?page=lecview&sid=57&read=0&lg=1376&kh=0.
(3) Raslān, Muḥammad Saʿīd (audio): http://www.rslan.com/vad/items.php?chain_id=164; or: https://www.youtube.com/watch?v=LJifWbH1ItA.
(4) Al-Muṣliḥ, Khālid (audio): https://www.almosleh.com/ar/index-ar-section-797.html.

---

43 Linked to the Saudi Brotherhood. Lacroix, *Awakening Islam* 166.

APPENDIX II

List of Traditions Transmitted on the Authority of Ghulām Khalīl

Appendix II assembles 22 traditions[1] transmitted on the authority of Ghulām Khalīl, as collected from the Arabic sources. These traditions are presented here for the first time in English translation. The texts offer insights not only into the thematic issues they relate, but also into the geographical areas where they were circulating and the sources that preserved them. These various pieces of information help us to draw a more comprehensive picture of Ghulām Khalīl's scholarship and its reception in later times.

Apparently, Ghulām Khalīl transmitted hundreds of *ḥadīth*s. However, Abū Dāwūd al-Sijistānī (d. 275/889) states in this regard that he had examined Ghulām Khalīl's traditions and found four hundred of them "entirely forged" (*kadhib kulluhā*) in terms of both the chains of transmissions (*asānīd*) and the texts (*mutūn*).[2] Several other medieval authors also highlight that Ghulām Khalīl had been accused of "lying" and "fabricating traditions." Generally, the authors of the medieval sources who included *ḥadīth*s transmitted from Ghulām Khalīl in their works question the veracity of the respective texts.

Most of the 22 traditions listed below circulated in eastern Iran (i.e., in cities such as Qazvin, Marv, Isfahan, Sarakhs, Nishapur, Gorgan; and two in Balkh in Transoxiana). The Baghdadi scholar Ibn Kāmil—who was, as we have seen, the first transmitter of *K. Sharḥ al-sunna* from Ghulām Khalīl—appears as the transmitter of four traditions.

The subjects addressed in the *ḥadīth*s vary. One tradition is concerned with God's establishment of the Throne, others with the hereafter, and yet others deal with the uncanny. Three *ḥadīth*s concern legal issues such as the Friday prayer and lawful slaughter; one with pederasty and three with supplications.

Two traditions transmitted from Ghulām Khalīl were not included here in translation, as they are quite long and thematically rather unrelated to the core of the present study. One of these *ḥadīth*s concerns the incantation of Abū Dujāna (d. 12/632), remembered as one of Muhammad's most skilled warriors; the other concerns the miracle[3] of the uromastyx lizard.[4]

---

1 The numbering takes into consideration that no. 10 includes two traditions with different transmission chains and a comparable *matn*.

2 Al-Khaṭīb al-Baghdādī, *Tārīkh* vi, 247–248.

3 For this miracle, see no. 17 below.

4 "Spiny-tailed agamas are small to medium-sized, ground- or rock-dwelling lizards. Most

 | DOI:10.1163/9789004429055_010

The terms of transmission used in the *ḥadīth*s to specify the mode of their diffusion are replaced in the following list by an arrow (←) to make these texts more easily accessible. Likewise, the expression *qāla*, "he said," used frequently in these traditions, was sometimes rendered as "he asked" or "he replied." The references of the respective traditions are given at the end of each *ḥadīth*. Thematic headings were assigned to them to facilitate their appraisal.

1 The Throne

(1) ʿAbdallāh b. Salam[5] ← Aḥmad b. Muḥammad b. Ghālib b. Khālid al-Bāhilī ← Muḥammad b. Ibrāhīm b. al-ʿAlāʾ[6] ← Ismāʿīl b. ʿAbd al-Karīm al-Ṣanʿānī[7] ← ʿAbd al-Ṣamad b. Maʿqil[8] ← Wahb b. Munabbih,[9] he said,

> I found in the Torah, "God was; and nothing was there before Him during his absence from creation."

Reference: Abū l-Shaykh al-Iṣbahānī, *al-ʿAẓama* i, 705–708; 709, 753. Al-Dhahabī gives the first text in abridged form, *K. al-ʿArsh* ii, 161–163. There are three *ḥadīth*s with the same *isnād*, all of which depict the establishment of the Throne, its description, and its bearers. Most probably, they all belong to one and the same long text that extends over 103 lines in print.

---

species reach a maximum length of 25–50 cm, and only the Uromastyx aegyptia group can reach a total length of up to 70 cm or more. The animals have a bulku, depressed body and strong, short limbs. The tail is covered by spiny scales, arranged in distinct whorls." Wilms and Böhme, Review, 435.

5 Died 294/906; cf. Abū Nuʿaym, *Dhikr akhbār Iṣbahān* ii, 20, no. 970.

6 Ibn Ḥibbān, *K. al-Majrūḥīn* ii, 301; Ibn Ḥajar, *Tahdhīb* ix, 14.

7 Ibn Ḥajar, *Tahdhīb* i, 315–316.

8 The nephew of Wahb b. Munabbih (d. 183/799 or 195/811); cf. al-Mizzī, *Tahdhīb* xviii, 104.

9 Died circa 114/732; cf. Khoury, *Wahb b. Munabbih* 189.

2 The Throne and the Merit of Marjoram

(2) Al-Ṭuraythīthī[10] ← al-Qāḍī Hannād[11] ← ʿAbdallāh b. al-Qāsim al-Ṣawwāf[12] in al-Mawṣil ← ʿAbdallāh b. Ziyād b. Abī Sufyān [!][13] ← Aḥmad b. Muḥammad b. Ghālib ← Dīnār b. ʿAbdallāh ← Anas b. Mālik,[14] the Prophet—God bless him and grant him peace—said,

> There appealed to me a plant which I saw sprouting around the Throne on the night when I was made to travel by night (*laylata usriya bī*). It was the marjoram plant (*al-marzanjūsh*).[15] Whenever marjoram was brought to the Prophet—God bless him and grant him peace—, and he smelled it and appreciated it, used to say, "I saw it sprouting around the Throne."

Reference: al-Ṭuraythīthī, *Musalsalāt* 125b; al-Ṣāliḥī, *Subul al-hudā* vii, 538.

3 Muḥammad's Intercession

(3) Abū Yaʿqūb ← Usayd b. Muḥammad (in Balkh) ← Aḥmad b. Muḥammad al-Bāqillānī [*sic*], known as Ghulām Khalīl[16] ← Dīnār b. ʿAbdallāh ← Anas b. Mālik, the Messenger of God—God bless him and grant him peace—said,

> By Him who sent me as prophet with certitude and righteousness, I will [surely] mediate on the Day of Judgment till I intercede for anyone whose heart had contained the weight of a mosquito's wing of belief.

Reference: al-Ḥakīm al-Samarqandī, *al-Sawād al-aʿẓam*, MS American University of Beirut, fol. 29. The *matn* is mentioned by al-Muttaqī al-Hindī, *Kanz* xiv, 390, no. 39043.

---

10 Aḥmad b. ʿAlī al-Ṣūfī (d. 497/1103); cf. al-Dhahabī, *Siyar* xix, 160, no. 87.

11 Most probably, he is Hannād b. Ibrāhīm al-Nasafī, judge of Baʿqūba in Iraq (d. 465/1072); cf. al-Khaṭīb al-Baghdādī, *Tārīkh* xvi, 149, no. 7393; Ibn Ḥajar, *Lisān* viii, 345, no. 8280.

12 Ibn al-Athīr, *al-Lubāb* ii, 249.

13 Amended above the line as ʿAbdallāh b. Zayd b. Sufyān.

14 Each narrator states in his narration, "And his narration (*ḥadīthuhu*) appealed to me." It is one of the conditions of *al-aḥādīth al-musalsalāt* that each narrator in the chain of transmission repeats the same sentence, which finds an echo in the text itself.

15 Al-Dīnawarī, *al-Nabāt* 209–210; the botanical name is *Origanum maiorana*.

16 See chapter 1, "Image as Scholar and Preacher," on the question of this name form.

4 Signs of the End Days

(4) Abū Ṭāhir Muḥammad b. Aḥmad b. ʿAlī b. Ḥamdān[17] ← Abū l-Qāsim Jaʿfar b. ʿAbdallāh b. Yaʿqūb al-Fannākī[18] ← Abū ʿĪsā ← Aḥmad b. Muḥammad b. Ghālib ← ʿAbdallāh b. Yazīd al-Ramlī ←Muḥammad b. ʿAbdallāh ← ʿAbd al-Raḥmān b. ʿAbdallāh ← al-Ḍaḥḥāk b. Muzāḥim ← Ibn ʿAbbās, the Messenger of God—God bless him and grant him peace—said,

> A planet will appear at the end of time from the East. In that year, a shriek will occur in Ramadan which will cause the death of seventy thousand, seventy thousand will become blinded, seventy thousand will go astray, seventy thousand will become dumb, seventy thousand virgins will become violated, seventy thousand will become struck, and seventy thousand will become deaf.
>
> Someone said, "O Messenger of God! What do you order us to do when this happens?" He answered, "Adhere to almsgiving, prayer, praising God and exclaiming His greatness, and reading the Quran." It was said, "O Messenger of God, what is the sign that would not happen in that year?" He answered, "Should the fifteenth of Ramadan pass away without having occured, then that year will be peaceful."

Reference: al-Shajarī, *al-Amālī al-khamīsiyya* ii, 21, no. 1443.

(5) Ghulām Khalīl ← Muḥammad b. Ibrāhīm al-Bayyāḍī ← Yaḥyā b. Saʿīd al-ʿAṭṭār[19] ← Abū l-Muhājir ← al-Awzāʿī,[20] the Messenger of God—God bless him and grant him peace—said,

> There will be a shriek in Ramadan! They asked in response, "O Messenger of God! Will it be at the beginning, the middle, or the end?" He said, "Rather in the middle of Ramadan. On the middle night of Ramadan, there will be a shriek as a consequence of which seventy thousand will be struck, seventy thousand will become dumb, and seventy thousand will become blinded." They said, "O Messenger of God, who will remain unharmed from among your community?" He replied, "He

---

17 Died after 441/1049; cf. al-Dhahabī, *Siyar* xvii, 663, no. 455.

18 From al-Rayy; he died 383/993; cf. al-Khalīlī al-Qazwīnī, *al-Irshād* 691, no. 462; al-Dhahabī, *Siyar* xvi, 430, no. 319.

19 Ibn ʿAsākir, *Tārīkh* lxiv, 266.

20 Ibn al-Jawzī quotes the text (*matn*) of the *ḥadīth* as given by Fayrūz al-Daylami (Companion; cf. Ibn ʿAbd al-Barr, *al-Istīʿāb* iii, 1264, no. 2085) with a different transmission chain. He mentions, however, the transmission chain of Ghulām Khalīl at the end of the quotation and comments on it.

who remains in his house, seeks refuge in prostration, and speaks out loud the exclamation that God is great. There will follow then another shriek. The first shriek is the voice of Gabriel, the second that of Satan, the third is in Ramadan, the turmoil in Shawwāl, the judging (or distinguishing, *tamyīz*) among the tribes in Dhū l-Qaʿda. The pilgrims will be raided in Dhū l-Ḥijja and al-Muḥarram. As for al-Muḥarram, its beginning brings forth affliction upon my community, [whereas] its end [will bring forth] happiness upon my community. A riding camel that a believer acquires in order to escape at that time will be better than a village whose revenue is a hundred thousand [dinars]."[21]

References: Ibn al-Jawzī, *al-Mawḍūʿāt* iii, 192–193; al-Dānī, *al-Sunan fī l-fitan* 238–239, no. 519. Both sources indicate the transmission chain by Ghulām Khalīl.

5 Angels of Hellfire

(6) Aḥmad b. Marwān al-Dīnawarī[22] ← Aḥmad b. Muḥammad b. Ghālib Ghulām Khalīl ← Thawbān b. Saʿīd[23] ← Ismāʿīl b. Ibrāhīm ← al-Jarīrī ← Kaʿb, who said,

There is a distance of a year's travel between the two shoulders of each keeper among the keepers of Hell, and with each angel among them there is a column with which he pushes the people of Hell into Hell, so that when he gives with it a push, seven hundred thousand fall into Hell.

References: al-Dīnawarī al-Mālikī, *al-Mujālasa* vii, 236.

6 The Merit of Abū Bakr and ʿUmar

(7) Ghulām Khalīl ← Muḥammad b. ʿAbdallāh al-ʿUmarī[24] ← Mālik ← Nāfiʿ ← Ibn ʿUmar, the Messenger of God—God bless him and grant him peace—said,

Follow the example of those two who will come after me, Abū Bakr and ʿUmar.[25]

---

21 The last sentence is unclear in Ibn al-Jawzī, *al-Mawḍūʿāt* iii, 193. It was amended here according to the text of al-Dānī, *al-Sunan* 239.

22 From al-Dīnawar in western Iran; he lived in Egypt and died there after 330/941; cf. the introduction to al-Dīnawarī, *al-Mujālasa* i, 11–25.

23 Died after 245/859; cf. Ibn Abī Ḥātim, *al-Jarḥ* ii, 470, no. 1909.

24 Ibn Ḥibbān, *K. al-Majrūḥīn* ii, 282.

25 For the *matn*, cf. al-Muttaqī al-Hindī, *Kanz* xi, 562, no. 32656.

References: al-Dhahabī, *Mīzān* i, 142; Ibn Ḥajar, *Lisān* i, 618. Neither, however, gives the chain of transmission that connects them with Ghulām Khalīl.

7 The Merit of ʿUrwa b. al-Zubayr / Supplication

(8) Abū Naṣr b. al-Qushayrī[26] wrote to me ← Abū Bakr al-Bayhaqī[27] ← al-Ḥākim Abū ʿAbdallāh,[28] I read in the handwriting of Abū ʿAmr al-Mustamlī[29] ← Abū l-Ḥusayn Aḥmad b. Muḥammad b. Hammām, at the door of his shop in Ramadan 282/December 895 ← Aḥmad b. Muḥammad b. Ghālib al-Bāhilī ← ʿAlī b. Ḥammād ← Jisr b. Farqad al-Qaṣṣāb[30] ← Hishām b. ʿUrwa,

> ʿUmar b. ʿAbd al-ʿAzīz, before he became caliph, went to ʿUrwa[31] b. al-Zubayr and said to him, "I saw yesterday the oddest thing [I have ever seen]. I was on the roof lying down on my mattress when I heard a commotion, so I looked on and thought I saw the watch guards. All of a sudden, there came the demons (*al-shayāṭīn*), one group after the other, till they gathered in a pit behind my house." He added, "Then came Satan (*Iblīs*), and when they all had gathered, Satan yelled in a loud voice, so they resorted to him. Satan then said, 'Who would bring me over ʿUrwa b. al-Zubayr?' A group from them responded, 'We will.' They went off and then returned and said, 'We were able to do nothing with him.'"
>
> He [i.e., ʿUmar] said, "He then yelled a second time louder than the first yell and said, 'Who would bring me over ʿUrwa b. al-Zubayr?' Another group responded, 'We will.' They went off and stayed for a long interval of time. When they came back, they said, 'We were able to do nothing with him.' He yelled for a third time, a shriek from which I thought the earth had been open split, so they resorted to him. He said, 'Who would bring me over ʿUrwa b. al-Zubayr?' They all responded, 'We will.' They went and stayed for a long interval of time. Then they came back and said, 'We were able to do nothing with him.' Satan went off, filled with wrath, and they followed him."

---

26 From Nishapur; son of the mystic Abū l-Qāsim ʿAbd al-Karīm (d. 514/1120); cf. al-Fārisī, *al-Muntakhab*, 498, no. 1073; al-Dhahabī, *Siyar* xix, 424, no. 247.

27 Celebrated traditionist; d. 458/1065; cf. al-Dhahabī, *Siyar* xviii, 163, no. 86.

28 Celebrated traditionist; d. 403/1012; cf. al-Dhahabī, *Siyar* xvii, 162–175, no. 100.

29 Abū ʿAmr Aḥmad b. al-Mubārak (d. 284/897); cf. al-Dhahabī, *Siyar* xiii, 373, no. 175.

30 Ibn Ḥibbān, *K. al-Majrūḥīn* i, 217.

31 In the original: "Abī ʿUrwa," which is a mistake since the author specifies in the text that ʿUrwa b. al-Zubayr is the addressee.

ʿUrwa b. al-Zubayr told ʿUmar b. ʿAbd al-ʿAzīz then, "My father, al-Zubayr b. al-ʿAwwām told me, 'I heard the Messenger of God—God bless him and grant him peace—say, "No man who supplicates God with the following prayer at the beginning of the night and the beginning of the day, but God will safeguard him from Satan and his soldiers. In the name of God the most eminent, He whose evidence is great, and whose power is rigorous, whatever God wills will be, I take refuge in God from Satan (*al-shayṭān*)".' "

Reference: Ibn ʿAsākir, *Tārīkh* xl, 267–268.

8 Supplications

(9) ʿAbd al-Raḥmān b. Muḥammad al-Yaḥmudī[32] (or al-Tamīmī) ← Aḥmad b. Muḥammad b. Ghālib, known as Ghulām Khalīl,

A man said, "O, Messenger of God, the world has turned away from me." The Messenger of God asked him, "Where do you stand vis-à-vis the prayer of the angels and their praise of God, through which you are endowed with your livelihood? Say at the outset of dawn one hundred times, 'Glory and thanks to God, the Greatest. Glory to God, the Greatest! I ask God for forgiveness." The world would then come to you submissively, and forcibly.

Reference: Ibn Ḥajar, *Lisān* v, 133, no. 4695.

(10)
(a) Muḥammad b. Aḥmad b. Rizq ← Aḥmad b. Kāmil al-Qāḍī ← Aḥmad b. Muḥammad b. Ghālib Ghulām Khalīl ← Dīnār b. ʿAbdallāh, the servant of Anas b. Mālik ← Anas b. Mālik, the Messenger of God—God bless him and grant him peace—said,

Should the servant of God say, "I ask God, no other god exists but He, Living and Everlasting, and I ask Him for forgiveness," he would be forgiven even if he were running away from the column [*in Jihād*].

References: al-Khaṭīb al-Baghdādī, *Tārīkh* ix, 359; Ibn al-Jawzī, *al-ʿIlal al-mutanāhiya* ii, 834, no. 1395.

---

32 The editor vocalizes the name as "al-Yuḥmidī."

(b) Al-Shaykh al-Imām Abū Bakr Muḥammad b. al-Khalīl ← his father [Abū Muḥammad al-Khalīl] in Dhū l-Ḥijja 448 [Februar 1057] ← Abū Muḥammad ʿAbdallāh b. ʿAmr b. Muslim al-Ṭarsūsī in a reading session in 392 [1001–1002] ← Abū Bakr Aḥmad b. Kāmil b. Khalaf al-Qāḍī in Shawwāl 349 [November 960] ← Abū ʿAbdallāh Aḥmad b. Muḥammad b. Ghālib ← Dīnār b. ʿAbdallāh ← Anas b. Mālik, the Messenger of God—God bless him and grant him peace—said,

> Should the servant of God say, "I ask forgiveness from God," he would be forgiven even if he were running away from the column [in *Jihād*].

Reference: al-Nasafī, *al-Qand* 143–144.

(11) Abū Muḥammad b. al-Ḥusayn b. Jāmiʿ b. Abī Sāj ← Abū l-Faḍl al-ʿAbbās b. Abī l-ʿAbbās al-Shaqqānī[33] ← Aḥmad b. Manṣūr b. Khalaf al-Maghribī[34] ← Abū ʿAbd al-Raḥmān Muḥammad b. al-Ḥusayn b. Muḥammad b. Mūsā l-Sulamī[35] ← Abū l-Fatḥ Yūsuf b. ʿUmar b. Masrūq al-Qawwās al-Zāhid [in Baghdad][36] ← Abū Bakr ʿUmar b. Muḥammad b. al-Ṣabbāḥ al-Muqriʾ ← Aḥmad b. Muḥammad b. Ghālib Ghulām al-Khalīl ← Yazīd b. Ṣāliḥ ← [Shuʿba] Ibn al-Ḥajjāj[37] ← ʿUmar b. Muḥammad b. ʿAmr b. Murra ← ʿAbdallāh b. Salama ← ʿAlī b. Abī Ṭālib,

> Abū Dujāna complained to the Prophet—God bless him and grant him peace. He said, "O Messenger of God—may my father and mother be sacrifice to you—I went out one night, when suddenly a night visitor (*ṭāriq*) came upon me. I touched and I found it was a hedgehog." The Prophet, then, turned around to ʿAlī b. Abī Ṭālib and said, "Write an incantation (*ḥirz*) for Abū Dujāna al-Anṣārī, and for those of my community who would come after him; those who fear accidents, and [the *jinn*] servant." Thereupon, follows a long incantation.

References: al-Majlisī, *Biḥār* xci, 220–223. Al-Majlisī gives two transmission chains; one of them, however, does not mention Ghulām al-Khalīl (although he does not specify his source for this). Compare also with al-Bayhaqī, *Dalāʾil* vii, 218–220; Ibn al-Jawzī, *al-Mawḍūʿāt* iii, 168–169; al-Suyūṭī, *Laʾāliʾ* ii, 347–348. Al-Dhahabī, *Mīzān* iv, 429, no. 9712, states, "The incantation of Abū Dujāna is made up (*makdhūb*), as if it were fabricated

33 Died 506/1112; cf. al-Fārisī, *al-Muntakhab* 665, no. 1373; al-Samʿānī, *al-Ansāb* vii, 360.
34 Sufi, from Naysābūr (d. 462/1069), al-Fārisī, *al-Muntakhab* 127, no. 233.
35 Famous Sufi; d. 412/1021; cf. al-Dhahabī, *Siyar* xvii, 247, no. 152.
36 Died 385/995; cf. al-Khaṭīb al-Baghdādī, *Tārīkh* xvi, 476, no. 7602.
37 Died 160/776; cf. al-Dhahabī, *Siyar* vii, 203–228; Juynboll, *Encyclopedia of canonical ḥadīth* 471–566.

by Ghulām Khalīl who transmits it insolently from Shuʿba with a sound transmission chain." Nonetheless, al-Dhahabī states in *Siyar* i, 245, "The incantation of Abū Dujāna is something that is not valid. I am not aware of its fabricator." See also Ibn Ḥajar, *Lisān* viii, 498, no. 8571.

9 The Journey in Pursuit of Knowledge

(12) Abū Yazīd Ṭayfūr b. Abī Isḥāq al-Mīshaqī;[38]—Abū Saʿīd Ismāʿīl b. Ibrāhīm al-Suwaydī[39] ← Ismāʿīl b. al-Faraj ← Aḥmad b. Muḥammad b. Ghālib Ghulām al-Khalīl ← Dīnār ← Anas b. Mālik, the Messenger of God—God bless him and grant him peace—said,

> Whoever sets out aiming to seek knowledge (*ṭalab al-ʿilm*), angels will surround him with their wings, birds in the sky and fish in the water will pray over him, and he will dwell in Heaven in the ranks of seventy martyrs.

Reference: al-Sahmī, *Tārīkh Jurjān* i, 109–110.

10 Friday Prayer

(13) Al-Dāraquṭnī, most probably in his book *al-Afrād*,[40] mentioned a tradition from Aḥmad b. Muḥammad b. Ghālib al-Bāhilī ← Muḥammad b. ʿAbdallāh Abū Zayd al-Madanī ← al-Mughīra b. ʿAbd al-Raḥmān ← Mālik ← al-Zuhrī ← ʿUbayd Allāh b. ʿAbdallāh ← Ibn ʿAbbās,

> The Messenger of God—God bless him and grant him peace—sanctioned the Friday prayer before he undertook the migration (*qabla an yuhājir*). He was not able to perform the Friday prayer in Mecca, or to demonstrate it for them. He wrote to Muṣʿab b. ʿUmayr, "Then (*ammā baʿd*), verify the day on which the Jews get together for their Sabbath. Gather, then, your women folk and children, and thereupon when the day turns away from its middle, at noon of Friday, seek favour with God by performing two prostrations."

---

38 From the city of Gorgan; cf. Ibn al-Athīr, *al-Lubāb* iii, 283.

39 Al-Sahmī, *Tārīkh Jurjān* i, 109, no. 172.

40 The book is reported to consist of more than 100 volumes. Volumes 2, 3, and 83, revised by Ibn al-Qaysarānī (d. 507/1113), are edited. The tradition is not included there.

He—Muṣʿab b. ʿUmayr—was the first to have performed the Friday prayer till the Messenger of God—God bless him and grant him peace—arrived in Medina. He then performed the Friday prayer at noon and made it (this rule).

Reference: Ibn Rajab, *Fatḥ al-bārī* viii, 65.

(14) ʿAbdallāh b. Muḥammad al-Qāḍī ← Muḥammad b. ʿAbdallāh al-Ḥākim ← Aḥmad b. Kāmil ← Aḥmad b. Muḥammad b. Ghālib ← Qurra b. Ḥabīb[41] ← Shuʿba ← Ibn ʿAwn ← Nāfiʿ ← Ibn ʿUmar,

He who joins the Friday prayer, let him take a bath.[42]

References: al-Khaṭīb al-Baghdādī, *Tārīkh* vi, 246; al-Khalīlī al-Qazwīnī, *al-Irshād* 503.

11 Lawful Slaughter

(15) Muḥammad b. Isḥāq b. Muḥammad al-Kaysānī[43] and Muḥammad b. Aḥmad b. Maymūn al-Kātib[44] ← Isḥāq b. Muḥammad al-Kaysānī[45] ← Aḥmad b. Muḥammad b. Ghālib ← Muḥammad b. Sulaymān ← Mālik b. Anas ←Ḥammād b. Salama, said,

O Messenger of God! Is lawful slaughter restricted only to the throat and the upper part of the chest? He answered, "Even piercing in the thigh and mentioning the name of God will do."

References: al-Khalīlī al-Qazwīnī, *al-Irshād* 503.

12 Pederasty

(16) Abū Jaʿfar, "the story-teller" (*al-qāṣṣ*) ← Aḥmad b. Muḥammad b. Ghālib ← Shaybān[46] ← al-Rabīʿ b. Badr ← Abū Hārūn ← Abū Saʿīd, The Messenger of God—God bless him and grant him peace—said,

---

41 From Basra (d. 224/838); cf. al-Dhahabī, *Siyar* x, 426, no. 128.
42 For the *matn*, cf. al-Muttaqī al-Hindī, *Kanz* vii, 752, no. 2137.
43 Died 383/993; cf. al-Khalīlī al-Qazwīnī, *al-Irshād*, 695, no. 472; al-Qazwīnī, *al-Tadwīn* i, 219.
44 Ibid., i, 191.
45 Died 319/931; cf. al-Qazwīnī, *al-Tadwīn* ii, 281.
46 Ibn Farrūkh al-Baṣrī (d. 236/850); cf. al-Dhahabī, *Siyar* xi, 101.

God will curse whoever kisses a lad (*ghulām*) when driven by desire. Should he shake hands with him driven by desire, his prayer will not be accepted. Should he hug him with gusto, he will be beaten with whips of fire on the Day of Judgment. Should he act immorally with him, God will make him enter Hell fire.

References: Ibn ʿAdī, *al-Kāmil* i, 322; al-Dhahabī, *Mīzān* i, 141, no. 557; Ibn Ḥajar, *Lisān* i, 618; Ibn ʿArrāq, *Tanzīh* ii, 221.

13 The Miracle of the Uromastyces-Lizard

(17) Al-Ṭuraythīthī [in Rabīʿ I 491/February 1098, in al-Ribāṭ mosque on the east side of Baghdād] ← Karīma bnt. Aḥmad b. Muḥammad b. Ḥātim al-Marwazī[47] ← Abū ʿAlī Zāhir b. Aḥmad al-Faqīh [in Sarakhs][48] ← Muʿādh b. Yūsuf al-Jurjānī ← Aḥmad b. Muḥammad b. Ghālib ← ʿUthmān b. Abī Shayba[49] ← Ibn ʿUmar [?] ← Mujāhid ← Ibn ʿAbbās,

who cites the text of the tradition about the Bedouin from Banū Sulaym and the uromastyces-lizard (*al-ḍabb*) that spoke out in clear Arabic tongue (*takallam bi-lisān ʿarabī faṣīḥ*) in order to ascertain the prophethood of Muhammad.

References: al-Ṭuraythīthī, *Musalsalāt* 127a. See the *matn* with a different chain of transmission that goes back to Ibn ʿUmar, al-Ṭabarānī, *al-Muʿjam al-ṣaghīr* ii, 153, no. 948; Abū Nuʿaym, *Dalāʾil* 279–280; al-Bayhaqī, *Dalāʾil* vi, 36–38.

14 Pleasing the Parents

(18) Al-Shaykh al-Ḥāfiẓ Abū ʿAlī al-Ḥasan b. ʿAbd al-Malik al-Nasafī ← al-Imām al-Khaṭīb Abū l-ʿAbbās Jaʿfar b. Muḥammad al-Nasafī ← Abū l-Ḥasan ʿAlī b. Aḥmad. Muḥammad b. Zakariyyāʾ b. Mubashshir in the town of Warkī[50] ← Abū Bakr Muḥammad b. Bakr b. Khalaf b. Muslim b. ʿAbbād ← al-Rabīʿ b. Muḥammad b. al-Ḍaḥḥāk b. Muzāḥim al-Kassī ← Yaʿqūb b. Muḥammad al-Balkhī ← Ghulām al-Khalīl Aḥmad b. Muḥammad b. Ghālib al-Baṣrī ← Dīnār ← Anas; the Prophet—God bless him and grant him peace—said,

47 Died 463/1070, cf. al-Dhahabī, *Siyar* xviii, 233, no. 110.

48 Died 389/998; cf. al-Dhahabī, *Siyar* xvi, 476, no. 352.

49 Celebrated traditionist (d. 239/853); cf. al-Dhahabī, *Siyar* xi, 151, no. 58.

50 Died 380/990; cf. al-Samʿānī, *Ansāb* xii, 251.

> Whoever pleases his parents has pleased God; and whoever enrages his parents has enraged God.

Reference: al-Nasafī, *al-Qand* 165–166.

15 Sustenance

(19) Abū Yaḥyā Aḥmad b. Muḥammad b. Mūsā b. ʿĪsā l-Samarqandī ← Saʿīd b. Muḥsin al-Ṣaffār al-Kassī ← Ilyās b. Idrīs al-Kassī ← Aḥmad b. Muḥammad b. Ghālib Ghulām al-Khalīl ← Dīnār ← Anas; the Prophet—God bless him and grant him peace—said,

> If a human being flew away from his sustenance, his sustenance would search for him the same way that death would.

Reference: al-Nasafī, *al-Qand* 197.

16 Reviving the Sunna

(20) Al-Ḥākim Abū Muḥammad ʿAbd al-Ghaffār b. Muḥammad b. al-Ḥusayn al-Kasbawī al-Nasafī ← Abū l-Maʿālī Muḥammad b. Muḥammad b. Zayd al-Baghdādī[51] ← Abū ʿAlī b. Shādhān[52] ← Aḥmad b. Kāmil ← Aḥmad b. Muḥammad b. Ghālib ← Dīnār ← Anas; the Prophet—God bless him and grant him peace—said,

> Whoever revives my Sunna really loves me; and whoever loves me will be with me on the Day of Resurrection.

Reference: al-Nasafī, *al-Qand* 407.

17 Good Progeny and Good Works

(21) Al-Imām al-Ḥākim Abū l-Ḥasn ʿAlī b. ʿĀlim b. Bakr al-Fāghī al-Ṣakkāk[53] in Samarqand ← Abū l-Ḥasan ʿAlī b. Isḥāq al-Tirmidhī [by way of dictation] in Shawwāl 447 [December 1055] ← Abū Muḥammad al-Ḥasan b. Muḥammad b. Maḥfūẓ al-Banākitī

51 Died after 476/1083; cf. al-Dhahabī, *Siyar* xviii, 520–524.
52 Died 425/1033; cf. al-Dhahabī, *Siyar* xvii, 415–418.
53 Died 511/1117; cf. al-Nasafī, *al-Qand* 564.

← Abū Bakr Muḥammad b. Jaʿfar b. Jābir ← Aḥmad b. Kāmil ← Aḥmad b. Muḥammad b. Ghālib ← Dīnār ← Anas; the Messenger of God—God bless him and grant him peace—said,

> Any Muslim who dies and leaves behind good progeny, God will bestow on him the same amount of the good works that his progeny performs, without this leading to a decrease in their rewards.

Reference: al-Nasafī, *al-Qand* 540–541.

18 Weavers and Teachers

(22) Abū Manṣūr al-Qazzāz ← Abū Bakr Aḥmad b. ʿAlī ← al-Ḥasan b. ʿAlī al-Jawharī[54] ← ʿAbd al-ʿAzīz b. Jaʿfar al-Khiraqī[55] ← ʿAlī b. Yūsuf b. Ayyūb al-Daqqāq[56] ← Aḥmad b. Muḥammad b. Ghālib Ghulām Khalīl ← Maḥmūd b. Ghaylān[57] ← al-Walīd b. Muslim ← Muʿādh[58] b. Rifāʿa ← ʿAlī b. Yazīd ← al-Qāsim ← Abū Umāma; the Messenger of God—God bless him and grant him peace—said,

> Do not consult weavers or teachers.

References: al-Khaṭīb al-Baghdādī, *Tārīkh* xiii, 617; Ibn al-Jawzī, *al-Mawḍūʿāt* i, 224. Cf. also a similar saying by the Seventh Imam, Mūsā b. Jaʿfar al-Kāẓim, in al-Majlisī, *Biḥār* c, 78.

---

54 Died 454/1062, cf. al-Dhahabī, *Siyar* xviii, 68.

55 Died 375/985; cf. al-Khaṭīb al-Baghdādī, *Tārīkh* xii, 235–236.

56 See chapter 1, under Ghulām Khalīl's students, no. 8.

57 Died 249/863; cf. al-Dhahabī, *Siyar* xii, 223–224.

58 Ibn al-Jawzī, *al-Mawḍūʿāt* i, 224, "*bin*," instead of "*ʿan*"; and in al-Khaṭīb al-Baghdādī, *Tārīkh* xiii, 617. Muʿān, however, cannot be identical with the Companion Muʿādh b. Rifāʿa: cf. Ibn Ḥajar, *al-Iṣāba* x, 210.

General Bibliography

Arabic-Language Sources

ʿAbd al-Razzāq, Aḥmad Muḥammad Jād, *Falsafat al-mashrūʿ l-ḥaḍārī: Bayn al-iḥyāʾ al-Islāmī wa-l-taḥdīth al-gharbī*, 2 vols., Herndon 1416/1995.

Abū Dāwūd, Sulaymān b. al-Ashʿath, *Masāʾil al-imām Aḥmad*, ed. Ṭāriq b. ʿAwaḍ Allāh b. Muḥammad, Cairo 1420/1999.

Abū Dāwūd, Sulaymān b. al-Ashʿath, *al-Sunan*, ed. Shuʿayb al-Arnāʾūṭ, 7 vols., Damascus 2009.

Abū Ḥanīfa, al-Nuʿmān b. Thābit, *al-ʿĀlim wa-l-mutaʿallim*, ed. Muḥammad Zāhid al-Kawtharī, Cairo 1368/1948.

Abū Ḥanīfa, al-Nuʿmān b. Thābit, *al-Fiqh al-akbar*, Hyderabad 1342/1923.

Abū Nuʿaym al-Iṣfahānī, Aḥmad b. ʿAbdallāh, *Dhikr akhbār Iṣbahān*, ed. S. Dedering, 2 vols., Leiden 1931–1932.

Abū Nuʿaym al-Iṣfahānī, Aḥmad b. ʿAbdallāh, *Ḥilyat al-awliyāʾ wa-ṭabaqāt al-aṣfiyāʾ*, 10 vols., Cairo 1357/1938.

Abū ʿUbayda, Maʿmar b. al-Muthannā, *Majāz al-Qurʾān*, ed. Muḥammad Fuʾād Sezgin, 2 vols., Cairo 1988.

Abū Yaʿlā al-Farrāʾ, Muḥammad b. al-Ḥusayn, *Ibṭāl al-taʾwīlāt li-akhbār al-ṣifāt*, ed. Abū ʿAbdallāh Muḥammad b. Ḥamad al-Najdī, vol. 1, Kuwait n.d.

Abū Yaʿlā al-Farrāʾ, Muḥammad b. al-Ḥusayn, *al-ʿIdda fī uṣūl al-fiqh*, ed. Aḥmad b. ʿAlī al-Mubārakī, Riyadh 1414/1993.

Abū Yaʿlā al-Farrāʾ, Muḥammad b. al-Ḥusayn, *Masāʾil al-īmān*, ed. Saʿūd b. ʿAbd al-ʿAzīz al-Khalaf, Riyadh 1410/1989.

Abū Yaʿlā al-Farrāʾ, Muḥammad b. al-Ḥusayn, *al-Masāʾil al-uṣūliyya min kitāb al-riwāyatayn wa-l-wajhayn*, ed. ʿAbd al-Karīm Muḥammad al-Lāḥim, Riyadh 1405/1985.

Abū Yaʿlā al-Farrāʾ, Muḥammad b. al-Ḥusayn, *al-Muʿtamad fī uṣūl al-dīn*, ed. Wadīʿ Zaydān Ḥaddād, Beirut 1974.

Abū Yūsuf, Yaʿqūb b. Ibrāhīm, *K. al-Kharāj*, ed. Iḥsān ʿAbbās, Beirut 1985.

Aḥmad b. ʿĪsā, *Raʾb al-ṣadʿ*, ed. ʿAlī b. Ismāʿīl al-Muʾyyad al-Ṣanʿānī, 3 vols., Beirut 1410/1990.

al-Ājurrī, Abū ʿUbayd Muḥammad b. ʿAlī, *Suʾālāt li-Abī Dāwūd al-Sijistānī*, ed. ʿAbd al-ʿAlīm ʿAbd al-ʿAẓīm al-Bastawī, Mecca and Beirut 1418/1997.

al-Akhfash, Saʿīd b. Masʿada, *Maʿānī al-Qurʾān*, ed. Zuhdī Maḥmūd Qarāʿa, 2 vols., Cairo 1411/1990.

al-Albānī, Muḥammad Nāṣir al-Dīn, *Fihris makhṭūṭāt Dār al-Kutub al-Ẓāhiriyya: al-muntakhab min makhṭūṭāt al-ḥadīth*, ed. Mashhūr Āl Sulymān, Riyadh 1422/2001.

al-ʿAlī, Ṣāliḥ, *Khiṭaṭ al-Baṣra*, Baghdad 1986.

al-Ashʿarī, ʿAlī b. Ismāʿīl, *Maqālāt al-Islāmiyyīn wa-khtilāf al-muṣallīn*, ed. H. Ritter, Wiesbaden 1963.
al-Ashʿarī, ʿAlī b. Ismāʿīl, *Risāla ilā ahl al-thaghr*, ʿAbdallāh Shākir Muḥammad al-Junaydī, Medina 1422/2002.
Anonymous, *Akhbār al-dawla al-ʿAbbāsiyya*, ed. ʿAbd al-ʿAzīz al-Dūrī and ʿAbd al-Jabbār al-Muṭṭalibī, Beirut 1971.
al-Azdī, Abū Yazīd b. Muḥammad, *Tārīkh al-Mawṣil*, ed. ʿAlī Ḥabība, Cairo 1387/1967.
Badawī, ʿAbd al-Raḥmān, *Madhāhib al-Islāmiyyīn*, vol. 1, Beirut 1979.
al-Barqī, Aḥmad b. Muḥammad, *al-Maḥāsin*, ed. Jalāl al-Dīn al-Ḥusaynī, Qum 1371.
al-Bayhaqī, Aḥmad b. al-Ḥusayn, *Manāqib al-Shāfiʿī*, ed. Aḥmad Saqr, 2 vols., Cairo 1390/1970.
al-Bukhārī, Muḥammad b. Ismāʿīl, *al-Jāmiʿ al-ṣaḥīḥ*, Damascus 1423/2002.
al-Bukhārī, Muḥammad b. Ismāʿīl, *Khalq afʿāl al-ʿibād wa-l-radd ʿalā l-jahmiyya wa-aṣḥāb al-taʿṭīl*, Beirut 1411/1990.
al-Dāraquṭnī, ʿAlī b. ʿUmar, K. *al-Ḍuʿafāʾ wa-l-matrūkīn*, ed. Muwaffaq b. ʿAbdallāh b. ʿAbd al-Qādir, Riyadh 1404/1984.
al-Dārimī, ʿUthmān b. Saʿīd, *al-Radd ʿalā l-jahmiyya*, ed. Badr al-Badr, Kuwait 1405/1985.
al-Dāwūdī, Muḥammad b. ʿAlī, *Ṭabaqāt al-mufassirīn*, 2 vols., Beirut 1403/1983.
al-Dhahabī, Muḥammad b. Aḥmad, *al-ʿArsh*, ed. Muḥammad b. Khalīfa l-Tamīmī, 2 vols., Medina 1420/1999.
al-Dhahabī, Muḥammad b. Aḥmad, *al-ʿIbar fī kabar man ghabar*, ed. Muḥammad al-Saʿīd b. Basyūnī Zaghlūl, 4 vols., Beirut 1405/1985.
al-Dhahabī, Muḥammad b. Aḥmad, *Maʿrifat al-qurrāʾ al-kibār*, ed. Bashshār ʿAwwād Maʿrūf et al., 2 vols., Beirut 1408/1988.
al-Dhahabī, Muḥammad b. Aḥmad, *Mīzān al-iʿtidāl fī naqd al-rijāl*, ʿAlī Muḥammad al-Bijāwī, 4 vols., Cairo 1382–1384/1963–1965.
al-Dhahabī, Muḥammad b. Aḥmad, *Siyar aʿlām al-nubalāʾ*, ed. Shuʿayb al-Arnāʾūṭ et al., 25 vols., Beirut 1417/1996.
al-Dhahabī, Muḥammad b. Aḥmad, *Tārīkh al-Islām*, ed. Bashshār ʿAwwād Maʿrūf, 17 vols., Beirut 1424/2003.
al-Dhahabī, Muḥammad b. Aḥmad, *al-ʿUluww lil-ʿaliyy al-ghaffār*, ed. Ashraf b. ʿAbd al-Maqṣūd, Riyadh 1416/1995.
al-Dimyāṭī, Aḥmad b. Aybak, *al-Mustafād min dhayl Tārīkh Baghdād*, ed. Qayṣar Abū Faraḥ, Beirut 1971.
al-Dīnawarī, Abū Ḥanīfa Aḥmad, *K. al-Nabāt*, ed. B. Levin, Wiesbaden 1974.
al-Dīnawarī, Aḥmad b. Marwān, *al-Mujālasa wa-jawāhir al-ʿilm*, ed. Abū ʿUbayda Mashhūr Āl Salmān, Beirut 1419/1998.
Fakhr al-Dīn al-Rāzī, Muḥammad b. ʿUmar, *Muḥaṣṣal afkār al-mutaqaddimīn wa-l-mutaʾakhkhirīn*, ed. Samīḥ Dughaym, Beirut 1992.
al-Farāhīdī, al-Khalīl b. Aḥmad, *K. al-ʿAyn*, ed. ʿAbd al-Ḥamīd Hindāwī, 4 vols., Beirut 1424/2003.

al-Fārisī, Abū l-Ḥasan, *al-Muntakhab min al-siyāq li-Tārīkh Naysābūr*, ed. Muḥammad Kāẓim al-Maḥmūdī, Tehran 1433/2013.
al-Fawzān, Ṣāliḥ, *al-Irshād ilā ṣaḥīḥ al-iʿtiqād wa-l-radd ʿalā ahl al-shirk wa-l-ilḥād*, Riyadh 1411/1990.
al-Ghassānī, Muḥammad b. Fayḍ, *Akhbār wa-ḥikāyāt*, ed. Ibrāhīm Ṣāliḥ, Damascus 1994.
al-Ghazālī, Abū Ḥāmid Muḥammad, *Iḥyāʾ ʿulūm al-dīn*, ed. Aḥmad ʿInāya and Aḥmad Zahwa, Beirut 2005.
al-Ghazālī, Abū Ḥāmid Muḥammad, *Miʿyār al-ʿilm*, ed. Sulaymān Dunyā, Cairo 1961.
al-Hādī ilā l-Ḥaqq, Yaḥyā b. al-Ḥusayn, *al-Aḥkām fī l-ḥalāl wa-l-ḥarm*, ed. al-Murtaḍā b. Zayd al-Maḥaṭwarī, 2 vols., Ṣanʿāʾ 1435/2014.
al-Ḥākim, al-Naysābūrī Muḥammad b. ʿAbdallāh, *al-Madkhal ilā l-ṣaḥīḥ*, Rabīʿ b. Hādī ʿUmayr al-Madkhalī, 4 vols., Cairo 1430/2009.
al-Ḥākim, al-Naysābūrī Muḥammad b. ʿAbdallāh, *al-Musnad al-mustakhraj ʿalā Ṣaḥīḥ Muslim*, ed. Muḥammad Ḥasan Ismāʿīl al-Shāfiʿī, 4 vols., Beirut 1996.
al-Ḥākim, al-Naysābūrī Muḥammad b. ʿAbdallāh, *Suʾālāt al-Dāraquṭnī*, ed. Muwaffaq b. ʿAbdallāh b. ʿAbd al-Qādir, Riyadh 1404/1984.
al-Ḥakīm al-Samarqandī, *al-Sawād al-aʿẓam*, MS. American University of Beirut, no. 227.
al-Hamdānī, Ḥasan b. Aḥmad, *al-Iklīl*, vol. 8., ed. Nabih Amin Faris, Princeton 1940.
Ḥanbal ibn Isḥāq, *Dhikr miḥnat al-Imām Aḥmad b. Ḥanbal*, ed. Muḥammad Naghash, Cairo 1398/1977.
Ḥanbal b. Isḥāq, Juzʾ Ḥanbal, in ʿĀmir Ḥasan Ṣabrī (ed.), *K. al-Fitan*, Beirut 1419/1998.
Ḥarb b. Ismāʿīl al-Kirmānī, *K. al-Sunna*, ed. ʿĀdil b. ʿAbdallāh Āl Ḥamdān, Beirut 1435/2014.
al-Ḥimṣī, Asmāʾ, al-Madrasa l-Ẓāhiriyya, *Majallat majmaʿ al-lugha al-ʿarabiyya bi-Dimashq* 41.4 (1966), 661–690; 42.2 (1967), 125–149; 42.3 (1967), 320–341; 42.4 (1967), 551–569.
al-Hujwīrī, ʿAlī b. ʿUthmān, *Kashf al-maḥjūb*, trans. Suʿād ʿAbd al-Hādī Qindīl, Beirut 1980.
al-Ḥumaydī, ʿAbdallāh b. al-Zubayr, *al-Musnad*, ed. Ḥabīb al-Raḥmān al-Aʿẓamī, 2 vols., Beirut 1382/1963.
Ibn ʿAbd al-Barr, Yūsuf b. ʿAbdallāh, *al-Istīʿāb fī maʿrifat al-aṣḥāb*, ed. ʿAlī Muḥammad al-Bijāwī, 4 vols., Beirut 1412/1992.
Ibn ʿAbd al-Barr, Yūsuf b. ʿAbdallāh, *Jāmiʿ bayān al-ʿilm wa-ahlih*, Cairo n.d.
Ibn ʿAbd al-Barr, Yūsuf b. ʿAbdallāh, *al-Tamhīd li-mā fī l-Muwaṭṭaʾ min al-maʿānī wa-l-asānīd*, 26 vols., Rabat 1387–1412/1967–1992.
Ibn Abī al-Dunyā, ʿAbdallāh b. Muḥammad, *al-ʿAql*, ed. Muḥammad Zāhid al-Kawtharī, Cairo 1365/1946.
Ibn Abī Ḥātim, ʿAbd al-Raḥmān b. Muḥammad, *al-ʿIlal*, ed. Saʿd b. ʿAbdallāh al-Ḥumayyid and Khālid b. ʿAbd al-Raḥmān al-Juraysī, 7 vols., Riyadh 1327/2006.

Ibn Abī Ḥātim, ʿAbd al-Raḥmān b. Muḥammad, *al-Jarḥ wa-l-taʿdīl*, 9 vols., Hyderabad 1371–1372/1952–1953.

Ibn Abī Ḥātim, ʿAbd al-Raḥmān b. Muḥammad, *Tafsīr al-Qurʾ ān al-ʿaẓīm*, ed. Asʿad Muḥammad al-Ṭayyib, 10 vols., Mecca 1417/1997.

Ibn Abī al-Wafāʾ, Muḥyī l-Dīn ʿAbd al-Qādir, *al-Jawāhir al-muḍiyya fī ṭabaqāt al-Ḥanafiyya*, ed. ʿAbd al-Fattāḥ Muḥammad al-Ḥilū, 6 vols., Cairo 1413/1993.

Ibn Abī Yaʿlā, Muḥammad b. Muḥammad, *al-Iʿtiqād*, ed. Muḥammad b. ʿAbd al-Raḥmān al-Kamīs, Riyadh 1423/2002.

Ibn Abī Yaʿlā, Muḥammad b. Muḥammad, *Ṭabaqāt al-Ḥanābila*, ed. Muḥammad Ḥāmid al-Fiqī, 2 vols., Cairo 1371/1952.

Ibn Abī Yaʿlā, Muḥammad b. Muḥammad, *Ṭabaqāt al-Ḥanābila*, ed. ʿAbd al-Raḥmān b. Sulaymān al-ʿUthaymīn, 3 vols., Riyadh 1419/1998.

Ibn ʿAdī, ʿAbdallāh, *al-Kāmil fī l-ḍuʿf ā*ʾ, ed. ʿĀdil Aḥmad ʿAbd al-Mawjūd et al., 9 vols., Beirut n.d.

Ibn al-Anbārī, ʿAbd al-Raḥmān b. Muḥammad, *Nuzhat al-alibbāʾ fī ṭabaqāt al-aṭṭibā*ʾ, ed. Ibrāhīm al-Samarrāʾ ī, al-Zarqāʾ 1405/1985.

Ibn ʿAsākir, ʿAlī b. Ḥasan, *Tabyīn kadhib al-muftarī*, Damascus 1347/1928.

Ibn ʿAsākir, ʿAlī b. Ḥasan, *Tārīkh madīnat Dimashq*, ed. ʿUmar b. Gharāma al-ʿUmrawī, 80 vols., Beirut 1415–1421/1995–2000.

Ibn al-Athīr, ʿAlī b. Muḥammad, *al-Kāmil*, ed. Abū l-Fidāʾ ʿAbdallāh al-Qāḍī and Muḥammad Yūsuf al-Daqqāq, 11 vols., Beirut 1407–1424/1987–2002.

Ibn al-Athīr, ʿAlī b. Muḥammad, *al-Lubāb fī tahdhīb al-ansāb*, 3 vols., Beirut 1400/1980.

Ibn Bābawayh al-Qummī, see: al-Ṣadūq.

Ibn al-Bannāʾ, ʿAlī b. Aḥmad, al-Mukhtār min uṣūl al-sunna, in Aḥmad Farīd al-Mazyadī (ed.), *Uṣūl al-sunna*, Beirut 1433/2012.

Ibn Baṭṭa ʿUkbarī, ʿUbaydallāh b. Muḥammad, *al-Sharḥ wa-l-ibāna ʿalā ūṣūl al-sunna wa-l-diyāna*, ed. H. Lauost, Damascus 1958.

Ibn al-Dubaythī, Muḥammad b. Saʿīd, *Dhayl Tārīkh madīnat al-salām*, ed. Bashshār ʿAwwād Maʿrūf, 5 vols., Beirut 1427/2006.

Ibn al-Faraḍī, ʿAbdallāh, *Tārīkh ʿulamāʾ al-andalus*, ed. Franciscus Codera, 2 vols., Madrid 1890–1892.

Ibn al-Fuwaṭī, ʿAbd al-Razzāq b. Aḥmad, *Majmaʿ al-ādāb fī muʿjam al-alqāb*, ed. Muḥammad al-Kāẓim, 6 vols., Tehran 1415/1994.

Ibn Ḥajar al-ʿAsqalānī, Aḥmad b. ʿAlī, *Fatḥ al-bārī bi-sharḥ Ṣaḥīḥ al-Bukhārī*, 13 vols., Beirut 1379/1959.

Ibn Ḥajar al-ʿAsqalānī, Aḥmad b. ʿAlī, *Lisān al-mīzān*, ed. ʿAbd al-Fattāḥ Abū Ghudda, 10 vols., Beirut 2002.

Ibn Ḥajar al-ʿAsqalānī, Aḥmad b. ʿAlī, *Tahdhīb al-tahdhīb*, 12 vols., Hyderabad 1325–1327/1907–1909.

Ibn Ḥamdān al-Ḥarrānī al-Ḥanbalī, Aḥmad, *Nihāyat al-mubtadiʾīn fī uṣūl al-dīn*, ed. Nāṣir b. Saʿūd al-Salāma, Riyadh 1425/2004.

Ibn Ḥāmid, Abū ʿAbdallāh al-Ḥasan, *Tahdhīb al-ajwiba*, ed. Ṣubḥī al-Samarrāʾī, Beirut 1408/1988.
Ibn Ḥanbal, ʿAbdallāh b. Aḥmad, *K. al-Sunna*, ed. Muḥammad b. Saʿīd al-Qaḥṭānī, 2 vols., Dammam 1406/1986.
Ibn Ḥanbal, Aḥmad, *al-Musnad*, ed. Shuʿayb al-Arnāʾūṭ and ʿĀdil Murshid, 50 vols., Beirut 1995–2005.
Ibn Ḥanbal, see also: ʿAbdallāh b. Aḥmad b. Ḥanbal, and Ṣāliḥ b. Aḥmad b. Ḥanbal.
Ibn Hāniʾ al-Naysābūrī, Isḥāq b. Ibrāhīm, *Masāʾil al-Imām Aḥmad b. Ḥanbal*, ed. Zuhayr al-Shāwīsh, 2 vols., Beirut 1394–1400/1974–1979.
Ibn Ḥazm, ʿAlī b. Aḥmad, *al-Iḥkām fī uṣūl al-aḥkām*, ed. Aḥmad Shākir, 8 vols., Cairo 1345/1926.
Ibn Ḥazm, ʿAlī b. Aḥmad, *Jamharat ansāb al-ʿArab*, ed. ʿAbd al-Salām Muḥammad Hārūn, Cairo 1391/1971.
Ibn Ḥibbān, Muḥammad, *K. al-Majrūḥīn min al-muḥaddithīn wa-l-ḍuʿafāʾ wa-l-matrūkīn*, Muḥammad Ibrāhīm Zāyid, 3 vols., Aleppo 1395–1396/1975–1976.
Ibn al-ʿImīd ʿAbd al-Ḥayy al-Ḥanbalī, *Shadharāt al-dhahab fī khabar man dhahab*, ed. Maḥmūd al-Arnāʾūṭ, 10 vols., Damascus 1406–1414/1986–1993.
Ibn Isḥāq, Muḥammad, *Sīra*, ed. Muḥammad Ḥamīdullāh, Fas 1396/1976.
Ibn al-Jawzī, ʿAbd al-Raḥmān b. ʿAlī, *al-Ḍuʿafāʾ wa-l-matrūkīn*, ed. Abū l-Fidā ʿAbdallāh al-Qāḍī, 3 vols., Beirut 1406/1986.
Ibn al-Jawzī, ʿAbd al-Raḥmān b. ʿAlī, *Manāqib al-Imām Aḥmad b. Ḥanbal*, trans. M. Cooperson, 2 vols., New York 2013–2015.
Ibn al-Jawzī, ʿAbd al-Raḥmān b. ʿAlī, *al-Mashyakha*, ed. Muḥammad Maḥfūẓ, Beirut 2006.
Ibn al-Jawzī, ʿAbd al-Raḥmān b. ʿAlī, *al-Mawḍūʿāt*, ed. ʿAbd al-Raḥmān Muḥammad ʿUthmān, 3 vols., Medina 1386–1388/1966–1968.
Ibn al-Jawzī, ʿAbd al-Raḥmān b. ʿAlī, *al-Muntaẓam fī tārīkh al-mulūk wa-l-umam*, ed. Muḥammad and Muṣṭafā ʿAbd al-Qādir ʿAṭā, 19 vols., Beirut 1992–1993.
Ibn al-Jawzī, ʿAbd al-Raḥmān b. ʿAlī, *K. al-Quṣṣāṣ wa-l-mudhakkirīn*, ed. Muḥammad b. Luṭfī al-Ṣabbāgh, Beirut 1403/1983.
Ibn al-Jawzī, ʿAbd al-Raḥmān b. ʿAlī, *Talbīs iblīs*, ed. ʿUthmān al-Mazyad, Riyadh 1423/2002.
Ibn al-Jazarī, Muḥammad b. Muḥammad, *Ghāyat al-nihāya fī ṭabaqāt al-qurrāʾ*, ed. G. Bergsträsser, Beirut 1427/2006.
Ibn Kathīr, Abū l-Fidāʾ Ismāʿīl b. ʿUmar, *al-Bidāya wa-l-nihāya*, 20 vols., Damascus 1431/2010.
Ibn Kathīr, Abū l-Fidāʾ Ismāʿīl b. ʿUmar, *Sīra*, ed. Muṣṭafā ʿAbd al-Wāḥid, 4 vols., Beirut 1395–1396/1979.
Ibn Manẓūr, Muḥammad b. Mukarram, *Lisān al-ʿArab*, ed. Aḥmad Fāris al-Shidyāq, 15 vols., Beirut 1956.

Ibn Mufliḥ, Ibrāhīm b. Muḥammad, *al-Maqsad al-arshad fī dhikr aṣḥāb al-Imām Aḥmad*, ed. ʿAbd al-Raḥmān b. Sulaymān al-ʿUthaymīn, 3 vols., Riyadh 1410/1990.

Ibn al-Mundhir al-Naysābūrī, Muḥammad b. Ibrāhīm, *al-Ishrāf ʿalā madhāhib al-ʿulamāʾ*, ed. Ṣaghīr Aḥmad al-Anṣārī, 10 vols., Ras al-Khayma 1425/2004.

Ibn al-Murtaḍā, Aḥmad b. Yaḥyā, *al-Baḥr al-zakhkhār al-jāmiʿ li-madhāhib ʿulamāʾ al-amṣār*, 5 vols., Ṣanʿāʾ 1409/1988.

Ibn al-Nadīm, Muḥammad b. Isḥāq, *al-Fihrist*, ed. G. Flügel, 2 vols., Leipzig 1871–1872.

Ibn al-Nadīm, Muḥammad b. Isḥāq, *al-Fihrist*, ed. R. Tajaddud, Beirut 1972.

Ibn Nuqṭa, Muḥammad b. ʿAbd al-Ghanī, *Takmilat al-Ikmāl*, ed. ʿAbd al-Qayyūm ʿAbd Rabb al-Nabī, 6 vols., Mecca 1406/1986.

Ibn Qayyim al-Jawziyya, Muḥammad b. Abī Bakr, *Ḥādī al-arwāḥ ilā bilād al-afrāḥ*, ed. Muḥammad b. ʿAlī b. Ḥalāwa, Cairo 1426/2005.

Ibn Qayyim al-Jawziyya, Muḥammad b. Abī Bakr, *Majmūʿ al-rasāʾil*, Jidda n.d.

Ibn Qudāma al-Maqdisī ʿAbdallāh, *al-Mughnī*, ed. ʿAbdallāh b. ʿAbd al-Muḥsin al-Turkī and ʿAbd al-Fattāḥ Muḥammad al-Ḥilū, 15 vols., Riyadh 1417/1997.

Ibn Qutayba, ʿAbdallāh b. Muslim, *Taʾwīl mukhtalif al-ḥadīth*, ed. Muḥammad Zuhrī al-Najjār, Cairo n.d.

Ibn Rajab al-Ḥanbalī, ʿAbd al-Raḥmān b. Aḥmad, *al-Dhayl ʿalā ṭabaqāt al-Ḥanābila*, ed. ʿAbd al-Raḥmān b. Sulaymān al-ʿUthaymīn, 5 vols., Riyadh 1425/2005.

Ibn Rajab al-Ḥanbalī, ʿAbd al-Raḥmān b. Aḥmad, *Fatḥ al-bārī: Sharḥ Ṣaḥīḥ al-Bukhārī*, 10 vols., Cairo 1417/1996.

Ibn Rajab al-Ḥanbalī, ʿAbd al-Raḥmān b. Aḥmad, *Jāmiʿ al-ulūm wa-l-ḥikam*, ed. Shuʿayb al-Arnāʾūṭ and Ibrāhīm Bājis, 2 vols., Beirut 1419/1999.

Ibn Saʿd, Muḥammad, *K. al-Ṭabaqāt al-kabīr*, ed. E. Sachau, 9 vols., Leiden 1912–1928.

Ibn Saʿd, Muḥammad, *K. al-Ṭabaqāt al-kabīr: al-Qism al-mutammim*, ed. Ziyād Muḥammad Manṣūr, Medina 1408/1987.

Ibn Taymiyya, Aḥmad b. ʿAbd al-Ḥalīm, *al-ʿAqīda al-wāsiṭiyya*, ed. Muḥammad Khalīl Harrās, Riyadh 1422/2001.

Ibn Taymiyya, Aḥmad b. ʿAbd al-Ḥalīm, *Bughyat al-murtād fī l-radd ʿalā al-mutafalsifa wa-l-qarāmiṭa wa-l-bāṭiniyya wa-ahl al-ilḥād*, ed. Mūsā b. Sulaymān al-Duwaysh, Medina 1423/2001.

Ibn Taymiyya, Aḥmad b. ʿAbd al-Ḥalīm, *K. al-Īmān*, Damascus 1381/1961.

Ibn Taymiyya, Aḥmad b. ʿAbd al-Ḥalīm, *al-Istighātha fī l-radd ʿalā l-Bakrī*, ed. ʿAbdallāh b. Dujayn al-Suhaylī, Riyadh 1417/1997.

Ibn Taymiyya, Aḥmad b. ʿAbd al-Ḥalīm, *al-Istiqāma*, ed. Muḥammad Rashād Sālim, 2 vols., Riyadh 1411/1991.

Ibn Taymiyya, Aḥmad b. ʿAbd al-Ḥalīm, *Majmūʿ al-rasāʾil al-kubrā*, 2 vols., Cairo 1323/1905

Ibn Taymiyya, Aḥmad b. ʿAbd al-Ḥalīm, *al-Radd ʿalā l-manṭiqyīn*, Lahore 1396/1976.

Ibn Taymiyya, Aḥmad b. ʿAbd al-Ḥalīm, *al-Ṣārim al-maslūl ʿalā shātim al-rasūl*, Hyderabad 1322/1904.

Ibn Taymiyya, Aḥmad b. ʿAbd al-Ḥalīm, *Sharḥ al-ʿaqīda al-aṣfahāniyya*, ed. Saʿīd b. Naṣr b. Muḥammad, Riyadh 1422/2001.

Ibn Taymiyya, Aḥmad b. ʿAbd al-Ḥalīm, *Sharḥ ḥadīth al-nuzūl*, ed. Muḥammad b. ʿAbd al-Raḥmān al-Khamīs, Riyadh 1414/1993.

Ibn Wahb al-Kātib, Isḥāq b. Ibrāhīm, *al-Burhān fī wujūh al-bayān*, ed. Ḥafnī Muḥammad Sharaf, Cairo 1969.

al-Ījī, ʿAḍud al-Dīn, *Sharḥ al-Mawāqif*, ed. Maḥmūd ʿUmar al-Dimyāṭī, Beirut 1419/1998.

ʿImād al-Dīn Idrīs b. ʿAlī, *Tārīkh al-Yaman min kitāb Kanz al-akhyār*, ed. ʿAbd al-Muḥsin Mudʿaj al-Mudʿaj, Kuwait 1992.

al-Isfarāyīnī, Abū l-Muẓaffar Shāhfūr, *al-Tabṣīr fī l-dīn*, ed. Kamāl Yūsuf al-Ḥūt, Beirut 1403/1983.

ʿIyāḍ, see: al-Qāḍī ʿIyāḍ.

Jadʿān, Fahmī, *al-Miḥna: Bath fī jadaliyyat al-dīnī wa-l-siyāsī fī l-Islām*, Amman 1989.

al-Jāḥiẓ, ʿAmr b. Baḥr, *al-Bayān wa-l-tabyīn*, ed. ʿAbd al-Salām Muḥammad Hārūn, 4 vols., Cairo 1968.

al-Jāḥiẓ, ʿAmr b. Baḥr, *K. al-Buldān*, ed. Ṣāliḥ Aḥmad al-ʿAlī, Baghdad 1970.

al-Jāḥiẓ, ʿAmr b. Baḥr, *al-Ḥayawān*, ed. ʿAbd al-Salām Muḥammad Hārūn, 8 vols., Cairo 1356–1364/1938–1945.

al-Jāḥiẓ, ʿAmr b. Baḥr, Istiḥqāq al-imāma, in ʿAbd al-Salām Muḥammad Hārūn (ed.), *Rasāʾil al-Jāḥiẓ*, 4 vols., iv, Cairo 1385–1399/1965–1979, 307–315.

al-Jāḥiẓ, ʿAmr b. Baḥr, Risāla fī l-radd ʿalā l-Naṣārā, in ʿAbd al-Salām Muḥammad Hārūn (ed.), *Rasāʾil al-Jāḥiẓ*, 4 vols., iii, Cairo 1385–1399/1965–1979, 301–351.

al-Jaṣṣāṣ, Abū Bakr al-Rāzī, *Sharḥ mukhtaṣar al-Ṭaḥāwī*, ed. ʿIṣmatallāh ʿInāyatallāh Muḥammad et al., 8 vols., Beirut 1431/2010.

al-Jīlānī, ʿAbd al-Qādir, *al-Ghunya li-ṭālibī ṭarīq al-ḥaqq*, ed. Ṣalāḥ b. Muḥammad b. ʿUwayḍa, 2 vols., Beirut 1417/1997.

al-Karābīsī, Muḥammad b. Muḥammad, *Shiʿār aṣḥāb al-ḥadīth*, ed. ʿAbd al-ʿAzīz Muḥammad al-Sadḥān, Beirut 1405/1985.

al-Kāsānī, Abū Bakr b. Masʿūd, *Badāʾiʿ al-ṣanāʾiʿ fī tartīb al-sharāʾiʿ*, 7 vols., Cairo 1327–1328/1909–1910.

al-Kawsaj, Isḥāq b. Manṣūr, *Masāʾil al-Imām Aḥmad b. Ḥanbal wa-Isḥāq b. Rāhawayh*, 10 vols., Medina 1425/2004.

Khalīfa b. Khayyāṭ, *Tārīkh*, ed. Akram Ḍiyāʾ al-ʿUmarī, Beirut 1397/1977.

al-Khalīlī al-Qazwīnī, al-Khalīl b. ʿAbdallāh, *al-Irshād fī maʿrifat ʿulamāʾ al-ḥadīth*, ed. Muḥammad Saʿīd b. ʿUmar Idrīs, Riyadh 1409/1988.

al-Khallāl, Aḥmad b. Muḥammad, *K. al-Sunna*, ed. ʿAṭiyya al-Zahrānī, 2 vols., Riyadh 1410/1989.

al-Khaṭīb al-Baghdādī, Aḥmad b. ʿAlī, *Tārīkh Baghdād = Tārīkh madīnat al-salām*, ed. Bashshār ʿAwwād Maʿrūf, 17 vols., Beirut 2001.

al-Kirmānī, see: Ḥarb b. Ismāʿīl.

al-Lālakāʾī, Hibatallāh b. al-Ḥasan, *Sharḥ uṣūl iʿtiqād ahl al-sunna*, ed. Aḥmad b. Saʿd b. Ḥamdān al-Ghāmidī, 5 vols., Riyadh 1415/1994.

Makḥūl al-Nasafī, Abū Muṭīʿ, *al-Radd ʿalā ahl al-bidaʿ wa-l-ahwāʾ*, ed. M. Bernand, *Annales Islamogiques* 16 (1980), 39–126.

al-Makkī, Abū Ṭālib Muḥammad, *Qūt al-qulūb fī muʿāmalat al-maḥbūb*, ed. Maḥmūd Ibrāhīm Muḥammad al-Riḍwānī, 2 vols., Cairo 1422/2001.

al-Makkī, Abū Ṭālib Muḥammad, *Qūt al-qulūb*, see: Gramlich, R., *Die Nahrung*.

al-Malaṭī, Muḥammad b. Aḥmad, *al-Tanbīh wa-l-radd ʿalā ahl al-ahwāʾ wa-l-bidaʿ*, ed. S. Dedering, Beirut 2009.

al-Malaṭī, Muḥammad b. Aḥmad, *al-Tanbīh wa-l-radd ʿalā ahl al-ahwāʾ wa-l-bidaʿ*, ed. Muḥammad Zāhid al-Kawtharī, Cairo 1428/2007.

al-Maqḥafī, Ibrāhīm Aḥmad, *Muʿjam al-buldān wa-l-qabāʾil al-Yamaniyya*, Beirut 1422/2002.

al-Marwazī, Muḥammad b. Naṣr, *Ikhtilāf al-fuqahāʾ*, ed. Muḥammad Ṭāhir Ḥakīm, Riyadh 1420/2000.

al-Marwazī, Muḥammad b. Naṣr, *Taʿẓīm qadr al-ṣalāt*, ed. ʿAbd al-Raḥmān ʿAbd al-Jabbār al-Firaywāʾī, Medina 1406/1986.

al-Masʿūdī, ʿAlī b. al-Ḥusayn, *Murūj al-dhahab wa-maʿādin al-jawhar*, ed. C. Pellat, 7 vols., Beirut 1966–1979.

al-Masʿūdī, ʿAlī b. al-Ḥusayn, *al-Tanbīh wa-l-ishāf*, ed. M.J. de Goeje, Leiden 1893.

al-Māturīdī, Abū Manṣūr Muḥammad, *Taʾwīlāt ahl al-sunna*, ed. Fāṭima Yūsuf al-Khiyamī, 5 vols., Beirut 1425/2004.

al-Māturīdī, *K. al-Tawḥīd*, ed. Bekir Topaloğlu and Muhammed Aruçi. Istanbul 2010.

al-Mizzī, Yūsuf, *Tahdhīb al-Kamāl fī asmāʾ l-rijāl*, ed. Bashshār ʿAwwād Maʿrūf, 35 vols., Beirut 1983–1992.

al-Mufīd, Muḥammad b. Muḥammad, *al-Masāʾil al-sarawiyya*, ed. Ṣāʾib ʿAbd al-Ḥamīd, Qum 1415/1992.

al-Muḥāsibī, al-Ḥārith b. Asad, *Māʾiyyat al-ʿaql*, in Ḥusayn al-Quwwatlī (ed.), *al-ʿAql wa-fahm al-Qurʾān*, Beirut 1983.

al-Muḥāsibī, al-Ḥārith b. Asad, *al-Waṣāyā*, ed. ʿAbd al-Qādir Aḥmad ʿAṭā, Cairo 1384/1965.

Muqātil b. Sulaymān, *Tafsīr*, ed. ʿAbdallāh Maḥmūd Shiḥāta, 5 vols., Cairo 1979–1987.

al-Muttaqī al-Hindī, ʿAlī b. Ḥusām, *Kanz al-ʿummāl fī sunan al-aqwāl wa-l-afʿāl*, ed. Shaykh Bakrī Ḥayyānī, 18 vols., Beirut 1405/1985.

al-Naʿʿāl, Muḥammad b. al-Anjab, *Min Mashyakhat al-Naʿʿāl al-Baghdādī*, ed. Nājī Maʿrūf and Bashshār ʿAwwād Maʿrūf, Baghdad 1395/1975.

al-Nasafī, ʿUmar b. Muḥammad, *al-Qand fī dhikr ʿulamāʾ Samarqand*, ed. Yūsuf al-Hādī, Tehran 1999.

al-Qāḍī ʿIyāḍ b. Mūsā, *Tartīb al-madārik wa-taqrīb al-masālik li-maʿrifat aʿlām madhhab Mālik*, 8 vols., Rabat 1965–1983.
Qawwām al-Sunna, *al-Ḥujja fī bayān al-maḥajja wa-sharḥ ʿaqīdat ahl al-sunna*, ed. Muḥammad b. Rabīʿ b. Hādī al-Madkhalī and Muḥammad b. Maḥmūd Abū Raḥīm, 2 vols., Riyadh 1990.
al-Qaysī, Nāhiḍ ʿAbd al-Razzāq Daftr, *al-Dīnār al-ʿarabī al-Islāmī*, Amman 1426/2006.
al-Qazwīnī, ʿAbd al-Karīm b. Muḥammad, *al-Tadwīn fī akhbār Qazwīn*, ed. ʿAzīzallāh al-ʿUṭāridī, Beirut 1408/1987.
Ps.-Qudāma, *Naqd al-nathr*, ed. ʿAbd al-Ḥamīd al-ʿAbbādī, Cairo 1948.
al-Qummī, Saʿd b. ʿAbdallāh, *al-Maqālāt wa-l-firaq*, ed. Muḥammad Jawād Mashkūr, Tehran 1381/1960.
al-Qushayrī, ʿAbd al-Karīm b. Hawāzin, *al-Risāla*, ed. ʿAbd al-Ḥalīm Maḥamūd, 2 vols., Cairo 1994–1995.
al-Rāmahurmuzī, al-Ḥasan b. ʿAbd al-Raḥmān, *al-Muḥaddith al-fāṣil bayn al-rāwī wa-l-wāʿī*, ed. ʿAjjāj al-Khaṭīb, Beirut 1391/1971.
al-Rāzī, see: Fakhr al-Dīn.
al-Ṣadūq, Ibn Bābawayh al-Qummī Muḥammad b. ʿAlī, *Man lā yaḥḍurhu l-faqīh*, 4 vols., Beirut 1406/1986.
al-Ṣafadī, Khalīl b. Aybak, *al-Wāfī bi-l-wafayāt*, 30 vols., Beirut 1962–2004.
al-Sahmī, Ḥamza b. Yūsuf, *Suʾālāt al-Sahmī lil-Dāraquṭnī*, ed. Muwaffaq b. ʿAbdallāh b. ʿAbd al-Qādir, Riyadh 1404/1984.
al-Sahmī, Ḥamza b. Yūsuf, *Tārīkh Jurjān*, 2 vols., Hyderabad 1950.
al-Sakhāwī, ʿAlī b. Muḥammad, *Jamāl al-qurrāʾ wa-kamāl al-iqrāʾ*, ed. ʿAlī Ḥusayn al-Bawwāb, Mecca 1409/1987.
Ṣāliḥ b. Aḥmad b. Ḥanbal, *Masāʾil al-Imām Aḥmad b. Ḥanbal*, ed. Fuʾād ʿAbd al-Munʿim Aḥmad, Riyadh 1415/1995.
al-Samʿānī, ʿAbd al-Karīm b. Muḥammad, *al-Ansāb*, 12 vols., Cairo 1400–1404/1980–1984.
al-Ṣanʿānī, Isḥāq b. Yaḥyā, *Tārīkh Ṣanʿāʾ*, ed. ʿAbdallāh Muḥammad al-Ḥibshī, Ṣanʿāʾ n.d.
al-Sarrāj, Abū Naṣr ʿAbdallāh, *al-Lumaʿ*, ed. ʿAbd al-Ḥalīm Maḥamūd and Ṭāhā ʿAbd al-Bāqī Surūr, Cairo 2008.
al-Sawwās, Yāsīn Muḥammad, *Fihris majāmīʿ al-madrasa al-ʿumariyya fī Dār al-Kutub al-Ẓāhiriyya bi-Dimashq*, Kuwait 1408/1987.
al-Shāfiʿī, Muḥammad b. Idrīs, *al-Risāla*, ed. Aḥmad Muḥammad Shākir, Cairo 1940.
al-Shāfiʿī, Muḥammad b. Idrīs, *al-Umm*, ed. Rifʿat Fawzī ʿAbd al-Muṭṭalib, 11 vols., Cairo 1422/2001.
al-Shahristānī, Muḥammad b. ʿAbd al-Karīm, *al-Milal wa-l-niḥal*, Beirut 1981.
al-Silafī, Abū Ṭāhir Aḥmad, *al-Wajīz fī dhikr al-mujāz wa-l-mujīz*, ed. Muḥammad Khayr al-Biqāʿī, Beirut 1411/1991.
al-Sīrjānī, ʿAlī b. al-Ḥasan, *al-Bayāḍ wa-l-sawād min khaṣāʾiṣ ḥikam al-ʿibād fī naʿt al-murīd wa-l-murād*, ed. M. Pourmokhtar, Berlin 2011.

al-Subkī, Abū Naṣr ʿAbd al-Wahhāb, *Ṭabaqāt al-Shāfiʿiyya al-kubrā*, ed. Maḥmūd Muḥammad al-Ṭanāḥī and ʿAbd al-Fattāḥ Muḥammad al-Ḥilū, 10 vols., Cairo 1964–1976.

al-Sulamī, Muḥammad b. al-Ḥusayn, *Masāʾil wa-taʾwīlāt al-Ṣūfiyya*, ed. G. Böwering and B. Orfali, Beirut 2010.

al-Ṣūlī, Muḥammad b. Yaḥyā, *Ashʿār awlād al-khulafāʾ wa-akhbāruhum*, ed. J. Heyworth Dunne, Cairo 1935.

al-Suyūṭī, ʿAbd al-Raḥmān, *al-Durr al-manthūr fī l-tafsīr bi-l-maʾthūr*, ed. ʿAbdallāh b. ʿAbd al-Muḥsin al-Turkī, 17 vols., Cairo 1424/2003.

al-Suyūṭī, ʿAbd al-Raḥmān, *al-Muḥāḍarāt wa-l-muḥāwarāt*, ed. Yaḥyā l-Jubūrī, Beirut 2003.

al-Ṭabarī, Muḥammad b. Jarīr, *Tafsīr = Jāmiʿ al-bayān ʿan tawīl āy al-Qurʾān*, ed. ʿAbdallāh b. ʿAbd al-Muḥsin al-Turkī, 26 vols., Cairo 1422/2001.

al-Ṭabarī, Muḥammad b. Jarīr, *Tārīkh al-rusul wa-l-mulūk*, ed. Muḥammad Abū l-Faḍl Ibrāhīm, 11 vols., Cairo 1968–1977.

al-Thaʿlabī, Aḥmad b. Muḥammad, *ʿArāʾis al-majālis*, Cairo n.d.

al-Tamīmī, Taqiyy al-Dīn b. ʿAbd al-Qādir, *al-Ṭabaqāt al-Saniyya fī tarājim al-Ḥanafiyya*, ed. ʿAbd al-Fattāḥ Muḥammad al-Ḥilū, 4 vols., Cairo 1970.

al-Ṭarṭūshī, Muḥammad b. al-Walīd, *Sirāj al-mulūk*, ed. Muḥammad Fatḥī Abū Bakr, 2 vols., Cairo 1414/1994.

al-Ṭuraythīthī, Aḥmad b. ʿAlī, *Musalsalāt wa-ḥadīth al-ḍabb*, MS. al-Ẓāhiriyya, majmūʿ, no. 3747.

Turkī, ʿAbd al-Majīd, *Munāẓarāt fī uṣūl al-sharīʿa l-Islāmiyya bayn Ibn Ḥazm wa-l-Bājī*, trans. ʿAbd al-Ṣabūr Shāhīn, Beirut 1406/1986.

al-Ṭūsī, Muḥammad b. al-Ḥasan, *al-Istibṣār*, ed. ʿAlī al-Ākhundi, 4 vols., Tehran 1363/1985.

al-Ṭuyūrī, al-Mubārak b. ʿAbd al-Jabbār, *al-Ṭuyūriyyāt*, ed. Dasmān Yaḥyā Maʿālī and ʿAbbās Ṣakhr al-Ḥusayn, 2 vols., Riyadh 1425/2004.

al-ʿUlaymī, Mujīr al-Dīn ʿAbd al-Raḥmān, *al-Manhaj al-aḥmad fī tarājim aṣḥāb al-Imām Aḥmad*, ed. ʿAbd al-Qādir al-Arnāʾūṭ et al., 6 vols., Beirut 1997.

al-ʿUqaylī, Muḥammad b. ʿAmr, *K. al-Ḍuʿafāʾ al-kabīr*, ed. ʿAbd al-Muʿṭī Amīn Qalʿajī, 4 vols., Beirut 1404/1984.

Wakīʿ, Muḥammad b. Khalaf, *Akhbār al-quḍāt*, ed. ʿAbd al-ʿAzīz Muṣṭafā al-Marāghī, 3 vols., Cairo 1947–1950.

Yaḥyā b. al-Ḥusayn, *Anbāʾ al-zaman fī akhbar al-Yaman*, ed. Muḥammad ʿAbdallāh Māḍī, Leipzig 1963.

al-Yaʿqūbī, Aḥmad b. Abī Yaʿqūb, *Tārīkh*, ed. T. Houtsma, 2 vols., Leiden 1883.

Yāqūt b. ʿAbdallāh, *Muʿjam al-udabāʾ: Irshād al-arīb ilā maʿrifat al-adīb*, ed. Iḥsān ʿAbbās, 7 vols., Beirut 1993.

Yāqūt b. ʿAbdallāh, *Muʿjam al-buldān*, 5 vols., Beirut 1979.

al-Yūsī, al-Ḥasan, *Zahr al-akam fī l-amthāl wa-l-ḥikam*, ed. Muḥammad Ḥajjī and Muḥammad al-Akhḍar, 3 vols., al-Dar al-Bayda' 1401/1981.

European-Language Sources

Abbott, N., *Studies in Arabic literary papyri. I. Historical texts*, Chicago 1957.

Abdel-Kader, A.H., *The life, personality and writings of al-Junayd*, London 1962.

Abou El Fadl, K., *Rebellion and violence in Islamic law*, Cambridge 2001.

Abrahamov, B., *Anthropomorphism and interpretation of the Qur'ān in the theology of al-Qāsim ibn Ibrāhīm: Kitāb al-Mustarshid*, Leiden 1996.

Abrahamov, B., The "bi-lākayfa" doctrine and its foundations in Islamic theology, in *Arabica* 42 (1995), 365–379.

Adang, C., H. Ansari, M. Fierro, and S. Schmidtke, *Accusations of unbelief in Islam*, Leiden 2015.

Afsaruddin, A., *Excellence and precedence: Medieval Islamic discourse on legitimate leadership*, Leiden 2002.

Aguadé, J., *Messianismus zur Zeit der frühen 'Abbāsiden: Das Kitāb al-fitan des Nu'aim Ibn Ḥammād*, Diss., Tübingen 1979.

Ahmad, Z., Abū Bakr al-Khallāl: The compiler of the teachings of Aḥmad b. Ḥanbal, in *Islamic Studies* 9 (1970), 245–254.

Ahmad, Z., Aḥmad b. Ḥanbal and the problems of īmān, in *Islamic Studies* 12.4 (1973), 261–270.

Ahmed, Z., Some aspects of the political theology of Aḥmad b. Ḥanbal, in *Islamic Studies* 12.1 (1973), 53–66.

Allard, M., Un pamphlet contre al-Aš'arī, in *BEO* 23 (1970), 129–165.

Allard, M., *Le problème des attributs divins dans la doctrine d'al-Aš'arī et de ses premiers grands disciples*, Beirut 1965.

Alshamsi, M.J., *Islam and political reform in Saudi Arabia: The quest for political change and reform*, New York 2011.

Amir-Moezzi, M.A., Raj'a, in *EIr*.

Arjomand, S.A., The consolation of theology: Absence of the imam and transition from chiliasm to law in Shi'ism, in *The Journal of Religion* 76.4 (1996), 548–571.

Arjomand, S.A., The crisis of the imamate and the institution of occultation in Twelver Shiism: A sociohistorical perspective, in *IJMES* 28.4 (1996), 491–515.

Armstrong, L.R., *The quṣṣāṣ of early Islam*, Leiden 2017.

Atawneh, M., Is Saudi Arabia a theocracy? Religion and governance in contemporary Saudi Arabia, in *MES* 45.5 (2009), 721–737.

Atawneh, M., Wahhābī legal theory as reflected in modern official Saudi *fatwās*: *Ijtihād*, *taqlīd*, sources, and methodology, in *ILS* 18 (2010), 1–29.

ʿAthamina, K., al-Qasas: Its emergence, religious origin and its socio-political impact on early Muslim society, in *SI* 76 (1992), 53–74.
Baldick, J., *Mystical Islam: An introduction to Sufism*, London 1989.
Bedir, M., An early response to Shāfiʿī: ʿĪsā b. Abān on the prophetic report (khabar), in *ILS* 9.3 (2002), 285–311.
Bell, J.N., *Love theory in late Hanbalite Islam*, Albany, NY 1979.
Bell, J.N., and H. Al Shafie, *Al Daylami's treatise on mystical Love*, Edinburgh 2005.
Ben Achour, Y., *Aux fondements de l'orthodoxie Sunnite*, Paris 2008.
Bin Ali, M., *The roots of religious extremism: Understanding the Salafi doctrine of al-wala' wal bara'*, London 2016.
Bin Ramli, H., From tradition to institution: Sunna in the early Ḥanbalī school, in A. Duderija (ed.), *The Sunna and its status in Islamic law*, New York 2015, 163–194.
Björkmann, W., Kāfir, in *EI*², iv, 407–409.
Bligh, Alexander, The Saudi religious elite (ulama) as participant in the political system of the kingdom, in *IJMES* 17.1 (1985), 37–50.
Boekhoff-van der Voort, N., The concept of *sunna* based on the analysis of *sīra* and historical works from the first three centuries of Islam, in A. Duderija (ed.), *The Sunna and its status in Islamic law*, New York 2015, 13–38.
Bonnefoy, L., *Salafism in Yemen: Transnationalism and religious identity*, London 2011.
Bonnefoy, L., Violence in contemporary Yemen: State, society and Salafis, in *MW* 101.2 (2011), 324–346.
Bonner, M., The *Kitāb al-Kasb* attributed to al-Shaybānī: Poverty, surplus, and the circulation of wealth, in *JAOS* 121.3 (2001), 410–427.
Bonner, M., The waning of empire, 861–945, in C. Robinson (ed.), *The new Cambridge history of Islam*. I. *The formation of the Islamic world, sixth to eleventh centuries*, Cambridge 2010, 305–359.
Bosworth, C.E., Ṣaffārids, in *EI*², viii, 795–798.
Bosworth, C.E., Ṭāhirids, in *EI*², x, 104–105.
Böwering, G., Early Sufism between persecution and heresy, in F. de Jong and B. Ratke (eds.), *Islamic mysticism contested: Thirteen centuries of controversies and polemics*, Leiden 1999, 45–67.
Böwering, G., *The mystical vision of existence in classical Islam: The Qurʾānic hermeneutics of the Ṣūfī Sahl al-Tustarī (d. 283/896)*, Berlin 1980.
Bravmann, M.M., *Spiritual background of early Islam*, Leiden 1972.
Brentjes, S., The vocabulary of "unbelief" in three biographical dictionaries and two historical chronicles of the 7th/13th and 8th/14th centuries, in C. Adang, H. Ansari, M. Fierro, and S. Schmidtke (eds.), *Accusations of unbelief in Islam*, Leiden 2015, 105–154.
Brodeur, P.C., Religion, in *EQ*, iv, 395–398.

Brown, J.A.C., *The canonization of al-Bukhārī and Muslim: The formation and function of the Sunnī ḥadīth canon*, Leiden 2007.

Brown, J.A.C., Faithful dissenters: Sunni scepticism about the miracles of saints, in *Journal of Sufi Studies* 1 (2012), 123–168.

Brown, J.A.C., *Hadith: Muhammad's legacy in the medieval and modern world*, Oxford 2009.

Brown, J.A.C., Is the devil in the details? Tension between minimalism and comprehensiveness in the shariah, in *Journal of Religious Ethics* 39.3 (2011), 458–472.

Brown, V., Classical and global jihad: al-Qa'ida's franchising frustrations, in A. Moghadam and B. Fishman (eds.), *Fault lines in global jihad: Organizational, strategic, and ideological fissures*, London 2011, 88–116.

Bulliet, R.W., *Conversion to Islam in the medieval period: An essay in quantitative history*, Cambridge, MA 1979.

Bulliet, R.W., *Cotton, climate, and camels in early Islamic Iran: A moment in world history*, New York 2009.

Cahen, Cl., Kasb, in *EI*², iv, 690–692.

Canard, M., Daʿwa, in *EI*², ii, 168–170.

Caskel, W., Bāhila, in *EI*², i, 920–921.

Chabbi, J., ʿAbd Qādir al-Jīlānī, in *EI*³.

Colby, F.S., *Narrating Muḥammad's night journey: Tracing the development of Ibn ʿAbbas ascension discourse*, Albany, NY 2008.

Cook, M., Activism and quietism in Islam: The case of the early Murji'a, in A.S. Cudsi and A.E. Hillal Dessouki (eds.), *Islam and power*, London 1981, 15–23.

Cook, M., *Commanding right and forbidding wrong in Islamic thought*, Cambridge 2000.

Cook, M., Ibn Qutayba and the monkeys, in *SI* 89 (1999), 43–74.

Coope, J.A., With heart, tongue and limbs: Ibn Ḥazm and the essence of faith, in *Medieval Encounters* 6.1–3 (2000), 101–113.

Cooperson, M., *al-Ma'mun*, Oxford 2005.

Cooperson, M., *Classical Arabic biography: The heirs of the Prophet in the age of al-Ma'mūn*, Cambridge 2000.

Cooperson, M.: See Ibn al-Jawzi.

Crone, P., *God's rule: Government and Islam*, New York 2004.

Crone, P., and M. Hinds, *God's caliph: Religious authority in the first century of Islam*, Cambridge 1986.

Crow, D.K., The death of al-Ḥusayn b. ʿAlī and early Shīʿī views of the imamate, in E. Kohlberg (ed.), *Shīʿism*, Aldershot 2003, 41–86.

Daiber, H., The creed (ʿaqīda) of the Ḥanbalite Ibn Qudāma al-Maqdisī: A newly discovered text, in W. al-Qāḍī (ed.), *Studia arabica et islamica: Festschrift for Iḥsān ʿAbbās*, Beirut 1981, 105–125 (see also Arabic bibliography Ibn Qudāma, *Lumʿat al-iʿtiqād*).

Daiber, H., *The Islamic concept of belief in the 4th/10th century: Abū l-Laiṯ as-Samarqan-*

dī's commentary on Abū Ḥanīfa (died 150/767) al-Fiqh al-absaṭ. Introduction, text and commentary, Tokyo 1995.

Daiber, H., Masāʾil wa-adjwiba, in *EI*², vi, 636–639.

Dakake, M.M., *The charismatic community: Shiʿite identity in early Islam*, Albany, NY 2007.

Dallal, A., Ghazali and the perils of interpretation, in *JAOS* 122.4 (2002), 773–787.

Dallal, A., The origins and objectives of Islamic revivalist thought, 1750–1850, in *JAOS* 113.3 (1993), 341–359.

Daniel, E.L., The anonymous "History of the Abbāsid family" and its place in Islamic historiography, in *IJMES* 14.4 (1982), 419–439.

de Crussol, Y., *Le role de la raison dans la réflexion éthique d'al-Muḥāsibī: ʿAql et conversion chez al-Muḥāsibī (165–243/782–857)*, Paris 2002.

Demichelis, M., *Fanāʾ al-nār* within early kalām and mysticism: An analysis covering the eighth and ninth centuries, in *Archiv orientální* 83.3 (2015), 385–410.

Dickinson, E., *The development of early Sunnite ḥadīth criticism: The Taqdima of Ibn Abī Ḥātim al-Rāzī (240/854–327/938)*, Leiden 2001.

Duderija, A., Evolution in the canonical Sunni ḥadith body of literature and the concept of an authentic ḥadith during the formative period of Islamic thought as based on recent Western scholarship, in *Arab Law Quarterly* 23 (2009), 1–27.

Duderija, A., Evolution of the concept of sunnah during the first four centuries of Muslims relation to the development of the concept of authentic ḥadīth as based on recent scholarship, in *Arab Law Quarterly* 26 (2012), 393–437.

Duderija, A., Neo-traditional Salafi Qurʾan-sunna hermeneutics and its interpretational implications, in *Religion Compass* 5.7 (2011), 314–325.

Duderija, A. (ed.), *The Sunna and its status in Islamic law*, New York 2015.

al-Dūrī, ʿA., al-Fikra al-mahdiyyabayn al-daʿwa al-ʿAbbāsiyya wa-l-ʿaṣral-ʿAbbāsī al-awwal, in W. al-Qāḍī (ed.), *Studia arabica et islamica: Festschrift for Iḥsān ʿAbbās*, Beirut 1981, 123–132.

Dutton, Y., *The origins of Islamic law: The Qurʾan, the Muwaṭṭaʾ and Madinan ʿAmal*, Richmond 1999.

Dutton, Y., Sunna, ḥadīth, and madinan ʿamal, in *JIS* 4.1 (1993), 1–31.

El-Hibri, T., *Reinterpreting Islamic historiography: Hārūn al-Rashīd and the narrative of the ʿAbbāsid caliphate*, Cambridge 2004.

El-Hibri, T., *Parable and politics in early Islamic history: The Rashidun caliphs*, New York 2010.

El Omari, R., Accommodation and resistance: Classical Muʿtazilites on ḥadīth, in *JNES* 71.2 (2012), 231–256.

El Omari, R., *The theology of Abū l-Qāsim al-Balkhī/al-Kaʿbī (d. 319/931)*, Leiden 2016.

El Shamsy, A., *The canonization of Islamic law: A social and intellectual history*, Cambridge 2013.

El Shamsy, A., Rethinking "taqlīd" in the early Shāfiʿī school, in *JAOS* 128.1 (2008), 1–23.

Ende, W., Salafiyya, in *EI*², viii, 906–909.

Ernst, C.W., *Words of ecstasy in Sufism*, Albany 1985.

Fierro, M., La polémique à propos de *Rafʿ al-yadayn fī l-ṣalat* dans al-Andalus, in *SI* 65 (1987), 69–90.

Fierro, M., The treatise against innovations (*Kutub al-Bidaʿ*), in *Der Islam* 69 (1992), 204–246.

Frank, R.M., al-Ashʿarī's *"Kitāb al-ḥathth ʿalā al-baḥth,"* in *MIDEO* 18 (1988), 83–152.

Frank, R.M., Elements in the development of the teaching of al-Ashʿarī, in *Muséon* 104 (1991), 141–190.

Frank, R.M., Knowledge and *taqlīd*: The foundations of religious belief in classical Ashʿarism, in *JAOS* 109 (1989), 37–62.

Gardet, L., Dīn, in *EI*², ii, 293–296.

Gilliot, C., La représentation arabo-musulmane des premières fractures religieuses et politiques (Ier–IVe/VIIe–Xe siècles), et la théologie, in T. Bianquis, P. Guichard, and M. Tillier (eds.), *Les débuts du monde musulman: De Muhammad aux dynasties autonomes*, Paris 2012, 137–159.

Gilliot, C., Textes arabes anciens édités en Égypte au cours des années 1996 à 1999, in *MIDEO* 24 (2000), 115–345.

Gimaret, D., Un document majeur pour l'histoire du kalām: Le Muǧarrad maqālāt al-Ašʿarī d'Ibn Fūrak, in *Arabica* 32.2 (1985), 185–218.

Gordon, M.S., *The breaking of a thousand swords: A history of the Turkish military of Samarra (A.H. 200–275/815–889 C.E.)*, Albany, NY 2001.

Gozashteh, N., and J. Estos, al-Barbahārī, in *Encyclopaedia Islamica Online* (http://referenceworks.brillonline.com/entries/encyclopaedia-islamica/al-barbahari-COM_00000078?s.num=0&s.f.s2_parent=s.f.book.encyclopaedia-islamica&s.q=al-Barbahārī, last accessed 05 September 2018).

Graham, W.A., *Divine word and prophetic word in early Islam*, The Hague 1977.

Gramlich, R., *Alte Vorbilder des Sufitums*, 2 vols., Wiesbaden 1995–1996.

Gramlich, R., *Die Lebensweise der Könige: Adab al-Mulūk. Ein Handbuch zur islamischen Mystik*, Stuttgart 1993.

Gramlich, R., *Muḥammad al-Ghazzālīs Lehre von den Stufen zur Gottesliebe*, Wiesbaden 1984.

Gramlich, R., *Die Nahrung der Herzen*, 4 vols., Stuttgart 1992–1995.

Gribetz, A., *Strange bedfellows: Mutʿat al-nisāʾ and Mutʿat al-ḥajj—A study based on Sunnī and Shīʿī sources of tafsīr, ḥadīth and fiqh*, Berlin 1994.

Guillemin-Puteaux, A., The religious legitimacy of the Saudi state, in Cercle des chercheurs sur le Moyen-Orient (https://cerclechercheursmoyenorient.wordpress.com/2018/10/09/the-religious-legitimacy-of-the-saudi-state/).

Günther, S., As the angels stretch out their hands (Quran 6:93): The work of heavenly agents according to Muslim eschatology, in S. Leder, S. Kuehn, and H.-P. Pökel (eds.), *Angels and mankind: Nature, role and function of celestial beings in Near Eastern and Islamic traditions*, Beirut 2020, 309–348.

Günther, S., "Eine Erkenntnis durch die keine Gewissheit entsteht, ist keine sichere Erkenntnis": Arabische Schriften zur klassischen islamischen Pädagogik, in Y. Sarıkaya and F.-J. Bäumer (eds.), *Aufbruch zu neuen Ufern: Aufgaben, Problemlagen und Profile einer islamischen Religionspädagogik im europäischen Kontext*, Münster 2016, 69–92.

Günther, S., In our days, religion has once again become something alien: al-Khattabi's critique of the state of religious learning in tenth-century Islam, in *AJISS* 25.3 (2008), 1–30.

Haider, N., Muʿāwiya in the Ḥijāz, in M. Cook, N. Haider, I. Rabb, and A. Sayeed (eds.), *Law and tradition in classical Islamic thought: Studies in honor of Professor Hossein Modarressi*, New York 2013, 43–64.

Haider, N., *The origins of the Shīʿa: Identity, ritual, and sacred space in eighth-century Kūfa*, Cambridge 2011.

Halkin, A.S., The Ḥashwiyya, in *JAOS* 54.1 (1934), 1–28.

Hallaq, W.B., On the authoritativeness of Sunni consensus, in *IJMES* 18 (1986), 427–454.

Hallaq, W.B., *The origins and evolution of Islamic law*, Cambridge 2004.

Halm, H., *Die Ausbreitung der šāfiʿitischen Rechtsschule von den Anfängen bis zum 8./14. Jahrhundert*, Wiesbaden 1974.

Heffining, W., al-Muzanī, in *EI²*, vii, 822.

Hellige, W., *Die Regenschaft al-Muwaffaqs: Ein Wendepunkt in der ʿAbbasidengeschichte*, Berlin 1936.

Hillenbrand, C., al-Mustars͟hid, in *EI²*, vii, 733–735.

Hinds, M., Miḥna, in *EI²*, vii, 3–6.

Hinds, M., Muʿāwiya I, in *EI²*, vii, 263–268.

Hirschler, K., *The written word in the medieval Arabic lands: A social and cultural history of reading practices*, Edinburgh 2012.

Hodgson, M.G.S., How did the early Shîʿa become sectarian?, in *JAOS* 75.1 (1955), 1–13.

Hodgson, M.G.S., *The venture of Islam*. I. *The classical age of Islam*, Chicago 1977.

Hodgson, M.G.S., and D.B. Macdonald, Ghayba, in *EI²*, ii, 1026.

Holtzman, L., Aḥmad b. Ḥanbal, in *EI³*.

Holtzman, L., *Anthropomorphism in Islam: The challenge of traditionalism (700–1350)*, Edinburgh 2018.

Hoover, J., Creed, in *EI³* (*Online*).

Hoover, J., Islamic universalism: Ibn Qayyim al-Jawziyya's Salaf? Deliberations on the duration of hell-fire, in *MW* 99.1 (2009), 181–201.

Hurvitz, N., Authority within the Hanbali madhhab: The case of al-Barbahari, in D. Ep-

hart and M. Hatina (eds.), *Religious knowledge, authority, and charisma: Islamic and Jewish perspectives*, Salt Lake City 2013, 36–49.
Hurvitz, N., *The formation of Ḥanbalism: Piety into power*, London 2002.
Hurvitz, N., Miḥna and self-defense, in *SI* 92 (2001), 93–111.
Hussain, J.M., *The occultation of the Twelfth Imam: A historical background*, London 1982.
Ibn al-Jawzī, *Virtues of the Imām Aḥmad ibn Ḥanbal*, ed. and trans. M. Cooperson, 2 vols., New York 2013–2015.
Izutsu, T., *The concept of belief in Islamic theology*, New York 1980.
Izutsu, T., *God and man in the Koran*, New York 1980.
Jackson, S.A., *On the boundaries of theological tolerance in Islam: Abū Ḥāmid al-Ghazālī's Fayṣal al-tafriqa bayna al-Islām wa al-zandaqa*, Oxford 2002.
Jafri, S.H.M., *The origins and early development of Shi'a Islam*, London 1981.
Jarrar, M., Exegetical designs of the Sīra: Tafsīr and sīra, in M. Shah and M. Abdel Haleem (eds.), *The Oxford Handbook of Qur'anic Studies*, Oxford (forthcoming).
Jarrar, M., Ghulām Khalīl, in *EI*^{3} (*Online*).
Jarrar, M., Ibn Abī Yaḥyā: A controversial Medinan akhbārī of the 2nd/8thcentury, in N. Boekhoff-van der Voort, K. Versteegh, and J. Wagemakers (eds.), *The transmission and dynamics of the textual sources of Islam: Essays in honour of Harald Motzki*, Leiden 2011, 197–227.
Jarrar, M., The martyrdom of passionate lovers: Holy war as a sacred wedding, in H. Motzki (ed.), *Ḥadīth: Origins and developments*, Aldershot 2004, 317–337.
Jarrar, M., *Die Prophetenbiographie im islamischen Spanien: Ein Beitrag zur Überlieferungs- und Redaktionsgeschichte*, Frankfurt am Main 1989.
Jarrar, M., and S. Günther, Ġulām Ḫalīl und das *K. Šarḥ as-sunna*: Erste Ergebnisse einer Studie zum Konservatismus Ḥanbalitischer Färbung im 3./9. Jahrhundert, in *ZDMG* 153.1 (2003), 11–36.
Jones, L.G., *The power of oratory in medieval Muslim world*, Cambridge 2012.
Judd, S.C., Competitive hagiography in biographies of al-Awzāʿī and Sufyān al-Thawrī, in *JAOS* 122.1 (2002), 25–37.
Juynboll, G.H.A., *Encyclopedia of canonical ḥadīth*, Leiden 2007.
Juynboll, G.H.A., An excursus on the *ahl al-sunna* in connection with van Ess, *Theologie und Gesellschaft*, vol. IV, in *Der Islam* 75 (1998), 318–330.
Juynboll, G.H.A., *Muslim tradition: Studies in chronology, provenance and authorship of early ḥadīth*, Cambridge 1983.
Juynboll, G.H.A., (Re)Appraisal of some technical terms in ḥadīth science, in *ILS* 8.3 (2001), 303–349.
Juynboll, G.H.A., Some new ideas on the development of sunna as a technical term in early Islam, in *JSAI* 10 (1987), 97–118.
Juynboll, G.H.A., Sunna, in *EI*^{2}, ix, 878–881.
Juynboll, T.W., Iḳāma, in *EI*^{2}, iii, 1057.

Kamrava, M., Contextualizing innovation in Islam, in M. Kamrava (ed.), *Innovation in Islam: Traditions and contributions*, Berkeley, CA 2011, 1–20.
Karamustafa, A.T., *Sufism: The formative period*, Edinburgh 2007.
Kelsay, J., Comparison and history in the study of religious ethics: An essay on Michael Cook's *Commanding right and forbidding wrong in Islamic thought*, in *Journal of Religious Ethics* 35.2 (2007), 349–373.
Kelsay, J., Divine command ethics in early Islam: al-Shafiʿi and the problem of guidance, in *Journal of Religious Ethics* 22.1 (1994), 101–126.
Kennedy, H., *The armies of the caliphs: Military and society in the early Islamic state warfare and history*, London 2001.
Kennedy, H., Caliphs and their chroniclers in the middle Abbasid period (third/ninth century), in C. Robinson (ed.), *Texts, documents, and artefacts: Islamic studies in honor of D.S. Richards*, Leiden 2003, 17–35.
Kennedy, H., Muʿtamid ʿAlāʾllāh, in *EI*², vii, 765.
Kennedy, H., al-Muwaffaḳ, in *EI*², vii, 801.
Kennedy, H., *The Prophet and the age of the caliphates*, London 2004.
Kern, L.L., Companions of the Prophet, in *EQ*, i, 386–390.
Khalidi, T., *Arabic historical thought in the classical period*, Cambridge 1994.
Khalidi, T., *The Qurʾan: A new translation*, New York 2008.
Khoury, R.G., *Wahb b. Munabbih*, i, Wiesbaden 1972.
Kilito, A., *Les séances: Récits et codes culturels chez Hamadhanî et Harîrî*, Paris 1983.
Knysh, A., *Islamic mysticism: A short history*, Leiden 2000.
Knysh, A., "Orthodoxy" and "heresy" in medieval Islam: An essay in reassessment, in *MW* 83.1 (1993), 48–67.
Kohlberg, E., From Imāmiyya to Ithnā-ʿashariyya, in *BSOAS* 39.3 (1976), 521–534.
Kohlberg, E., Rad͟jʿa, in *EI*², viii, 371–373.
Kohlberg, E. (ed.), *Shīʿism*, Aldershot 2003.
Kohlberg, E., Some Imāmī Shīʿī views on the ṣaḥāba, in *JSAI* 5 (1984), 143–175.
Lacroix, S., *Awakening Islam: The politics of religious dissent in contemporary Saudi Arabia*, trans. G. Holoch, Cambridge, MA 2011.
Lacroix, S., Between revolution and apoliticism: Nasir al-Din al-Albani and his impact on the shaping of contemporary Salafism, in R. Meijer (ed.), *Global Salafism: Islam's new religious movement*, London 2009, 58–80.
Laoust, H., al-Barbahārī, in *EI*², i, 1039–1040.
Laoust, H., Ibn al-Farrāʾ, in *EI*², iii, 765–766.
Laoust, H., Le Hanbalisme sous le califat de Bagdad (241/855–656/1258), in *REI* 27 (1959), 67–128.
Laoust, H., Les premières professions de foi Hanbalites, in *Mélanges Louis Massignon* 3 (1957), 7–35.
Laoust, H., *La profession de foi d'Ibn Baṭṭa: Traditioniste et jurisconsulte musulman d'école Ḥanbalite, mort en Irak à ʿUkbara en 387/997*, Damascus 1958.

Laoust, H., *Les schismes dans l'Islam: Introduction à une étude de la religion musulmane*, Paris 1983.

Lapidus, I.M., State and religion in Islamic societies, in *Past & Present* 151 (1996), 3–27.

Lauzière, H., *The making of Salafism: Islamic reform in the twentieth century*, New York 2016.

Leaman, O., *An introduction to classical Islamic philosophy*, Cambridge 2002.

Leder, S., Dokumente zum Ḥadīṯ in Schrifttum und Unterricht aus Damaskus im 6./12. Jhdt., in *Oriens* 34 (1994), 57–75.

Le Strange, G., *Baghdad during the Abbasid caliphate*, Oxford 1900.

Levanoni, A., *Takfīr* in Egypt and Syria during the Mamlūk period, in C. Adang, H. Ansari, M. Fierro, and S. Schmidtke (eds.), *Accusations of unbelief in Islam*, Leiden 2015, 155–188.

Lewinstein, K., Notes on eastern Hanafite heresiography, in *JAOS* 114.4 (1994), 583–598.

Lewis, B., Some observations on the significance of heresy in the history of Islam, in *SI* 1 (1953), 43–63.

Lindroos, K., *Now-time, image space: Temporalization of politics in Walter Benjamin's philosophy of history and art*, Jyväskylä 1998.

Lowry, J.E., *Early Islamic legal theory: The Risāla of Muḥammad ibn Idrīs al-Shāfiʿī*, Leiden 2007.

Lowry, J.E., The legal hermeneutics of al-Shāfiʿī and Ibn Qutayba: A reconsideration, in *ILS* 11.1 (2004), 1–41.

Lucas, S.C., *Constructive critics, ḥadīth literature, and the articulation of Sunnī Islam: The legacy of the generation of Ibn Saʿd, and Ibn Ḥanbal*, Leiden 2004.

Lumbard, J.E.B., From *ḥubb* to *ʿishq*: The development of love in early Sufism, in *JIS* 18.3 (2007), 345–385.

Madelung, W., ʿAbd Allāh b. al-Zubayr and the Mahdi, in *JNES* 40.4 (1981), 291–305.

Madelung, W., Early Murjiʾa in Khurāsān and Transoxania and the spread of Ḥanafism, in *Der Islam* 59 (1982), 32–39.

Madelung, W., Early Sunnī doctrine concerning faith as reflected in the "*Kitāb al-Īmān*" of Abū ʿUbayd al-Qāsim b. Sallām (d. 224/839), in *SI* 32 (1970), 233–254.

Madelung, W., Frühe muʿtazilitische Häresiographie: Das *Kitāb al-Uṣūl* des Ǧaʿfar b. Ḥarb?, in *Der Islam* 57 (1980), 220–236.

Madelung, W., al-Ḳāʾim, in *EI*², iv, 456–457.

Madelung, W., al-Kharrāz, in *EI*², iv, 1083–1084.

Madelung, W., New documents concerning al-Maʾmūn, al-Faḍl b. Sahl, and ʿAlī al-Riḍā, in W. al-Qāḍī (ed.), *Studia arabica et islamica: Festschrift for Iḥsān ʿAbbās*, Beirut 1981, 333–346.

Madelung, W., The origins of the controversy concerning the creation of the Koran, in J.M. Barral (ed.), *Orientalia Hispanica sive studia F.M. Pareja octogenario dicta*, Leiden 1974, 504–525.

Madelung, W., *Religious trends in early Islamic Iran*, Albany, NY 1988.

Madelung, W., *The succession to Muḥammad: A study of the early caliphate*, Cambridge 1997.

Madelung, W., The vigilante movement of Sahl b. Salāma al-Khurāsānī and the origins of Ḥanbalism reconsidered, in *Journal of Turkish Studies* 14 (1990), 331–337.

Makdisi, G., Ashʿarī and the Ashʿarites in Islamic religious history I, in *SI* 17 (1962), 37–80.

Makdisi, G., *Censure of speculative theology: An edition and translation of Ibn Qudāma's Taḥrīm al-naẓar fī kutub al-kalām*, London 1985.

Makdisi, G., The diary in Islamic historiography: Some notes, in *History and Theory* 25.2 (1986), 173–185.

Makdisi, G., The Hanbali school of Sufism, in *Humaniora Islamica* 2 (1974), 61–72.

Makdisi, G., Hanbalite Islam, in M. Swartz, *Studies on Islam*, New York 1981.

Makdisi, G., *Ibn ʿAqīl et la résurgence de l'Islam traditionaliste au XI. siècle*, Damascus 1963.

Makdisi, G., *Ibn ʿAqīl and culture in classical Islam*, Edinburgh 1997.

Makdisi, G., *The rise of colleges: Institutions of learning in Islam and the West*, Edinburgh 1981.

Makdisi, G., The significance of the Sunni schools of law in Islamic religious history, in *IJMES* 10 (1979), 1–8.

Martin, R., Createdness of the Qurʾān, in *EQ*, i, 467–471.

Massignon, L., *Essai sur les origines du lexique technique de la mystique musulmane*, Paris 1922.

Massignon, L., Explication du plan de Basra (Irak), in Y. Moubarac (ed.), *Opera minora: Textes recueillis, classes et présents avec une bibliographie*, iii, Beirut 1963, 61–87.

Massignon, L., Explication du plan de Kufa (Irak), in Y. Moubarac (ed.), *Opera minora: Textes recueillis, classes et présents avec une bibliographie*, iii, Beirut 1963, 35–60.

Massignon, L., *The passion of al-Hallaj: Mystic and martyr of Islam*, trans. H. Mason, 4 vols., Princeton, NJ 1982.

Massignon, L., *Recueil des textes inédits concernant l'histoire de la mystique en pays d'Islam, réunis, classés, annotés et publiés*, Paris 1929.

McCarthy, R.J., *The theology of al-Ashʿarī*, Beirut 1953.

Meijer, R. (ed.), *Global Salafism: Islam's new religious movement*, London 2009.

Meijer, R., Politicising *al-jarḥ wa-l-taʿdīl*: Rabīʿ b. Hādī al-Madkhalī and the transitional battle for religious authority, in N. Boekhoff-van der Voort, K. Versteegh, and J. Wagemakers (eds.), *The transmission and dynamics of the textual sources of Islam: Essays in honour of Harald Motzki*, Leiden 2011, 375–399.

Melchert, C., The adversaries of Aḥmad Ibn Ḥanbal, in *Arabica* 44.2 (1997), 234–253.

Melchert, C., *Ahmad ibn Hanbal*, Oxford 2006.

Melchert, C., al-Barbahārī, in *EI*^{3} (*Online*).

Melchert, C., Basran origins of classical Sufism, in *Der Islam* 82.2 (2005), 221–240.
Melchert, C., The early Ḥanafiyya and Kufa, in *Journal of Abbasid Studies* 1 (2014), 23–45.
Melchert, C., *The formation of the Sunni schools of law, 9th–10th centuries C.E.*, Leiden 1997.
Melchert, C., The Ḥanābila and the early Sufis, in *Arabica* 48.3 (2001), 352–367.
Melchert, C., The *Musnad* of Ahmad ibn Hanbal: How it was composed and what distinguishes it from the Six Books, in *Der Islam* 82 (2005), 32–51.
Melchert, C., The piety of the hadith folk, in *IJMES* 34.3 (2002), 425–439.
Melchert, C., Religious policies of the caliphs from al-Mutawakkil to al-Muqtadir, in *ILS* 3.3 (1996), 316–342.
Melchert, C., Sufis and competing movements of Nishapur, in *Iran* 39 (2001), 237–247.
Melchert, C., Traditionist-jurisprudents and the framing of Islamic law, in *ILS* 8.3 (2001), 383–406.
Melchert, C., The transition from asceticism to mysticism at the middle of the ninth century C.E., in *SI* 83 (1996), 51–70.
Minorsky, V., Abū Dulaf, in *EI*², i, 116.
Modarressi, H., *Crisis and consolidation in the formative period of Shiʿite Islam*, Princeton, NJ 1993.
Modarressi, H., *An introduction to Shīʿī law: A biographical study*, London 1984.
Modarressi, H., *Tradition and survival: A biographical survey of early Shīʿite literature*, Oxford 2003.
Moosa, E., Muslim political theology: Defamation, apostasy and anathema, Heinrich-Böll-Stiftung—Middle East Office, 2012 (https://lb.boell.org/en/2014/03/03/muslim-political-theology-conflict-intl-politics).
Motzki, H., *The origins of Islamic jurisprudence: Meccan fiqh before the classical schools*, trans. M.H. Katz, Leiden 2002.
Mughni, S.A., *Ḥanbalī movements in Baghdād from Abū Muḥammad al-Barbahārī (d. 329/941) to Abū Jaʿfar al-Hāshimī (d. 470/1077)*, Diss., Los Angeles 1990.
Murad, H.Q., Sunnah and ḥadīth in ʿUmar's epistle against the Qadariyya, in *Islamic Studies* 35.3 (1996), 283–291.
Muranyi, M., Ṣaḥāba, in *EI*², viii, 827–829.
Mustafa, A.-R., *On taqlīd: Ibn al-Qayyim's critique of authority in Islamic law*, Oxford 2013.
Nagel, T., Das Problem der Orthodoxie im frühen Islam, in *Studien zum Minderheitenproblem im Islam* 1 (1973), 7–44.
Nagel, T., *Rechtleitung und Kalifat: Versuch über eine Grundfrage der islamischen Geschichte*, Bonn 1975.
Nagel, T., *Staat und Glaubensgemeinschaft im Islam: Geschichte der politischen Ordnungsvorstellungen der Muslime*, 2 vols., Zürich 1981.

Nawas, J.A., The appellation *Ṣāḥib sunna* in classical Islam: How Sunnism came to be, in *ILS* 23 (2016), 1–22.
Nawas, J.A., The miḥna of 218 A.H./833 A.D. revisited: An empirical study, in *JAOS* 116.4 (1996), 698–708.
Nawas, J.A., A reexamination of three current explanations for al-Mamun's introduction of the mihna, in *IJMES* 26.4 (1994), 615–629.
Nwyia, P., *Exégèse coranique et langage mystique: Nouvel essai sur le lexique technique des mystiques musulmans*, Beirut 1970.
Pellat, C., al-Masḥ ʿalā ʾl-khuffayn, in *EI*², vi, 709–710.
Pellat, C., *Le milieu baṣrien et la formation de Ǧāḥiz*, Paris 1953.
Pessagno, J., Irāda, ikhtiyār, qudra, kasb: The view of Abū Manṣūr al-Māturīdī, in *JAOS* 104 (1984), 177–191.
Pessagno, J., Meric, intellect and religious assent: The view of Abū Manṣūr al-Māturīdī, in *MW* 69 (1979), 18–27.
Pessagno, J., The Murjiʾa, īmān and Abū ʿUbayd, in *JAOS* 95 (1975), 382–394.
Peters, R., Islamischer Fundamentalismus: Glaube, Handeln, Führung, in W. Schluchter (ed.), *Max Webers Sicht des Islams: Interpretation und Kritik*, Frankfurt am Main 1987, 217–241.
Picken, G., Ibn Ḥanbal and al-Muḥāsibī: A study of early conflicting scholarly methodologies, in *Arabica* 55 (2008), 337–361.
Popovic, A., *The revolt of African slaves in Iraq in the 3rd/9th century*, trans. L. King, Princeton 1998.
al-Qāḍī, W., The earliest "Nābita" and the paradigmatic "Nawābit," in *SI* 78 (1993), 27–61.
Radtke, B., Theologien und Mystiker in Ḫurāsān und Transoxanien, in *ZDMG* 136.3 (1986), 536–569.
Reinert, B., *Die Lehre vom Tawakkul in der klassischen Sufik*, Berlin 1968.
Rentz, G., Barahūt, in *EI*², 1, 1045.
Reynolds, G.S., Jesus, the qāʾim and the end of the world, in *RSO* 75.1/4 (2001), 55–86.
Rispler, V., Toward a new understanding of the term *bidʿa*, in *Der Islam* 68 (1991), 320–328.
Ritter, H., Studien zur Geschichte des islamischen Frömmigkeit, in *Der Islam* 21 (1933), 1–83.
Rosenthal, F., *The History of al-Ṭabarī.* I. *General introduction and from the creation to the flood*, Albany 1989.
Rudolph, U., *al-Māturīdī and the development of Sunnī theology in Samarqand*, trans. R. Adem, Leiden 2015.
Sachedina, A.A., *Islamic messianism: The idea of Mahdi in Twelver Shiʿism*, Albany 1981.
Sadan, J., Kursī, in *EI*², v, 509.
Salem, F., *The emergence of early Sufi piety and Sunnī scholasticism: ʿAbdallāh b. al*

Mubārak and the formation of Sunnī identity in the second Islamic century, Leiden 2016.
Schacht, J., An early Murciʾi treatise: Kitab al-ʿAlim wa-l-mutaʿallim, in *Oriens* 17 (1964), 96–117.
Schacht, J., Abū Thawr, in *EI*², i, 155a.
Schacht, J., al-Awzāʿī, in *EI*², i, 772–773.
Schacht, J., *Der Islam: Mit Ausschluss des Qorʾāns*, Tübingen 1931.
Schimmel, A., Abū'l-Ḥusayn al-Nūrī: Qibla of the lights, in L. Lewisohn (ed.), *The heritage of Sufism*. I. *Classical Persian Sufism from its origins to Rumi (700–1300)*, Oxford 1999, 59–64.
Schmidtke, S., Creeds, in *EQ*, i, 480–486.
Shah, M., Trajectories in the development of Islamic theological thought: The synthesis of kalām, in *Religion Compass* 1.4 (2007), 430–454.
Shinar, P., Salafiyya, in *EI*², viii, 900–906.
Smith, W.C., *On understanding Islam*, The Hague 1981.
Sobieroj, F., *Ibn Ḫafīf al-Šīrāzī und seine Schrift zur Novizenerziehung (Kitāb al-iqtiṣād)*, Beirut 1998.
Spectorsky, S.A., Sufyān al-Thawrī, in *EI*², ix, 770–772.
Spectorsky, S.A., Sunna in the responses of Isḥāq b. Rāhwayh, in B. Weiss (ed.), *Studies in Islamic legal theory*, Leiden 2002, 51–74.
Stewart, D., Developments within the religious sciences during the rise and decline of empire, in A. Salvatore, R. Tottoli, et al. (eds.), *The Wiley Blackwell History of Islam*, Oxford 2018, 137–157.
Streck, M., and S. El-Ali, al-Baṭīḥa, in *EI*², i, 1093–1097.
Strothmann, R., *Kultus der Zaiditen*, Strasbourg 1912.
Takim, L.N., *The heirs of the prophet: Charisma and religious authority in Shiʿite Islam*, Albany 2006.
Temel, A., Uṣūl al-sunna: The tenets of Islamic orthodoxy and orthopraxy according to the traditionalists (ahl al-ḥadīth), in A. Duderija (ed.), *The Sunna and its status in Islamic law*, New York 2015, 39–57.
Tillier, M., Qāḍīs and the political use of the maẓālim jurisdiction under the ʿAbbāsids, in C. Lange and M. Fierro (eds.), *Public violence in Islamic societies: Power, discipline, and the construction of the public sphere, 7th–19th centuries CE*, Edinburgh 2009, 42–66.
Turner, C.P., *Islam without Allah? The rise of religious externalism in Safavid Iran*, Richmond 2000.
Turner, C.P., The "Tradition of Mufaḍḍal" and the doctrine of the Rajʿa: Evidence of "ghuluww" in the eschatology of Twelver Shiʿism?, in *Iran* 44 (2006), 175–195.
Turner, J.P., The abnāʾ al-dawla: The definition and legitimation of identity in response to the fourth fitna, in *JAOS* 124.1 (2004), 1–22.

Turner, J.P., *Inquisition in early Islam: The competition for political and religious authority in the Abbasid empire*, London 2013.

van Bekkum, W., Many nations and one God: Abraham in Hebrew hymns, in M. Goodman, G.H. van Kooten, and J.T.A.G.M. van Ruiten (eds.), *Abraham, the nations, and the Hagarites: Jewish, Christian, and Islamic perspectives on kinship with Abraham*, Leiden 2010, 275–288.

van Ess, J., Abū'l-Layṯ Naṣr b. Moḥammad b. Aḥmad Samarqandī, in *EIr*, i, 332–333.

van Ess, J., *Anfänge muslimischer Theologie: Zwei antiqadaritische Traktate aus dem ersten Jahrhundert der Hiǧra*, Beirut 1977.

van Ess, J., Bibliographische Notizen zur islamischen Theologie, in *WO* 11 (1980), 122–134.

van Ess, J., Constructing Islam in the "classical" period: Maqalat literature and the seventy-two sects, in A. Filali-Ansary and A. Esmail (eds.), *The construction of belief: Reflections on the thought of Mohammed Arkoun*, London 2012, 63–74.

van Ess, J., *Der Eine und das Andere: Beobachtungen an islamischen häresiographischen Texten*, 2 vols., Berlin 2011.

van Ess, J., Kritisches zum Fiqh Akbar, in *REI* 45 (1986), 327–338.

van Ess, J., Political ideas in early Islamic religious thought, in *BJMES* 28.2 (2001), 151–164.

van Ess, J., Sufism and its opponents: Reflections on topoi, tribulations, and transformations, in F. de Jong and B. Ratke (eds.), *Islamic mysticism contested: Thirteen centuries of controversies and polemics*, Leiden 1999, 22–44.

van Ess, J., Tas̲h̲bīh, in *EI*², x, 341–344.

van Ess, J., *Theologie und Gesellschaft im 2. und 3. Jahrhundert Hidschra: Eine Geschichte des religiösen Denkens im frühen Islam*, 6 vols., Berlin 1991–1996.

van Ess, J., *Ungenützte Texte zur Karramiyya: Eine Materialsammlung*, Heidelberg 1980.

von Grunebaum, G.E., *Der Islam im Mittelalter*, Zurich 1963.

Waines, D., The third century internal crisis of the Abbasids, in *JESHO* 20.3 (1977), 282–306.

Ward, R.B., The works of Abraham James 2:14–26, in *The Harvard Theological Review* 61.2 (1968), 283–290.

Watt, W.M., ʿAḳīda, in *EI*², i, 332–336.

Watt, W.M., *The formative period of Islamic thought*, Oxford 1998.

Watt, W.M., *Islam and the integration of society*, London 2000.

Watt, W.M., *Islamic creeds*, Edinburgh 1994.

Watt, W.M., *Islamic fundamentalism and modernity*, London 2013.

Wensinck, A.J., al-ʿAs̲h̲ara al-mubas̲h̲s̲h̲ara, in *EI*², i, 693.

Wensinck, A.J., *The Muslim creed: Its genesis and historical development*, New Delhi 1979.

Widengren, G., *The ascension of the apostle of God and the heavenly book*, Uppsala 1950.

Wiederhold, L., Blasphemy against the Prophet Muḥammad and his companions (*sabb al-Rasūl, sabb al-ṣaḥābah*): The introduction of the topic into Shāfiʿī legal literature and its relevance for legal practice under Mamluk rule, in *JSS* 42.1 (1997), 39–70.

Wiktorowicz, Q., Anatomy of the Salafi movement, in *Studies in Conflict & Terrorism* 29 (2006), 207–239.

Williams, W., Aspects of the creed of Imam Ahmad Ibn Hanbal: A study of anthropomorphism in early Islamic discourse, in *IJMES* 34.3 (2002), 441–463.

Williams, W., A body unlike bodies: Transcendent anthropomorphism in ancient Semitic tradition and early Islam, in *JAOS* 129.1 (2009), 19–43.

Wilms, T.M., and W. Böhme, Review of the taxonomy of the spiny-tailed lizards of Arabia, in *Fauna of Arabia* 23 (2007), 435–468.

Yazigi, M., Ḥadīth al-ʿashara or the political uses of a tradition, in *Studia Islamica* 86 (1997), 159–167.

Yücesoy, H., *Messianic beliefs and imperial politics in medieval Islam: The ʿAbbāsid caliphate in the early ninth century*, Columbia, SC 2009.

Zahniser, M., Insights from the ʿUthmāniyya of al-Jāḥiẓ into the religious policy of al-Maʾmūn, in *MW* 69.1 (1979), 8–16.

Zaman, M.Q., *Religion and politics under the early ʿAbbāsids: The emergence of the proto-Sunnī elite*, Leiden 1997.

Zettersteén, K.V., Ṣadaḳa b. Manṣūr, in *EI*^{2}, viii, 716.

General Index

ʿAbbādān 11, 17
al-ʿAbbās b. ʿAbd al-ʿAẓīm 11
al-ʿAbbās b. Abī l-ʿAbbās al-Shaqqānī, Abū l-Faḍl 208
ʿAbbasid ideology 60–61, 63, 65, 144, 149
ʿAbbasids 7, 8, 63, 65, 143, 144, 149, 150
ʿAbd al-ʿAzīz al-Azajī 76, 77
ʿAbd al-ʿAzīz b. Jaʿfar al-Khiraqī 213
ʿAbd al-Ghaffār b. Muḥammad b. al-Ḥusayn al-Kasbawī, Al-Ḥākim 212
ʿAbd al-Ghanī al-Maqdisī 29
ʿAbd al-Ḥaqq b. ʿAbd al-Khāliq 30, 32, 33, 35, 37, 153
ʿAbd al-Jabbār b. Shīrān al-ʿAbdī, Abū l-Qāsim 81
ʿAbd al-Khāliq b. Aḥmad b. ʿAbd al-Qādir 32, 33, 35
ʿAbdallāh b. ʿAbbās 168, 204, 209, 211
ʿAbdallāh b. Aḥmad b. al-Faraj al-Daqqāq 32
ʿ Abdallāh b. Aḥmad b. Ḥanbal 10, 50, 53, 61, 77
ʿAbdallāh b. ʿAmr b. Muslim al-Ṭarsūsī, Abū Muḥammad 208
ʿAbdallāh b. ʿAwn 69, 184, 190
ʿAbdallāh b. al-Faraj al-Daqqāq 32, 34
ʿAbdallāh b. Ḥamza b. Abī Ṭāhir b. Sānū 32, 33
ʿAbdallāh b. Idrīs al-Awdī 184
ʿAbdallāh b. Masarra 18
ʿAbdallāh b. al-Mubārak 5, 69, 70, 97, 98, 183, 188
ʿAbdallāh b. al-Qāsim al-Ṣawwāf 203
ʿAbdallāh b. Salam 202
ʿAbdallāh b. Salama 208
ʿAbdallāh b. al-Ṣāmiṭ 52
ʿAbdallāh b. Shabīb 21
ʿAbdallāh b. Sulaymān b. Abī Dāwūd al-Sijistānī 41
ʿAbdallāh b. ʿUmar 52, 120, 121, 158, 187, 205, 210
ʿAbdallāh b. Yazīd al-Ramlī 17, 204
ʿAbdallāh b. Ziyād b. Abī Sufyān [!] 203
ʿAbd al-Malik al-Maymūnī 40
ʿAbd al-Qādir b. Muḥammad b. Yūsuf, Abū Ṭālib 30, 36, 37, 153
ʿAbd al-Qādir al-Jīlī 36, 37
ʿAbd al-Raḥmān b. ʿAwf 86, 92, 120, 158
ʿAbd al-Raḥmān b. Muḥammad al-Yaḥmudī al-Tamīmī 19, 207
ʿAbd al-Raḥīm b. ʿAbd al-Razzāq al-Jīlī 37
ʿAbd al-Razzāq b. ʿAbd al-Qādir b. Abī Ṣāliḥ al-Jīlī 36, 37, 38
ʿAbd al-Ṣamad b. Maʿqil 202
ʿAbd al-Wāḥid b. Zayd 55
ʿAbdak al-Ṣūfī 137
ʿAbdūs b. Mālik 40, 74, 76, 77, 90, 91, 92, 93, 94, 95, 99, 111, 128, 145
Abnāʾ (*Abnāʾ al-dawla*) 65, 66
Abraham 13, 91
Abū l-ʿAbbās al-Sarrāj 80
Abū ʿAbdallāh al-Ḥumrānī 42
Abū Aḥmad b. Abī Usāma al-Qurashī al-Harawī 81
AbūʿAlī b. Shādhān 212
Abū l-ʿĀliya 190
Abū ʿAmr al-Mustamlī 206
Abū Bakr (first caliph) 83, 85, 86, 92, 99, 120, 158, 176, 180, 188, 205
Abū Bakr al-Aʿyan 80
Abū Bakr b. ʿAyyāsh 98–99
Abū Bakr al-Bayhaqī 206
Abū Bakr al-Mufīd 76
Abū Bakr Ibn Abī Shayba 80
Abū l-Bayān b. al-Ḥawrānī 38
Abū Dāwūd al-Sijistānī, Sulaymān 16, 21, 41, 78, 98, 99, 201
Abū Dharr 159
Abū Dujāna 16, 201, 208
Abū l-Dulaf 33
Abū l-Dulaf Muḥammad b. Hibatallāh b. ʿAlī 35
Abū l-Faḍl al-Mukharramī, see: ʿAlī b. al-Mubārak
Abū l-Faḍl b. Nāṣir al-Salāmī, see: Muḥammad b. Nāṣir
Abū l-Fatḥ Yūsuf b. Aḥmad, see: Yūsuf b. Aḥmad b. al-Faraj al-Daqqāq
Abū Ḥafs al-Barmakī 31, 41
Abū Ḥamza (sufi) 26
Abū Ḥanīfa [al-Nuʿmān b. Thābit] 69, 82, 83, 86, 110, 118

Abū l-Ḥasan b. Bashshār 39
Abū Ḥātim al-Rāzī, Muḥammad b. Idrīs 74, 81, 90, 91, 92, 94, 95, 112, 145
Abū l-Hudhayl al-ʿAllāf 52, 140, 185
Abū Hurayra 184
Abū l-Ḥusayn al-Nūrī 26
Abū l-Ḥusayn b. Wahb al-Kātib 140
Abū Isḥāq al-Fazārī 70, 72, 73
Abū Jaʿfar al-Khawwāṣ 11, 16–17
Abū l-Maʿālī Muḥammad b. Aḥmad, see: Muḥammad b. Aḥmad b. al-Faraj al-Daqqāq Abū Manṣūr al-Jawālīqī 33, 34, 37
Abū Manṣūr al-Qazzāz 213
Abū Muḥammad b. al-Ḥusayn b. Jāmiʿ b. Abī Sāj 208
Abū Muqātil al-Samarqandī 110
Abū Muṭīʿ al-Balkhī 82
Abū Naṣr b. al-Qushayrī 206
Abū l-Qāsim al-Balkhī al-Kaʿbī 75, 145
Abū Saʿd al-Mukharramī 35–36
Abū Saʿīd Ibn al-Aʿrābī 25
Abū l-Shaykh al-Iṣbahānī 19
Abū Ṭālib al-Makkī 41
Abū Thawr, see: Ibrāhīm b. Khālid,
Abū ʿUbayd al-Harawī, see: Aḥmad al-Harawī al-Fāshānī
Abū ʿUbayda b. al-Jarrāḥ 86, 92
Abū Umāma 213
Abū l-Wafāʾ b. ʿAqīl 33, 37
Abū Yaʿlā al-Farrāʾ 31, 39, 50, 51, 59, 62
Abū Zurʿa al-Rāzī, ʿUbayd Allāh b. ʿAbd al-Karīm 74, 81, 90, 91, 92, 94, 95, 112, 145
Adam 91, 130, 131, 157, 161
Adultery 5, 103, 104, 160, 162
ahl al-āthār 25, 102, 169, 179
ahl al-ḥadīth 51, 66, 67, 83, 96, 97, 133, (see also: *aṣḥāb al-ḥadīth*)
ahl al-ḥaqq wa-l-sunna 175
ahl al-Qibla (People of the Qibla) 109, 115, 160, 161, 173, 178
ahl al-sunna 47, 68, 70, 74, 76, 81, 84, 87, 89, 96, 97, 99, 108, 115, 120, 121, 127, 136, 142, 143, 144, 145, 152, 154, 193, 196
ahl al-sunna wa-l-jamāʿa 3, 5, 28, 67, 68, 79, 86, 96–98, 101, 103, 104, 109, 118, 153
Aḥmad b. al-Faraj al-Daqqāq 32, 34
Aḥmad b. Ḥanbal 1, 4, 9, 10, 16, 17, 31, 34, 35, 37, 38, 39, 40, 47, 53, 56, 61, 65, 66, 72, 74, 75, 77, 78, 80, 86, 88, 89, 109, 121, 122, 123, 124, 125, 127, 128, 129, 132, 133, 138, 142, 144, 145, 151, 152, 156, 159, 164, 173, 184
Aḥmad al-Harawī al-Fāshānī 34
Aḥmad b. Ḥarb 138
Aḥmad b. Isḥāq al-Sukkarī 78
Aḥmad b. Jaʿfar b. Yaʿqūb, Abū l-ʿAbbās al-Iṣṭakhrī (see also: Ḥarb al-Kirmānī) 40, 53, 68, 71, 72, 74, 75, 76, 89, 90, 91, 92, 93, 94, 95, 111, 114, 125, 131, 132, 138
Aḥmad b. Kāmil b. Khalaf b. Shajara 11, 12, 15, 17, 18, 20, 27, 29, 30, 37, 39, 62, 153, 182, 194, 201, 208, 210, 212, 213
Aḥmad b. Manṣūr b. Khalaf al-Maghribī 208
Aḥmad b. Marwān al-Dīnawarī 15, 19, 205
Aḥmad b. Muḥammad al-Fayrūmī 33
Aḥmad b. Muḥammad b. Hammām, Abū l-Ḥusayn 19, 206
Aḥmad b.Muḥammad al-Marrūdhī, Abū Bakr 10, 40, 61
Aḥmad b. Muḥammad b. Mūsā b. ʿĪsā l-Samarqandī, Abū Yaḥyā 212
Aḥmad b. Muḥammad al-Tamīmī al-Zarandī (al-Bardhaʿī) 77
Aḥmad b. Naṣr 184
Aḥmad b. Ṣāliḥ (grandson of Aḥmad b. Ḥanbal) 41
Aḥmad al-Sinjī 40
al-Ahwāz 15, 35
ʿĀʾisha 6, 119, 179, 180
Āl al-Shaykh, ʿA.ʿA. (Muftī of the Arab Kingdom of Saudi Arabia) 195
Āl al-Shaykh, ʿA.Ḥ. 195
al-Albānī, N. 196
ʿAlī b. ʿAbdallāh al-Madīnī 11, 80, 90, 91, 92, 93, 94, 95, 111, 145
ʿAlī b. Abī Ṭālib 6, 84, 86, 92, 98, 113, 119, 120, 121, 122, 134, 135, 158, 179, 188, 208
ʿAlī b. Aḥmad. Muḥammad b. Zakariyyāʾ b. Mubashshir 211
ʿAlī b. ʿĀlim b. Bakr al-Fāghī al-Ṣakkāk 212
ʿAlī b. Bushrān 77
ʿAlī b. Dāwūd Abū l-Ḥasan al-Warthānī 19
ʿAlī b. Ḥammād 17, 206
ʿAlī b. Isḥāq al-Tirmidhī 212
ʿAlī b. al-Mubārak al-Mukharramī 33, 35, 38
ʿAlī b. Mūsā b. al-Simsār 79

ʿAlī al-Qurashī 42
ʿAlī al-Riḍā (eighth ʿAlid imam) 65
ʿAlī b. Yazīd 213
ʿAlī b. Yūsuf b. Ayyūb al-Daqqāq 19, 213
ʿām al-jamāʿa (the year of the unification of the community) 127
al-Amīn (ʿAbbasid caliph) 8, 65
al-ʿāmma (common people), see: rabble
al-amr bi-l-maʿrūf wa-l-nahy ʿan al-munkar (commanding right and forbidding wrong) 45, 53, 54, 63, 89, 151, 181
Anas b. Mālik 15, 184
al-ʿAnnābī, Abū ʿAbd al-Muḥsin 197, 198
Anṣār (Supporters of Muḥammad) 92, 120, 158, 159, 172
Anthropomorphism/Anthropomorphists 41, 42, 47, 48, 49, 56, 61, 63, 64, 71, 74, 91, 106, 113, 114, 129–133, 143, 183
Antichrist 60, 157
Apocalyptic expectations 23, 60, 149
ʿaqīda, iʿtiqād, see: Creed
al-ʿaql 39, 138–141, 167
Arabs (their excellence and precedence) 91, 172
ʿArafa (Day of) 130, 161
aṣḥāb, ṣaḥāba, see: Companions
aṣḥāb al-athar 89, 115 (see also: *ahl al-athar*)
aṣḥāb al-ḥadīth 68, 70, 103, 104, 115, 132
aṣḥāb al-raʾy 69, 73, 76
al-ʿashara al-mubashshara bi-l-janna 85, 121, 189
al-Ashʿarī, Abū l-Ḥasan ʿAlī b. Ismāʿīl 42, 44, 46, 47, 48, 49, 54, 55, 62, 63, 133
Ashʿaris 34, 192
al-Aṣmaʿī 13
āthār 101, 102, 110, 161
al-Athram al-Iskāfī (Ibn Hāniʾ) 40
al-Awzāʿī, ʿAbd al-Raḥmān b. ʿAmr 52, 69, 70, 72, 73, 82, 83, 85, 96, 123, 133
Ayyūb al-Sakhtiyānī 69, 70, 184
Azerbaijan 19

Bāb al-Azaj 35, 38
Bāb Ḥarb 35
Badr (place, battle) 92, 164, 180
Baghdad 7, 8, 23, 27, 31, 34, 35, 37, 51, 61, 65, 66, 80, 89, 97, 143, 145, 146, 147, 148, 208, 211
Bāhila 10
Bakr, the nephew of ʿAbd al-Wāḥid 164
Bakr b. al-Faraj 73
Balkh 19, 77, 80, 144, 201, 203
Banū Hāshim (the line of) 60, 172
Banū Miskī 22
Banū Budhayl 22
Banū Ḥarb 22
Baqiyya b. al-Walīd 72, 96
Barahūt [well] 166
al-Barbahārī, see: al-Ḥasan b. ʿAlī
al-Barmakī, see: Ibrāhīm b. ʿUmar b. Aḥmad
basmala 87
Basra 8, 10, 12, 13, 15, 20, 22, 23, 24, 25, 27, 55, 79, 80, 82, 89, 97, 117, 143, 146, 148, 184
Beatific Vision 95, 112, 131, 157, 168
bidʿa (novelty, innovation) 90, 116, 117, 118, 154
  ṣāḥib bidʿa 72, 96, 115
bi-lā kayfa 132, 133
Bishr b. al-Ḥārith al-Ḥāfī 101, 190
Bishr al-Marīsī 185
Bukhārā 80, 144, 146
al-Bukhārī, Muḥammad b. Ismāʿīl 16, 52, 59, 74, 78, 80, 81, 89, 90, 91, 92, 125, 144
Burbank, Abu Talhah D. 199

Companions 1, 4, 5, 6, 7, 11, 52, 68, 70, 78, 84, 85, 86, 88, 89, 90, 91, 92, 100, 101, 102, 107, 111, 118, 119, 120, 121, 122, 123, 124, 125, 127, 135, 136, 154, 155, 156, 158, 165, 170, 171, 172, 173, 174, 176, 177, 178, 180, 182, 185, 188, 189, 190, 194, 196
  Disparaging the Companions 180, 182, 185, 189
  Consensus of the Companions 6, 119, 122, 176
Commanding right and forbidding wrong, see: *al-amr bi-l-maʿrūf*
Community 2, 3, 4, 6, 8, 28, 46, 53, 54, 67, 68, 69, 70, 71, 85, 90, 91, 92, 96, 100, 101, 103, 106, 107, 108, 115, 117, 118, 119, 120, 122, 123, 127, 136, 144, 151
Conversion 146
Council of Senior Ulema in the Kingdom of Saudi Arabia 8, 150, 191
Creed (*ʿaqīda, iʿtiqād*) 1, 2, 3, 7, 28, 40–41, 63, 68, 69, 70–88, 90–95, 100–101, 146, 197

Daghrīrī, Ḥ.M. 195
al-Ḍaḥḥāk b. Muzāḥim 204
Damascus 19, 28, 38, 147
Dammāj (North Yemen) 198
David 11
daʿwa (Islamic mission) 60, 65, 149
Saudi Arabian *daʿwa* institutions 8, 152, 192
Dāwūd b. al-Muḥabbar 19
Darb al-Khabbāzīn 35
Day of Judgment 4, 61, 63, 87, 95, 174, 187, 203, 211
al-Dhahabī 11, 16, 20, 23, 42, 49, 59, 63, 73, 74, 98, 147, 194
dīn 4, 13, 50, 67, 90, 100, 101, 104, 111, 114, 117, 123, 125, 126, 154, 155, 175, 178
dīn ʿatīq 6, 126, 176
uṣūl al-dīn 74, 99
Dīnār b. ʿAbdallāh 15, 203, 207, 208, 209, 211, 212, 213
Disputes, controversy, argumentation (prohibition of) 93, 100, 122, 156, 165, 168–169, 187
Divorce 94, 162

Egypt 89
Eschatological signs and notions 63, 94, 134
Esoteric knowledge (*ʿilm al-bāṭin*) 182
Evil times (*zamān sūʾ; iḥdhar zamānak*) 171, 178, 185
Excommunication, see: *Takfīr*

faḍl (excellence and virtue) 60, 172
Faith (*īmān*) 1, 3, 4, 69, 82–83, 90, 101–106, 119, 157, 158, 165, 166, 169, 188
Faith/belief (increases and decreases) 83, 104–105, 109, 157, 188
faqīh (pl. *fuqahāʾ*) 31, 37, 78, 80, 87
al-Farāhīdī, see: al-Khalīl b. Aḥmad
al-Farghānī (historian) 24
Fasting 92, 109, 160
Fate (*al-qadar*) 4, 83, 90, 163, 165
al-Fawzān, Ṣ.F. 150, 151, 191, 197, 198, 199
Fear (*khawf*—God) 25, see: hope
fitna/fitan (civil strife) 6, 83, 92, 127, 179
Friday prayer 6, 86, 92, 127, 128, 159, 173, 180, 181, 182, 201, 209, 210
Fuḍayl [b. ʿIyāḍ] 182, 190
furqa (dissension) 6, 83

Gabriel (Archangel) 166, 205
Ghaylān al-Dimashqī 82
God
God's unicity 183
Nothing resembles His Likeness 130, 156
God's attributes 41, 91, 112, 130, 133, 156, 157, 161, 173, 180, 184, 196
God's anger 168
God's decree 4, 82, 90, 163
God's knowledge 112, 130, 156, 163
God's foot 130, 161
God's movement 130, 161, 164
God's speech 4, 84, 132, 167
God spoke to Moses 131–132
God's Throne 55, 61, 63, 91, 113, 130, 131, 133, 156, 157, 163, 166, 201, 202, 203
God's mercy 5, 108, 158, 159, 160, 164
God's will 175
Muḥammad saw God 95, 161
See also: Beatific Vision
Gorgan 201
The Grave (punishment in the grave) 4, 27, 95, 174
Torment (Munkar and Nakir) 157, 166

ḥadīth 2, 68, 69, 85
ḥadīth folk 37
Ḥāʾil (northwest of Medina) 195
al-Ḥajjāj b. al-Minhāl 184
al-Ḥajūrī, Y.ʿA. 198
al-Ḥajūrī al-Zuʿkurī, Abū Muḥammad ʿA. 198
al-Ḥākim Abū ʿAbdallāh [Muḥammad b. ʿAbdallāh al-Nīsābūrī] 206, 210
al-Ḥakīm al-Samarqandī 20, 149
al-Ḥakīm al-Tirmidhī 138
al-ḥalāl wa-l-ḥarām (lawful and unlawful things) 113, 137, 159, 162, 163, 170, 183, 210
Ḥamdān b. ʿAlī, Abū Jaʿfar 122
Ḥammād b. Salama 69, 184, 210
Ḥammād b. Zayd 69, 184
Ḥanābila (Hanbalis; ḥanbalite) 11, 12, 31, 34, 35, 37, 38, 44, 45, 46, 48, 53, 57, 58, 60, 61, 63, 71, 72, 131, 133, 147, 152
Ḥanbal b. Isḥāq 10
Ḥarb b. Ismāʿīl al-Kirmānī (see also: al-Iṣṭakhrī) 53, 68, 71, 72, 73, 75, 76, 89, 91, 92, 93, 94, 95, 111, 113, 114, 115, 125, 131, 132, 138, 145

Hārūn al-Rashīd (ʿAbbasid caliph) 65, 99
al-Ḥasan (unidentified) 187
al-Ḥasan b. ʿAbd al-Malik al-Nasafī 211
al-Ḥasan b. ʿAlī b. Abī Ṭālib 150
al-Ḥasan b. ʿAlī al-Ahwāzī 42, 43, 47, 48, 49, 62, 63, 194
al-Ḥasan b. ʿAlī al-Barbahārī 2, 7, 8, 9, 38, 39, 41, 42, 43, 44, 45, 46, 47, 48, 49, 50, 51, 52, 54, 55, 56, 58, 59, 60, 61, 62, 63, 64, 131, 142, 143, 150, 152, 191, 192–200
al-Ḥasan al-Baṣrī 52, 137, 187
al-Ḥasan b. ʿAlī al-Jawharī 213
al-Ḥasan b. Ismāʿīl al-Rabaʿī 76, 89, 90, 91, 92, 93
al-Ḥasan b. Muḥammad b. Maḥfūẓ al-Banākitī, Abū Muḥammad 212
al-Ḥasan b. Ṣāliḥ [b. Ḥayy] 164
al-Ḥasan al-Yūsī 13
ḥashwiyya 76
al-ḥawḍ (the Prophets' pool) 157
Hazārasb al-Harawī 33, 36, 37
Heaven 131, 157, 163, 164, 166, 174, 209
Hell 4, 94, 113, 114, 157, 163, 166, 169, 174, 205
Hell-fire (Hellfire) 24, 114, 117, 118, 119, 130, 154, 155, 161, 163, 205, 211
Heresy 3, 6, 25, 71, 82, 106, 112, 146, 168, 172, 179, 184, 185, 186
Hijaz 89, 115
al-Ḥilla 35
Hims 145
Hishām (Hišam) al-Fuwaṭī 52, 169, 185
Hishām b. ʿUrwa 206
Hope (*rajāʾ*) 70, 170
Hope and fear 25, 92, 108, 109, 114, 160, 170, 179
ḥubb/maḥabba 25, 51
Ḥulūlīya 45
al-Ḥumaydī, Abū Bakr ʿAbdallāh 73, 90, 91, 92, 99, 109
al-Ḥusayn b. ʿAlī b. Abī Ṭālib 151
al-Ḥusayn b. Muḥammad b. al-Ṭabarī 183

Ibāḍiyya 117
Iblīs 177, 206
Ibn ʿAbbās, see: ʿAbdallāh b. ʿAbbās
Ibn ʿAbd al-Barr 124
Ibn ʿAbduh, Abū Yaḥyā M. 199
Ibn Abī l-Dunyā 138
Ibn Abī Duʾād 185
Ibn Abī Ḥātim al-Rāzī 21, 74, 99, 133
Ibn Abī Shayba, see: Abū Bakr and ʿUthmān
Ibn Abī Yaʿlā 7, 31, 38, 39, 40, 41, 43, 44, 46, 49, 58, 59, 61, 62, 63, 72, 74, 76, 77, 111, 112, 113, 194
Ibn al-Aʿrābī, see: Abū Saʿīd Ibn al-Aʿrābī
Ibn ʿAsākir 42, 78, 79
Ibn ʿAwn, see: ʿAbdallāh b. ʿAwn
Ibn Baṭṭa al-ʿUkbarī 31, 44, 45, 99
Ibn al-Dubaythī 34
Ibn al-Furāt, see: Muḥammad b. al-ʿAbbās
Ibn Ḥajar al-ʿAsqalānī 59
Ibn Ḥamdān al-Ḥarrānī 58–59, 62–63
Ibn Ḥāmid, al-Ḥasan 31
Ibn Hāniʾ al-Naysābūrī 53
Ibn Ḥazm 120
Ibn al-Jawzī 11, 15, 16, 22, 32, 34, 36, 77
Ibn Kāmil, see: Aḥmad b. Kāmil
Ibn al-Madīnī, see: ʿAlī b. ʿAbdallāh al-Madīnī
Ibn Maʿīn 80
Ibn al-Mufriṭ 79
Ibn al-Munādī 27
Ibn Qayyim al-Jawziyya 196
Ibn Qutayba 53
Ibn Rajab al-Ḥanbalī 59
Ibn Ṣāliḥ, J. 197
Ibn Sānū, see: ʿAbdallāh b. Ḥamza b. Abī Ṭāhir
Ibn Sayyār al-Marwazī 80
Ibn Shāqillā 41
Ibn Shihāb al-Zuhrī 16, 52, 209
Ibn Sīrīn 69
Ibn Taymiyya 10, 21, 25, 59, 63, 75, 105, 194, 196
Ibn ʿUkāsha al-Kirmānī, see: Muḥammad b. ʿUkāsha
Ibn Zūrān (read Ibn Zūzān) 74
Ibrāhīm b. Ismāʿīl al-Qahmī 22
Ibrāhīm b. Khālid, Abū Thawr 79, 80, 111, 145
Ibrāhīm b. Muḥammad al-Burūdī, Abū Isḥāq 79
Ibrāhīm b. ʿUmar b. Aḥmad al-Barmakī, Abū Isḥāq 30, 31, 37, 153
ijmāʿ (consensus) 120, 122
Ilyās b. Idrīs al-Kassī 19, 212
Imami (Twelver) 60, 87, 135, 151, 183

Innovation (see also *bidʿa*; novelties) 1, 6, 55, 70, 75, 76, 85, 90, 97, 105, 106, 107, 113, 115, 116, 117, 118, 126, 133, 134, 145, 154, 155, 162, 168, 171, 174, 175, 177, 178, 181, 184, 185, 186, 188, 190
Intention (*niyya*) 83, 90, 105, 158, 182
Iraq 2, 10, 35, 65, 115, 137, 143, 145, 146
Iran 20, 67, 76, 137, 138, 140, 143, 145, 146, 201
irjāʾ 66, 184, 188
Isfahan 56, 63, 147, 201
Isḥāq b. Muḥammad al-Kaysānī 19, 210
Isḥāq b. Rāhawayh 123, 124
ʿishq 25
Islam 83, 99, 100, 101–106, 108, 109, 117, 119, 122, 126, 153, 154, 155–156, 160, 161, 165, 168, 169, 170, 171, 172, 174, 179, 182, 190
Ismāʿīl b. ʿAbd al-Karīm al-Ṣanʿānī 202
Ismāʿīl b. Abī Uways 16
Ismāʿīl b. Aḥmad (Samanid prince) 149
Ismāʿīl b. al-Faraj 19, 209
Ismāʿīl b. Ibrāhīm al-Suwaydī al-Jurjānī, Abū Saʿīd 209
Ismāʿīl b. Isḥāq al-Azdī 24, 26
Ismāʿīl b. Yaḥyā l-Muzanī 99
Ismaʿilis 60
al-Iṣṭakhrī, see: Aḥmad b. Jaʿfar b. Yaʿqūb
al-istiḥlāl 133, 172
ittibāʿ (blind adherence; compliance; see also *taqlīd*) 90, 124, 154, 196

Jaʿd b. Dirham 84
Jaʿfar b. ʿAbdallāh b. Yaʿqūb al-Fannākī, Abū l-Qāsim 204
Jaʿfar b. Muḥammad (al-Ṣādiq) 134, 135, 188
Jaʿfar b. Muḥammad al-Nasafī, Abū l-ʿAbbās 211
al-Jāḥiẓ 108, 129, 132, 139
al-Jahm b. Ṣafwān 84
Jahmi (Jahmiyya) 6, 61, 66, 106, 107, 108, 112, 113, 114, 130, 131, 161, 169, 172, 173, 174, 180, 183, 184, 186
Jesus 60, 94, 157, 159
Jihad 6, 70, 128, 174, 182, 188, 207
Jisr b. Farqad al-Qaṣṣāb 206
Job 11
al-Jummayzī, ʿA.A. 196, 198
al-Junayd, Abū l-Qāsim 26

Kahmas b. al-Ḥasan 55
Kalām 46, 55, 56, 165, 168
Kalawādhā 27
Karīma bnt. Aḥmad b. Muḥammad b. Ḥātim al-Marwazī 211
Karrāmiyya 138
al-kasb or *al-makāsib* (earnings for living or acquisition of profit) 5, 136, 137, 138, 180
al-Khalīl b. Aḥmad al-Farāhīdī 12–13
al-Khallāl, Abū Bakr Aḥmad b. Muḥammad 12, 41, 47, 53, 138
khārijī (dissident) 54, 159
al-Kharrāz 26
Al-Khaṭīb al-Baghdādī 15, 17, 31, 146
Khawārij (Kharijites) 5, 70, 92, 97, 106, 188
Khorasan 65, 79, 145, 184
Kingdom of Saudi Arabia 8
Kufa 17, 80, 89, 184
Kufr (*kāfir*; see also: unbelief) 84, 104, 106, 109, 110, 116, 117, 133

Lālakāʾī, Hibatallāh b. al-Ḥasan 73, 79, 80, 81, 84, 85
Layth b. Saʿd 133

Maʿbad al-Juhanī 82
al-Madkhalī, R.H.ʿU. 197, 198
al-Mahdī 94, 150, 151 (see also: *al-Qāʾim*)
Maḥmūd b. Ghaylān 17, 213
Mardawayh al-Ṣāʾigh 63, 182
Marjoram 203
Makḥūl al-Dimashqī 52, 82
Mālik b. Anas 15, 16, 69, 87, 105, 123, 131, 133, 157, 163, 187, 189, 209
Mālik b. Mighwal 184
al-Maʾmūn (ʿAbbasid caliph) 1, 8, 11, 65, 66, 67, 68, 107, 108, 134, 144, 149
al-Manṣūr mosque 31, 37
Marriage 5, 94, 133–134, 162, 171, 181
al-Marrūdhī, see: Aḥmad b.Muḥammad al-Marrūdhī
Martyrs 157, 166, 190, 209
Marv 201
al-Marwazī, Abū ʿAbdallāh, see: Muḥammad b. Naṣr
Mary 60, 157, 159
al-masḥ ʿalā l-khuffayn 86, 87, 93, 160
al-Mawṣil 203
Maysara b. ʿAbd Rabbih 19

Mecca 73, 89, 120, 158, 166, 184, 192, 209
Medina 80, 120, 184, 195, 210
miḥna (the inquisition against the traditionalists) 1, 4, 8, 11, 40, 66, 67, 68, 70, 73, 80, 84, 88, 89, 107, 122, 129, 144
miḥna against the Sufis 13, 20, 25–26, 118
al-Minqarī 77
al-Miʿrāj (the Nocturnal Journey) 95, 131, 166
al-Mīzān (The Balance on the Day of Resurrection) 157
Moses 91, 112, 113, 132, 141, 167
Mothers of the Believers 183
Muʿādh b. Muʿādh 184
Muʿādh b. Rifāʿa 213
Muʿādh b. Yūsuf al-Jurjānī 19, 211
Muʿāwiya 6, 119, 127, 150, 179
Muʿāwiya b. Qurra 140
al-Mughīra b. ʿAbd al-Raḥmān 209
al-Muhājirūn (Immigrants) 92, 120, 158
Muḥammad (Prophet, Messenger of God) 1, 4, 6, 16, 61, 63, 70, 78, 84, 85, 90, 101, 102, 107, 108, 110, 114, 116, 119, 120, 121, 125, 128, 131, 141, 150, 154, 156, 157, 160, 161, 162, 164, 165, 166, 168, 169, 170, 171, 172, 173, 174, 175, 177, 178, 179, 180, 181, 182, 185, 186, 188, 189, 190, 194, 204, 211
  Muḥammad's Household (Āl) 60, 157, 172, 189
  The chamber where he is buried 180
Muḥammad b. al-ʿAbbās b. al-Furāt 18, 29, 30, 31, 153
Muḥammad b. ʿAbdallāh, Abū Zayd al-Madanī 17, 209
Muḥammad b. ʿAbdallāh al-ʿUmarī 17, 120, 205
Muḥammad b. ʿAbd al-Qādir 31–32
Muḥammad b. ʿAbd al-Wahhāb 196
Muḥammad b. Aḥmad b. ʿAlī b. Ḥamdān, Abū Ṭāhir 204
Muḥammad b. Aḥmad b. al-Faraj al-Daqqāq, Abū l-Maʿālī 32, 34
Muḥammad b. Aḥmad al-Hāshimī 41
Muḥammad b. Aḥmad b. Maymūn al-Kātib 210
Muḥammad b. Aḥmad b. Muḥammad b. Dāwūd al-Iṣbahānī 33
Muḥammad b. Aḥmad al-Malaṭī 38, 78, 99
Muḥammad b. Aḥmad al-Qahmī al-Simsār 22
Muḥammad b. Aḥmad b. Rizq 207
Muḥammad b.ʿAlī (al-Bāqir) 134, 135, 141, 188
Muḥammad b. ʿAwf Abū Jaʿfar al-Ḥimṣī 40, 77, 90, 91, 92, 93, 94, 95, 113, 145
Muḥammad b. Bakr b. Khalaf b. Muslim b. ʿAbbād 211
Muḥammad b. Ḥabīb al-Andarābī 68, 77, 90, 91, 92, 93, 94, 95, 144
Muḥammad b. al-Ḥasan al-ʿAskarī (the twelfth Imam) 135, 151
Muḥammad b. al-Ḥasan al-Shaybānī 136, 137
Muḥammad b. al-Ḥusayn b. Muḥammad b. Mūsā l-Sulamī 208
Muḥammad b. Ibrāhīm al-Bayyāḍī 17, 204
Muḥammad b. Ibrāhīm b. al-ʿAlāʾ 17, 19, 202
Muḥammad b. Isḥāq b. Muḥammad al-Kaysānī 210
Muḥammad b. Isḥāq al-Thaqafī 73
Muḥammad b. Jaʿfar b. Jābir, Abū Bakr 213
Muḥammad b. Karrām 138
Muḥammad b. al-Khalīl, Abū Bakr 208
Muḥammad b. Makhlad 18
Muḥammad b. Maslama al-Madīnī 15
Muḥammad b. Muḥammad b. Zayd al-Baghdādī, Abū l-Maʿālī 212
Muḥammad b. Nāṣir b. Muḥammad b. ʿAlī, Abū l-Faḍl al-Salāmī 32, 33, 34, 37
Muḥammad b. Naṣr al-Marwazī, Abū ʿAbdallāh 103, 104, 105
Muḥammad b. Samāʿa 136
Muḥammad b. Sīrīn 186
Muḥammad b. Sulaymān 17, 210
Muḥammad b. Sulaymān al-Baṣrī Abū Jaʿfar 79
Muḥammad b. ʿUkāsha al-Kirmānī 71, 78, 79, 99
Muḥammad b. Yūnus al-Sarakhsī 40, 77
Muhannā b. Yaḥyā al-Shāmī 40
al-Muḥāsibī, al-Ḥārith b. Asad 137, 138, 139, 140
al-muḥtasib 26
Mujāhid b. Jabr 61
Munabbihb. ʿUthmān al-Dimashqī 78
Mujāhid 61, 211

Murji'a 5, 70, 83, 85, 97, 104, 112, 118, 136, 144, 145, 188
Mūsā b. Ja'far (al-Kāẓim) 134, 135, 188
Muṣ'ab b. 'Umayr 209, 210
Musaddad b. Musarhad al-Baṣrī 40, 68, 77, 90, 91, 92, 93, 94, 95, 112, 113, 114, 145
Muslim b. al-Ḥajjāj 16
al-Musta'īn ('Abbasid caliph) 143, 148
al-Mustarshid ('Abbasid caliph) 35
al-Mustaẓhir bi-Llāh ('Abbasid caliph) 35
mut'a (temporary marriage) 5, 94, 133, 134, 171
al-Mu'tamid ('Abbasid caliph) 8, 23, 25, 143, 147, 149
al-Mu'taṣim ('Abbasid caliph) 66
al-Mutawakkil ('Abbasid caliph) 17, 67, 78, 88, 122, 123, 143, 147, 174
al-Mu'tazz ('Abbasid caliph) 143, 148
Mu'tazila 6, 52, 53, 55, 66, 106, 107, 112, 117, 137, 138, 145, 184
al-Muwaffaq, Abū Aḥmad Ṭalḥa b. Ja'far ('Abbasid regent) 7, 8, 23, 24, 147, 149–151

nābita 76, 132–133
Nāfi' 205, 210
Al-Najmī, A.Y. 195, 198
Nasibi 183
Nishapur 81, 103, 201
Novelty (novelties; see also *bid'a*) 5, 72, 96, 117, 124, 126, 155, 156, 173, 177

Orthodoxy 4, 88, 144
Orthopraxy 3, 71, 86, 93, 106, 146

Paradise 4, 85, 94, 113, 114, 121, 157, 163, 164, 166, 168, 189
Pederasty 201, 210
People of the Qibla 109, 115, 160–161, 173, 178
Political quietism 68, 151
Prayers and communal prayers 4, 5, 6, 86, 92, 93, 94, 108, 109, 120, 127, 158, 159, 160, 166, 169, 181
 Prayer over the body of a deceased 160–161, 164
Proto-Sunnis 65–70, 82, 88, 97, 107, 108, 109, 127, 136
Qadari (Qadariyya) 5, 70, 82, 85, 97, 111, 112, 184, 188

al-Qāḍī Hannād 203
al-Qaḥṭānī, M.S. 191, 192, 193, 194, 196
al-Qā'im 60, 63, 149, 150, 151, 157, 192
Qalīb [dry well of Badr] 164
Qarmaṭians 23
Qāṣṣ (preacher) 2, 7, 13, 20, 21, 22, 23, 43, 54, 60, 63, 138, 142, 147
Qawwām al-Sunna, Abū l-Qāsim Ismā'īl 10, 56, 63, 71, 72, 73, 80, 140, 147
Qazvin 201
qiyās (reasoning by analogy) 6, 93, 107, 171, 172
Quran
 God's speech and revelation 4, 84, 156
 Authority of 90, 102, 115, 165, 178
 Created 11, 66, 107, 174
 Uncreated 4, 84, 91, 99, 111, 112, 113, 156
 lafẓ is created 81, 124, 173
 Doubt a letter of 116, 189
 Sunna explicates 90
Qudāma b. Ja'far 140
Quran as the Speech of God 4
Quraysh 85, 91, 159, 172
Qurra b. Ḥabīb al-Baṣrī 16, 210
Qutayba b. Sa'īd, Abū Rajā' 80, 144
Quṭb, M. 191

Rabble (riffraff) 65, 107, 108, 172, 175, 187
al-Rabī' b. Badr 210
al-Rabī' b. Muḥammad b. al-Ḍaḥḥāk b. Muzāḥim al-Kassī 211
al-Raddādī, Abū Yāsir Kh. Q. 192, 193–195, 196, 198
al-Rāḍī ('Abbasid caliph) 49, 131
Rāfiḍa (Rafidi) 111, 121, 183, 188
al-raj'a, (Return of the dead Imam) 113, 133–135, 188
Al-Rāmahurmuzī 75
al-ra'y (subjective opinion) 6, 80, 93, 107, 172
Rayy 81, 145
Reason, see: *al-'aql*
Religion, see also: *dīn*
 Consists of Quran, tradition and Sunna 90, 123, 154, 171
 Islam and *īmān* 104
 Strict obedience; servile imitation 1, 46, 74

No "why" and "how" in matters of 4, 49, 90, 100, 102, 113, 130, 133, 146, 156, 165, 173
Repentance 108, 160, 189
Resurrection 4, 94, 95, 113, 130, 132, 133, 134, 157, 159, 161, 163, 170, 171, 188, 212
al-Ribāṭ mosque (Baghdad) 211
Rightly guided caliphs (al-Rāshidūn) 173
Ritual ablution 3, 5, 86, 93, 160
Rulers (authority) 6, 7, 9, 53–54
Obedience to 6, 7, 9, 53, 54, 126–128, 151, 158–159, 182–183, 191
praying behind 86, 181
almsgiving to 109, 169
jihad with them 182–183
ruwaybiḍa (see, rabble) 107, 172
Ruwaym (sufi) 26

Sa'd b. Abī Waqqās 120, 158
Ṣadaqa b. Manṣūr al-Mazyadī 35
Saffarids 143
ṣāḥib hawā (sectarian) 115, 116, 158, 182, 189
ṣāḥib sunna (pl. *aṣḥāb sunna*) 7, 67, 72, 73, 76, 80, 96–98, 103, 177, 184
ṣāḥib sunna wa-jamā'a 67, 80, 96
Sahl al-Tustarī 55, 81, 90, 91, 92, 93
Ṣāfī al-Muṭayyin 33
Ṣaḥwa (political movement in Saudi Arabia) 191
Sa'īd b. Muḥsin al-Ṣaffār al-Kassī 212
Sa'īd b. Zayd b. Nufayl 120, 158
al-Sakhāwī 98
Salaf, salafi 2, 3, 8, 9, 150, 152, 191, 196, 198
al-salaf 69, 71, 89, 197
Ṣāliḥ (Prophet) 157
Ṣālih b. Aḥmad b. Ḥanbal 10
Ṣāliḥ b. Suwayd 82
Salmān al-Anṣārī, Abū l-Qāsim 48
sālimī (follower of the doctrine of the Baṣran Abū l-Ḥasan b. Sālim) 42, 48, 64
Samarra 143, 145
Samarqand 104, 212
Ṣāmiṭah (in Jāzān, Saudi Arabia) 195
Ṣan'ā' (Sanaa) 22–23
Sarakhs 201
ṣarf (exchange *in specie*) 184
al-Sarrāj, Abū Naṣr al-Ṭūsī 55
Satan 55, 155, 205, 206, 207
Saudi Arabia 8, 150, 152, 191, 192, 195
Saudi religious establishment 152, 192, 196
sawād of Dujayl 35
al-sawād al-a'ẓam (the vast majority) 104, 119, 154
al-sayf (rebellion) 92, 184
Seventy-two deviating sects 5, 70, 97, 99, 188
al-Sha'bī 184
Shādhān 21
shafā'a (Muḥammad's intercession on the Day of Judgment) 61, 62, 95, 157, 174, 203
al-Shafi'i, Muḥammad b. Idrīs 2, 74, 80, 99, 109
al-shahāda (the confession of faith) 83, 90
al-Shām (Syria) 89, 184
al-Shanqīṭī, M.A. 196
Shaqīq al-Balkhī 137
al-Sharīf Abū Ja'far 37
al-Shāsh 81
shawq 51
Shaybān b. Farrūkh al-Baṣrī 16, 210
Shi'a (Shi'is) 5, 60, 70, 79, 87, 133–135, 184, 188
Shibārū-Sinnū, H. 191, 192, 193
Shu'ayb b. Ḥarb 73, 84
[Shu'ba] Ibn al-Ḥajjāj 208
Singing 184
Sirjan 145
al-ṣirāṭ (Narrow Bridge stretched over Hell) 157
al-ṣirāṭ al-mustaqīm (the straight path) 117, 126, 155
Stoning 5, 94, 160
al-Ṣubayḥī (Sufi) 55
Successors 7, 52, 70, 78, 85, 89, 100, 121, 124, 178, 189, 194
Sufis 5, 7, 13, 20, 24, 25–26, 36, 55, 118, 135, 137, 147, 179
Sufyān al-Thawrī 67, 69, 73, 80, 82, 83, 84, 85, 86, 87, 97, 133
Sufyān b. 'Uyayna 69, 70, 73, 74, 82, 83, 84, 87, 109, 121, 158, 188
ṣūfiyyat al-Mu'tazila 137
Sulaymān b. Bilāl 21
Sulaymān b. Dāwūd al-Shādhakūnī al-Baṣrī 16
Sulaymān b. Jāmi' 10

Sulaymān b. Jarīr al-Raqqī 87
Sulaymān al-Sijzī 40
Sumnūn al-Muḥibb 26
Sunna 3, 4, 5, 6, 7, 8, 12, 24, 28, 32, 34, 36, 37, 38, 42, 47, 50, 51, 56, 67, 70, 72, 73, 74, 80, 85, 87, 88, 89, 90, 96, 97, 98, 99, 100, 101, 102, 103, 105, 106, 115, 116, 118, 119, 123, 124, 126, 128, 129, 153, 154, 156, 159, 160, 161, 165, 170, 171, 173, 174, 175, 176, 178, 180, 183, 184, 185, 187, 188, 189, 190
  khiṣāl al-sunna 97
  uṣūl *al-sunna* 31, 73, 74, 78, 79, 99
Sunnis 4, 6, 144
Syria 10, 82, 89, 115, 145, 184

al-Ṭabarī 17, 18, 62
al-Tabrīzī, Yaḥyā b. ʿAlī 34
Takfīr 106, 108, 115, 117, 118, 198
Ṭalḥa b. ʿUbaydallāh (Companion) 6, 92, 119, 120, 158, 179
Taqlīd 1, 46, 48, 67, 74, 90, 122–125, 173, 186, 196
ṭalab al-ʿilm 209
Ṭayfūr b. Abī Isḥāq al-Mīshaqī, Abū Yazīd 209
Thawbān b. Saʿīd 17, 205
Thumāma b. al-Ashras 185
Tigris 10, 27
Traditionalists 1, 8, 125, 130, 179
Transoxania 144, 149, 201
The Trumpet (Day of Resurrection) 163
Ṭuʿma b. ʿAmr 121, 188
al-Ṭūr (the Mount) 132, 167
Al-Ṭuraythīthī 203, 211
Turkish soldiers 143
al-Ṭuyūrī, al-Mubārak b. ʿAbd al-Jabbār 73, 76, 77, 84

al-ʿUbaylān, ʿA.Ṣ. 195, 196
Ubayy b. Kaʿb 52
ʿUkāsha al-Kirmānī, see: Muḥammad b. ʿUkāsha
ʿulamāʾ 66, 69, 70, 71, 82, 83, 89, 191, 192
ʿUmar b. ʿAbd al-ʿAzīz 206, 207
ʿUmar b. Ḥayyawayh 41
ʿUmar b. al-Khaṭṭāb 52, 83, 85, 86, 92, 99, 107, 120, 154, 158, 171, 176, 180, 187, 188, 205
ʿUmar b. Muḥammad b. ʿAmr b. Murra 208
ʿUmar b. Muḥammad b. al-Ṣabbāḥ al-Muqriʾ 208
Umayya b. ʿUthmān al-Dimashqī 78–79
Umayyads 68, 82
Umm Isḥāq (or Asḥar), mother of al-Muwaffaq 149, 147
Unbelief (see also: *kufr*) 3, 6, 52, 92, 93, 107, 110, 111, 112, 114, 115, 117, 132, 156, 160, 167, 168, 171, 172, 173, 178
ʿUrwa b. al-Zubayr 206–207
Usayd b. Ḥuḍayr 184
Usayd b. Muḥammad 19, 203
ʿUthmān b. Abī Shayba 17, 211
ʿUthmān b. ʿAffān 84, 86, 92, 106, 107, 120, 121, 126, 158, 171, 176, 188, 189
ʿUthmān b. Aḥmad b. al-Sammāk 18, 77
ʿUthmān al-Battī 110
al-ʿUthaymīn, M.Ṣ. 197

al-Wādiʿī, M.H. 198
Wahb b. Jarīr 184
Wahb b. Munabbih 202
Wahhabi 152, 191, 196
al-Walīd b. Muslim 213
Wāsiṭ 25, 26, 89
Works (*al-ʿamal*) 69, 82, 83, 90, 104, 105, 141, 158, 188, 213

Yaḥyā b. ʿAlī al-Ḥannāṭ 33
Yaḥyā b. Aktham 134
Yaʿqūb b. Muḥammad al-Balkhī 19, 211
Yaʿqūb b. Muḥammad al-Balkhī 211
Yaʿqūb al-Ṣaffār 143, 149
Yazīd b. Ṣāliḥ 16, 208
Yazīd b. Zurayʿ 184
Yemen 191, 198
Yūnus b. ʿUbayd 69, 184, 185, 190
Yūsuf b. Aḥmad b. al-Faraj al-Daqqāq, Abū l-Fatḥ 32, 34
Yūsuf b. ʿUmar b. Masrūq al-Qawwās al-Zāhid, Abū l-Fatḥ 208

Zāhir b. Aḥmad al-Faqīh, Abū ʿAlī 211
Zandaqa (zindīq) 25, 99, 112, 168, 184
Zanj (revolt of) 8, 10, 22, 23, 143, 148, 149
Zaydi 23, 87, 198
al-Zubayr [b. al-ʿAwwām] 6, 92, 119, 120, 158, 179, 207
al-Zuhrī, see: Ibn Shihāb al-Zuhrī

Index of Book Titles

al-Afrād, al-Dāraquṭnī 209
aḥādīth al-ṣifāt, Abū Sulaymān al-Dimashqī 41
Akhbār al-quḍāt, Aḥmad b. Kāmil 18
Akhbār al-shuʿarāʾ, Aḥmad b. Kāmil 18
K. al-ʿĀlim wa-l-mutaʿallim, Abū Ḥanīfa (put together by Abū Muqātil al-Samarqand) 110
ʿaqīda (*iʿtiqād*), ʿAbdūs b. Mālik 40, 74, 76, 99, 145
ʿaqīda (*iʿtiqād*), Abū l-ʿAbbās al-Iṣṭakhrī 40, 68, 71, 72, 74, 75
ʿaqīda (*iʿtiqād*), Abū ʿAlī Muḥammad b. Aḥmad al-Hāshimī 41
ʿaqīda (*iʿtiqād*), Abū Rajāʾ Qutayba b. Saʿīd 80, 144
ʿaqīda (*iʿtiqād*), Abū Thawr, Ibrāhīm b. Khālid 79, 145
ʿaqīda (*iʿtiqād*), ʿAlī b. ʿAbdallāh b. al-Madīnī 80, 145
ʿaqīda (*iʿtiqād*), Ḥarb al-Kirmānī 68, 72, 75, 89
ʿaqīda (*iʿtiqād*), al-Ḥasan b. Ismāʿīl al-Rabaʿī 76, 89
ʿaqīda (*iʿtiqād*), al-Awzāʿī 72
ʿaqīda (*iʿtiqād*), Muḥammad b. ʿAwf Abū Jaʿfar al-Ḥimṣī 40, 77, 145
ʿaqīda (*iʿtiqād*), Muḥammad b. Ḥabīb al-Andarābī 68, 77, 144
ʿaqīda (*iʿtiqād*), Muḥammad b. Ismāʿīl al-Bukhārī 80, 144
ʿaqīda (*iʿtiqād*), Muḥammad b. ʿUkāsha al-Kirmānī 71, 78–79, 99, 145
ʿaqīda (*iʿtiqād*), Muḥammad b. Yūnus al-Sarakhsī 40, 77
ʿaqīda (*iʿtiqād*), Musaddad b. Musarhad al-Baṣrī 40, 68, 77, 145
ʿaqīda (*iʿtiqād*), the two Rāzīs: Abū Zurʿa ʿUbayd Allāh and Abū Ḥātim Muḥammad 81, 145
ʿaqīda (*iʿtiqād*), Sufyān al-Thawrī 73
ʿaqīda (*iʿtiqād*), Sufyān b. ʿUyayna 73

K. al-Buldān, al-Jāḥiẓ 139
K. al-Burhān, Abū l-Ḥusayn b. Wahb al-Kātib 140

K. al-Duʿāʾ, Ghulām Khalīl 20

Fatḥ al-bārī, Ibn Ḥajar al-ʿAsqalānī 59
K. fī l-ṣalāt, attributed to Aḥmad b. Ḥanbal by Muhannā b. Yaḥyā al-Shāmī 40
al-Fiqh al-absaṭ, attributed to Abū Ḥanīfa (Abū Muṭīʿ al-Balkhī) 82, 86
al-Fiqh al-akbar II, attributed to Abū Ḥanīfa 110

gharīb al-ḥadīth, Abū ʿUbayd al-Harawī al-Fāshānī 34
K. Gharīb al-Quran, Aḥmad b. Kāmil 18

al-Ḥathth ʿalā al-baḥth, see: *Risāla fī istiḥsān al-khawḍ fī ʿilm al-kalām*
al-Haththʿalā l-tijāra, al-Khallāl 138
al-Ḥujja, Qawwām al-Sunna 56

K. al-Ibāna, Ibn Baṭṭa al-ʿUkbarī 44
K. al-Ibāna ʿan uṣūl al-diyāna, Abū l-Ḥasan al-Ashʿarī 42, 47, 62
K. Ibṭāl al-taʾwīlāt, Abū Yaʿlā l-Farrā 39
K. ilā l-thaghr (creed), al-Athram al-Iskāfī 40
K. al-Īmān, Ibn Taymiyya 105
K. al-Inqiṭāʿ ilā Allāh, Ghulām Khalīl 20

Juzʾ, Abū l-Ḥasan b. Bashshār 39

K. Māʾiyyat al-ʿaql, al-Muḥāsibī 139
al-Majmūʿ, Abū Ḥafṣ al-Barmakī 41
masāʾil, Abū Bakr Aḥmad b. Muḥammad al-Marrūdhī 40
masāʾil, ʿAbd al-Malik al-Maymūnī 40
masāʾil, Abdūs b. Mālik 77
masāʾil, al-Athram al-Iskāfī 40
masāʾil of Ḥarb b. Ismāʿīl al-Kirmānī 72, 115
masāʾil, Muḥammad b. ʿAwf al-Ḥimṣī 40
Mathālib *b. Abī Bishr*, al-Ḥasan b. ʿAlī al-Ahwāzī 42
K. al-Mawāʿiẓ, Ghulām Khalī l 20
miḥnat Ibn Ḥanbal, Sulaymān al-Sijzī 40
Musnad, Aḥmad b. Ḥanbal 34, 61

Musnad, al-Ḥumaydī, Abū Bakr ʿAbdallāh 73
Musnad, Musaddad b. Musarhad 78

Nihāyat al-mubtadiʾīn, Ibn Ḥamdān al-Ḥarrānī 58, 59

K. al-Qirāʾāt, Aḥmad b. Kāmil 18
Qūt al-qulūb, Abū Ṭālib al-Makkī 41

Risāla fī istiḥsān al-khawḍ fī ʿilm al-kalām (*Risāla II*), Abū l-Ḥasan al-Ashʿarī 46, 47, 48
Risāla fī nafy al-tashbīh, al-Jāḥiẓ 129

K. al-Ṣalāt, Ghulām Khalīl 20
al-Sharḥ wa-l-ibāna ʿalā uṣūl al-sunna wa-l-diyāna, Ibn Baṭṭa 31, 44
K. al-Shurūṭ, Aḥmad b. Kāmil 18
K. al-Shurūṭ al-ṣaghīr, Aḥmad b. Kāmil 18
K. al-Siyar, Aḥmad b. Kāmil 18
Kitāb al-Sunnah, ʿAbdallāh b. Aḥmad b. Ḥanbal 50
K. al-Sunna, Abū Dāwūd al-Sijistānī 99
K. al-Sunna, Ḥarb b. Ismāʿīl al-Kirmānī 72, 75, 76
K. al-Sunna, al-Khallāl 41

Ṭabaqāt al-Ḥanābila, Ibn Abī Yaʿlā 7, 11, 38, 39, 44, 50, 59, 62, 63, 76, 193
Ṭabaqāt al-nussāk, Abū Saʿīd Ibn al-Aʿrābī 25
K. al-Tanbīh, Muḥammad b. Nāṣir al-Salāmī 34
al-Tanbīh wa-l-radd ʿalā ahl al-ahwāʾ wa-l-bidaʿ, Muḥammad b. Aḥmad al-Malaṭī 38, 78, 99
Taʾwīl mukhtalif al-ḥadīth, Ibn Qutayba 53

K. al-ʿUdda, Abū Yaʿlā l-Farrāʾ 39
Uṣūl al-sunna, Abū Bakr ʿAbdallāh al-Ḥumaydī 73

al-Walāʾ wa-l-barāʾ fī l-Islām, Muḥammad Saʿīd al-Qaḥṭānī 191
K. al-Waqf, Aḥmad b. Kāmil 18

K. al-Zakāt, transmitted on the authority of ʿUmar b. Ḥayyawayh 41

المسيح الدجّال 13ي
المطر (مع كلّ قطرة ملك) 42
المعصية/المعاصي 21، 128، 148، 150
معصية آدم لربّه 13ط
المكاسب 103
الملائكة 13خ، 50
المناظرة 133، 136، 135، 140
المنسوخ 79
منكر ونكير 13ج، 52
مؤمن بالاسم 28
الميزان 13ب
النصيحة 57
النظر إلى الله (انظر: الرؤية)
النظر في النجوم 96
النفاق/المنافقون 25
النكاح 34، 112
النيّة 13ك
الهجرة 50
الهوامّ والسِّباع 32، (تُقاصصُ يومَ القيامة) 38
الهوى 14 (وانظر: الأهواء)
اليقين 92
يوم الطّور 54
يوم القيامة 36

الصلاة (تقصير الصلاة) 24، (بالسراويل) 24، (خلف كلّ برّ وفاجر) 144، (الصلاة خلف الجهميّ) 104، (على مَن مات من أهل القبلة) 26، 27، (فرض الصلاة) 50، (الصلاة المفروضة) 63، (الصلاة في السفر) 24، (الاقتداء بالإمام) 108
الصلاة على غير الرسول وآله 147
الصُّور 36
الصوم (في السفر) 24
الضلالة 2، 3، 5، 10، 61، 76، 79، 88، 99، 111، 133، 150
الطلاق 34
العتيق (انظر: الدين العتيق)
عذاب الله 46، 52، 69، (بالأغلال والسلاسل) 79ي
عذاب القبر 13ج، 52، (انكار عذاب القبر) 79ي
العرش 11، 31ح، 36، 50، 51
العشرة المبشّرة بالجنّة 147
العصبيّة 94
العقل (مولود) 55
علم الله 11، 13أ، 33، 40، 58
علم الباطن 111
العمل 13ك، 39، 55، 69، 144، 151
الغزو = الجهاد
الغلوّ 91
الغناء 120
الفاجر 15، 46، 52، 57، 128، 144
الفتنة 79، 94
الفرائض 115، 117
الفرقة 58، 71، 79هـ، 85
فضل الله/تفضّل (وتفضيله) 13هـ، 14، 55، 56، 58، 69، 100
الفقهاء 12، 41
الفكرة في الله (انظر: التفكّر)
القائم من آل محمّد 13ي
القبر 52 (وانظر: عذاب القبر)
قتل النفس المؤمنة 35
القدر 40، 49، 53، 120، 144
قدرة الله 71
القرآن 10، 48، 68، 124، 148
القرآن مخلوق (ليس بمخلوق) 12، 75، 79أ
القصاص (يوم القيامة) 38
قضاء الله 39
القلم 36
القياس 9، 71، 74، 77، 83، 133
كتاب الله 134، 139، (ردّ آية من) 28، 79ك
الكرسي 36، 50
الكفر/ كافر/ كفّار/تكفير 4، 12، 25، 30، 33، 54، 56، 60، 61، 71، 74، 77، 78، 79أ، 79ك، 90، 92
الكلام 9، 10، 49، 61، 79، 89، 97، 133
الكلام في الربّ 10
اللجاجة 93
لِمَ وكيف 9، 11، 47، 77ب
اللوح 36
المال 102
المتشابه في القرآن 79ز، 134
متعة النساء 72
المُحدث (المحدثة) 5، 9، 10، 76، 89، 119
المحكّ 93
المحنة/المحن 71، 131
المِراء 9، 12، 61، 133، 136، 142
المرتدّ 35 (وانظر: الردّة)
المرض/المريض 44، 108
المروق من الدين 4
المسح على الخفّين 24

الخصومة 9، 49، 61، 136
الخلق خلق الله 47
الخلافة 14، 15، 17
الخلافة في قُريش 17
الخوف 69، 98
الخير والشرّ 13ب
دار إسلام 26
الدار دار الله 47
الدنيا 19، 26، 30، 45، 56، 69، 71، 85، 94
الدين 3، 4، 19، 56، 57، 61، 71، 74، 77د، 79، 80، 83، 84، 91، 92، 93، 131، 133 (الدين العتيق) 85، (الأمر الأوّل العتيق) 92، (دين الله ودين رسول الله) 92
الذنب/الذنوب/المذنبون 13هـ، 22، 46، 69
الرأي 74، 77د، 83
الربّ 10، 11، 49، 71، 77أ
ربقة الإسلام 1
الرجاء 69
الرجعة 145
الرجم 23
رحمة الله 22، 46
الردّة 129، 130
الرضا 29، 61، (الرضا بقضاء الله) 39
الرفض 120، 146 (وانظر: الرافضة)
الرؤية يوم القيامة 13أ، 60، 135، الرؤية في الدنيا 30
الزكاة 64
الزندقة/الزنادقة 61، 96، 124، 125، 133
الزِّنا 35
السترة/المستور 110، 118، 157
السلطان = الإمام/الأئمّة
السماء السابعة 13ح
السماوات 40، 46، 50، 55
السنّة 1، 3، 4، 5، 9، 19، 48، 68، 71، 79، 81، 82، 83، 84، 86، 87، 92، 111، 128، 131، 143، 147، 148، 151، 152، 154، 155، 156، 157، 158، (علم السنّة) 79، (خصال السنّة) 143
السواد الأعظم 4
السيف 13ب، 106، 109، 120، 125، 144
الشبهة 118
الشراء والبيع 68
الشرائع 67
شرائع الإسلام 26
شفاعة رسول الله 13هـ، 79ي
الشفقة 69، 98
الشكّ/شاكّ 9، 31، 61، 79، 88، 92، 133، (الشكّ في حرف من كتاب الله) 148
شَهادة أنْ لا إله إلّا الله 65، 92
الشهيد/الشهداء 13هـ، 44، 51، 151
الشوق والمحبّة 99
شيطان 7
صاحب بدعة 56، 82، 92، 130، 150
صاحب جماعة 87
صاحب سنّة 87، 88، 104، 115، 117، 121، 122، 132، 143، 144، 148
صاحب هوًى 14، 114، 115، 117، 123، 128، 129، 148
الصالحون 13هـ، 151
الصحابة (انظر: أصحاب محمّد)
الصَّداق 34، 112
الصدّيقون 13هـ، 151، 157
الصِّراط 6.113هـ، 13و
الصِّراط المستقيم 5، 81
الصرف 120
الصفات 11

كِتَابُ شَرْحِ السنَّة

عن أبي عبد الله أحمد بن محمّد بن غالب الباهلي غُلام خليل، رحمه الله،

رواية أبي إسحاق إبراهيم بن عمر بن أحمد البرمكي الفقيه،[1]
إجازةً عن أبي الحسن محمّد بن العبّاس بن أحمد بن الفُرات،[2]
عن رواية أبي بكر أحمد بن كامل بن خلف بن شجرة القاضي.[3]
رواية الشيخ الأجلّ الأمين أبي طالب عبد القادر[4] بن محمّد بن عبد القادر بن محمّد بن يوسف،
عن أبي إسحاق البرمكي،
إجازةً عن ابن الفرات، إجازةً عنه.
رواية الشيخ الأجلّ الثقة أبي الحسين عبد الحقّ[5] بن عبد الخالق[6] بن أحمد بن عبد القادر بن محمّد بن يوسف عنه سماعًا.
[سمع][7] منه الشيخ الإمام الصالح أبو[8] القاسم عبد الله بن حمزة بن أبي طاهر بن سانو، نفعه الله وجميع المسلمين.

---

1 (1053/445–971/361)، الخطيب، **تاريخ بغداد** 63/7، الرقم 3133؛ ابن أبي يعلى، **طبقات** (الفقي) 190/2، الرقم 660، (العثيمين)، 352/3، الرقم 660؛ الذهبي، **سير** 607/17، الرقم 405.

2 (ت 931/319–994/384)، الخطيب، **تاريخ بغداد** 207/4، الرقم 1406؛ الصفدي، **الوافي** 196/3؛ الذهبي، **العبر** 167/1.

3 (961/350–873/260)، ابن النديم، **الفهرست** 39، 292؛ الخطيب، **تاريخ بغداد** 587/5، الرقم 2477؛ ياقوت، **معجم الأدباء** 421/1، الرقم 133؛ الصفدي، **الوافي** 299/7؛ ابن أبي الوفا، **الجواهر المضيّة** 238/1، الرقم 168.

4 (بعد 1038/430–1122/516)، ابن الجوزي، **المنتظم** 211/17؛ ابن نقطة، **التكملة** 308/6؛ الذهبي، **سير** 386/19، الرقم 228.

5 (1100/494–1179/575)، ابن الدبيثي، **ذيل**، 219/4، الرقم 2028 (وذكر أنّه سمع من ابن عمّ أبيه، أبي طالب عبد القادر بن محمّد بن يوسف)؛ ابن الجوزي، **المشيخة** 186–187، الرقم 79؛ الذهبي، **سير** 552/20، الرقم 353.

6 (1071/464–1153/548)؛ الذهبي، **سير** 279/20، الرقم 187.

7 غير واضحة في الأصل.

8 في الأصل: "أبي".

 | DOI:10.1163/9789004429055_013

بسم الله الرحمن الرحيم

ب 1 أخبرنا[9] الشيخ الإمام الثّقة أبو[10] الحسين عبد الحقّ بن عبد الخالق قراءةً، أخبركم[11] أبو[12] طالب عبد القادر بن محمّد بن عبد القادر بن يوسف بالمسجد الجامع ونحن نسمع،[13] قيل له: أخبركم الشيخ أبو إسحاق إ براهيم بن عمر بن أحمد البرمكي، فيما أذن لكم في روايته عنه، وأجازه لكم ما عُرف بذلك وقال نعم، قال: أنبأ أبو الحسن محمّد بن العبّاس بن أحمد بن الفرات، رحمه الله، في كتابه، ومن كتابه قُرِئ، قال: أخـ[ـبرنا][14] أبو بكر أحمد بن كامل بن خلف بن شجرة القاضي قراءةً عليه، قال: دفع إليّ أبو عبد الله أحمد بن محمّد بن غالب الباهلي هذا الكتاب وقال لي: اروِ[15] عنّي هذا الكتاب من أوّله إلى آخره، قال أبو عبد الله أحمد بن محمّد بن غالب الباهلي رضي الله عنه:

الحمدُ لله الذي هدانا للإسلام ومَنَّ علينا به وأخرجنا في خير أمّةٍ، فنسأله التوفيق لما يُحبُّ ويرضى والحفظَ ممّا يكره ويسخط.

(1) اعلموا أنّ الإسلام هو السنّة والسنّة هي الإسلام، ولا يقوم أحدهما إلّا[16] بالآخر. فمن السنّة لزومُ الجماعة، فمن رغب عن الجماعة وفارقها فقد خلع رِبْقَة الإسلام من عُنُقِه وصار ضالًّا مُضِلًّا.

---

9 في الأصل: "أنا".

10 في الأصل: "أبي".

11 "أخبركم": هذا ما يقوله القارئ (أو المستملي) الذي يقرأ على شيخه نصّ كتاب الشيخ (أو روايات من كتاب شيخه) في جلسة سماع يحضرها مجموعة من طلبة العلم، لأن الشيخ هو من "سمع وحُدّث وأُخبر وأُنبأ" وليس المستملي. وهذه هي الطريقة التي تدوّن في سماعات المجالس. انظر على سبيل المثال: الخطيب البغدادي، **الكفاية** 303–304؛ الخليلي القزويني، **الإرشاد** 849–850.

12 في الأصل: "أبي".

13 في الأصل: "وهويسمع"، ثمّ صحّحها في الهامش الأيمن.

14 في الأصل ما صورته: .

15 في الأصل: "اروي".

16 في الأصل "الا" فوق السطر.

"الإسلام هو السنّة والسنّة هي الإسلام"، انظر الفصل الرابع من الدراسة بالإنكليزية (3.1).

انظر في "خلع ربقة الإسلام"، أبو يوسف، **الخراج** 80–81؛ ابن أبي شيبة، **المصنّف** 242/13، الرقم 38171 (كتاب الفتن)؛ ابن حنبل، **المسند** 406/28، الرقم 17170، 336/29، الرقم 17800، كلاهما عن الحارث الأشعري؛ الترمذي، **الجامع** 149/5، الرقم 2863 (ربقة الإسلام)؛ المباركفوري، **تحفة الأحوذي** 162/8، الرقم 3023؛ ابن أبي عاصم، **السنّة** 154، الرقم 892؛ الدارمي، **المسند** 123، الرقم 103؛ مسلم، **الصحيح** 593/2، الرقم 867 (كتاب الجمعة، باب تخفيف الصلاة)؛ ابن قتيبة، **تأويل مختلف الحديث** 4 (والقاعد يقول..)؛ الخلّال، **السنّة** 87/1؛ الملطي، **التنبيه** 65؛ ابن بطّة، **الشرح والإبانة** 24، 28 (عن عليّ)؛ ابن بطّة، **الإبانة** (الإيمان) 289/1–295 (عن عليّ، وعن غيره)؛ 354، الرقم 234 (عن ابن عبّاس)؛ 389/1؛ الآجرّي، **الشريعة** 286/1؛ اللالكائي، **شرح** 120/1، الرقم 157 (عن الحارث الأشعري).

(2) والأساس الذي بُنِيَ[17] عليه الجماعةُ، وهم | أصحاب محمّد، صلّى الله عليه ورحمهم أجمعين، وهم أهل السنّة والجماعة، فمن لم يأخذ عنهم فقد ضلّ وابتدع، وكلّ بدعة ضلالة والضلالة وأهلها في النار. 2 أ

انظر في "كلّ بدعة ضلالة"، الآجرّي، **شرح السنّة** 205/1؛ ابن أبي زمنين، **أصول السنّة** 43؛ ابن بطّة، **الشرح والإبانة** 23؛ المباركفوري، **تحفة الأحوذي** 440/7، "من جوامع الكلم لا يخرج عنه شيء وهو أصل عظيم من أصول الدين"؛ السجزي، **الرد على من أنكر الحرف** 99–100؛ الشاطبي، **الاعتصام**، 66/1، 46/2–52 (مع شرح للحديث)، 256/2.

(3) وقال عمر بن الخطّاب، رحمه الله، "لا عُذرَ لأحدٍ في ضلالة ركبها حسبها هدىً، ولا في هدىً تركه حسبه ضلالة، فقد بُيِّنَتِ الأمورُ وثبّتتِ الحجّة وانقطع العُذرُ". وذلك أنّ السنّة والجماعة قد أَحكما أمرَ الدّين كلِّه وتبيَّن للناس، فعلى الناس الاتّباع.

انظر في قول عمر بن الخطّاب بسند عن الأوزاعي، الخطيب البغدادي، **الفقيه والمتفقّه** 383/1، الرقم 392؛ ابن بطّة، **الإبانة** (الإيمان) 320/1–321، الرقم 162؛ أبو نُعيم، **حلية** 346/5؛ وهو لعمر بن الخطاب في الرسالة المنسوبة لعمر بن عبد العزيز في الردّ على القدريّة (van Ess, *Anfänge*, 43)؛ قوّام السنّة، **الحجّة** 440/2؛ وهو معزوٌّ إلى عمر بن عبد العزيز في: المروزي، **السنّة** 44، الرقم 97.

"على الناس الاتّباع"، انظر في الاتباع في السنة قول محمد بن يوسف البنّا، قوّام السنّة، **الحجّة** 272/1.

17 في الأصل: "بنيا"، غير معجمة؛ "بنا"، في: *Massignon, Recueil*, 213.

(4) واعلم، رحمك الله، أنّ الذي جاء من قِبلِ الله، تبارك وتعالى، لم يُوضَع على عقول الرجال وآرائهم، وعلمُهُ عند الله وعند رسوله، فلا تتّبع شيئًا بهواك فتمرقَ من الدين فتخرجَ من الإسلام، فإنّه لا حجّةَ لك، فقد بيّن رسولُ الله، صلّى الله عليه وسلّم، لأُمّته السنّة وأوضحها لأصحابه، وهم الجماعة وهم السواد الأعظم، والسواد الأعظم الحقّ وأهله، فمن خالف أصحاب رسول الله، صلّى الله عليه وسلّم، في شيء من أمر الله فقد كفر.[18]

انظر في "فتمرق من الدين"، حديث عليّ بن أبي طالب، وحديث أبي سعيد الخدري، في البخاري، **الجامع** 1714، الرقم 6930 (باب قتال الخوارج)، و7562 (كتاب التوحيد، باب قراءة الفاجر)؛ مسلم، **الصحيح** 739/2، الرقم 1064، و 1066 (كتاب الزكاة، باب ذكر الخوارج)؛ النسائي، **الصحيح** 455/3–456، الرقم 3555، و3551 (كتاب المحارب، من شهر سيفه)؛ أبو نُعيم، **حلية** 83/5؛ وانظر ابن وضّاح، **البدع** 61–62.

انظر في "السواد الأعظم"، نصًّا في الآجرّي، **الشريعة** 302/1، وقارن بـ: 313، 433؛ وورد "السواد الأعظم" في جملة من الأحاديث عن افتراق الأمّة، كما في: أبو حنيفة [جمعه أبو مطيع البلخي]، **الفقه الأبسط** 52–53؛ ابن ماجة، **السنن** 1303/2، الرقم 3950 (كتاب الفتن، باب السواد الأعظم، بسنده عن أنس بن مالك "إن أمّتي لا تجتمع على ضلالة فإذا رأيتم اختلافًا فعليكم بالسواد الأعظم")؛ ابن أبي عاصم، **السنّة** 15، الرقم 80 (عن ابن عمر "ما كان الله ليجمع هذه الأمّة على الضلالة أبدًا، ويد الله على الجماعة، هكذا اتّبعوا السواد الأعظم فإنّ مَن شذّ شذّ في النار")؛ ابن بطّة، **الإبانة** (الإيمان) 288/1 (عن أنس)؛ والداني، **الرسالة الوافية** (في ذم أهل البدع ومذهبهم) 112، الرقم 200، والنصّ مضطرب في كلا المصدرين، وفي: أبو نعيم، **حلية** 37/3 "... أمّتي ويد الله مع الجماعة هكذا"؛ وانظره في اللالكائي، **شرح** 118/1، الرقم 154.

وورد بأحاديث عن أبي أمامة في سياق قصّة طويلة عن الخوارج زمن عبد الملك بن مروان، بصيغ مختلفة تطول وتقصر: ابن أبي شيبة، **المصنّف** 446/13، الرقم 38906 (ما ذكر في الخوارج)؛ المروزي، **السنّة**، 34 (الحديثان 56، 57)؛ ابن أبي عاصم، **السنّة**، 13–14؛ ابن حنبل، **المسند** 392/30، الرقم 18450؛ و96/32، الرقم 19351؛ اللالكائي، **شرح**، 114/1–118، الأرقام 151–154، بأسانيد مختلفة؛ ابن أبي زمنين، **أصول السنّة** 294–295؛ ابن حجر، **المطالب العالية** 494/12–497، الرقم 2974 (كتاب الإيمان والتوحيد، باب افتراق الأمّة).

كما وردت في حديث عن أبي أُمامة بنصّ: "إنّ بني إسرائيل افترقوا على ثنتين وسبعين فرقة وإنّ أمّتي تفترق على ثلاث وسبعين فرقة كلها ضالّ إلّا السواد الأعظم، قالوا يا رسول الله وما السواد الأعظم؟

18 لم ترد هذه الفقرة في **طبقات الحنابلة**.

قال: من لا يماري في دين الله ومن كان على ما أنا عليه اليوم وأصحابي، من لم يمارِ في دين الله ولم يكفّر أحدًا من أهل التوحيد بذنب"، وورد بألفاظ مختلفة في ابن بطّة، **الإبانة** (الإيمان) 1/369–370؛ 373، الرقم 271؛ الملطي، **التنبيه** 10؛ ابن عساكر، **تاريخ دمشق** 52/24، 368/33، 370؛ وقد توسّع الشّاطبي في مسألة حديث الفرقة الناجية، **الاعتصام** 2/189–289.

وانظر في "فمن خالف أصحاب رسول الله"، قوّام السنّة، **الحجّة** 2/440 (عن عمر في سياق حديث "إنّ لا عذر لأحد")، وفيه ".. في شيء من الدين فقد ضلّ".

(5) واعلم أنّ النّاس لم يبتدعوا بدعةً قطُّ حتّى تركوا من السنّة مثلها، فاحذر المُحدَثات من الأمور، فإنّ كلّ محدثةٍ بدعةٌ وكلَّ بدعةٍ ضلالة والضلالةُ وأهلُها | في النار. واحذر صغار المحدَثات من الأمور، ب 2 فإنّ صغير البدع يعود حتّى يصيرَ كبيرًا؛[19] ولذلك كلُّ بدعة أُحدِثت في هذه الأُمّة كان أوّلُها صغيرًا يُشبه الحقَّ، فاغترّ بذلك من دخل فيها ثمّ لم يستطع الخروجَ منها فعظُمت وصارت دينًا يُدان بها، فخالف الصراط[20] المستقيم فخرج من الإسلام.

انظر في "حتّى تركوا من السنّة مثلها"، قولًا للإمام عليّ في الشريف الرضي، **نهج البلاغة**، 202 (الخطبة 145)؛ والكليني، **الكافي** 1/58؛ وقارن بقولِ لحسّان بن عطيّة، ابن وضّاح، **البدع** 44؛ وعن خِلاس بن عمرو 45؛ وقارن بقول لغُضَيْف بن الحارث عن الرسول، صلّى الله عليه وسلّم، **الإبانة** (الإيمان) 1/349، الرقم 224؛ وفي ".. شرّ الأمور محدثاتها"، البخاري، **الجامع** 1797، الرقم 7277 (كتاب الاعتصام بالكتاب والسنّة، باب الاقتداء بسنن رسول الله)؛ مسلم، **الصحيح** 2/593، الرقم 867 (كتاب الجمعة، باب تخفيف الصلاة)؛ النسائي، **السنن** 2/308، الرقم 1799؛ أبو حنيفة [جمعه أبو مطيع البلخي]، **الفقه الأبسط** 53؛ ابن وضّاح، **البدع** 30، 36–37؛ الملطي، **التنبيه** 66؛ ابن بطّة، **الإبانة** (الإيمان) 1/177، الرقم 10؛ 307، الرقم 142، 313، الرقم 148؛ 325–326، 336؛ و(القدر) 2/85، الرقم 1492؛ البغوي، **شرح السنّة** 1/211–212؛ الآجرّي، **الشريعة** 1/398–399؛ أبو نعيم، **حلية** 3/189؛ قوّام السنّة، **الحجّة** 2/428؛ البيهقي، **الاعتقاد** 152. وفي "كلّ بدعة ضلالة"، ابن وضّاح، **البدع** 31.

(6) فانظر، رحمك الله، كلَّ من سمعت كلامه من أهل زمانك، فلا تعجلنَّ ولا تدخُلنّ في شيء حتّى تسألَ وتنظر هل تكلّم به أصحاب رسول الله، صلّى الله عليه وسلّم، فإنْ وجدتَ فيه أثرًا عنهم فتمسّك به ولا تجاوزه بشيء ولا تختر عليه شيئًا فتسقط في النّار.

---

19 **شذرات الذهب** 4/159 "فإنّ صغار البدع تعود حتّى تصير كبارًا".

20 في الأصل: "السراط"، غير أنّه يكتبها بالصاد في ما بعد.

(7) واعلم أنّ الخروج من الطريق على وجهين: أمّا أحدهما فرجلٌ زلَّ عن الطريق وهو لا يريد إلّا الخير، فلا يُقتدى بزَلّته فإنّه هالك،[21] وآخر عانَدَ الحقَّ وخالف من كان قبلَه من المتّقين وهو ضالٌّ مُضِلٌّ، شيطانٌ مَريد[22] في هذه الأمّة، حقيقٌ على من يعرفه أنْ يُحذّر النّاس منه ويبيّنَ للنّاس قصّته لِئلّا يقع أحدٌ في بدعته فيهلك.

انظر في "رجل عاند الحقّ"، الطبري، **تفسير** 184/5 (آل عمران 4/3)؛ ابن عبد البر، **التمهيد** 42/18 "وإنّما الكافر من عاند الحق لا من جهله"؛ 282/23 "ولما وجبت مجاهدة الكفار حتّى يظهر دين الحقّ فكذلك كلّ من عاند الحقّ من أهل الباطل واجب مجاهدته على من قدر عليه حتّى يظهر الحقّ". و"شيطان مَريد"، تعبير قرآني لمن جادل في الله بغير علم (النساء 117/4؛ الحج 3/22).

(8) واعلم، رحمك الله، أنّه لا يتمّ إسلامُ عبدٍ حتّى يكونَ مُتّبِعًا مصدّقًا مُسلّمًا، فمن زعم أنّه بقي شيءٌ من أمر | الإسلام لم يكْفوناه أصحابُ محمّد، صلّى الله عليه وسلّم، فقد كذّبهم، وكفى به فُرقةً[23] وطعنًا عليهم وهو مبتدع ضالٌّ مُضلٌّ مُحدِث في الإسلام ما ليس فيه. 3 أ

(9) واعلم، رحمك الله، أنّه ليس في السنّة قياسٌ، ولا تُضرب لها الأمثال، ولا تُتّبع فيها الأهواء. وهو التصديق بآثار رسول الله، صلّى الله عليه وسلّم، بلا كيف ولا شرح؛ لا يُقال: لما وكيف.

قارن بـ: قوّام السنّة، **الحجّة** 437/2؛ انظر في "ليس في السنّة قياس"، عن أحمد بن حنبل برواية عبدوس "وليس في السنّة قياس ولا تضرب لها الأمثال ولا تدرك بالعقول ولا الأهواء إنّما هي الاتّباع وترك الهوى"؛ اللالكائي، **شرح** 176/1؛ ابن مفلح، **المقصد الأرشد** 281/2؛ وذكر هذا القول الشافعي في **الأمّ** 287/3، في معرض ردّه على من اعترض على مسألة الحجّ عن الميت؛ وعن أبي هريرة "إذا حدّثتك عن رسول الله حديثًا فلا تضرب له الأمثال"، ابن ماجة، **السنن** 10/1، الرقم 22؛ ابن حامد، **تهذيب** 52–53؛ البغوي، **شرح السنّة** 203/1، عن أبي عبيد؛ ابن الجوزي، **مناقب أحمد** 286/1، 306، 316.

---

21 في الأصل "يُقيدا"، بألف طويلة رغم أنّ الناسخ يكتب الألف المقصورة في مواضعها. **طبقات** (الفقي) 19/2، (العثيمين) 38/3 "فإنّه لا يقتدى بزلله فإنّه هالك".

22 "مريد"، ليست في **طبقات الحنابلة**.

23 "مزقة"، في: *Massignon, Recueil*, 213.

وانظر في "لا يقال لما وكيف"، اعتقاد عليّ ابن المديني في اللالكائي، **شرح** 186/1؛ ابن أبي حاتم، **العلل** 468/5، الصابوني، **عقيدة السلف** 249؛ واللالكائي، **شرح**558/2، الرقم 875 (عن الأوزاعي وسفيان الثوري ومالك بن أنس والليث بن سعد "أمرّوها كما جاءت بلا كيف")؛ وانظر المروزي، **تعظيم قدر الصلاة** 494، الرقم 535 (وليس فيه "بلا كيف")؛ وعن أحمد "بلا كيف ولا حدّ"، اللالكائي، **شرح** 176/1 (اعتقاد عبدوس)، 502، الرقم 777؛ وانظر القول المنسوب إلى مالك بن أنس حول "الكيف والاستواء"، الدارمي، **الردّ على الجهميّة** 55، الرقم 104؛ الدارقطني، **الصفات** 59، 60؛ اللالكائي، **شرح**582/2، الرقم 930؛ ابن الجوزي، **مناقب أحمد** 316/1؛ وما يلي الرقم 11، 47، 77ب.

والكلام والخصومة والجدال والمِراء[24] مُحدَث يَقدَح الشكَّ في القلب وإنْ أصاب صاحبُه الحقَّ والسنّة.

انظر في "يقدح الشكّ في القلب"، قول منسوب إلى عليّ بن أبي طالب لكُميل بن زياد في اليعقوبي، **تاريخ** 243/2؛ وعن أحمد بن حنبل "من أحبّ الكلام لم يفلح لأنّه يؤول أمرهم إلى حيرة؛ عليكم بالسنّة والحديث وإيّاكم والخوض في الجدال والمراء. أدركنا الناس وما يعرفون هذا الكلام"، الذهبي، **سير** 291/11؛ وقال مالك "المراء في العلم يقسّي القلب"، الهروي، **ذمّ الكلام** 287/4 (عن الشافعي).

وفي النهي عن المماراة والخصومة، الدارمي، **المسند**، 174–175 (باب اجتناب أهل الأهواء)؛ ابن عساكر، **تاريخ** 367/33–368؛ ابن أبي زيد، **الرسالة** 22؛ ابن بطّة، **الشرح والإبانة** 66؛ ابن بطّة، **الإبانة** (الإيمان) 533/1 (عن ابن الماجشون)، 522/2–531؛ الآجرّي، **الشريعة** 429/1–435؛ وانظر نهي أحمد بن حنبل عن الجدال والخصومة، الخلّال، **السنّة** 23/4، 132/5؛ عياض، **ترتيب** 39/2 (عن مالك بن أنس)؛ قوّام السنّة، **الحجّة** 280/1 (عن الحسن "إياكم والمنازعة، إيّاكم والخصومة، يعني في الدين")؛ وسوف يتكرّر النهي عن الجدال والخصومة والمراء في السنّة والقرآن والصفات في أكثر من موضع من هذا الكتاب.

(10) واعلم، رحمك الله، أنّ الكلام في الربِّ مُحدث وهو بدعة وضلالة، ولا يُتكلّمُ في الربّ إلّا بما[25] وصف به نفسه في القرآن، وما بيّن رسولُ الله، صلّى الله عليه وسلّم، لأصحابه.

قارن بـ: قوّام السنّة، **الحجّة** 432/2؛ ابن بطّة، **الإبانة** (المختار) 326/3؛ ونقله الذهبي عن البربهاري، **العلوّ** 222–223؛ ونقل طرفًا منه مع كلام من مواضع أخرى، **سير** 91/15؛ وانظر ما نقله المروزي بسنده عن

24 في الأصل: "والمرى".

25 الذهبي، **تاريخ** 522/7، **العلوّ** 223: "... محدث وبدعة وضلالة، فلا نتكلّم في الربّ إلّا بما...".

أحمد بن حنبل في: ابن قدامة المقدسي، **ذمّ التأويل** 20، الرقم 33 "... لا يوصف الله تعالى بأكثر ممّا وصف به نفسه أو وصفه به رسوله بلا حدّ ولا غاية ..."؛ ابن قدامة، **لمعة الاعتقاد** 6؛ السفاريني، **لوامع** 24/1.

(11) وهو، جلّ ثناؤه، واحدٌ ﴿ليس كمِثْلِه شيءٌ وهوَ السَّميعُ البَصيرُ﴾ (الشورى 11/42)، ربُّنا أوّلٌ بلا متى، وآخِرٌ بلا مُنتهى، ﴿يَعلَمُ السِرَّ وأَخْفَى﴾ (طه 7/20)، وعلى[26] عرشه استوى، وعلمُه بكلِّ مكان لا يخلو من علمه مكان، ولا يقول في صفات الربّ كيف ولِمَ إلّا شاكٌّ في الله.

انظر في موقف أهل السنّة من الاستواء والصفات، الدارمي، **الردّ على الجهميّة** 13–14، 26–42؛ حرب الكرماني، **كتاب السنّة** 193–195؛ البغوي، **شرح السنّة** 168/1–171؛ ابن قدامة، **إثبات صفة العلوّ**؛ والذهبي، **العلوّ**، حيث أوردا أقوال التابعين وعلماء أهل السنّة في مسألة العلوّ والاستواء؛ القرطبي، **الإعلام** 444 "لا يتوجّه عليه متى، ولا أين، ولا لِمَ، ولا كيف"؛ وانظر في "لا يُقال لِمَ وكيفَ"، ابن بطّة، **الشرح والإبانة** 56؛ الجيلاني، **الغنية** 125/1؛ **الحجّة** 232/1 (من اعتقاد معمر بن أحمد)؛ وما تقدّم الرقم 9، وما يلي الرقم 47، 77ب.

(12) والقرآن كلام الله وتنـزيله ونوره، وليس بمخلوق لأنّ القرآن من الله وما كان من الله فليس بمخلوق، وهكذا قال مالك بن أنس وأحمد بن حنبل والفقهاء قبلهما وبعدهما،[27] والمِراء فيه كُفر.

قارن بـ: البخاري، **خلق أفعال العباد** 7–10؛ حرب الكرماني، **كتاب السنّة** 52، 201–209؛ عبد الله بن أحمد بن حنبل، **كتاب السنّة** 156، عن مالك؛ 155–157 عن ابن المبارك "القرآن كلام الله ليس بخالق ولا مخلوق"، أبو داود، **مسائل الإمام أحمد** 356، الرقم 1712؛ صالح بن أحمد، **سيرة** 71–72؛ وهو في ابن عساكر، **تاريخ** 409/32؛ وعن ابن مهدي "القرآن كلام الله ليس بمخلوق ولا خالق"؛ وعن ابن أبي إدريس "القرآن كلام الله ومن الله وما كان من الله فليس بمخلوق"؛ الدارمي، **الردّ على بشر المرّيسي** 116؛ الأشعري، **الإبانة** 53–61؛ الخلّال، **السنّة** 12/7/3، الرقم 1972، من قول عليّ بن الحسن، 13/7/3، 53–54، الرقم 1980 و2071، من قول جعفر الصادق؛ ابن بطّة، **الإبانة** (الردّ على الجهميّة) 6/2؛ ابن أبي زمنين، **أصول السنّة** 86؛ البغوي، **شرح السنّة** 186/1–187، عن سفيان الثوري وعن جعفر الصادق؛ وقول ابن المبارك وابن مهدي في اللالكائي، **شرح** 281/1، 287؛ وأبو نُعيم، **حلية** 325/6؛ عياض، **ترتيب** 43/2 (عن مالك بن أنس)؛ قوّام السنّة، **الحجّة** 331/1 (عن عليّ)؛ 339/1 (عمرو بن دينار)؛ ابن قدامة، "العقيدة"، 109

---

26 **طبقات** (الفقي) 19/2، (العثيمين) 39/3 "وهو على".

27 **طبقات** (الفقي) 20/2، (العثيمين) 39/3 "مالك بن أنس والفقهاء قبله وبعده".

(عن عليّ وابن عباس)؛ ابن مفلح، **المقصد الأرشد** 25/3 أنّ ابن حنبل قال لمسدّد في كتاب له ".. فإنّه بلغنا عن النبيّ، صلّى الله عليه وسلّم، أنّه قال إنّ الله ليدخل العبد الجنّة بالسنّة يتمسّك بها فأمركم أن لا تؤثروا على القرآن شيئاً فإنّه كلام الله وما تكلّم الله به فليس بمخلوق".

وانظر في "المراء فيه كفر"، ابن حنبل، **المسند** 85/29، الرقم 17542 (من حديث أبي جُهيم)، 355، الرقم 17821 (عمرو بن العاص)؛ صالح بن أحمد، **مسائل الإمام** 249 (رسالة أحمد إلى عبيد الله بن يحيى)؛ وذكره أحمد بن حنبل للخليفة المعتصم، حنبل، **ذكر محنة الإمام** 54؛ وفي رسالته إلى الخليفة المتوكّل، الخلّال، **السنّة** 102/6؛ صالح بن أحمد، **سيرة** 113 (عن أبي هريرة)؛ أبو داود، **السنن** 12/7 (كتاب السنّة)؛ حرب الكرماني، **كتاب السنّة** (الملحق)، 297؛ ابن بطّة، **الشرح والإبانة** 10؛ ابن بطّة، **الإبانة** (الإيمان) 611/2–612، الرقم 750 (عن أبي هريرة)؛ الآجرّي، **الشريعة** 466/1–467، وتعليق الآجرّي 475 وما يلي؛ ابن البنّا، **المختار** 205، الرقم 21 (عن أبي هريرة).

(13)

أ. والإيمان بالرؤية يوم القيامة، يَرَوْن الله بأبصارِ رؤوسهم، وهو مُحاسِبهم[28] | بلا حجاب ولا ترجمان. ب 3

انظر في الرؤية، ابن حنبل، **الردّ على الزنادقة** 259–264؛ الدارمي، **الردّ على بشر المرّيسي** 55–59، 187–188؛ ابن بطّة، **الشرح والإبانة** 54؛ الجيلاني، **الغنية** 123/1.

وفي "بلا حجاب ولا ترجمان"، المحاسبي، **التوهّم** 19؛ عن ابن حنبل في ابن الجوزي، مناقب أحمد 318/1 (مسدّد بن مسرهد)؛ الحافظ العدني، **الإيمان** 82، الرقم 16، 89، الرقم 24؛ البخاري، **الجامع** 343، الرقم 1413 (كتاب الزكاة، باب الصدقة)، 885، الرقم 3595 (كتاب المناقب)، 1624، الرقم 6539 (كتاب التوحيد، باب من نوقش الحساب)؛ السمرقندي، **السواد الأعظم**، الرقم 23؛ ابن بطّال، **شرح** 466/10–467؛ مسلم، **الصحيح** 703/2، الرقم 1016 (كتاب الزكاة، باب الحثّ على الصدقة)؛ عبد الله بن أحمد بن حنبل، **السنّة** 256؛ الطبري، **التبصير** 147–148؛ الأشعري، **الإبانة** 59؛ الطحاوي، **العقيدة** 26؛ ابن أبي العز، **شرح العقيدة** 208–211؛ ابن بطّة، **الإبانة** (الرد على الجهمية) 17/2/3–20؛ ابن أبي زمنين، **أصول السنّة** 119؛ الخلال، **السنّة** 81/6/3؛ الآجرّي، **التصديق بالنظر** 95–97؛ ابن خزيمة، **التوحيد** 167–190؛ الطبري، **تفسير** 67/10 (تفسير الأعراف 7/8)؛ الإسماعيلي، **اعتقاد** 174، الرقم 24؛ اللالكائي، **شرح** 372/1، الرقم 553؛ عياض، **ترتيب** 42/2؛ البيهقي، **شعب الإيمان** 418/1؛ قوّام السنّة، **الحجّة** 124/1، 357، 406/2.

---

28 **طبقات** (الفقي) 20/2، (العثيمين) 40/3 "يحاسبهم".

ب. والإيمان بالميزان يوم القيامة يوزن فيه الخير والشر، له كفّتان ولسان.

انظر الطبري، **تفسير** 69/10 (سورة الأعراف 8/7)؛ السيوطي، **الدرّ المنثور** 322/6؛ حرب الكرماني، **كتاب السنّة** 168 "له لسان وكفّتان"؛ الأشعري، **مقالات** 472؛ البيهقي، **شعب الإيمان** 447/1؛ الغزالي، **قواعد العقائد** 23؛ ابن قدامة المقدسي، **لمعة الاعتقاد** 33؛ و"العقيدة"، 110؛ السفاريني، **لوامع الأنوار** 184/2–185؛ ابن أبي زمنين، **أصول السنّة** 166؛ ابن قدامة، "العقيدة"، 110؛ ابن حجر العسقلاني، **فتح الباري** 538/13 "قال أبو إسحاق الزجّاج: أجمع أهل السنّة على الإيمان بالميزان وأنّ أعمال العباد توزن يوم القيامة وأنّ الميزان له لسان وكفّتان ويميل بالأعمال"، ولم نجده في الزجّاج، **معاني القرآن** 319/2 (الأعراف 7/8)، 396/4 (الشورى 17/42)، 95/5–96 (الرحمن 7/55).

ج. والإيمان بعذاب القبر ومُنكر ونكير.

انظر في مسألة عذاب القبر، **وصيّة أبي حنيفة** 637؛ ابن هانئ النيسابوري، **مسائل الإمام أحمد** 156/2؛ ابن أبي يعلى، **طبقات** (الفقي) 55/1 (أبو عبيد القاسم بن سلام عن أحمد)، 62/1 (المرّوذي عن أحمد)، 174/1 (البرمكي في كتاب **المجموع عن أحمد**)؛ البخاري، **الجامع** 322، الرقم 1338 (كتاب الجنائز، باب الميّت يسمع خفق النعال)، 332، الرقم 1374 (كتاب الجنائز، باب التعوّذ من عذاب القبر)؛ الترمذي، **الجامع** 374/3، الرقم 1071 (باب ما جاء في عذاب القبر)؛ السمرقندي، **السواد الأعظم**، الرقم 14؛ السرخسي، **شرح السير** 8/1 "عذاب القبر حقّ"؛ ابن أبي عاصم، **السنّة** 149–152 (باب في القبر وعذاب القبر)؛ أبو حنيفة [جمعه أبو مطيع البلخي]، **الفقه الأبسط** 56؛ حرب الكرماني، **كتاب السنّة** 46–47؛ الأشعري، **مقالات** 296؛ **الإبانة** 23؛ الطبري، **التبصير** 212–214؛ الطحاوي، **العقيدة** 50؛ ابن أبي العز، **شرح العقيدة** 572/2؛ الآجرّي، **الشريعة** 1288/3–1300 (باب ذكر الإيمان والتصديق بمسألة منكر ونكير)؛ الإسماعيلي، **اعتقاد** 177، الرقم 38 و 39؛ الملطي، **التنبيه** 94؛ ابن بطّة، **الشرح والإبانة** 53؛ ابن أبي زمنين، **أصول السنّة** 151، 157 (عذاب القبر)؛ ابن شاهين، **شرح** (اعتقاد ابن شاهين في آخر الكتاب) 320؛ اللالكائي، **شرح**1206/3، الرقم 2139؛ قوّام السنّة، **الحجّة** 450/1–452، 476، 93/2–95؛ المتولّي، **المغني** 56؛ ابن عبد البر، **التمهيد** 247/22؛ ابن أبي يعلى، **الاعتقاد** 32؛ البيهقي، **الاعتقاد** 145–150 (باب الإيمان بعذاب القبر)؛ البيهقي، **إثبات عذاب القبر**33–47؛ ابن قدامة، "العقيدة"، 110؛ القرطبي، **التذكرة** 180/1؛ وانظر:

Günther, "As the angels stretch out their hands," 35–38.

د. والإيمان بحوض رسول الله، صلّى الله عليه وسلّم، ولكلِّ نبيٍّ حوض إلّا صالح[ـًا]،[29] عليه السّلام، فإنّ حوضَه ضَرعُ ناقته.

انظر في الحوض، البخاري، **الجامع** 1631، الأرقام 6575–6593 (كتاب الرقائق، باب في الحوض)؛ ابن حجر، فتح الباري 369/11–467؛ مسلم، **الصحيح** 1792/2–1801، الأرقام 2289–2305 (كتاب الفضائل، باب إثبات حوض نبيّنا)؛ الترمذي، **الجامع** 628/4–630، الأرقام 2442–2445 (كتاب صفة القيامة، باب الحوض)؛ ابن أبي عاصم، **السنّة** 123–128؛ الطحاوي، **العقيدة** 30؛ ابن أبي العز، **شرح العقيدة** 277–282؛ ابن بطّة، **الشرح والإبانة** 54؛ ابن أبي زمنين، **السنّة** 157–161؛ اللالكائي، **شرح**3/1188–1198؛ الصابوني، **عقيدة السلف** 263؛ الجيلاني، **الغنية** 150/1.

وانظر في حوض صالح، القرطبي، **التذكرة** 413/1 "قال البكري المعروف بابن الواسطي لكلّ نبيّ حوض إلّا صالحاً فإنّ حوضه ضرع ناقته" وعنه المناوي، **فيض القدير** 516/2؛ وانظر حديثًا في هذا المعنى لعبد الكريم بن كيسان في العُقيلي، **الضعفاء** 64/3–65.

هـ. والإيمان بشفاعة رسول الله، صلّى الله عليه وسلّم، للمُذنبين الخاطئين في[30] القيامة، وعلى الصراط، ويُخرجهم من جوف جهنّم. وما من نبيٍّ إلّا له شفاعة، وكذلك الصدّيقين والشهداء والصالحين،[31] ولله بعد ذلك تفضُّلٌ كبير فيمن يشاء. والخروج من النار بعدما احترقوا وصاروا فحمًا.

روى غلام خليل قال حدثنا دينار بن عبد الله عن أنس بن مالك، رضي الله عنه، قال قال رسول الله، صلّى الله عليه وسلّم: "والذي بعثني بالحقّ نبيًّا لأشفعنّ يوم القيامة حتّى أشفع لمن كان في قلبه مثل جناح بعوضة من الإيمان"، الحكيم السمرقندي، **السواد الأعظم**، الرقم 16.

وانظر في "الشفاعة"، البخاري، **الجامع** 1573، الأرقام 6304–6305 (كتاب الدعوات، باب لكلّ نبيّ دعوة مستجابة)؛ الطبري، **تفسير** (البقرة 48/2).

وانظر في شفاعة الشهداء، أبو داود، **السنن** 176/4، الرقم 2522 (كتاب الجهاد، باب في الشهيد يشفع)؛ حنبل بن إسحاق، **الفتن** 162؛ ابن أبي عاصم، **السنّة** 149، الرقم 863؛ البيهقي، **السنن الكبرى**، 539/18، الرقم 18567 (كتاب السير، باب الشهيد يشفع)؛ الذهبي، **إثبات الشفاعة** 33 (حديث أبي بكرة الثقفي).

---

29 في الأصل "صالح"، وكذلك في **طبقات** (الفقي) 20/2، (العثيمين) 40/3.

30 **طبقات** (الفقي) 20/2، (العثيمين) 40/3 "يوم".

31 **طبقات** (الفقي) 20/2، (العثيمين) 40/3 "الصديقون والشهداء والصالحون".

وفي شفاعة الصدّيقين، حديث أبي بكر في الشفاعة، ابن حنبل، **المسند** 193/1–196، الرقم 15؛ الذهبي، **إثبات الشفاعة** 29–30.

وانظر في "الخروج من النار بعدما احترقوا"، مسلم، **الصحيح** 172/1، الرقم 306 (كتاب الإيمان، باب إثبات الشفاعة وإخراج الموحّدين من النار)؛ ابن حنبل، **المسند** 30/18 (الرقم 11441) "حدّثنا عبد الله حدّثني أبي ثنا وكيع حدّثني إسماعيل بن مسلم ثنا أبو المتوكّل عن أبي سعيد عن النبيّ، صلّى الله عليه وسلّم، قال ثمّ يخرج الناس من النار بعدما احترقوا وصاروا فحمًا فيدخلون الجنّة فينبتون فيها كما ينبت الغثاء في حَميل السَّيل"؛ المروزي، **تعظيم قدر الصلاة** 277 (حديث الرقاشي في المعراج)؛ حرب الكرماني، **كتاب السنّة** 47–48؛ ابن خزيمة، **التوحيد** 324؛ ابن أبي عاصم، **السنّة** 145؛ الأشعري، **مقالات** 294، **الإبانة** 15؛ الطحاوي، **العقيدة** 30؛ ابن أبي العز، **شرح العقيدة** 282 وما بعدها؛ الملطي، **التنبيه** 101–102؛ ابن مندة، **الإيمان** 813/2–814، الرقم 836؛ ابن أبي زمنين، **أصول السنّة** 180؛ اللالكائي، **شرح** 1163/3–1165، الأرقام 2048–2050؛ الجيلاني، **الغنية** 148/1؛ ابن الجوزي، **مناقب أحمد** 306/1، 320؛ الذهبي، **إثبات الشفاعة** 27، 35.؛ وقارن بردّ للقاضي عبد الجبّار، **شرح** 672.

و. والإيمان بالصراط على جهنّم، يأخذ الصراطُ من شاء الله، ويجوز من شاء الله، ويسقط في جهنّم من شاء الله، ولهم أنوارٌ على قدر إيمانهم.

انظر في الصراط حديث جابر بن عبد الله وفيه "وعلى جسر جهنّم كلاليب وحسك تأخذ من شاء الله"، مسلم، **الصحيح** 177/1–178، الرقم 191 (كتاب الإيمان، باب أدنى أهل الجنّة منزلةً فيها)؛ وحديث عائشة وفيه "ولجهنّم جسر أدقّ من الشعر وأحدّ من السيف عليه كلاليب وحسك يأخذون من شاء الله"، ابن حنبل، **المسند** 302/41، الرقم 24793؛ وحديث أبي سعيد الخدري، ابن المبارك، **الزهد** 448، الرقم 1268؛ ابن حنبل، **المسند** 141/17، الرقم 11081؛ المروزي، **تعظيم قدر الصلاة** 286–287؛ السمرقندي، **السواد الأعظم**، الرقم 21؛ الطحاوي، **العقيدة** 51؛ ابن أبي العز، **شرح العقيدة** 604–606؛ الملطي، **التنبيه** 84؛ ابن أبي زمنين، **أصول السنة** 168–170؛ قوّام السنّة، **الحجّة** 459/1؛ الجيلاني، **الغنية** 149/1؛ ابن حمدان، **نهاية المبتدئين** 56.

انظر في "ولهم أنوارٌ على قدر إيمانهم"، سورة الحديد 12/57–15؛ مسلم، **الصحيح** 177/1، الرقم 191؛ الطبري، **تفسير** 398/22–399؛ "ويعطون النور يومئذ على قدر أعمالهم وإيمانهم"؛ الحاكم، **المستدرك** 632/4، الرقم 8751، من حديث طويل عن أبي عبيدة عن مسروق عن عبد الله بن مسعود في كتاب الأهوال، وفيه ".. فيعطون نورهم على قدر أعمالهم".

ز. والإيمان بالأنبياء والملائكة.

انظر سورة البقرة2/285؛ الطحاوي، **العقيدة** 38؛ ابن أبي العز، **شرح العقيدة** 401؛ وقارن بـ: ابن بطّة، **الشرح والإبانة** 55؛ أبو يعلى الحنبلي، **مسائل الإيمان** 190–191 (نقلًا عن جزءٍ لأبي حفص ابن شاهين).

ح. والإيمان بأنّ الجنّة حقٌّ والنارَ حقٌّ، والجنّة والنار مخلوقتان،[32] الجنّة في السماء السابعة وسقفها العرش، والنار تحت [الـ]أرض السابعة السفلى وهما مخلوقتان. قد علم الله عدد أهل الجنّة ومن يدخلها وعدد أهل النار ومن يدخلها، لا تفنيان[33] أبدًا، هما مع بقاء الله،[34] تبارك وتعالى، أبد الآبدين ودهر الداهرين.

قارن بـ: قوّام السنّة، **الحجّة** 2/433؛ "الجنّة حقّ والنار حقّ"، انظر حديث عبادة بن الصامت، البخاري، **الجامع**851، الرقم 3435 (كتاب أحاديث الأنبياء)؛ أبو حنيفة [جمعه أبو مطيع البلخي]، **الفقه الأبسط** 56؛ **وصية أبي حنيفة** 54؛ حرب الكرماني، **كتاب السنّة** 48؛ الأشعري، **مقالات** 290، 296؛ **الإبانة** 23؛ ابن بطّة، **الإبانة** (الإيمان) 2/557 ؛ ابن أبي زيد، **الرسالة** 19؛ اللالكائي، **شرح** 1/197 (اعتقاد الرازيّين)؛ وابن حزم، **الدرّة** 206؛ ابن أبي يعلى، **الاعتقاد** 34؛ ابن حجر، **المطالب العالية** 14/148 (حديث أنس).

وفي "الجنّة والنار مخلوقتان"، ابن حنبل، **المسائل والرسائل** 2/225؛ السمرقندي، **السواد الأعظم**، الرقم 22؛ الأشعري، **مقالات** 475؛ الطحاوي، **العقيدة** 51؛ ابن أبي العزّ، **شرح العقيدة** 614–624؛ ابن أبي زمنين، **السنّة** 132؛ أبو يعلى الحنبلي، **المعتمد** 180؛ اللالكائي، **شرح** 1/199 (اعتقاد الرازيّين)؛ 3/1256؛ ابن حزم، **الفصل**، 4/68؛ الجيلاني، **الغنية** 1/154؛ ابن الجوزي، **مناقب أحمد** 1/322 (اعتقاد عبدوس عن أحمد)؛ ابن القيّم، **مفتاح** 45، "فإنّه قد اتّفق أهل السنّة والجماعة على أنّ الجنّة والنار مخلوقتان". انظر مسألة "الجنّة في السماء السابعة"، ابن القيّم، **حادي الأرواح** 81–84. انظر في "وسقفها العرش"، البخاري، **الجامع**1832، الرقم 7423، (كتاب التوحيد باب وكان عرشه على الماء). وفي "العرش سقف الجنّة"، ابن حنبل، **الردّ على الزنادقة** 327؛ وانظر في "النار تحت الأرض"، البيهقي، **البعث والنشور**265، الرقم 455.

وفي "لا تفنيان"، أبو حنيفة [جمعه أبو مطيع البلخي]، **الفقه الأبسط** 56؛ النسفي، **بحر الكلام** 219؛ "الجنّة والنار لا تفنيان"، الآجرّي، **الشريعة** 3/1343؛ القرطبي، **التذكرة** 1/240؛ وانظر:

Demichelis, "Fanā' al-Nār," 392–394; and Hoover, "Islamic Universalism".

---

32 **طبقات** (الفقي) 2/20، (العثيمين) 3/40 "والإيمان بالجنّة والنار أنّهما مخلوقتان".

33 **طبقات** (الفقي) 2/20، (العثيمين) 3/41 "يفنيان".

34 **طبقات** (الفقي) 2/20، (العثيمين) 3/41 "بقاؤهما مع بقاء الله".

وفي "أبد الآبدين ودهر الداهرين"، ورد التعبير في حديث عن "حملة العرش" يرويه أبو الشيخ بسند عن عبد الله بن سلم عن أحمد بن محمد بن غالب، وهو على الأرجح غلام خليل، انظر: أبو الشيخ، **كتاب العظمة** 755/1؛ وانظر ابن عبد ربّه، **العقد** 77/3؛ وعبد الجبّار، **شرح** 650، 666؛ ابن منظور، **لسان العرب** 68/3 (أبد).

ط. وآدم كان في الجنّة الباقية المخلوقة فأُخرِج منها بعد ما عصى الله.

سورة البقرة 35/2؛ وفي ابن عطيّة **المحرّر الوجيز** 338/1 (البقرة 253/2) "وقد تأوّل بعض الناس أنّ تكليم آدم كان في الجنّة"، والقرطبي، 264/3؛ ابن تيمية، **الفتاوى** 347/4؛ وقد ناقش ابن القيم المسألة بالتفصيل، **مفتاح** 49–87.

4أ ي. والإيمان بالمسيح الدجّال، وبنزول[35] عيسى بن مريم، ينزلُ فيقتل الدجّال | ويتزوّج ويصلّي خلف القائم من آل محمّد، صلّى الله عليه وسلّم، ويموت ويدفنه المسلمون.

انظر في زواج عيسى بن مريم عند نزوله، ابن حمّاد، **الفتن** 578، الرقم 1616؛ ابن الجوزي، **المنتظم** 39/2؛ السهروردي، **عوارف** 237/1؛ ابن حجر، **الإصابة** 596/7، الرقم 6179 (ترجمة عيسى بن مريم)؛ السيوطي، **نزول عيسى بن مريم** 85؛ السفاريني، **لوامع** 98/2.

ولم يُعرف عن "أهل السنّة والجماعة" قول في القائم، وعند بعض أهل الشام القول بالقائم من آل أبي سفيان، ابن عساكر، **تاريخ** 31/43؛ وقد قال العباسيون بـ"القائم"، **أخبار الدولة العباسيّة**، 51، 52، 199، 200، 238، 288، 317؛ وانظر:

Al-Dūrī, "al-Fikra al-mahdiyya," 124, 127, 128; Madelung, "New Documents," 343.

ك. والإيمان بأنّ الإيمان قولٌ وعملٌ، وعملٌ وقولٌ ونيّةٌ وإصابة، يزيد وينقص؛ يزيد ما شاء الله، وينقص حتّى لا يبقى منه شيء.

الكوسج، **مسائل الإمام أحمد** 4748/9، 4847؛ عبد الله بن أحمد بن حنبل، **السنّة** 314–318؛ صالح بن أحمد، **سيرة** 80؛ حرب الكرماني، **كتاب السنّة** 36؛ ابن أبي زمنين، **السنّة** 207، وفيه "إصابة السنّة"؛ وتوسّع الآجرّي في المسألة، **الشريعة** 580/2–643؛ كما ناقشها الحليمي بتفصيل، **المنهاج** 55/1–127. وانظر

---

35 **طبقات** (الفقي) 20/2، (العثيمين) 41/3 "الإيمان بنزول".

الحميدي، **المسند** (أصول السنّة) 547 (عن سفيان بن عيينة)؛ أبو عبيد القاسم، **الإيمان** 58 وما بعدها، 72–74؛ ابن أبي شيبة، **الإيمان** 35، 46؛ الحافظ العدني، **الإيمان** 94، الرقم 28 (عن سفيان بن عيينة)؛ حرب الكرماني، **كتاب السنّة** 35، 74–81، 152 (عن يوسف بن أسباط)؛ الطبري، **التبصير** 194–199؛ الأشعري، **الإبانة** 21؛ الملطي، **التنبيه** 116 (عن ابن عباس)؛ الإسماعيلي، **اعتقاد** 175، الرقم 25؛ ابن أبي زيد، **الرسالة** 21؛ ابن بطّة، **الإبانة** (الإيمان) 811/2–826 (وأورد قائمة عن أبي عبيد القاسم بن سلام في تسمية من كان يقول بهذا القول مرتّبة على الأمصار)، 844–852؛ الخلّال، **السنّة** 566/3 (ابن حنبل)، 580 (عبد الرحمن بن مهدي)؛ الأشعري، **مقالات** 293؛ ابن خفيف، **المعتقد** 355؛ وانظر تعليل أبي يعلى الحنبلي لمسألة الزيادة والنقصان، **مسائل الإيمان** 252–274، 395–408؛ البيهقي، **شعب الإيمان** 153/1–154؛ اللالكائي، **شرح** 179/1 (اعتقاد ابن حنبل)، 187/1 (اعتقاد ابن المديني)، 198/1 (اعتقاد الرازيّين)؛ ابن أبي زمنين، **أصول السنّة** 211؛ قوّام السنّة، **الحجّة** 406/1؛ 154/2 (هشام بن عمّار)؛ ابن عبد البر، **التمهيد** 252/9–254 (الأقوال عن مالك)؛ عياض، **ترتيب** 43/2 (مالك بن أنس)؛ أبو نُعيم، **حلية** 29/7 (سفيان الثوري)، 218 (مسعر)؛ البغوي، **شرح السنّة** 39/1، 41؛ ابن أبي يعلى، **الاعتقاد** 23؛ ابن قدامة، "العقيدة"، 109؛ الذهبي، **ميزانالاعتدال** 144/4 ، الرقم 8658 (معروف بن عبد الله)؛ وانظر قول الجُنيد، الكلاباذي، **التعرّف** 80.

(14) وخيرُ هذه الأُمّة بعد وفاة نبيّها: أبو بكر وعمر وعثمان،[36] هكذا رُوي لنا عن ابن عمر قال: "كنّا نقول ورسول الله، صلّى الله عليه وسلّم، بين أظهرنا إنّ خير النّاس بعد رسول الله، صلّى الله عليه وسلّم، أبو بكر وعمر وعثمان، ويسمع النبيّ، صلّى الله عليه وسلّم، بذلك فلا ينكره".

انظر في قول ابن عمر، ابن شاهين، **شرح** 312–313؛ أبو يعلى الموصلي، **المسند** 456/9، الرقم 5604؛ الطبراني، **الكبير** 285/12، الرقم 13132؛ ابن أبي يعلى، **طبقات** (الفقي) 313/1 (.. فيبلغ ذلك النبي...)؛ ابن عساكر، **تاريخ** 345/30، 346؛ الهيثمي، **مجمع الزوائد** 2/9، الرقم 14385؛ وبغير هذا اللفظ من دون ذكر "ويسمع النبي ..." في ابن هانئ، **مسائل** 170/2؛ البخاري، **الجامع** 899، الرقم 3655 (فضائل الصحابة، باب فضل أبي بكر بعد النبي)؛ الترمذي، **الجامع** 629/5، الرقم 3707؛ أبو داود، **السنن** 31/7، الرقم 4628؛ حرب الكرماني، **كتاب السنّة** 257–258؛ الخلّال، **السنّة** 398/2؛ ابن أبي زمنين، **أصول السنّة** 271؛ قوّام السنّة، **الحجّة** 347/2 (بلفظ مختلف).

---

36 **طبقات** (الفقي) 21/2، (العثيمين) 41/3.

ثمّ أفضل النّاس بعد هؤلاء عليٌّ،[37] وطلحة، والزُبير، وسعد وسعيد، وعبد الرحمن بن عوف، وكلّهم يصلح للخلافة.[38]

قارن بـ: أبو داود، **السنن** 44/7–45 (كتاب السنّة، باب في الخلفاء)؛ وبقول ابن المديني في اللالكائي، **شرح** 187/1؛ والواشحي في: الخلّال، **السنّة** 368/1 (وليس فيه "وكلّهم يصلح للخلافة"). "سعد وسعيد"، هما سعد بن أبي وقّاص (ابن عبد البرّ، **الاستيعاب** 606/2، الرقم 963)؛ وسعيد بن زيد بن نُفيل (**الاستيعاب** 614/2، الرقم 982)؛ الجيلاني، **الغنية** 157/1–158؛ ابن الجوزي، **مناقب أحمد** 296/1؛ ابن قدامة، "العقيدة"، 111؛ وترد أسماؤهم في حديث العشرة المبشّرة بالجنّة عند الترمذي، **الجامع** 647/5، الرقم 3747 (مع اسم أبي عبيدة بن الجرّاح، وفي رواية لا يرد اسم ابن عوف).

ثمّ أفضلُ النّاس بعد هؤلاء أصحابُ رسول الله، صلّى الله عليه وسلّم، القرنُ الأوّل الذين بُعث فيهم المهاجرون الأوّلون والأنصار، وهم من صلّى القِبلتين.[39]

انظر في تعبير "القرن"، الطبري، **تفسير** 213/3 (آل عمران 19/3)؛ الطبري، **صريح السنة** 31؛ وحديث عمران بن الحصين في البخاري، **الجامع** (كتاب فضائل الصحابة، باب فضائل أصحاب النبيّ، صلّى الله عليه وسلّم)؛ ومسلم، **الصحيح** (باب فضل الصحابة ثمّ الذين يلونهم ثمّ الذين يلونهم)؛ وابن حجر، **فتح الباري** 5/7–8.

"من صلّى القبلتين"، انظر الطبري، **تفسير** 638/11–640 (التوبة 100/9)؛ أبو نعيم، **معرفة الصحابة** 7/1–8؛ ابن عبد البرّ، **الاستيعاب** 2/1–3.

ثمّ أفضل النّاس بعد هؤلاء مَن صَحِبَ رسول الله، صلّى الله عليه وسلّم، يومًا أو شهرًا أو سنةً أو أقلَّ أو أكثر. تترحّم[40] عليه وتذكر فضله وتكُفّ عن زلّته، ولا تذكر أحدًا منهم إلّا بخير لقول رسول الله،

37 "علي"، ليس في **طبقات الحنابلة** (الفقي) 21/2، (العثيمين) 41/3.

38 في **شذرات الذهب** 161/4 "وأفضل هذه الأمّة والأمم كلّها بعد الأنبياء، صلوات الله عليهم، أبو بكر ثمّ عمر ثمّ عثمان ثمّ عليّ، ثمّ أفضل الناس بعد هؤلاء طلحة، والزبير، وسعد وسعيد، وعبد الرحمن بن عوف [وأبو عبيدة عامر بن الجرّاح] وكلّهم يصلح للخلافة".

39 في **شذرات الذهب** 161/4 "للقبلتين".

40 في الأصل: "ترحم".

صلّى الله عليه وسلّم، "إذا ذُكر أصحابي فأمسكوا"، وقال ابن عُيَيْنة "من نطق في أصحاب رسول الله، صلّى الله عليه وسلّم، بكلمة فهو صاحب هوًى".[41]

قال أحمد بن حنبل "إن صحبه ولو ساعة"، الكوسج، **مسائل الإمام أحمد** 4669/9، الرقم 3324؛ وفي الخطيب البغدادي، **الكفاية** 51 "... ثمّ أفضل الناس بعد هؤلاء أصحاب رسول الله، صلّى الله عليه وسلّم، القرن الذي بُعث فيهم، كلّ من صحبه سنةً أو شهرًا، أو يومًا، أو ساعةً، أو رآه، فهو من أصحابه، له من الصحبة على قدر ما صحبه، وكانت سابقته معه وسمع منه، ونظر إليه"؛ اللالكائي، **شرح** 179/1–180 (اعتقاد أحمد بن حنبل)؛ ابن الجوزي، **مناقب أحمد** 296/1 (اعتقاد عبدوس)؛ اللالكائي، **شرح** 188/1 (اعتقاد ابن المديني)؛ وانظر الأشعري، **رسالة** 302.

"ولا تذكر أحدًا منهم إلّا بخير"، قال الأشعري في حكاية قول أصحاب الحديث وأهل السنّة "... ويمسكون عمّا شجر بينهم كبيرهم وصغيرهم"، **مقالات** 294؛ **رسالة** 302–303. وانظر في "إذا ذكر أصحابي فأمسكوا"، أحاديث عن ابن مسعود وغيره، الطبراني، **المعجم الكبير** 243/10–244، الرقم 10448؛ ابن عدي، **الكامل**، 264/8–265 (ترجمة النضر بن معبد)؛ ابن أبي زمنين، **أصول السنة** 267، الرقم 186؛ اللالكائي، **شرح** 143/1، الرقم 210، 1323/4، الرقم 2351؛ وقارن بـ 152/1، الرقم 246؛ البيهقي، **القضاء والقدر** 711/3–712، الرقم 358؛ قوّام السنّة، **الترغيب** 367/1، الرقم 629، 206/3–207، الرقم 2360؛ ابن عساكر، **تاريخ** 40/49. وانظر قول ابن عيينة في الجيلاني، **الغنية** 164/1.

(15) والسمع والطاعة للأئمّة فيما يحبّ الله ويرضى.| ومن ولِيَ الخلافةَ بإجماع الناس عليه ورضاهم ب 4
به[42] فهو أمير المؤمنين؛ ولا يحِلُّ لأحد أنْ يبيتَ ليلةً ولا يرى أنّ عليه[43] إمامًا، برًّا كان أو فاجرًا.

"السمع والطاعة للأئمّة فيما يحبّ الله ويرضى"، البخاري، **الجامع** 1765، الرقم 7144 (كتاب الأحكام، باب السمع والطاعة للأئمّة)؛ مسلم، **الصحيح** 1469، الرقم 1839؛ وسائر أحاديث الباب (كتاب الإمارة، باب وجوب طاعة الأمراء)؛ الطبري، **تفسير** 183/7 (النساء 59/4). وانظر في "لا يحِلُّ لأحد أنْ يبيتَ ليلةً ولا يرى أنّ عليه إمامًا"، الأشعري، **رسالة** 296؛ الطحاوي، **العقيدة** 46؛ ابن أبي العزّ، **شرح**

41 **طبقات** (الفقي) 21/2، (العثيمين) 42/3 "وقال النبيّ صلى الله عليه وسلم أصحابي كالنجوم بأيّهم اقتديتم اهتديتم".

42 **طبقات** (الفقي) 21/2 "باجماعهم عليه ورضاهم به"، (العثيمين) 42/3 "باجماع عليه ورضاهم به".

43 **طبقات** (الفقي) 21/2، (العثيمين) 42/3 "ليس عليه".

العقيدة 528–531؛ ابن أبي زمنين، **السنّة** 275–276؛ اللالكائي، **شرح** 180/1 (اعتقاد ابن حنبل)؛ 188/1 (اعتقاد عليّ بن المديني)؛ أبو يعلى الحنبلي، **الأحكام السلطانيّة** 23 (عن أحمد برواية عبدوس)؛ ابن قدامة، "العقيدة"، 111؛ وقارن بـ: حنبل، **ذكر محنة الإمام** 75 وما بعدها؛ وانظر ما يلي الرقم 144.

(16) والحجُّ والغزوُ مع الإمام ماضٍ، وصلاة[44] الجمعة خلفهم جائزةٌ، ويصلّي بعدها ستّ ركعاتٍ يفصِل بين كلّ ركعتين، هكذا قال أحمد بن حنبل.

انظر في الصلاة خلف كلّ إمام، المزني، **شرح السنّة** 87؛ حرب الكرماني، **كتاب السنّة** 40؛ الإسماعيلي، **اعتقاد** 179، الرقم 43، ولم يذكر صلاةً بعدها؛ الأشعري، **رسالة** 297؛ الخلّال، **السنّة** 75/1–82؛ الطحاوي، **العقيدة** 34؛ ابن قدامة، **المغني** 22/3، عن أحمد؛ ابن أبي زمنين، **السنّة** 288–292 (الحجّ والغزو)؛ اللالكائي، **شرح** 180/1–181، (اعتقاد أحمد بن حنبل؛ مع إضافة "من أعادهما فهو مبتدع تارك للآثار مخالف للسنّة")؛ ابن أبي يعلى، **طبقات** (الفقي) 123/1؛ وقارن بـ: المحاسبي، **المكاسب** 83؛ ابن حزم، **الفصل**، 135/4.

(17) والخلافةُ في قريش إلى أنْ ينزلَ عيسى بن مريم.

انظر في فضائل قريش وأنّ الأئمّة من قريش، ابن أبي شيبة، **المصنّف** 550/10–555 (كتاب الفضائل، ما ذكر من فضل قريش)؛ "الخلافة في قريش"، ابن حنبل، **المسند** 200/29، الرقم 17654 (طرف حديث طويل عن عتبة بن عبد)؛ الترمذي، **الجامع** 503/4 (كتاب الفتن، باب ما جاء أنّ الخلفاء من قريش إلى أن تقوم الساعة)؛ وحديث "استقيموا لقريش"، حرب الكرماني، **كتاب السنّة** 39، 134–135؛ الخلّال، **السنّة** 94/1–96، 126–129.

"نزول عيسى بن مريم"، البخاري، **الجامع** 855، الرقم 3449 (كتاب الأنبياء، باب نزول عيسى بن مريم) "كيف أنتم إذا نزل ابن مريم فيكم وإمامكم منكم". وانظر أحاديث الفتن.

(18) ومَن خرج على إمام من أئمّة المسلمين فهو خارجيّ، وقد شقّ عصا المسلمين وخالف الآثار وميتته ميتةُ جاهليّة.

قارن باعتقاد عبدوس بن مالك عن ابن حنبل، ابن أبي يعلى، **طبقات** (الفقي)، 244/1، (العثيمين)، 171/2؛ وبقول أحمد بن حنبل في اللالكائي، **شرح** 181/1؛ وانظر الخلّال، **السنّة** 131/1–132.

---

44 في الأصل: "وصلا".

(19) ولا يحلُّ قتال السلطان والخروج عليهم[45] وإنْ جاروا،[46] وذلك قولُ رسول الله، صلّى الله عليه وسلّم، لأبي ذرٍّ "اِصبرْ وإنْ كان عبداً حبشيًّا"، وقوله للأنصار "اِصبروا حتّى تلْقَوني على الحوض".

انظر في "لا يحلّ قتال السلطان"، ابن الجوزي، **مناقب أحمد** 306/1، 324 (اعتقاد عبدوس عن أحمد)؛ وفي قول أبي ذر، ابن بطّة، **الشرح والإبانة** 67؛ وفي معناه "إنّ خليلي، صلّى الله عليه وسلّم، أوصاني أنْ أسمعَ وأطيعَ وإن كان عبدًا مُجَدَّعَ الأطراف"، مسلم، **الصحيح** 1467/3، الرقم 1837، (وما يليه من أحاديث في كتاب الإمارة، باب وجوب الطاعة)؛ البيهقي، **السنن** 555/16، الرقم 16685 (كتاب قتال أهل البغي)؛ وعن أنس بن مالك قال قال رسول الله، صلّى الله عليه وسلّم، "اسمعوا وأطيعوا وإن استعمل عليكم عبد حبشيّ كأنّ رأسه زبيبة"، البخاري، **الجامع**1765، الرقم 7142 (كتاب الأحكام، باب السمع والطاعة)؛ وقارن بـ: حنبل، **ذكر محنة الإمام** 72.

وفي قوله للأنصار، البخاري، **الجامع** 1381/3 (باب قول النبيّ، صلّى الله عليه وسلّم، للأنصار اصبروا حتّى تلقوني على الحوض) وانظر البيهقي، **شعب الإيمان** 128/7.

وليس من السنّة قتالُ السلطان، فإنّ فيه فَسادَ الدين والدنيا.

انظر اللالكائي، **شرح** 181/1 (اعتقاد ابن حنبل)، 189/1 (اعتقاد ابن المديني)؛ المزني، **شرح السنّة** 85 "وترك الخروج عند تعديهم وجورهم"؛ النووي، **المنهاج** 317/12–318.

(20) ويحلُّ قتالُ الخوارج إذا عرضوا للمسلمين في أنفسهم وأموالهم وأهاليهم.[47] وليس له إذا فارقوه أنْ يطلبهم ولا [يُجهِز][48] على جريحهم ولا يأخذ فَيْئَهم[49] ولا يقتل أسيرهم ولا يتتبّع مُدبرهم.

عن عليّ بن أبي طالب يوم البصرة "لا يُتَّبَع مُدبر ولا يذفّف على جريح ولا يُقتل أسير ومن أغلق بابه فهو آمن ولم يأخذ من متاعهم شيئًا"، ابن أبي شيبة، **المصنّف** 155/11، الرقم 33850 (كتاب السير، في الإجازة على الجرحى)؛ البيهقي، **السنن** 49/17، الرقم 16827 (وما يليه)، وانظر أثرًا عن ابن عمر، البزّار، **المسند** 231/12، الرقم 5954.

45 **طبقات** (الفقي) 21/2 "ولا الخروج عليه وإن جار"، (العثيمين) 43/3 "ولا الخروج عليهم وإن جاروا".

46 هكذا في الأصل "السلطان" مفرد ثم جمع.

47 **طبقات** (الفقي) 22/2، (العثيمين) 43/3 "وأهليهم".

48 في الأصل: "يجير".

49 **طبقات** (الفقي) 21/2، (العثيمين) 43/3 "فيهم".

وفي "عدم جواز قتال السلطان، وقتال الخوارج"، اللالكائي، **شرح** 180/1 (اعتقاد ابن حنبل برواية عبدوس)، 189/1 (اعتقاد عليّ بن المديني).

(21) واعلم، رحمك الله، أنْ لا طاعة لِبشر في معصية الله عزّ وجلّ.

انظر ابن حنبل، **مسند** 128/2، الرقم 724، 318/2، الرقم 1065 (عن عليّ بن أبي طالب)؛ الكرماني، **السنّة** 147 (.. في معصية الله)؛ ابن حبّان، **الصحيح** 792، الرقم 4549 (كتاب السير، عن عليّ)؛ "لا طاعة لمخلوق في معصية الخالق"، من كلام طويل لعلي، الصدوق، **الخصال** 166–167، الرقم 158 (باب الثلاثة).

(22) مَن كان من أهل الإسلام ولم يشهد على أحدٍ، ولم يشهد له بعمل خير ولا شرّ،[50] فإنّك لا تدري بما يُختم له؛ نرجو له ونخاف عليه ولا ندري ما يسبق[51] له عند الموت إلى الله من النَّدَم، وما | أحدث الله في ذلك الوقت إذا مات على الإسلام، ونرجو له رحمةَ الله، ونخاف عليه[52] ذنوبه؛ وما من ذنب إلا وللعبد منه توبة. 5 أ

قارن بعبد الله بن مسعود، ابن المبارك، **الزهد** 313 (باب رحمة الله)؛ "ما يسبق إليه عند الموت"، انظر حديث عبد الله بن عمر "إنّ الله يقبل توبة العبد ما لم يغرغر"، ابن حنبل، **المسند** 300/10، الرقم 6160، 461، الرقم 6408؛ 239/39، الرقم 23816؛ ابن ماجة، **السنن** 1420/2، الرقم 4253 (كتاب الزهد، باب ذكر التوبة)؛ الأشعري، **الإبانة** 21؛ الطحاوي، **العقيدة** 31 "الأعمال بالخواتيم"؛ ابن أبي العزّ، **شرح العقيدة** 318–319؛ البغوي، **شرح السنّة** 90/5؛ "نرجو له ونخاف عليه"، أبو حنيفة [جمعه أبو مقاتل السَّمرقندي]، **العالم والمتعلّم** 23؛ وقارن بقول ابن حنبل، اللالكائي، **شرح** 182/1 (اعتقاد أحمد بن حنبل)؛ ابن بطّة، **الشرح والإبانة** 63؛ البغوي، **شرح السنّة** 90/5؛ الطحاوي، **العقيدة** 41؛ ابن أبي العزّ، **شرح العقيدة** 537/2–539؛ الإسماعيلي، **اعتقاد** 175، الرقم 26؛ اللالكائي، **شرح** 189/1 (اعتقاد ابن المديني)؛ ابن أبي زمنين، **أصول السنّة** 222–223، 225؛ وانظر قول سفيان الثوري، قوّام السنّة، **الحجّة** 491/2؛ ابن الجوزي، **مناقب أحمد** 316/1؛ 322 (اعتقاد عبدوس عن أحمد)؛ المقدسي، **الاقتصاد** 205؛ القرطبي، **تفسير** 20/1 (المقدّمة).

50 **طبقات** (الفقي) 22/2، (العثيمين) 43/3 "من كان من أهل الإسلام فلا تشهد له بعمل خير ولا شرّ".

51 **طبقات** (الفقي) 22/2، (العثيمين) 43/3 "ترجو.. تدري .. سبق".

52 **طبقات** (الفقي) 22/2، (العثيمين) 44/3 "ترجو له الرحمة وتخاف عليه ذنوبه".

(23) والرَّجم حقّ.

البخاري، **الجامع** 1688، الرقم 6829 ("ألا وإنّ الرجمَ حقّ"، كتاب الحدود، باب الاعتراف بالزنى)؛ ابن ماجه **السنن** 1317/2، الرقم 1691 ("إنّ الرجم في كتاب الله حقّ"، كتاب الحدود، باب الرجم)؛ الترمذي، **الجامع** 39/4، الرقم 1432 (كتاب الحدود، باب ما جاء في تحقيق الرجم)؛ ابن أبي يعلى، **طبقات** (الفقي)، 245/1، وابن الجوزي، **مناقب أحمد** 322/1 ؛ اللالكائي، **شرح** 182/1 (اعتقاد أحمد بن حنبل)؛ الآجرّي، **الشريعة** 1195/4، الرقم 868؛ قوّام السنّة، **الحجّة** 266/2؛ ابن عبد البر، **التمهيد** 69/19، 98/23.

(24) والمسح على الخفّين سنّة.

"المسح على الخفّين"، دار النقاش بين العلماء حول ما إذا كانت سورة المائدة 6/5 قد نسخت المسح على الخفّين (مسلم، **الصحيح** 227/1؛ الترمذي، **الجامع** 155/1–157؛ القرطبي، **تفسير** 93/6)؛ أبو حنيفة، **الوصية** 49؛ وعن الكاساني أنّ أبا حنيفة رآه "من شرائط السنّة والجماعة"، **بدائع** 7/1؛ الشافعي، **الأمّ** 357/2؛ 760/8–761 (كتاب اختلاف مالك والشافعي)؛ صالح بن أحمد، **مسائل الإمام** 79 (الرقم 271)، 151–152 (الرقم 544)؛ ابن حنبل، **المسائل والرسائل** 421/2؛ ابن الجوزي، **مناقب أحمد** 306/1، 314؛ المروزي، **السنّة** 119؛ المروزي، **اختلاف الفقهاء** 149–151؛ السمرقندي، **السواد الأعظم**، الرقم 8؛ الأشعري، **مقالات** 295، **الإبانة** 23؛ ابن بطّة، **الإبانة** (الإيمان) 362/1–363؛ ابن بطّة، **الشرح والإبانة** 69؛ الطحاوي، **العقيدة** 49؛ ابن أبي العز، **شرح العقيدة** 551/2–555؛ ابن شاهين، **شرح** (اعتقاد ابن شاهين في آخر الكتاب) 321؛ اللالكائي، **شرح** 205/1 (اعتقاد سهل التستري)، 189/1 (اعتقاد ابن المديني)؛ قوّام السنّة، **الحجّة** 266/2؛ وترى سائر مذاهب السنّة المسح على الخفّين وأنكره سواهم، الأشعري، **مقالات** 470. وانظر نقاشًا مستفيضًا في ابن عبد البرّ، **التمهيد** 122/11–161؛ ويعلّق على حديث المغيرة بن شعبة بقوله "وفيه الحكم الجليل الذي فرّق بين أهل السنّة وأهل البدع وهو المسح على الخفّين لا ينكره إلّا مخذول أو مبتدع خارج عن جماعة المسلمين"، **التمهيد**، 134/11؛ الزيلعي، **نصب الراية** 183/1–191؛ ويروي حفص بن غياث عن سفيان الثوري قوله "من لم يشرب النبيذ ولم يأكل الجِرِّي ولم يمسح على الخفين فاتّهموه على دينكم"، أبو نُعيم، **حلية** 32/7، والجِرِّي نوع من السمك يُشْبه الحَيّات (الخطّابي، **غريب الحديث** 185/2–186؛ ابن منظور، **لسان العرب** 128/2).

ولا يقرّ الفقه الزيدي والإمامي بالمسح على الخفّين (الإمام زيد، **مسند** 73؛ الكليني، **الكافي** 32/3)؛ إلّا أنّ الحسن بن صالح بن حيّ من الزيديّة كان يقول به (أبو نُعيم، **حلية** 334/7؛ القرطبي، **تفسير** 102/6).

وتقصير الصلاة في السفر سنّة، والصوم في السفر من شاء صام ومن شاء أفطر.

الكوسج، **مسائل الإمام أحمد** 674، الأرقام 312–314؛ صالح بن أحمد، **مسائل الإمام** 22، الأرقام 15–18؛ المزني، **شرح السنّة** 88؛ عن أبي حنيفة "من أتمّ الصلاة في السفر فقد أساء وخالف السنّة"، الكاساني، **بدائع** 91/1؛ وقال الشافعي "والقصر في السفر بلا خوف سنّة"، **الأمّ** 355/2؛ وانظر، مسلم، **الصحيح** 310/1 (كتاب صلاة المسافرين وقصرها)؛ ابن قدامة، **المغني** 104/3؛ ابن تيمية، **مجموع الفتاوي** 24/7–8.

و"في الصوم في السفر"، البخاري، **الجامع** 467، الرقم 1943 (باب الصوم في السفر)، 468، الرقم 1948 (باب من أفطر في السفر ليراه الناس)؛ المزني، **السنة** 88؛ الطبري، **تفسير** 164/3 (البقرة 184/2).

ولا بأس بالصلاة في السراويل.

قال الشافعي "ويصلّي الرجل في السراويل إذا وارى ما بين السرّة والركبة، والإزار أستر وأحبّ منه"، **الأمّ** 202/3؛ عبد الله بن أحمد بن حنبل، **السنّة** 200/1، الرقم 297 (جابر بن زيد عن ابن عبّاس عن الرسول، صلّى الله عليه وسلّم، "السراويل لمن لم يجد الإزار، والخفّين لمن لم يجد النعلين")؛ أبو داوود، **السنن** 474/1، الرقم 636 (عن أبي بريدة .. "ونهى أن يصلّي الرجل في سراويل وليس عليه رداء")؛ والبيهقي، **السنن** 227/4، الرقم 3319 (كتاب الصلاة، باب ما يستحبّ أن يصلّي فيه...)؛ وانظر السرخسي، **الأصل** 78/1؛ وقال ابن نُجيم الحنفي "والمكروه أن يصلّي في سراويل واحد"، **البحر الرائق** 283/1.

(25) والنفاق أنْ تُظهر الإسلام وتخفي الكفر.[53]

قارن بـ الطبري، **تفسير** 277/1 (البقرة 8/2)؛ العدني، **الإيمان** 74؛ ابن بطّة، **الإبانة** 690/2–693؛ وقارن بـاللالكائي، **شرح** 182/1 (اعتقاد أحمد بن حنبل)؛ ابن الجوزي، **مناقب أحمد** 320/1 (اعتقاد عبدوس عن أحمد)؛ ابن الأثير، **النهاية** 98/5 "الذي يستر كفره ويظهر إيمانه".

(26) واعلم أنّ الدنيا دار إيمان وإسلام، فأُمّةُ محمّد، صلّى الله عليه وسلّم، فيها مؤمنون مسلمون في أحكامهم ومواريثهم والصلاة عليهم.[54] لا نشهد لأحدٍ بحقيقة الإيمان حتّى يأتيَ بجميع شرائع الإسلام،

53 **طبقات** (الفقي) 22/2، (العثيمين) 44/3 "أن يظهر الإسلام باللسان ويخفي الكفر بالضمير".

54 **طبقات** (الفقي) 22/2، (العثيمين) 44/3 "ومواريثهم وذبائحهم".

فإنْ قصَّر في شيءٍ من ذلك كان ناقصَ الإيمان حتّى يموت،[55] وعِلْمُ[56] إيمانه إلى الله تعالى، تامّ الإيمان أو ناقص الإيمان، إلّا ما ظهر من ذلك[57] من تضييع شرائع الإسلام.

"الدنيا دار إيمان"، المصطلح المعروف هو "الدار دار إيمان"، غير أنّه ورد عند الدبّوسي الحنفي، "الأصل عندنا أنّ الدنيا كلّها داران، دار إسلام ودار حرب، وعند الإمام الشافعي الدنيا كلّها دار واحدة"، **تأسيس النظر** 119؛ وانظر في "دار الإسلام ودار الكفر"، الشافعي، **الأمّ** 599/5، 601، 606، 621 (وغيرها من المواضع في كتاب السير، والردّ على الشيباني، والتدبير)؛ الإسماعيلي، **اعتقاد** 180، الرقم 49 (ويرون الدار دار إسلام لا دار كفر كما رأته المعتزلة ما دام النداء بالصلاة والإقامة بها ظاهرين وأهلها ممكّنين منها آمنين)؛ السرخسي، **المبسوط** 113/10–114؛ الكاساني، **بدائع** 130/7–131؛ أبو يعلى الحنبلي، **المعتمد** 276.

وانظر في "ناقص الإيمان"، قول سفيان بن عيينة في خبر طويل، أبو نعيم، **حلية** 295/7–296؛ وانظر في "ناقصي الإيمان"، ابن عبد البرّ، **التمهيد** 243/9؛ وعن الشافعي في البيهقي، **مناقب الشافعي** 392/1: وقد خصّص ابن تيمية اللفظَ لمن سمّاه بـ "الفاسق الملّي"، **شرح العقيدة الواسطية** 268–269.

(27) والصلاة على من مات من أهل القِبلة سُنّة، المرجوم والزاني والزانية والذي يقتل نفسَه، وغيرهم من أهل القبلة والسكران وغيره، الصلاة عليهم سنّة.

"يصلي على من مات من أهل القبلة"، السمرقندي، **السواد الأعظم**، الرقم 5؛ وانظر السرخسي، **شرح السير** 110/1–111 "لا تكفّروا أهل ملّتكم وإن عملوا الكبائر، الصلاة مع كلّ إمام، الصلاة على كلّ ميت، الجهاد مع كلّ أمير"، الأشعري، **الإبانة** 20؛ **مقالات** 294، 296؛ الطحاوي، **العقيدة** 46؛ ابن أبي العزّ، **شرح العقيدة** 529/2–531؛ ابن أبي زمنين، **أصول السنّة** 224؛ ابن عبد البرّ، **التمهيد** 130/24–131؛ ابن قدامة، **المغني** 508/3؛ واختلف في "الصلاة على المرجوم"، انظر الصنعاني، **المصنّف** 534/3–536، الأرقام 6614–6624؛ البيهقي، **السنن** 171/17–176 (كتاب الحدود، باب المرجوم)؛ ابن حزم، **المحلّى** 170/5–171.

---

55 **طبقات** (الفقي) 22/2، (العثيمين) 44/3 "يتوب".

56 **طبقات** (الفقي) 22/2، (العثيمين) 44/3 "واعلم أن إيمانه".

57 **طبقات** (الفقي) 22/2، (العثيمين) 44/3 "إلا ما أظهر لك".

(28) ولا تُخرِج أحدًا من أهل القبلة من الإسلام حتّى يرُدَّ آيةً من كتاب الله، أو يردّ شيئًا من آثار رسول الله، صلّى الله عليه وسلّم، أو يذبح لغير الله، أو يصلّي لغير الله. وإذا [فعل شيئًا من ذلك فقد وجب عليك أن تُخرجه من الإسلام، وإذا][58] لم يفعل من ذلك شيئًا فهو مؤمن مسلم[59] بالاسم لا بالحقيقة.

"بالاسم لا بالحقيقة"، كأنه ردٌّ على قول أبي حنيفة [جمعه أبو مقاتل السمرقندي]، **العالم والمتعلّم** 13؛ وأبو حنيفة [منسوب] **الفقه الأكبر** 9: ".. ولا نُزيل عنه اسم الإيمان، ونسميه مؤمنًا حقيقة" (Wensinck, *Muslim Creed*, 192, art. 11)؛ المعاملة تكون بحسب ما ظهر، وبحسب قول الجصّاص الحنفي "أن تكون العبادة علينا في اعتبار إظهار الاسم دون الضمير، ألا ترى أنّ من أظهر القول بالتوحيد وتصديق الرسول، صلّى الله عليه وسلّم، كان حكمه حكم المسلمين مع جواز اعتقاده للتشبيه المضادّ للتوحيد"، **أحكام القرآن** 155/1؛ ابن عبد البرّ، **التمهيد** 157/10 "وقد أجمعوا أنّ أحكام الدنيا على الظاهر وأنّ السرائر إلى الله عزّ وجلّ".

ب 5 (29) وكلّ ما سمعت من الآثار ممّا لم | يبلغه عقلُك،[60] نحو قول رسول الله، صلّى الله عليه وسلّم،

المقصود هنا هو التفويض في مسألة الصفات وإمرارها كما جاءت، انظر قول الزهري ومكحول، قوّام السنّة، **الحجّة** 173/1–174، 285–289، 436؛ ابن حجر، **فتح الباري** 383/13؛ قارن بـ: الكوسج، **مسائل الإمام أحمد** 4675/9–4676؛ عبد الله بن أحمد بن حنبل، **السنّة** 268/1، الرقم 496؛ الأشعري، **الإبانة** 22–23؛ **مقالات** 211.

أ. "قلوب العباد بين إصبعين من أصابع الرحمن".

ابن قتيبة، **تأويل مختلف الحديث** 8 ، 77، 217؛ ابن أبي عاصم ، **السنّة** 37؛ حرب الكرماني، **كتاب السنّة** 51؛ الأشعري، **الإبانة** 21؛ ابن بطّة، **الإبانة** (الرد على الجهميّة) 270/3–279؛ الدارقطني، **الصفات** 35، الرقم 29؛ الآجرّي، **الشريعة** 731/2، الرقم 321؛ ابن أبي يعلى، **الاعتقاد** 26؛ ابن الجوزي، **مناقب أحمد** 312/1؛ الذهبي، **سير** 467/8 "قال سفيان هي كما جاءت نقرّ بها ونحدّث بها بلا كيف".

58 أضافها الناسخ في الهامش الأيسر.

59 **طبقات** (الفقي) 23/2، (العثيمين) 45/3 "مؤمن ومسلم".

60 **طبقات** (الفقي) 23/2، (العثيمين) 45/3 "من الآثار شيئًا لم يبلغه عقلك".

ب. وقوله "إنّ الله تبارك وتعالى ينـزل إلى سماء الدنيا وينـزل يوم عرفة ويوم القيامة".

الترمذي، **الجامع** 50/3، الرقم 662 "ونزول الربّ تبارك وتعالى كلّ ليلة إلى السماء الدنيا، قالوا قد ثبت الروايات في هذا ويؤمن بها ولا يتوهّم ولا يقال كيف هكذا. روي عن مالك وسفيان بن عيينة وعبد الله بن المبارك أنّهم قالوا في هذه الأحاديث: أمرّوها بلا كيف وهكذا قول أهل العلم من أهل السنّة والجماعة"؛ الدارمي، **الردّ على الجهميّة** 63–71؛ الدارمي، **الردّ على بشر المرّيسي** 19–22؛ وحرب الكرماني، **كتاب السنّة** 199–200؛ ابن أبي عاصم، **السنّة** 78–79. وانظر في أحاديث النزول، ابن خزيمة، **التوحيد** 126–136؛ ابن بطّة، **الإبانة** (الردّ على الجهميّة) 201/3–243؛ الملطي، **التنبيه** 86–87؛ ابن أبي زمنين، **أصول السنّة** 110–113؛ ابن أبي يعلى، **الاعتقاد** 25؛ ابن قدامة، "العقيدة"، 110؛ ابن رجب، **فتح الباري** 248–277/9.

ج. و"إنّ جهنّم لا يزال يطرح فيها حتّى يضع عليها قدمه، جلّ ثناؤه".

قارن بـ: ابن حنبل، **المسند** 373/19، الرقم 12380، 428، الرقم 12440 (كلاهما عن أنس)، وانظر في "إنّ الله يضع قدمه في النار":

Graham, *Divine Word*, 139.

د. وقول الله للعبد "إن مشيت إليَّ هرولت إليك".

قارن بـ:

Graham, *Divine Word*, 127–128.

هـ. وقوله "إنّ الله، تبارك وتعالى، ينـزل يوم عرفة".[61]

و. وقوله "إنّ الله خلق آدم على صورته".

الصنعاني، **المصنّف** 384/10، الرقم 19435؛ الغطفاني، **التحريش** 136؛ البخاري، **الجامع**1554، الرقم 6227 (كتاب الاستئذان)؛ ابن حجر، **فتح الباري** 3/11–4؛ مسلم، **الصحيح** 2183/4، الرقم 2841 (كتاب الجنّة)، 2017/4، الرقم 2612 (كتاب البرّ والصلة، باب النهي عن ضرب الوجه)؛ حرب الكرماني، **كتاب**

61 مرّ سابقًا، وواضح أنّه تكرار لا ضرورة له، أو سهو من الناسخ.

السنّة 51، و(الملحق)، 302؛ ابن قتيبة، **تأويل مختلف الحديث** 217؛ ابن أبي عاصم، **السنّة** 81–82؛ ابن بطّة، **الشرح والإبانة** 57؛ ابن بطّة، **الإبانة** (الرد على الجهمية) 3/244–269؛ الدارقطني، **الصفات** 49–52، الأرقام 44–50؛ عبد الله بن أحمد بن حنبل، **السنّة** 2/268، الرقم 498، 2/478–479، الرقم 1100، 2/490، الرقم 1122؛ ابن أبي يعلى، **طبقات** (الفقي) 1/212؛ قوّام السنّة، **الحجّة** 1/286، 2/290، 2/435؛ البغوي، **شرح السنّة** 12/254؛ أبو يعلى الحنبلي، **إبطال التأويلات** 1/77–80؛ وانظر استنكار مالك لحديث "خلق آدم على صورته"، الذهبي، **ميزان الاعتدال** 2/419 (الرقم 4301).

ز. وقول النبيّ، صلّى الله عليه وسلّم، "إنّي رأيت ربّي في أحسن صورة".

عن عبد الرحمن بن عائش الحضرمي، أحمد بن حنبل، **المسند** 27/171، الرقم 16621؛ الترّمذي، **الجامع** 5/366، الرقم 3233 (تفسير القرآن، باب من سورة ص).

وأشباه هذه الأحاديث، فعليك بالتسليم والتصديق والتفويض والرضا، لا تفسّر شيئًا[62] بهواك. فإنّ الإيمانَ بهذا واجبٌ، فمن فسّر شيئًا من هذا بهواه أو ردّه فهو جَهْميّ.

وانظر أيضًا في هذه الأحاديث: البغوي، **شرح السنّة** 1/168–171.

(30) ومن زعم أنّه يرى ربّه في دار الدنيا فهو كافر بالله.

عن عبادة بن الصامت "لن تروا ربّكم حتى تموتوا"، ابن حنبل، **المسند** 37/424، الرقم 22864؛ وحديث ابن ثابت الأنصاري "تعلموا أنّه لن يرى أحد ربّه، عزّ وجلّ، حتّى يموت"؛ مسلم، **الصحيح** 4/2245، الرقم 2930 (كتاب الفتن، باب ذكر ابن صياد)؛ الدارمي، **الردّ على الجهميّة** 93، الرقم 182؛ الدارمي، **الردّ على بشر المريسي** 17 ".. وأقررتم برؤية الخلق كلّهم إيّاه في الدنيا مؤمنهم وكافرهم، لما أنّهم جميعًا لا يزالون يرون أموره وآياته آناء الليل والنهار، فخالفتم بسلوك هذه الحجّة جميع العالمين ورددتم قول الله ﴿لا تدركه الأبصار﴾، إذ ادّعيتم أنّ رؤيته، يعني إدراك آياته وأموره وأفعاله"، وانظر 58؛ الباقلاني، **الإنصاف** 224.

وانظر في قول بكر ابن أخت عبد الواحد وبعض متصوّفة البصرة، الطبري، **التبصير** 217–218؛ الأشعري، **مقالات** 213–214؛ السرّاج 544–545؛ القشيري، **الرسالة** 524؛ الشهرستاني، **الملل والنحل** 45 (قول الكعبي عن مشبّهة الحشويّة).

62 **طبقات** (الفقي) 2/23، (العثيمين) 3/45 "شيئا من هذه".

(31) والفكرة في الله، تبارك وتعالى، بدعةٌ، لقول رسول الله، صلّى الله عليه وسلّم، "تفكّروا في الخلق ولا تفكّروا في الله"، فإنّ الفكرة في الله تقدح الشكّ في القلب.

حرب الكرماني، **كتاب السنة** 229؛ أبو الشيخ، **كتاب العظمة** 218 "لا فكرة في الربّ"؛ ابن كثير، **تفسير** 281/13 (النجم /42–55)؛ وانظر الملطي، **التنبيه** 73 (في طائفة الروحانيّة أو الفكريّة).

وانظر في "تفكّروا في الخلق ولا تفكّروا في الله"، **تخريج أحاديث إحياء علوم الدين** 2457، الرقم 3880؛ ويرد بصيغة "تفكّروا في آلاء الله ولا تفكّروا في الله" عند البيهقي، **شعب الإيمان**، 263/1، الرقم 119؛ ابن بطّة، **الإبانة** (الردّ على الجهميّة) 86/2/3؛ أبو الشيخ، **كتاب العظمة** 309؛ ابن أبي زمنين، **أصول السنّة** 79؛ اللالكائي، **شرح** 580/2، الرقم 927؛ وقارن بـ أبو نعيم، **حلية** 67/6؛ الذهبي، **ميزان الاعتدال** 327/4، الرقم 9320؛ الهيثمي، **مجمع الزوائد** 106/1، الرقم 260. الطبراني، **الأوسط** 250/6، الرقم 6319 (عن ابن عمر)؛ قوّام السنّة، **الحجّة** 98/1 (عن عبد الله بن سلام).

(32) واعلم أنّ الهوام والسباع والدواب كلَّها، نحو الذرّ والنمل، كلّها مأمورة[63] لا يعملون شيئًا إلّا بإذن الله تبارك وتعالى.

قارن بـ: ابن قتيبة، **تأويل مختلف الحديث** 137–138.

(33) والإيمان بأنّ الله، تبارك وتعالى، قد علم ما كان من أوّل الدهر وما لم يكن ممّا هو كائنٌ،[64] أحصاه الله وعدّه عدًّا، ومن قال إنّه لا يعلم ما كان وما هو كائن فقد كفر بالله العظيم.

قارن بـ: ابن كثير، **تفسير** 493/10 (العنكبوت 3/29) "والله سبحانه يعلم ما كان وما يكون وما لم يكن لو كان كيف يكون، وهذا مُجمع عليه عند أهل السنّة والجماعة".

(34) ولا نكاح إلّا بوليّ وشاهِدَيْ عدلٍ | وصَداق، قلَّ أو كثُر، ومَن لم يكن له[65] وليٌّ فالسلطان وليُّ أ 6
مَن لا وليَّ له.

63 **طبقات** (الفقي) 23/2، (العثيمين) 45/3 "كلها، نحو الذر والذباب والنمل مأمورة".

64 **طبقات** (الفقي) 23/2، (العثيمين) 45/3 "وما لم يكن وما هو كائن".

65 **طبقات** (الفقي) 23/2، (العثيمين) 46/3 "لها".

انظر البيهقي، **السنن** 141/14، الرقم 13836، و 86/14–88، الأرقام 13732–13735؛ وقارن بـ: ابن أبي شيبة، **المصنّف** 11/6، الرقم 16160، 13/4، الرقم 16170؛ ابن حنبل، **المسند** 482/32، الرقم 19710 "لا نكاح إلّا بوليّ"؛ أبو داود، **السنن،** 425/3 (كتاب النكاح، باب في الوليّ)؛ الترمذي، **الجامع**، الرقم 1101، 1102؛ الدارمي، **السنن**575/2؛ أبو يعلى الموصلي، **المسند**195/13؛ ابن حبّان، **الصحيح** 705، الرقم 4063؛ ابن الجوزي، **مناقب أحمد** 14/1 3 (عقيدة مسدّد بن مسرهد)؛ وقارن بـ: ابن بطّة، **الشرح والإبانة** 74.

وإذا طلّق الرجلُ امرأته ثلاثًا فقد حَرُمت عليه ولا تحقُّ له حتّى تنكح زوجًا غيره.

البقرة 230/2؛ الشافعي، **الأمّ** 66/1، 399/6، 467؛ الصنعاني، **المصنّف** 311/6، الرقم 10964؛ البخاري، **الجامع**1341، الرقم 5264، و5265 (كتاب الطلاق، باب من قال لامرأته أنت عَلَيَّ حرام)؛ الطبري، **تفسير** 166/4–167؛ ابن بطّة، **الشرح والإبانة** 69–70؛ السرخسي، **المبسوط** 8/6–9؛ البيهقي، **السنن** 238/15 (كتاب الخلع والطلاق، باب إمضاء الطلاق)؛ قوّام السنّة، **الحجّة** 438/2؛ ابن قدامة، **المغني** 332/10، 334.

(35) ولا يحلُّ دمُ امرئٍ مسلم يشهد أن لا إله إلّا الله، ويشهد أنّ محمّدًا[66] رسول الله، وعبده ورسوله[67] إلّا بإحدى ثلاث: زانٍ بعد إحصان، أو مرتدٌّ بعد إيمان، أو قَتْلُ نفسٍ[68] مؤمنة فيقتل به؛[69] وما سوى ذلك فدم المسلم على المسلم حرام[70] حتّى تقومَ الساعة.

قارن بـ: الشافعي، **الأمّ** 534/5، 6/7، 371–372، 393–394؛ ابن سعد، **الطبقات** 46/3، 48 (عثمان بن عفّان يوم الدار)؛ البخاري، **الجامع**1701، الرقم 6878 (كتاب الديات، باب إذا قتل بحجر أو بعصا)؛ ابن حجر، **فتح الباري** 201/12–202، قال "وفي حديث ابن عبّاس مرتدّ بعد إيمان"؛ مسلم، **الصحيح** 1302/3، الرقم 1676 (كتاب القسامة، باب ما يباح به دم المسلم)؛ النسائي، **السنن** 427/3، الرقم 3466 (المحاربة)، 324/6، الرقم 6897 (القسامة، باب القود)؛ ابن الأثير، **جامع الأصول** 213/10–215؛ الهيثمي، **مجمع** 276/6، الرقم 10520، عن عمّار بن ياسر وفيه ".. والمرتدّ عن الإيمان".

66 في الأصل: "محمّد".

67 زادها في الأصل فوق السطر، وهي ليست في **طبقات الحنابلة**.

68 في الأصل: "نفسا".

69 كذا بالأصل: "به".

70 **طبقات** (الفقي) 24/2، (العثيمين) 46/3 "حرام أبدا".

"دم المسلم على المسلم حرام حتّى تقوم السّاعة"، قارن بـ البخاري، **الجامع** 419، الرقم 1739 (كتاب الحجّ، باب الخطبة أيّام منى)؛ مسلم، **الصحيح** 1986/4، الرقم 2564 (كتاب البرّ والصلة، باب تحريم ظلم المسلم).

(36) وكلُّ شيءٍ ممّا أوجب الله عليه الفناء يَفنى، إلّا الجنّة والنّار والعرش والكرسي واللوح والقلم والصُّور،[71] ليس يفنى شيء من هذا أبدًا.

قارن بـ قوّام السنّة، **الحجّة** 436/2؛ قال أبو المعين النسفي الماتريدي، "قال أهل السنّة والجماعة: سبعة لا تفنى العرش والكرسي والقلم والجنة والنار وأهلهما والأرواح" (باب فيما لا يفنى عند النفخ في الصُّور)، انظر **بحر الكلام** 219.

(37) ثمّ يبعث الله الخلقَ على ما ماتوا عليه يوم القيامة، ويحاسبهم بما شاء، فريقٌ في الجنّة وفريقٌ في السعير ويقول لسائر الخلق[72] كونوا ترابًا.

"يبعث كلّ عبد على ما مات عليه"، مسلم، **الصحيح** 2206/4، الرقم 2878 (عن جابر، كتاب الجنّة وصفة نعيمها وأهلها)؛ سفيان الثوري، **تفسير** 112، الرقم 285 (الأعراف 23/7)؛ ابن أبي زمنين، **أصول السنّة** 153.

﴿فريقٌ في الجنّة وفريقٌ في السَّعير﴾، الشورى 7/42.

"يقول لسائر الخلق كونوا ترابًا"، الصنعاني، **تفسير** 344/2، عن أبي هريرة "إنّ الله يحشر الخلق كلّهم من دابّة وطائر والإنسان ثمّ يقول للبهائم والطير والدوابّ كوني ترابًا" (النبأ 40/78)؛ السيوطي، **الدر المنثور** 147/4 (الأنعام 38/6).

(38) والإيمان بالقِصاص يوم القيامة بين الخلق كلّهم، بني آدم والسباع والهوامّ،[73] حتّى للذرّة من الذرّة، حتّى يأخذَ الله لبعضهم من بعض، [لأهل الجنّة من أهل النار ولأهل النار من أهل الجنّة، وأهل الجنّة بعضهم من بعض وأهل النّار بعضهم من بعض].[74]

---

71 **طبقات** (الفقي) 24/2، (العثيمين) 46/3 "والصور والقلم واللوح".

72 **طبقات** (الفقي) 24/2، (العثيمين) 46/3 "لسائر الخلق ممن لم يخلق للبقاء".

73 **طبقات** (الفقي) 24/2، (العثيمين) 46/3 "من الخلق كلهم وبين بني آدم".

74 زادها في الهامش الأيسر طولًا.

نقله ابن حمدان، **نهاية المبتدئين** 56 (وقال: "والقصاص بين بني آدم وسائر الحيوانات حقّ، حتّى الذرّة من الذرّة، ومن الحجر لمنكب إصبع الرجل حقّ". ذكره البربهاري)؛ عن أبي هريرة "يقتصّ للخلق بعضهم من بعض، حتى للجمّاء من القرناء، وحتى للذرّة من الذرة"، ابن حنبل، **المسند** 365/14، الرقم 8756، وقارن بـ: 345/35، الرقم 21438 (عن أبي ذرّ)؛ مسلم، **الصحيح** 1997/4، الرقم 2582 (كتاب البرّ والصلة، باب تحريم المظالم)؛ النووي، **المنهاج** 205/16 ("هذا تصريح بحشر البهائم يوم القيامة وإعادته يوم القيامة كما يعاد أهل التكليف ... ليس هو قصاص تكليف إذ لا تكليف عليها بل قصاص مقاربة")؛ الطبري، **تفسير** 54/24–55 (النبأ 40/78)؛ قوّام السنّة، **الحجّة** 313/1–314؛ وانظر أقوالًا في العوض على البهائم والهوامّ، الأشعري، **مقالات** 254.

(39) وإخلاص العمل لله، والرضا بقضاء الله، والصبر على حكم الله، والإيمان بما قال الله، عزّ وجلّ.

قارن بـ: ابن المبارك، **الزهد** (زيادات نعيم بن حمّاد)31، الرقم 123 (عن أبي الدرداء، ذروة الإيمان أربع خلال...)؛ الأشعري، **رسالة** 244؛ **مقالات** 296؛ ابن الجوزي، **مناقب أحمد** 326/1.

(40) والإيمان بأقدار الله[75] كلِّها خيرها وشرِّها وحلوها ومرّها.

أبو حنيفة [جمعه أبو مطيع البلخي]، **الفقه الأبسط** 56؛ الحميدي، **المسند** (أصول السنّة) 546؛ أبو داود، **السنن** 80/7، الرقم 4695 في حديث طويل عن يحيى بن يعمر "وتؤمن بالقدر خيره وشرّه" (كتاب السنّة، باب القدر)؛ والبيهقي، **السنن** 73/21، الرقم 20913 (كتاب الشهادات، باب ما ترد به شهادة أهل الأهواء)؛ ابن أبي عاصم، **السنّة**، 22–23، الرقم 133–135؛ 28، الرقم 178؛ الإسماعيلي، **اعتقاد** 174، الرقم 21؛ الأشعري، **مقالات** 291، 292، 293؛ الطحاوي، **العقيدة** 44؛ ابن مندة، **الإيمان** 131/1–132؛ ابن أبي زيد، **الرسالة** 8؛ ابن أبي زمنين، **أصول السنّة** 197–198؛ ابن بطّة، **الشرح والإبانة** 52؛ ابن أبي يعلى، **الاعتقاد** 31؛ قوّام السنّة، **الحجّة** 417/1؛ ابن حمدان، **نهاية المبتدئين** 53؛ الجيلاني، **الغنية** 140/1؛ ابن قدامة، "العقيدة"، 109.

وانظر مسلم، **الصحيح** 150/1، الرقم (كتاب الإيمان، باب بيان الإسلام والإحسان).

---

75 **طبقات** (الفقي) 24/2، (العثيمين) 47/3 "بما قدّر الله".

قد علم الله ما العبادُ عاملون وإلى ما هم صائرون، لا يخرجون من علم الله، ولا يكون في الأَرَضِين | ب 6
ولا في السماوات[76] إلّا ما علم الله.

رسالة عمر بن عبد العزيز في الردّ على القدريّة (van Ess, *Anfänge*, 44)؛ الأشعري، **الإبانة** ؛ الأزهري، **تهذيب اللغة** 59/11 ("المرجئة"، عن أبي عبيد)

وتعلمُ أنّ ما أصابك لم يكن ليخطئك وما أخطأك لم يكن ليصيبك، ولا خالق مع الله.

انظر في "ما أصابك لم يكن ليخطئك وما أخطأك لم يكن ليصيبك"، أبو حنيفة [جمعه أبو مطيع البلخي]، **الفقه الأبسط** 40؛ الحميدي، **المسند** (أصول السنّة) 546، 547 (عن سفيان بن عيينة)؛ الحافظ العدني، **الإيمان** 81، الرقم 14؛ أبو داود، **السنن** 84/7، الرقم 4699، و4700 (كتاب السنّة، باب في القدر)؛ ابن ماجة، **السنن** 29/1، الرقم 77 (المقدمة)؛ ابن حنبل، **المسند** 182/5، 185، 189، 205؛ عبد الله بن أحمد بن حنبل، **السنّة** 388/2، الرقم 843؛ ابن أبي عاصم، **السنّة** 40، الرقم 245؛ الأشعري، **مقالات** 293، **الإبانة** 20؛ الطبري، **صريح السنّة** 29؛ الطبراني، **المعجم الكبير** 123/11، الرقم 11243؛ ابن حبان، **الصحيح** 174، الرقم 724 (كتاب الرقائق، باب الورع والتوكّل)؛ الخلّال، **السنّة** 537/3، الرقم 886؛ الفريابي، **القدر** 140–141، الرقم 199، 200؛ النيسابوري، **المستدرك** 624/3، الرقم 6304 (عن عبد الله بن عبّاس في كتاب معرفة الصحابة)؛ قوّام السنّة، **الحجّة** 156/2 (من قول لابن مسعود)؛ البيهقي، **السنن** 73/21، الرقم 20913 (كتاب الشهادات، باب ما تردّ به شهادة أهل الأهواء)؛ وفيه "أنّ الله تبارك وتعالى لو عذّب أهل السموات والأرض..."، انظر ما يلي الرقم 46، حيث ورد الحديث نفسه في النصّ؛ ابن قدامة، "العقيدة"، 109.

(41) والتكبير على الجنائز أربع، وهو قول مالك بن أنس، وسفيان الثوري، والحسن بن صالح، وأحمد بن حنبل، والفقهاء؛ وهكذا قال رسول الله، صلّى الله عليه وسلّم.

وهو قول مالك، **الموطأ**، 226/1، الرقم 14، 15 (كتاب الجنائز)؛ الشافعي، **الأمّ** 646/2 (باب التكبير على الجنائز)، 413/8 (اختلاف عليّ وعبد الله بن مسعود)؛ الصنعاني، **المصنّف** 479/3–484؛ البخاري، **الجامع** 321، الرقم 1333، 1334 (باب التكبير على الجنازة أربعًا)؛ مسلم، **الصحيح** 656/2–657، الرقم 951، 952 (باب في التكبير على الجنازة)؛ الترمذي، **الجامع** 333/3، الرقم 1022–1023 (ما جاء في التكبير على

76 في الأصل: "السموات".

الجنازة)، وعلّق: "ثمّ أكثر أهل العلم من أصحاب النبيّ، صلّى الله عليه وسلّم، يرَوْن التكبير على الجنازة أربع تكبيرات وهو قول سفيان الثوري ومالك بن أنس وابن المبارك والشافعي وأحمد وإسحاق"؛ وعن أحمد بن حنبل في رواية الكوسج "من أربع ولا يزاد على سبع"، **مسائل الإمام أحمد** 808، الرقم 447؛ وعن صالح بن أحمد "أعجب إليَّ أن يقف بعد الرابعة قليلاً، ثمّ يُسلّم"، **مسائل الإمام** 38 ، الرقم 111؛ المروزي، **اختلاف الفقهاء** 212–213؛ ابن بطّة، **الشرح والإبانة** 70؛ ابن الجوزي، **مناقب أحمد** 1/314–315 (وذكر أحمد خلاف الشافعي له)؛ وذكر البيهقي، **السنن** 7/378–387، ثم أفرد بابًا في من روى أنّه كبّر على جنازة خمسًا؛ وانظر الطحاوي، **شرح معاني الآثار** 1/493–495؛ والزيلعي، **نصب الراية** 2/267–270. وقال ابن عبد البرّ، **التمهيد** 6/332–337 "قال أبو عمر اختلف السلف في عدد التكبير على الجنازة ثمّ اتّفقوا على أربع تكبيرات وما خالف ذلك شذوذ يشبه البدعة والحدث"؛ أمّا ابن حزم، **المحلّى** 5/125–127، فيقول بخمس تكبيرات ويجيز الأربع ويناقش أسانيد الأحاديث. وفي **مسندالإمام زيد**، 149، خمس تكبيرات، وفي رواية عن عليّ أنه كبّر أربعًا وخمسًا وستًّا وسبعًا. وعند الشيعة الإماميّة خمس تكبيرات، كما في الكليني، **الكافي** 3/181–182، وروى بسنده عن أبي عبد الله "إذا كبّر على رجل أربعًا اتُّهم"، يعني بالنفاق.

ولم نجد أنّ الحسن بن صالح بن حيّ كان يقول بأربع تكبيرات، والحسن كان صهرًا لعيسى بن زيد، وكان عيسى يقول بخمس تكبيرات (الأصفهاني، **مقاتل** 288، 343) ؛ وأهل السنّة يوثّقون الحسن بن صالح سوى في قوله في ترك الجمعة وبالسيف- أي بجواز الخروج على السلطان الجائر، قال الذهبي "له أقوال تحكى في الخلافيّات"، **تاريخ الإسلام** 4/337.

(42) والإيمان أنّ مع كلِّ قطرةٍ ملكًا ينزل من السماء حتّى يضعها حيث أمره الله عزّ وجلّ.

انظر ابن أبي الدنيا، **كتاب المطر** 55، الرقم 10؛ الطبري، **تفسير** 14/40–41 (الحجر 15/21)؛ أبو الشيخ، **كتاب العظمة** 968، الرقم 493، 1274، الرقم 762؛ البغوي، **تفسير** 4/375؛ الثعلبي، **تفسير** 5/336؛ وقارن بـ: الطبري، **تاريخ** 8/518؛ المقدسي، **البدء والتاريخ** 174–175 (أبو حذيفة عن مقاتل عن عطاء)؛ السيوطي، **الدرّ المنثور** 1/185 (البقرة 2/22).

(43) والإيمان أنّ النبيّ، صلّى الله عليه وسلّم، حين كلّم أهل القليب يوم بَدرٍ، أنّ[77] المشركين كانوا يسمعون كلامه.

---

77 **طبقات** (الفقي) 2/25، (العثيمين) 3/46 "أي".

في خبر "أهل القليب"، انظر ابن هشام، **سيرة** 453/2؛ الواقدي، **مغازي** 112/1؛ البيهقي، **دلائل النبوّة** 92/3، 117؛ الصنعاني، **المصنّف** 352/5؛ ابن حنبل، **المسند** 468/8، الرقم 4864؛ **ابن أبي شيبة** 70/13، الرقم 37720، 71/13، الرقم 137724؛ البخاري، **الجامع** 331، الرقم 1370 (كتاب الجنائز، باب ما جاء في عذاب القبر)؛ مسلم، **الصحيح** 643/2، الرقم 932 (كتاب الجنائز، باب الميت يعذّب ببكاء أهله عليه)؛ الطبري، **تاريخ** 456/2؛ الطبراني، **المعجم الكبير** 198/10، الرقم 10320؛ القرطبي، **التذكرة** 163/1؛ **تفسير** 377/7 (الأنفال 11/8)؛ ابن عبد البرّ، **التمهيد** 240/20.

(44) والإيمان أنّ الرجل إذا مرض يأجره[78] اللّٰهُ على مرضه.

انظر في أجر المريض، ابن حنبل، **المسند** 19/11، الرقم 6482 (عن عبد الله بن عمرو)، 422/11، الرقم 6825 (عن عبد الله بن عمرو)، 150/21، الرقم 13501 (عن أنس)، 343/28، الرقم 17118 (عن أبي الأشعث الصنعاني)؛ ابن أبي الدنيا، **كتاب المرض**؛ ابن حجر، **المطالب العالية** 54/12–84 (كتاب الطبّ، باب كفّارات المرض)؛ وعن الحسن البصري "المرض زكاة البدن"، ابن الجوزي، **آداب الحسن** 60.

والشهيد يأجره الله على القتل.

انظر على سبيل المثال، ابن حنبل، **المسند** 419/28، الرقم 17182 (عن المقدام بن معدي كرب)، 294/36، الرقم 21962 (عن عبد الرحمن بن يزيد بن جابر)؛ البخاري، **الجامع** 691–692 (كتاب الجهاد والسير، باب درجات المجاهدين، وما يليه)؛ مسلم، **الصحيح** 1495–1498 (كتاب الإمارة، باب فضل الجهاد)؛ الترمذي، **الجامع** 175/4–178 (كتاب الجهاد، باب ما جاء في ثواب الشهداء).

(45) والإيمان بأنّ الأطفال إذا أصابهم شيءٌ في دار الدنيا يألمون، وذلك أنّ بكر ابن أخت عبد الواحد قال "لا يألمون"، وكذب.

ابن قتيبة، **تأويل مختلف الحديث**، 47؛ الأشعري، **مقالات** 286–287؛ عبد الجبّار ، **شرح** 483؛ البغدادي، **الفرق** 213؛ الإسفرايني، **التبصير** 110؛ وانظر:

van Ess, *TuG*ii, 115.

ونسب ابن حزم القول إلى عبد الله بن عيسى تلميذ بكر، **الفصل** 146/4.

78 **طبقات** (الفقي) 25/2، (العثيمين) 46/3 "آجره".

(46) واعلم أنّه لا يدخل الجنّة أحدٌ إلّا برحمة الله.

البخاري، **الجامع** 1439، الرقم 5673 (كتاب المرضى، باب تمني المريض الموت)؛ 1609، الرقم 6467 (كتاب الرقاق، باب القصد والمداومة في العمل)؛ مسلم، **الصحيح** 2168/4، الرقم 2816 (كتاب صفات المنافقين، باب لن يدخل أحد الجنّة بعمله).

ولا يعذّبُ الله أحدًا إلّا بذنوبه، بقدر ذنوبه.[79] ولو عذّب الله أهلَ السماوات والأَرَضين، برّهم وفاجرهم، عذّبهم غيرَ ظالمٍ لهم.

"لو عذّب"، انظر، ابن حنبل، **المسند** 465/35، الرقم 21589، 486/35، الرقم 21611، 511/35، الرقم 21653 (من حديث ابن الديلمي)؛ عبدالله بن أحمد بن حنبل، **السنّة** 389، الرقم 843؛ أبو داود، **السنن** 85/7، الرقم 4699 (عن الديلمي، كتاب السنّة، باب في القدر)؛ ابن ماجة، **السنن** 29/1–30، الرقم 77 (المقدّمة)؛ الطبراني، **المعجم الكبير** 186/10، الرقم 10564 (عن أبي الأسود الدؤلي)؛ الفريابي، **القدر** 138، الرقم 192 (ابن الديلمي)؛ البيهقي، **السنن** 73/21، الرقم 20913 (كتاب الشهادات، باب ما تردّ به شهادة أهل الأهواء)؛ البيهقي، **القضاء والقدر** 425/2.

(47) لا يجوز أن يُقال لله، تبارك وتعالى، إنّه يظلم؛[80] وإنّما يظلم من يأخذ ما ليس له، والله جلّ ثناؤه،
7أ له الخلق والأمر، الخلقُ خلقُهُ والدارُ دارُه ﴿لا يُسَئَلُ عمّا يفّعلُ وهم يُسئلون﴾ (الأنبياء 23/21).[81] |
ولا يُقال لِمَ وكيفَ، لا يدخل أحدٌ بين الله وبين خلقه.

"إنّما يظلم من يأخذ ما ليس له"، انظر، الآجرّي، **الشريعة** 701/2؛ "لا يُقال لِمَ وكيفَ"، وانظر ما تقدم الرقم 9، 11، وما يلي الرقم 47، 77أ.

(48) وإذا سمعت الرجل يطعنُ على الآثار[82] فاتّهمه على الإسلام، فإنّه رجلٌ رديء القول والمذهب، وإنّما طعن على رسول الله، صلّى الله عليه وسلّم، وأصحابه. لأنّه إنّما عرفنا الله وعرفنا رسول الله، صلّى

79 **طبقات** (الفقي) 25/2 "إلا بذنوب بعد ذنوب"، (العثيمين) 48/3 "إلا بذنوب بعد الذنوب".

80 **طبقات** (الفقي) 25/2، (العثيمين) 48/3 "ظلم".

81 في الأصل: "يفعل بخلقه"، ثمّ ضبّب عليها وزاد "يسئلون".

82 **طبقات** (الفقي) 25/2، (العثيمين) 48/3 "يطعن على الآثار ولا يقبلها أو ينكر شيئا من أخبار رسول الله".

الله عليه وسلّم، وعرفنا القرآن، وعرفنا الخير والشرّ والدنيا والآخرة، بالآثار. فإنّ القرآن إلى السنّة أحوجُ من السنّة إلى القرآن.

"إذا سمعت رجلًا يطعن على الإسلام..."، قوّام السنّة، **الحجّة** 428/2؛ وعن سفيان الثوري "إنّما الدين الآثار"، قوّام السنّة، **الحجّة** 206/1.

وانظر في "القرآن إلى السنّة أحوج..."، خبر ينسب إلى مكحول في: المروزي، **السنة** 45، الرقم 106؛ حرب الكرماني، **كتاب السنّة** (الملحق)، 313 (الأوزاعي عن يحيى بن أبي كثير)؛ وللأوزاعي، ابن بطّة، **الإبانة** (الإيمان)، 253/1، الرقم 88 (الأوزاعي عن مكحول)؛ والرقم 254 (الأوزاعي عن يحيى بن أبي كثير)؛ ابن عبد البرّ، **جامع بيان العلم** 191/2 (مرّةً عن الأوزاعي وأُخرى الأوزاعي عن مكحول)؛ الهروي، **ذمّ الكلام** 148/2؛ الزركشي، **البحر المحيط** 167/4 (عن الأوزاعي).

(49) والكلام والجدال والخصومةُ في القدر خاصّةً منهيٌّ عنه [عند] جميع الفرق.[83] لأنّ القدر سرُّ الله، ونهى الربُّ، تبارك وتعالى، الأنبياء عن الكلام في القدر؛ ونهى رسول الله، صلّى الله عليه وسلّم، عن الخصومةُ في القدر، وكرهه العلماء وأهل الورع ونَهَوْا عن الجدال في القدر. فعليك بالتسليم والإقرار والإيمان واعتقاد ما قال رسول الله، صلّى الله عليه وسلّم، في جملة الأشياء وتسكت[84] عمّا سوى ذلك.

"القدر سرّ الله"، الأشعري، **مقالات** 294؛ الطحاوي، **العقيدة** 32؛ ابن أبي العز، **شرح العقيدة** 320–321؛ ابن بطّة، **الإبانة** (القدر) 243/1، الرقم 1281 (عن يحيى بن معاذ)؛ ابن عبد البر، **التمهيد** 139/3؛ وهو من قول عليّ بن أبي طالب، ابن بابويه، **الاعتقادات** 41.

وانظر في النهي عن الجدال والخصومات في القدر، ابن بطّة، **الإبانة** (القدر) 307/2–310؛ وفي النهي عن الجدال في الصّفات، البغوي، **شرح السنّة** 216/1–218؛ البيهقي، **القضاء والقدر** 705/2–724 (الباب 27، ما ورد في النهي عن مجالسة القدريّة ومفاتحتهم والنهي عن الخصومة في القدر).

(50) والإيمان بأنّ رسول الله، صلّى الله عليه وسلّم، أُسرِيَ به إلى السماء، وصار إلى العرش وكلّم

83 النصُّ مضطربٌ في الأصل: "..جميع الفرق لان القدر خاصة منهي جميع الفرق لان القدر سر الله".

84 **طبقات** (الفقي) 25/2، (العثيمين) 49/3 "واسكت".

الله،[85] تبارك وتعالى، ودخل الجنّة، واطّلع إلى النار، ورأى الملائكة، ونُشرت له[86] الأنبياء، ورأى
ب 7 سُرادِقات العرش والكرسي وجميعَ ما في السماوات [وما في الأَرَضين في اليقظة. حمله جبريل | على
البُراق حتّى أداره في السموات]،[87] وفُرِضَت له الصلاةُ[88] في تلك الليلة،[89] ورجع إلى مكّة في تلك
الليلة، وذلك قبل الهجرة.

كثيرة هي أحاديث الإسراء والمعراج وتشتمل على تفاصيل متنوّعة، انظر مثلًا، مسلم، **الصحيح** 157/1، الرقم 173 (كتاب الإيمان، في ذكر سدرة المنتهى)؛ النسائي، **السنن** 197/1، الرقم 309 (كتاب الصلاة، فرض الصلاة)، 199/1، الرقم 310 (عن أبي ذر) "راجعت ربي"؛ ابن بطّة، **الشرح والإبانة** 60؛ ويبدو لنا أنّ غلام خليل يعتمد على أكثر من أثر.

"وكلّم الله"، انظر، ابن أبي حاتم، **تفسير** 2313/7 (الإسراء 1/17)؛ "فكلمه الله تعالى عند ذلك"، من حديث طويل في المعراج)؛ الطبري، **تفسير** 432/14 (الإسراء 1/17 من حديث أبي العالية عن أبي هريرة أو غيره، والنصّ كما في تفسير ابن أبي حاتم)؛ قوّام السنّة، **الحجّة** 491/1–492 (عن أبي حامد أحمد بن محمد المقرئ في شرح ﴿فأوحى إلى عبدِه ما أوحى﴾، قال "تكليمًا منه")؛ ابن خفيف، **المعتقد** 353 (وأنّه رأى ربّه وكلّمه وأوصاه)؛ ابن أبي يعلى، **الاعتقاد** 25، 37؛ وانظر:

Colby, *Narrating Muḥammad's Night Journey*, 84, 90–98.

وورد ذكر "سرادقات العرش" في حديث الضحّاك بن مُزاحم، القشيري، **المعراج** 53 (ونصّ الضحّاك مبكر بحسب فان أس، **بدايات الفكر الإسلامي** 56–60)؛ وانظر في نفي الرؤية والكلام: مسلم، **الصحيح** 159/1، الرقم 177 (مسروق عن عائشة)؛ الفزاري الإباضي، **كتاب الفتيا** 131؛ وانظر في أنّ الإسراء كان في اليقظة، الطبري، **تفسير** 420/14، 447؛ قوّام السنّة، **الحجّة** 512/1، 253/2؛ وانظر فان أس، **بدايات الفكر الإسلامي** 39–62.

وفي "وذلك قبل الهجرة"، ثمّة اختلاف في تحديد تاريخ الإسراء والمعراج، انظر، ابن حجر، **فتح** 203/7–204؛ وانظر:

Jarrar, *Prophetenbiographie*, 185, 194.

Colby, *Narrating Muḥammad's Night Journey*, 24, 57.

---

85 **طبقات** (الفقي) 26/2، (العثيمين) 49/3 "وسمع كلام الله".

86 **طبقات** (الفقي) 26/2، (العثيمين) 49/3 "وبشرت به".

87 [ ] ليس في **طبقات الحنابلة**.

88 **طبقات** (الفقي) 26/2، (العثيمين) 49/3 "وفرضت عليه الصلوات الخمس".

89 **طبقات** (الفقي) 26/2، (العثيمين) 49/3 "ليلته".

(51) واعلم أنّ أرواحَ الشهداء في قناديلَ تحت العرش تسرح في الجنّة، وأرواح المؤمنين تحت العرش،[90] وأرواح الكفّار والفجّار في بَرَهوت.

انظر، مسلم، **الصحيح** 1502/3، الرقم 1887 (كتاب الإمارة، باب بيان أنّ أرواح الشهداء في الجنّة)؛ الطبري، **تفسير** 228/6–229 (169/3)؛ ابن عبد البرّ، **التمهيد** 62/11–65.

وانظر في أنّ "أرواح الكفار في برهوت"، الصنعاني، **المصنّف** 116/5، الرقم 9118؛ ياقوت الحموي، **معجم البلدان** 405/1، 92/2؛ الزمخشري، **الفائق** 101/1؛ ابن حمدان، **نهاية المبتدئين** 54؛ الهيثمي، **مجمع** 467/3، الرقم 5712؛ وقارن بـ: ابن الجوزي، **آداب الحسن** 57.

(52) والإيمان بأنّ الميّت يُقعد في قبره ويُرسل الله فيه الروح حتّى يسألَه منكرٌ ونكير عن الإيمان وشرائعه، ثمّ تُسَلُّ روحُه بلا ألم، ويعرف الميّتُ الزائرَ إذا أتاه، ويَنعم في القبر المؤمنُ ويعذّب الفاجرُ كيف شاء الله.

"يُقعد في قبره"، البخاري، **الجامع** 322، الرقم 1338 (كتاب الجنائز، باب الميّت يسمع خفق النعال)؛ ابن بطّة، **الشرح والإبانة** 53؛ "يُرسل الله فيه الروح"، أبو نعيم، **حلية** 190/3؛ الجيلاني، **الغنية** 142/1؛ القرطبي، **التذكرة** 165/1، 169، 181؛ "يعرف الميّتُ الزائرَ إذا أتاه"، انظر حديث عبد الله بن عمير عن ابن عبّاس، الطبراني، **المعجم الكبير** 364/20، الرقم 850؛ وعن عبد الله بن عمير عن ابن عبّاس، ابن عبد البرّ، **الاستذكار** 185/1؛ وحديث أبي هريرة، البيهقي، **شعب الإيمان** 473/11، الرقم 8857؛ وقد أنكرت عائشة هذا المعنى، القرطبي، **التذكرة** 204/1؛ ابن القيم، **الروح** 5–10؛ وقارن بـ: ابن عبد البرّ، **التمهيد** 239/20–240؛ وابن حمدان، **نهاية المبتدئين** 55.

(53) واعلم أنّ التزويج بقضاء الله وقدره.[91]

لعلّه يشير إلى سورة الشورى 50/42 ﴿أَوْ يُزَوِّجُهُمْ ذُكْرَانًا وَإِنَاثًا وَيَجْعَلُ مَن يَشَآءُ عَقِيمًا﴾، قال الفرّاء "يجعل بعضهم بنين ويجعل بعضهم بنات، ذلك التزويج في هذا الموضع"، **معاني القرآن** 26/3؛ الطبري "بأن يجعل حَمل زوجته مرّةً ذكرًا ومرّةً أنثى، فذلك هو التزويج"، **تفسير** 537/20؛ الزمخشري، **الكشّاف** 420/5.

90 **طبقات** (الفقي) 26/2، (العثيمين) 49/3 "في حواصل طير خضر تسرح في الجنة وتأوي إلى قناديل".

91 ليس في **طبقات الحنابلة**.

(54) والإيمان بأنّ الله، تبارك وتعالى، هو الذي كلّم موسى بن عمران يوم الطُّور وموسى يسمع من الله الكلامَ بصوت وقع في مسامعه، منه لا من غيره؛ فمن قال غيرَ هذا فقد كَفَر.[92]

قارن بـ: عبد الله بن أحمد بن حنبل، **السنّة** 208/1، الرقم 328، 280/1–283؛ أبو داود، **مسائل الإمام أحمد** 353، الرقم 1695؛ الإصطخري، "العقيدة" في ابن أبي يعلى، **طبقات** (الفقي) 29/1 "وكلّم الله موسى من فيه..."؛ حرب الكرماني، **كتاب السنّة** 53 (بلفظ مختلف)، 220–222؛ السجزي، **الردّ** 114، 161–163؛ الملطي، **التنبيه** 100؛ ابن بطّة، **الإبانة** (الردّ على الجهميّة) 314/2/3–322؛ الآجرّي، **الشريعة** 1109/3؛ الجيلاني، **الغنية** 123/1؛ ابن قدامة، **لمعة الاعتقاد** 15–16؛ ابن قدامة، "العقيدة"، 109 ؛ وقارن بـ: قوّام السنّة، **الحجّة** 214/1–215.

(55) والعقل مولودٌ. أُعطي كلُّ إنسانٍ من العقل ما أراد الله، يتفاوتون في العقول مثل الذرّة في السماوات؛ ويُطلب من كلِّ إنسانٍ من العمل على قدر ما أعطاه الله من العقل. وليس العقل باكتسابٍ إنّما هو فضلٌ من الله تبارك وتعالى.

النصّ في: أبو يعلى الحنبلي، **العدّة** 83/1–84، 94 (فقال أبو محمد البربهاري في شرح السنّة)؛ "ليس العقل باكتساب"، قوّام السنّة، **الحجّة** 429/2 (ولم يذكر مصدره، غير أنّه ذكر أنّ غلام خليل من مصادره 475/2)؛ ابن تيمية، **بغية المرتاد** 258 (وذُكر عن أبي محمد البربهاري أنّه قال...)؛ وقد ذكر الجاحظ أنّ "العقل المولود متناهي الحدود، وعقل التجارب لا يوقف منه على حدّ"، **البلدان** 465.وانظر، قوّام السنّة، **الحجّة** 320/1 (العقل على ثلاثة أوجه، عقل مولود مطبوع وهو عقل ابن آدم الذي فُضِّل به على أهل الأرض، وهو محلّ التكليف والأمر والنهي، وبه يكون التمييز والتدبير ... عقلُ التأييد الذي يكون مع الإيمان معًا... وعقل التجارب والعبر...). ونقل أبو يعلى الحنبلي، **العدّة** 85/1–86 عن ابن حنبل أنّه غريزة، وقارن بـ: المحاسبي الذي عدّه غريزة ونورًا، **العقل** 201–207، وانظر:

van Ess, *TuG* iv, 206.

"يتفاوتون في العقول مثل الذرّة في السماوات"، قارن بحديث لسعيد بن أبي عروبة عن سعيد بن جبير، عمارة بن وثيمة، **بدء الخلق** 128 (.. ولكنّ الناس يتفاضلون في عقولهم ويتفاوتون [في] ذلك بينهم كبعد ما بين السماء والأرض...)؛ و أبو حيّان التوحيدي، **الإمتاع والمؤانسة** 204/2 (عن ابن زرعة الفيلسوف "والعقل بين أصحابه ذو عرضٍ واسع، وبقدر ذلك يتفاضلون التفاضل الذي لا سبيل إلى حصره").

92 **طبقات** (الفقي) 26/2، (العثيمين) 50/3 "كفر بالله العظيم".

وانظر في "يطلب من كلِّ إنسانٍ من العمل على قدر ما أعطاه الله من العقل"، أحاديث مشابهة في البيهقي، **شعب الإيمان** 351/6، الرقم 4315 وما يليه؛ وفي حديث عن أبي جعفر الباقر في خبر عن موسى النبيّ "أنا أؤاخذ عبادي على قدر ما أعطيتهم من العقل"، البرقي، **المحاسن** 194 (باب العقل)؛ وقارن بـ الكليني، **الكافي** 14/1–15 (كتاب العقل)؛ وابن أبي الدنيا، **العقل وفضله** 42؛ وأبو نعيم، **حلية** 223/3؛ والهيثمي، **بغية الباحث** 802/2–804.

(56) واعلم أنّ الله فضّل العبادَ بعضَهم على بعض في الدين والدنيا، عدلٌ منه؛ لا يُقال جارَ[93] ولا حابَى؛ فمن | قال بأنّ فضلَ الله على المؤمن والكافر سَواءٌ فهو صاحبُ بدعة. بل فضّل اللهُ المؤمنين أ 8
على الكافرين،[94] والطائعَ على العاصي، والمعصومَ على المخذول، عدلٌ منه هو فضلُه؛ يُعطِي من يشاء ويمنع من يشاء.

في "يعطي من يشاء"، انظر، الطبري، **تفسير** 302/5 (آل عمران 27/3)؛ ابن كثير، **تفسير** 122/4 (الشورى 293/12)؛ الزرقاني، **أوجز المسالك** 39/16–40.

(57) ولا يحِلُّ أنْ تكتمَ النصيحةَ للمسلمين،[95] برِّهم وفاجرِهم، في أمرِ الدين، فمن كتم فقد غشّ [المسلمين، ومن غشّ المسلمين فقد غشّ][96] الدينَ، ومن غشّ الدين فقد خان اللهَ ورسولَه والمؤمنين.

"النصح لكلّ مسلم"، وردت في بيعة النبيّ، ابن مندة، **الإيمان** 426/1–429؛ وعن تميم الداري أنّ النبيّ، صلّى الله عليه وسلّم، قال "الدين النصيحة"، الشافعي، **الرسالة** 50–51؛ المروزي، **تعظيم قدر الصلاة** 680–694؛ الحافظ العدني، **الإيمان** 132، الرقم 96؛ مسلم، **الصحيح** 74/1، الرقم 55 (كتاب الإيمان)؛ الأشعري، **رسالة** 319؛ **مقالات** 297؛ ابن بطّة، **الشرح والإبانة** 68؛ الملطي، **التنبيه** 65؛ ابن حبّان، **روضة العقلاء** 194–198؛ عياض، **الشفا** 508–510. وانظر في حديث "من غشّ المسلمين"، أبو يعلى الموصلي، **المسند** 233/2 (قيس بن أبي غرزة عن الرسول، بلفظ من غشّ المسلمين فليس منهم).

93 **طبقات** (الفقي) 26/2 "جاد".

94 **طبقات** (الفقي) 26/2، (العثيمين) 50/3 "المؤمن على الكافر".

95 **طبقات** (الفقي) 26/2، (العثيمين) 51/3 "أحدا من المسلمين".

96 زادها في الهامش الأيسر طولا.

(58) والله، تبارك وتعالى، ﴿سميعٌ بصير﴾، ﴿سميعٌ عليم﴾،[97] ﴿يداه مَبسوطتان﴾. قد علم الله أنّ الخلقَ يعصونه قبل أنْ يخلقهم، عِلْمُه نافذٌ فيهم، فلم يمنعه علمُه فيهم أنْ هداهم للإسلام ومنَّ به عليهم كرمًا وجودًا وتفضّلًا، فله الحمْدُ.

تتكرّر مفردات ﴿سميع بصير﴾، الحجّ 61/22، وآيات أُخرى؛ ﴿سميعٌ عليمٌ﴾، البقرة 181/2، وآيات أُخرى، مرارًا في القرآن الكريم، والشاهد هنا هو في الردّ على من عطّل الصفات، الأشعري، **الإبانة** 94–95.

أمّا ﴿يداه مبسوطتان﴾ فمن سورة المائدة 64/5. انظر، البخاري، **الجامع** 1824، الرقم 7386 (كتاب التوحيد، باب وكان الله سميعًا بصيرا)؛ الدارمي، **الردّ على بشر المرّيسي** 30؛ الإسماعيلي، **اعتقاد** 171 "ويداه مبسوطتان ينفق كيف يشاء، بلا اعتقاد كيف"، 172، الرقم 12؛ الأشعري، **رسالة** 224؛ **مقالات** 290؛ ابن قدامة، "العقيدة"، 110.

قال الطبري "الصواب من هذا القول عندنا أن نثبت حقائقها على ما نعرف من جهة الإثبات ونفي التشبيه، كما نفى ذلك عن نفسه جلّ ثناؤه"، فمعناه "الإثبات على ما يُعقل من معنى الإثبات لا على النفي، وكذلك سائر الأسماء والمعاني التي ذكرنا"، **التبصير** 140، 142؛ وحديث "إنّ الله ينزل إلى السماء الدنيا ثمّ يبسط يده..."، ابن حنبل، **المسند** 191/6، الرقم 3673 (عن ابن مسعود)؛ قوّام السنّة، **الحجّة** 168/1.

(59) واعلم أنّ البِشارةَ عند الموت ثلاثُ بِشارات: يُقال أَبْشِرْ يا حبيبَ الله برضا الله والجنّة، ويُقال أبشر يا عدوَّ الله بغضب الله والنار، ويُقال أبشر يا عبدَ الله بالجنّة بعد الإسلام؛[98] هذا قولُ ابن عبّاس.

قارن بحديث طويل للبراء بن عازب فيه ذكر لبشائر الموت، الطيالسي، **المسند** 114/2–119، الرقم 789؛ وانظر المحاسبي، **التوهّم** 2؛ البيهقي، **إثبات عذاب القبر** 44–45؛ القرطبي، **التذكرة** 84/1–85؛ السيوطي، **الدر المنثور** 240/14 (عن سلمان).

(60) واعلم أنّ أوّلَ من ينظر إلى الله في الجنّة الأضرّاءُ، ثمّ الرجال، ثمّ النساء بأعين رؤوسهم؛ كما قال رسول الله، صلّى الله عليه وسلّم، "سترَوْن ربّكم كما ترَوْن القمرَ ليلةَ البدر لا تضامون في رؤيته"؛ والإيمانُ بهذا واجبٌ | وإنكاره كُفر. ب 8

97 **طبقات** (الفقي) 27/2، (العثيمين) 51/3 "سميع بصير عليم".

98 **طبقات** (الفقي) 27/2، (العثيمين) 51/3 "يا عبد الله بالجنّة بعد الانتقام، ويقال أبشر يا عدوّ الله بغضب الله والنار".

"أوّل من ينظر الأضرّاء"، قارن بـ اللالكائي، **شرح** 578/2، الرقم 923 و924.

انظر في حديث "الرؤية"، الحميدي، **المسند** 350، الرقم 799؛ البخاري، **الجامع** 143/1، الرقم 554 (باب فضل صلاة العصر)؛ مسلم، **الصحيح** 439/1، الرقم 633 (باب فضل صلاتي الصبح والعصر)؛ ابن حنبل، **المسند** 526/31، الرقم 19190؛ عبد الله بن أحمد بن حنبل، **السنة** 229–236؛ ابن أبي عاصم، **السنّة** 69–71؛ ابن خُزيمة، **كتاب التوحيد** 173–179؛ حرب الكرماني، **كتاب السنة** 53؛ الأشعري، **رسالة**، 237–238؛ **مقالات** 292؛ **الإبانة** 25–38؛ ابن حبان، **الصحيح** 1302، الرقم 7399 (رؤية المؤمنين ربّهم)؛ الملطي، **التنبيه** 89–90؛ ابن بطّة، **الإبانة** (الإيمان) 557/2؛ الآجرّي، **التصديق بالنظر** 60–61، الرقم 25، 26؛ ابن مندة، **الإيمان** 779/1–782؛ البيهقي، **السنن** 9/3 (كتاب الصلاة، باب أول فرض الصلاة)؛ القرطبي، **تفسير** 211/3 (البقرة 237/2).

(61) واعلم، رحمك الله، أنّه ما كانت[99] زندقةً قطُّ، ولا كفر، ولا شكّ،[100] ولا بدعة، ولا ضلالة، ولا حَيْرة في الدين، إلّا من الكلام وأصحاب[101] الكلام والجدال والمِراء[102] والخصومة. والعجبُ[103] كيف يجترىء الرجل على المِراء والخصومة والجدال والله تعالى يقول ﴿ما يُجادِلُ في آياتِ اللهِ إلّا الذين كَفَروا﴾ (غافر 4/40). فعليك بالتسليم والرضا بالآثار وأهل الآثار، والكفِّ والسكوت.

قارن بـ الاسماعيلي، **اعتقاد** 177، الرقم 40؛ والهروي، **ذمّ الكلام** 400/4 (عن إبراهيم الخوّاص).

(62) والإيمان بأنّ الله، تبارك وتعالى، يعذِّبُ الخلقَ في النار في الأغلال والأنكال والسلاسل، والنار في أجوافهم وفوقهم وتحتهم. وذلك أنّ الجَهميّةَ—منهم هشام الفُوَطي—قال "يعذّب عند النار"، ردًّا[ا] على الله وعلى رسوله.

انظر الرعد 5/13؛ سبأ 33/34؛ يس 8/36؛ غافر 71/40؛ الحاقة 30/69–38؛ المزمّل 12/73؛ الإنسان 4/76، وغيرها من الآيات. وانظر في عذاب النار، المحاسبي، **كتاب التوهّم**؛ ابن أبي الدنيا، **كتاب صفة النار**؛ الدارمي، **الردّ على بشر المرّيسي** 16–17؛ الجيلاني، **الغنية** 285/1–300.

---

99 **طبقات** (الفقي) 27/2، (العثيمين) 51/3 "أنّها لم تكن".

100 **طبقات** (الفقي) 27/2، (العثيمين) 51/3 "شكوك".

101 **طبقات** (الفقي) 27/2، (العثيمين) 52/3 "أهل".

102 من "الكلام"، كتبها في الهامش الأيمن طولًا و كتب بعده "صح".

103 **طبقات** (الفقي) 27/2، (العثيمين) 52/3 "وكيف".

وانظر في قول الفوطي، الأشعري، **مقالات** 488؛ الذهبي، **سير** 547/10؛ وانظر الشهرستاني، **الملل** 31؛ وانظر:

van Ess, *TuG* iv, 8.

(63) واعلم أنّ الصلاةَ الفريضة خمسٌ،[104] لا يزاد فيهنّ ولا يُنقص في مواقيتها. وفي السفر ركعتان[105] إلّا المغربَ؛ فمن قال "أكثر من خمس" فقد ابتدع، ومن قال "أقلّ من خمس" فقد ابتدع. لا يقبل الله شيئًا منها إلّا لوقتها، إلّا أنْ يكونَ نِسيان، فإنّه معذور يأتي بها إذا ذكرها،[106] أو يكون مسافرًا فيجمع بين الصلاتين إنْ شاءَ.

روى الشافعي "وسئل رسول الله عن الإسلام فقال خمس صلوات في اليوم والليلة، فقال السائل: هل عليّ غيرها؟ قال: لا إلّا أن تطوّع"، **الأمّ** 149/2 (أوّل كتاب الصلاة).

"إلّا المغرب"، الكاساني، **بدائع** 91/1–93؛ ابن قدامة، **المغني** 121/3–122.

"لا يقبل الله شيئًا منها إلّا لوقتها"، نقله ابن رجب عن البربهاري، **فتح الباري** 135/5 (كتاب مواقيت الصلاة، باب من نسي صلاةً فليصلِّ إذا ذكر)؛ وقارن بـ: ابن حزم، **المحلّى** 235/2؛ انظر في فوات الصلاة، قال ابن حنبل "يعيده" وانظر التفصيل برواية أبي داود، **مسائل الإمام أحمد** 72، وبرواية ابن هانئ النيسابوري، **مسائل الإمام أحمد** 73/1؛ الشيباني، **الأصل** 135/1؛ الشافعي، **الأمّ** 170/2–171؛ وفصّل المروزي في وجوه المسألة وآراء العلماء، **تعظيم قدر الصلاة** 894–926، 980 وما بعدها؛ الإسماعيلي، **اعتقاد** 175، الرقم 27؛ ابن عبد البرّ، **الاستذكار** 76/1–78، قال "وقد شذّ بعض أهل الظاهر، وأقدم على خلاف جمهور علماء المسلمين وسبيل المؤمنين، فقال ليس على المتعمّد لترك الصلاة في وقتها أن يأتي بها في غير وقتها، لأنّه غير نائم ولا ناس" 78؛ وقال ابن قدامة ، **المغني** 357/3 "ولا نعلم بين المسلمين خلافًا في أنّ تارك الصلاة يجب عليه قضاؤها".

9أ (64) والزكاة من الذهب والفضّة والتَّمر والحبوب والدوابّ، على ما قال رسول | الله، صلّى الله عليه وسلّم؛ فإنْ قَسَمَها فجائزٌ وإنْ أعطاها الإمامَ[107] فجائز.

104 **طبقات** (الفقي) 27/2، (العثيمين) 52/3 "خمس صلوات".

105 في الأصل "ركعتين".

106 ابن رجب، **فتح الباري**، 135/5.

107 **طبقات** (الفقي) 27/2، (العثيمين) 52/3: "دفعها إلى الإمام".

"إنْ قَسَمَها فجائزٌ وإنْ أعطاها الإمامَ فجائز"، وهو رأي الحسن في ما رواه ابن أبي شيبة عن هشام عنه "إن دفعها إليهم أجزأ عنه وإن قسمها أجزأ عنه"، **المصنّف** 235/4، الرقم 10306، ويرى حرب الكرماني دفعها للأمراء "عدلوا فيها أم جاروا"، **كتاب السنّة** 40؛ وانظر الأحاديث في هذه المسألة وآراء الفقهاء في **المصنّف** 232/4–236 (كتاب الزكاة، البابان 84 و49)؛ ويرى الشافعي "أن يتولّى الرجل قسمتها عن نفسه فيكون على يقين من أداءها"، **الأمّ** 57/3–58؛ وللتفصيل في المسألة، ابن قدامة، **المغني** 90/4–95.

(65) واعلم أنّ أوّلَ الإسلام شهادةُ "أنْ لا إله إلّا الله وأنّ محمّدًا عبده ورسوله".

الشهادة هي الركن الأوّل من الإسلام، وانظر حديث "بُني الإسلام على خمس"، ابن حنبل، **المسند** 417/8، 4798 (عن عبد الله بن عمر)؛ 550/31، الرقم 19220 (عن جابر بن عبد الله)؛ مسلم، **الصحيح** 45/1، الرقم 16 (كتاب الإيمان، باب بيان أركان الإسلام).

(66) وأنّ ما قال الله كما قال، ولا[108] خُلفَ لما قال وهو عند ما قال.

(67) والإيمان بالشرائع كلِّها.

البقرة 136/2 و285؛ وحديث عمر "أنّ جبريل سأل النبيّ، صلّى الله عليه وسلّم، فقال: أخبرني عن الإيمان، قال: أن تؤمن بالله، وملائكته، وكتبه، ورسله، واليوم الآخر، وتؤمن بالقدر خيره وشرّه"، البخاري، **الجامع** 23، الرقم 50 (كتاب الإيمان، باب سؤال جبريل)؛ مسلم، **الصحيح** 37/1–39، الرقم 8 و9 (كتاب الإيمان)؛ وقارن بـ الرازي، **مفاتح** 91/4.

(68) واعلم أنّ الشراءَ والبيع—ما بِيعَ في أسواق المسلمين—حلالٌ،[109] ما بيع على حكم الكتاب والإسلام والسنّة من غير أنْ يدخله تغرير[110] أو ظلم أوجَوْر[111] أو خلاف للقرآن أو خلاف للعلم.

108 الأصل: "ولا".

109 **طبقات** (الفقي) 27/2، (العثيمين) 53/3 "حلال إذا بيع في أسواق المسلمين".

110 تغيير؛ والتغرير الخداع والغشّ.

111 **طبقات** (الفقي) 28/2، (العثيمين) 53/3 "من غير أن يدخله ظلم أو غدر".

"أصل البيوع كلّها مباح إذا كانت برضا المتبايعين الجائزي الأمر فيما تبايعا، إلّا ما نهى عنه رسول الله منها وما كان في معنى ما نهى عنه"، الشافعي، **الأمّ** 5/4 (كتاب البيوع)؛ وقارن بقول لأحمد بن حنبل عند ابن الجوزي، **مناقب أحمد** 306/1 (اعتقاد أحمد رواية الأندرابي)؛ والخلّال، **الحثّ على التجارة** 25–26؛ وفي النهي عن بيع الغرر، ابن بطّة، **الشرح والإبانة** 78.

(69) واعلم، رحمك الله، أنّه ينبغي للعبد أن تصحَبَه الشفقةُ[112] أبدًا ما صحبَ الدنيا، لأنّه لا يدري على ما يموت، وبما يُختَم له، وعلى ما يَلقى اللهَ، وإنْ عمل كلَّ عملٍ من الخير. وينبغي للرجل المُسرِف على نفسه ألّا يقطعَ رجاءَه من الله تعالى عند[113] الموت، ويُحسِنَ ظنَّه بالله تبارك وتعالى، ويخافَ ذنوبه، فإنْ رحِمَه الله فبفضل وإنْ عذّبه فبذنبٍ.

"أن تصحبه الشفقة"، قال يحيى بن جعدة "إعمل وأنت مشفق، ودع العمل وأنت تحبّه، عمل صالح دائم وإن قلّ"، ابن المبارك، **الزهد** 392؛ وانظر المحاسبي، **شرح المعرفة** 52؛ والإشفاق "دوام الحذر مقرونًا بالترحّم..."، الهروي، **منازل السائرين** 27–28.

"لا يدري على ما يموت، وبما يُختَم له"، انظر حديث أنس، ابن حنبل، **المسند** 246/19، الرقم 12214؛ وقارن بـ: الإسماعيلي، **اعتقاد** 176، الرقم 36؛ الصابوني، **عقيدة السلف** 286؛ القرطبي، **تفسير** 323/7 (الأعراف 176/8)؛ ابن بطّال، **شرح** 203/10؛ ابن حجر، **فتح الباري** 330/11 (باب الأعمال بالخواتيم).

"ويحسن ظنّه بالله"، انظر حديث جابر بن عبد الله في ابن حنبل، **المسند** 28/22، الرقم 1425، 366/22، الرقم 14481؛ مسلم، **الصحيح** 2205/4، الرقم 2877 (كتاب الجنّة، باب الأمر بحسن الظنّ)؛ ابن أبي الدنيا، **حسن الظنّ بالله** 12، و15 (إنّ حسن الظنّ بالله من حسن العبادة)؛ ابن حبّان، **الصحيح** 159، الرقم 630 (كتاب الرقائق، باب حسن الظنّ).

(70) والإيمان بأنّ الله، تبارك وتعالى، أطْلعَ نبيَّهُ على ما يكون في أُمّته إلى يوم القيامة.

قارن بحديث عمرو بن أخطب "... فأعلمنا بما كان وما هو كائن"، مسلم، **الصحيح** /2216، الرقم 2891، 2892 (كتاب الفتن، باب إخبار النبيّ، صلّى الله عليه وسلّم، فيما يكون إلى قيام الساعة)؛ وانظر، عياض، **الشفا** 413 وما بعدها.

112 في الأصل: "السفقة".

113 **طبقات** (الفقي) 28/2، (العثيمين) 53/3 "رجاءه عند الموت".

(71) واعلم أنّ رسول الله، صلّى الله عليه وسلّم، قال "ستفترق أُمّتي على ثلاثٍ وسبعين فرقةً، كلُّها في النار إلّا واحدةً وهي الجماعةُ، قيل يا رسول الله مَنْ هم؟[114] قال ما أنا عليه اليوم وأصحابي".

حديث "ستفترق أمّتي" عدد كبير من الروايات والأسانيد، انظره بهذا اللفظ في الترمذي، **الجامع** 26/5، الرقم2641 (من حديث عبد الله بن عمرو، كتاب الإيمان، باب ما جاء في افتراق الأمّة)؛ المباركفوري، **تحفة الأحوذي** 399/7–400؛ ابن وضّاح، **البدع** 92؛ ابن بطّة، **الإبانة** 176/1، الرقم 1 (عن عبد الله بن عمرو)؛ 369/1–370، الرقم 264 و265 (عن عبد الله بن عمرو) ؛ اللالكائي، **شرح** 114/1–119؛ قوّام السنّة، **الحجّة** 108/1؛ وقارن بـالطبراني، **المعجم الأوسط** 137/5، الرقم 4886 (عن أنس بن مالك)؛ الهيثمي، **مجمع الزوائد** 257/1، الرقم 899 (عن أنس بن مالك)؛ وانظر:

van Ess, *Der Eine*, 1:7–64.

وهكذا كان الدين إلى خلافة عمر،[115] وهكذا | كان[116] في زمن عثمان، فلمّا قُتِلَ عثمانُ جاء الاختلافُ والبدع وصار الناسُ أحزابًا وصاروا فرقًا؛[117] فمن الناس من ثَبَتَ على الحقّ عند أوّل التغيير وقال به[118] ودعا الناس إليه. فكان الأمر مستقيمًا حتّى كانت الطبقة الرابعة في خلافة بني فلان، [فـ]انقلب الزمان[119] وتغيّر الناس جدًّا، وفشت البدعُ، وكثرتِ الدعاةُ إلى غير سبيل الحقِّ والجماعة، و[كثر]ت[120] المحن في شيءٍ[121] [لم يقل به][122] رسول الله، صلّى الله عليه وسلّم، ولا أصحابه.[123] ودعوا ب 9

114 **طبقات** (الفقي) 28/2، (العثيمين) 53/3 "من هم يا رسول الله".

115 في الأصل: "كلها والاجماع كلها"، ثم ضبّب عليها؛ **طبقات** (الفقي) 28/2، (العثيمين) 53/3 "عمر بن الخطاب الجماعة كلها".

116 ليست في **طبقات الحنابلة**.

117 **طبقات** (الفقي) 28/2، (العثيمين) 53/3 "وصار الناس فرقا".

118 **طبقات** (الفقي) 28/2، (العثيمين) 53/3 "وقال به وعمل به".

119 **طبقات** (الفقي) 28/2، (العثيمين) 53/3 "الطبقة الرابعة انقلب الزمان".

120 ممحوّة في الأصل، وفي **طبقات الحنابلة** (الفقي) 28/2، (العثيمين) 53/3 "ووقعت".

121 **طبقات** (الفقي) 28/2، (العثيمين) 53/3 "في كل شيئ".

122 غير واضحة في الأصل وفي **طبقات الحنابلة** (الفقي) 28/2، (العثيمين) 53/3 "لم يتكلّم"، وما بقي من الرسم في الأصل لا يرجّح هذه القراءة؛ وورد تعبير "لم يتكلّم فيه" في ما يلي الرقم 79.

123 **طبقات** (الفقي) 28/2، (العثيمين) 53/3 "ولا أحد من الصحابة".

إلى الفرقة—ونهى رسول الله عن الفرقة—وكفّر بعضُهم بعضًا، وكلُّ داعٍ[124] إلى رأيه وإلى تكفير من خالفه، فَضَلَّ الجاهلُ والرَّعاع ومن لا علم له، وأطمعوا الناس في شيءٍ من أمر الدنيا، وخَوَّفوهم عقاب الدنيا، فاتّبعهمُ الخلق على خوف دنياهم،[125] ورغبةً في دنياهم.

فصارت السنّة وأهلها[126] مكتومين، وظهرت البدع وفشت، فكفَروا من حيث لا يَعلمون من وجوهٍ شتّى، ووضعوا القياس، وحملوا قدرة الربّ في آياته[127] وأحكامه وأمره ونهيه على قَدْر عقولهم؛[128] فما وافق عقولَهم قبلوه وما لم يوافق[129] عقولهم ردّوه. فصار الإسلام غريبًا والسنّة غريبة وأهل السنّة غرباء في خوف في دنياهم.[130]

انظر في تعبير "فصارت السنّة وأهلها مكتومين"، ما ذكره الذهبي في ترجمة المستنصر الفاطمي (ت 1094/487)، **سير**، 196/15 "وكان سبّ الصحابة فاشيًا في أيّامه والسنّة غريبة مكتومة".

وانظر في وصف أهل السنّة بالغرباء، وفيأحاديث الغربة والإسلام، ابن حنبل، **المسند** 157/3، الرقم 1604 (عن سعد بن أبي وقّاص)، 325/6، الرقم 3784 (عن عبد الله بن مسعود)، 231/11، الرقم 6650 (عبد الله بن عمرو، طوبى للغرباء)، 22/15، الرقم 9054 (عن أبي هريرة، إنّ الدين بدأ غريبًا)، 237/27، الرقم 16690 (عن عبد الرحمن بن سَنّة)؛ مسلم، **الصحيح** 130/2، الرقم 232 (كتاب الإيمان، باب بدأ الإسلام غريبًا)؛ النووي، **المنهاج** 233/2–235؛ ابن ماجة، **السنن**، 1320/2، الرقم 3988 (كتاب الفتن، باب بدأ الإسلام غريبًا)؛ ابن قتيبة، **الاختلاف في اللفظ** 18؛ ابن وضّاح، **البدع** 72–73؛ البزار، **المسند** 209/11، الرقم 5898 (عن ابن عمر)؛ ابن بطّة، **الشرح والإبانة** 13؛ ابن بطّة، **الإبانة** (الإيمان) 196/1–197، الرقم 32؛ الآجرّي، **الغرباء** 16–20؛ ابن مندة، **الإيمان** 520/1–522؛ الطحاوي، **مشكل الآثار** 169/2–172؛ اللالكائي، **شرح** 126/1، الرقم 173 و174؛ قوّام السنّة، **الحجّة** 231/1 (من اعتقاد معمر بن أحمد)؛ وقول

124 في الأصل: "داعي"، **طبقات** (الفقي) 28/2، (العثيمين) 54/3 "كل دعا".

125 هكذا في الأصل.

126 **طبقات** (الفقي) 29/2، (العثيمين) 54/3 "وأهل السنّة".

127 **طبقات** (الفقي) 29/2، (العثيمين) 54/3 "وآياته".

128 **طبقات** (الفقي) 29/2، (العثيمين) 54/3 "على عقولهم".

129 **طبقات** (الفقي) 29/2، (العثيمين) 54/3 "وما خالف".

130 **طبقات** (الفقي) 29/2، (العثيمين) 54/3 "في جوف ديارهم".

لعليّ في ابن أبي الحديد، **شرح** 10/97–98؛ الطرطوشي، **الحوادث والبدع** 93–94؛ الذهبي، **سير** 7/273 (سفيان الثوري)؛ وانظر:

Günther, *al-Khattabi's Critique*, 11.

(72) واعلم أنّ المتعة، متعةَ النساء، | والاستحلالَ حرامٌ إلى يوم القيامة. 10 أ

انظر، الشافعي، **الأمّ** 10/208–209 (كتاب اختلاف الحديث، باب الاختلاف في نكاح المتعة)؛ أبو عبيد، **الناسخ والمنسوخ** 73، الرقم 122؛ مسلم، **الصحيح** 1/1025، الرقم 1406 (عن الربيع بن سبرة الجهني، كتاب النكاح، باب نكاح المتعة)؛ الطبراني، **المعجم الكبير** 7/126، الرقم 6513؛ ابن بطّة، **الشرح والإبانة** 74؛ البيهقي، **السنن** 14/376، الرقم 14259 (كتاب النكاح، باب نكاح المتعة)؛ ابن حنبل، **المسند** 42/40؛ ابن بطّة، **الشرح والإبانة** 74؛ الملطي، **التنبيه** 124؛ والاستحلال هو استحلال زواج المحارم (سورة النساء 4/23)؛ والاستحلال بعد التطليقة الثالثة هو الزواج من مُستحلّ وهو حيلة منهيّ عنها لما روي عن النبيّ، صلّى الله عليه وسلّم، أنّه قال "لعن الله المُحَلِّل والمُحَلَّل له"، الترمذي، **الجامع** 3/418 (كتاب النكاح، باب ما جاء في المحلّ)؛ الصنعاني، **المصنّف** 6/265–266؛ وانظر ابن قدامة، ابن شاهين، **شرح** (اعتقاد ابن شاهين في آخر الكتاب) 321؛ **المغني** 10/49–54، 549–550؛ ابن تيمية، **مجموع الفتاوي** 32/151–154.

(73) واعرف[131] لبني هاشم فضلَهم لقرابتهم من رسول الله، صلّى الله عليه وسلّم، وتعرف فضلَ قريشٍ والعرب وجميعَ الأفخاذ، فاعرف قدرهم في الإسلام؛[132] و"مولى القوم منهم". وتعرف لسائر الناس حقّهم في الإسلام،[133] والأنصار[134] ووصيّة رسول الله، صلّى الله عليه وسلّم، فيهم. وآل الرسول فلا تنسهم، تعرفُ[135] فضلهم؛ وجيرانه[136] من أهل المدينة فاعرف فضلهم.

الزهري عن أبي سلمة عن عائشة، قال رسول الله، صلّى الله عليه وسلّم، "قال لي جبريل، عليه السلام، قلّبت الأرض مشارقها ومغاربها، فلم أجد رجلًا أفضل من محمد، عليه الصلاة والسلام، وقلّبت الأرض

131 **طبقات** (الفقي) 2/29، (العثيمين) 3/54 "وتعرف".

132 **طبقات** (الفقي) 2/29، (العثيمين) 3/54 "واعرف قدرهم وحقوقهم في الإسلام".

133 **طبقات** (الفقي) 2/29، (العثيمين) 3/54 "للناس حقوقهم في الإسلام".

134 **طبقات** (الفقي) 2/29، (العثيمين) 3/54 "وتعرف فضل الأنصار".

135 في الأصل "فلا ينساهم يعرف فضلهم".

136 في الأصل "وجرانه"؛ **طبقات** (الفقي) 2/29، (العثيمين) 3/55 "وكراماتهم".

مشارقها ومغاربها، فلم أجد بني أب أفضل من بني هاشم"، ابن أبي عاصم، **السنّة** 253؛ وعن عليّ بن أبي طالب "إنّ الأئمّة من قريش غرسوا فيهذا البطن من هاشم، لا تصلح على سواه أو لا تصلح الولاة من غيرهم"، ابن أبي الحديد، **شرح** 84/9؛ ابن أبي عاصم، **السنّة** 253، الرقم 1494، وما يليه؛ وانظر في فضائل قريش، ابن أبي شيبة، **المصنّف** 551/10–555؛ الرامهرمزي، **أمثال** 234–235.

انظر في فضل العرب، حرب الكرماني، **كتاب السنّة** 265–268؛ وفي "مولى القوم منهم"، ابن حنبل، **المسند** 478/24، الرقم 15708؛ البخاري، **الجامع** 872، الرقم 3528 (كتاب المناقب، باب ابن أخت القوم منهم)؛ القرطبي، **تفسير** 167/5 (النساء، 7/4)؛ الزيلعي، **نصب الراية** 148/4، الرقم 6880 (كتاب الولاء)؛ والحديث يرد في أحاديث الزكاة؛ ويردّ الجاحظ على "ناجمة من الموالي ونابتة" تزعم أنّ المولى بولاية قد صار عربيًّا لقول النبي، صلى الله عليه وسلّم، "مولى القوم منهم"، **رسائل الجاحظ** 21/2.

وانظر في "وصية الرسول للأنصار"، ابن هشام، **سيرة** 1007/2؛ ابن حنبل، **فضائل الصحابة** 809/2 (الرقم 1461)؛ أبويعلى الموصلي، **المسند** 73/7، الرقم 3998 (عن أنس بن مالك)؛ الطبراني، **المعجم الكبير** 208/6، الرقم 6028 (قدامة بن أبراهيم)؛ ابن عساكر، **تاريخ دمشق** 264/26 "أوصى أن يُحسَن إلى مُحسِن الأنصار ويُعفى عن مسيئهم".

(74) واعلم، رحمك الله، أنّ أهل العلم لم يزالوا يردّون قول الجهميّة حتّى كان في خلافة بني فلان،[137] تكلّم[138] الرُّوَيْبِضَة في أمر العامّة، وطعنوا على آثار رسول الله، صلّى الله عليه وسلّم، وأخذوا بالقياس والرأي وكفّروا من خالفهم.

انظر في "الرويبضة"، الصنعاني، **المصنّف** 382/11، الرقم 20803 (جامع معمر) "عن عبد الله بن دينار قال، قال رسول الله، صلّى الله عليه وسلّم، بين يدي الساعة سنين خوادع يخون فيها الأمين ويؤتمن فيها الخائن وتنطق الرويبضة في أمر العامّة، قال، قيل: وما الرويبضة يا رسول الله؟ قال سفلة الناس"؛ ابن حنبل، **المسند** 171/14، الرقم 8459 (عن أبي هريرة)؛ ابن ماجة، **السنن** 1339/2، الرقم 4036 (كتاب الفتن، باب شدّة الزمان)؛ النيسابوري، **المستدرك** 512/4، الرقم 8439، 557–558، الرقم 8564 (كلاهما عن أبي هريرة)؛ البغوي، **شرح السنّة** 11/1–12 "ويتكلّم فيهم الرويبضة، وهو الرجل التافهينطق في أمور العامّة. وقيل الرويبضة، تصغير الرابضة، وهو راعي الربيض، والربيض الغنم، والهاء للمبالغة"؛ ابن الجوزي، **غريب الحديث** 375/1.

137 **طبقات** (الفقي) 29/2، (العثيمين) 55/3 "بني العباس".

138 **طبقات** (الفقي) 29/2، (العثيمين) 55/3 "تكلّمت".

فدخل في قولهم الجاهل والمغفّل والذي لا علم له، حتّى كفروا من حيث لا يعلمون، فهلكت الأُمّة من وجوه، وكفرت من وجوه، وتزندقت من وجوه، وظلمت من وجوه، وابتدعت من وجوه،[139] إلّا من ثبَت على قول رسول الله، صلّى الله عليه وسلّم، وأمرِه وأمر أصحابه،[140] ولم يُخطِّىء أحداً[141] منهم، ولم يجاوز[142] أمرَهم، ووسِعه ما وسعهم، ولم يرغب عن طريقهم ومذهبهم، وعلم أنّهم[143] كانوا على الإسلام الصحيح | والإيمان الصحيح فقلّدَهم دينَه، وعلم[144] أنّ الدين إنّما هو بالتقليد، والتقليدُ لأصحاب محمّد، صلّى الله عليه وسلّم. ب 10

"إنّ الدين هو التقليد لأصحاب محمد"، روى الإصطخري/حرب الكرماني في عقيدة عن ابن حنبل "ومن زعم أنّه لا يرى التقليد ولا يقلّد دينه أحداً، فهو قول فاسق عند الله ورسوله، صلّى الله عليه وسلّم، إنّما يريد بذلك إبطال الأثر وتعطيل العلم والسنّة والتفرّد بالرأي والكلام والبدعة والخلاف"، ابن أبي يعلى، **طبقات** (الفقي) 31/1، (العثيمين) 65/1، وحرب الكرماني، **كتاب السنّة** 60–61؛ ويقول قوّام السنّة، **الحجّة** 116/2 "أمّا لفظ التقليد فلا نعرفه، جاء في شيء من الأحاديث وأقوال السلف فيما يرجع إلى الدين، وإنّما ورد الكتاب والسنّة بالاتّباع".

وكانت مسألة التقليد موضع نقاش بين العلماء في مسائل أصول الفقه، انظر على سبيل المثال قول الشافعي، **الأمّ** 763/8–764 (كتاب اختلاف مالك والشافعي)؛ الشوكاني، **إرشاد** 998/2–1000 (المقصد الخامس، في قول الصحابي)؛ وانظر رأي ابن حزم في النهي عن التقليد، **النبذة الكافية** 70–71.

(75) واعلم أنّ من قال "لفظي بالقرآن مخلوق"[145] فهو مبتدِع،[146] ومن سكت فلم يقُل مخلوق ولا غير مخلوق فهو جَهْمي؛ هكذا قال أحمد بن حنبل.

139 **طبقات** (الفقي) 29/2، (العثيمين) 55/3 "وكفرت من وجوه وتفرّقت وابتدعت من وجوه".

140 **طبقات** (الفقي) 29/2، (العثيمين) 55/3 "من ثبت على أمر رسول الله صلى الله عليه وسلم وأصحابه".

141 **طبقات** (الفقي) 29/2 "يتخطّ واحداً"، (العثيمين) 55/3 "يخطّ واحداً".

142 في الأصل: "يجاوزوا".

143 **طبقات** (الفقي) 29/2، (العثيمين) 55/3 "لأنّهم على".

144 **طبقات** (الفقي) 29/2، (العثيمين) 55/3 "واعلم".

145 **طبقات** (الفقي) 30/2، (العثيمين) 55/3 "ومن قال لفظه".

146 **طبقات** (الفقي) 30/2، (العثيمين) 55/3 "جهمي".

"من قال لفظي بالقرآن مخلوق"، هو من قول الكرابيسي (ت 245/858)، الأشعري، **مقالات** 602؛ انظر: van Ess, *TuGi*, 140; iv, 214–218.

وانظر، ابن هانئ النيسابوري، **مسائل الإمام أحمد** 152/2؛ عبد الله بن أحمد، **السنّة** 163/1–164؛ الأشعري، **مقالات** 292؛ الطبري، **صريح السنّة** 37 (عن أحمد بن حنبل)؛ ابن بطّة، **الإبانة** 331/3–335؛ اللالكائي، **شرح** 385/1، وما بعدها؛ ابن أبي يعلى، **طبقات** (الفقي) 120/1؛ قوّام السنّة، **الحجّة** 223/1، 195/2–196؛ الجيلاني، **الغنية** 128/1؛ ابن الجوزي، **مناقب أحمد** 290؛ ابن مفلح، **المقصد الأرشد** 377/2 (ترجمة البخاري)؛ الذهبي، **سير** 288/11، 289، 510، 456/12–459.

(76) وقال رسول الله، صلّى الله عليه وسلّم، "مَن[147] يعِشْ منكم بعدي فَسَيَرَى اختلافًا كبيرًا، فإيّاكم ومحدثاتِ الأمور فإنّها ضلالة، وعليكم بسنّتي وسنّة الخلفاء الراشدين المهدِيّين عضّوا عليها بالنواجذ".

حديث العِرْباض بن سارية "من يعش منكم بعدي"، في ابن حنبل، **المسند** 372/28–375، الرقم 17144، 17145؛ الترمذي، **الجامع** 44/5، الرقم 2676 (كتاب العلم، باب ما جاء في الأخذ بالسنّة)؛ أبو داود، **السنن** 16/7، الرقم 4607؛ الدارمي، **السنن** 123/1، الرقم 103 (كتاب العلم، باب اتباع السنّة)؛ المروزي، **السنّة** 26–27؛ ابن أبي عاصم، **السنّة** 11، الرقم 54؛ ابن حِبّان، **الصحيح** 43/1، الرقم 5 (المقدّمة، باب الاعتصام بالسنّة)؛ ابن بطّة، **الإبانة** 304/1؛ اللالكائي، **شرح** 22/1، 82–83، الرقم 79–80؛ البيهقي، **السنن** 334/20، الرقم 20364 (كتاب أدب القاضي)؛ ابن عبد البرّ، **التمهيد** 279/21؛ أبو نُعيم، **حلية** 220/5؛ البغوي، **شرح السنّة** 205/1.

(77) واعلم أنّه إنّما جاء هلاكُ الجهميّة

أ. أنّهم تفكّروا[148] في الربّ،

ب. فأدخلوا لِمَ وكيفَ،

ج. وتركوا الأثر،

---

147 **طبقات** (الفقي) 30/2، (العثيمين) 55/3 "إنّه من".

148 في الأصل "تكفروا"؛ **طبقات** (الفقي) 30/2، (العثيمين) 56/3 "فكّروا".

د. ووضعوا القياس، وقاسوا الدين على رأيهم،

فجاؤوا بالكفر عَيانًا لا يخفى أنّه كفر،[149] وأكفروا الخلقَ واضطرّهم الأمر حتّى قالوا[150] بالتعطيل.

انظر في التفكّر في الربّ وفي "لِمَ وكيف"، ما تقدّم الرقم 3، 9، 11، 47؛ "قالوا بالتعطيل"، لتعطيلهم الصفات، انظر البخاري، **خلق أفعال العباد** 15؛ الدارمي، **الردّ على الجهميّة** 17–25.

(78) وقال بعض العلماء، منهم أحمد بن حنبل رضي الله عنه "الجهميّ كافر ليس من أهل القبلة، حلالُ الدم لا يَرِثُ ولا يورَث لأنّه قال لا جمعةَ ولا جماعةَ ولا صدقةَ".[151]

ابن هانئ النيسابوري، **مسائل الإمام أحمد** 154/2؛ وقد ذكر ابنه عبد الله تكفيره للجهميّة، **السنّة** 102–103؛ وانظر أقوالًا في تكفيرهم لابن حنبل وغيره، ابن بطّة، **الإبانة** (الردّ على الجهميّة) 77/2–79، 93–100؛ الخلّال، **السنّة** 131/5–132، 138–139؛ ابن الجوزي، **مناقب أحمد** 290/1، 310؛ والقياس في أنّ الجهميّ لا يرث ولا يورث هو في اعتباره مرتدًّا أو زنديقًا، قارن بـ: ابن قدامة، **المغني** 159/9–160 (كتاب الفرائض).

(79) وقالوا:

أ. إنّ من[152] لم يقل "القرآنُ مخلوق" فهو كافر،

ب. واستحلّوا السيف على أُمّة محمّد، صلّى الله عليه وسلّم، وخالفوا من كان قَبلَهم، وامتحنوا النّاس بشيءٍ لم يتكلّم فيه رسول الله، صلّى الله عليه وسلّم، ولا أحدٌ من أصحابه،

ج. | وأرادوا تعطيل المساجد والجوامع، وأوهنوا الإسلام، 11 أ

د. وعطّلوا الجهاد،

149 **طبقات** (الفقي) 30/2، (العثيمين) 56/3 "انهم كفروا".

150 **طبقات** (الفقي) 30/2، (العثيمين) 56/3 "إلى أن قالوا".

151 **طبقات** (الفقي) 30/2، (العثيمين) 56/3 "عيدين".

152 **طبقات** (الفقي) 30/2، (العثيمين) 56/3 "وقالوا من".

هـ. وعملوا في الفُرقة،

و. وخالفوا الآثار،

ز. وتكلّموا بالمنسوخ واحتجّوا بالمتشابِه،

ح. فشكّكوا الناس في آرائهم وأديانهم،

ط. واختصموا في ربّهم،

ي. وقالوا ليس[153] عذابُ قبرٍ ولا حوضٌ ولا شفاعةٌ، والجنّة والنار لم يُخلقا.

قارن بـ: حرب الكرماني، **كتاب السنّة** 64؛ والمروزي، **السنّة** 245.

إنكار عذاب القبر هو من قول ضرار بن عمرو، القاضي عبد الجبّار، **فضل الاعتزال** 201، ابن حزم، **الفصل** 117/4؛ وانظر في إنكار عذاب القبر والحوض والشفاعة وأنّ الجنّة والنار لم تُخلقا، الأشعري، **مقالات** 472–475، **الإبانة** 13، 141–144؛ ابن بطّة، **الإبانة** (الردّ على الجهميّة) 215/2/3، الملطي، **التنبيه** 77؛ البغدادي، **أصول الدين** 238–246؛ البغدادي، **الفرق** 164؛ ابن عبد البرّ، **جامع بيان العلم** 138/2؛ مانكديم، **شرح الأصول الخمسة** 730–738؛ وانظر، الجيلاني، **الغنية** 185/1؛ ابن البنّا، **المختار** 230، الرقم 59؛ وانظر الطبري، **التبصير** 208–211؛ القرطبي، **التذكرة** 181/1–186؛ وانظر أبو مطيع النسفي، **الردّ** 112 (باب القبريّة).

ك. وأنكروا كثيرًا ممّا قال رسول الله، صلّى الله عليه وسلّم، فاستحلَّ مَنِ استحلَّ تكفيرهم ودماءَهم من هذا الوجه، لأنّ مَنْ ردَّ آيةً من كتاب الله فقد ردَّ الكتابَ كلَّه، ومن ردَّ أثرًا[154] عن رسول الله، صلّى الله عليه وسلّم، فقد ردَّ الأثرَ كلَّه وهو كافرٌ بالله العظيم.

من قول إبراهيم بن يزيد النخعي "من كفر بآية من القرآن فقد كفر به كلّه"، سعيد بن منصور، **السنن** 483، الرقم 143؛ وعن أحمد بن حنبل "من ردّ حديث رسول الله، صلّى الله عليه وسلّم، فهو على شفا

153 **طبقات** (الفقي) 30/2، (العثيمين) 56/3 "ليس هناك".

154 **طبقات** (الفقي) 30/2، (العثيمين) 57/3 "حديثا".

هلكة"، ابن الجوزي، **مناقب أحمد** 338/1؛ الذهبي، **سير** 297/11؛ وانظر قول أبي عاصم خشيش في ردّه على من أنكر العرش "من كفر بآية من كتاب الله فقد كفر به أجمع"، الملطي، **التنبيه** 78.

فدامت لهم المدّة ووجدوا من السلطان مَعونةً على ذلك،[155] ووضعوا السيفَ والسوط دون ذلك،[156] فدرس علمُ السنّة والجماعة وصارتا[157] مكتومين، لإظهار البدع والكلام فيها، ولكثرتهم. واتّخذوا المجالس وأظهروا رأيهم، ووضعوا فيه[158] الكتب، وأطمعوا الناس، وطلبوا لهم الرئاسة، وكانت فتنة عظيمة لم ينجُ منها إلّا من عصَمَ الله. فأدنى ما كان نصيبُ الرجل من مجالستهم أنْ يَشُكَّ في دينه أو يتابعَهم أو يزعم أنّهم على الحقّ، ولا يدري أنّه على[159] الحقّ أو على الباطل، فصار شاكًّا.[160]

فهلَكَ الخلقُ حتّى كان[161] أيّام | جعفر، الذي يُقال له المتوكِّل، فأطفأ الله به البدع، وأظهر به الحقَّ وأظهر به أهلَ السنّة وطالت ألسنتُهم مع قلّتهم وكثرة أهل البدع إلى يومنا. والرسم وأعلام الضلالة[162] قد بقي قوم يعملون بها ويدعون إليها، لا مانع يمنعهم ولا أحدَ يحجِزهم عمّا يقولون ويعملون. ب 11

وقارن بقول في المتوكّل لابن حنبل عند الخلّال، **السنّة** 87/1–88، الرقم 24؛ وحنبل، **ذكر محنة الإمام** 73؛ الدارمي، **الردّ على بشر المرّيسي** 108؛ والمعنيّ هو الخليفة جعفر بن محمد المتوكّل على الله (846/232–861/246) الذي أمر برفع المحنة سنة 848/234؛ انظر المسعودي، **مروج** 5/5؛ المقدسي، **البدء والتاريخ** 121/6؛ ابن الجوزي، **المنتظم** 206/11–208؛ ابن الجوزي، **مناقب أحمد** 166/2–170.

155 **طبقات** (الفقي) 30/2، (العثيمين) 57/3 "في ذلك معونة".

156 **طبقات** (الفقي) 30/2، (العثيمين) 57/3 "على ذلك".

157 **طبقات** (الفقي) 30/2، (العثيمين) 57/3 "وأوهنوهما فصاروا".

158 **طبقات** (الفقي) 31/2، (العثيمين) 57/3 "آرائهم ووضعوا فيها".

159 **طبقات** (الفقي) 31/2، (العثيمين) 57/3 "أويرى رأيهم على الحق ولا يدري أنهم".

160 **طبقات** (الفقي) 31/2، (العثيمين) 57/3 "صاكا شاكا".

161 **طبقات** (الفقي) 31/2، (العثيمين) 57/3 "كانت".

162 **طبقات** (الفقي) 31/2، (العثيمين) 57/3 "فالرسم والبدع وأهل الضلالة قد بقي منهم قوم".

(80) واعلم أنّه لم تجئ بدعةٌ[163] قطُّ إلّا من "الهمَج الرَّعاع أتباع[164] كلِّ ناعقٍ يميلون مع كُلِّ ريح"، فمَن كان هكذا فلا دين له، قال الله تبارك وتعالى ﴿فما اختلفوا إلّا مِن بَعْدِ ما جاءَهُمُ العِلمُ بغياً بيْنَهم﴾ (الجاثية 17/45)؛ وهم علماء السوء، أصحاب الطمع والبدع.

"الهمج الرعاع ..."، جزءٌ من كلام لعليّ بن أبي طالب يروى عن كُميل النخعي، انظر، اليعقوبي، **تاريخ** 243/2؛ المسعودي، **مروج الذهب** 226/3؛ **نهج البلاغة**، 496 (147)؛ الخطيب البغدادي، **تاريخ بغداد** 379/6؛ أبو نُعيم، **حلية** 80/1؛ ابن عبد البرّ، **جامع بيان العلم** 112/2؛ ابن عساكر، **تاريخ** 18/14، 252/50.

(81) واعلم أنّه لا يزال الناس في عصابةٍ من أهل الحقِّ والسنّة يهديهِم الله ويهدي بهم غيرَهم ويحيي بهم السنن، فهم الذين وصفهم الله مع قلّتهم عند الاختلاف وقال[165] ﴿الذين أُوتوه مِن بَعدِ ما جاءَتْهُمُ البيِّناتُ بغياً بيْنَهم﴾، فاستثناهم فقال ﴿فهَدَى اللهُ الذين آمنوا لِمَا اخْتلَفوا فيه مِن الحقِّ [بِإِذْنِه][166] واللّهُ يَهدي مَن يَشاء إلى صِراطٍ[167] مُسْتَقيم﴾ (البقرة 213/2)، وقال رسول الله، صلّى الله عليه وسلّم، "لا تزال عصبةٌ[168] من أُمّتي ظاهرين على الحقِّ لا يضرّهم من خذلهم حتّى يأتيَ أمرُ الله".[169]

وردت أحاديث كثيرة بألفاظ مختلفة يرد فيها تعبيرا "عصابة" و"طائفة" وبعضها يشير إلى الشام أو إلى بيت المقدس؛ انظره بلفظ "لا تزال طائفة... على الحقّ ظاهرين"، ابن حنبل، **المسند** 88/37، الرقم 22403 (عن ثوبان)؛ "لا تزال طائفة... ظاهرين على الحقّ"، مسلم، **الصحيح** 1523/3، الرقم 1920 (عن ثوبان، كتاب الإمارة، باب لا تزال طائفة من أمّتي)؛ "لا تزال طائفة... ظاهرين على الحقّ" كجزء من حديث أطول عن ثوبان، الترمذي، **الجامع** 504/4، الرقم 2229 (كتاب الفتن، باب ما جاء في الأئمّة المضلّين)؛ "لا تزال طائفة... على الحقّ منصورين"، ابن ماجة، **السنن** 5/1، الرقم 10 (عن ثوبان، المقدّمة)؛ وقارن بـ

163 **طبقات** (الفقي) 31/2، (العثيمين) 57/3 "لم تجئ زندقة".

164 **طبقات** (الفقي) 31/2، (العثيمين) 57/3 "وأتباع".

165 أوّل الآية: "وما اختلف فيه إلّا الذين ...".

166 ليست في الأصل.

167 في الأصل: "سراط"، واعتاد أن يكتبها بالصاد.

168 **طبقات** (الفقي) 31/2، (العثيمين) 58/3 "عصابة".

169 **طبقات** (الفقي) 31/2، (العثيمين) 58/3 "أمر الله وهم ظاهرون".

الداني، **السنن في الفتن** 174، الرقم 360؛ الحاكم، **المستدرك** 503/4، الرقم 8409 (عن يزيد بن أبي حبيب، كتاب الفتن)؛ ابن عساكر، **تاريخ** 295/1–263، 263/31؛ النووي، **المنهاج** 99/13؛ ابن حجر، **فتح الباري** 293/13.

(82) واعلم، رحمك الله، أنّ العلم | ليس بكثرة الرواية،[170] إنّما العالم من اتّبع العلم والسنن وإنْ كان قليلَ العلم،[171] ومن خالف الكتاب والسنّة فهو صاحب بدعة وإنْ كان كثير العلم.[172] أ 12

من قول إبراهيم الخوّاص، كما في: الخطيب، **اقتضاء العلم العمل** 169، الرقم 24؛ وعن ابن مسعود "ليس العلم بكثرة الرواية إنّما العلم الخشية"، ابن حنبل، **الزهد** 106/2؛ ابن عبد البر، **جامع بيان العلم** 25/2؛ وعن مالك "ليس العلم بكثرة الرواية ولكنّه نور جعله الله في القلوب"، **جامع بيان العلم** 25/2؛ عياض، **ترتيب** 60/2؛ وروى ابن وهب عن مالك "العلم حيث شاء الله جعله ليس هو بكثرة الرواية"، الذهبي، **سير** 107/8؛ وعن إبراهيم الخوّاص "ليس العلم بكثرة الرواية إنّما العالم من اتّبع العلم واستعمله واقتدى بالسنن وإن كان قليل العلم"، البيهقي، **شعب الإيمان** 293/3، الرقم 1684.

(83) واعلم رحمك الله، أنّ من قال في دين الله برأيه وقياسه وتأويله[173] من غير حجّة من السنّة والجماعة، فقد قال على الله ما لا يعلم؛ ومن قال على الله ما لا يعلم فهو من المتكلّفين.

في إشارةٍ إلى آية ﴿وما أنا من المُتَكَلِّفين﴾ (ص 86/38)؛ عن ابن زيد "أتخرّص وأتكلّف ما لم يأمرني الله به"، الطبري، **تفسير** 150/20؛ وقال الرازي "إنّ هذا الذي أدعوكم إليه لا يحتاج في معرفة صحّته إلى التكلّفات الكثيرة"، **مفاتيح الغيب** 236/26.

(84) والحقُّ ما جاء من عند الله، والسنّة سنّة[174] رسول الله، صلّى الله عليه وسلّم، والجماعةُ ما اجتمع عليه أصحابُ رسول الله، صلّى الله عليه وسلّم، في خلافة أبي بكر وعمر.[175] ومن اقتصر على سنّة رسول

170 **طبقات** (الفقي) 31/2، (العثيمين) 58/3 "الرواية والكتب".

171 **طبقات** (الفقي) 31/2، (العثيمين) 58/3 "والسنّة وإن كان قليل العلم والكتب".

172 **طبقات** (الفقي) 31/2، (العثيمين) 58/3 "الرواية والكتب".

173 **طبقات** (الفقي) 31/2، (العثيمين) 58/3 "وتأوله".

174 **طبقات** (الفقي) 32/2، (العثيمين) 58/3 "ما سنّه".

175 **طبقات** (الفقي) 32/2، (العثيمين) 58/3 "وعمر وعثمان".

الله، صلّى الله عليه وسلّم، وما كان عليه الجماعةُ[176] فَلَجَ على أهل البدع كلّها، واستراح بَدَنُه وسلم له دينُه، إنْ شاء الله، لأنّ رسول الله، صلّى الله عليه وسلّم، قال "ستفترق أُمّتي"، وبيّن لنا رسول الله، صلّى الله عليه وسلّم، الناجي[177] منها فقال "ما كنتُ أنا عليه اليوم[178] وأصحابي"؛ فهذا هو الشفاء والبيان والأمر الواضح والمنار المستنير.[179]

عن ابن المبارك "من الجماعة؟ فقال أبو بكر وعمر"، الترمذي، **الجامع** 466/4 (كتاب الفتن، باب لزوم الجماعة)؛ روى حرملة بن يحيى عن سفيان الثوري "الجماعة ما اجتمع عليه أصحاب محمد، صلّى الله عليه وسلّم، من بيعة أبي بكر وعمر"، ابن الحطّاب، **المشيخة** 116، الرقم 25؛ وانظر في حديث "ستفترق أمّتي"، ما تقدّم الرقم 71.

(85) وقال رسول الله، صلّى الله عليه وسلّم، "إيّاكم والتعمّق وإيّاكم والتنطّع وعليكم بدينكم العتيق"؛[180] واعلم أنّ العتيق[181] ما كان من وفاة رسول الله، صلّى الله عليه وسلّم، إلى قتْلِ عثمانَ بن عفّان. فكان قتلُه أوّلَ الفُرقة وأوّل الاختلاف، فتحاربت الأُمّة وتفرّقت واتّبعت الطمع والأهواء[182] والمَـيْل إلى الدنيا.

"إيّاكم والتّعمّقَ وإيّاكم والتنطّع وعليكم بدينكم العتيق"، يعزى لابن مسعود، انظر، الصنعاني، **المصنّف** 252/11، الرقم 20365؛ المروزي، **السنّة** 41–42، الرقم 86؛ الدارمي، **المسند** 130، الرقم 152 (كتاب العلم، باب من هاب الفتيا)؛ ابن وضّاح، **البدع** 32–33؛ ابن بطّة، **الإبانة** (الإيمان) 324/1، الرقم 168 و169، 332، الرقم 189؛ 333، الرقم 192؛ 419، الرقم 338؛ 881/2–882، الرقم 1214، 1216 (الأوزاعي)؛ الملطي، **التنبيه** 66–67 (عزاه مرة لابن مسعود وأُخرى لمعاذ بن جبل)؛ والمقدسي، أحسن التقاسيم 127 ("عليكم بالعتيق"، عن ابن مسعود)؛ اللالكائي، **شرح** 97/1، الرقم 108؛ ابن أبي يعلى، **طبقات** (الفقي) 71/1 (عن

176 **طبقات** (الفقي) 32/2، (العثيمين) 58/3 "أصحابه والجماعة".

177 **طبقات** (الفقي) 32/2، (العثيمين) 58/3 "الناجية".

178 **طبقات** (الفقي) 32/2، (العثيمين) 58/3 "ما أنا عليه وأصحابي".

179 **طبقات** (الفقي) 32/2، (العثيمين) 59/3 "المستقيم".

180 **طبقات** (الفقي) 32/2، (العثيمين) 59/3 "إيّاكم والتنطّع وإيّاكم والتعمّق".

181 **طبقات** (الفقي) 32/2، (العثيمين) 59/3 "الدين العتيق".

182 **طبقات** (الفقي) 32/2، (العثيمين) 59/3 "والهوى".

معاذ بن جبل)؛ قوّام السنّة، **الحجّة** 304/1 (معاذ بن جبل)، 347؛ وورد نهي عن التعمّق للأوزاعي، قوّام السنّة، **الحجّة** 6/2، وكذلك في رسالة لابن الماجشون في القدر، ابن بطّة، **الإبانة** (القدر) 242/2، ورسالته في اتّباع السنة 248/2. ابن الأثير، **النهاية** 179/3 "والعتيق، القديم ومنه الحديث "عليكم بالأمر العتيق"، أي القديم الأول"؛ ابن سعد، **طبقات** 183/5، عن عبد الملك بن مروان، "يا أهل المدينة إنّ أحق الناس أن يلزمَ الأمرَ الأوّلَ لأنتمُ ..."؛ وانظر الزرنوجي، **تعليم المتعلّم** 71 "ويختار العتيق دون المحدَثات"، وقارن بـ: قوّام السنّة، **الحجّة** 195/1 (العتيق)؛ 183/2 (التعمّق).

(86) فليس | لأحد رخصةٌ في شيء أحدثه[183] ممّا لم يكن عليه أصحابُ محمّدٍ، رسولِ الله، صلّى الله عليه وسلّم؛ أو يكونَ رجلًا يدعو إلى شيء أحدثه مَنْ قَبْلَه[184] مِن أهل البدع فهو كمن أحدثه؛ فمن زعم ذلك أو قال به فقد ردّ السنّةَ، وخالف الجماعة،[185] وأباح البدع،[186] وهو أضرُّ[187] على هذه الأمّة من إبليس. ب 12

(87) ومن عرف ما ترك أصحابُ البدع من السنّة وما فارقوا فيه[188] فتَمَسَّك به، فهو صاحب سنّة وصاحب جماعة وحقيقٌ أنْ يُتّبع وأنْ يُعان وأنْ يُحفظ،[189] وهو ممّن أوصى به رسول الله، صلّى الله عليه وسلّم.

(88) واعلموا، رحمكم الله، أنّ أصول البدع أربعةُ أبوابٍ، انشعب[190] من هذه الأربعةِ اثنان وسبعون[191] هوًى، ثمّ يصير[192] كلّ واحدٍ من البدع [يتشعّب]،[193] حتّى تَصير كلُّها ألفين وثمان مائة

183 **طبقات** (الفقي) 32/2، (العثيمين) 59/3 "أخذ به".

184 **طبقات** (الفقي) 32/2، (العثيمين) 59/3 "أخذ به من قبله أو من قبل رجل من أهل البدع".

185 **طبقات** (الفقي) 32/2، (العثيمين) 59/3 "الحقّ والجماعة".

186 **طبقات** (الفقي) 32/2، (العثيمين) 59/3 "الهوى".

187 **طبقات** (الفقي) 32/2، (العثيمين) 59/3 "أشرّ".

188 **طبقات** (الفقي) 32/2، (العثيمين) 59/3 "منها".

189 **طبقات** (الفقي) 32/2، (العثيمين) 59/3 "وأن يعان ويحفظ".

190 **طبقات** (الفقي) 32/2، (العثيمين) 59/3 "يتشعّب".

191 في الأصل: "اثنان وسبعين".

192 **طبقات** (الفقي) 32/2، (العثيمين) 59/3 "ويصير".

193 ليست في الأصل، والزيادة عن **الطبقات** (الفقي) 32/2، (العثيمين) 59/3.

مقالة، وكلّها ضلالة[194] وكلّها في النار إلّا واحدة، وهو من آمَنَ بما في هذا الكتاب واعتقده من غير رِيبة في قلبه ولا شكوك فهو صاحب سنّة، وهو الناجي[195] إنْ شاء الله.

ينسب القول إلى يوسف بن أسباط ومثله لعبد الله بن المبارك، ابن أبي عاصم، **السنّة** 167، الرقم 953؛ ابن بطّة، **الإبانة** (الإيمان) 1/377–380؛ الآجرّي، **الشريعة** 1/304، الرقم 20؛ قال الطرطوشي "اعلم أنّ علماءنا قالوا: أصول البدع أربعة وسائر الأصناف الاثنتين وسبعين فرقة عن هؤلاء تفرّقوا وتشعّبوا"، **الحوادث والبدع** 97، الرقم 20.

(89) واعلم، رحمك الله، لوأنّ النّاس[196] وقفوا عند محدثاتِ الأمور ولم يتجاوزوها[197] بشيءٍ [و]لم يولّدوا كلامًا ممّا لم يجيء فيه أثرٌ عن رسول الله، صلّى الله عليه وسلّم، ولا عن أصحابه، لم تكن بدعة.

13أ (90) واعلم، رحمك الله، أنّه ليس بين العبد وبين | أنْ يكون مؤمنًا حتّى يَصيرَ كافرًا إلّا أنْ يجحد شيئًا ممّا أنزله الله تعالى، أويزيدَ في كلامه، أو يُنقص أو ينكرَ شيئًا[198] ممّا قال الله، أو شيئًا ممّا تكلّم به رسول الله، صلّى الله عليه وسلّم.

فاتّقِ[199] الله، رحمك الله، وانظر لنفسك وإيّاك والغلوَّ في الدين فإنّه ليس من طريق الحقّ في شيء. وجميع ما وصفت لك في هذا الكتاب، فهو عن الله[200] وعن رسول الله، صلّى الله عليه وسلّم، وعن أصحابه، وعن التابعين، والقرن الثالث إلى القرن الرابع.

عن ابن عبّاس "إيّاكم والغلوّ في الدين، فإنّما هلك من قبلكم بالغلو"، ابن حنبل، **المسند** 3/350، الرقم 1851؛ انظر حديث سعيد بن المسيّب عن جابر بن عبد الله، وفيه "واختار من أمّتي أربعة قرون من بعد أصحابي، القرن الأوّل والثاني والثالث تترى، والقرن الرابع فردًا"، الطبري، **صريح السنّة** 31.

194 **طبقات** (الفقي) 2/32، (العثيمين) 3/59 "مقالة كلّها ضلالة".

195 **طبقات** (الفقي) 2/32، (العثيمين) 3/59 "ناج".

196 **طبقات** (الفقي) 2/33، (العثيمين) 3/60 "أنّ الناس لو".

197 **طبقات** (الفقي) 2/33، (العثيمين) 3/60 "يجاوزوها".

198 **طبقات** (الفقي) 2/33، (العثيمين) 3/60 "أويزيد في كلام الله أو ينقص أو ينكر شيئًا".

199 في الأصل: "فاتقي" حيثما وردت.

200 زادها في الأصل في الهامش الأيسر.

(91) فاتّقِ الله يا عبدَ الله وعليك بالتصديق والتسليم والتفويض لما[201] في هذا الكتاب، ولا تكتم ما في هذا[202] الكتاب أحدًا من أهل القبلة فعَسَى يردُّ اللهُ به حَيْرانًا[ـــ] عن حَيْرَته، أو صاحبَ بدعة عن[203] بدعته، أو ضالًّا عن ضلالته فينجو به.

(92) فاتّقِ الله وعليك بالأمر الأوّل العتيق، وهو ما وصفت لك في هذا الكتاب. فرحم الله عبدًا ورحم والديه، قرأ هذا الكتاب وبثّه وعمل به ودعا إليه واحتجّ به، فإنّه دين الله ودين رسول الله، صلّى الله عليه وسلّم، فإنّه من انتحل[204] شيئًا خلاف ما في هذا الكتاب، فإنّه ليس بدين الله يدين وقد ردّه كلّه. كما لو أنّ عبدًا آمَنَ بجميع ما قال الله، تبارك وتعالى، | إلّا أنّه يشكُّ[205] في حرف، فقد ردَّ جميعَ ما قال الله تعالى وهو كافر. كما أنّ شهادة "أنْ لا إله إلّا الله"، لا تُقبل من صاحبها إلّا بصدق النيّة وخالص اليقين، كذلك لا يقبل الله شيئًا من السنّة في ترك بعض، ومن ترك من السنّة شيئًا فقد ترك السنّة[206] كلّها. ب 13

(93) فعليك بالقَبول ودع عنك المَحْك واللَّجاجة[207] فإنّه ليس من دين الله في شيء، وزمانُك خاصّةً زمان سوء.

"الأمر العتيق الأوّل"، من قول لابن مسعود "... وإيّاكم والتبدّع، وإيّاكم والتنطّع، وإياكم والتعمّق، وعليكم بالعتيق"، الدارمي، **السنن** 130، الرقم 152 153 (كتاب العلم، باب من هاب الفتيا)؛ المرّوذي، **أخبار الشيوخ** 185 ("فعليك بالأمر الأول"، من كتاب سفيان الثوري إلى عبّاد بن عبّاد)؛ اللالكائي، **شرح** 97/1، الرقم 108؛ ابن بطّة، **الإبانة** (الإيمان) 330/1، الرقم 182 و 183 "إنّكم ستحدثون ويحدث لكم، فإذا رأيتم محدثةً فعليكم بالأمر الأوّل"؛ وانظر ما تقدّم، الرقم 85.

"لا يقبل الله شيئًا من السنّة في ترك بعض" قارن بقول لسفيان بن عيينة "السنّة عشرة، فمن كُنّ فيه فقد استكمل السنّة، ومن ترك منها شيئًا فقد ترك السنّة، إثبات القدر، وتقديم أبي بكر وعمر، والحوض

201 **طبقات** (الفقي) 33/2، (العثيمين) 60/3 "والتفويض والرضى بما".

202 **طبقات** (الفقي) 33/2، (العثيمين) 60/3 "لا تكتم هذا".

203 **طبقات** (الفقي) 33/2، (العثيمين) 61/3 "من حيرته... من بدعته".

204 **طبقات** (الفقي) 33/2، (العثيمين) 61/3 "استحلّ".

205 **طبقات** (الفقي) 33/2، (العثيمين) 61/3 "شكّ".

206 **طبقات** (الفقي) 33/2، (العثيمين) 62/3 "ومن خالف وردّ من السنة شيئًا فقد ردّ".

207 **طبقات** (الفقي) 33/2، (العثيمين) 62/3 "اللجاج".

والشفاعة، والميزان، والصراط، والإيمان قول وعمل، والقرآن كلام الله، وعذاب القبر، والبعث يوم القيامة، ولا تقطعوا بالشهادة على مسلم"، اللالكائي، **شرح** 175/1.

(94) فاتّقِ الله وحدَه؛[208] وإذا وقعت الفتنة فالزم جوف بيتك، وفِرّ من جوار الفتنة وإيّاك والعصبيّة، وكلّ ما كان من قتال بين المسلمين على الدنيا فهو فتنة.

"فالزم جوف بيتك"، من حديث حذيفة بن اليمان؛ وورد في أحاديث الفتن عدد من العبارات تأمر بلزوم البيوت والاعتزال في الفتنة، قارن بـ: ابن حمّاد، **الفتن** 143–144. وورد بلفظ ".. الزموا أجواف بيوتكم"، ابن أبي شيبة، **المصنّف** 234/13، الرقم 38138 (عن أبي موسى)؛ ".. كونوا أحلاس بيوتكم"، 234/13، الرقم 38136 (عن أبي موسى)؛ "كن حِلس بيتك"، ابن قتيبة، **تأويل مختلف الحديث** 4 ؛ "اِلزم بيتك"، 232/13، الرقم 38131 (عكرمة عن عبد الله بن عمرو)؛ "تكفّ لسانك ويدك وتكون حِلسًا من أحلاس بيتك"، أبو داود، **السنن** 314/6، الرقم 4258 (عن ابن مسعود، كتاب الفتن)؛ و 318/6، الرقم 4261 (أبو ذر)؛ "ادخلوا بيوتكم وأخملوا ذكركم"، حرب الكرماني، **كتاب السنّة** 149–150؛ "تلزم بيتك"، ابن وضّاح، **البدع** 40–41 (عن حذيفة، "فاعتزل تلك الفرق كلها")؛ أبو يعلى الموصلي، **المسند** 91/3–92، الرقم 1523 (جندب بن سفيان عن رجل من بجيلة)؛ وانظر، ابن بطّة، **الإبانة** 578/2–594؛ القرطبي، **التذكرة** 716/2–718؛ ابن حجر، **فتح الباري** 29/13–30؛ وانظر في الحِلسيّة، الغطفاني، **التحريش** 58–59 (وترد خطأ "الجلسيّة")؛ جعفر بن حرب (منسوب للناشئ)، **مسائل الإمامة** 17، 19، 20.

(95) فاتّق الله وحده لا شريك له، ولا تخرج فيها، ولا تقاتل فيها، ولا تهوَ، ولا تُشايع، ولا تأمل،[209] ولا تحبَّ شيئًا من أمورهم؛ فإنّه يُقال "من أحبّ فَعالَ قوم خيرًا كان أم شرًّا كان كمن عمله"، وفّقنا الله وإيّاكم لمرضاته وجنّبنا وإيّاكم معصيته.

جعفر بن محمد عن أبيه عن عليّ بن أبي طالب "من أحبّ عمل قوم خيرًا كان أو شرًا كان كمن عمله"، القضاعي، **مسند الشهاب** 259/1، الرقم 420.

(96) وأقِلَّ النظرَ في النجوم إلّا ما تستعين به على [أوقات][210] الصلاة؛ والهُ عمّا سوى ذلك، فإنّه يدعو إلى الزندقة.

---

208 "وحده"، ليست في **الطبقات**.

209 غير واضحة في الأصل، وقد تُقرأ "تمايل"، كما في **طبقات** (الفقي) 33/2، (العثيمين) 62/3.

210 مطموسة في الأصل ولم يبق منها سوى "ت".

عن إبراهيم النخعي "لا بأس أن نتعلم من النجوم والقمر ما يهتدى به"، ابن أبي شيبة، **المصنّف** 434/8، الرقم 26145 (كتاب الأدب، في تعليم النجوم)؛ وعن عمر "تعلّموا من هذه النجوم ما تهتدون به في ظلمة البرّ والبحر ثم أمسكوا"، ابن أبي شيبة، **المصنّف** 434/8، الرقم 26147؛ ابن عبد البرّ، **جامع** 38/2؛ وانظر الخطّابي، **معالم السنن** 230/4 (كتاب الطب)؛ البغوي، **شرح السنّة** 183/12؛ الزرنوجي، **تعليم المتعلّم** 64؛ وقارن بـ: ابن بطّة، **الشرح والإبانة** 85؛ **الإبانة** (القدر)، 244/1/2.

(97) وإيّاك والنظرَ في الكلام والجلوس إلى أصحاب الكلام، وعليك بالآثار وأهل الآثار، وإيّاهم فاسأل ومعهم فاجلس ومنهم فاقتبس.

"إيّاك والنظر في الكلام"، عن معاوية بن قرّة، أبي الفضل المقرئ، **أحاديث في ذم الكلام** 101–102.

(98) واعلم أنّه ما عُبِد اللهُ بمثل[211] الخوف من الله، وطريقِ الخوف والحزن[212] | والشفقات والحياء من الله تبارك وتعالى. 14 أ

عن وهب بن منبه "ما عُبد الله بمثل الخوف"، ابن رجب، **التخويف من النار** 9؛ وعن الحسن "ما عُبد الله بمثل طول الحزن"، ابن المبارك، **الزهد** 41، الرقم 126؛ وعن أحمد بن عاصم الأنطاكي "مَن كان بالله أعرف، كان مِن الله أخوف"، المروزي، **تعظيم قدر الصلاة** 728.

(99) واحذر أنْ تجلس مع مَن يدعو إلى الشوق والمحبّة ومَن يخلو مع النساء، وطريقِ المذهب،[213] فإنّ هؤلاء كلّهم على الضلالة.

انظر موقف غلام خليل من "العشق" عند المتصوّفة وما سبّبه لهم من محنة، السرّاج، **اللمع** 492، 498–499؛ الغزالي، **إحياء** 1797؛ وذكر أبو مطيع النسفي "زعمت الشمراخيّة أنّ النساء هنّ الرياحين لا بأس على من يشمّهن بغير نكاح ولا مُلك، وهم صنف من الحبّيّة"، **الردّ** 75.

---

211 **طبقات** (الفقي) 34/2، (العثيمين) 62/3 "بشيئ مثل".

212 **طبقات** (الفقي) 34/2، (العثيمين) 62/3 "والحذر".

213 يعني مذهب التصوّف.

(100) واعلم، رحمك الله، أنّ الله، تبارك وتعالى، دعا الخلق كلّهم إلى عبادته ومَنَّ بعد[214] ذلك على من شاء بالإسلام تفضُّلًا منه.

(101) والكفَّ عن حربِ عليٍّ ومعاوية وعائشة وطلحة والزبير[215] ومن كان معهم، ولا تُخاصِم فيهم وكِلْ أمرَهم إلى الله، تبارك وتعالى، فإنّ رسول الله، صلّى الله عليه وسلّم، قال "إيّاكم وذكرِ أصحابي وأصهاري وأختاني"، وقوله "إنّ الله، تبارك وتعالى، نظر إلى أهل بَدْرٍ فقال اعملوا ما شئتم فإنّي قد[216] غفرت لكم".

في الإمساك والكفّ عن أحداث الفتنة وما شجر بين الصحابة، انظر ابن حنبل، **المسائل والرسائل** 399/1–400، حرب الكرماني، **كتابالسنّة** 40، الخلّال، **السنة** (الإيمان) 460/1–467؛ الإسماعيلي، **اعتقاد** 180، الرقم 47؛ ابن أبي زيد، **الرسالة** 22؛ ابن بطّة، **الإبانة** (الإيمان) 558/2؛ ابن بطّة، **الشرح والإبانة** 63–64؛ قوّام السنّة، **الحجّة** 506/2 (الكفّ عن مساوئ الصحابة).

"إيّاكم وذكر أصحابي..."، قارن بـ ابن حنبل، **فضائل الصحابة** 412/1–413، الرقم 640 "احفظوني في أصحابي وأزواجي وأصهاري"؛ الأشعري، **رسالة** 303 (الكفّ عن ذكر الصحابة)؛ الطبراني، **المعجم الكبير** 104/6، الرقم 5640 "أيّها الناس احفظوني في أصحابي وأصهاري وأختاني لا يطلبنّكم الله في مظلمة" (عن سهل بن مالك ابن أخي كعب)، 369/17، الرقم 1012؛ الآجرّي، **الشريعة** 2507/5، الرقم 2002؛ أبو نعيم، **معرفة الصحابة** 1317/3، الرقم 1191؛ ابن عساكر، **تاريخ** 132/30–133.

وفي "نظر إلى أهل بدر"، انظر ابن حنبل، **المسند** 322/13، الرقم 7940 (عن أبي هريرة)؛ ابن أبي شيبة، **المصنّف** 543/10، الرقم 32946؛ وانظر حديث حاطب بن أبي بلتعة بلفظ ".. وما يدريك لعلّ الله عزّ وجل اطّلع على أهل بدر..."، البخاري، **الجامع** 1236، الرقم 4890 (كتاب التفسير، باب ﴿لا تَتَّخِذوا عدوي وعدوَّكُم أولياءَ﴾)؛ ابن حجر، **فتح الباري** 634/8–635؛ مسلم، **الصحيح** 1941/4، الرقم 2494 (فضائل الصحابة، باب فضائل أهل بدر)؛ أبو داود، **السنن** 49/7، الرقم 4654 (كتاب السنّة، عن أبي هريرة).

214 **طبقات** (الفقي) 34/2، (العثيمين) 62/3 "من بعد".

215 **طبقات** (الفقي) 34/2، (العثيمين) 62/3 "رحمهم الله أجمعين".

216 **طبقات** (الفقي) 34/2، (العثيمين) 63/3 "فقد".

(102) واعلم، رحمك الله، أنّه لا يحلُّ مالُ امرىءٍ مسلمٍ إلّا بطيبة نفسه؛[217] وإنْ كان مع رجلٍ مالٌ[218] حرام فقد ضمِنه، لا يحِلُّ لأحدٍ أنْ يأخذَ منه شيئًا إلّا بإذنه؛ فإنّه عسى أنْ يتوب هذا فيريد أن يردّه على أربابه، فأخذتَ حرامًا.

ابن حنبل، **المسند** 239/24 "ولا يحلّ لامرئ من مال أخيه إلّا ما أعطاه عن طيب نفس" (عمرو بن يثربي الضمري)؛ الجصّاص، **شرح** 140/3 (كتاب السَّلَم)؛ **الحاكم**، المستدرك 171/1، الرقم 318 (عكرمة عن ابن عباس).

(103) والمكاسب، ما بان لك صحّته فهو مُطلق[219] إلّا ما ظهر فساده؛ وإن كان فاسدًا يأخذ من الفساد مَسيكةَ[220] نفسه. لا تقول "أترك المكاسب وآخذ ما أعطوني"، ما فعل هذا الصحابة ولا العلماء إلى زماننا هذا. وقال عمر،[221] رضي الله عنه | "كسبٌ فيه بعض الدنّيةِ خيرٌ من الحاجة إلى الناس". ب 14

يقول أبو طالب المكي، **قوت القلوب** 220/4 "الأصل في ذلك حديث النعمان بن بشير: الحلال بيّن والحرام بيّن، والشبهات بين ذلك..."، والحديث في مسلم، **الصحيح** 1219/3، الرقم 1599 (كتاب المساقاة، باب أخذ الحلال). وقد ورد النّهي عن تحريم المكاسب في عدد من عقائد أهل السنة، انظر مثلا عقيدة حرب الكرماني/الإصطخري، **كتاب السنة** للكرماني، 57، الرقم 85؛ ابن أبي يعلى، **طبقات** (الفقي)، 30/1، (العثيمين)، 64/1؛ السمرقندي، **السواد الأعظم**، الرقم 48.

وذكر المحاسبي أنّ الحركات في طلب الرزق هي "إقامة الحقّ والوقوف على تجاوز الحدود وتصحيح الورع في المتجر وفي الصناعات وفي كلّ المضطرب فيه"، **المكاسب** 47، 51، وانظر في تفصيل القول في من قال بترك الكسب 61–65؛ وانظر في مسألة الحضّ على الكسب، السرخسي، **المبسوط** 245/30–286.

217 كتب في الأصل: "قلبه"، ثمّ كتب في الحاشية اليسرى: "صوابه نفسه".

218 في الأصل: "مالا".

219 **طبقات** (الفقي) 34/2، (العثيمين) 62/3 "والمكاسب مطلقة ما بان لك صحّته مطلق".

220 أو "مُسَيْكَة"، تصغير مُسكة، وهي ما يُمسك الأبدان، والمُسكة القوة (ابن منظور، **لسان العرب** 488/10). **طبقات** (الفقي) 34/2، (العثيمين) 62/3 "يأخذ من الفاسد ممسكة".

221 **طبقات** (الفقي) 35/2، (العثيمين) 63/3 "بن الخطاب".

"لا تقول أترك المكاسب وآخذ ما أعطوني"، عن النبيّ، صلّى الله عليه وسلّم، "إنّ أطيب ما أكل الرجل من كسبه"، المحاسبي، **المكاسب** 48؛ الخلّال، **الحثّ على التجارة** 27؛ وقد ردّ المحاسبي على شقيق البلخي وغيره من الزهّاد الذين قالوا بترك المكاسب، 61–67، وانظر الكلاباذي، **التعرّف** 85–86.

انظر في "كسب فيه بعض الدنيّة"، ابن أبي الدنيا، **إصلاح المال** 97، الرقم 323؛ ابن الجوزي، **مناقب عمر** 194؛ ابن حجر، **فتح الباري** 276/11–277 (وهو يشير إلى البربهاري، فلعلّ كتاب "شرح السنّة" وصله معزوًّا إليه—انظر الدراسة بالإنكليزية).

"يأخذ من الفساد مَسيكة نفسه"، هي مسألة من مسائل البيوع والسَّلَم، وفي لفظ غلام خليل عدم وضوح وتبسيط، إذ فرّع الفقهاء في مسائل الكسب والبيوع وفي كلّ مذهب أقوال تختصّ بأنواع البيوع والسّلم وغير ذلك؛ ويبدو لي أنّ ما يجيز غلام خليل أخذه "مسيكة نفسه" هو من نماء ماله الأصليّ.

(104) والصلواتُ الخمس جائزة خلف [من] صلّيت[222] خلفه إلّا أنْ يكون جهميًّا،[223] فإنّه مُعَطِّل، فإن صلّيتَ خلفه فأعد صلاتك. وإن كان إمامُك يومَ الجمعة جهمياً وهو سلطان، فصلِّ خلفه وأعِد صلاتك. وإنْ كان إمامك، من السلطان وغيره، صاحبَ سُنّة فصلِّ خلفه ولا تُعد صلاتك.

أبو داود، **مسائل الإمام أحمد** 64، الرقم 305 (قلت لأحمد أيّام كان يصلّي الجمعَ الجهميّةُ، قلت له الجمعة؟ قال أنا أعيد ومتى ما صلّيت خلف أحد ممّن يقول القرآن مخلوق فأعد. قلت وبِعَرَفَة؟ قال نعم)؛ حرب الكرماني، **كتاب السنّة** 46 "ولا أحبّ الصلاة خلف أهل البدع"، 98 "ولا يصلّي خلف المرجئ"، 155، وعن أبي عبيد "ما أبالي صلّيت خلف الجهميّ والرافضيّ، أم صلّيت خلف اليهوديّ والنصرانيّ"، وانظر أقوالًا في النهي عن الصلاة خلفهم 156–157؛ ابن بطّة، **الإبانة** (الردّ على الجهميّة) 61/2/3، الرقم 267؛ 196/3، الرقم 152؛ البغدادي، **الفرق** 358؛ ابن الجوزي، **مناقب أحمد** 288/1 "إذا صلّيت وبجنبك جهميّ فأعد"؛ ابن قدامة، **المغني** 17/3؛ ونهى مالك عن الصلاة خلف أهل الأهواء، عياض، **ترتيب** 47/2.

(105) والإيمان بأنّ أبا بكرٍ وعمرَ في حجرة عائشةَ مع رسول الله، صلّى الله عليه وسلّم، دُفنا[224] هناك معه، فإذا أتيتَ القبر فالتسليم عليهما واجبٌ بعد رسول الله، صلّى الله عليه وسلّم.[225]

222 **طبقات** (الفقي) 35/2، (العثيمين) 63/3 "خلف من صليت".

223 في الأصل: "جهمي".

224 في الأصل: "دهنا".

225 **طبقات** (الفقي) 35/2، (العثيمين) 63/3 "بعد رسول الله واجب".

قارن بـ: ابن الجوزي، **مناقب أحمد** 312/1 (عقيدة مسدّد بن مسرهد)؛ الطبري، **تاريخ** 422/3، 193/4؛ الحاكم، **المستدرك** 99/3، الرقم 4520 "اطّلعت في القبر، قبر رسول الله، صلّى الله عليه وسلّم، وأبي بكر وعمر من حجرة عائشة رضي الله عنها فرأيت عليه حصباء حمراء" (عن القاسم بن محمد).

عن نافع "كان ابن عمر إذا قدم من سفر أتى قبر النبيّ، صلّى الله عليه وسلّم، فقال، السلام عليك يا رسول الله، السلام عليك يا أبا بكر، السلام عليك يا أبتِ"، الصنعاني، **المصنّف** 576/3، الرقم 6724.

(106) والأمرُ بالمعروف والنهي عن المنكر واجبٌ، إلّا من خِفْتَ سيفَه أو عصاه.

ابن هانئ النيسابوري عن ابن حنبل "متى يجب عليّ الأمر؟ قال، ما لم تخف سوطًا ولا عصا"، **مسائل الإمام أحمد** 173/2، الرقم 1949؛ عن وكيع "مُروا بها من لا يُخاف سيفُه ولا سوطه"، الخلّال، **الأمر بالمعروف** 41، الرقم 19؛ ابن حمدان، **نهاية المبتدئين** 67؛ وعن جعفر الصادق "إنّما يؤمر بالمعروف وينهى عن المنكر مؤمن فيتّعظ أو جاهل فيتعلّم، وأمّا صاحب سيف أو سوط فلا"، الكليني، **الكافي** 60/5؛ وقارن بـ:

Cook, *Commanding Right*, 50–55.

(107) والتسليم[226] على عباد الله أجمعين.

فالتسليم وإفشاء السلام من المعروف. انظر الأحاديث في البخاري، **الجامع** 1554، الرقم 6229 (كتاب الاستئذان، باب بدء السلام)، الرقم 6235 (باب إفشاء السلام)؛ مسلم، **الصحيح** 1703/4–1705 (كتاب السلام)؛ المروزي، **تعظيم قدر الصلاة** 411 (في حديث "إن للإسلام صُوًى")، 448 (باب إفشاء السلام)؛ ابن أبي زيد، **الرسالة** 206.

(108) ومَنْ تَرَكَ الجمعة[227] والجماعةَ في المسجد من غير عُذرٍ فهو مبتدعٌ، والعذرُ لمرضٍ،[228] لا طاقة له بالخروج إلى المسجد، أو خوفٍ من سلطان ظالم، وما سوى ذلك فلا عذر له. ومن صلّى خلف إمامه فلم يقتدِ به[229] فلا صلاةَ له.

---

226 **طبقات** (الفقي) 35/2، (العثيمين) 63/3 "والسلام".

227 **طبقات** (الفقي) 35/2، (العثيمين) 63/3 "صلاة الجمعة".

228 **طبقات** (الفقي) 35/2، (العثيمين) 63/3 "المريض".

229 **طبقات** (الفقي) 35/2، (العثيمين) 64/3 "لا يقتدى به".

انظر، الشافعي، **الأمّ** 430/2 (التشديد في ترك الجمعة)؛ عن أبي قتادة "من ترك الجمعة ثلاث مرات من غير ضرورة طُبع على قلبه"، ابن حنبل، **المسند** 250/37، الرقم 22558؛ أبو عثمان عن أسامة بن زيد "من ترك ثلاث جمعات من غير عذر كتب من المنافقين"، الطبراني، **المعجم الكبير** 170/1، الرقم 422؛ السرخسي، **المبسوط** 21/2–22.

"من صلّى خلف إمامه فلم يقتدِ به فلا صلاةَ له"، اتّفق جمهور الفقهاء من المذاهب الأربعة على تحريم سبق المأموم للإمام.

(109) والأمرُ بالمعروف والنهيُ عن المنكر باليد واللسان والقلب بلا سيف.

وذلك خلافاً للمعتزلة والزيدية الذين قالوا بالسيف.

قارن بـ أبو حنيفة [جمعه أبو مطيع البلخي]، **الفقه الأبسط** 44؛ وبقول حذيفة "ليس من السنّة أن تشهر السلاح على إمامك"، أبو يوسف، **الخراج** 83؛ ابن حمّاد، **الفتن** 153؛ الأشعري، **رسالة** 295؛ الخلّال، **الأمر بالمعروف** 39–45؛ ابن حزم، **الفصل** 132/4؛ ابن حمدان، **نهاية المبتدئين** 70 "ولا ينكر أحد بسيف إلّا مع السلطان"؛ وانظر ما تقدّم، الرقم 106.

(110) والمستور من المسلمين من لم تظهر له[230] رِيبة.

عن إبراهيم النخعي وسأله منصور "ما العدل من المسلمين؟ قال، الذين لم تظهر لهم رِيبة"، الصنعاني، **المصنّف** 319/8، الرقم 15361 (كتاب الشهادات)؛ ابن المنذر النيسابوري الشافعي، **الإشراف** 300/4 (وقال أحمد بن حنبل وإسحاق والنخعي، "العدل في المسلمين الذي لم تظهر له ريبة").

(111) وكلُّ علمٍ ادّعاه العباد من علم الباطن لم يوجد في الكتاب والسنّة | فهو بدعةٌ وضلالة ولا ينبغي لأحدٍ [أن] يعمل به ولا يدعو إليه.[231] 15أ

انظر ردّ السرّاج على قول أهل الظاهر في علم الباطن، **اللمع** 43–44؛ السيرجاني، **البياض والسواد** 24 (سهل التستري)، 77 (يحيى بن معاذ عن ورع الباطن وورع الظاهر)، 79، 225–226.

---

230 **طبقات** (الفقي) 35/2، (العثيمين) 64/3 "يظهر منه".

231 الملطي، **التنبيه** (ملحق) 144، وليس فيه "من علم الباطن".

(112) وأيّما امرأةٍ وهبت نفسها لرجلٍ فإنّها لا تحلُّ له، يُعاقبان إنْ نال منها شيئًا، إلّا بوليٍّ وشاهدَيْن[232] وصَداق.

انظر تعليق البغوي على مسألة "أيّما امرأة وهبت نفسها"، في **شرح السنّة**، 9/52–53.

(113) وإذا رأيت الرجلَ يطعن على أحدٍ من أصحاب رسول الله، صلّى الله عليه وسلّم، فاعلم أنّه صاحبُ قول سوءٍ وهوًى[233] لقول رسول الله، صلّى الله عليه وسلّم، "إذا ذُكر أصحابي فأمسكوا". قد علم النبيّ، صلّى الله عليه وسلّم، ما يكون منهم من الزَّلل بعد موته فلم يقل فيهم إلّا خيرًا؛ وقوله "ذروا أصحابي لا تقولوا فيهم إلّا خيرًا". ولا تُحدّث بشيء من زللهم ولا حربهم[234] ولا ما غاب عنك علمُه؛ ولا تسمعْه من أحدٍ يُحدِّث به، فإنّه لا يسلم لك قلبُك إنْ سمعتَ.

قارن بقول لابن حنبل عند ابن الجوزي، **مناقب أحمد** 1/296؛ وانظر في حديث "إذا ذُكر أصحابي فأمسكوا"، الغطفاني، **التحريش** 84؛ الطبراني، **المعجم الكبير** 2/96، 10/198 "حدّثنا أحمد بن محمّد بن يحيى بن حمزة الدمشقي ثنا إسحاق بن إبراهيم ثنا يزيد بن ربيعة ثنا أبو الأشعث عن ثوبان عن النبيّ، صلّى الله عليه وسلّم، قال، ثمّ إذا ذُكر أصحابي فأمسكوا، وإذا ذُكرتِ النجوم فأمسكوا، وإذا ذُكر القدر فأمسكوا"؛ ابن بطّة، **الإبانة** (القدر) 1/239، الرقم 1275 (عن أبي ذرّ)؛ وتعليل الحديث 245–246؛ وانظر أيضًا الهيثمي، **مجمع الزوائد** 7/202؛ 1427.

(114) وإذا سمعتَ الرجل يَطعن على الآثار أو يريد غير الآثار[235] فاتّهمه على الإسلام ولا تشكَّ أنّه صاحبُ هوًى مُبتدع.

انظر الفقرة 48 أعلاه.

(115) واعلم أنّ جَوْر السلطان لا يُنقِصُ فريضَةً من فرائض الله، عزّ وجلّ، التي افترضها على لسان نبيّه، صلّى الله عليه وسلّم. جَوْرُهُ على نفسِه، وتطوُّعُك وبِرُّك معه تامٌّ لك إنْ شاء الله. يعني الجمعةَ معهم

232 **طبقات** (الفقي) 2/35، (العثيمين) 3/64 "شاهدي عدل".

233 **طبقات** (الفقي) 2/35، (العثيمين) 3/64 "صاحب هوى".

234 **طبقات** (الفقي) 2/36، (العثيمين) 3/64 "خبرهم".

235 **طبقات** (الفقي) 2/36، (العثيمين) 3/65 "أو يردّ الآثار أو يريد غير الآثار".

والجهادَ[236] معهم، وكلّ شيءٍ من الطاعات فشاركْ فيه، فلك نيّتُك.[237] وإذا رأيت الرجلَ يدعو على
ب 15 السلطان فاعلم أنّه صاحبُ هوًى، وإذا رأيت[238] الرجل يدعو للسلطان بالصلاح | فاعلم أنّه صاحبُ
سنّةٍ إنْ شاء الله، لقول فُضيل "لو كانت لي دعوةٌ ما جعلتها إلّا في السلطان".

"جور السلطان لا ينقص فريضة"، قارن بحديث عوف بن مالك الأشجعي ".. أفلا ننابذهم يا رسول الله عند ذلك؟ قال لا، ما أقاموا فيكم الصلاة، إلّا من ولي عليه والٍ فرآه يأتي شيئًا من معصية الله، فليكره ما يأتي من معصية الله ولا ينزعنّ يدًا من طاعة"، الدارمي، **المسند** 669، الرقم 3004 (الرقاق، باب في الطاعة ولزوم الجماعة)؛ وانظر في قول فُضيل بن عياض، المحاسبي، **المكاسب** 109؛ اللالكائي، **شرح** 197/1 (اعتقاد البخاري)؛ الثعالبي، **آداب الملوك** 42؛ ابن كثير، **البداية والنهاية** 476/10.

أمّا **أحمد بن كامل**، [فـ]ـقال: أخبرني الحسين بن محمّد الطبري، أخبرني مردويه الصائغ[239] قال، سمعت فُضيلاً يقول "لو أنّ لي دعوةً مستجابةً ما جعلتها إلّا في السلطان، قيل له: يا أبا عليّ فسِّر لنا هذا، قال: إذا جعلتها في نفسي لم تَعْدُني، وإذا جعلتها في السلطان صلحَ، فصلح بصلاحه العباد والبلاد".[240]

انظر الخبر في، أبو نعيم، **حلية** 91/8–92 (وفيه "ما صيّرتها إلّا في الإمام ...")؛ ابن عساكر، **تاريخ** 447/48.

فأُمِرنا أنْ ندعو لهم[241] ولم نُؤمر أنْ ندعو عليهم وإن ظلموا وإن جاروا، لأنّ ظلمهم وجوْرَهُم على أنفُسِهم وصلاحَهم لأنفسهم وللمسلمين.

236 **طبقات** (الفقي) 36/2، (العثيمين) 65/3 "يعني الجماعة والجمعة والجهاد معهم".

237 **طبقات** (الفقي) 36/2، (العثيمين) 65/3 "فشاركهم فيه".

238 **طبقات** (الفقي) 36/2، (العثيمين) 65/3 "سمعت".

239 هو عبد الصمد بن يزيد، خادم الفضيل بن عياض (ت 235/849)، **تاريخ بغداد** 305/12، الرقم 5668.

240 من "أما أحمد بن كامل"، حتى آخر هذا المقطع، لم يرد في **طبقات الحنابلة**.

241 **طبقات** (الفقي) 36/2، (العثيمين) 65/3 "لهم بالصلاح".

قارن بـ الطحاوي، **العقيدة** 46–47؛ وقول الحسن البصري، ابن الجوزي، **آداب الحسن** 123.

(116) ولا تذكُر أحدًا من أُمّهاتِ المؤمنين[242] إلّا بخير.

انظر الحديث عن أمّ سلمة "إنّ الذي يحنو عليكنّ بعدي لهو الصادق البارّ"، ابن حنبل، **المسند** 183/44، الرقم 26559 (مسند النساء)؛ الجيلاني، **الغنية** 162/1.

(117) وإذا رأيتَ الرجل يتعاهدُ الفرائضَ في جماعةٍ مع السلطان وغيره فاعلم أنّه صاحبُ سنّة إنْ شاء الله، وإذا رأيتَ الرجل يتهاون بالفرائض في جماعةٍ وإنْ كان مع السلطان، فاعلم أنّه صاحبُ هوًى.

(118) والحلال ما شهدتَ عليه وحلفتَ عليه أنّه حلال وكذلك الحرام، وما حاكَ في صدرك فهو شُبهةٌ. والمستور من بَانَ ستره والمهتوك من بان هتكه.

(119) وإنْ سمعتَ الرجل يقول فلان[243] مُشبِّه وفلان يتكلّم في التشبيه فاتّهمه واعلم أنّه جهميّ | ؛[244] أ 16 وإذا سمعت الرجل يقول فلان ناصبيّ فاعلم أنّه رافضي، وإذا سمعت الرجل يقول[245] تَكَلَّمْ بالتوحيد أو اشرح لي التوحيد فاعلم أنّه معتزلي؛[246] [وإذا سمعت الرجل يقول][247] فلان مُجبِر أو يتكلّم بالإجبار أو يتكلّم بالعدل فاعلم أنّه قدريّ، لأنّ هذه الأسماء مُحدَثة أحدَثها أهل الأهواء.

قارن بـ اللالكائي، **شرح** 166/1، الرقم 306 (عن عليّ بن المديني).

242 **طبقات** (الفقي) 36/2، (العثيمين) 65/3 "أمّهات المسلمين".

243 في الأصل: "فلانا".

244 جاء ترتيب الجمل مختلفًا في **طبقات الحنابلة**.

245 زادها في الهامش الأيمن.

246 في الأصل: "معتزلي"، ثم كتب فوقها "خارجي"، **طبقات** (الفقي) 37/2، (العثيمين) 66/3؛ الملطي، **التنبيه** (ملحق) 144 "خارجي معتزلي".

247 ليست في الأصل.

(120) قال عبد الله بن المبارك "لا تأخذوا عن أهل [الكوفة قطُّ في الرفض،[248] ولا عن أهل الشام في السيف، ولا عن أهل][249] البصرة في القدر، ولا عن أهل خراسان في الإرجاء، ولا عن أهل مكّة في الصرف، ولا عن أهل المدينة في الغناء، لا تأخذوا عنهم في هذه الأشياء شيئًا".

انظر قولًا مشابهًا للأوزاعي، الزركشي، **البحر المحيط** 326/6؛ ولابن حنبل عن محمد بن يحيى القطان، وعن معمر، الخلّال، **الأمر بالمعروف** 99؛ و"الصرف، هو بيع الذهب بالفضة وبالعكس"، وقال به ابن عبّاس، ابن قدامة، **المغني** 52/6؛ الصنعاني، **المصنّف** 117/8، الرقم 14546؛ المباركفوري، **تحفة الأحوذي** 441/4 (كتاب البيوع، باب الصرف)؛ ابن حجر، **فتح الباري** 381/4 (كتاب البيوع، بيع الدينار بالدينار).

(121) وإذا رأيتَ الرّجل يُحبُّ أبا هُريرة، وأنسَ بن مالك، وأُسيد بن حُضير، فاعلم أنّه صاحبُ سُنّة إنْ شاء الله.[250]

إذ يعدّهم الشيعة الإمامية في جملة المنحرفين عن عليّ المبغضين له، انظر (في أبي هريرة)، ابن أبي الحديد، **شرح** 64/4، 67–70؛ و(في أنس)، أبو نعيم، **حلية** 26/5–27؛ ابن أبي الحديد، **شرح** 74/4، 19، 217–218؛ و(في أُسيد بن حُضير)، ابن أبي الحديد، **شرح** 48/6؛ كما طعن النظّام في أبي هريرة وروايته للحديث، البغدادي، **الفرق** 147؛ وكذلك فعل بشر المريّسي، الدارمي، **الردّ على بشر المريّسي** 132، وما بعدها. وقارن بـ اللالكائي، شرح 191/1–192 (اعتقاد ابن المديني).

---

248 **طبقات** (الفقي) 37/2، (العثيمين) 66/3؛ والملطي، **التنبيه** (ملحق) 144 "عن أهل الكوفة في الرفض شيئا"، مع إضافة "شيئا" بعد ذكر كل موضع.

249 "اهل ... اهل" زادها في الهامش الأيسر طول.

250 **طبقات** (الفقي) 37/2، (العثيمين) 66/3 "وإذا رأيت الرجل يحب مالك بن أنس ويتولّاه فاعلم أنّه صاحب سنّة إن شاء الله، واذا رأيت الرجل يحب أبا هريرة رضي الله عنه وأسيدًا فاعلم أنّه صاحب سنّة إن شاء الله."

(122) وإذا رأيتَ الرجل يُحبُّ أيّوب[ـا]،[251] وابن عون،[252] ويونسَ بن عُبيد،[253] وعبد الله بن إدريس الأَوْدي،[254] والشَّعبي،[255] ومالك بن مِغْول،[256] ويزيد بن زُريع،[257] ومُعاذ بن معاذ،[258] ووهب بن جرير،[259] وحمّاد بن سَلَمة،[260] وحمّاد بن زيد،[261] [(262)]، والحجّاج بن المِنْهال،[263] وأحمد بن حنبل، وأحمد بن نصر،[264] فاعلم أنّه صاحبُ سنّة إنْ شاء الله، إذا ذكرهم بخير وقال بقولهم.[265]

من المستغرب أن لا يذكر بينهم عبد الله بن المبارك. وقارن بقائمة الهروي، **ذمّ الكلام** 327/4؛ والصابوني، **عقيدة السلف** 308–309، نقلًا عن اعتقاد قتيبة بن سعيد (ت 854/240)، ويرد فيه اسم عبد الله بن المبارك؛ اللالكائي، **شرح** 69/1، الرقم 40، و74/1، الرقم 59؛ و192/1–193 (اعتقاد ابن المديني). كان كلّ واحد من هؤلاء ملتزمًا بالسنّة أو آخذًا على أهل البدع، أيّوب "أفضل من جالسته وأشدّه اتّباعًا

251 هو السَّختياني البصري (ت 748/131)، المزّي، **تهذيب** 457/3، الرقم 607.

252 عبد الله بن عون البصري (ت 768/151)، المزّي، **تهذيب** 394/15، الرقم 3469.

253 البصري (ت 756/139 أو 757/140)، المزّي، **تهذيب** 517/32، الرقم 7189.

254 الكوفي (ت 807/192)، المزّي، **تهذيب** 293/14، الرقم 3159.

255 عامر بن شراحيل الكوفي (ت 721/103 أو 722/104)، المزّي، **تهذيب** 28/14، الرقم 3042.

256 الكوفي (ت 773/157 أو 775/159)، المزّي، **تهذيب** 158/27، الرقم 5753.

257 البصري (ت 798/182)، المزّي، **تهذيب** 124/32، الرقم 6987.

258 البصري (ت 811/196)، المزّي، **تهذيب** 132/28، الرقم 6036.

259 البصري (ت 821/206)، المزّي، **تهذيب** 121/31، الرقم 6753.

260 البصري (ت 783/167)، المزّي، **تهذيب** 253/7، الرقم 1482.

261 البصري (ت 795/179)، المزّي، **تهذيب** 239/7، الرقم 1481.

262 **طبقات** (الفقي) 37/2، (العثيمين) 67/3، و**شذرات الذهب** 162/4 "وحمّاد بن زيد وحماد بن سلمة ومالك بن أنس والأوزاعي وزائدة بن قدامة"؛ وجاء ما يليها بتقديم "وإذا رأيت الرجل...".

263 البصري (ت 831/216)، المزّي، **تهذيب** 457/5، الرقم 1128.

264 البغدادي (ت 845/231)، المزّي، **تهذيب** 505/1، الرقم 119.

265 في **شذرات الذهب** 162/4–163 "واعلم أنّ من اتّبع جنازة مبتدع لم يزل في سخط الله، عزّ وجلّ، حتى يرجع. وقال فضيل بن عياض: آكل مع اليهودي والنصراني ولا آكل مع مبتدع، وأحبّ أن يكون بيني وبين صاحب بدعة حصن من حديد"؛ ومن غير المرجّح أن يكون هذا موضعها في النصّ، إذ إنّ ابن العماد ينتقي ويجمع ويلخّص.

للسنة"، المزّي، تهذيب 461/3 (عن حمّاد بن زيد)؛ "ما كان بالعراق أحد أعلم بالسنة من ابن عون"، تهذيب 400/15؛ ابن عبيد "كان يعمل على سنّة"، تهذيب 523/32، 530؛ الأودي "آخذٌ في السنة"، تهذيب 298/14؛ الشَّعبي "قال ابن عيينة كان الناس بعد أصحاب النبيّ، صلّى الله عليه وسلّم، ابن عبّاس في زمانه والشعبي في زمانه والثوري في زمانه"، تهذيب 34/14؛ مالك بن مِغول "من خيار المسلمين" ووثّقه ابن حنبل، تهذيب 161/27؛ ابن زُريع "قال ابن حنبل، إليه المنتهى في التثبّت في البصرة"، تهذيب 127/32؛ حمّاد بن سلمة، قوّام السنّة، الحجّة 439/1؛ وقال فيه ابن حنبل "لا أعلم أحدًا أروى في الردّ على أهل البدع منه"، تهذيب 259/7؛ ووصفه ابن حِبّان بـ "الصلابة في السنّة والقمع لأهل البدع"، تهذيب 267/7؛ حمّاد بن زيد، قال فيه ابن مهدي "لم أر أحدًا قطّ أعلم بالسنة ولا بالحديث الذي يدخل في السنّة من حماد بن زيد"، تهذيب 246/7؛ الحجّاج بن المنهال "كان صاحب سنّة يظهرها"، تهذيب 459/5؛ أحمد بن نصر الشهيد، صاحب أحمد بن حنبل، قُتل في خلافة الواثق لامتناعه عن القول بخلق القرآن.

(123) وإذا رأيتَ الرّجل جالسًـ[ـا][266] مع رجلٍ من أهل الأهواء فحَذِّره وعرِّفه، فإنْ عاد فجلس معه بعدما علم، فاتّقِه فإنّه صاحبُ هوًى.

(124) وإذا سمعتَ الرّجل تأتيه بالأثر فلا يريده ويريد القرآنَ، فلا تشكَّ أنّه رجلٌ قد احتوى على
ب 16 الزندقة | فقُم من عنده.[267]

قارن بـ: الجيلاني، **الغنية** 166/1.

(125) واعلم أنّ الأهواء كلَّها رديّةٌ تدعو كلُّها إلى السيف، وأرداها وأكفرُها الروافضُ والمعتزلة والجهميّة، فإنّهم يدورون[268] على التعطيل والزندقة.

266 في الأصل: "جالس"، **طبقات** (الفقي) 37/2، (العثيمين) 67/3 "يجلس".

267 **طبقات** (الفقي) 37/2، (العثيمين) 67/3 "من عنده ودعه".

268 في الأصل "يدرون"، **طبقات** (الفقي) 37/2، (العثيمين) 67/3 "يريدون الناس".

(126) واعلم أنّ من تناول أحدًا من أصحاب محمّد،[269] صلّى الله عليه وسلّم، فاعلم أنّه إنّما أراد محمّدًا، صلّى الله عليه وسلّم، وقد آذاه في قبره.

(127) وإذا ظهر لك من إنسان شيءٌ من البدع فاحذره، فإنّ الذي أخفى أكثر ممّا أظهر.[270]

(128) وإذا رأيتَ الرجل من أهل السنّة رديَّ الطريق[271] والمذهب فاسقًا فاجرًا، صاحب معاصٍ، ضالًّا وهو على السنّة، فاصحبْه واجلس معه، فإنّه ليس يضرّك معصيته. وإذا رأيتَ الرجل مجتهدًا عابدًا،[272] مُتقشّفًا مُحترِقًا[273] بالعبادة صاحبَ هوى، فلا تُجالسه ولا تقعد معه ولا تسمع كلامه ولا تمشِ معه في طريق، فإنّي لا آمن أنْ تستحليَ طريقته فتهلك معه.

قارن بـ: ابن بطّة، **الشرح والإبانة** 21.

(129) ورأى يونس بن عُبيد ابنه خرج[274] من عند صاحب هوى فقال "يا بُنيَّ من أين جئت؟ قال: من عند فلان،[275] قال: يا بُنيّ لئن أراك تخرج من بيت خَنى[276] أحبّ إليَّ من أنْ أراك تخرج من بيت فلان، ولئن تلقى الله يا بنيّ زانيًا سارقًا[277] فاسقًا خائنًا أحبّ إليَّ من أنْ تلقاه بقول فلان وفلان". ألا ترى[278] أنّ يونسَ بن عُبيد علم أنّ الخَنى لا يضلُّ ابنه عن دينه وأنّ صاحب البدعة يضلّه حتّى يُكْفِرَه.

269 الملطي، **التنبيه** (ملحق) 144 "من أصحاب رسول الله".

270 الملطي، **التنبيه** (ملحق) 144 "... أكثر من الذي أظهر".

271 **طبقات** (الفقي) 38/2 "وإذا رأيت الرجل ردّ من الطريق"، (العثيمين) 67/3 "وإذا رأيت الرجل رديء الطريق".

272 في الأصل: "مجتهدا في العبادة" ثم ضبّب عليها وكتب في الهامش الأيمن "صوابه عابدا".

273 **طبقات** (الفقي) 38/2، (العثيمين) 68/3 "محترفا".

274 **طبقات** (الفقي) 38/2، (العثيمين) 68/3 "وقد خرج".

275 **طبقات** (الفقي) 38/2، (العثيمين) 68/3 "من عند عمرو بن عبيد".

276 **طبقات** (الفقي) 38/2 "هيتي"، (العثيمين) 68/3 "خنثى"، وكذلك في الموضع الذي يليه.

277 "سارقا" في الهامش الأيمن.

278 **طبقات** (الفقي) 38/2، (العثيمين) 68/3 "أفلا تعلم".

أ17 واحذر ثُمّ احذر| زمانَك[279] خاصّة، وانظر مَن تُجالس وممّن تسمع ومَن تُصاحب، فإنّ الخلقَ كأنّهم في رِدّةٍ[280] إلّا من عصَمه الله منهم.

حرب الكرماني، **كتاب السنّة** (الملحق)، 318؛ العقيلي، **الضعفاء** 285/3 ("يا بُنيّ ... أنهاك عن الزنا والسرقة وشرب الخمر، ولأن تلقى الله، عزّ وجلّ، بهنّ أحبّ إليّ من أن تلقاه برأي عمرو وأصحاب عمرو"، يعني عمرو بن عُبيد)؛ الآجرّي، **الشريعة**2551/5، الرقم 2061؛ ابن بطّة، **الإبانة** 466/2 ؛ اللالكائي، **شرح**817/2، الرقم 1378؛ أبو نعيم، **حلية** 20/3–21؛ الخطيب البغدادي، **تاريخ بغداد** 70/14. حرب الكرماني، **كتاب السنّة** (الملحق) 321، الرقم 617، يصف محمد بن عبيد أخي عمرو بن عبيد بأنه كان "صاحب سنّة".

(130) وانظر إذا سمعتَ[281] الرجل يذكر ابن أبي دُؤاد، وبِشرًا المرّيسي، وثُمامة، أو أبا الهُذَيل،[282] أو هشا[مًا] الفُوَطي، أو أحدًا من أشْياعهم،[283] فاحذره فإنّه صاحبُ بدعة؛ فإنّ هؤلاء كانوا على الردّة، واترك هذا الرجل الذي ذكرهم بخير [ومن ذُكِر منهم][284] بمنزلتهم.

(131) والمحنةُ في الإسلام بدعةٌ، وأمّا اليوم فيُمتَحنُ بالسنّة، لقوله "إنّ هذا العلم دين فانظروا عمّن تأخذون دينكم".

عن أنس بن مالك، قال رسول الله، صلّى الله عليه وسلّم، "إنّ هذا العلم دين فلينظر أحدكم ممّن يأخذ دينه"، ابن عدي، **الضعفاء** 251/1 (المقدّمة، نهي الرجل أن يأخذ العلم إلّا عمّن يرضاه)، وهو معزوّ إلى ابن سيرين عند مسلم، **الصحيح** 14/1 (المقدّمة، باب بيان أن الإسناد من الدين)؛ ولا بن سيرين وغيره،

279 **طبقات** (الفقي) 38/2، (العثيمين) 69/3 "أهل زمانك"؛ الملطي، **التنبيه** (ملحق) 144 "واحذر ثُمّ احذر أهل زمانَك خاصّة، وانظر مَن تجالسه وممّن تسمع ومَن تصحب"، وتأتي هناك في سياق مختلف.

280 **طبقات** (الفقي) 38/2، (العثيمين) 69/3 " كلّهم في ضلالة".

281 **طبقات** (الفقي) 38/2، (العثيمين) 69/3 "وإذا رأيت".

282 **طبقات** (الفقي) 38/2، (العثيمين) 69/3 "يذكر المرّيسي أو ثمامة وأبا الهذيل".

283 **طبقات** (الفقي) 38/2، (العثيمين) 69/3 "واحدًا من أتباعهم وأشياعهم".

284 كتبها في الأصل في الهامش الأيسر طولا. **طبقات** (الفقي) 38/2، (العثيمين) 69/3 "واترك هذا الرجل الذي ذكرهم بخير منزلتهم".

الرامهرمزي، **المحدّث** 414–416؛ ابن عدي، **الضعفاء** 252/1–255؛ ابن عبد البرّ، **التمهيد** 47/1، 67 (عن أبي هريرة وعن مالك وغيرهما)؛ الهروي، **ذمّ الكلام**125/4، 54/5–62؛ عياض، **ترتيب** 136/1 (عن مالك بن أنس)؛ ابن خير الإشبيلي، **الفهرسة** 42–43؛ وذكره الدارمي عن ابن سيرين بلفظ "إنّ هذا الحديث دين..."، الدارمي، **الردّ على بشر المرّيسي** 137.

(132) ولا تقبلوا الحديث إلّا ممّن تقبلون شهادتَه، فتنظرَ فإن كان صاحبَ سنّة، له معرفةٌ، صدوقًا، كتبتَ عنه وإلّا تركته.[285]

"لا تقبلوا الحديث إلّا ممّن تقبلون شهادته"، الرامهرمزي، **المحدّث** 411 "قال ابن عبّاس لا تأخذوا العلم إلّا ممّن تجيزون شهادته"، ابن عدي، **الكامل** 255/1–256؛ ابن خير الإشبيلي، **الفهرسة** 44؛ وقارن بقول لابن حنبل عن يزيد بن هارون، **التمهيد** 29/1.

(133) وإذا أردتَ الاستقامةَ على الحقّ، وطريق أهلِ السنّة قبلك، فاحذر الكلام وأصحاب الكلام والجدال والمِراء والقياس والمناظرة في الدين، فإنّ استماعك منهم—وإنْ لم تَقبَل منهم—يَقْدَحُ الشكَّ في القلب، وكفى به قَبولًا.[286] وما كانت زندقةٌ قطُّ ولا بدعة ولا هوًى ولا ضلالة إلّا من الكلام والجدال والمِراء والقياس. وهي[287] أبواب البدعة والشكوك والزندقة،[288] فاللهَ اللهَ في نفسك وعليك بالأثر وأصحاب الأثر والتقليد، فإنّ الدينَ إنّما هو بالتقليد،[289] ومَنْ قبلَنا لم يَدَعونا في لَبْس فقلِّدهم واسترح ولا تجاوز | الأثرَ وأهلَ الأثر. ب 17

تقدّم الكلام في النهي عن المراء والجدال؛ "ما كانت زندقة قطّ" حرب الكرماني، **كتاب السنّة** 113، الرقم 216 ("..إلّا كان أصلها الكذب بالقدر"؛ "الدين بالتقليد..."، قارن بـ: حرب الكرماني، **كتاب السنّة** 60–61؛ الخطيب البغدادي، **الكفاية** 421.

285 الملطي، **التنبيه** (ملحق) 144 وفيه ".. وإلّا تركته لقوله، عليه السلام، إنّ هذا العلم دين فانظروا ممّن تأخذون دينكم"؛ وقارن بالرقم 80 فيما تقدم.

286 **طبقات** (الفقي) 38/2، (العثيمين) 69/3 "قبولًا فتهلك".

287 في الأصل: "وهو".

288 **طبقات** (الفقي) 38/2، (العثيمين) 70/3 "البدع والشكّ والزندقة".

289 **طبقات** (الفقي) 39/2، (العثيمين) 70/3 "يعني للنبيّ صلّى الله عليه وسلّم وأصحابه رضوان الله عليهم".

(134) وقِفْ عند المتشابه[290] ولا تقسْ[291] شيئًا، ولا تطلب من عندك حيلةً تردّ[292] على أهل البدع، فإنّك أُمرتَ بالسكوت عنهم ولا تُمكّنهم من نفسك. أما علمتَ أنّ محمّد بن سيرين، في[293] فضله، لم يُجب رجلًا من أهل البدع في مسألة واحدة ولا سمع منه آيةً من كتاب الله، فقيل له، فقال "أخاف أنْ يُحرِّفها فيَقع في قلبي شيء".

انظر في قول ابن سيرين، عبد الله بن أحمد بن حنبل، **السنّة** 24؛ صالح بن أحمد، **سيرة** 115.

(135) وإذا سمعتَ الرجل يقول "إنّا نحن نُعظِّمُ الله"، إذا سمع آثار رسول الله، صلّى الله عليه وسلّم، فاعلم أنّه جهميّ يريد أنْ يردَّ أثَرَ رسول الله، صلّى الله عليه وسلّم، [ويدفع بهذه الكلمة آثار رسول الله، صلّى الله عليه وسلّم]؛[294] وهو يزعم أنّه يعظّم الله وينزّهه[295] إذا سمع حديث الرؤية وحديث النزول وغيره، أفليس يرُدُّ[296] أثر رسول الله، صلّى الله عليه وسلّم؟ وإذا قال "إنّا[297] نعظّم الله أنْ يزولَ من موضعٍ إلى موضع"، فقد زعم أنّه أعلمُ بالله من غيره، فاحذر هؤلاء، فإنّ جمهور النّاس من السُّوْقَة وغيرهم على هذا.[298]

قارن بـ: الدارمي، **الردّ على بشر المرّيسي** 79–82؛ ابن تيمية، **شرح العقيدة الأصفهانيّة** 61.

290 **طبقات** (الفقي) 39/2، (العثيمين) 70/3 "متشابه القرآن والحديث".

291 **طبقات** (الفقي) 39/2، (العثيمين) 70/3 "تفسر".

292 **طبقات** (الفقي) 39/2، (العثيمين) 70/3 "تردّ بها".

293 **طبقات** (الفقي) 39/2، (العثيمين) 70/3 "مع".

294 كتبها في الهامش الأيمن طولا وهي غير واضحة؛ **طبقات** (الفقي) 39/2، (العثيمين) 70/3 "ويدفعه بهذه الكلمة".

295 **طبقات** (الفقي) 39/2، (العثيمين) 70/3 "ويتزهّد".

296 **طبقات** (الفقي) 39/2، (العثيمين) 70/3 "قد ردّ".

297 **طبقات** (الفقي) 39/2، (العثيمين) 70/3 "إذ قال إنّا نحن".

298 **طبقات** (الفقي) 39/2، (العثيمين) 70/3 "على هذا الحال وحذّر الناس منهم".

(136) وإذا سألك أحدٌ عن مسألةٍ في هذا الكتاب[299] وهو مسترسلٌ[300] فكلّمه وأرشده، وإذا جاءك يناظرك فاحذره، فإنّ في المناظرة المِراءَ[301] والجدال والمغالبة والخصومة والغضب، وقد نُهيت عن هذا جدًّا،[302] تُخرج[303] جميعًا من طريق الحقِّ. ولم يبلغنا عن أحدٍ من فقهائنا وعلمائنا أنّه | ناظر أو جادل أو خاصم. أ 18

(137) قال الحسن البصريّ[304] "الحكيم لا يماري ولا يداري، حكمته ينشرها[305] إنْ قُبلت حَمَدَ الله وإنْ رُدّت حَمَدَ الله".

انظر قول الحسن في ابن المبارك، **الزهد** (زيادات نعيم بن حمّاد) 8، الرقم 30؛ ابن أبي يعلى، **طبقات** (الفقي) 150/2، (العثيمين) 267/3؛ ابن الجوزي، **آداب الحسن** 36.

(138) وجاء رجل إلى الحسن فقال له "أناظرك[306] في الدين؟"، فقال الحسن "أنا عرفت ديني، فإنْ ضلَّ دينُك فاذهب فاطلبه".[307]

قارن بـ: ابن بطّة، **الإبانة** (الإيمان) 509/2، الرقم 586 (هشام بن حسّان عن الحسن)؛ الآجرّي، **الشريعة** 438/1، 454؛ ابن أبي يعلى، **طبقات** (الفقي) 236/1، (العثيمين) 156/2؛ اللالكائي، **شرح** 144/1، الرقم 215؛ قوّام السنّة، **الحجّة** 280/1–281؛ في المجلسي، **بحار الأنوار** 303/2، الرقم 32 "قال رجل للحسين بن عليّ بن أبي طالب، اِجلس حتّى نتناظر في الدين، فقال يا هذا، أنا بصير بديني مكشوفٌ عليَّ هُداي، فإن كنت جاهلًا بدينك فاذهب فاطلبه، ما لي وللمماراة".

---

299 **طبقات** (الفقي) 39/2، (العثيمين) 70/3 "الرجل عن مسألة في هذا الباب".

300 **طبقات** (الفقي) 39/2، (العثيمين) 70/3 "مسترشد"، ولعلها أصحّ.

301 في الأصل "والمراء"؛ وقراءة **الطبقات** على ما أثبتنا.

302 **طبقات** (الفقي) 39/2، (العثيمين) 71/3 "عن جميع هذا وهو يزيل عن طريق الحقّ".

303 في الأصل: "يخرجان".

304 **طبقات** (الفقي) 39/2، (العثيمين) 71/3 "وقال الحسن".

305 **طبقات** (الفقي) 39/2، (العثيمين) 71/3 "في حكمته أن ينشرها".

306 **طبقات** (الفقي) 39/2، (العثيمين) 71/3 "أنا أناظرك".

307 **طبقات** (الفقي) 39/2، (العثيمين) 71/3 "أنا قد عرفت ديني فإن كان دينك قد ضلّ منك فاذهب فاطلبه".

(139) وسمع رسول الله، صلّى الله عليه وسلّم، قومًا على باب حجرته يقول أحدُهم "ألم يقل الله كذا؟"، وقال الآخر "ألم يقلِ الله كذا؟"، فخرج مُغضبًا فقال "أبهذا أُمِرتم أم بهذا بُعِثت إليكم، أنْ تضربوا كتابَ الله بعضه ببعض"؟ فنهى[308] عن الجدال.

انظر في حديث النهي عن الجدل، ابن حنبل، **المسند** 433/11، الرقم 6845: "حدّثنا عبد الله حدّثني أبي ثنا إسماعيل ثنا داود بن أبي هند عن عمرو بن شعيب عن أبيه عن جدّه إنّ نفرًا كانوا جلوسًا بباب النبيّ، صلّى الله عليه وسلّم، فقال بعضهم، ألم يقل الله كذا وكذا؟ وقال بعضهم، ألم يقل الله كذا وكذا؟ فسمع ذلك رسول الله، صلّى الله عليه وسلّم، فخرج كأنّما فُقِئ في وجهه حبّ الرمان فقال، بهذا أمرتم أو بهذا بعثتم أن تضربوا كتاب الله بعضه ببعض؟ إنّما ضلت الأمم قبلكم في مثل هذا، أنّكم لستم ممّا ههنا في شيء. انظروا الذي أمرتم به فاعملوا به والذي نهيتم عنه فانتهوا"؛ ابن بطّة، **الشرح والإبانة** 9؛ ابن بطّة، **الإبانة** (الإيمان) 493/2، الرقم 538.

(140) وكان ابن عمر يكره المناظرة، ومالكُ بن أنس، ومن فوقه ومن دونه إلى يومنا هذا. وقول الله أكبر من قول الخلق، قال الله تبارك وتعالى[309] ﴿ما يُجادل في آياتِ اللهِ إلّا الذين كَفروا﴾ (غافر 4/40).

(141) وسأل رجل عمر فقال ما ﴿النَّاشِطاتِ نَشْطًا﴾ s(النازعات 2/79)، فقال "لو كنت محلوقًا لضربت عنقَك".[310]

انظر في خبر عمر، المرّوذي، **الورع** 192؛ ابن بطّة، **الإبانة** (الإيمان) 416/1 (وفيه: "لضربت الذي فيه عيناك")؛ ابن رستم الطبري، **المسترشد** 542؛ الجيلاني، **الغنية** 46/1؛ ابن أبي الحديد، **شرح** 102/12؛ ابن عساكر، **تاريخ** 408/23 وما بعدها في ترجمة صَبيغ بن عِسل.

(142) وقال النبيّ، صلّى الله عليه وسلّم، "المؤمن لا يُماري، ولا انتفع المماري يوم القيامة فدعوا المِراء".[311]

---

308 **طبقات** (الفقي) 39/2، (العثيمين) 71/3 "فنهاهم".

309 الملطي، **التنبيه** (ملحق) 143 "إذ يقول عزّ وجل".

310 الملطي، **التنبيه** (ملحق) 143.

311 **طبقات** (الفقي) 40/2، (العثيمين) 71/3 ".. ولا أشفع للمماري يوم القيامة، دعوا المراء لقلّة خيره".

انظر، الطبراني، **المعجم الكبير** 178/8، الرقم 7659؛ وقارن بـ الآجرّي، **الغرباء** 81 (وفيه "المؤمن يداري ولا يماري")؛ من قول النبي، صلّى الله عليه وسلّم، للسائب "كان لا يداري ولا يماري"، ابن حنبل، **المسند** 263/24، الرقم 15505؛ النسائي، **السنن** 125/9، الرقم 10071 (كتاب عمل يوم وليلة، ما يقول للقادم)؛ وما تقدّم الرقم 137 (من قول الحسن البصري).

(143) ولا يحلُّ لرجل مسلم[312] أنْ يقول فلان صاحب سنّة، حتّى يعلم منه أنّه[313] قد اجتمعت فيه خصال السنّة؛ [و]لا يقال له صاحب سنّة، حتّى تجتمع فيه السنّة كلُّها.

(144) وقال عبد الله بن المبارك "أصْلُ اثنين وسبعين هوًى[314] منها؛[315] أربعةُ أهواءٍ، | فمن هذه الأربعة أهواءٍ انشعبت[316] هذه الاثنانوسبعون هوًى، القدريّة والمرجئة والشيعة والخوارج". ب 18

قارن بـ ابن بطّة، **الإبانة** (الإيمان) 379/1–380، الرقم 278؛ وما تقدّم الرقم 88؛ وانظر تعليق ابن تيمية، **شرح العقيدة الأصفهانية** 237.

فمن قدّم أبا بكر وعمر وعثمان[317] على جميع أصحاب رسول الله، صلّى الله عليه وسلّم، ولم يتكلّم في الباقي إلّا بخيرٍ ودعا لهم، فقد خرج من التشيّع أوّلِه وآخره.

انظر ما تقدّم الرقم 14 (حديث ابن عمر)؛ الخلّال، **السنّة** 396/2–404؛ وقارن بـ السرخسي، **شرح السير** 111/1؛ ابن الصلاح، **علوم الحديث** 298–299.

ومن قال "الإيمان قول وعمل يزيد وينقص"، فقد خرج من الإرجاء[318] كلِّه أوّلِه وآخره.

---

312 **طبقات** (الفقي) 40/2، (العثيمين) 71/3؛ الملطي، **التنبيه** (ملحق) 143–144 "لرجل".

313 **طبقات** (الفقي) 40/2، (العثيمين) 71/3؛ الملطي، **التنبيه** (ملحق) 143 "يعلم أنّه".

314 الملطي، **التنبيه** (ملحق) 143 "أصل الاثنين والسبعين فرقة هو أربعة أهواء فمن هذه الأربعة أهواء...".

315 "منها"، ليست في **طبقات الحنابلة** (الفقي) 40/2، (العثيمين) 71/3.

316 **طبقات** (الفقي) 40/2، (العثيمين) 72/3 "تشعّبت".

317 **طبقات** (الفقي) 40/2 ؛ (العثيمين) 72/3، أضاف "وعليًّا".

318 الملطي، **التنبيه** (ملحق) 143 "خرج من قول المرجئة".

"الإيمان قول وعمل يزيد وينقص"، انظر ما تقدّم الرقم 13ك؛ وانظر في أقوال فرق المرجئة في الإيمان، الأشعري، **مقالات**، 132–141؛ الملطي، **التنبيه** 110–117؛ ابن عبد البرّ، **التمهيد** 238/9؛ وانظر ردّ المروزي على قول المرجئة في الإيمان، **تعظيم قدر الصلاة** 641–651، 700–709.

ومن قال "الصلاةُ خلف كلِّ برٍّ وفاجر والجهاد مع كلِّ خليفة"، ولم يرَ الخروجَ على السلطان بالسيف ودعا لهم بالصلاح، فقد خرج من قول الخوارج أوّلِه وآخره.

"الصلاة خلف كلّ برّ وفاجر"، الغطفاني، **التحريش** 84؛ أبو حنيفة [جمعه أبو مطيع البلخي]، **الفقه الأبسط** 52؛ ابن هانئ النيسابوري، **مسائل الإمام أحمد** 156/2؛ ابن حنبل، **المسائل والرسائل** 6؛ ابن قتيبة، **تأويل مختلف الحديث** 4؛ السمرقندي، **السواد الأعظم**، الرقم 3؛ ابن الجوزي، **مناقب أحمد** 306/1؛ أبو داود، **السنن**، 186/4، الرقم 2533 (كتاب الجهاد، باب الغزو مع أئمّة الجور)؛ حرب الكرماني، **كتاب السنّة** 40؛ الطحاوي، **العقيدة** 46؛ ابن أبي العزّ، **شرح العقيدة** 528–529؛ الدارقطني، **السنن** 404/2، الرقم 1768 (كتاب الصلاة، باب صفة من تجوز الصلاة معه)؛ ابن بطّة، **الشرح والإبانة** 67؛ البيهقي، **السنن** 325/7 (كتاب الجنائز، باب الصلاة على من قتل نفسه)؛ ابن قدامة، "العقيدة"، 111؛ الزيلعي، **نصب الراية** 26/2–29؛ وانظر ما تقدّم الرقم 15 و16.

"النهي عن الخروج على السلطان" يرد النهي في بعض العقائد السنّيّة المبكّرة؛ السمرقندي، **السواد الأعظم**، الرقم 7؛ وانظر ابن حنبل، **المسائل والرسائل** 5؛ ابن حمّاد، **الفتن** 151؛ وانظر:

Aguadé, *Messianismus*, 87–92.

ابن الجوزي، **مناقب أحمد** 306/1 (عقيدة مسدّد بن مسرهد)؛ حرب الكرماني، **كتاب السنّة** 138–139؛ الأشعري، **الإبانة** 23؛ الإسماعيلي، **اعتقاد** 180، الرقم 46؛ 151–152 (عن يوسف بن أسباط)؛ الأشعري، **مقالات** 294؛ الطحاوي، **العقيدة** 46–47؛ ابن أبي زمنين، **أصول السنّة** 281، 288؛ ابن خفيف، **المعتقد** 358. وفي قول الخوارج بالسيف، الأشعري، **مقالات** 125.

ومن قال "المقاديرُ كُلُّها [من] الله خيرها وشرِّها ﴿يُضِلُّ من يشاء ويهدي من يشاء﴾ (المدّثر 31/74)، فقد خرج من قول القدريّة أوّله وآخره وهو صاحب سُنّة".

قارن بما تقدّم الرقم 40.

(145) وبدعةٌ[319] ظهرت هي كُفرٌ بالله العظيم ومن قال بها هو كافرٌ لا شكَّ فيه، من يؤمن[320] بالرجعة ويقول عليّ بن أبي طالب حيٌّ وسيرجع قبل يوم القيامة، ومحمّد بن عليّ، وجعفر بن محمّد، وموسى بن جعفر؛ وتكلّموا[321] في الإمامة وأنّهم يعلمون الغيب، فاحذرهم فإنّهم كفّارٌ بالله العظيم ومن قال بهذا القول.[322]

في القول بالرجعة، قارن بـ: حرب الكرماني، **كتاب السنّة** 250 (رجعة عليّ)؛ ابن قتيبة، **تأويل مختلف الحديث** 10؛ جعفر بن حرب (منسوب للناشئ)، **مسائل الإمامة** 26، 29، 41، 46–48؛ الأشعري، **مقالات** 46؛ الملطي، **التنبيه** 14؛ وانظر:

Modarressi, *Crisis and Consolidation*, 47fn, 57, 60–62, 88–91.

(146) قال طعمة بن عمرو[323] وسفيان بن عُيَيْنة "من وقف عند عثمان وعليّ، فهو شيعي لا يُعدّل ولا يُكلّم ولا يُجالس". | 19 أ

ومن قدّم عليًّا على عثمان، فهو رافضيّ قد رفض أمر[324] أصحاب رسول الله، صلّى الله عليه وسلّم، ومن قدّم الثلاثة على جماعتهم[325] وترحّم على الباقين وكفّ عن زللهم فهو على طريق الهدى في هذا الكتاب.[326]

قارن بـ: الخلّال، **السنّة** 378–383؛ ابن عبد البرّ، **الاستيعاب** 3/1115–1118؛ قال ابن حجر معلّقًا على مسألة مشابهة "وهذا ظلم بيّنٌ فإنّ هذا مذهب جماعة من أهل السنّة، أعني التوقّف في تفضيل أحدهما على الآخر، وإن كان الأكثر على تقديم عثمان؛ بل كان جماعة من أهل السنّة يقدّمون عليًّا على عثمان، منهم سفيان الثوري وابن خزيمة"، **لسان الميزان** 1/312، الرقم 197.

---

319 **طبقات** (الفقي) 2/40، (العثيمين) 3/72 "وكل بدعة".

320 **طبقات** (الفقي) 2/40، (العثيمين) 3/72 "والذين يؤمنون".

321 **طبقات** (الفقي) 2/40، (العثيمين) 3/72 "ويتكلمون".

322 "ومن قال بهذا القول"، ليست في **طبقات الحنابلة**.

323 الكوفي (ت 169/785 أو 178/794)، المزّي، **تهذيب** 13/383، الرقم 2963.

324 **طبقات** (الفقي) 2/40، (العثيمين) 3/73 "آثار".

325 **طبقات** (الفقي) 2/40، (العثيمين) 3/73 "الأربعة على جميعهم".

326 **طبقات** (الفقي) 2/40، (العثيمين) 3/73 "هذا الباب".

(147) والسنّة أنْ تشهد أنّ العشَرةَ الذين شهد لهم رسول الله، صلّى الله عليه وسلّم، بالجنّة أنّهم في الجنّة لا تشُكّ.[327]

الترمذي، **الجامع** 5/647–648، الرقم 3747 و3748 (المناقب، باب مناقب عبد الرحمن بن عوف)، 5/651، الرقم 3757 (مناقب سعيد بن زيد)؛ الطحاوي، **العقيدة** 58؛ السمرقندي، **السواد الأعظم**، الرقم 24؛ ابن أبي العزّ، **شرح العقيدة** 728–733؛ ابن حبّان، **الصحيح** 1211، الرقم 6954 (كتاب التاريخ، ذكر سعيد بن زيد)؛ ابن بطّة، **الشرح والإبانة** 62؛ ابن أبي يعلى، **الاعتقاد** 41–42؛ وقارن بما تقدّم الرقم 14.

ولا تفرد بالصلاة[328] على أحدٍ، إلّا لرسول الله، صلّى الله عليه وسلّم، وعلى آله فقط.

عن ابن عبَّاس "لا أعلم الصلاة تنبغي من أحدٍ على أحدٍ إلّا على النَّبي، صلّى الله عليه وسلّم"، ابن أبي شيبة، **المصنّف** 3/535، الرقم 8806؛ الطبراني، **المعجم الكبير** 11/305، الرقم 11813؛ الهروي، **ذمّ الكلام** 5/117؛ اللالكائي، **شرح** 4/1478، الرقم 2676. غير أنّ القائلين بجواز الصلاة على غير النبيّ من الصحابة احتجّوا بعدد من الآثار منها حديثا جابر وابن أبي أوفى، ابن أبي شيبة، **المصنّف** 3/535، الأرقام 8806–8808، وقول عليّ لعمر وهو مسجّى "صلّى الله عليك"، انظر ابن سعد، **الطبقات** 3/1/269؛ ابن شبّة، **تاريخ المدينة** 4/940؛ أبو داود، **مسائل الإمام أحمد** 1/113، الرقم 54؛ الكوسج، **مسائل الإمام أحمد** 9/470؛ البيهقي، **السنن** 3/685؛ وانظر اللقاني، **شرح** 1/110–111.

وتعلم أنّ عثمان بن عفّان قُتِلَ مظلومًا ومَن قتله كان ظالـمًا.

ابن شبّة، **تاريخ المدينة** 4/1157؛ ابن عساكر، **تاريخ** 39/415 (كلاهما برواية الزهري عن ابن المسيّب).

(148) فمن أقرَّ بما في هذا الكتاب وآمن به واتّخذه إمامًا ولم يشكّ في حرفٍ منه ولم يجحد حرفًا واحدًا، فهو صاحب سنّةٍ وجماعةٍ، كاملٌ قد كَمُلت فيه السنّة؛[329] ومن جحد حرفًا ممّا في هذا الكتاب أو شكّ

327 **طبقات** (الفقي) 2/40، (العثيمين) 3/73 "أنّهم من أهل الجنّة لا شكّ فيه".

328 **طبقات** (الفقي) 2/41 "ولا نصلّي على أحد إلّا..."، (العثيمين) 3/73 "ولا نفرد الصلاة"، وهي قراءة المحقّق.

329 **طبقات** (الفقي) 2/41، (العثيمين) 3/73 "الجماعة".

أو وقف فهو صاحب هوًى؛ ومن جحد أو شكَّ في حرفٍ من القرآن أو في شيءٍ جاء عن رسول الله، صلّى الله عليه وسلّم، لقي الله تعالى مُكَذِّبًا، فاتّقِ الله واحذ[ره][330] وتعاهد إيمانك.

"من جحد ..."، قارن بـ الهروي، **ذمّ الكلام** 90/4، 97.

(149) ومن السنّة أنْ لا تُعِين أحدًا على[331] معصية الله، ولا أولي الخير ولا الخلقَ أجمعين، لا طاعة [لبشرٍ][332] في معصية الله ولا تُحِب عليه، واكْرَه ذلك كلّه لله تبارك وتعالى.

عن عليّ بن أبي طالب "لا طاعة لبشر في معصية الله جلّ وعلا"، ابن حبان، **الصحيح** 792، الرقم 4550 و 4549 (كتاب السير، ذكر الزجر عن طاعة المرء لمن دعاه...)؛ ابن حزم، **المحلّى** 361/9؛ وعن عليّ بلفظ "لا طاعة في معصية الله، إنّما الطاعة في المعروف"، ابن حنبل، **المسند** 128/2، الرقم 724؛ البخاري، **الجامع** 1793، الرقم 7257 (كتاب الآحاد)؛ مسلم، **الصحيح** 1469/3، الرقم 1840 (كتاب الإمارة، باب وجوب طاعة الأمراء)؛ وقارن بـ حنبل، **ذكر محنة الإمام** 66.

(150) والإيمان بأنّ التوبة فريضةٌ، على العباد أنْ[333] يتوبوا من كبير المعاصي وصغيرها.

قارن بـ ابن أبي زيد، **الرسالة** 201.

(151) ومن لم يشهد لمن شهد له رسول الله، صلّى الله عليه وسلّم، بالجنّة، فهو صاحب بدعة | وضلالة، ب 19
شاكٌّ فيما قال رسول الله، صلّى الله عليه وسلّم.

انظر الرقم 147 في ما تقدّم.

330 **طبقات** (الفقي) 41/2، (العثيمين) 74/3 "واحذر".

331 **طبقات** (الفقي) 41/2، (العثيمين) 74/3 "تطع أحدا في".

332 كتبها في الهامش الأيسر.

333 **طبقات** (الفقي) 41/2، (العثيمين) 74/3 "..فرض على العباد وأن يتوبوا".

(152) وقال مالك بن أنس "من لزم السنّة وسَلِم منه أصحاب[334] رسول الله، صلّى الله عليه وسلّم، ثُمّ مات كان مع النبيّين[335] والصدّيقين والشهداء والصالحين، وإن كان له تقصير في العمل".[336]

(153) وقال بشر [بن] الحارث "الإسلام هو السنّة والسنّة هي الإسلام".

قارن بـالرقم 1 في ما تقدّم.

(154) وقال فُضيل بن عِياض "إذا رأيت رجلًا من أهل السنّة فكأنّما أرى[337] رجلًا من أصحاب رسول الله، صلّى الله عليه وسلّم، وإذا رأيت رجلًا من أهل البدع فكأنّما أرى رجلًا من المنافقين".

(155) وقال يونس بن عُبَيد "العجب ممّن يدعو اليوم إلى السنّة وأعجب منه من يُجيب إلى السنّة فيقبل".[338]

أبو نعيم، **حلية** 21/3؛ المزّي، **تهذيب** 527/32.

(156) وكان ابن عون[339] يقول عند الموت "السنّة السنّة وإيّاكم والبدعَ"، حتى مات.

---

334 **طبقات** (الفقي) 41/2، (العثيمين) 74/3 "أصهار".

335 "النبيين"، ليست في **طبقات الحنابلة**؛ الملطي، **التنبيه** (ملحق) 144 "كان من الذين انعم الله عليهم من النبيين...".

336 **طبقات** (الفقي) 41/2، (العثيمين) 74/3 "وإن قصر في العمل"؛ الملطي، **التنبيه** (ملحق) 144 "وإن كان مقصرا في العمل".

337 **طبقات** (الفقي) 42/2، (العثيمين) 74/3 "رأيت" في الموضعين.

338 **طبقات** (الفقي) 42/2، (العثيمين) 74/3 "وأعجب منهم المجيب إلى السنّة"؛ الملطي، **التنبيه** (ملحق) 144 "والأعجب منه من يدعى فيقبل".

339 الملطي، **التنبيه** (ملحق) 143 "وكان أيّوب يقول عند الموت" (لعلّه يعني السختياني).

(157) قال أبو عبد الله غُلام خليل[340] "ومات رجلٌ من أصحابي فرُئي في المنام، فقال قولوا لأبي عبد الله عليك بالسنّة، فإنّ أوّلَ ما سألني الله سألني عن السنّة".

(158) وقال أبو العالية "من مات على السنّة مستورًا[341] فهو صِدّيقٌ".

(159) ويقال[342] "الاعتصام بالسنّة نجاة".[343]

انظر في هذا الأثر الرسالة المنسوبة لعمر بن عبد العزيز في الردّ على القدرية (van Ess, *Anfänge*, 43)؛ وهو عن الزهري عند ابن المبارك، **الزهد** 281 (باب ما جاء في قبض العلم)؛ الدارمي، **المسند** 123، الرقم 104 (كتاب العلم، باب اتّباع السنة)؛ ابن بطّة، **الشرح والإبانة** 26؛ ابن بطّة، **الإبانة** (الإيمان) 320/1؛ أبو نُعيم، **حلية** 369/3؛ اللالكائي، **شرح** 62/1، الرقم 15، 106، الرقم 136؛ الهروي، **ذمّ الكلام** 405/2، 110/4؛ قوّام السنّة، **الحجّة** 110/1، 246؛ ابن الجوزي، **مناقب أحمد** 310/1 (اتّباع السنّة نجاة)؛ ابن تيمية، **شرح العقيدة الأصفهانيّة** 214.

340 **طبقات** (الفقي) 41/2، (العثيمين) 74/3 "وقال أحمد بن حنبل"؛ الملطي، **التنبيه** (ملحق) 143: "قال أبو عبد الله أحمد بن حنبل".

341 الملطي، **التنبيه** (ملحق) 143 "مستور".

342 الملطي، **التنبيه** (ملحق) 143؛ "يقال"، ليست في **طبقات الحنابلة**.

343 ترد أخبار إضافية في نص **طبقات الحنابلة**.

آخرُ الكتاب

والحمد لله ربّ العالمين وصلّى الله على محمّد[344]

صورة السماع من الأصل نقلته:
كتب عبد الله بن حمزة بن سانو
سمع جميعَه على الشيخ أبي طالب[345] أمدّه الله—بقراءة محمّد بن ناصر بن محمّد بن عليّ[346]—أولادُ أخته:
أبو القاسم عبد الله
وأبو المعالي،[347]
وأبو الفتح يوسف، بنو[ا] أحمد ابن الفرج الدقاق
والأديب أبو منصور الجواليقي،[348]
وأبو الدلف،[349]
وأبو الفا[350] الخنّاط المقرئ،
وأبو الفرج عبد الخالق بن أحمد بن عبد القادر،[351]

---

344 في الأصل بداية كلمة بقي منها "اب".

345 أبو طالب عبد القادر بن محمّد بن عبد القادر، مرّت ترجمته في الهامش 4 في ما تقدّم.

346 أبو الفضل محمّد بن ناصر بن محمّد بن عليّ بن عمر السلامي البغدادي (467/1074–550/1155). الذهبي، **سير** 265/20، الرقم 180؛ ابن رجب، **ذيل** 51/2، الرقم 122.

347 مهملة النقط في الأصل، وهو محمّد بن أحمد بن الفرج الدقاق أبو المعالي (ت 564/1168)، ابن أخت أبي الفضل محمّد بن ناصر، ابن الدبيثي، **ذيل** 177/1، الرقم 23.

348 موهوب بن أحمد (ت 540/1145)، اللغوي النحوي البغدادي، ابن خلكان، **وفيات** 342/5، الرقم751؛ الذهبي، **سير** 89/20، الرقم 50؛ ابن رجب، **ذيل** 1/2، الرقم 95.

349 انظر التعليق على السماع في الدراسة بالإنكليزية.

350 الكلمة غير واضحة في الأصل.

351 مرّت ترجمته في الهامش 6 في ما تقدّم.

وابنه عبد الحقّ،[352]

وابن أخيه يحيى بن عليّ الحنّاط،[353]

وأبو الفضل المخرمي،[354]

وصافي المطيّن،[355]

وهزارسب الهروي،[356]

وأحمد بن محمّد الفيرومي،

وحسين بن إبراهيم (أدهم)،

وجماعة آخرين.

وسمع محمّد بن أحمد بن محمّد بن داود الأصبهاني،

وذلك في سنة ستٍّ أو أكثر وخمسمائة.

352 مرّت ترجمته في الهامش 5 في ما تقدّم.

353 أو "الخيّاط".

354 مهملة النقط في الأصل، ولعلّه أبو الفضل عليّ بن المبارك المخرِّمي (ت 552/1172)، ابن الدبيثي، **ذيل** 520/4، الرقم 2418.

355 الكلمة غير واضحة في الأصل.

356 ابن عوض بن الحسن (ت 515/1121)، وهو شيخ الحافظ أبي طاهر السِّلَفي (السلفي، **الوجيز** 74، 76–77)، سمع من طراد الزينبي ببغداد، ابن الجوزي، **المنتظم** 202/17، الرقم 3908؛ الذهبي، **العبر** 405/2؛ ابن العماد، **شذرات** 78/6؛ Makdisi, The diary, 178–179

ب 20 سُمع جميع كتاب "شرح السنّة" على الشيخ الاما ...
بن عبد القادر بن محمّد بن يوسف نحو سماعه من أبي طال ...
الرزاق بن[357] عبد القادر بن أبي صالح الجيلي،[358] ابنه أبو القاسم[359] عبد الرحيم[360] وأبو ... بن مسعود
ابن حمزة النهرواني وأبو الحسن عليّ بن هلال ...
وذلك في تاسع شهر محرّم سنة ثمان وستين وخمسمائة بمدرسة - ...[361]

حمدلله ...
قال أبو الغمر فقرأ عليه قراءة حمزة في دار مخول فمات
بعض أصحابه، فرآه الشيخ في النوم فقال له: "ما فعل الله بك؟"، قال: "غفر لي"، قال فما حال
متكبر و يا أستاذنا من ربك من

357 لعبد الرزاق بن عبد القادر بن أبي صالح الجيلي (528/1133–603/1206) ترجمة في ابن الدبيثي، **ذيل** 184/4، الرقم 1990، سمع من أبي الفضل محمّد بن ناصر البغدادي؛ ابن رجب، **ذيل** 75/3، الرقم 247.

358 شيخ الطريقة (ت 561/1165)، ابن رجب، **ذيل** 187/2، الرقم 144؛ الذهبي، **سير** 439/20، الرقم 286.

359 غير واضحة في الأصل، وقد تقرأ "العمر".

360 أبو القاسم عبد الرحيم بن عبد الرزاق الجيلي (ت 606/1209)، ابن الدبيثي، **ذيل** 89/4، الرقم 1884.

361 كلمة غير واضحة في الأصل، قد تقرأ "مدرس..."، ثم ينقطع النصّ.

ثبت المصادر

الآجرّي، أبو بكر محمّد بن الحسين (ت 970/360). **التصديق بالنظر إلى الله تعالى**، بيروت: مؤسّسة الرسالة، 1988.

الآجرّي، أبو بكر محمّد بن الحسين (ت 970/360). **الشريعة**، تحقيق عبد الله بن عمر بن سليمان الدميجي، 1–6. الرياض: دار الوطن، 1997/1418.

الآجرّي، أبو بكر محمّد بن الحسين (ت 970/360). **الغرباء**، تحقيق بدر البدر. الكويت: دار الخلفاء، 1983/1403.

الآجرّي، أبو عبيد محمّد بن عليّ (القرن الرابع/العاشر). **سؤالات أبي عبيد الآجرّي لأبي داود سليمان بن الأشعث السجستاني**، تحقيق عبد العليم عبد العظيم البستوي، 1–2. مكّة وبيروت: دار الاستقامة ومؤسّسة الريّان، 1997/1418.

ابن أبي حاتم، عبد الرحمن بن محمّد (ت 938/327). **أصل السنّة واعتقاد الدين**، تحقيق أحمد فريد المزيدي، ضمن مجموعة بعنوان **أصول السنّة للإمام أحمد بن حنبل الشيباني**. بيروت: دار الكتب العلميّة، 2012/1433.

ابن أبي حاتم، عبد الرحمن بن محمّد (ت 938/327). **تفسير القرآن العظيم**، تحقيق أسعد محمّد الطيّب، 1–10. مكّة والرياض: مكتبة نزار مصطفى الباز، 1997/1417.

ابن أبي حاتم، عبد الرحمن بن محمّد (ت 938/327). **الجرح والتعديل**، 1–9. حيدر أباد الدكن: دائرة المعارف العثمانيّة، 1952/1371–1953/1372.

ابن أبي حاتم، عبد الرحمن بن محمّد (ت 938/327). **العلل**، تحقيق سعد بن عبد الله الحميّد وخالد بن عبد الرحمن الجريسي، 1–7. الرياض: الجريسي، 2006/1427.

ابن أبي الحديد، أبو حامد بن هبة الله (ت 1257/655). **شرح نهج البلاغة**، تحقيق محمّد أبو الفضل إبراهيم، 1–20. القاهرة: دار إحياء الكتب العربيّة، 1964–1965.

ابن أبي الدنيا، أبو بكر عبد الله بن محمّد (ت 894/281). **إصلاح المال**، تحقيق محمّد عبد القادر عطا. بيروت: مؤسّسة الكتب الثقافيّة، 1993/1414.

ابن أبي الدنيا، أبو بكر عبد الله بن محمّد (ت 894/281). **حسن الظنّ بالله**، تحقيق عبد الحميد شانوحة. بيروت: مؤسّسة الكتب الثقافيّة، 1993/1413.

ابن أبي الدنيا، أبو بكر عبد الله بن محمّد (ت 894/281). **صفة النار**، تحقيق محمّد خير رمضان يوسف. بيروت: دار ابن حزم، 1997/1417.

ابن أبي الدنيا، أبو بكر عبد الله بن محمّد (ت 894/281). **العقل وفضله**، تحقيق محمّد زاهد الكوثري. القاهرة: مكتبة نشر الثقافة الإسلاميّة، 1946/1365.

ابن أبي الدنيا، أبو بكر عبد الله بن محمّد (ت 894/281). **المرض والكفّارت**، تحقيق عبد الوكيل الندوي. بومباي: الدار السلفيّة، 1991/1411.

ابن أبي الدنيا، أبو بكر عبد الله بن محمّد (ت 894/281). **كتاب المطر**، تحقيق طارق محمّد سكلوع العمودي. الدمّام: دار ابن الجوزي، 1997/1418.

ابن أبي زمنين، أبو عبد الله محمّد بن عبد الله (ت 1008/399). **أصول السنّة = رياض الجنّة بتخريج أصول السنّة**، تحقيق عبد الله بن محمّد بن عبد الرحيم البخاري. المدينة النبويّة: مكتبة الغرباء الأثريّة، 1994/1415.

ابن أبي زيد القيرواني (ت 996/386). **الرسالة**، تحقيق أحمد مصطفى قاسم الطهطاوي. القاهرة: دار الفضيلة، 2005.

ابن أبي شيبة، أبو بكر عبد الله بن محمّد (ت 849/235). **كتاب الإيمان**، تحقيق محمّد ناصر الدين الألباني. الكويت: دار الأرقم، 1985.

ابن أبي شيبة، أبو بكر عبد الله بن محمّد (ت 849/235). **المصنّف**، تحقيق أبي محمّد أسامة بن إبراهيم، 1–15. القاهرة: الفاروق الحديثة، 2007.

ابن أبي عاصم، أبو بكر أحمد بن عمرو (ت 900/287). **السنّة**، تحقيق يحيى مراد. بيروت: دار الكتب العلميّة، 2004/1424.

ابن أبي العزّ الحنفي، عليّ (ت 1389/792). **شرح العقيدة الطحاويّة**، تحقيق عبد الله بن عبد المحسن التركي وشعيب الأرنؤوط، 1–2. بيروت: مؤسّسة الرسالة، 1992.

ابن أبي الوفا القرشي، محيي الدين عبد القادر (ت 1373/775). **الجواهر المضيّة في طبقات الحنفيّة**، تحقيق عبد الفتّاح محمّد الحلو، 1–6. القاهرة: هجر للطباعة والنشر، 1993/1413.

ابن أبي يعلى، أبو الحسين محمّد بن محمّد (ت 1131/526). **الاعتقاد**، تحقيق محمّد بن عبد الرحمن الخميس. الرياض: دار أطلس الخضراء، 2002/1423.

ابن أبي يعلى، أبو الحسين محمّد بن محمّد (ت 1131/526). **طبقات الحنابلة**، تحقيق محمّد حامد الفقي، 1–2. القاهرة: مطبعة السنّة المحمّدية، 1952.

ابن أبي يعلى، أبو الحسين محمّد بن محمّد (ت 1131/526). **طبقات الحنابلة**، تحقيق عبد الرحمن بن سليمان العثيمين. الرياض: الأمانة العامّة، 1998/1419.

ابن الأثير، عزّ الدين عليّ بن محمّد (ت 1232/630). **اللباب في تهذيب الأنساب**، 1–3. بيروت: دار صادر، 1980.

ابن الأثير، مجد الدين المبارك بن محمّد (ت 1209/606). **جامع الأصول في أحاديث الرسول**، تحقيق عبد القادر الأرناؤوط، 1–12. دمشق: مكتبة الحلواني، 1969/1389–1972/1392.

ابن إسحاق، محمّد (ت 768/151). **سيرة ابن إسحاق**، تحقيق محمّد حميد الله. فاس: معهد الدراسات للأبحاث والتعريب، 1976/1396.

ابن بابويه القمي، الشيخ الصدوق أبو جعفر محمّد (ت 991/381). **الاعتقادات**، ضمن **مجموع مصنّفات الشيخ الصدوق**. قم: مكتبة بارسا، 2008.

ابن بابويه القمي، الشيخ الصدوق أبو جعفر محمّد (ت 991/381). **من لا يحضره الفقيه**، 1–4. بيروت: مؤسّسة الأعلمي، 1986/1406.

ابن بطّال، أبو الحسين عليّ بن خلف (ت 1057/449). **شرح صحيح البخاري**، تحقيق أبو تميم ياسر بن إبراهيم، 1–11. الرياض: مكتبة الرشد، 2003/1423.

ابن بطّة العكبري، أبو عبد الله عبيد الله بن محمّد (ت 997/387). **الإبانة عن شريعة الفرقة الناجية**، تحقيق رضا بن نعسان معطي وآخرين، 1–6. الرياض: دار الراية، 1995/1415–2005/1462.

ابن بطّة العكبري، أبو عبد الله عبيد الله بن محمّد (ت 997/387). **الشرح والإبانة على أصول السنّة والديانة**، تحقيق هنري لاوست. دمشق: المعهد الفرنسي للدراسات العربيّة، 1958.

ابن البنّا، أبو عليّ الحسن بن أحمد (ت 1078/471). **المختار في أصول السنّة**، تحقيق أحمد فريد المزيدي، ضمن مجموعة بعنوان **أصول السنّة للإمام أحمد بن حنبل الشيباني**. بيروت: دار الكتب العلميّة، 2012/1433.

ابن تيمية الحرّاني، أحمد بن عبد الحليم (ت 1337/728). **الاستغاثة في الردّ على البكري**، تحقيق عبد الله بن دجين السهيلي. الرياض: دار الوطن، 1997/1417.

ابن تيمية الحرّاني، أحمد بن عبد الحليم (ت 1337/728). **الإيمان**. دمشق: منشورات المكتب الإسلامي، 1961/1381.

ابن تيمية الحرّاني، أحمد بن عبد الحليم (ت 1337/728). **بغية المرتاد في الردّ على المتفلسفة والقرامطة والباطنيّة وأهل الإلحاد**، تحقيق موسى بن سليمان الدويش. المدينة المنوّرة: مكتبة العلوم والحكم، 2001/1423.

ابن تيمية الحرّاني، أحمد بن عبد الحليم (ت 1337/728). **درء تعارض العقل والنقل**، تحقيق محمّد رشاد سالم. الرياض: جامعة الإمام محمّد بن سعود، 1991/1411.

ابن تيمية الحرّاني، أحمد بن عبد الحليم (ت 1337/728). **شرح حديث النزول**، تحقيق محمّد بن عبد الرحمن الخمسي، الرياض: دار العاصمة، 1993/1414.

ابن تيمية الحرّاني، أحمد بن عبد الحليم (ت 1337/728). **شرح العقيدة الأصفهانيّة**، تحقيق سعيد بن نصر بن محمّد. الرياض: مكتبة الرشد، 2001/1422.

ابن تيمية الحرّاني، أحمد بن عبد الحليم (ت 1337/728). **شرح العقيدة الواسطيّة**، باعتناء محمّد خليل هراس، ضبط نصّه علوي بن عبد القادر السقاف. الرياض: دار الهجرة، 1422/2001.

ابن تيمية الحرّاني، أحمد بن عبد الحليم (ت 1337/728). **السياسة الشرعيّة في إصلاح الراعي والرعيّة**، تحقيق عصام فارس الحرستاني. بيروت: دار الجيل، 1993.

ابن تيمية الحرّاني، أحمد بن عبد الحليم (ت 1337/728). **الصارم المسلول على شاتم الرسول**، حيدر أباد الدكن: مجلس دائرة المعارف، 1904/1322.

ابن تيمية الحرّاني، أحمد بن عبد الحليم (ت 1337/728). **العصيان المسلّح أو قتال أهل البغي في دولة الإسلام وموقف الحاكم منه**، تحقيق عبد الرحمن عميرة. بيروت: دار الجيل، 1992.

ابن تيمية الحرّاني، أحمد بن عبد الحليم (ت 1337/728). **مجموع الرسائل الكبرى**، 1–2. القاهرة: شركة طبع الكتب العلميّة، 1905/1323.

ابن تيمية الحرّاني، أحمد بن عبد الحليم (ت 1337/728). **مجموع فتاوى شيخ الإسلام أحمد بن تيمية**، الجزء الخامس. المدينة المنوّرة: مجمّع الملك فهد، 2003/1424.

ابن تيمية الحرّاني، أحمد بن عبد الحليم (ت 1337/728). **منهاج السنّة النبوية في نقض كلام الشيعة القدريّة**، تحقيق محمّد رشاد سالم، 1–9. الرياض: جامعة الإمام محمّد بن سعود الإسلاميّة، 1986/1406.

ابن الجزري، شمس الدين محمّد بن محمّد (ت 1429/833). **غاية النهاية في طبقات القرّاء**، تحقيق ج. برجستراسر و، 1–2. بيروت: دار الكتب العلميّة، 2006/1427.

ابن الجوزي، عبد الرحمن بن عليّ (ت 1201/597). **آداب الحسن البصري وزهده ومواعظه**، تحقيق أحمد عبد الوهّاب الشرقاوي. بيروت: دار الكتب العلميّة، 2015.

ابن الجوزي، عبد الرحمن بن عليّ (ت 1201/597). **التبصرة**، تحقيق مصطفى عبد الواحد، 1–2. بيروت: دار الكتب العلميّة، لا.ت.

ابن الجوزي، عبد الرحمن بن عليّ (ت 1201/597). **تلبيس إبليس**، تحقيق أحمد عثمان المزيد، 1–2. الرياض: دار الوطن، 2002/1423.

ابن الجوزي، عبد الرحمن بن عليّ (ت 1201/597). **الضعفاء والمتروكين**، تحقيق أبي الفدا عبد الله القاضي، 1–3. بيروت: دار الكتب العلميّة، 1986/1406.

ابن الجوزي، عبد الرحمن بن عليّ (ت 1201/597). **العلل المتناهية في الأحاديث الواهية**، تحقيق خليل الميس، 1–2. بيروت: دار الكتب العلميّة، 1983/1403.

ابن الجوزي، عبد الرحمن بن عليّ (ت 1201/597). **غريب الحديث**، تحقيق عبد المعطي أمين قلعجي، 1–2. بيروت: دار الكتب العلميّة، 2004/1425.

ابن الجوزي، عبد الرحمن بن عليّ (ت 1201/597). **كتاب القصّاص والمذكّرين**، تحقيق محمّد لطفي الصبّاغ. بيروت ودمشق: المكتب الإسلامي، 1983/1403.

ابن الجوزي، عبد الرحمن بن عليّ (ت 1201/597). **المشيخة**، تحقيق محمّد محفوظ. بيروت: دار الغرب الإسلامي، 2006.

ابن الجوزي، عبد الرحمن بن عليّ (ت 1201/597). **مناقب الإمام أحمد بن حنبل**، تحقيق وترجمة مايكل كوبرسون، 1–2. نيويورك 2013–2015.

ابن الجوزي، عبد الرحمن بن عليّ (ت 1201/597). **مناقب عمر بن الخطّاب**، تحقيق حلمي بن محمّد إسماعيل. الإسكندريّة: دار ابن خلدون، 1996/1416.

ابن الجوزي، عبد الرحمن بن عليّ (ت 1201/597). **المنتظم في تاريخ الملوك والأمم**، تحقيق محمّد عبد القادر عطا ومصطفى عبد القادر عطا، 1–19. بيروت: دار الكتب العلميّة، 1992–1993.

ابن الجوزي، عبد الرحمن بن عليّ (ت 1201/597). **المنتظم في تاريخ الملوك والأمم**، 1–9. حيدر أباد الدكن: دائرة المعارف العثمانيّة، 1938/1357–1940/1359.

ابن الجوزي، عبد الرحمن بن عليّ (ت 1201/597). **المشيخة**، تحقيق محمّد محفوظ. بيروت: دار الغرب الإسلامي، 2006.

ابن الجوزي، عبد الرحمن بن عليّ (ت 1201/597). **كتاب الموضوعات**، تحقيق عبد الرحمن محمّد عثمان، 1–3. المدينة المنورة: المكتبة السلفية، 1966/1386–1968/1388.

ابن حامد، أبو عبد الله الحسن (ت 1012/403). **تهذيب الأجوبة**، تحقيق صبحي السامرّائي. بيروت: عالم الكتب، 1988/1408.

ابن حبّان البستي، محمّد (ت 965/354). **روضة العقلاء ونزهة الفضلاء**، تحقيق محمّد حامد الفقي. القاهرة: مطبعة السنّة المحمّديّة، 1374.

ابن حبّان البستي، محمّد (ت 965/354). **الصحيح**، بترتيب علاء الدين عليّ بن بلبان، تحقيق جاد الله بن حسن الخدّاش. عمّان: بيت الأفكار الدوليّة، 2004.

ابن حبّان البستي، محمّد (ت 965/354). **كتاب المجروحين من المحدّثين والضعفاء والمتروكين**، تحقيق محمّد إبراهيم زايد، 1–3. حلب: دار الوعي، 1395/1975–1396/1976.

ابن حجر العسقلاني، أحمد بن عليّ (ت 1448/852). **الإصابة في تمييز الصحابة**، تحقيق عبد الله بن عبد المحسن التركي، 1–14. القاهرة: مركز هجر للبحوث، 1429/2008.

ابن حجر العسقلاني، أحمد بن عليّ (ت 1448/852). **فتح الباري بشرح صحيح البخاري**، 1–13. بيروت: دار المعرفة، 1379/1959.

ابن حجر العسقلاني، أحمد بن عليّ (ت 1448/852). **لسان الميزان**، تحقيق عبد الفتاح أبو غدّة، 1–10. بيروت: مكتب المطبوعات الإسلاميّة، 2002.

ابن حجر العسقلاني، أحمد بن عليّ (ت 1448/852). **المطالب العالية بزوائد المسانيد الثمانية**، 1–19. الرياض: دار العاصمة ودار الغيب، 1419/1998.

ابن حزم، عليّ بن أحمد بن سعيد (ت 1063/456). **الإحكام في أصول الأحكام**، تحقيق أحمد محمّد شاكر، 1–8. القاهرة، 1345/1926–1347/1928.

ابن حزم، عليّ بن أحمد بن سعيد (ت 1063/456). **جمهرة أنساب العرب**، تحقيق عبد السلام محمّد هارون. القاهرة: دار المعارف، 1971/1391.

ابن حزم، عليّ بن أحمد بن سعيد (ت 1063/456). **الدرّة فيما يجب اعتقاده**، تحقيق أحمد بن ناصر بن محمّد الحمد وسعيد بن عبد الرحمن بن موسى القزقي. مكّة المكرّمة: مكتبة التراث، 1988/1408.

ابن حزم، عليّ بن أحمد بن سعيد (ت 1063/456). **الفصل في الملل والأهواء والنحل**، 1–5. القاهرة: محمّد عليّ صبيح، 1348.

ابن حزم، عليّ بن أحمد بن سعيد (ت 1063/456). **المحلّى**، 1–11. القاهرة: إدارة الطباعة المنيريّة، 1348–1352.

ابن حزم، عليّ بن أحمد بن سعيد (ت 1063/456). **النبذة الكافية في أحكام أصول الدين**، تحقيق محمّد أحمد عبد العزيز. بيروت: دار الكتب العلميّة، 1405/1985.

ابن الحطّاب الرازي، أبو عبد الله محمّد بن أحمد (ت 1130/525) **مشيخة ابن الحطّاب وثبت مسموعاته**، بانتقاء أبي طاهر السلفي، وبذيله **ثلاث حكايات غريبة لأبي عبد الله الرازي**، تحقيق الشريف حاتم بن عارف العوني. الرياض: دار الهجرة، 1415/1994.

ابن حمّاد، نُعيم (ت 898/288). **كتاب الفتن**، تحقيق سمير بن أمين الزهيري. القاهرة: مكتبة التوحيد، 1991.

ابن حمدان، أحمد الحرّاني (ت 1295/695). **نهاية المبتدئين في أصول الدين**، تحقيق ناصر بن سعود بن عبد الله السلامة. الرياض: مكتبة الرشد، 2004/1425.

ابن حنبل، أحمد (ت 855/241). **أصول السنّة**، ويليه **اعتقادات أُخرى في السنّة**. تحقيق أحمد فريد المزيدي. بيروت: دار الكتب العلميّة، 2012/1433.

ابن حنبل، أحمد (ت 855/241). **الردّ على الزنادقة والجهميّة**، تحقيق دغيش بن شبيب العجمي. الكويت: غراس، 2005/1426.

ابن حنبل، أحمد (ت 855/241). **الزهد**، تحقيق محمّد جلال شرف، 1–2. بيروت دار النهضة العربيّة، لا.ت.

ابن حنبل، أحمد (ت 855/241). **فضائل الصحابة**، تحقيق وصيّ الله بن محمّد عبّاس، 1–2. مكّة المكرّمة: جامعة أمّ القرى، 1983/1403.

ابن حنبل، أحمد (ت 855/241). **المسائل والرسائل المرويّة عن الإمام أحمد في العقيدة**، جمع وتحقيق ودراسة عبد الإله بن سلمان بن سالم الأحمدي، 1–2. الرياض: دار طيبة، 1991/1412.

ابن حنبل، أحمد (ت 855/241). **المسند**، تحقيق شعيب الأرنؤوط وعادل مرشد، 1–50. بيروت: مؤسّسة الرسالة، 1995–2001.

ابن حنبل، صالح بن أحمد (ت 878/265). **سيرة الإمام أحمد بن حنبل**، تحقيق فؤاد بن عبد المنعم أحمد. الرياض: دار السلف 1995/1415.

ابن حنبل، صالح بن أحمد (ت 878/265). **مسائل الإمام أحمد بن حنبل**، تحقيق طارق بن عوض الله بن محمّد. الرياض: دار الوطن، 1999/1420.

ابن حنبل، عبد الله بن أحمد (ت 902/290). **كتاب السنّة**، تحقيق محمّد بن سعيد بن سالم القحطاني، 1–2. الدمّام: دار ابن القيم، 1986/1406.

ابن خزيمة، محمّد بن إسحاق (ت 923/311). **كتاب التوحيد وإثبات صفات الربّ عزّ وجلّ**، راجعه خليل هراس. القاهرة: مكتبة الكلّيّات الأزهرية، 1968/1388.

ابن خفيف الشيرازي، أبو عبد الله محمّد (ت 982/371). **معتقد ابن خفيف**، في **سيرة الشيخ الكبير** لركن الدين يحيى بن جنيد الشيرازي، ترجمها عن الفارسيّة إبراهيم الدسوقي شتا. القاهرة: الهيئة العامّة لشؤون المطابع الأميريّة، 1977/1397.

ابن خلدون، عبد الرحمن بن محمّد (ت 1406/808). **لُباب المحصّل في أصول الدين**، تحقيق رفيق العجم. بيروت: دار المشرق، 1995.

ابن خلّكان، أبو العباس أحمد بن محمّد (ت 1282/681)، **وفيات الأعيان وأنباء أبناء الزمان**، تحقيق إحسان عبّاس، 1–7. بيروت: دار صادر، 1969–1972.

ابن خير الإشبيلي، أبو بكر محمّد (ت 1179/575). **فهرسة ما رواه عن شيوخه**، تحقيق بشّار عوّاد معروف ومحمود بشّار عوّاد. تونس: دار الغرب الإسلامي، 2009.

ابن الدبيثي، أبو عبد الله محمّد بن سعيد (ت 1239/637). **ذيل تاريخ مدينة السلام**، تحقيق بشّار عوّاد معروف، 1–5. بيروت: دار الغرب الإسلامي، 1427/2006.

ابن راهويه، إسحاق بن إبراهيم (ت 852/238). **المسند**، تحقيق عبد الغفور عبد الحقّ حسين البلوشي، 1–3. المدينة المنوّرة: مكتبة الإيمان، 1412/1991.

ابن رجب الحنبلي، عبد الرحمن بن أحمد (ت 1392/795). **التخويف من النار**، تحقيق بشير محمّد عون. دمشق: مكتبة دار البيان، 1409/1988.

ابن رجب الحنبلي، عبد الرحمن بن أحمد (ت 1392/795). **جامع العلوم والحكم**، تحقيق شعيب الأرناؤوط وإبراهيم باجس، 1–2. بيروت: مؤسّسة الرسالة، 1419/1999.

ابن رجب الحنبلي، عبد الرحمن بن أحمد (ت 1392/795). **الذيل على طبقات الحنابلة**، تحقيق عبد الرحمن بن سليمان العثيمين، 1–5. الرياض: مكتبة العبيكان، 1425/2005.

ابن رجب الحنبلي، عبد الرحمن بن أحمد (ت 1392/795). **فضل علم السلف على علم الخلف**، تحقيق يحيى مختار غزّاوي. بيروت: دار البشائر الإسلامية، 1983.

ابن رستم الطبري، محمّد بن جرير (ت أوائل القرن الرابع/العاشر). **المسترشد في إمامة أمير المؤمنين عليّ بن أبي طالب**، تحقيق أحمد المحمودي. طهران: مؤسّسة الثقافة لكوشانبور، 1415.

ابن سعد، محمّد (ت 844/230). **كتاب الطبقات الكبير**، تحقيق إدوارد سخو، 1–9. ليدن: بريل 1912–1928.

ابن شاهين، أبو حفص عمر بن أحمد (ت 995/385). **شرح مذاهب أهل السنّة ومعرفة شرائع الدين والتمسّك بالسنن**، تحقيق عادل بن محمّد. القاهرة: مؤسّسة قرطبة 1415/1995.

ابن شبّة، أبو زيد عمر النُميري البصري (ت 875/262). **تاريخ المدينة المنوّرة**، تحقيق فهيم محمّد شلتوت، 1–2. قم: دار الفكر، 1410/1989.

ابن الصلاح، أبو عمرو عثمان بن عبد الرحمن (ت 1245/643). **علوم الحديث**، تحقيق نور الدين العتر. دمشق: دار الفكر، 1986.

ابن عبد البرّ، أبو عمر يوسف بن عبد الله (ت 463/1070). **الاستيعاب في معرفة الأصحاب**، تحقيق عليّ محمّد البجاوي، 1–4. بيروت: دار الجيل، 1412/1992.

ابن عبد البرّ، أبو عمر يوسف بن عبد الله (ت 463/1070). **التمهيد لما في الموطّأ من المعاني والأسانيد**، 1–26. الرباط: وزارة الأوقاف والشؤون الإسلاميّة، 1387/1967–1412/1992.

ابن عبد البرّ، أبو عمر يوسف بن عبد الله (ت 463/1070). **جامع بيان العلم وأهله**. القاهرة: المطبعة المنيريّة، لا.ت.

ابن عبد ربّه، أحمد بن محمّد (ت 328/940). **العقد الفريد**، تحقيق مفيد محمّد قميحة وعبد المجيد الترحيني، 1–9. بيروت: دار الكتب العلميّة، 1404/1983.

ابن عدي، عبد الله (ت 365/975). **الكامل في الضعفاء**، تحقيق عادل أحمد عبد الموجود وآخرين، 1–9. بيروت: دار الكتب العلميّة، لا.ت.

ابن عرّاق الكناني، عليّ بن محمّد (ت 963/1555). **تنزيه الشريعة المرفوعة عن الأخبار الشنيعة الموضوعة**، تحقيق عبد الوهاب عبد اللطيف وعبد الله محمّد الصدّيق، 1–2. بيروت: دار الكتب العلميّة 1401/1981.

ابن عساكر، أبو القاسم عليّ بن الحسن (ت 571/1175). **كتاب الأربعين في مناقب أمّهات المؤمنين**، تحقيق محمّد مطيع الحافظ وغزوة بدير. دمشق: دار الفكر، 1406/1986.

ابن عساكر، أبو القاسم عليّ بن الحسن (ت 571/1175). **تاريخ مدينة دمشق**، تحقيق محبّ الدين عمر بن غرامة العمروي. بيروت: دار الفكر، 1415/1995–1421/2000.

ابن عساكر، أبو القاسم عليّ بن الحسن (ت 571/1175). **تبيين كذب المفتري**، باعتناء القدسي. دمشق: مطبعة التوفيق، 1347/1928.

ابن عطيّة، أبو محمّد عبد الحقّ (ت 546/1151). **المحرّر الوجيز في تفسير الكتاب العزيز**، تحقيق عبد السلام عبد الشافي محمّد. بيروت: دار الكتب العلميّة، 2001.

ابن العماد الحنبلي، عبد الحيّ بن أحمد (ت 1089/1678). **شذرات الذهب في أخبار من ذهب**، تحقيق محمود الأرناؤوط. دمشق: دار ابن كثير، 1406/1986–1414/1993.

ابن الفرضي، أبو الوليد عبد الله (ت 403/1012). **تاريخ علماء الأندلس**، تحقيق فرنثيسكو كوديرا، 1–2. مدريد: مطبعة بلاغرنلده، 1890–1892.

ابن الفوطي، أبو الفضل عبد الرزّاق بن أحمد (ت 723/1323). **مجمع الآداب في معجم الألقاب**، تحقيق محمد الكاظم، 1–6. تهران: وزارة فرهنگ وارشاد اسلامي، 1415/1994.

ابن قتيبة، أبو محمّد عبد الله بن مسلم (ت 276/889). **تأويل مختلف الحديث**، تحقيق محمّد زهري النجّار. القاهرة: مكتبة الكلّيّات الأزهريّة، لا.ت.

ابن قتيبة، أبو محمّد عبد الله بن مسلم (ت 276/889). **تأويل مشكل القرآن**، تحقيق السيّد أحمد صقر. القاهرة: ، 1973.

ابن قدامة المقدسي، أبو محمّد عبد الله (ت 620/1223). **إثبات صفة العلوّ**، تحقيق أحمد بن عطيّة بن عليّ الغامدي. بيروت: مؤسّسة علوم القرآن، 1409/1988.

ابن قدامة المقدسي، أبو محمّد عبد الله (ت 620/1223). **ذمّ التأويل**، تحقيق بدر بن عبد الله البدر. الشارقة: دار الفتح، 1414/1994.

ابن قدامة المقدسي، أبو محمّد عبد الله (ت 620/1223). "العقيدة"، انظر: Daiber, H.

ابن قدامة المقدسي، أبو محمّد عبد الله (ت 620/1223). **لمعة الاعتقاد**. بيروت: المكتب الإسلامي، 1395/1975.

ابن قدامة المقدسي، أبو محمّد عبد الله (ت 620/1223). **المغني**، تحقيق عبد الله عبد المحسن التركي وعبد الفتاّح محمّد الحلو، 1–15. الرياض: دار عالم الكتب، 1417/1997.

ابن قيّم الجوزية، أبو عبد الله محمّد بن أبي بكر (ت 751/1450). **اجتماع الجيوش الإسلامية على غزو المعطّلة والجهمية**، تحقيق عوّاد عبد الله المعتق، 1–2. الرياض: مطابع الفرزدق، 1988.

ابن قيّم الجوزية، أبو عبد الله محمّد بن أبي بكر (ت 751/1450). **حادي الأرواح إلى بلاد الأفراح**، تحقيق محمّد بن عليّ بن حلاوة. القاهرة: مكتبة عباد الرحمن، 1426/2005.

ابن قيّم الجوزية، أبو عبد الله محمّد بن أبي بكر (ت 751/1450). **الروح**، تحقيق محمّد أجمل أيوب الإصلاحي وكمال بن محمّد قالمي، 1–2. مكّة المكرّمة: دار عالم الفوائد، 1432.

ابن قيّم الجوزية، أبو عبد الله محمّد بن أبي بكر (ت 751/1450). **مجموع الرسائل**، تحقيق مجموعة من الباحثين، جدّة: دار عالم الفوائد، لا.ت.

ابن قيّم الجوزية، أبو عبد الله محمّد بن أبي بكر (ت 751/1450). **مفتاح دار السعادة**، تحقيق عبد الرحمن بن حسن بن قائد. مكّة المكرّمة: دار عالم الفوائد، 1432.

ابن كثير، عماد الدين أبو الفداء (ت 774/1372). **البداية والنهاية**، 1–20. دمشق: دار ابن كثير، 1431/2010.

ابن كثير، عماد الدين أبو الفداء (ت 774/1372). **تفسير ابن كثير**، 1–15. القاهرة: مؤسّسة قرطبة، 1421/2000.

ابن كثير، عماد الدين أبو الفداء (ت 774/1372). **السيرة النبوية**، تحقيق مصطفى عبد الواحد، 1–4. بيروت: دار المعرفة، 1395–1396/1979.

ابن ماجة، أبو عبد الله محمّد بن يزيد (ت 888/275). **السنن**، تحقيق محمّد فؤاد عبد الباقي، 1–2. القاهرة: دار إحياء الكتب العربيّة، 1372/1952–1373/1953.

ابن المبارك، عبد الله (ت 181/797). **كتاب الزهد ويليه الرقائق**، تحقيق حبيب الرحمن الأعظمي. بيروت: دار الكتب العلميّة، 1385/1965.

ابن المرتضى، أحمد بن يحيى (ت 840/1436). **البحر الزخّار الجامع لمذاهب علماء الأمصار**، 1–5. صنعاء: دار الحكمة اليمانيّة، 1409/1988.

ابن مفلح، إبراهيم بن محمّد (ت 884/1479). **المقصد الأرشد في ذكر أصحاب الإمام أحمد**، تحقيق عبد الرحمن بن سليمان العثيمين، 1–3. الرياض: مكتبة الرشد، 1410/1990.

ابن الملقّن، أبو حفص عمر (ت 804/1401). **طبقات الأولياء**، تحقيق نور الدين شريبة. القاهرة: مكتبة الخانجي، 1994.

ابن مندة، محمّد بن إسحاق (ت 395/1004). **كتاب الإيمان**، تحقيق عليّ بن محمّد بن ناصر الفقيهي، 1–2. بيروت: مؤسّسة الرسالة، 1985.

ابن مندة، محمّد بن إسحاق (ت 395/1004). **كتاب التوحيد ومعرفة أسماء الله عزّ وجلّ وصفاته**، تحقيق عليّ بن محمّد بن ناصر الفقيهي، 1–3. المدينة المنوّرة: الجامعة الإسلاميّة، 1413/1992.

ابن المنذر النيسابوري، أبو بكر محمّد بن إبراهيم (ت 319/931). **الإشراف على مذاهب العلماء**، تحقيق أبو حمّاد صغير أحمد الأنصاري، 1–10. الإمارات العربيّة المتحدة: مكتبة مكّة، 1425/2004.

ابن منظور، جمال الدين محمد بن مكرّم (ت 711/1311). **لسان العرب**، باعتناء أحمد فارس الشدياق، 1–15. بيروت: دار صادر، 1956.

ابن نُجيم الحنفي، زين الدين بن إبراهيم (ت 969/1561). **البحر الرائق شرح كنز الدقائق**، تحقيق زكرياء عميرات، 1–9. بيروت: دار الكتب العلميّة، 1418/1997.

ابن النديم، محمّد بن إسحاق (ت حوالي 388/998). **الفهرست**، تحقيق غوستاف فلوجل، 1–2. لايبزغ: فلوجل، 1871–1872.

ابن النديم، محمّد بن إسحاق (ت حوالي 388/998). **الفهرست**، تحقيق رضا تجدّد. بيروت: 1972.

ابن نقطة، أبو بكر محمّد بن عبد الغني (ت 629/1231). **تكملة الإكمال**، تحقيق عبد القيّوم عبد ربّ النبي، 1–6. مكّة: جامعة أم القرى، 1408/1986.

ابن هانئ النيسابوري، إسحاق بن إبراهيم (ت 275/888). **مسائل الإمام أحمد بن حنبل**، تحقيق زهير الشاويش، 1–2. بيروت: المكتب الإسلامي، 1394/1974–1400/1979.

ابن هشام، أبو محمّد عبد الملك (ت 826/211). **سيرة سيّدنا محمّد رسول الله صلى الله عليه وسلم**، تحقيق فستنفلد، 1–2. غوتنجن، 1858–1860.

ابن وضّاح القرطبي، (ت 286/900). **البدع والنهي عنها**، تحقيق محمّد أحمد دهمان. القاهرة: دار الصفا، 1411/1990.

أبو حنيفة، النعمان ين ثابت (ت 150/767). **العالم والمتعلم** [جمعه أبو مقاتل السَّمَرقندي، ت 208/823]، ويليه **رسالة أبي حنيفة إلى عثمان البتّي**، و**الفقه الأبسط** [جمعه أبو مطيع البلخي، ت 199/814]، تحقيق محمد زاهد الكوثري. القاهرة: مكتبة الخانجي، 1368/1948.

أبو حنيفة، النعمان ين ثابت (ت 150/767) [منسوب].**الفقه الأكبر**. حيدر أباد الدكن: دائرة المعارف النظامية، 1342/1923.

أبو حنيفة، النعمان ين ثابت (ت 150/767). **الوصيّة**، تحقيق أبي معاذ محمد بن عبد الحي عوينة. بيروت: دار ابن حزم، 1418/1997.

أبو داود، سليمان بن الأشعث (ت 275/888). **السنن**، تحقيق شعيب الأرنؤوط ومحمّد كامل قره بللي، 1–7. دمشق: دار الرسالة العالميّة، 2009.

أبو داود، سليمان بن الأشعث (ت 275/888). **مسائل الإمام أحمد**، تحقيق طارق بن عوض الله بن محمّد. القاهرة: مكتبة ابن تيمية، 1420/1999.

أبو شامة المقدسي، عبد الرحمن بن إسماعيل (ت 665/1266). **الباعث على إنكار البدع والحوادث**، تحقيق محمّد محبّ الدين أبو زيد. القاهرة: دار مجد الإسلام، 2007.

أبو الشيخ الأصبهاني، أبو محمّد عبد الله (ت 369/979). **كتاب العظمة**، تحقيق رضاء الله بن محمّد المباركفوري. الرياض: دار العاصمة، 1411/1990.

أبو عبيد، القاسم بن سلام الهروي (ت 224/838). **كتاب الإيمان**، تحقيق محمّد ناصر الدين الألباني. الكويت: دار الأرقم، 1985.

أبو عبيد، القاسم بن سلام الهروي (ت 224/838). **الناسخ والمنسوخ في الكتاب العزيز**، تحقيق محمّد صالح المديفر. الرياض: مكتبة الرشد، لا.ت.

أبو عبيدة، معمر بن المثنّى (ت 210/825). **مجاز القرآن**، تحقيق محمّد فؤاد سزكين، 1–2. القاهرة: مكتبة الخانجي، 1988.

أبو مطيع، انظر: النسفي.

أبو معين النَّسَفي، ميمون بن محمد (ت 1114/508). **بحر الكلام**، تحقيق ولي الدين محمد صالح الفرفور. دمشق: دار الفرفور، 200/1421.

أبو نعيم الأصفهاني، أحمد بن عبد الله (ت 1038/430). **ذكر أخبار إصبهان**، تحقيق ديدرينغ، 1–2. لايدن: بريل، 1931–1932.

أبو نعيم الأصفهاني، أحمد بن عبد الله (ت 1038/430). **حلية الأولياء وطبقات الأصفياء**، 1–10. القاهرة: مكتبة الخانجي، 1938/1357.

أبو نعيم الأصفهاني، أحمد بن عبد الله (ت 1038/430). **دلائل النبوة**. بيروت: عالم الكتب، 1988/1409.

أبو يعلى الحنبلي الفرّاء، محمّد بن الحسين (ت 1066/458). **إبطال التأويلات لأخبار الصفات**، تحقيق محمّد بن حمد الحمود النجدي. الكويت: دار إيلاف الدوليّة، لا.ت.

أبو يعلى الحنبلي الفرّاء، محمّد بن الحسين (ت 1066/458). **الأحكام السلطانية**، تحقيق محمّد حامد الفقي. بيروت: دار الكتب العلميّة، 2000/1421.

أبو يعلى الحنبلي الفرّاء، محمّد بن الحسين (ت 1066/458). **الحثّ على التجارة**، ومعه **المنارة على التجارة والكسب المستطاب**، تحقيق محمود بن محمّد الحدّاد. الرياض: دار العاصمة، 1986/1407.

أبو يعلى الحنبلي الفرّاء، محمّد بن الحسين (ت 1066/458). **العدّة في أصول الفقه**، تحقيق أحمد بن عليّ سير المباركي. الرياض، 1993/1414.

أبو يعلى الحنبلي الفرّاء، محمّد بن الحسين (ت 1066/458). **مسائل الإيمان**، تحقيق سعود بن عبد العزيز الخلف. الرياض: دار العاصمة، 1989/1410.

أبو يعلى الحنبلي الفرّاء، محمّد بن الحسين (ت 1066/458). **المعتمد في أصول الدين**، تحقيق وديع زيدان حدّاد. بيروت: دار المشرق، 1974.

أبو يعلى الموصلي، أحمد بن عليّ (ت 919/307). **المسند**، تحقيق حسين سليم أسد، 1–16. دمشق: دار المأمون، 1987.

أبو يوسف، يعقوب بن إبراهيم (ت 798/182). **كتاب الخراج**، تحقيق إحسان عبّاس. بيروت: دار الشروق، 1985.

أخبار الدولة العباسية (مؤلف مجهول من القرن 9/3)، تحقيق عبد العزيز الدوري وعبد الجبّار المطلبي. بيروت: دار الطليعة، 1971.

الأخفش، سعيد بن مسعدة (ت 830/215). **معاني القرآن**، تحقيق زهدي محمود قراعة، 1–3. القاهرة: مكتبة الخانجي، 1411/1990.

الأزهري، أبو منصور محمّد بن أحمد (ت 981/370). **تهذيب اللغة**، تحقيق عبد السلام هارون، 1–15. القاهرة: المؤسّسة المصريّة العامّة، 1964–1967.

الإسفرايني، أبو المظفّر شاهفور بن طاهر (ت 1078/471). **التبصير في الدين وتمييز الفرقة الناجية عن الفرق الهالكين**، تحقيق كمال يوسف الحوت. بيروت: عالم الكتب، 1983/1403.

الإسماعيلي، أبو بكر أحمد بن إبراهيم (ت 981/371). **كتاب اعتقاد أهل السنّة والجماعة**، تحقيق أحمد فريد المزيدي، ضمن مجموعة بعنوان **أصول السنّة للإمام أحمد بن حنبل الشيباني**. بيروت: دار الكتب العلميّة، 2012/1433.

الأشعري، أبو الحسن عليّ بن إسماعيل (ت 935/324). **الإبانة عن أصول الديانة**. بيروت: دار الكتاب العربي، 1990.

الأشعري، أبو الحسن عليّ بن إسماعيل (ت 935/324). **رسالة إلى أهل الثغر**، تحقيق عبد الله شاكر محمّد الجنيدي. المدينة المنوّرة: مكتبة العلوم والحكم، 2002/1422.

الأشعري، أبو الحسن عليّ بن إسماعيل (ت 935/324). **مقالات الإسلاميّين واختلاف المصلّين**، باعتناء هلموت ريتر. فيسبادن: فرانز شتاينر، 1963.

الأصفهاني، أبو الفرج عليّ بن الحسين (ت 966/356). **مقاتل الطالبيّين**، تحقيق السيّد أحمد صقر. بيروت: مؤسّسة الأعلمي، 1987/1408.

الألباني، محمّد ناصر الدين. **فهرس مخطوطات دار الكتب الظاهريّة: المنتخب من مخطوطات الحديث**، باعتناء مشهور حسن آل سلمان. الرياض: مكتبة المعارف، 2001/1422.

الأنصاري النيسابوري، أبو القاسم سلمان بن ناصر (ت 1118/512). **الغنية في الكلام**، تحقيق مصطفى حسنين عبد الهادي، 1–2. القاهرة: دار السلام، 2010/1431.

الإيجي، عضد الدين عبد الرحمن (ت 1355/756). **شرح المواقف** للسيّد الشريف عليّ بن محمّد الجرجاني، شرحه وضبطه محمود عمر الدمياطي، 1–8. بيروت: دار الكتب العلميّة، 1998/1419.

الباقلّاني، أبو بكر ابن الطيب (ت 1012/403). **الإنصاف فيما يجب اعتقاده ولا يجوز الجهل به**، تحقيق محمّد زاهد الكوثري، ضمن **العقيدة وعلم الكلام**. بيروت: دار الكتب العلميّة، 2009.

البخاري، أبو عبد الله محمّد بن إسماعيل (ت 869/256). **الجامع الصحيح**، دمشق وبيروت: دار ابن كثير، 2002.

البخاري، أبو عبد الله محمّد بن إسماعيل (ت 869/256). **خلق أفعال العباد والردّ على الجهميّة وأصحاب التعطيل**. بيروت: مؤسّسة الرسالة، 1990/1411.

البخاري، أبو عبد الله محمّد بن إسماعيل (ت 869/256). **رفع اليدين في الصلاة**. بيروت: دار ابن حزم، 1996/1416.

البربهاري، أبو محمّد الحسن بن عليّ (ت 940/329). [منسوب] **شرح السنّة**، تحقيق خالد بن قاسم الردّادي. الرياض: دار السلف ودار الصميعي، 2000.

البربهاري، أبو محمّد الحسن بن عليّ (ت 940/329). **النبذ على شرح السنّة**، تحقيق عبد الله بن صالح العبيلان، راجعه وصححه سماحة الشيخ عبد العزيز بن عبد الله آل الشيخ. الكويت: غراس للنشر، 2003/1423.

البربهاري، أبو محمّد الحسن بن عليّ (ت 940/329). **غاية المنّة على شرح السنّة**، تحقيق جمعة بن صالح. القاهرة: مكتب ألفا، 2007.

البربهاري، أبو محمّد الحسن بن عليّ (ت 940/329). **فتح الباري على شرح السنّة للبربهاري**، للزُعكري، عبد الحميد بن يحيى بن زيد الحجوري. صعدة: دار الحديث بدماج، 2011/1433.

البرقي، أحمد بن محمّد بن خالد (ت 887/274 أو 893/280). **المحاسن**، تحقيق جلال الدين الحسني. قم: دار الكتب الإسلاميّة، 1371.

البزّار، أبو بكر أحمد بن عمرو (ت 904/292). **البحر الزخّار بمسند البزّار**، تحقيق محفوظ الرحمن زين الله وآخرين، 1–20. بيروت: مؤسّسة علوم القرآن، 1988/1409–2009/1430.

البغدادي، أبو منصور عبد القاهر (ت 1037/429). **كتاب أصول الدين**. بيروت: دار الآفاق الجديدة، 1981.

البغدادي، أبو منصور عبد القاهر (ت 1037/429). **الفرق بين الفرق وبيان الفرقة الناجية منهم**، تحقيق محمّد محيي الدين عبد الحميد. القاهرة: مكتبة صبيح، 1964.

البغوي، الحسين بن مسعود (ت 1122/516). **شرح السنّة**، تحقيق شعيب الأرنؤوط ومحمّد زهير الجاويش، 1–16. بيروت: المكتب الإسلامي، 1983.

البغوي، عبد الله بن محمّد (ت 855/241). **جزء في مسائل عن أبي عبد الله أحمد بن حنبل الشيباني**، تحقيق محمود بن محمّد الحدّاد. الرياض: دار العاصمة، 1407.

البلخي الكعبي، أبو القاسم عبد الله بن أحمد (ت 931/319). **قبول الأخبار ومعرفة الرجال**، تحقيق أبي عمرو الحسيني بن عمر بن عبد الرحيم. بيروت: دار الكتب العلميّة، 2000/1421.

بهاء الدين زاده (ت 1545/952). **القول الفصل. شرح الفقه الأكبر للإمام أبي حنيفة**، تحقيق رفيق العجم. بيروت: دار المنتخب العربي، 1998.

البيهقي، أبو بكر أحمد بن الحسين (ت 1066/458). **إثبات عذاب القبر**، تحقيق شرف محمود القضاة. عمّان: دار الفرقان، 1983/1403.

البيهقي، أبو بكر أحمد بن الحسين (ت 1066/458). **الأسماء والصفات**، تحقيق عبد الله بن محمّد الحاشدي، 1–2. جدّة: مكتبة السوادي، 1993/1413.

البيهقي، أبو بكر أحمد بن الحسين (ت 1066/458). **الاعتقاد والهداية إلى سبيل الرشاد**، صحّحه كمال يوسف الحوت. بيروت: عالم الكتب، 1983/1403.

البيهقي، أبو بكر أحمد بن الحسين (ت 1066/458). **البعث والنشور**، تحقيق عامر أحمد حيدر. القاهرة: مركز الأبحاث والخدمات الثقافيّة، 1986/1406.

البيهقي، أبو بكر أحمد بن الحسين (ت 1066/458). **دلائل النبوّة ومعرفة أحوال صاحب الشريعة**، تحقيق عبد المعطي قلعجي، 1–7. بيروت: دار الكتب العلميّة، 1985.

البيهقي، أبو بكر أحمد بن الحسين (ت 1066/458). **السنن الكبرى**، 1–24. القاهرة: دار هجر، 2011.

البيهقي، أبو بكر أحمد بن الحسين (ت 1066/458). **شعب الإيمان**، 1–14. الرياض: مكتبة الرشد، 2003/1423.

البيهقي، أبو بكر أحمد بن الحسين (ت 1066/458). **القضاء والقدر**، تحقيق صلاح الدين بن عبّاس شكر، 1–3. الرياض: مكتبة الرشد 1425.

البيهقي، أبو بكر أحمد بن الحسين (ت 1066/458). **مناقب الشافعي**، تحقيق السيّد أحمد صقر، 1–2. القاهرة: مكتبة دار التراث، 1970/1390.

تخريج أحاديث إحياء علوم الدين، للعراقي وابن السبكي والزبيدي، استخراج أبي عبد الله محمود بن محمّد الحدّاد، 1–7. الرياض: دار العاصمة، 1987/1408.

تركي، عبد المجيد. **مناظرات في أصول الشريعة الإسلاميّة بين ابن حزم والباجي**، ترجمة عبد الصبور شاهين. بيروت: دار الغرب الإسلامي، 1986/1406.

الترمذي، أبو عيسى محمّد بن عيسى (ت 909/297). **الجامع الصحيح**، تحقيق أحمد محمّد شاكر ومحمّد فؤاد عبد الباقي وإبراهيم عطوه عوض، 1–5. القاهرة: مصطفى البابي الحلبي، 1968–1975.

التوحيدي، أبو حيّان عليّ بن محمّد (ت 1023/414). **الإمتاع والمؤانسة**، تحقيق أحمد أمين وأحمد الزين، 1–3. القاهرة: 1939–1944.

الثعالبي، أبو منصور عبد الملك (ت 1038/429). **آداب الملوك**، تحقيق جليل العطيّة. بيروت: دار الغرب الإسلامي، 1990.

الثعلبي، أبو إسحاق أحمد بن محمّد (ت 1035/427). **عرائس المجالس**، القاهرة: مكتبة الجمهوريّة العربيّة، لا.ت.

الثعلبي، أبو إسحاق أحمد بن محمّد (ت 1035/427). **الكشف والبيان عن تفسير القرآن**، تحقيق أبو محمّد ابن عاشور، 1–10. بيروت: دار إحياء التراث العربي، 2002/1422.

ثلاث وثائق في محاربة الأهواء والبدع في الأندلس، تحقيق محمّد عبد الوهاب خلاف. القاهرة: المركز العربي الدولي للإعلام، 1981.

الجاحظ، عمرو بن بحر (ت 255/869). **البيان والتبيين**، تحقيق عبد السلام محمّد هارون، 1–4. القاهرة: مكتبة الخانجي، 1968.

الجاحظ، عمرو بن بحر (ت 255/869). **كتاب الحيوان**، تحقيق عبد السلام محمّد هارون، 1–8. القاهرة: البابي الحلبي، 1356/1938–1364/1945.

الجاحظ، عمرو بن بحر (ت 255/869). **رسائل الجاحظ**، تحقيق عبد السلام محمّد هارون، 1–4. القاهرة: مكتبة الخانجي، 1384/1964–1400/1979.

الجاحظ، عمرو بن بحر (ت 255/869). **كتاب البلدان**، مستلّة من **مجلة كلية الآداب**، تحقيق صالح أحمد العلي. بغداد: 1970.

جدعان، فهمي. **المحنة: بحث في جدلية الديني والسياسي في الإسلام**. عمان: دار الشروق، 1989.

الجيلاني، عبد القادر بن أبي صالح (ت 561/1165). **الغنية لطالبي طريق الحقّ**، تحقيق أبو عبد الرحمن صلاح بن محمّد بن عويضة، 1–2. بيروت: دار الكتب العلميّة، 1417/1997.

الحافظ العدني، أبو عمر محمّد بن يحيى (ت 243/857). **الإيمان**، تحقيق حمد بن حمدي الجابري الحربي. الكويت: الدار السلفيّة، 1407/1986.

الحاكم النيسابوري، أبو عبد الله محمّد بن عبد الله (ت 405/1014). **سؤالات الحاكم النيسابوري للدارقطني**، تحقيق موفّق بن عبد الله بن عبد القادر. الرياض: مكتبة المعارف، 1404/1984.

الحاكم النيسابوري، أبو عبد الله محمّد بن عبد الله (ت 405/1014). **المدخل إلى الصحيح**، تحقيق ربيع بن هادي عمير المدخلي، 1–4. القاهرة: دار الإمام أحمد 1430/2009.

الحاكم النيسابوري، أبو عبد الله محمّد بن عبد الله (ت 405/1014). **المستدرك على الصحيحين**، تحقيق مصطفى عبد القادر عطا، 1–5. بيروت: دار الكتب العلميّة، 1422/2002.

الحاكم النيسابوري، أبو عبد الله محمّد بن عبد الله (ت 405/1014). **المسند المستخرج على صحيح مسلم**، تحقيق محمّد حسن إسماعيل الشافعي، 1–4. بيروت: دار الكتب العلميّة، 1996.

حرب بن إسماعيل الكرماني (ت 280/893). **كتاب السنّة (من مسائل حرب بن إسماعيل)**، تحقيق عادل بن عبد الله آل حمدان. بيروت: دار اللؤلؤة، 1435/2014.

الحربي، إبراهيم بن إسحاق (ت 285/898). **رسالة في أنّ القرآن غير مخلوق ويليه رسالة الإمام أحمد بن حنبل إلى الخليفة المتوكّل في مسألة القرآن**، تحقيق عليّ بن عبد العزيز بن عليّ الشبل. الرياض: دار العاصمة 1416/1995.

الحكيم السمرقندي، أبو إسحاق محمّد بن إسماعيل (ت 953/342). **السواد الأعظم على مذهب الإمام الأعظم أبي حنيفة.** مخطوط الجامعة الأميركيّة في بيروت، الرقم 227 (انظر: الخوري، **المخطوطات العربيّة الموجودة في مكتبة الجامعة الأميركيّة في بيروت**، ص 90)، تحقيق ماهر جرّار (قيد الطبع).

الحليمي، أبو عبد الله الحسين (ت 1012/403). **المنهاج في شعب الإيمان**، تحقيق حلمي محمّد فودة، 1–3. دار الفكر، 1979.

الحمصي، أسماء. "المدرسة الظاهريّة"، 1–4، **مجلّة مجمع اللغة العربيّة بدمشق**، المجلّدات 41.4 (1966)، 661–690؛ 42.2 (1967)، 125–149؛ 42.3 (1967)، 320–341؛ 42.4 (1967)، 551–569.

الحميدي، أبو بكر عبد الله (ت 834/219). **أصول السنّة**، تحقيق مشعل محمّد الحدّاري. الكويت: دار ابن الأثير، 1997/1418.

حنبل بن إسحاق (ت 886/273). **ذكر محنة الإمام أحمد بن حنبل**، تحقيق محمّد نغش. القاهرة: 1977/1398.

حنبل بن إسحاق (ت 886/273). **كتاب الفتن، وجزء حنبل بن إسحاق**، تحقيق عامر حسن صبري: بيروت: دار البشائر الإسلاميّة، 1998/1419.

الخطّابي، أبو سليمان حمد بن محمّد (ت 998/388). **غريب الحديث**، تحقيق عبد الكريم إبراهيم العزباوي، 1–3. دمشق: دار الفكر، 1983/1403.

الخطّابي، أبو سليمان حمد بن محمّد (ت 998/388). **معالم السنن**، تحقيق محمّد راغب الطبّاخ، 1–4. حلب: المطبعة العلميّة، 1934/1352.

الخطيب البغداي، أحمد بن عليّ (ت 1069/462). **اقتضاء العلم العمل**، تحقيق محمّد ناصر الدين الألباني. الكويت: دار الأرقم، 1985.

الخطيب البغداي، أحمد بن عليّ (ت 1069/462). **تاريخ بغداد =تاريخ مدينة السلام**، تحقيق بشّار عوّاد معروف، 1–17. بيروت: دار الغرب الإسلامي، 2001.

الخطيب البغداي، أحمد بن عليّ (ت 1069/462). **الفقيه والمتفقّه**، تحقيق عادل بن يوسف العَزَازي، 1–2. الدمّام والرياض: دار ابن الجوزي، 1996/1417.

الخطيب البغداي، أحمد بن عليّ (ت 1069/462). **الكفاية في علم الرواية**. حيدر أباد الدكن: دائرة المعارف العثمانيّة، 1357.

الخلّال، أبو بكر أحمد بن محمّد (ت 923/311). **الأمر بالمعروف والنهي عن المنكر**، تحقيق عبد القادر أحمد عطا. بيروت: دار الكتب العلميّة، 1986/1406.

الخلّال، أبو بكر أحمد بن محمّد (ت 923/311). **السنّة**، تحقيق عطيّة الزهراني، 1–5. الرياض: دار الراية، 1989/1410.

خليفة بن خيّاط (ت 854/240). **تاريخ**، تحقيق أكرم ضياء العمري. بيروت: مؤسّسة الرسالة، 1977/1397.

الخليلي القزويني، أبو يعلى الخليل بن عبد الله (ت 1054/446). **الإرشاد في معرفة علماء الحديث**، تحقيق محمّد سعيد بن عمر إدريس. الرياض: مكتبة الرشد، 1988/1409.

الخوري، يوسف قزما. **المخطوطات العربيّة الموجودة في مكتبة الجامعة الأميركيّة في بيروت**. بيروت: الجامعة الأميركيّة في بيروت، 1982.

الخيّاط، أبو الحسين عبد الرحيم بن محمّد (ت 912/300). **كتاب الانتصار والردّ على ابن الروندي الملحد**، تحقيق نيبرج. القاهرة: دار الكتب المصريّة، 1925.

الدارقطني، عليّ بن عمر (ت 995/385). **السنن**، تحقيق شعيب الأرنؤوط وآخرين، 1–6. بيروت: مؤسّسة الرسالة، 2004.

الدارقطني، عليّ بن عمر (ت 995/385). **كتاب الصفات**، تحقيق عبد الله بن محمّد الغنيمان. الدمّام والرياض: دار ابن الجوزي، 2008/1429.

الدارقطني، عليّ بن عمر (ت 995/385). **كتاب الضعفاء والمتروكين**، تحقيق موفّق بن عبد الله بن عبد القادر. الرياض: مكتبة المعارف، 1984/1404.

الدارمي، عثمان بن سعيد (ت 893/280). **الردّ على بشر المرّيسي**، تحقيق محمّد حامد الفقي. بيروت: دار الكتب العلميّة، لا.ت.

الدارمي، عثمان بن سعيد (ت 893/280). **الردّ على الجهميّة**، تحقيق بدر البدر. الكويت: الدار السلفية، 1985/1405.

الدارمي، عثمان بن سعيد (ت 893/280). **المسند الجامع**، تحقيق نبيل بن هاشم الباعلوي. بيروت: دار البشائر الإسلاميّة، 1983/1403.

الداني، أبو عمرو عثمان بن سعيد (ت 1052/444). **الرسالة الوافية لمذهب أهل السنّة في الاعتقادات وأصول الديانات**، تحقيق أبي أنس حلمي بن محمّد الرشيدي. الإسكندريّة: دار البصيرة، 2005.

الداني، أبو عمرو عثمان بن سعيد (ت 1052/444). **السنن الواردة في الفتن**، تحقيق أبو نضال عيسى العبوشي. عمّان: بيت الأفكار الدوليّة، لا.ت.

الداودي، شمس الدين محمّد بن عليّ (ت 1538/945). **طبقات المفسّرين**، 1–2. بيروت: دار الكتب العلميّة، 1983/1403.

الدبّوسي، أبو زيد عبد الله بن عمر (ت 1038/430 أو 1040/432). **تأسيس النظر**، تحقيق مصطفى محمّد القبّاني الدمشقي. بيروت والقاهرة: دار ابن زيدون ومكتبة الكلّيّات الأزهريّة، لا.ت.

الدمياطي، أحمد بن أيبك (ت 1348/749). **المستفاد من ذيل تاريخ بغداد**، تحقيق قيصر أبو فرح. بيروت: دار الكتاب العربي، 1971.

الدينوري، أبو بكر أحمد بن مروان (ت 944/333). **المجالسة وجواهر العلم**، تحقيق أبو عبيدة مشهور آل سلمان، 1–10. بيروت: دار ابن حزم، 1998/1419.

الدينوري، أبو حنيفة أحمد بن داوود (ت حوالي 895/282). **كتاب النبات**، تحقيق برنهارد لڤين. فيسبادن: فرانز شتاينر، 1974.

الذهبي، شمس الدين محمّد بن أحمد (ت 1347/748). **إثبات الشفاعة**، تحقيق إبراهيم باجس عبد المجيد. الرياض: أضواء السلف، 2000/1420.

الذهبي، شمس الدين محمّد بن أحمد (ت 1347/748). **تاريخ الإسلام ووفيات المشاهير والأعلام**، تحقيق بشّار عوّاد معروف، 1–17. بيروت: دار الغرب الإسلامي، 2003/1424.

الذهبي، شمس الدين محمّد بن أحمد (ت 1347/748). **سير أعلام النبلاء**، تحقيق شعيب الأرنؤوط وآخرين، 1–25. بيروت: مؤسّسة الرسالة، 1996/1417.

الذهبي، شمس الدين محمّد بن أحمد (ت 1347/748). **العِبر في خَبر من غَبر**، تحقيق أبي هاجر محمّد السعيد بن بسيوني زغلول، 1–4. بيروت: دار الكتب العلميّة، 1985/1405.

الذهبي، شمس الدين محمّد بن أحمد (ت 1347/748). **العرش**، تحقيق محمّد بن خليفة التميمي، 1–2. المدينة المنوّرة: الجامعة الإسلاميّة، 1999/1420.

الذهبي، شمس الدين محمّد بن أحمد (ت 1347/748). **العلوّ للعليّ الغفّار في إيضاح صحيح الأخبار وسقيمها**، تحقيق أبو محمّد أشرف بن عبد المقصود. الرياض: مكتبة أضواء السلف، 1995/1416.

الذهبي، شمس الدين محمّد بن أحمد (ت 1347/748). **معرفة القرّاء الكبار على الطبقات والأعصار**، تحقيق بشّار عوّاد معروف وشعيب الأرناؤوط وصالح مهدي عبّاس، 1–2. بيروت: مؤسّسة الرسالة، 1988/1408.

الذهبي، شمس الدين محمّد بن أحمد (ت 1347/748). **ميزان الاعتدال في نقد الرجال**، تحقيق عليّ محمّد البجاوي، 1–4. القاهرة: دار النهضة، 1963/1382.

الرازي، فخر الدين (ت 1209/606). **محصّل أفكار المتقدّمين والمتأخّرين من العلماء والحكماء والمتكلّمين**، تحقيق سميح دغيم. بيروت: دار الفكر اللبناني، 1992.

الرازي، فخر الدين (ت 606/1209). **مفاتيح الغيب**، 1–32. بيروت: دار الفكر، 1401/1981.

الرامهرمزي، الحسن بن عبد الرحمن (ت 360/970). **أمثال الحديث**، تحقيق عبد العليّ عبد الحميد الأعظمي. بومبائي: الدار السلفيّة، 1404/1983.

الرامهرمزي، الحسن بن عبد الرحمن (ت 360/970). **المحدّث الفاصل بين الراوي والواعي**، تحقيق عجّاج الخطيب. بيروت: دار الفكر، 1391/1971.

الزجّاج، أبو إسحاق إبراهيم بن السري (ت 311/923). **معاني القرآن وإعرابه**، تحقيق عبد الجليل عبده شلبي، 1–5. بيروت: عالم الكتب، 1408/1988.

الزركشي، بدر الدين محمّد (ت 794/1391). **البحر المحيط**، 1–6. الكويت: وزارة الأوقاف والشؤون الإسلاميّة، 1413/1992.

الزرنوجي الحنفي، برهان الإسلام (ت 591/1194 أو 597/1200). **تعليم المتعلّم طريق التعلّم**، تحقيق مروان قبّاني. بيروت: المكتب الإسلامي، 1401/1981.

الزمخشري، جار الله محمود بن عمر (ت 538/1143). **الفائق في غريب الحديث**، تحقيق عليّ محمّد البجاوي ومحمّد أبو الفضل إبراهيم، 1–4. القاهرة: عيسى البابي الحلبي، 1971.

زيد بن عليّ بن الحسين (ت 121/738–739 أو 122/739). **مسند الإمام زيد**. بيروت: دار الكتب العلميّة، لا.ت.

الزيلعي، جمال الدين عبد الله بن يوسف (ت 762/1360). **نصب الراية في أحاديث الهداية**، تحقيق محمّد عوامة، 1–5. جدّة: دار القبلة 1418/1997.

سبط ابن الجوزي، أبو المظفّر يوسف (ت 654/1256). **مرآة الزمان في تواريخ الأعيان**، 1–23. دمشق: دار الرسالة العالميّة، 1434/2013.

السبكي، تاج الدين أبو نصر عبد الوهّاب (ت 771/1369). **طبقات الشافعيّة الكبرى**، تحقيق محمود محمّد الطناحي وعبد الفتاح محمّد الحلو، 1–10. القاهرة: دار إحياء الكتب العربيّة، 1964–1976.

السجزي، أبو نصر عبيد الله (ت 444/1052). **الردّ على من أنكر الحرف والصوت**، تحقيق محمّد باكريم باعبد الله. الرياض: دار الراية، 1414/1994.

السخاوي، علم الدين عليّ بن محمّد (ت 643/1245). **جمال القرّاء وكمال الإقراء**، تحقيق عليّ حسين البوّاب، 1–2. مكّة المكرّمة: مكتبة التراث، 1409/1987.

السرّاج، أبو نصر عبد الله بن عليّ الطوسي (ت378/988). **اللُّمَع**، تحقيق عبد الحليم محمود وطه عبد الباقي سرور. القاهرة: مكتبة الثقافة الدينيّة، 2008.

السرخسي، أبو بكر محمّد بن أحمد (ت 1089/482). **شرح كتاب السير الكبير** لمحمّد بن الحسن الشيباني (ت 804/189)، تحقيق صلاح الدين المنجّد، 1–3. القاهرة: معهد المخطوطات بجامعة الدول العربيّة، 1958.

السرخسي، أبو بكر محمّد بن أحمد (ت 1089/482). **شرح كتاب السير الكبير.** تحقيق محمّد بن حسن الشافعي، 1–5. بيروت: دار الكتب العلميّة، 1997.

السرخسي، أبو بكر محمّد بن أحمد (ت 1089/482). **المبسوط**، 1–31. بيروت: دار المعرفة، 1989 (مصوّرة عن طبعة القاهرة: دار السعادة، 1912/1331).

سعيد بن منصور (ت 841/227). **السنن**، تحقيق سعد بن عبد الله آل حميد وآخرين، 1–8. الرياض: دار الصميعي ودار الألوكة، 2012/1433.

السفاريني النابلسي الحنبلي، محمّد بن أحمد (ت 1775/1189). **لوامع الأنوار البهيّة وسواطع الأسرار الأثريّة. شرح الدرّة المضيّة في عقيدة الفرقة المرضيّة**، 1–2. بيروت: المكتب الإسلامي، 1991.

السِّلَفي، أبو طاهر أحمد بن محمّد (ت 1180/576). **الوجيز في ذكر المُجاز والمُجيز**، تحقيق محمّد خير البقاعي. بيروت: دار الغرب الإسلامي، 1991/1411.

السِّلَفي، أبو طاهر أحمد بن محمّد (ت 1180/576). **الطيوريّات**، انظر: الطيوري.

السُّلمي، أبو عبد الرحمن محمّد بن الحسين (ت 1021/412). **مسائل وتأويلات الصوفيّة**، تحقيق غيرهارد بورينغ وبلال الأورفه لي. بيروت: دار المشرق، 2010.

السمعاني، أبو سعد عبد الكريم بن محمّد (ت 1166/562). **الأنساب**، تحقيق عبد الرحمن بن يحيى المعلمي اليماني وآخرين، 1–12. القاهرة: مكتبة ابن تيمية، 1980/1400.

السهروردي، أبو حفص عمر بن محمد (ت 1234/632): **عوارف المعارف**، 1–2، تحقيق عبد الحليم محمود ومحمود بن الشريف، دار المعارف، القاهرة 1993–2000.

السهمي، أبو القاسم حمزة بن يوسف (ت 1035/427). **تاريخ جرجان**، 1–2. حيدر أباد الدكن: دائرة المعارف العثمانيّة، 1950.

السهمي، أبو القاسم حمزة بن يوسف (ت 1035/427). **سؤالات حمزة بن يوسف السهمي للدارقطني**، تحقيق موفق بن عبد الله بن عبد القادر. الرياض: مكتبة المعارف، 1984/1404.

السوّاس، ياسين محمّد. **فهرس مجاميع المدرسة العمريّة في دار الكتب الظاهريّة بدمشق.** الكويت: المنظّمة العربيّة للتربية والثقافة والعلوم، 1987/1408.

السيرجاني، أبو الحسن عليّ (ت حوالي 1077/470). **البياض والسواد من خصائص حكم العباد في نعت المريد والمراد**، تحقيق محسن پورمختار. تهران: مؤسسهء پژهشي حكمت وفلسفهء إيران، 1390هـ.ق./2011.

السيوطي، جلال الدين عبد الرحمن (ت 1505/911). **الدرّ المنثور في التفسير بالمأثور**، تحقيق عبد الله بن عبد المحسن التركي، 1–17. القاهرة: دار هجر، 2003/1424.

السيوطي، جلال الدين عبد الرحمن (ت 1505/911). **اللآلئ المصنوعة في الأحاديث الموضوعة**، 1–2. بيروت: دار المعرفة، لا.ت.

السيوطي، جلال الدين عبد الرحمن (ت 1505/911). **المحاضرات والمحاورات**، تحقيق يحيى الجبوري. بيروت: دار الغرب الإسلامي، 2003.

السيوطي، جلال الدين عبد الرحمن (ت 1505/911). **نزول عيسى بن مريم آخر الزمان**، تحقيق عبد القادر عطا. بيروت: دار الكتب العلميّة، لا.ت.

الشاطبي، أبو إسحاق إبراهيم بن موسى (ت 1388/790). **الاعتصام**، تحقيق محمد رشيد رضا، 1–2. القاهرة: المكتبة التجارية الكبرى، لا.ت.

الشافعي، محمّد بن إدريس (ت 819/204). **الأمّ**، تحقيق رفعت فوزي عبد المطّلب، 1–11. القاهرة: دار الوفاء، 2001/1422.

الشافعي، محمّد بن إدريس (ت 819/204). **الرسالة**، تحقيق أحمد محمّد شاكر. القاهرة: مصطفى البابي الحلبي، 1940.

شبارو-سِنّو، هبة. **أبو محمّد البربهاري. عقيدته ومساهمته في الحياة العامّة (233/847–329/941)**، رسالة مقدّمة لنيل درجة الماجيستير. بيروت: جامعة القدّيس يوسف، 1980.

الشجري، المرشد بالله يحيى بن الحسين (ت 1226/623). **الأمالي الخميسيّة**، ترتيب محيي الدين محمّد بن أحمد العبشمي، محمّد حسن محمّد حسن إسماعيل، 1–2. بيروت: دار الكتب العلميّة، 2001/1422.

الشريف الرضي، أبو الحسن محمّد بن الحسن (ت 1013/404). **نهج البلاغة**، تحقيق صبحي الصالح. بيروت والقاهرة: دار الكتاب اللبناني ودار الكتاب المصري، 1980.

الشهرستاني، أبو الفتح محمّد بن عبد الكريم (ت 1153/548). **الملل والنحل**. بيروت: مؤسّسة ناصر للثقافة، 1981.

الشيرازي، أبو إسحاق إبراهيم بن عليّ (ت 1083/476). **الإشارة إلى مذهب أهل الحقّ وعقيدة السلف**، دراسة وتحقيق ماري برنار. القاهرة: المعهد الفرنسي للآثار، 1987.

صالح بن أحمد = ابن حنبل، صالح بن أحمد.

الصابوني، أبو عثمان إسماعيل بن عبد الرحمن (ت 1057/449). **عقيدة السلف وأصحاب الحديث أو الرسالة في اعتقاد أهل السنّة**، تحقيق ناصر بن عبد الرحمن بن محمّد الجديع. الرياض: دار العاصمة، 1998/1419.

الصفدي، صلاح الدين خليل بن أيبك (ت 764/1362). **الوافي بالوفيات**، 1–30. بيروت: المعهد الألماني للدراسات الشرقيّة، 1381/1962–1425/2004.

الصنعاني، عبد الرزاق بن همّام (ت 211/826). **المصنّف**، تحقيق حبيب الرحم الأعظمي، 1–12. جوهانسبرغ: المجلس العلمي، 1983.

الصنعاني الطبري، إسحاق بن يحيى (ت حوالي 450/1058). **تاريخ صنعاء**، تحقيق عبد الله محمّد الحبشي. صنعاء: مكتبة السنحاني، لا.ت.

الصولي، أبو بكر محمّد بن يحيى (ت 335/946). **أخبار الراضي والمتّقي لله**، تحقيق هيورث دُن. القاهرة: مطبعة الصاوي، 1935.

الصولي، أبو بكر محمّد بن يحيى (ت 335/946). **أشعار أولاد الخلفاء وأخبارهم**، تحقيق هيورث دُن. لندن: لوزاك، 1936.

الطبراني، أبو القاسم سليمان بن أحمد (ت 360/970). **المعجم الأوسط**، تحقيق طارق بن عوض الله وعبد المحسن بن إبراهيم الحسيني، 1–10. القاهرة: دار الحرمين، 1415/1995.

الطبراني، أبو القاسم سليمان بن أحمد (ت 360/970). **المعجم الصغير، الروض الداني إلى المعجم الصغير**، تحقيق محمّد شكور محمود الحاج أمرير، 1–2. بيروت: المكتب الإسلامي، 1405/1985.

الطبراني، أبو القاسم سليمان بن أحمد (ت 360/970). **المعجم الكبير**، تحقيق حمدي عبد المجيد السلفي، 1–25. القاهرة: مكتبة ابن تيمية، 1379.

الطبري، أبو جعفر محمّد بن جرير (ت 310/922). **التبصير في معالم الدين**، تحقيق عليّ بن عبد العزيز الشبل. الرياض: دار العاصمة، 1416/1996.

الطبري، أبو جعفر محمّد بن جرير (ت 310/922). **جامع البيان عن تأويل آي القرأن**، تحقيق عبد الله بن عبد المحسن التركي، 1–26. القاهرة: دار هجر، 1422/2001.

الطبري، أبو جعفر محمّد بن جرير (ت 310/922). **صريح السنّة**، تحقيق بدر بن يوسف المعتوق. الكويت: مكتبة أهل الأثر، 1426/2005.

الطحاوي، أبو جعفر أحمد بن محمّد (ت 321/933). **العقيدة الطحاوية**، شرح وتعليق محمّد ناصر الألباني. بيروت: المكتب الإسلامي، 1978.

الطرطوشي، أبو بكر محمّد بن الوليد (ت 520/1126). **الحوادث والبدع**، تحقيق عبد المجيد تركي. بيروت: دار الغرب الإسلامي، 1410/1990.

الطرطوشي، أبو بكر محمّد بن الوليد (ت 1126/520). **سراج الملوك**، تحقيق محمّد فتحي أبو بكر، 1–2. القاهرة: الدار المصريّة اللبنانيّة، 1994/1414.

الطريثيثي، أبو بكر أحمد بن عليّ (ت 1103/497). **مسلسلات الطريثيثي وحديث الضبّ**. مخطوط المكتبة الظاهريّة بدمشق، انظر: السوّاس، **فهرس مجاميع المدرسة العمريّة**، ص 50.

الطوسي شيخ الطائفة، أبو جعفر محمّد بن الحسن (ت 1067/460). **الاستبصار**، تحقيق الشيخ عليّ الآخوندي، 1–4. تهران: دار الكتب الإسلامية، 1985/1363.

الطيّب، أحمد (شيخ الأزهر). **أهل السنّة والجماعة**. القاهرة: دار القدس العربي، 2018/1439.

الطيوري، أبو الحسين المبارك بن عبد الجبار (ت 1106/500). **الطيوريّات**، انتخاب أبي طاهر أحمد بن محمّد السلفي (ت 1180/576)، تحقيق دسمان يحيى معالي وعباس صخر الحسين، 1–2. الرياض: مكتبة أضواء السلف، 2004/1425.

عبد الجبّار، القاضي أبو الحسن بن أحمد (ت 1024/415). **شرح الأصول الخمسة**، تعليق مانكديم، أحمد بن أبي هاشم (ت 1034/425)، تحقيق عبد الكريم عثمان، الهيئة المصرية العامة للكتّاب، القاهرة 2009.

عبد الجبّار، القاضي أبو الحسن بن أحمد (ت 1024/415). **فضل الاعتزال وطبقات المعتزلة**، لأبي القاسم البلخي والقاضي عبد الجبّار والحاكم الجشمي، تحقيق فؤاد سيّد. تونس: الدار التونسيّة للنشر، 1974.

عبد الرزّاق، أحمد محمّد جاد. **فلسفة المشروع الحضاري بين الإحياء الإسلامي والتحديث الغربي**، 1–2. هيرندن، فرجينيا: المعهد العالمي للفكر الإسلامي، 1995.

العجلي، أبو الحسن أحمد (ت 874/261). **تاريخ الثقات**، تحقيق عبد المعطي قلعجي، بيروت: دار الكتب العلميّة، 1984/1405.

عطّار، فريد الدين (ت حوالي 1192/589). **تذكرة الأولياء**، تحقيق نيكلسون، 1–2. لندن وليدن: بريل، 1905–1907.

العقيلي، أبو جعفر محمّد بن عمرو (ت 933/322). **كتاب الضعفاء الكبير**، تحقيق عبد المعطي أمين قلعجي، 1–4. بيروت: دار الكتب العلميّة، 1984/1404

العلي، صالح. **خطط البصرة ومنطقتها: دراسة في أحوالها العمرانية والمالية في العهود الإسلامية الأولى**. بغداد: المجمع العلمي العراقي، 1986.

العليمي، مجير الدين عبد الرحمن (ت 1521/928). **المنهج الأحمد في تراجم أصحاب الإمام أحمد**، تحقيق عبد القادر الأرناؤوط وآخرين، 1–6. بيروت: دار صادر، 1997.

عماد الدين إدريس بن عليّ الحمزي (ت714/1314). **تاريخ اليمن من كتاب كنز الأخيار في معرفة السير والأخبار**، تحقيق عبد المحسن مدعج المدعج. الكويت: مؤسّسة الشراع العربي، 1992.

عمارة بن وثيمة، أبو رفاعة (ت 289/902). **كتاب بدء الخلق وقصص الأنبياء**، تحقيق رئيف جورج خوري. فيسبادن: هرسوفتس، 1978.

عياض بن موسى اليحصُبي (ت 544/1149). **ترتيب المدارك وتقريب المسالك لمعرفة أعلام مذهب مالك**، مجموعة من المحقّقين، 1–8. الرباط: وزارة الأوقاف والشؤون الإسلامية، 1965–1983.

عياض بن موسى اليحصُبي (ت 544/1149). **الشفا بتعريف حقوق المصطفى**، تحقيق عبده عليّ كوشك. بيروت: دار البشائر الإسلاميّة، 1434/2013.

الغزالي، أبو حامد محمّد (ت 505/1111). **إحياء علوم الدين**، تحقيق أحمد عناية وأحمد زهوة. بيروت: دار الكتاب العربي، 2005.

الغزالي، أبو حامد محمّد (ت 505/1111). **الاقتصاد في الاعتقاد**، تحقيق إنصاف رمضان. دمشق وبيروت: دار قتيبة، 2003.

الغزالي، أبو حامد محمّد (ت 505/1111). **عقيدة أهل السنّة**، وبهامشه **الحصن والجنّة على عقيدة أهل السنّة**، وهو شرح محمّد بن يوسف الكافي التونسي (ت 1380/1960). القاهرة: مكتبة الكلّيّات الأزهريّة، لا.ت.

الغزالي، أبو حامد محمّد (ت 505/1111). **قواعد العقائد في التوحيد**، تحقيق السيّد محمّد عقيل بن عليّ المهدلي. القاهرة: دار الحديث، لا.ت.

الغسّاني، أبو الحسن محمّد بن الفيض (ت 315/927). **أخبار وحكايات**، تحقيق إبراهيم صالح. دمشق: دار البشائر 1994.

الغطفاني، ضرار بن عمرو (ت 200/815). **كتاب التحريش**، تحقيق حسين خانصو ومحمّد گسكين. استانبول وبيروت: دار الإرشاد ودار ابن حزم، 1435/2014.

الفارسي، أبو الحسن (ت 529/1134). **المنتخب من السياق لتاريخ نيسابور**، انتخاب إبراهيم بن محمّد الأزهر الصرفيني (ت 641/1243)، تحقيق محمّد كاظم المحمودي. طهران: مركز وثائق مجلس الشورى الإسلامي، 1391ش/1433ق/2013.

فان أس، يوسف. **بدايات الفكر الإسلامي: الأنساق والأبعاد**، ترجمة عبد المجيد الصغير. الدار البيضاء: الفنك 2000.

الفراهيدي، الخليل بن أحمد (ت حوالي 170/786). **كتاب العين**، تحقيق عبد الحميد هنداوي، 1–4. بيروت: دار الكتب العلميّة، 1424/2003.

الفريابي، أبو بكر جعفر بن محمّد (ت 913/301). **كتاب القدر**، تحقيق عبد الله بن حمد المنصور. الرياض: مكتبة أضواء السلف، 1997/1418.

الفزاري الإباضي، عبد الله بن يزيد (ت بعد 795/179). **كتاب الفتيا في علم الكلام الإباضي المبكر**، تحقيق عبد الرحمن السالمي وولفرد مادلونغ. ليدن وبوسطن: بريل، 2014.

[منسوب]قدامة بن جعفر (ت 948/337). **نقد النثر أو كتاب البيان**، تحقيق عبد الحميد العبادي وتمهيد طه حسين. القاهرة: مطبعة الاعتماد، 1948.

القرطبي، أبو عبد الله محمّد بن أحمد (ت 1272/671). **الإعلام بما في دين النصارى من الفساد والأوهام**، تحقيق أحمد حجازي السقا. القاهرة: دار التراث العربي، 1980.

القرطبي، أبو عبد الله محمّد بن أحمد (ت 1272/671). **التذكرة بأحوال الموتى وأمور الآخرة**، تحقيق السيّد الجميلي، 1–2. بيروت والقاهرة: دار ابن زيدون ومكتبة مدبولي، 1986.

القرطبي، أبو عبد الله محمّد بن أحمد (ت 1272/671). **التفسير = الجامع لأحكام القرآن**، 1–20. القاهرة: دار الكتب المصريّة، 1935/1353–1950/1369.

القزويني، عبد الكريم بن محمّد الرافعي (ق 12/6). **التدوين في أخبار قزوين**، تحقيق الشيخ عزيز الله العطاردي، 1–4. بيروت: دار الكتب العلميّة، 1987/1408.

القشيري، عبد الكريم بن هوازن (ت 1072/465). **الرسالة القشيريّة**، تحقيق عبد الحليم محمود ومحمود بن الشريف، 1–2. القاهرة: دار المعارف، 1994–1995.

القشيري، عبد الكريم بن هوازن (ت 1072/465). **المعراج ويليه معراج أبي يزيد البسطامي**، تحقيق عليّ حسن عبد القادر. القاهرة: دار الكتب الحديثة، 1960 (مصوّرة دار بيبليون، باريس).

القضاعي، محمّد بن سلامة (ت 1062/454). **مسند الشهاب**، تحقيق حمدي عبد المجيد السلفي، 1–2. بيروت: مؤسّسة الرسالة، 1985/1405.

القمّي الأشعري، سعد بن عبد الله (ت299/912 أو 301/914). **المقالات والفرق**، تحقيق محمّد جواد مشكور. تهران: مركز انتشارات علمي وفرهنكي، 1981/1360.

قوّام السنّة الأصبهاني، أبو القاسم إسماعيل (ت 1140/535). **الترغيب والترهيب**، تحقيق أيمن بن صالح بن شعبان، 1–3. القاهرة: دار الحديث، 1993/1414.

قوّام السنّة الأصبهاني، أبو القاسم إسماعيل (ت 1140/535). **الحجّة في بيان المحجّة وشرح عقيدة أهل السنّة**، تحقيق محمّد بن ربيع بن هادي المدخلي ومحمّد بن محمود أبو رحيم، 1–2. الرياض: دار الراية، 1990.

القيسي، ناهض عبد الرزاق. **الدينار العربي الإسلامي**. عمّان: دار المنهاج، 2006/1426.

الكاساني، أبو بكر بن مسعود الحنفي (ت 587/1192). **بدائع الصنائع في ترتيب الشرائع**، 1–7. القاهرة: 1327/ 1328–1909/1910.

الكاندهلوي المدني، محمّد زكرياء. **أوجز المسالك إلى موطّأ مالك**، باعتناء تقيّ الدين الندوي، 1–17. دمشق: دار القلم، 1424/2003.

الكرماني = حرب بن إسماعيل الكرماني.

الكليني، أبو جعفر محمّد بن يعقوب (ت 329/940). **كتاب الكافي**، 1–8. بيروت: دار الأضواء، 1405/1985.

الكوسج، إسحاق بن منصور المروزي (ت 251/865). **مسائل الإمام أحمد بن حنبل وإسحاق بن راهويه**، 1–10. المدينة المنوّرة: الجامعة الإسلاميّة، 1425/2004.

اللالكائي، أبو القاسم هبة الله بن الحسن (ت 418/1027). **شرح أصول اعتقاد أهل السنّة**، تحقيق أحمد بن سعد بن حمدان الغامدي، 1–5. الرياض: دار طيبة، 1415/1994.

اللَّقاني، برهان الدين إبراهيم (ت 1041/1631). **شرح الناظم على جوهرة التوحيد وهو الشرح الصغير المسمّى هداية المريد لجوهرة التوحيد**، تحقيق مروان حسين عبد الصالحين البجاوي، 1–2. القاهرة: دار البصائر، 1430/2009.

الماتريدي، أبو منصور محمّد بن محمّد (ت 333/944). **تأويلات أهل السنّة (تفسير)**، تحقيق فاطمة يوسف الخيمي، 1–5. بيروت: مؤسّسة الرسالة ناشرون، 1425/2004.

الماتريدي، أبو منصور محمّد بن محمّد (ت 333/944). **كتاب التوحيد**، تحقيق بكر طوبال أوغلي ومحمّد آروشي، بيروت واستانبول: دار صادر ومكتبة الإرشاد، 2010.

مالك بن أنس (ت 179/795). **الموطّأ**، تحقيق محمّد فؤاد عبد الباقي، 1–2. بيروت: دار إحياء التراث العربي، 1406/1985.

مانكديم، أحمد بن أبي هاشم (ت 425/1034). **شرح الأصول الخمسة**، تحقيق عبد الكريم عثمان. القاهرة: الهيئة المصريّة العامّة للكتّاب، 2009.

المباركفوري، أبو العلى محمّد بن عبد الرحمن (ت 1353/1934). **تحفة الأحوذي بشرح جامع الترمذي**، تحقيق عبد الوهاب عبد اللطيف وعبد الرحمن محمّد عثمان، 1–10. القاهرة 1967 (مصوّرة دار الفكر).

المتّقي الهندي، علاء الدين عليّ بن حسام (ت 975/1567). **كنز العمّال في سنن الأقوال والأفعال**، تحقيق الشيخ بكري حيّاني، 1–18. بيروت: مؤسّسة الرسالة، 1405/1985.

المتولّي، عبد الرحمن بن مأمون النيسابوري الشافعي الأشعري (ت 478/1085). **كتاب المغني**، تحقيق ماري برنان. القاهرة: ملحق حوليّات إسلاميّة، 7، 1986.

المجلسي، محمّد باقر (ت 1602/1111). **بحار الأنوار الجامعة لدرر أخبار الأئمّة الأطهار**. 1–110، بيروت: مؤسّسة الأعلمي، 2008/1429.

المحاسبي، أسد بن حارث (ت 857/243). **كتاب التوهّم**، تحقيق آربري. القاهرة: مطبعة لجنة التأليف والترجمة والنشر، 1937.

المحاسبي، أسد بن حارث (ت 857/243). **شرح المعرفة وبذل النصيحة**، تحقيق أبو مريم مجدي فتحي السيّد. طنطا: دار الصحابة، 1993/1413.

المحاسبي، أسد بن حارث (ت 857/243). **العقل وفهم القرآن**، تحقيق حسين القوّتلي. بيروت: دار الكندي، 1983.

المحاسبي، أسد بن حارث (ت 857/243). **المكاسب**، تحقيق عبد القادر أحمد عطا. بيروت: مؤسّسة الكتب الثقافيّة، 1987/1407.

المرّوذي، أبو بكر أحمد بن محمّد (ت 888/275). **أخبار الشيوخ وأخلاقهم**، تحقيق عامر حسن صبري. بيروت: دار البشائر الإسلاميّة، 2005/1426.

المرّوذي، أبو بكر أحمد بن محمّد (ت 888/275). **كتاب الورع**، تحقيق سمير بن أمين الزهيري. الرياض: دار الصيمعي، 1997/1418.

المروزي، أبو عبد الله محمّد بن نصر (ت 906/294). **اختلاف الفقهاء**، تحقيق محمّد طاهر حكيم. الرياض: مكتبة أضواء السلف، 2000/1420.

المروزي، أبو عبد الله محمّد بن نصر (ت 906/294). **تعظيم قدر الصلاة**، تحقيق عبد الرحمن بن عبد الجبّار الفِرَيْوائي. المدينة المنوّرة: مكتبة الدار، 1985/1406.

المروزي، أبو عبد الله محمّد بن نصر (ت 906/294). **السنّة**، تحقيق أحمد فريد المزيدي، ضمن مجموعة بعنوان **أصول السنّة للإمام أحمد بن حنبل الشيباني**. بيروت: دار الكتب العلميّة، 2012/1433.

المزني، إسماعيل بن يحيى (ت 877/264). **شرح السنّة**، تحقيق جمال عزّون. المدينة النبويّة: مكتبة الغرباء الأثريّة، 1995/1415.

المزني، إسماعيل بن يحيى (ت 877/264). **الردّ على بشر المرّيسي**، تحقيق محمّد حامد الفقي. بيروت: دار الكتب العلميّة، لا.ت.

المزّي، أبو الحجّاج يوسف (ت 1341/742). **تهذيب الكمال في أسماء الرجال**، تحقيق بشّار عوّاد معروف، 1–35. بيروت: مؤسّسة الرسالة، 1983–1992.

المسعودي، عليّ بن الحسين (ت 956/345). **التنبيه والإشراف**، تحقيق دي خويه. ليدن: بريل، 1893.

المسعودي، عليّ بن الحسين (ت 345/956). *مروج الذهب ومعادن الجوهر*، تحقيق شارل بلّا، 1–7. بيروت: منشورات الجامعة اللبنانيّة، 1966–1979.

مسلم بن الحجاج النيسابوري (ت 261/874). *المسند الصحيح*، تحقيق محمّد فؤاد عبد الباقي، 1–5. بيروت: دار الكتب العلميّة، 1991.

الشيخ المفيد، محمّد بن محمّد بن النعمان (ت 413/1022). *المسائل السرويّة*، تحقيق صائب عبد الحميد. المؤتمر العالمي بمناسبة ألفيّة الشيخ المفيد، 1413/1992.

المقحفي، إبراهيم أحمد. *معجم البلدان والقبائل اليمنيّة*، 1–2. صنعاء وبيروت: دار الكلمة، 1422/2002.

المقدسي، أبو محمّد تقي الدين بن عبد الواحد (ت 600/1203). *الاقتصاد في الاعتقاد*، تحقيق أحمد بن عطيّة بن عليّ الغامدي. المدينة المنوّرة: مكتبة العلوم والحكم، 1414/1993.

المقدسي، أبو حامد محمّد (ت 888/1483). *رسالة في الردّ على الرافضة*، تحقيق عبد الوهاب خليل الرحمن. بومباي: الدار السلفيّة، 1403/1983.

المقدّسي، محمّد بن أحمد البشاري (ت 380/990). *أحسن التقاسيم في معرفة الأقاليم*، تحقيق دي خويه. ليدن: بريل 1877.

المقدسي، المطهّر بن طاهر (ت بعد 355/966). *البدء والتاريخ*، تحقيق هورات، 1–6. باريس: 1899–1919.

المكّي، أبو طالب محمّد بن عليّ (ت 386/996). *قوت القلوب في معاملة المحبوب*، تحقيق محمود إبراهيم محمّد الرضواني، 1–3. القاهرة: مكتبة دار التراث، 1422/2001.

الملطي، أبو الحسين محمّد بن أحمد (ت 377/987). *التنبيه والردّ على أهل الأهواء والبدع*، تحقيق س. ديدرينغ. بيروت: المعهد الألماني للأبحاث الشرقيّة، 2009.

الملطي، أبو الحسين محمّد بن أحمد (ت 377/987). *التنبيه والردّ على أهل الأهواء والبدع*، تحقيق محمّد زاهد بن الحسن الكوثري. القاهرة: المكتبة الأزهريّة للتراث، 1428/2007.

المناوي، عبد الرؤوف محمّد (ت 1031/1621). *فيض القدير شرح الجامع الصغير*، 1–6. بيروت: دار المعرفة، 1391/1972.

النسائي، أبو عبد الرحمن أحمد بن شعيب (ت 303/915). *السنن الكبرى*، تحقيق شعيب الأرنؤوط وآخرين، 1–12. بيروت: مؤسّسة الرسالة، 1421/2001.

النسفي، أبو مطيع مكحول (ت 318/930). *الردّ على أهل البدع والأهواء*، تحقيق ماري برناند، في: *Annales Islamogiques*, 16 (1980): 39–126.

النسفي، أبو معين ميمون بن محمّد (ت 1114/508). **بحر الكلام**، تحقيق وليّ الدين محمّد صالح الفرفور. دمشق: دار الفرفور، 2000/1421.

النسفي، نجم الدين عمر بن محمّد (ت 1142/537). **القند في ذكر علماء سمرقند**، تحقيق يوسف الهادي. تهران: دفتر نشري تراث مكتوب، 1378ش/1999.

النعّال، صائن الدين محمّد بن الأنجب (ت 1245/659). **من مشيخة النعّال البغدادي**، تخريج المنذري، تحقيق ناجي معروف وبشّار عوّاد معروف. بغداد: مطبعة المجمع العلمي العراقي، 1975/1395.

النووي، أبو زكرياء يحيى بن شرف (ت 1277/676). **المنهاج في شرح صحيح مسلم بن الحجاج**، 1–18. القاهرة: مؤسّسة قرطبة، 1994/1414.

الهادي إلى الحقّ، يحيى بن الحسين (ت 910/298). **الأحكام في الحلال والحرام**، جمع وترتيب أبي الحسن ابن أبي حريصة، تحقيق المرتضى بن زيد المَحَطْوَري الحسني، 1–2. صنعاء: مكتبة بدر، 2014/1435.

الهجويري، أبو الحسن عليّ بن عثمان (ت 1072/465). **كشف المحجوب**، دراسة وترجمة وتعليق إسعاد عبد الهادي قنديل. بيروت: دار النهضة العربيّة، 1980.

الهروي، أبو إسماعيل عبد الله بن محمّد الأنصاري (ت 1088/481). **ذمّ الكلام وأهله**، تحقيق عبد الله بن محمّد بن عثمان الأنصاري، 1–5. المدينة النبويّة: مكتبة الغرباء الأثريّة، 1998.

الهروي، أبو إسماعيل عبد الله بن محمّد الأنصاري (ت 1088/481). **منازل السائرين**. بيروت: دار الكتب العلميّة، 1988/1408.

الهمداني، أبو محمّد الحسن (ت 945/334). **الإكليل**، تحقيق نبيه أمين فارس. برنستون: مطبعة جامعة برنستون، 1940.

الهيثمي، نور الدين عليّ بن أبي بكر (ت 1404/807). **مجمع الزوائد ومنبع الفوائد**، تحقيق محمّد عبد القادر أحمد عطا، 1–12. بيروت: دار الكتب العلميّة، 2001/1422.

الواقدي، محمّد بن عمر (ت 822/207). **كتاب المغازي**، تحقيق مارسدن جونس، 1–3. لندن: مطبعة جامعة أوكسفورد، 1966.

وكيع، محمّد بن خلف (ت 918/306). **أخبار القضاة**، تحقيق عبد العزيز مصطفى المراغي، 1–3. القاهرة: مطبعة الاستقامة، 1947–1950.

ياقوت الحموي، شهاب الدين ابن عبد الله (ت 1228/626). **معجم الأدباء: إرشاد الأريب إلى معرفة الأديب**، تحقيق إحسان عبّاس، 1–7. بيروت: دار الغرب الإسلامي، 1993.

ياقوت الحموي، شهاب الدين ابن عبد الله (ت 1228/626). **معجم البلدان**، 1–5. بيروت: دار صادر ودار بيروت، 1979.

يحي بن الحسين (ت نحو 1688/1100). **أنباء الزمن في أخبار اليمن**، تحقيق محمّد عبد الله ماضي. لايبزغ، 1936.

اليعقوبي، أحمد بن أبي يعقوب ابن واضح (ت حوالي 904/292). **التاريخ**، 1–2، تحقيق هوتسما. ليدن: بريل، 1883.

اليوسي، الحسن (ت 1691/1102). **زهر الأكم في الأمثال والحكم**، تحقيق محمّد حجّي ومحمّد الأخضر، 1–3. الدار البيضاء: دار الثقافة، 1981/1401.

الفهارس

الإشارة إلى أرقام الفقرات.

الآيات القرآنيّة

﴿الذين أوتوه من بعد ما جاءتهم البيّنات بغيًا بينهم ... فهدى الله الذين آمنوا لما اختلفوا فيه من الحقّ [بإذنه] والله يهدي من يشاء إلى صراط مستقيم﴾ (البقرة 213/2) 81

﴿يعلم السرّ وأخفى﴾ (طه 7/20) 11

﴿ليس كمثله شيء و هو السميع البصير﴾ (الشورى 42/11) 11

﴿لا يُسئل عمّا يفعل وهم يُسئلون﴾ (الأنبياء 23/21) 47

﴿ما يجادل في آيات الله إلّا الذين كفروا﴾ (غافر 4/40) 61، 140

﴿فما اختلفوا إلّا من بعد ما جاءهم العلم بغيًا بينهم﴾ (الجاثية 17/45) 80

﴿الناشطات نشطا﴾ (النازعات 2/79) 141

الحديث والآثار

"إذا ذُكر أصحابي فأمسكوا" 14، 113

"اِصبرْ وإنْ كان عبدًا حبشيًّا" 19

"اِصبروا حتى تلقَوني على الحوض" 19

"إنْ مشيت إليّ هرولت إليك" 29د

"إنّ الله، تبارك وتعالى، نظر إلى أهل بدر فقال اعملوا ما شئتم فإنّي قد غفرت لكم" 101

"إنّ الله، تبارك وتعالى، ينزل إلى سماء الدنيا وينزل يوم عرفة ويوم القيامة" 29ب

"إنّ الله، تبارك وتعالى، ينزل يوم عرفة" 29هـ

"إنّ الله خلق آدم على صورته" 29و

"إنّ جهنّم لا يزال يطرح فيها حتّى يضع عليها قدمه، جلّ ثناؤه" 29ج

"إنّ هذا العلم دين فانظروا عمّن تأخذون دينكم"

"إنّي رأيت ربّي في أحسن صورة" 29ز

"إيّاكم والتعمّق وإيّاكم والتنطّع وعليكم بدينكم العتيق" 85

"إيّاكم وذكر أصحابي وأصهاري وأختاني" 101

"تفكّروا في الخلق ولا تفكّروا في الله" 31

"ذروا أصحابي لا تقولوا فيهم إلّا خيرًا" 113

"ستَرَوْن ربّكم كما ترون القمرَ ليلةَ البدر لا تضامون في رؤيته" 60

"ستفترق أُمّتي على ثلاث وسبعين فرقة، كلُّها في النار إلّا واحدة وهي الجماعة، قيل يا رسول الله مَنْ هم؟ قال: ما أنا عليه اليوم وأصحابي" 71، 84

سمع رسول الله، صلّى الله عليه وسلّم، قومًا على باب حجرته يقول أحدهم: "ألم يقل اللهُ كذا"، وقال

الآخر: "ألم يقلِ اللهُ كذا"، نخرج مُغضباً فقال: "أبهذا أُمِرتم أم بهذا بُعِثت إليكم أنْ تضربوا كتابَ الله بعضه ببعض؟" 139
"قلوب العباد بين إصبعين من أصابع الرحمن" 29أ
"لا تزال عصبةٌ من أُمّتي ظاهرين على الحقّ لا يضرّهم من خذلهم حتّى يأتيَ أمرُ الله" 81
"من يعش منكم بعدي فسيرى اختلافاً كبيراً فإيّاكم ومحدَثات الأمور فإنّها ضلالة وعليكم بسنّتي وسنّة الخلفاء الراشدين المهديّين وعضّوا عليها بالنواجذ" 76
"مولى القوم منهم" 73
"المؤمن لا يُماري ولا انتفع المماري يوم القيامة فدعوا المِراء" 142

الآثار عن الصحابة وأقوال العلماء

"إذا رأيت رجلاً من أهل السنّة فكأنّما أرى رجلاً من أصحاب رسول الله وإذا رأيت رجلاً من أهل البدع فكأنّما أرى رجلاً من المنافقين" (فُضيل بن عِياض) 153
"الإسلام هو السنّة والسنّة هي الإسلام" (بشر [بن] الحارث) 152
"الجهميّ كافر ليس من أهل القبلة، حلالُ الدم لا يرث ولا يورّث لأنّه قال لا جمعة ولا جماعة ولا صدقة" (أحمد بن حنبل وغيره) 78
"الحكيم لا يماري ولا يداري حكمته، ينشرها إنْ قُبلت حمد الله وإنْ رُدّت حمد الله" (الحسن البصري) 137
"أخاف أنْ يُحرِّفَها فيقع في قلبي شيء" (محمّد بن سيرين) 134
"أصل اثنين وسبعين هوًى..." (عبد الله بن المبارك) 144
"الاعتصام بالسنّة نجاة"، [الزهري] 158
"أنا عرفت ديني فإنْ ضلَّ دينُك فاذهب فاطلبه" (الحسن) 138
"أوّل ما سألني الله سألني عن السنّة" (منام، عن غلام خليل) 156
"الإيمان قول وعمل يزيد وينقص" 13ك، 144
"السنّة السنّة وإيّاكم والبدع حتّى مات" (ابن عون عند الموت) 155
"الصلاةُ خلف كلِّ برٍّ وفاجر والجهاد مع كلِّ خليفة" 144
"العجب ممّن يدعو اليوم إلى السُنّة وأعجب منه من يُجيب إلى السنّة فيقبل" (يونس بن عُبَيد) 154
"القرآن إلى السنّة أحوج من السنّة إلى القرآن" [الأوزاعي/مكحول] 48
"كسبٌ فيه بعض الدنيّةِ خيرٌ من الحاجة إلى النّاس" عمر[بن الخطّاب] 103
"كلّ محدثة بدعة وكلّ بدعة ضلالة" 5
"كنّا نقول ورسول الله، صلّى الله عليه وسلّم، بين أظهرنا أنّ خير النّاس بعد رسول الله، صلّى الله عليه وسلّم، أبو بكر وعمر وعثمان ويسمع النبيّ، صلّى الله عليه وسلّم، بذلك فلا ينكره"، (عبد الله بن عمر) 14
"لا تأخذوا عن أهل الكوفة قطُّ في الرفض، ولا عن أهل الشام في السيف، ولا عن أهل البصرة في القدر، ولا عن أهل خراسان في الإرجاء، ولا عن أهل مكّة في الصرف، ولا عن أهل المدينة في الغناء، لا تأخذوا عنهم في هذه الأشياء شيئاً" (عبد الله بن المبارك) 120

"لا طاعة لبشر في معصية الله" [عليّ بن أبي طالب] 21، 149
"لا عُذرَ لأحد في ضلالة ركبها حسبها هدًى، ولا في هدًى تركه حسبه ضلالة، فقد بُيّنَتِ الأمورُ وثبّتتِ الحجّة وانقطع العُذرُ" (عمر بن الخطّاب) 3
"لو أنّ لي (أو: لو كان لي) دعوة مستجابة ما جعلتها إلّا في السلطان..." (الفضيل بن عياض) 115
"لو كنت محلوقًا لضربت عنقك"، (عمر بن الخطّاب) 141
"ما أصابك لم يكن ليخطئك، وما أخطأك لم يكن ليصيبك"، [أُبَي بن كعب وعبادة بن الصامت وغيرهما] 40
"المقاديرُ كُلُّها من الله خيرها وشرّها" 144
"من أحبّ فعال قوم خيرًا كان أم شرًّا كان كمن عمله" 95
"من لزم السنّة وسَلِم منه أصحاب رسول الله، صلّى الله عليه وسلّم، ثُمّ مات كان مع النبيّين والصّدّيقين والشهداء والصالحين، وإن كان له تقصير في العمل" (مالك بن أنس) 151
"من مات على السنّة مستورًا فهو صِدّيقٌ" (أبو العالية) 157
"من نطق في أصحاب رسول الله، صلّى الله عليه وسلّم، بكلمة فهو صاحب هوًى" (سفيان بن عُيينة) 14
"الهمج الرَّعاع أتباع كلّ ناعق يميلون مع كلّ ريح" [عليّ بن أبي طالب] 80

الأعلام

1 الأعلام المذكورون في سماعات رواية الكتاب

إبراهيم بن عمر بن أحمد البرمكي، أبو إسحاق ص 251، 252
أبو الفتح يوسف (بن محمّد بن أحمد بن الفرج الدقاق) ص 336
أبو الفضل المخرمي ص 337
أبو القاسم عبد الرحيم: انظر عبد الرحيم بن عبد القادر
أبو القاسم عبد الله (بن محمّد بن أحمد بن الفرج الدقّاق) ص 336
أبو المعالي (بن محمّد بن أحمد بن الفرج الدقّاق) ص 336
أبو منصور الجواليقي، (موهوب بن أحمد اللغوي) ص 336
أبو الدلف ص 336
أحمد بن كامل بن خلف بن شجرة، أبو بكر ص 251، 252
أحمد بن محمّد الفيرومي ص 337
حسين بن إبراهيم ص 337
صافي المطيّن ص 337
عبد الحقّ بن عبد الخالق بن أحمد، أبو الحسين ص 251، 337
عبد الخالق بن أحمد بن عبد القادر بن محمّد بن يوسف، أبو الفرج ص 251، 336
(عبد الرزاق) بن عبد القادر بن أبي صالح الجيلي ص 338
عبد الرحيم بن عبد القادر الجيلي، أبو القاسم ص 338

عبد القادر بن أبي صالح الجيلي (شيخ الطريقة) ص 338
عبد القادر بن محمّد بن عبد القادر، أبو طالب ص 251، 252، 336
عبد الله بن حمزة بن أبي طاهر، أبو القاسم ص 251، 336
عليّ بن هلال، أبو الحسن ص 338
محمّد بن أحمد ابن الفرج الدقاق ص 336
محمّد بن أحمد بن محمّد بن داود الأصبهاني ص 337
محمّد بن العبّاس بن أحمد بن الفُرات، أبو الحسن ص 251، 252
محمّد بن ناصر بن محمّد بن عليّ، (أبو الفضل السلامي) ص 337
هزارسب (بن عوض بن الحسن) الهروي ص 337
يحيى بن عليّ الخنّاط (أو الخيّاط) ص 337

2 الأعلام المذكورون في متن الكتاب

آدم 13ط
إبليس 86
ابن أبي دُؤاد 130
ابن عون 122، 155
أبو بكر 14، 84، 105، 144
أبو ذرّ 19
أبو العالية 157
أبو الهُذَيل 130
أبو هُريرة 121
أحمد بن حنبل 12، 16، 41، 75، 78، 122
أحمد بن كامل 115
أحمد بن نصر 122
أسيد بن حُضير 121
أنس بن مالك 121
أيّوب [السَّخْتياني] 122
بشر بن الحارث 152
بشر المرّيسي 130
بكر ابن أخت عبد الواحد 45
ثمامة بن الأشرس 130
جبريل 50
جعفر المتوكِّل على الله 79
جعفر بن محمّد [الإمام الصادق] 145
الحجّاج بن المنهال 122
الحسن 138
الحسن البصري 137
الحسن بن صالح [بن حيّ] 41
الحسين بن محمّد الطبري 115
حمّاد بن زيد 122
حمّاد بن سلمة 122
الزُبير [بن العوّام] 14، 101
سعد [بن بن أبي وقّاص] 14
سعيد [بن زيد بن نُفَيل] 14
سفيان ابن عُيَيْنة 14، 146
سفيان الثوري 41
الشَّعبي 122
صالح [النّبي] 13د
طعمة بن عمرو 146
طلحة [بن عُبيدالله] 14، 101
عائشة 101، 105
عبد الله بن إدريس الأوْدي 122
عبد الله بن العبّاس 59
عبد الله بن عمر 14، 140

عبد الله بن المبارك 120، 144
عبدالرحمن بن عوف 14
عثمان 14، 71، 85، 144، 146، 147
عليّ 14، 101، 145، 146
عمر بن الخطّاب 3، 14، 71، 84، 103، 105، 141، 144
عيسى بن مريم 13ي، 17
غُلام خليل 156
الفضيل بن عياض 115، 153
مالك بن أنس 12، 41، 140، 151
مالك بن مِغْول 122
المتوكِّل = جعفر
محمّد بن سيرين 134
محمّد بن عليّ 145
مردويه الصائغ 115
معاذ بن معاذ 122
معاوية 101
موسى بن جعفر [الإمام الكاظم] 145
موسى بن عمران 54
هشام الفُوَطي 62، 130
وهب بن جرير 122
يزيد بن زريع 122
يونس بن عبيد 122، 129، 154

3 الأماكن

بدر 43، 101
بَرَهوت 51
البصرة 120
الشّام 120
الطّور 54
قبر الرسول 105
الكوفة 120
المدينة 73، 120
مكّة 50

4 الفرق والجماعات والقبائل

آل الرسول 73، 147
أصحاب الأثر 133
أصحاب الكلام 61، 97
أصحاب محمّد 2، 4، 6، 8، 10، 14، 48، 71، 74، 79، 84، 86، 89، 90، 153 (الطعن على الصحابة) 101، 103، 113، 126، 144، 146، 151
أمهات المؤمنين 116
الأنصار 14، 19، 73
أهل الآثار 61، 97
أهل الأهواء 119، 123
أهل بدر 101
أهل البدع 79، 84، 86، 134، 153
أهل البصرة 120
أهل الحقّ 81
أهل خراسان 120

أهل القليب 43
أهل السنّة 71، 84، 86، 134، 153
أهل السنّة والجماعة 2
أهل الشام 120
أهل العلم 74
أهل القِبلة 27، 78، 92
أهل الكوفة 120
أهل المدينة 73، 120
أهل مكّة 120
بنو هاشم 73
التابعون 90
الجهميّة/جَهْميّ 29، 62، 74، 75، 77، 78، 104، 119، 125، 135
الخلفاء الراشدون 76
الخوارج/خارجيّ 18، 20، 144
الرافضة/رافضي 119، 125، 146
الرعاع 71، 80
السوقة 135
الشيعة 144
الطبقة الرابعة 71
العامّة 74
العرب 73
العلماء 49، 78، 103
علماء السوء 80
القدريّة/قدريّ 119، 144
القرن الأول 14
القرن الثالث إلى القرن الرابع 91
قريش 73
المجبرة 119
المرجئة/مرجىء 144 (وانظر: الإرجاء)
المعتزلة/معتزليّ 119، 125
المشركون 43
المنافقون 153
من صلّى القبلتين 14
المهاجرون 14
النّاصبة/ناصبيّ 119

5 المواضيع والمصطلحات

الاتّباع 3
الأثر (الآثار) 6، 9، 18، 28، 29، 61، 93، 135 (الطعن على الآثار وردها) 48، 74، 79، 114، 124
الإرجاء 120، 144 (وانظر: المرجئة)
الأَرَضين 40، 46، 50
أرواح الشهداء 51
أرواح الكفّار 51
الاستحلال 72
الإسراء 50
الإسلام 1، 8، 22، 25، 26، 28، 48، 59، 65، 68، 71، 73، 74، 79، 100، 114، 131، 152 (شرائع الإسلام) 26 (الخروج من الإسلام) 4، 5، 8، 28
الإقرار 49
ألم الأطفال 45
الأمثال 3
الإمام/الأئمّة (السلطان): طاعة السلطان 15، (الجهاد مع السلطان) 115، 144، (الجمعة مع السلطان) 16، 104، 115، (جورهم على أنفسهم) 115، (الخروج على) 18، 144، (السلطان وليّ مَن لا وليّ له) 34 (والزكاة) 64

الأمّة (أمّة محمّد) 4، 5، 6، 26، 74، 79
أمر الإسلام 8
أمر الدين 3، 57
أمر الرسول 74
أمر الصحابة 74، 146
أمر الله 104
الأمر الأوّل العتيق (= الدّين العتيق)
الأمرُ بالمعروف والنهي عن المنكر 106، 107
أمير المؤمنين 15
الأنبياء 13خ، 49، 50، 151
الأهواء (الهوى) 9، 14، 85، 88، 113، 114، 115، 117، 119، 123، 125، 128، 129، 133، 144، 148
الإيمان 13ك، 26، 29، 52، 144 (ويتكرّر مصطلح الإيمان مرارًا)
الإيمان قول وعمل يزيد وينقص 13ك، 144
البدعة/ البدع/المبتدع 2، 5، 7، 8، 10، 31، 56، 61، 71، 75، 79، 80، 82، 84، 86، 87، 88، 89، 92، 108، 111، 114، 127، 129، 130، 131، 133، 134، 145، 150، 153، 155
البُراق 50
البشارة (عند الموت) 59
البعث 36
بلا حجاب ولا ترجمان 13أ
بلا كيف 9، 11
بلا متى 11
بلا منتهى 11
التأويل 83
التزويج 53
التسليم 49، 61، 91
(التسليم، بمعنى السلام على) 107
التشبيه 119
التشيّع 144، 146 (وانظر: الشيعة)
التصديق 9، 29، 91
التّعطيل 77، 125
تعطيل المساجد 79
التعمّق 85
التفكّر في الله 31، 77
التفويض 29، 92
التقليد 74، 133
التكبير عل الجنائز 41
التنطّع 85
التوبة 22، 150
التوحيد 119
الجدال 9، 49، 61، 133، 136، 139
الجماعة 1، 2، 3، 4، 71، 78، 84، 86، 87، 108 (علم السنة والجماعة) 79
الجمعة 16، 104، 108، 115
الجنّة 13ح، 13ط، 36، 37، 38، 46، 50، 51، 59، 60، 79ي، 147، 150
الجنة والنار مخلوقتان 13ح، (لا تفنيان) 36، (لم تخلقا) 79
الجهاد 16، (تعطيله) 79و، (وجوبه مع السلطان) 16، 144
جهنم 13هـ، 13و
الحجّ 16
حديث النزول 135
حُسن الظنّ بالله 69
الحقّ 4، 5، 7، 9، 71، 79، 81، 82، 84، 91، 133، 136
الحلال والحرام 118
الحوض 13د، 79ي
الحيوانات = الهوامّ
الختام (ما يُختم للعبد عند الموت) 22، 69
الخروج بالسيف 144 (وانظر: السيف)
الخروج من الإسلام 28